APPLIED MULTIVARIATE STATISTICS FOR THE SOCIAL SCIENCES

Third Edition

JAMES STEVENS

University of Cincinnati

LAWRENCE ERLBAUM ASSOCIATES, PUBLISHERS
1996   Mahwah, New Jersey

Lawrence Erlbaum Associates, Inc., Publishers
10 Industrial Avenue
Mahwah, New Jersey 07430

Books published by Lawrence Erlbaum Associates are printed on acid-free paper,
and their bindings are chosen for strength and durability.

Library of Congress Cataloging-in-Publication Data

Stevens, James.
    Applied multivariate statistics for the social sciences / James
Stevens . — 3rd ed.
      p.   cm.
    Includes bibliographical references and indexes.
    ISBN 0-8058-1670-4 (cloth : alk. paper). — ISBN 0-8058-1671-2
(pbk. : alk. paper)
    1. Multivariate analysis. 2. Social sciences—Statistical
methods. I. Title.
QA278.S74 1995   95-39716
519.5'35'0243—dc20   CIP

Printed in the United States of America
10 9 8 7 6 5 4 3 2 1

Table of Contents

Preface

The first two editions of this text have been received very warmly, and I am grateful for that. The objectives for this third edition are essentially the same as for the two previous editions.

1. The most significant change has been the major expansion and revision of chapter 11 to include *both* exploratory and confirmatory factor analysis. This has been done to modernize the book, and bring in one important facet of structural equation modeling. Both major software packages (LISREL and EQS) are illustrated.

2. Chapter 6 on assumptions in ANOVA and MANOVA has been substantially rewritten and shortened. I have integrated the relatively new EXAMINE procedure from SPSSX. This is a very nice procedure for exploring your data, and has some quite useful statistical tests (Levene test and Shapiro-Wilks test).

3. I have added a section on the *doubly multivariate* problem in the repeated measures chapter. Although this is fairly complicated, it is common in many research situations. The subjects are measured on several dependent (outcome) variables at each point in time, or for each treatment/ condition.

4. Many exercises have been added to chapter 14 on categorical data analysis, and the answers have been included for the more difficult problems. This chapter was new to the second edition.

In common with the second edition, I decided to continue to feature the SPSSX and SAS statistical packages. Again, all printouts are indicated with a gray screen. Also, all data sets (except for the very small ones), along with two large real data sets, are available on a 3.5 inch disk. This disk can be obtained free of charge for those adopting the text by simply writing to the publisher.

I am pleased to note that Dr. Deborah Bandalos of the University of Nebraska wrote the material on confirmatory factor analysis. Her lucid writing style should help to make this inherently difficult material more accessible. Also, Dr. David Cole of the University of Notre Dame, as the external expert reviewer on confirmatory factor analysis, provided many useful comments.

A few comments on how a course(s) might be structured from this book. For the past several years I have offered a three quarter sequence on multivariate methods at the University of Cincinnati. The first quarter, as of this past year, focuses on multiple regression and factor analysis (both exploratory and confirmatory), for which chapters 3 and 11 are appropriate. I used to cover canonical correlation, but have dropped it because of sample size requirements for reliable results, and because of difficulty in interpreting the many canonical variates. The second quarter of the sequence deals with multivariate tests of group differences, for which chapters 4, 5, and 6 (dealing with MANOVA), chapter 7 (discriminant analysis) and chapter 9 (analysis of covariance) are appropriate. The first half of the third quarter focuses on repeated measures analysis and the second half is devoted to categorical data analysis. There is sufficient material in the text for three quarters work. I recommend that instructors stay with the *same* software and hardware if offering a two or three quarter sequence, unless there is some compelling reason to do otherwise. This minimizes confusion that can result from switching software and/or hardware operating environments, and enables students to become very familiar and facile with either SAS or SPSSX.

In the preface to the second edition I indicated three books that I thought were exemplary. In this edition I wish to note five texts that are exemplary and certainly seminal works in their respective areas. Myers (1990) text on regression analysis is an excellent modern approach to the topic. Johnson and Wichern's (1992) book is a very good general, but more mathematical, source on multivariate methods, with an especially good treatment of the classification problem. The text by Bollen (1989) is excellent on structural equation modeling. Maxwell and Delaney (1990) have, in my opinion, the most modern and comprehensive treatment of repeated measures analysis (about 250 pages). Finally, the text by Agresti (1990) is one of the definitive works on categorical data analysis. Much can be learned from each of these texts, although the mathematical level required increases fairly substantially for all except the Maxwell and Delaney text.

In closing, once again I wish to thank Larry Erlbaum for his continued encouragement and support, and Art Lizza for a very professional job in producing this third edition. I again encourage users of this text to write and/or call me with any comments. I really would appreciate hearing from you.

James Stevens

1 Introduction

1.1 INTRODUCTION

Studies in the social sciences comparing two or more groups very often measure their subjects on several criterion variables. The following are some examples. A researcher is comparing two methods of teaching second grade reading. On a posttest he measures the subjects on the following basic elements related to reading: syllabication, blending, sound discrimination, reading rate, and comprehension. A social psychologist is testing the relative efficacy of 3 treatments on self concept, and measures the subjects on the academic, emotional, and social aspects of self concept. Two different approaches to stress management are being compared. The investigator employs a couple of paper and pencil measures of anxiety (say the State-Trait Scale and the Subjective Stress Scale) and some physiological measures. Another example would be comparing two types of counseling (Rogerian and Adlerian) on client satisfaction and client self acceptance. A major part of this text involves the statistical analysis of several groups on a set of criterion measures simultaneously, i.e., multivariate analysis of variance, the multivariate referring to the multiple dependent variables.

Cronbach and Snow (1977), writing on aptitude-treatment interaction research, have echoed the need for multiple criterion measures:

> Learning is multivariate, however. Within any one task a person's perfor-
> mance at a point in time can be represented by a set of scores describing
> aspects of the performance . . . even in laboratory research on rote learning,
> performance can be assessed by multiple indices: errors, latencies and

1

resistance to extinction, for example. These are only moderately correlated, and do not necessarily develop at the same rate. In the paired associates task, subskills have to be acquired: discriminating among and becoming familiar with the stimulus terms, being able to produce the response terms, and tying response to stimulus. If these attainments were separately measured, each would generate a learning curve, and there is no reason to think that the curves would echo each other. (p. 116)

There are three good reasons why the use of multiple criterion measures in a study comparing treatments (such as teaching methods, counseling methods, types of reinforcement, diets, etc.) is very sensible:

1. Any worthwhile treatment will affect the subjects in more than one way. Hence the problem for the investigator is to determine in which specific ways the subjects will be affected, and then find sensitive measurement techniques for those variables.
2. Through the use of multiple criterion measures we can obtain a more complete and detailed description of the phenomenon under investigation, whether it is teacher method effectiveness, counselor effectiveness, diet effectiveness, stress management technique effectiveness, etc.
3. Treatments can be expensive to implement, while the cost of obtaining data on several dependent variables is relatively small, and maximizes information gain.

Since we define a multivariate study as one with several dependent variables, multiple regression (where there is only one dependent variable) and principal components analysis would not be considered multivariate techniques. However, our distinction is more semantic than substantive. Therefore, since regression and components analysis are so important and frequently used in social science research, we include them in this text.

We have four major objectives for the remainder of this chapter:

1. To review some basic concepts (e.g., type I error and power) and some issues associated with univariate analysis, but that are equally important in multivariate analysis.
2. To discuss the importance of identifying outliers, i.e., points which split off from the rest of the data, and deciding what to do about them. We give some examples to show the considerable impact outliers can have on the results in univariate analysis.
3. To give research examples of some of the multivariate analyses to be covered later in the text, and to indicate how these analyses involve generalizations of what the student has previously learned.
4. To introduce the SPSSX and SAS statistical packages, whose outputs are discussed throughout the text.

1.2   TYPE I ERROR, TYPE II ERROR AND POWER

Suppose we have randomly assigned 15 subjects to a treatment group and 15 subjects to a control group, and are comparing them on a single measure of task performance (a univariate study, since a single dependent variable). The reader may recall that the t test for independent samples is appropriate here. We wish to determine whether the difference in the sample means is large enough, given sampling error, to suggest that the underlying population means are different. Since the sample means estimate the population means, they will generally be in error (i.e., they will not hit the population values right "on the nose"), and this is called sampling error. We wish to test the null hypothesis (H_0) that the population means are equal:

$$H_o{:}\mu_1 = \mu_2$$

It is called the null hypothesis because saying the population means are equal is equivalent to saying that the difference in the means is 0, i.e., $\mu_1 - \mu_2 = 0$, or that the difference is null.

Now, statisticians have determined that if we had populations with equal means and drew samples of size 15 repeatedly and computed a t statistic each time, then 95% of the time we would obtain t values in the range -2.048 to 2.048. The so-called sampling distribution of t under H_0 would look like:

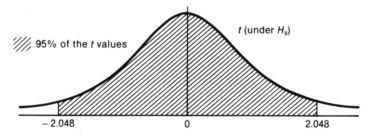

This sampling distribution is extremely important for it gives us a frame of reference for judging what is a large value of t. Thus, if our t value was 2.56 it would be very plausible to reject the H_0, since obtaining such a large t value is *very unlikely* when H_0 is true. Note, however, that if we do so there is a chance we have made an error, since it is possible (although very improbable) to obtain such a large value for t, even when the population means are equal. In practice, one must decide how much of a risk of making the above type of error (called a type I error) they wish to take. Of course, one would want that risk to be small, and many have decided a 5% risk is small. This is formalized in hypothesis testing by saying that we set our level of significance (α) at the .05 level. That is, we are willing to take a 5% chance of making a type I error. In other words, *type I error (level of significance) is the probability of rejecting the null hypothesis when it is true.*

Recall that the formula for degrees of freedom for the t test is $(n_1 + n_2 - 2)$; hence for this problem $df = 28$. If we had set $\alpha = .05$, then reference to Table B in the Appendix of this book shows that the critical values are -2.048 and 2.048. They are called critical values since they are critical to the decision we will make on H_0. These critical values define critical regions in the sampling distribution. If the value of t falls in the critical region we reject H_0; otherwise we fail to reject:

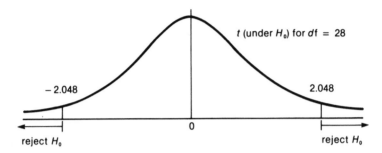

Type I error is equivalent to saying the groups differ when in fact they don't. The α level set by the experimenter is a subjective decision, but is usually set at .05 or .01 by most researchers. There are situations, however, when it makes sense to use α levels other than .05 or .01. For example, if making a type I error will not have serious substantive consequences, or if sample size is small, setting $\alpha = .10$ or $.15$ is quite reasonable. Why this is reasonable for small sample size will be made clear shortly. On the other hand, suppose we are in a medical situation where the null hypothesis is equivalent to saying a drug is unsafe, and the alternative is that the drug is safe. Here making a type I error could be quite serious, for we would be declaring the drug safe when it is not safe. This could cause some people to be permanently damaged or perhaps even killed. In this case it would make sense to take α very small, perhaps .001.

There is another type of error that can be made in conducting a statistical test, and this is called a type II error. Type II error, denoted by β, is the probability of accepting H_0, when it is false, i.e., saying the groups don't differ when they do. Now, not only can either type of error occur, but in addition they are inversely related. Thus, as we control on type I error, type II error increases. This is illustrated below for a two group problem with 15 subjects per group:

α	β	$1 - \beta$
.10	.37	.63
.05	.52	.48
.01	.78	.22

Notice that as we control on α more severely (from .10 to .01), type II error increases fairly sharply (from .37 to .78). Therefore, the problem for the experimental planner is achieving an appropriate balance between the two types of errors. While we do not intend to minimize the seriousness of making a type I error, we hope to convince the reader throughout the course of this text that much more attention should be paid to type II error. Now, the quantity in the last column of the above table $(1 - \beta)$ is the *power of a statistical test, which is the probability of rejecting the null hypothesis when it is false.* Thus, power is the probability of making a correct decision, or saying the groups differ when in fact they do. Notice from the above table that as the α level decreases, power also decreases. The diagram in Figure 1.1 should help to make clear why this happens.

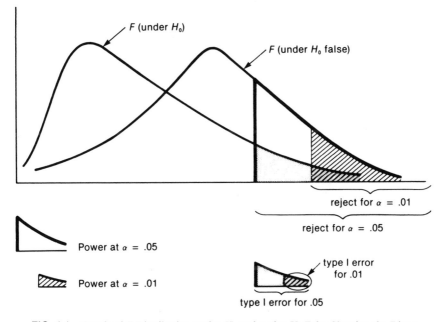

FIG. 1.1 Graph of F Distribution under H_0 and under H_0 False Showing the Direct Relationship Between Type I Error and Power. Since type I error is the probability of rejecting H_0 when true, it is the area underneath the F distribution in critical region for H_0 true. Power is the probability of rejecting H_0 when false; therefore it is the area underneath the F distribution in critical region when H_0 is false.

The power of a statistical test is dependent on three factors:

1. The α level set by the experimenter.
2. Sample size

3. Effect size—How much of a difference the treatments make, or the extent to which the groups differ in the population on the dependent variable(s).

Figure 1.1 has already demonstrated that power is directly dependent on the α level. Power is *heavily* dependent on sample size. Consider a two-tailed test at the .05 level for the t test for independent samples. Estimated effect size for the t test, as defined by Cohen (1977), is simply $\hat{d} = (x_1 - x_2)/s$, where s is the standard deviation. That is, effect size expresses the difference between the means in standard deviation units. Thus, if $x_1 = 6$ and $x_2 = 3$ and $s = 6$, then $\hat{d} = (6 - 3)/3 = .5$, or the means differ by ½ standard deviation. Suppose for the above problem we have an effect size of .5 standard deviations. Power changes dramatically as sample size increases (power values from Cohen, 1977):

n (subjects per group)	power
10	.18
20	.33
50	.70
100	.94

As the table suggests, when sample size is large (say 100 or more subjects per group) power is not an issue. It is when one is conducting a study where the group sizes will be small ($n \leq 20$), or when one is evaluating a completed study that had small group size, that it is imperative to be very sensitive to the possibility of poor power (or equivalently, a type II error). Thus, in studies with small group size it can make sense to test at a more liberal level (.10 or .15) to improve power, since (as mentioned earlier) power is directly related to the α level. We explore the power issue in considerably more detail in Chapter 4.

1.3 MULTIPLE STATISTICAL TESTS AND THE PROBABILITY OF SPURIOUS RESULTS

If a researcher sets his $\alpha = .05$ in conducting a single statistical test (say a t test), then the probability of rejecting falsely (a spurious result) is undercontrol. Now consider a five group problem in which the researcher wishes to determine whether the groups differ significantly on some dependent variable. The reader may recall from a previous statistics course that a one way ANOVA is appropriate here. But suppose our researcher is unaware of ANOVA and decides to do 10 tests, each at the .05 level, comparing each pair of groups. His probability of a false rejection is no longer under control for the *set* of 10 *t* tests. We define the *overall α for a set of tests as the probability of at least one false rejection when the null hypothesis is true.* There is an important inequality, called the *Bonferroni Inequality* which gives an upper bound on overall α:

$$\text{overall } \alpha \leq .05 + .05 + \ldots + .05 = .50$$

Thus, the probability of a few false rejections here could easily be 30 or 35%, i.e., much too high.

In general then, if we are testing k hypotheses at the $\alpha_1, \alpha_2, \ldots, \alpha_k$ levels, the Bonferroni inequality guarantees that

$$\text{overall } \alpha \leq \alpha_1 + \alpha_2 + \ldots + \alpha_k$$

If the hypotheses are each tested at the same alpha level, say α', then the Bonferroni upper bound becomes

$$\text{overall } \alpha \leq k\alpha'$$

This Bonferroni upper bound is conservative, and how to obtain a sharper (tighter) upper bound is discussed below.

If the tests are independent, then an *exact* calculation for overall α is available.

First, $(1 - \alpha_1)$ is the probability of no type I error for the first comparison. Similarly, $(1 - \alpha_2)$ is the probability of no type I error for the second, $(1 - \alpha_3)$ the probability of no type I error for the third, etc. If the tests are independent, then we can multiply probabilities. Therefore, $(1 - \alpha_1)(1 - \alpha_2) \ldots (1 - \alpha_k)$ is the probability of *no* type I errors for all k tests. Thus,

$$\text{overall } \alpha = 1 - (1 - \alpha_1)(1 - \alpha_2) \ldots (1 - \alpha_k)$$

is the probability of at least one type I error. If the tests are not independent, then overall α will still be *less* than given above, although it is very difficult to calculate. If we set the alpha levels equal, say to α' for each test, then the above expression becomes

$$\text{overall } \alpha = 1 - (1 - \alpha')(1 - \alpha') \ldots (1 - \alpha') = 1 - (1 - \alpha')^k$$

This expression, that is, $1 - (1 - \alpha')^k$ is approximately equal to $k\alpha'$ for small α'. The table below compares the two for $\alpha' = .05, .01$ and $.001$ for number of tests ranging from 5 to 100.

	$\alpha' = .05$		$\alpha' = .01$		$\alpha' = .001$	
	$1 - (1 - \alpha')^k$	$k\alpha'$	$1 - (1 - \alpha')^k$	$k\alpha'$	$1 - (1 - \alpha')^k$	$k\alpha'$
No. of Tests						
5	.226	.25	.049	.05	.00499	.005
10	.401	.50	.096	.10	.00990	.010
15	.537	.75	.140	.15	.0149	.015
30	.785	1.50	.260	.30	.0296	.030
50	.923	2.50	.395	.50	.0488	.050
100	.994	5.00	.634	1.00	.0952	.100

First, the numbers in the table greater than 1 don't represent probabilities, since a probability can't be greater than 1. Second, note that if we are testing each of a large number of hypotheses at the .001 level, the difference between $1 - (1 - \alpha')^k$ and the Bonferroni upper bound of $k\alpha'$ is very small and of no practical consequence. Also, the differences between $1 - (1 - \alpha')^k$ and $k\alpha'$ when testing at $\alpha' = .01$ are also small for up to about 30 tests. For more than about 30 tests $1 - (1 - \alpha')^k$ provides a tighter bound and should be used. When testing at the $\alpha' = .05$ level, $k\alpha'$ is okay for up to about 10 tests, but beyond that $1 - (1 - \alpha')^k$ is much tighter and should be used.

The reader may have been alert to the possibility of spurious results in the above example with multiple t tests, since this problem is pointed out in texts on intermediate statistical methods. Another frequently occurring example of multiple t tests, where overall α gets completely out of control is in comparing two groups on *each* item of a scale (test). For example, comparing males and females on each of 30 items, doing 30 t tests, each at the .05 level.

Multiple statistical tests also arise in various other contexts in which the reader may not readily recognize that the same problem of spurious results exists. And the fact that the researcher may be using a more sophisticated design or more complex statistical tests doesn't mitigate the problem.

As our first illustration, consider a researcher who runs a 4-way ANOVA ($A \times B \times C \times D$). Then 15 statistical tests are being done, one for each effect in the design: A, B, C and D main effects, and AB, AC, AD, BC, BD, CD, ABC, ABD, ACD, BCD, and $ABCD$ interactions. If each of these effects is tested at the .05 level, then all we know from the Bonferroni inequality is that overall $\alpha \leq 15 (.05) = .75$; not very reassuring: Hence, two or three significant results from such a study (if they were *not* predicted ahead of time) could very well be type I errors, i.e., spurious results.

Let us take another common example. Suppose an investigator has a two way ANOVA design ($A \times B$) with 7 dependent variables. Then, there are three effects being tested for significance: A main effect, B main effect and the $A \times B$ interaction. The investigator does separate two-way ANOVAs for each dependent variable. Therefore, the investigator has done a total of

21 statistical tests, and if each of them was conducted at the .05 level, then the overall α has gotten completely out of control. This type of thing is done *very frequently* in the literature, and the reader should be aware of it in interpreting the results of such studies. Little faith should be placed in scattered significant results from these studies.

A third example comes from survey research, where investigators are often interested in relating demographic characteristics of the subjects (sex, age, religion, SES, etc.) to responses to items on a questionnaire. The statistical test for relating each demographic characteristic to response on each item is a two-way χ^2. Often in such studies 20 or 30 (or many more) two-way χ^2's are run (and it is so easy to get them run on SPSSX). The investigators often seem to be able to explain the frequent small number of significant results perfectly, although seldom have the significant results been predicted a priori.

A fourth fairly common example of multiple statistical tests is in examining the elements of a correlation matrix for significance. Suppose there were 10 variables in one set being related to 15 variables in another set. In this case there are 150 between correlations, and if each of these is tested for significance at the .05 level, then $150 (.05) = 7.5$, or about 8 significant results could be expected by chance. Thus, if 10 or 12 of the between correlations are significant, most of them could be chance results, and it is very difficult to separate out the chance effects from the real associations. A way of circumventing this problem is to simply test each correlation for significance at a much more stringent level, say $\alpha = .001$. Then, by the Bonferroni inequality overall $\alpha \leq 150 (.001) = .15$. Naturally, this will cause a power problem (unless n is large), and only those associations that are quite strong will be declared significant. Of course, one could argue that it is only such strong associations that may be of practical significance anyways.

A fifth case of multiple statistical tests occurs when comparing the results of many studies in a given content area. Suppose, for example, that 20 studies have been reviewed in the area of programmed instruction and its effect on math achievement in the elementary grades, and that only 5 studies show significance. Since at least 20 statistical tests were done (there would be more if there was more than a single criterion variable in some of the studies), most of these significant results could be spurious, i.e., type I errors.

1.4   STATISTICAL SIGNIFICANCE VERSUS PRACTICAL SIGNIFICANCE

The reader probably was exposed to the statistical significance versus practical significance issue in a previous course in statistics, but it is so important that we review it here. Recall from our earlier discussion of power (probability of rejecting the null hypothesis when it is false), that power is heavily dependent on sample size. Thus, given very large sample size (say group sizes > 200), most effects will be declared statistically significant at the .05 level. If significance is found, then we must decide whether the difference in means is large enough to be of practical significance. There are several ways of getting at practical significance; among them are

1. confidence intervals
2. effect size measures
3. measures of association (variance accounted for)

Suppose you are comparing two teaching methods and decide ahead of time that the achievement for one method must be *at least* 5 points higher on the average for practical significance. The results are significant, but the 95% confidence interval for the difference in the population means is (1.61, 9.45). You do not have practical significance, because although the difference could be as large 9 or slightly more it could also be less than 2.

You can calculate an effect size measure, and see if the effect is large relative to what others have found in the same area of research. As a simple example, recall that the Cohen effect size measure for two groups is $\hat{d} = (\bar{x}_1 - \bar{x}_2)/s$, that is, it indicates how many standard deviations the groups differ by. Suppose your t test was significant and the estimated effect size measure was $\hat{d} = .63$ (in the medium range according to Cohen's rough characterization). If this is large relative to what others have found, then it probably is practically significant. As Light, Singer, and Willett indicate in their excellent text *By Design* (1990), "Because practical significance depends upon the research context, only *you* can judge if an effect is large enough to be important" (p. 195).

Measures of association or strength of relationship, such as Hay's $\hat{\omega}^2$, can also be used to assess practical significance because they are essentially independent of sample size. However, there are limitations associated with these measures, as O'Grady (1982) has pointed out in an excellent review on measures of explained variance. He discusses three basic reasons why such measures should be interpreted with caution: measurement, methodological and theoretical. We limit ourselves here to a theoretical point O'Grady mentions that should be kept in mind before casting asperations on a "low" amount of variance accounted. The point is that most behaviors have *multiple causes,* and hence it will be difficult in these cases to account for a large amount of variance with just a single cause such as treatments. We give an example in Chapter 4 to show that treatments only accounting for

10% of the variance on the dependent variable can indeed be practically significant.

Sometimes practical significance can be judged by simply looking at the means and thinking about the range of possible values. Consider the following example.

Example

A survey researcher compares four religious groups on their attitude toward education. The survey is sent out to 1200 subjects, of which 823 eventually respond. Ten items, Likert scaled from 1 to 5, are used to assess attitude. There are only 800 usable responses. The Protestants are split into two groups for analysis purposes. The group sizes, along with the means and standard deviations, are given below:

	Protestant1	Catholic	Jewish	Protestant2
n_i	238	182	130	250
$\bar{x}$	32.0	33.1	34.0	31.0
s_i	7.09	7.62	7.80	7.49

An analysis of variance on these groups yields $F = 5.61$, which is significant at the .001 level. The results are "highly significant," but do we have practical significance? Very probably not. Look at the size of the mean differences for a scale which has a range from 10 to 50. The mean differences for all pairs of groups, except for Jewish and Protestant 2, are about 2 or less. These are trivial differences on a scale with a range of 40.

Now recall from our earlier discussion of power, the problem of finding statistical significance with small sample size. Thus, *results in the literature that are not significant may be simply due to poor or inadequate power, while results that are significant, but have been obtained with huge sample sizes, may not be practically significant.* We illustrate this statement with two examples.

First, consider a two-group study with 8 subjects per group and an effect size of .8 standard deviations. This is a large effect size (Cohen, 1977), and most researchers would consider this result to be practically significant. However, if testing for significance at the .05 level (two tailed test), then the chances of finding significance are only about 1 in 3 (.31 from Cohen's power tables). The danger of not being sensitive to the power problem in such a study is that a researcher may abort a promising line of research, perhaps an effective diet or type of psychotherapy, because significance is not found. And it may also discourage other researchers.

On the other hand, now consider a two-group study with 300 subjects per group and an effect size of .20 standard deviations. In this case, when testing at the .05 level, the researcher is likely to find significance (power = .70 from Cohen's tables). To use a domestic analogy, this is like using a sledgehammer to "pound out" significance. Yet the effect size here would probably not be considered practically significant in most cases. Based on these results, for example, a school system may decide to implement an expensive program that may yield only very small gains in achievement.

For further perspective on the practical significance issue, there is a nice article by Haase, Ellis, and Ladany (1989). Although that article is in the *Journal of Counseling Psychology,* the implications are much broader. They suggest five different ways of assessing the practical and/or clinical significance of findings:

1. reference to previous research — the importance of *context* in determining whether a result is practically important;
2. conventional definitions of magnitude of effect — Cohen's (1977) definitions of small, medium and large effect sizes.
3. normative definitions of clinical significance — here they reference a special issue of *Behavioral Assessment* (Jacobson, 1988) that should be of considerable interest to clinicians.
4. cost benefit analysis
5. the good enough principle — here the idea is to posit a form of the null hypothesis that is more difficult to reject. For example, rather than testing whether two population means are equal, testing whether the difference between them is at least 3.

Finally, although in a somewhat different vein, with various multivariate procedures we consider in this text (such as discriminant analysis and canonical correlation), unless sample size is large relative to the number of variables, the results will not be reliable, that is, they will not generalize. A major point of the discussion in this section is that *it is critically important to take sample size into account in interpreting results in the literature.*

1.5 OUTLIERS

Outliers are data points that split off or are very different from the rest of the data. Specific examples of outliers would be an I.Q. of 160, or a weight of 350 lbs. in a group for which the median weight is 180 lbs. Outliers can occur because of two fundamental reasons: (1) a data recording or entry error was made, or (2) the subjects are simply different from the rest. The first type of outlier can be identified by always listing the data and checking to make sure the data has been read in accurately.

The importance of listing the data was brought home to me many years ago as a graduate student. A regression problem with 5 predictors, one of which was a set of random scores, was run without checking the data. This was a textbook problem to show the student that the random number predictor would not be related to the dependent variable. However, the random number predictor was significant, and accounted for a fairly large part of the variance on y. This all resulted simply because one of the scores for the random number predictor was mispunched as a 300 rather than as a 3. In this case it was obvious that something was wrong. But, with large data sets the situation will not be so transparent, and the results of an analysis could be completely thrown off by 1 or 2 errant points. The amount of time it takes to list and check the data for accuracy (even if there are 1,000 or 2,000 subjects) is well worth the effort, and the computer cost is minimal.

Statistical procedures in general can be quite sensitive to outliers. This is particularly true for the multivariate procedures that will be considered in this text. *It is very important to be able to identify such outliers and then decide what to do about them.* Why? Because we want the results of our statistical analysis to reflect most of the data, and not to be highly influenced by just 1 or 2 errant data points.

In small data sets with just 1 or 2 variables, such outliers can be relatively easy to spot. We now consider some examples.

Example 1

Consider the following small data set with two variables:

Case Number	x_1	x_2
1	111	68
2	92	46
3	90	50
4	107	59
5	98	50
6	150	66
7	118	54
8	110	51
9	117	59
10	94	97

Cases 6 and 10 are both outliers, but for different reasons. Case 6 is an outlier because the score for Case 6 on x_1 (150) is deviant, while Case 10 is an outlier because the score for that subject on x_2 (97) splits off from the other scores on x_2. The graphical split off of cases 6 and 10 is quite vivid and is given in Figure 1.2.

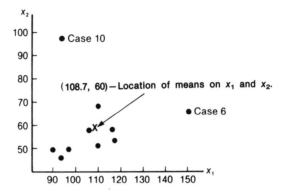

FIG. 1.2.   Plot of Outliers for Two Variable Example

In large data sets involving many variables, however, some outliers are not so easy to spot and could go easily undetected. Now, we give an example of a somewhat more subtle outlier.

Example 2

Consider the following data set on four variables:

Case	x_1	x_2	x_3	x_4
1	111	68	17	81
2	92	46	28	67
3	90	50	19	83
4	107	59	25	71
5	98	50	13	92
6	150	66	20	90
7	118	54	11	101
8	110	51	26	82
9	117	59	18	87
10	94	67	12	69
11	130	57	16	97
12	118	51	19	78
13	155	40	9	58
14	118	61	20	103
15	109	66	13	88

The somewhat subtle outlier here is case 13. Notice that the scores for case 13 on none of the x's really split off dramatically from the other subjects scores. Yet, the scores tend to be low on x_2, x_3, and x_4 and high on

x_1, and the cumulative effect of all this is to isolate case 13 from the rest of the cases. We indicate shortly a statistic that is quite useful in detecting multivariate outliers and pursue outliers in more detail in Chapter 3.

Now let us consider three more examples, involving material learned in previous statistics courses, to show the effect outliers can have on some simple statistics.

Example 3

Consider the following small set of data: 2, 3, 5, 6, 44. The last number, 44, is an obvious outlier, that is, it splits off sharply from the rest of the data. If we were to use the mean of 12 as the measure of central tendency for this data, it would be quite misleading, as there are no scores around 12. That is why you were told to use the median as the measure of central tendency when there are extreme values (outliers in our terminology), because the median is unaffected by outliers. That is, it is a robust measure of central tendency.

Example 4

To show the dramatic effect an outlier can have on a correlation, consider the two scatterplots in Figure 1.3. Notice how the inclusion of the outlier in each case *drastically* changes the interpretation of the results. For Case A there is no relationship without the outlier but there is a strong relationship with the outlier, while for Case B the relationship changes from strong (without the outlier) to weak when the outlier is included.

Example 5

As our final example, consider the following data:

GROUP 1		GROUP 2		GROUP 3	
15	21	17	36	6	26
18	27	22	41	9	31
12	32	15	31	12	38
12	29	12	28	11	24
9	18	20	47	11	35
10	34	14	29	8	29
12	18	15	33	13	30
20	36	20	38	30	16
		21	25	7	23

For now, ignore the second column of numbers in each group. Then we have a one-way ANOVA for the first variable.

The score of 30 in group 3 is an outlier. With that case in the ANOVA we

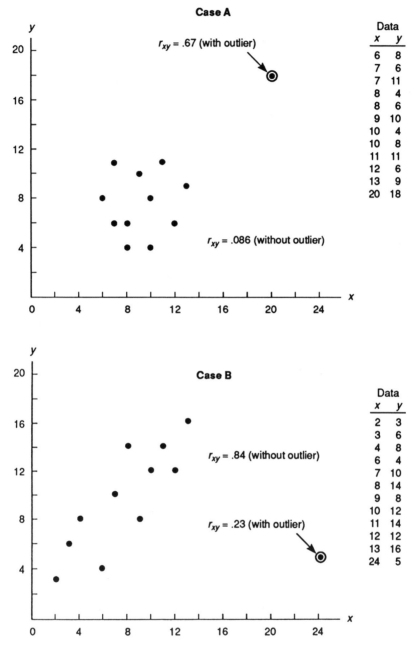

FIG. 1.3. The Effect of an Outlier on a Correlation Coefficient

16

do not find significance ($F = 2.61$, $p < .095$) at the .05 level, while with the case deleted we do find significance well beyond the .01 level ($F = 11.18$, p < .0004). Deleting the case has the effect of producing greater separation among the three means, because the means with the case included are 13.5, 17.33, and 11.89 while with the case deleted the means are 13.5, 17.33, and 9.63. It also has the effect of reducing the within variability in group 3 substantially, and hence the pooled within variability (error term for ANOVA) will be much smaller.

Detecting Outliers

If the variable is approximately normally distributed, then z scores around 3 in absolute value should be considered as potential outliers. Why? Because in an approximate normal distribution about 99% of the scores should lie within three standard deviations of the mean. Therefore, any z value > 3 indicates a value very unlikely to occur. Of course, if n is large, (say > 100), then simply by chance we might expect a few subjects to have z scores > 3 and this should be kept in mind. However, even for *any type of distribution* the above rule is reasonable, although we might consider extending the rule to $z > 4$. It was shown many years ago that regardless of how the data is distributed the percentage of observations that are contained within k standard deviations of the mean must be *at least* $(1 - 1/k^2)$ 100%. The above holds only for $k > 1$ and yields the following percentages for $k = 2$ through 5:

Number of standard deviations	Percentage of observations
2	at least 75%
3	at least 88.89%
4	at least 93.75%
5	at least 96%

Shiffler (1988) has shown that the largest possible z value in a data set of size n is bounded by $(n - 1)/\sqrt{n}$. This means for $n = 10$ the largest possible z is 2.846 and for $n = 11$ the largest possible z is 3.015. Thus, for small sample size any data point with a z around 2.5 should be seriously considered as a possible outlier.

Multivariate outliers can occur in more subtle ways. For instance, as shown in Example 2, a case may be an outlier because the subject is somewhat deviant on several of the variables, although not markedly deviant on any of them. Of course, in some instances, mu' 'variate outliers might be detected by simply examining z scores on each variable. For example, a subject may be a multivariate outlier because he(she) is very deviant on one of the variables, or on a few of the variables. Fortunately, however, there is a statistic (called Mahalanobis Distance) which has an approximate chi-square distribution for large N, which can be used to detect multivariate outliers of any type. It is available in the BMDPAM program.

In Table 1.1 we show the control lines for running the data in Example 2, and the Mahalanobis distances and probabilities associated with each case. As alluded to earlier, the probability associated with case 13 is quite small ($p = .020$), indicating that it splits of markedly from the vector of means for the 4 variables. Thus, this subject is quite different from what is average for the set of subjects.

The BMDPAM program can also be used to detect multivariate outliers when two or more groups of subjects are being compared. To illustrate this, consider Example 5, which is a three-group multivariate analysis of variance. The control lines and selected output for this run are given in Table 1.2. The output shows that the case in group three with scores of 30 and 16 is an outlier since the probability associated with that case is very small (.0006).

After the outliers are identified, what should be done with them? The action to be taken is not to automatically drop the outlier(s) from the analysis. If one finds after further investigation of the outlying points that an outlier was due to a recording or entry error, then of course one would correct the data value and redo the analysis. Or if it is found that the errant data value is due to an instrumentation error or that the process that generated the data for that subject was different, then it is legitimate to drop the outlier. If, however, none of these appear to be the case then one should *not* drop the outlier, but perhaps report two analyses (one including the outlier and the other excluding it). Outliers should not necessarily be regarded as "bad." As a matter of fact, it has been argued that outliers can provide some of the most interesting cases for further study.

In summary then, always listing the data to check for possible recording errors and running the data through BMDPAM to check for potential multivariate outliers are both essential parts of the *preliminary data screening* process investigators should routinely do.

1.6   RESEARCH EXAMPLES FOR SOME ANALYSES CONSIDERED IN THIS TEXT

To give the reader somewhat of a feel for several of the statistical analyses considered in succeeding chapters, we present the objectives in doing a multiple regression analysis, a multivariate analysis of variance and cova-riance, and a canonical correlation analysis, along with illustrative studies from the literature that used each of these analyses.

TABLE 1.1

BMDPAM Control Lines for Assessing Multivariate Outliers for a
Single Group of Subjects

	/PROBLEM TITLE IS ' OBTAINING MAHALANOBIS DISTANCES FOR IDENTIFYING MULTIVARIATE OUTLIERS'.
	/INPUT VARIABLES ARE 4. FORMAT IS STREAM.
	/VARIABLE NAMES ARE X1,X2,X3,X4.
①	/ESTIMATE METHOD IS REGR.
②	/PRINT CASE = 15. MATRICES ARE CORR,DIS.
	/END

111	68	17	81
92	46	28	67
90	50	19	83
107	59	25	71
98	50	13	92
150	66	20	90
118	54	11	101
110	51	26	82
117	59	18	87
94	67	12	69
130	57	16	97
118	51	19	78
155	40	9	58
118	61	20	103
109	66	13	88

③

CASE NUMBER	CHI—SQ ↓	CHISQ/DF	D.F.	SIGNIFICANCE
1	2.428	0.607	4	0.6576
2	5.619	1.405	4	0.2294
3	2.497	0.624	4	0.6452
4	2.820	0.705	4	0.5883
5	3.825	0.956	4	0.4301
6	6.264	1.566	4	0.1803
7	3.772	0.943	4	0.4378
8	2.561	0.640	4	0.6337
9	0.178	0.044	4	0.9963
10	7.146	1.787	4	0.1284
11	1.805	0.451	4	0.7716
12	0.515	0.129	4	0.9720
13	11.630	2.908	4	0.0203 ④
14	2.790	0.698	4	0.5935
15	2.149	0.537	4	0.7084

①The ESTIMATE paragraph is necessary in order for the Mahalanobis distances to be printed.

②To obtain the correlation matrix for the variables and the distances, we specify MATRICES ARE CORR,DIS. in the PRINT paragraph. The CASE = 15. is necessary to get all the data printed; otherwise the program will just print out the first 5 cases.

③This is Mahalanobis distance.

④Case 13 splits off significantly, at the .05 level, from the measure of central tendency for the 4 variables, i.e., the vector of means. Since statistical distance, as measured by Mahalanobis distance, is different from ordinary (Euclidean) distance, we indicate in the Appendix of this chapter some of the considerations needed in defining a measure of statistical distance.

TABLE 1.2
BMDPAM Control Lines for Assessing Multivariate Outliers in a
Three Group Multivariate Analysis of Variance

```
/PROBLEM TITLE IS ' MULTIVARIATE OUTLIERS
  FOR MULTIVARIATE ANOVA.' .
/INPUT VARIABLES ARE 3. FORMAT IS STREAM.
/VARIABLE NAMES ARE GPID,Y1,Y2. GROUPING IS GPID.
/GROUP CODES(1) ARE 1,2,3. NAMES(1) ARE GP1,GP2,GP3.
/ESTIMATE METHOD IS REGR.
/PRINT CASE = 26. MATRICES ARE CORR,DIS.
/END
```

The control lines here are very similar to those in Table 1.1, except here we must indicate which variable is the grouping variable. This is done in the VARIABLE paragraph by specifying GROUPING IS GPID. Also, there is a GROUP paragraph where a numerical code (1, 2, or 3) and name is given to each group. The 1 in parenthesis refers to the location of the grouping variable in the variable list. Here the grouping variable is the first variable in the list.

CASE NUMBER	GROUP	CHI—SQ	CHISG/DF	D.F.	SIGNIFICANCE
1	GP1	0.794	0.397	2	0.6724
2	GP1	0.757	0.378	2	0.6850
3	GP1	0.623	0.311	2	0.7324
4	GP1	0.174	0.087	2	0.9168
5	GP1	2.466	1.233	2	0.2914
6	GP1	1.483	0.742	2	0.4763
7	GP1	1.754	0.877	2	0.4159
8	GP1	3.410	1.705	2	0.1817
9	GP2	0.069	0.035	2	0.9659
10	GP2	1.823	0.911	2	0.4020
11	GP2	0.432	0.216	2	0.8057
12	GP2	1.923	0.961	2	0.3824
13	GP2	3.738	1.869	2	0.1543
14	GP2	1.012	0.506	2	0.6028
15	GP2	0.239	0.119	2	0.8875
16	GP2	0.580	0.290	2	0.7484
17	GP2	2.233	1.116	2	0.3274
18	GP3	1.395	0.698	2	0.4977
19	GP3	0.487	0.243	2	0.7839
20	GP3	2.098	1.049	2	0.3504
21	GP3	0.370	0.185	2	0.8311
22	GP3	1.047	0.523	2	0.5925
23	GP3	0.579	0.290	2	0.7485
24	GP3	0.133	0.067	2	0.9356
25	GP3	14.929	7.464	2	0.0006*
26	GP3	1.452	0.726	2	0.4837

*There is only one case here which is significantly separated at the .05 level, ie, case 25. The program, however, only specifically flags those observations which have really extreme probabilities ($p < .001$).

Multiple Regression

In a previous course simple linear regression was covered, where a dependent variable (say chemistry achievement) is predicted from just one predictor, like I. Q. Now it is certainly reasonable that other factors would also be related to chemistry achievement and that we could obtain better prediction by making use of these other factors, such as previous average grade in science courses, attitude toward education and math ability. Thus, the objective in multiple regression (called multiple since we have multiple predictors) is:

Objective: Predict a dependent variable from a set of independent variables.

Example

Feshbach, Adelman, and Fuller (1977) conducted a longitudinal study on 850 middle class kindergarten children. The children were administered a psychometric battery that included the Wechsler Preschool and Primary Scale of Intelligence, the deHirsch-Jansky Predictive Index (assessing various linguistic and perceptual motor skills) and the Bender Motor Gestalt test. The students were also assessed on a Student Rating Scale (SRS) developed by the authors, which measured various cognitive and affective behaviors and skills. These various predictors were used to predict reading achievement in grades 1, 2, and 3. Reading achievement was measured with the Cooperative Reading Test. The major thrust of the study in the authors words was

> The present investigation evaluates and contrasts one major psychometric predictive index, that developed by deHirsch . . . with an alternative strategy based on a systematic behavioral analysis and ratings made by the kindergarten teacher of academically relevant cognitive and affective behaviors and skills (assessed by the SRS). . . . This approach, in addition to being easier to implement and less costly than psychometric testing, yields assessment data which are more closely linked to intervention and remedial procedures. (p. 300)

The SRS scale proved equal to the deHirsch in predicting reading achievement, and because of the above rationale might well be preferred.

One Way Multivariate Analysis of Variance

In univariate analysis of variance, several groups of subjects were compared to determine whether they differed on the average on a single dependent variable. But, as was mentioned earlier in this chapter, any good treatment(s) generally affects the subjects in several ways. Hence, it makes sense to measure the subjects on those variables and then test whether they differ on the average on the set of variables. This gives a more accurate assessment of the true efficacy of the treatments. Thus, the objective in multivariate analysis of variance is:

Objective: Determine whether several groups differ on the average on a set of dependent variables.

Example

Stevens (1972) conducted a study on National Merit scholars. The classification variable was the educational level of both parents of the scholars. Four groups were formed:

1. Students for whom at least one parent had an eighth grade education or less
2. Students whose both parents were high school graduates
3. Students both of whose parents had gone to college, with at most one graduating
4. Students for whom both parents had at least one college degree

The dependent variables were a subset of the Vocational Personality Inventory: realistic, intellectual, social, conventional, enterprising, artistic, status, and aggression. He found that the parents' educational level was related to their children's personality characteristics, with conventional and enterprising being the key variables. Specifically, scholars whose parents had gone to college tended to be more enterprising and less conventional than scholars whose parents had not gone to college. This example is considered in detail in the chapter on discriminant analysis.

Multivariate Analysis of Covariance

Objective: Determine whether several groups differ on a set of dependent variables after the posttest means have been adjusted for any initial differences on the covariates (which are often pretests).

Example

Friedman, Lehrer, and Stevens (1983) examined the effect of two stress management strategies, directed lecture discussion and self-directed, and the locus of control of teachers on their scores on the State-Trait Anxiety Inventory and on the Subjective Stress Scale. Eighty-five teachers were pretested and posttested on the above measures, with the treatment extending five weeks. Those subjects who received the stress management programs reduced their stress and anxiety more than those in a control group. However, subjects who were in a stress management program compatiable with their locus of control (i.e., externals with lectures and internals with the self-directed) did not reduce stress significantly more than those subjects in the unmatched stress management groups.

Canonical Correlation

With a simple correlation we analyzed the nature of the association between two variables, like anxiety and performance. However, there are many situations where one may want to examine the nature of the association between two *sets* of variables. For example, we may wish to relate a set of interest variables to a set of academic achievement variables, or a set of biological variables to a set of behavioral variables, or a set of stimulus variables to a set of response variables. Canonical correlation is a procedure for breaking down the complex association present in such situations into additive pieces. Thus, the objective in canonical correlation is:

Objective: Determine the number and nature of independent relationships existing between two sets of variables.

Example

Tetenbaum (1975), in a study of the validity of student ratings of teachers, hypothesized that specified student needs would be related to ratings of specific teacher orientations congruent with those needs. Student needs were assessed by the Personality Research Form, and fell into four broad categories: need for control, need for intellectual striving, need for gregariousness, and need for ascendancy. There were a total of 12 need variables. There were also 12 teacher-rating variables. These two sets of variables were analyzed using canonical correlation. The first canonical dimension revealed quite cleanly the intellectual striving—rating correspondence and the ascendancy need—rating correspondence. The second canonical dimension revealed the control need-rating correspondence, and the third the gregariousness need-rating correspondence. This example is considered in detail in the chapter on canonical correlation.

1.7   THE SAS AND SPSSX STATISTICAL PACKAGES

The Statistical Analysis System (SAS) and the Statistical Package for the Social Sciences (SPSSX) were selected for use in this text for several reasons:

1. They are very widely distributed.
2. They are easy to use.
3. They do a very wide range of analyses — from simple descriptive statistics to various analysis of variance designs to all kinds of complex multivariate analyses (factor analysis, multivariate analysis of variance, discriminant analysis, multiple regression, etc.).
4. They are well documented, having been in development for over two decades.

The control language that is used by both packages is quite natural, and you will see that with a little practice complex analyses are run quite easily, and with a small set of control line instructions. Getting output is relatively easy; however, this can be a mixed blessing. Because it is so easy to get output, it is also easy to get "garbage." Hence, although we illustrate the complete control lines in this text for running various analyses, there are several other facets that are much more important, such as interpretation of printout (in particular, knowing what to focus on in the printout), careful selection of variables, adequate sample size for reliable results, checking for outliers, and knowing what assumptions are important to check for a given analysis.

It is assumed that the reader will be accessing the packages through use of a terminal (on a system such as the VAX) or a microcomputer. Also, we limit our attention to examples where the data is part of the control lines (inline data, as SPSSX refers to it). It is true that fairly often in practice data will be accessed from disk or tape. However, accessing data from tape or disk, along with data management (e.g., interleaving or matching files) is a whole other arena we do not wish to enter. For those who are interested, however, SAS is very nicely set up for ease of file manipulation.

Structurally, a SAS program is composed of three fundamental blocks:

1. statements setting up the data
2. the data lines
3. procedure (PROC) statements — procedures are SAS computer programs which read the data and do various statistical analyses.

To illustrate how to set up the control lines, suppose we wish to compute the correlations between locus of control, achievement motivation and achievement in language for a hypothetical set of 9 subjects. First we create a data set and give it a name. The name *must* begin with a letter and be 8 or less characters. Let us call the data set LOCUS. Now, each SAS statement *must* end with a semicolon. So our first SAS line looks like this

DATA LOCUS;

The next statement needed is called an INPUT statement. This is where we give names for our variables and indicate the format of the data (i.e., how the data is arranged on each line). We will use what is called free format. With this format the scores for each variable do not have to be in specific columns. However, at least one blank column must separate the score for each variable from the next variable. Furthermore, we will put in our INPUT statement the following symbols @@. In SAS this set of symbols allows you to put the data for more than one subject on the same line.

In SAS, as with the other packages, there are certain rules for variable names. Each variable name must begin with a letter and be 8 or less characters. The variable name can contain numbers, but *not* special characters or an imbedded blank(s). For example, I.Q., $x1 + x2$ and also SOC CLAS, are not valid variable names. We have special characters in the first two names (periods in I.Q. and the $+$ in $x1 + x2$) and there is an imbedded blank in the abbreviation for social class.

Our INPUT statement is as follows:

INPUT LOCUS ACHMOT ACHLANG @@;

Following the INPUT statement there is a CARDS statement, which tells SAS that the data is to follow. Thus, the first three statements here setting up the data look like this:

DATA LOCUS;
INPUT LOCUS ACHMOT ACHLANG @@;
CARDS;

Recall that the next structural part of a SAS program is the set of data lines. Remember there are three variables, so we have three scores for each subject. We will put the scores for three subjects on each data line. Adding the data lines to the above three statements, we now have the following part of the SAS program:

```
DATA LOCUS;
INPUT LOCUS ACHMOT ACHLANG @@;
CARDS;
11   23   31   13   25   38   21   28   29
21   34   28   14   36   37   29   20   37
17   24   39   19   30   39   23   28   41
```

The first 3 scores (11, 23, and 31) are the scores on locus of control, achievement motivation, and achievement in language for the first subject, the next 3 numbers (13, 25, and 38) are the scores on these variables for subject 2, etc.

Now we come to the last structural part of a SAS program, calling up some SAS procedure(s) to do whatever statistical analysis(es) we desire. In this case we want correlations, and the SAS procedure for that is called CORR. Also, as mentioned earlier, we should always print the data. For this we use PROC PRINT. Adding these lines we get our complete SAS program:

```
DATA LOCUS;
INPUT LOCUS ACHMOT ACHLANG @@;
CARDS;
11  23  31  13  25  38  21  28  29
21  34  28  14  36  37  29  20  37
17  24  39  19  30  39  23  28  41
PROC CORR;
PROC PRINT;
```

Note there is a semicolon at the end of each statement, but *not* for the data lines.

In Table 1.3 we present some of the basic rules of the control language for SAS, and in Table 1.4 give the complete SAS control lines for obtaining a set of correlations (this is the example we just went over in detail), a *t* test, a one way ANOVA and a simple regression. Although the rules are basic, they are important. For example, failing to end a statement in SAS with a semicolon, or using a variable name longer than 8 characters will cause the program to terminate. The four sets of control lines in Table 1.4 show the structural similarity of the control line flow for different types of analyses. Notice in each case we start with the DATA statement, than an INPUT statement (naming the variables being read in and describing the format of the data), and then the CARDS statement preceding the data. Then, after the data, one or more PROC statements are used to perform the wanted statistical analysis, or to print the data (PROC PRINT).

These 4 sets of control lines serve as useful models for running analyses of the same type, where only the variable names change and/or the names and number of variables change. For example, suppose you want all correlations on 5 attitudinal variables (call them X1, X2, X3, X4 and X5). Then the control lines are:

```
DATA ATTITUDE;
INPUT X1 X2 X3 X4 X5 @@;
CARDS;
DATA LINES
PROC CORR;
PROC PRINT;
```

TABLE 1.3
Some Basic Elements of the SAS Control Language

Non-column oriented. Columns only relevant when using column input.

SAS statements give instructions. Each statement *must* end with a semicolon.

Structurally a SAS program composed of three fundamental blocks:

1) statements setting up the data (2) the data lines and (3) procedure (PROC) statements — procedures are SAS computer programs which read the data and do various statistical analyses.

DATA SETUP — First there is the DATA statement where you are creating a data set. The name for the data set must begin with a letter and be 8 or less characters.

VARIABLE NAMES — must be 8 or less characters, must begin with a letter, and can not have special characters or blanks.

COLUMN INPUT — scores for the variables go in specific columns.

If the variable is non-numeric then we need to put a $ after the variable name.

EXAMPLE — Suppose we have a group of subjects measured on IQ, attitude toward education, and grade point average (GPA), and will label them as M for male and F for female.

SEX $ 1 IQ 3–5 ATTITUDE 7–8 GPA 10–12.2

This tells SAS that sex (M or F) is in column 1, IQ in columns 3 to 5, ATTITUDE in columns 7 and 8 and GPA in columns 10 to 12.

The .2 is to insert a decimal point *before* the last two digits.

FREE FORMAT — the scores for the variables do not have to be in specific columns, they simply need to be separated from each other by at least one blank.

The CARDS statement follows the DATA and INPUT statements and precedes the data lines.

ANALYSIS ON SUBSET OF VARIABLES — analysis on a subset of variables from the INPUT statement is done through the VAR (abbreviation for VARIABLE) statement. For example if we had 6 variables (X1 X2 X3 X4 X5 X6) on the INPUT statement and only wished correlations for the first three, then we would insert VAR X1 X2 X3 after the PROC CORR statement.

STATISTICS FOR SUBGROUPS — obtained through use of BY statement Suppose we want the correlations for males and females on variables X, Y and Z. If the subjects have not been sorted on sex, then we sort them first using PROC SORT, and the control lines are   PROC CORR;
                          PROC SORT;
                          BY SEX;

MISSING VALUES — these are represented with either periods or blanks. If you are using FIXED format (i.e., data for variables in specific columns), then use blanks for missing data. If you are using FREE format, then you must use periods to represent missing data.

CREATING NEW VARIABLES — put the name for the new variable on the left and insert the statement after the INPUT statement. For example, to create a subtest score for the first 3 items on a test, use TOTAL = ITEM1 + ITEM2 + ITEM3. Or, to create a difference score from pretest and posttest data, use

DIFF = POSTTEST-PRETEST

Some basic elements of the SPSSX control language are given in Table 1.5, and the *complete* control lines for obtaining a set of correlations, a *t* test, a one-way ANOVA and a simple regression analysis with this package are presented in Table 1.6.

TABLE 1.4
SAS Control Lines for Set of Correlations, *t* Test, One-Way ANOVA and a Simple Regression

CORRELATIONS		*T* TEST
①	DATA LOCUS;	DATA ATTITUDE;
②	INPUT LOCUS ACHMOT;	⑤ INPUT TREAT $ ATT @@;
	ACHLANG @@;	CARDS;
③	CARDS;	C 82 C 95 C 89 C 99 C 87
	11 23 31 13 25 38 21 28 29	C 79 C 98 C 86
	21 34 28 14 36 37 29 20 27	T 94 T 97 T 98 T 93 T 96
	17 24 39 19 30 39 23 28 41	T 99 T 88 T 92 T 94 T 90
④	PROC CORR;	⑥ PROC TTEST;
	PROC PRINT;	CLASS TREAT;

ONE WAY ANOVA		SIMPLE REGRESSION
	DATA ONEWAY;	DATA REGRESS;
	INPUT GPID Y @@;	INPUT Y X @@;
	CARDS;	CARDS;
⑦	1 2 1 3 1 5 1 6	34 8 23 11 26 12
	2 7 2 9 2 11	31 9 27 14 37 15
	3 4 3 5 3 8 3 11 3 12	19 6 25 13 33 18
⑧	PROC MEANS;	PROC REG SIMPLE CORR;
	BY GPID;	MODEL Y = X;
⑨	PROC ANOVA;	SELECTION=STEPWISE;
	CLASS GPID;	
	MEANS GPID/TUKEY;	

① Here we are giving a name to the data set. Remember it must be eight or less letters and must begin with a letter. Note that there is a semicolon at the end of the line, and at the end of *every* line for all 4 examples (except for the data lines).

② Note that the names for the variables all begin with a letter and are less than or equal to 8 characters. The double @@ is needed in order to put the data for more than one subject on the same data line; here we have data for 3 subjects on each line.

③ When the data is part of the control lines, as here, then this CARDS command always precedes the data.

④ PROC (short for procedure) CORR yields the correlations, and PROC PRINT gives a listing of the data.

⑤ The $ after TREAT is used to denote a non-numeric variable; note in the data lines that TREAT is either *C*(control) or *T*(treatment).

⑥ We call up the t test procedure and tell it that TREAT is the grouping variable.

⑦ The first number of each pair is the group identification of the subject and the second number is the score on the dependent variable.

⑧ This PROC MEANS is necessary to obtain the means on the dependent variable in each group.

⑨ The ANOVA procedure is called and GPID is identified as the grouping (independent) variable through this CLASS statement.

TABLE 1.5
Some Basic Elements of the SPSSX Control Language

SPSSX operates on commands and subcommands.

It is column oriented to the extent that each command begins in column 1 and continues for as many lines as needed. All continuation lines are indented at least one column.

Examples of Commands: TITLE, DATA LIST, BEGIN DATA, COMPUTE

The title may be put in apostrophes, and may be up to 60 characters.

All subcommands begin with a keyword followed by an equal sign, then the specifications, and are terminated with a slash.

Each subcommand is indented at least one column.

Subcommands are further specifications for the commands.

For example, if the command is DATA LIST, then DATA LIST FREE involves the subcommand FREE which indicates the data will be in free format.

FIXED FORMAT – this is the default format for data

EXAMPLE – We have a group of subjects measured on IQ, attitude toward education, and grade point average (GPA), and will label them as M for male and F for female.

DATA LIST FIXED/SEX 1(A) IQ 3 – 5 ATTITUDE 7-8 GPA 10-12(2)

A non-numeric variable is indicated in SPSSX by specifying (A) after the variable name and location.

The rest of the statement indicates IQ is in columns 3 through 5, attitude is in columns 7 and 8, and GPA in columns 10 through 12.

An *implied* decimal point is indicated by specifying the implied number of decimal places in parentheses; here that is two.

FREE FORMAT – the variable must be in the same order for each case but do not have to be in the same location. Also, multiple cases can go on the same line, with the values for the variables separated by blanks or commas.

When that data is part of the command file, then the BEGIN DATA command precedes the data and the END DATA follows the last line of data.

We can use the keyword TO in specifying a set of consecutive variables, rather than listing all the variables. For example, if we had the six variables X1,X2,X3,X4,X5,X6, the following subcommands are equivalent:

VARIABLES = X1,X2,X3,X4,X5,X6/ or VARIABLES = X1 TO X6/

MISSING VALUES – The missing values command consists of a variables names(s) with value for each variable in parentheses:

Examples: MISSING VALUES X (8) Y (9)

Here 8 is used to denote missing for variable X and 9 to denote missing for variable Y.

If you want the same missing value designation for all variables, then use the keyword ALL, followed by the missing value designation, e.g., MISSING VALUES ALL (0)

If you are using FREE format, do *not* use a blank to indicate a missing value, rather assign some number to indicate missing.

CREATING NEW VARIABLES – THE COMPUTE COMMAND

The COMPUTE command is used to create a new variable, or to transform an existing variable.

Examples: COMPUTE TOTAL = ITEM1 + ITEM2 + ITEM3 + ITEM4

COMPUTE NEWTIME = SQRT(TIME)

SELECTING A SAMPLE OF CASES –

To obtain a *random* sample of cases, select an approximate percentage of cases desired (say 10%) and use SAMPLE .10

If you want an exact 10% sample, say exactly 100 cases from 1000, then use SAMPLE 100 FROM 1000

You can also select a sample(s) based on logical criteria.

For example, suppose you only want to use females from a data set, and they are coded as 2's. You can accomplish this with SELECT IF (SEX EQ 2)

TABLE 1.6
SPSSX Control Lines for Set of Correlations, *t* Test, One-Way ANOVA and Simple Regression

CORRELATIONS		*T* TEST
	TITLE 'CORRELATIONS FOR 3 VARS'	TITLE 'T TEST'
		DATA LIST FREE/TREAT ATT
①	DATA LIST FREE/LOCUS ACMOT ACHLANG	BEGIN DATA
②	BEGIN DATA	⑥ 1 82 1 95 1 89 1 99
	11 23 31 13 25 38 21 28 29	1 87 1 79 1 98 1 86
	11 34 28 14 36 37 29 20 37	2 94 2 97 2 98 2 93
	17 24 39 19 30 39 23 28 41	2 96 2 99 2 88 2 92
	END DATA	2 94 2 90
③	CORRELATIONS	END DATA
	VARIABLES = LOCUS ACHMOT ACHLANG/	⑦ T-TEST GROUPS = TREAT(1,2)/
	PRINT = TWOTAIL/	VARIABLES = ATT/
④	STATISTICS = DESCRIPTIVES/	

ONE WAY		SIMPLE REGRESSION
	TITLE 'ONE WAY ANOVA'	TITLE 'ONE PREDICTOR'
	DATA LIST FREE/GPID Y	DATA LIST FREE/Y X
	BEGIN DATA	⑤ LIST
	1 2 1 3 1 5 1 6	BEGIN DATA
	2 7 2 9 2 11	34 8 23 11 26 12
	3 4 3 5 3 8 3 11 3 12	31 9 27 14 37 15
	END DATA	19 6 25 13 33 18
⑧	ONEWAY Y BY GPID(1,3)/	END DATA
	RANGES = TUKEY/	REGRESSION DESCRIPTIVES =
⑨	STATISTICS ALL	DEFAULT/
		VARIABLES = Y X/
		DEPENDENT = Y/STEPWISE/

①The FREE on this DATA LIST command is a further specification, indicating that the data will be in free format.

②When the data is part of the command file, it is preceded by BEGIN DATA and terminated by END DATA.

③This VARIABLES subcommand specifies the variables to be analyzed.

④This yields the means and standard deviations for all variables.

⑤This LIST command gives a listing of the data.

⑥The first number for each pair is the group identification and the second is the score for the dependent variable. Thus, 82 is the score for the first subject in group 1 and 97 is the score for the second subject in group 2.

⑦The t test procedure is called and the number of levels for the grouping variables is put in parentheses.

⑧ONEWAY is the code name for the one way analysis of variance procedure in SPSSX. The numbers in parentheses indicate the levels of the groups being compared, in this case levels 1 through 3. If there were 6 groups, this would become GPID(1,6).

⑨This yields the means, standard deviations and the homogeneity of variance tests.

A More Complex Example Using SPSSX

Often in data analysis things are not as neat or clean as in the previous examples. There may be missing data, or we may need to do some recoding, we may need to create new variables, and we may wish to obtain some reliability information on the variables which will be used in the analysis. We now consider an example in which we deal with 3 of the above 4 issues. I will not deal with recoding in this example; readers interested may refer to the second edition of this text for the details.

Before we get to the example, it is important for the reader to understand that there are different types of reliability, and they will not necessarily be of similar order of magnitude. First, there is test-retest (or parallel or alternate forms) reliability where the same subjects are measured at two different points in time. There is also interrater reliability, where you examine the consistency of judges or raters. And there is internal consistency reliability, where you are measuring the subjects at a single point in time as to how their responses on different items correlate or "hang together". The following comments from the excellent *By Design* book by Light, Singer, and Willett, are important to keep in mind, "Because different reliability estimators are sensitive to different sources of error, they will not necessarily agree. An instrument can have high internal consistency, for example, but low test-retest reliability . . . This means you must examine several different reliability estimates before deciding whether your instrument is really reliable. Each separate estimate presents an incomplete picture." (p. 167)

Now, let us consider the example. A survey researcher is conducting a pilot study on a 12-item scale to check out possible ambiguous working, whether any items are sensitive, whether they discriminate, etc. She administers the scale to 16 subjects. The items are scaled from 1 to 5, with 1 representing strongly agree and 5 representing strongly disagree. There is some missing data, which is coded as a 0. The data is presented below:

ID	1	2	3	4	5	6	7	8	9	10	11	12	SEX
1	1	2	2	3	3	1	1	2	2	1	2	2	1
2	1	2	2	3	3	3	1	2	2	1	1	1	1
3	1	2	1	3	3	2	3	3	2	1	2	3	1
4	2	2	4	2	3	3	2	2	3	3	2	3	1
5	2	3	2	4	2	1	2	3	0	3	4	0	1
6	2	3	2	3	3	2	3	4	3	2	4	2	1
7	3	4	4	3	5	2	2	1	2	3	3	4	1
8	3	2	3	4	4	3	4	3	3	3	4	2	1
9	3	3	4	2	4	3	3	4	5	3	5	3	2
10	4	4	5	5	3	3	5	4	4	4	5	3	2
11	4	4	0	5	5	5	4	3	0	5	4	4	2
12	4	4	4	5	5	4	3	3	5	4	4	5	2
13	4	4	0	4	3	2	5	1	3	3	0	4	2
14	5	5	3	4	4	4	4	5	3	5	5	3	2
15	5	5	4	5	3	5	5	4	4	5	3	5	2
16	5	4	3	4	3	5	4	4	3	2	2	3	2

Again, the 0 indicates missing data. Thus, we see that subject 5 did not respond to items 9 and 12, subject 11 didn't respond to items 3 and 9, and finally subject 13 didn't respond to items 3 and 11. If data is missing on any variable for a subject, it is dropped from the analysis by SPSSX.

Suppose the first 8 subjects in the above file are male and the last 8 are female. The researcher wishes to compare males and females on 3 subtests of this scale obtained as follows:

SUBTEST1 = I1 + I2 + I3 + I4 + I5

SUBTEST2 = I6 + I7 + I8 + I9

SUBTEST3 = I10 + I11 + I12

To create these new variables we make use of three COMPUTE statements (cf Table 1.3). For example, for SUBTEST3, we have

COMPUTE SUBTEST3 = I10 + I11 + I12

To determine the internal consistency of the above 3 subscales, we access the RELIABILITY program and tell it to compute Cronbach's alpha for each of the three subscales with three subcommands. Finally, suppose the researcher uses three t tests for independent samples to compare males and females on these 3 subtests. The complete control lines for doing all of the above are:

```
TITLE 'SURVEY RESEARCH WITH MISSING DATA'
DATA LIST FREE/ID I1 I2 I3 I4 I5 I6 I7 I8 I9 I10 I11 I12 SEX
BEGIN DATA
1 1 2 2 3 3 1 1 2 2 1 2 2 1
        DATA LINES CONTINUE
16 5 4 3 4 3 5 4 4 3 2 2 3 2
END DATA
MISSING VALUES ALL (0)
COMPUTE SUBTEST1 = I1 + I2 + I3 + I4 + I5
COMPUTE SUBTEST2 = I6 + I7 + I8 + I9
COMPUTE SUBTEST3 = I10 + I11 + I12
RELIABILITY VARIABLES=I1 TO I12/
   SCALE(SUBTEST1)=I1 TO I5/
   SCALE(SUBTEST2)=I6 TO I9/
   SCALE(SUBTEST3)=I10 I11 I12/
   STATISTICS=CORR/
T-TEST GROUPS=SEX(1,2)/
   VARIABLES=SUBTEST1 SUBTEST2 SUBTEST3/
```

Before leaving this example, we wish to note that missing data is a fairly common occurrence in certain areas of research, and there is no simple solution for this problem. If it can be assumed that the data is missing *at random,* then there is a sophisticated procedure available for obtaining good estimates (Johnson & Wichern, 1988, pp 197–202). On the other hand, if the random missing data assumption is not tenable (usually the case), then there is no general consensus as to what should be done. There are various suggestions, like using the mean of the scores on the variable as an estimate, or using regression analysis (Frane, 1976). Probably the "best" solution is to make every attempt to minimize the problem before and during the study, rather than having to manufacture data. The statistical packages SAS and SPSSX have various ways of handling missing data. The default option for both, however, is to delete the case if there is missing data on any variable for the subject.

Examining the *pattern* of missing values is important. If, for example, there is at least a moderate amount of missing data, and most of it is concentrated on just a few variables, it might be wise to drop those variables from the analysis. Otherwise, you will suffer too large a loss of subjects.

SAS and SPSSX Statistical Manuals

The two most recent statistical manuals from SAS that the reader should be aware of are *SAS/STAT USER'S GUIDE (VOLUME 1, ANOVA-FREO,* Version 6, 4th Ed., 1990) and *SAS/STAT USER'S GUIDE (VOLUME 2, GLM-VARCOMP,* Version 6, 4th Ed., 1990). The major statistical procedures contained in Volume 1 are clustering techniques, structural equation modeling (a very extensive program called CALIS), categorical data analysis (another very extensive program called CATMOD), discriminant analysis, and factor analysis. One of the major statistical procedures that is included in Volume 2 is the GLM (General Linear Models) program, which is quite comprehensive and handles equal and unequal factorial ANOVA designs, does analysis of covariance, multivariate analysis of variance, and repeated measures analysis. Also contained in Volume 2 are several fundamental regression procedures, including REG and RSREG, a procedure called (LOGISTIC) for fitting regression models to data where the dependent variable is binary, and PROC NLIN, which fits nonlinear regression models using the least squares method.

These two volumes replaced *SAS USER'S GUIDE: STATISTICS,* Version 5, 1985. Any frequent statistical user of SAS should have both of these manuals. Based on the past record of SAS, these two volumes will probably remain the main statistical guides for several years.

With respect to statistical manuals for SPSSX, the most comprehensive is *SPSSX USER'S GUIDE* (3rd Ed., 1988). This manual does not tend to serve that well as a pedagogical aid to a multivariate course(s) based on my two years of experience with it. It is recommended here that instructors consider *SPSS INTRODUCTORY STATISTICS STUDENT GUIDE*

(1990) as a manual supplement for a multivariate course(s). This manual is much more readable, much less expensive, and in fact has several chapters on multivariate techniques (the title is somewhat of a misnomer). The *SPSSX USER'S GUIDE* is still important to have available for reference, probably on library reserve and/or from the instructor.

The introductory guide has chapters on multiple regression, discriminant analysis, factor analysis, cluster analysis, and multivariate analysis of variance. This guide has nice introductory chapters on preparing and defining data and data transformations and selection. In addition, there is a very nice treatment of a newer SPSSX procedure called EXAMINE (not documented in the 1988 *USERS GUIDE*). This procedure provides a variety of descriptive plots and statistics for exploring your data (to spot outliers, to check assumptions) before jumping into tests of significance. Among some of the important features in EXAMINE are stem and leaf plots, boxplots, the Levene test for homogeneity of variance (one of the better tests), and the Shapiro-Wilks test for normality (a quite powerful test for detecting lack of normality in small samples).

It should be understood that although we have given some very important, basic elements of the packages in Tables 1.3 and 1.5, and present complete control lines for running various analyses in this text, our treatment is in no sense a substitute for the SAS and SPSSX manuals. All the contingencies one might encounter in a practical problem can't be covered in this text; however, a way of dealing with them undoubtedly will be found in the manuals. Also, although certain analyses are done with one package (e.g., SPSSX) while other analyses are done with SAS, this does *not* mean we are advocating that particular package for that analysis. The choice is simply illustrative, unless otherwise indicated.

Finally, it should be kept in mind that SAS and SPSSX execute their programs within some type of *operating system*. The operating system controls all work done by the computer, such as allocating computer resources and storing data. There are different operating systems for different types of computers. Some of the more common operating systems are described in the *SAS USER'S GUIDE: STATISTICS (VERSION 5, 1985)* in Appendix 3. For example, CMS and TSO for IBM and compatible mainframes, and VMS for the DIGITAL VAX. It is assumed in this text that the reader knows CMS, or whatever is necessary, to run SAS or SPSSX.

1.8 MICRO & NOTEBOOK COMPUTERS, WINDOWS AND THE PACKAGES

The SAS and SPSS statistical packages were developed in the 1960's, and they were in widespread use during the 1970's on mainframe computers.

The emergence of microcomputers in the late 1970's had implications for the way in which data is processed today. Vastly increased memory capacity and more sophisticated microprocessors made it possible for the packages to become available on microcomputers by the mid 1980's.

I made the statement in the first edition of this text (1986) that, "The days of dependence on the mainframe computer, even for the powerful statistical packages, will probably diminish considerably within the next 5 to 10 years. We are truly entering a new era in data processing." In the second edition (1992) I noted that this has certainly come true in at least two ways. Individuals were either running SAS or SPSS on their personal computers, or were accessing the packages via minicomputers, such as the VAX.

Rapid changes in computer technology have brought us to the point now where "windows" versions of the packages are available, and sophisticated analyses can be run by simply clicking a series of buttons. About one year ago I purchased a Compaq Contura 4/25C notebook computer with passive color. It had 4meg of RAM, a 120 megabyte hard disk drive, ran at 25 megaherz and had a built in math co-processor. By adding 4 megs of RAM, and establishing a "swap file" of 15 megs, I am able to run analyses smoothly and quickly for SPSS WINDOWS, Release 6.1 and LISREL 8.10 (to do structural equation modeling; confirmatory factor analysis, path analysis, etc.).

The reader needs to be aware, however, that because of the way SPSS for windows is structured you will need the base package (for multiple regression) *and* PROFESSIONAL STATISTICS module (to do factor analysis and discriminant analysis), *and* the ADVANCED STATISTICS module (to do MANOVA, MANCOVA, repeated measures and loglinear analysis) to run all the analyses in this book (except for confirmatory factor analysis. Relevant books are *SPSS for Windows: Base System User's Guide, Release 6.0* (1993); *SPSS Advanced Statistics 6.1* (1994) and *SPSS Professional Statistics 6.1* (1994).

Also, if you wish to do structural equation modeling, you will need LISREL, which is a separate module sold through SPSS. An excellent book here is *LISREL 8: The Simplis Command Language* by Joreskog and Sorbom (1993). Readers who have struggled with earlier versions of LISREL may find it difficult to believe, but the SIMPLIS language in LISREL 8 makes running analyses very easy. The above text has several nice examples to illustrate this fact.

A couple of other comments that will be helpful for readers using SPSS for windows. If you are using *matrix* data (like feeding in a correlation or covariance matrix to do a factor analysis), you can't run the analysis by just clicking buttons. Instead you must run the analysis from the SYNTAX WINDOW. That is, you insert the matrix as part of the command file, and run it as such.

How to run command syntax in a syntax window is far from obvious. First, you must highlight the commands you wish to run, and then click on the run syntax tool ⊡ (this is underneath UTILITIES). See pages 345–346 in *SPSS Advanced Statistics 6.1*.

The syntax to be used in running either package on microcomputers is essentially identical to that used on the mainframe computer or a minicomputer such as the VAX. What changes is the operating system within which the package is embedded. For SAS this is the SAS Display Manager, which is described in detail in *SAS Language Guide for Personal Computers* (Version 6, 1985). However, the first book to read when using SAS on the microcomputer (personal computer) is the *SAS Introductory Guide for Personal Computers* (Version 6, 1985). In my opinion, this book does a better job than some of the more recent manuals that have followed.

The SAS display manager divides the screen into three windows (in different colors): an output window, a log window, and a program editor window. The output window is where the output from a SAS run would scroll by. The log window displays messages (including error messages in red) from SAS as well as the SAS statements as they are executed. The program window is where you enter the SAS statements to run a particular analysis. We will not describe the operating system further, as the best way to learn SAS PC is while working at the personal coputer with a knowledgable instructor guiding you.

Factorial ANOVA on SAS PC—Accessing Data from Disk

Although the major focus in this text is the use of inline data as part of the command file, it is very easy to access data from disk with SAS PC. To illustrate we consider data from a study by Philips and Jahanshahi of the London University Institute of Psychiatry. The study examined the effectiveness of 4 different treatments for two types of headache sufferers: migraine and tension. The design was thus a 2 (sufferer type) × 4 (treatments) factorial. The subjects were pretested and posttested on two measures. We consider a factorial ANOVA on one of the posttests (POSTU). This data set was on a 3.5 inch disk, along with several other data sets. The factorial ANOVA was run on SAS PC, that is, on the personal computer version of SAS for microcomputers. The complete control lines for the run are given below:

```
TITLE 'HEADACHE STUDY';
DATA TWOWAY;
INFILE 'A: HEADACHE';
INPUT HEADACHE TREAT PREU PREUP POSTU POSTUP @@;
PROC GLM;
CLASS HEADACHE TREAT;
MODEL POSTU = HEADACHE TREAT HEADACHE*TREAT;
RUN;
```

We wish to elaborate on the INFILE statement. In all previous runs of SAS, the data was *part* of the command file. In this case the data are external to the control lines. As noted in the *SAS Introductory Guide for Personal Computers, Version 6,* 1985: "If your data are stored on your fixed disk (the hard drive) or a diskette, then they are ready to read using your PC. If they are stored on disk or tape on the main computer, then they must be downloaded to a file on your PC" (p. 24). We use the INFILE statement to point to the data, that is, to tell SAS where the data is located. I called the data HEADACHE and it was on a disk that I put in drive A on my IBM Personal System computer. Note that the drive information and file name are put in apostrophes after the INFILE designation, with a colon after the drive name. If the data had been on the hard drive, denoted by C, then the INFILE statement becomes INFILE 'C: HEADACHE';.

1.9.   SOME ISSUES UNIQUE TO MULTIVARIATE ANALYSIS

Many of the techniques discussed in this text are *mathematical maximization procedures,* and hence there is great opportunity for capitalization on chance. Often, as the reader will see as we move along in the text, the results "look great" on a given sample, but do not generalize to other samples. Thus, the results are sample-specific and of limited scientific utility. Reliability of results is a real concern.

The notion of a *linear combination* of variables is fundamental to all of the types of analysis we discuss. A general linear combination for p variables is given by:

$$y = a_1x_1 + a_2x_2 + a_3x_3 + \ldots + a_px_p,$$

where $a_1, a_2, a_3, \ldots, a_p$ are the coefficients for the variables. The above definition is abstract; however, we give some simple examples of linear combinations that the reader will be familiar with.

Suppose we have a treatment vs. control group design with the subjects pretested and posttested on some variable. Then sometimes analysis is done on the difference scores (gain scores), i.e., posttest-pretest. If we denote the pretest variable by x_1 and the posttest variable by x_2, then the difference variable $y = x_2 - x_1$ is a simple linear combination, where $a_1 = -1$ and $a_2 = 1$.

As another example of a simple linear combination, suppose we wished to sum three subtest scores on a test (x_1, x_2, and x_3). Then the newly created sum variable $y = x_1 + x_2 + x_3$ is a linear combination, where $a_1 = a_2 = a_3 = 1$.

Still another example of linear combinations that the reader has encountered in an intermediate statistics course is that of contrasts among means, as in the Scheffe' post hoc procedure or in planned comparisons. Consider the following 4-group ANOVA, where T_3 is a combination treatment, and T_4 is a control group.

T_1	T_2	T_3	T_4
μ_1	μ_2	μ_3	μ_4

Then the following meaningful contrast

$$L_1 = \frac{\mu_1 + \mu_2}{2} - \mu_3$$

is a linear combination, where $a_1 = a_2 = \frac{1}{2}$ and $a_3 = -1$, while the following contrast among means

$$L_1 = \frac{\mu_1 + \mu_2 + \mu_3}{3} - \mu_4$$

is also a linear combination, where $a_1 = a_2 = a_3 = \frac{1}{3}$ and $a_4 = -1$. The notions of mathematical maximization and linear combinations are combined in many of the multivariate procedures. For example, in multiple regression we talk about the linear combination of the predictors that is maximally correlated with the dependent variable, and in principal components analysis the linear combinations of the variables which account for maximum portions of the total variance are considered.

APPENDIX:
DEFINING A MEASURE OF STATISTICAL DISTANCE

Consider two points (x_1, y_1) and (x_2, y_2) in the plane. Then the ordinary (sometimes called Euclidean) distance between them is obtained by use of the Pythagorean theorem, which states that the square of the hypotenuse (side opposite the right angle) is equal to the sum of the squares of the two legs. This is shown below:

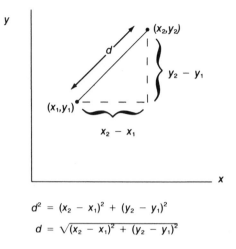

$$d^2 = (x_2 - x_1)^2 + (y_2 - y_1)^2$$

$$d = \sqrt{(x_2 - x_1)^2 + (y_2 - y_1)^2}$$

For example, if the two points were (2,3) and (4,6), then the distance would be $d = \sqrt{(4 - 2)^2 + (6 - 3)^2} = \sqrt{13}. = 3.606$.

As Johnson and Wichern (1982) note, "Straight line or Euclidean distance is unsatisfactory for most statistical purposes. This is because each coordinate (variable) contributes equally to the calculation of the Euclidean distance. When the coordinates represent measurements that are subject to random fluctuations of differing magnitudes, it is often desirable to weight coordinates subject to a great deal of variability less heavily than those that are not highly variable (p. 20)." In defining a statistical measure of distance then we must take into account two factors: (1) differing variability for the variables, which can occur simply because the variables have been scaled differently, and (2) the correlation between the variables.

The squared, standardized distance which adjusts for differing variability on the variables is given by:

$$d^2 = \frac{(x_{i1} - \bar{x}_1)^2}{s_1^2} + \frac{(x_{i2} - \bar{x}_2)^2}{s_2^2}$$

where x_{i1} and x_{i2} represent the scores for subject i on variables 1 and 2 and $\bar{x}_1$ and $\bar{x}_2$ represent the means on the variables.

To illustrate the above formula, suppose we have two variables x_1 and x_2 with variances of 36 and 100 and that the means are 4 and 6. For the moment, assume that x_1 and x_2 are uncorrelated. We wish to determine the distance of a subject with scores (2,3) from the vector of means, i.e., from (4,6).

$$d^{*2} = \frac{(2-4)^2}{36} + \frac{(3-6)^2}{100} = .11 + .09 = .20$$

These are the same two points we considered earlier with the unstandardized Euclidean distance formula. It is important to note that using the unstandardized formula it was found that a greater portion of the squared distance (9) was due to x_2 (denoted by y earlier). After appropriate standardization for the different variances, we find that the greater portion of the distance is due to x_1 (.11 of .20).

Now, suppose the variables are moderately correlated, i.e., $r_{x1x2} = .50$. The Mahalanobis distance, which takes correlation into account, is given by

$$D^2 = \frac{1}{1-r^2} \left[\frac{(x_{i1} - \bar{x}_1)^2}{s_1^2} + \frac{(x_{i2} - \bar{x}_2)^2}{s_2^2} - \frac{2r(x_{i1} - \bar{x}_1)(x_{i2} - \bar{x}_2)}{s_1 s_2} \right]$$

Note that if the correlation is positive then the distance is reduced by an amount related to the third term inside the brackets. This is because some of the distance along the second dimension (on the second variable) is predictable from x_2's correlation with x_1.

Now we calculate the distance from (2,3) to (4,6), assuming a correlation of .50:

$$D^2 = \frac{1}{1-.25} \left[\frac{(2-4)^2}{36} + \frac{(3-6)^2}{100} - \frac{2(.5)(2-4)(3-6)}{6(10)} \right]$$

If the correlation is strong (e.g., .71), then the Mahalanobis distance is even smaller:

$$D^2 = \frac{1}{1-.50} \left[.11 + .09 - \frac{2(.71)(-2)(-3)}{60} \right] = .116$$

On the other hand, if the correlation is negative, then the distance will be *greater* than what it was when the variables were uncorrelated. To illustrate, suppose in the above example that the correlation between x_1 and x_2 was $-.50$. Then the distance is

$$D^2 = \frac{1}{1-.25} (.11 + .09 + .10) = .40$$

After we have covered matrices in Chapter 2, we define the Mahalanobis distance in terms of matrices for the general case of p variables in Chapter 3.

2 Matrix Algebra

2.1. INTRODUCTION

A matrix is simply a rectangular array of elements. The following are examples of matrices:

$$
\begin{bmatrix} 1 & 2 & 3 & 4 \\ 4 & 5 & 6 & 9 \end{bmatrix} \quad \begin{bmatrix} 1 & 2 & 1 \\ 2 & 3 & 5 \\ 5 & 6 & 8 \\ 1 & 4 & 10 \end{bmatrix} \quad \begin{bmatrix} 1 & 2 \\ 2 & 4 \end{bmatrix}
$$

$$
2 \times 4 \qquad\qquad 4 \times 3 \qquad 2 \times 2
$$

The numbers underneath each matrix are the dimensions of the matrix, and indicate the size of the matrix. The first number is the number of rows and the second number the number of columns. Thus, the first matrix is a 2×4 since it has 2 rows and 4 columns.

A familiar matrix in educational research is the score matrix. For example, suppose we had measured six subjects on three variables. We could represent all the scores as a matrix:

Variables

	1	2	3
1	10	4	18
2	12	6	21
3	13	2	20
4	16	8	16
5	12	3	14
6	15	9	13

Subjects (rows 1–6)

This is a 6×3 matrix. More generally, we can represent the scores of N subjects on p variables in a $N \times p$ matrix as follows:

Variables

$$
\begin{array}{c}
\\
1 \\
2 \\
\\
N
\end{array}
\begin{array}{cccccc}
1 & 2 & 3 & & & p \\
\left[\begin{array}{ccccc}
x_{11} & x_{12} & x_{13} & \cdots & x_{1p} \\
x_{21} & x_{22} & x_{23} & \cdots & x_{2p} \\
\vdots & \vdots & \vdots & & \vdots \\
x_{N1} & x_{N2} & x_{N3} & \cdots & x_{Np}
\end{array}\right]
\end{array}
$$

Subjects

The first subscript indicates the row and the second subscript the column. Thus, x_{12} represents the score of subject 1 on variable 2 and x_{2p} represents the score of subject 2 on variable p.

The *transpose* A' of a matrix A is simply the matrix obtained by interchanging rows and columns.

Examples

$$
A = \begin{bmatrix} 2 & 3 & 6 \\ 5 & 4 & 8 \end{bmatrix} \Rightarrow A' = \begin{bmatrix} 2 & 5 \\ 3 & 4 \\ 6 & 8 \end{bmatrix}
$$

The first row of A has become the first column of A' and the second row of A has become the second column of A'.

$$
B = \begin{bmatrix} 3 & 4 & 2 \\ 5 & 6 & 5 \\ 1 & 3 & 8 \end{bmatrix} \rightarrow B' = \begin{bmatrix} 3 & 5 & 1 \\ 4 & 6 & 3 \\ 2 & 5 & 8 \end{bmatrix}
$$

In general, if a matrix **A** has dimensions $r \times s$, then the dimensions of the transpose are $s \times r$.

A matrix with a single row is called a row vector, and a matrix with a single column is called a column vector. Vectors are always indicated by small letters and a row vector by a transpose, i.e., **x′**, **y′** etc. Throughout this text a matrix or vector will be denoted by boldface letters.

Examples

$$\mathbf{x'} = (1, 2, 3)$$

1×3 row vector

$$\mathbf{y} = \begin{bmatrix} 4 \\ 6 \\ 8 \\ 7 \end{bmatrix} \quad 4 \times 1 \text{ column vector}$$

A row vector that is of particular interest to us later is the vector of means for a group of subjects on several variables. For example, suppose we have measured 100 subjects on the California Psychological Inventory and have obtained their average scores on 5 of the subscales. We could represent their 5 means as a column vector, and the transpose of this column vector is a row vector **x′**.

$$\mathbf{x} = \begin{bmatrix} 24 \\ 31 \\ 22 \\ 27 \\ 30 \end{bmatrix} \rightarrow \mathbf{x'} = (24, 31, 22, 27, 30)$$

The elements on the diagonal running from upper left to lower right are said to be on the main diagonal of a matrix. A matrix **A** is said to be *symmetric* if the elements below the main diagonal are a mirror reflection of the corresponding elements above the main diagonal. This is saying $a_{12} = a_{21}$, $a_{13} = a_{31}$ and $a_{23} = a_{32}$ for a 3×3 matrix, since these are the corresponding pairs. This is illustrated below:

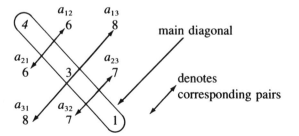

In general, a matrix $\mathbf{A}$ is symmetric if $a_{ij} = a_{ji}, i \neq j$, i.e., if all corresponding pairs of elements above and below the main diagonal are equal.

An example of a symmetric matrix that is frequently encountered in statistical work is that of a correlation matrix. For example, below is the matrix of intercorrelations for 4 subtests of the Differential Aptitude Test for boys:

	VR	NA	Cler.	Mech.
Verbal Reas.	1.00	.70	.19	.55
Numerical Abil.	.70	1.00	.36	.50
Clerical Speed	.19	.36	1.00	.16
Mechan. Reas.	.55	.50	.16	1.00

This matrix is obviously symmetric since, for example, the correlation between VR and NA is the same as the correlation between NA and VR.

Two matrices $\mathbf{A}$ and $\mathbf{B}$ are equal if and only if all corresponding elements are equal. That is to say, 2 matrices are equal only if they are identical.

2.2. ADDITION, SUBTRACTION, AND MULTIPLICATION OF A MATRIX BY A SCALAR

Two matrices $\mathbf{A}$ and $\mathbf{B}$ are added by adding corresponding elements

Example

$$\mathbf{A} = \begin{bmatrix} 2 & 3 \\ 3 & 4 \end{bmatrix} \quad \mathbf{B} = \begin{bmatrix} 6 & 2 \\ 2 & 5 \end{bmatrix}$$

$$\mathbf{A} + \mathbf{B} = \begin{bmatrix} 2+6 & 3+2 \\ 3+2 & 4+5 \end{bmatrix} = \begin{bmatrix} 8 & 5 \\ 5 & 9 \end{bmatrix}$$

Notice the elements in the (1, 1) positions, i.e., 2 and 6 have been added, etc.

Only matrices of the same dimensions can be added. Thus addition would not be defined for the matrices below:

$$\begin{bmatrix} 2 & 3 & 1 \\ 1 & 4 & 6 \end{bmatrix} + \begin{bmatrix} 1 & 4 \\ 5 & 6 \end{bmatrix} \quad \text{not defined}$$

Two matrices, of the same dimensions, are subtracted by subtracting corresponding elements.

$$
\underset{\mathbf{A}}{\begin{bmatrix} 2 & 1 & 5 \\ 3 & 2 & 6 \end{bmatrix}} - \underset{\mathbf{B}}{\begin{bmatrix} 1 & 4 & 2 \\ 1 & 2 & 5 \end{bmatrix}} = \underset{\mathbf{A} - \mathbf{B}}{\begin{bmatrix} 1 & -3 & 3 \\ 2 & 0 & 1 \end{bmatrix}}
$$

Multiplication of a matrix or a vector by a scalar (number) is accomplished by multiplying each element of the matrix or vector by the scalar.

Examples

$$
2\,(3, 1, 4) = (6, 2, 8) \qquad 1/3 \begin{bmatrix} 4 \\ 3 \end{bmatrix} = \begin{bmatrix} 4/3 \\ 1 \end{bmatrix}
$$

$$
4 \begin{bmatrix} 2 & 1 \\ 1 & 5 \end{bmatrix} = \begin{bmatrix} 8 & 4 \\ 4 & 20 \end{bmatrix}
$$

Multiplication of Matrices

In order to multiply two matrices they do not necessarily have to be of the same dimensions, however, there is a restriction as to when two matrices can be multiplied. Consider the product **AB**. Then *the number of columns in* **A** *must equal the number of rows in* **B**. For example, if **A** is 2 × 3, then **B** must have 3 rows, although **B** could have any number of columns. If two matrices can be multiplied they are said to be *conformable*. The dimensions of the product matrix, call it **C**, is simply the number of rows of **A** by number of columns of **B**. In the above example, if **B** were 3 × 4, then **C** would be a 2 × 4 matrix. In general then, if **A** is an $r \times s$ matrix and **B** is an $s \times t$ matrix, then the dimensions of the product **AB** are $r \times t$.

Example

$$
\underset{2 \times 3}{\overset{\mathbf{A}}{\begin{bmatrix} 2 & 1 & 3 \\ 4 & 5 & 6 \end{bmatrix}}} \quad \underset{3 \times 2}{\overset{\mathbf{B}}{\begin{bmatrix} 1 & 0 \\ 2 & 4 \\ -1 & 5 \end{bmatrix}}} = \underset{2 \times 2}{\overset{\mathbf{C}}{\begin{bmatrix} c_{11} & c_{12} \\ c_{21} & c_{22} \end{bmatrix}}}
$$

Notice first that **A** and **B** can be multiplied since the number of columns in **A** is 3 which is equal to the number of rows in **B**. The product matrix **C** is a 2×2, i.e., the outer dimensions of **A** and **B**. To obtain the element c_{11} (in the first row and first column), we multiply corresponding elements of the first row of **A** by the elements of the first column of **B**. Then, we simply add the sum of these products. To obtain c_{12} we take the sum of products of the corresponding elements of the first row of **A** by the second column of **B**. This procedure is presented below for all four elements of **C**:

Element

$$c_{11} \quad (2, 1, 3) \begin{pmatrix} 1 \\ 2 \\ -1 \end{pmatrix} = 2\,(1) + 1\,(2) + 3\,(-1) = 1$$

$$c_{12} \quad (2, 1, 3) \begin{pmatrix} 0 \\ 4 \\ 5 \end{pmatrix} = 2\,(0) + 1\,(4) + 3\,(5) = 19$$

$$c_{21} \quad (4, 5, 6) \begin{pmatrix} 1 \\ 2 \\ -1 \end{pmatrix} = 4\,(1) + 5\,(2) + 6\,(-1) = 8$$

$$c_{22} \quad (4, 5, 6) \begin{pmatrix} 0 \\ 4 \\ 5 \end{pmatrix} = 4\,(0) + 5\,(4) + 6\,(5) = 50$$

Therefore, the product matrix **C** is: $\mathbf{C} = \begin{bmatrix} 1 & 19 \\ 8 & 50 \end{bmatrix}$

Now we multiply two more matrices to illustrate an important property concerning matrix multiplication

Example

$$\overset{\mathbf{A}}{\begin{bmatrix} 2 & 1 \\ 1 & 4 \end{bmatrix}} \overset{\mathbf{B}}{\begin{bmatrix} 3 & 5 \\ 5 & 6 \end{bmatrix}} = \begin{bmatrix} 2 \cdot 3 + 1 \cdot 5 & 2 \cdot 5 + 1 \cdot 6 \\ 1 \cdot 3 + 4 \cdot 5 & 1 \cdot 5 + 4 \cdot 6 \end{bmatrix} = \overset{\mathbf{AB}}{\begin{bmatrix} 11 & 16 \\ 23 & 29 \end{bmatrix}}$$

$$\overset{\mathbf{B}}{\begin{bmatrix} 3 & 5 \\ 5 & 6 \end{bmatrix}} \overset{\mathbf{A}}{\begin{bmatrix} 2 & 1 \\ 1 & 4 \end{bmatrix}} = \begin{bmatrix} 3 \cdot 2 + 5 \cdot 1 & 3 \cdot 1 + 5 \cdot 4 \\ 5 \cdot 2 + 6 \cdot 1 & 5 \cdot 1 + 6 \cdot 4 \end{bmatrix} = \overset{\mathbf{BA}}{\begin{bmatrix} 11 & 23 \\ 16 & 29 \end{bmatrix}}$$

Notice that $\mathbf{AB} \neq \mathbf{BA}$, i.e., the *order* in which matrices are multiplied makes a difference. The mathematical statement of this is to say that multiplication of matrices is not commutative. Multiplying matrices in two different orders (assuming they are conformable both ways) in general yields different results.

Example

$$
\begin{array}{ccc}
\mathbf{A} & \mathbf{x} & \mathbf{Ax} \\
\begin{bmatrix} 3 & 1 & 2 \\ 1 & 4 & 5 \\ 2 & 5 & 2 \end{bmatrix} &
\begin{bmatrix} 2 \\ 6 \\ 3 \end{bmatrix} = &
\begin{bmatrix} 18 \\ 41 \\ 40 \end{bmatrix} \\
(3 \times 3) & (3 \times 1) & (3 \times 1)
\end{array}
$$

Notice that multiplying a matrix on the right by a column vector takes the matrix into a column vector.

$$
(2, 5) \begin{bmatrix} 3 & 1 \\ 1 & 4 \end{bmatrix} = (11, 22)
$$

Multiplying a matrix on the left by a row vector results in a row vector. If we are multiplying more than two matrices, then we may *group at will*. The mathematical statement of this is that multiplication of matrices is associative. Thus, if we are considering the matrix product $\mathbf{ABC}$, we get the same result if we multiply $\mathbf{A}$ and $\mathbf{B}$ first (and then the result of that by $\mathbf{C}$) as if we multiply $\mathbf{B}$ and $\mathbf{C}$ first (and then the result of that by $\mathbf{A}$), i.e.,

$$
\mathbf{A} \, \mathbf{B} \, \mathbf{C} = (\mathbf{A} \, \mathbf{B}) \, \mathbf{C} = \mathbf{A} \, (\mathbf{B} \, \mathbf{C})
$$

A matrix product that is of particular interest to us in Chapter 4 is of the following form:

$$
\begin{array}{ccc}
\mathbf{x}' & \mathbf{S} & \mathbf{x} \\
1 \times p & p \times p & p \times 1
\end{array}
$$

Note that this product yields a number, i.e., the product matrix is 1×1 or a number. The multivariate test statistic for 2 groups is of this form (except for a scalar constant in front).

Example

$$
(4, 2) \begin{bmatrix} 10 & 3 \\ 3 & 4 \end{bmatrix} \begin{bmatrix} 4 \\ 2 \end{bmatrix} = (46, 20) \begin{bmatrix} 4 \\ 2 \end{bmatrix} = 184 + 40 = 224
$$

2.3.   OBTAINING THE MATRIX OF VARIANCES AND COVARIANCES

Now, we show how various matrix operations introduced thus far can be used to obtain a very important quantity in statistical work, i.e., the matrix of variances and covariances for a set of variables. Consider the following set of data

x_1	x_2
1	1
3	4
2	7

$$\bar{x}_1 = 2 \quad \bar{x}_2 = 4$$

First, we form the matrix X_d of deviation scores, i.e., how much each score deviates from the mean on that variable:

$$\mathbf{X}_d = \overset{\mathbf{X}}{\begin{bmatrix} 1 & 1 \\ 3 & 4 \\ 2 & 7 \end{bmatrix}} - \overset{\bar{\mathbf{X}}}{\begin{bmatrix} 2 & 4 \\ 2 & 4 \\ 2 & 4 \end{bmatrix}} = \begin{bmatrix} -1 & -3 \\ 1 & 0 \\ 0 & 3 \end{bmatrix}$$

Next we take the transpose of X_d:

$$\mathbf{X}_d' = \begin{bmatrix} -1 & 1 & 0 \\ -3 & 0 & 3 \end{bmatrix}$$

Now we can obtain the so-called matrix of sums of squares and cross products (SSCP) as the product of X_d' and X_d:

deviation scores for x_1 — $\mathbf{X}_d'$ $\mathbf{X}_d$ — deviation scores for x_2

$$\mathbf{SSCP} = \begin{bmatrix} \boxed{-1 & 1 & 0} \\ -3 & 0 & 3 \end{bmatrix} \begin{bmatrix} -1 & \boxed{-3} \\ 1 & 0 \\ 0 & 3 \end{bmatrix} = \begin{bmatrix} ss_1 & ss_{12} \\ ss_{21} & ss_2 \end{bmatrix}$$

The diagonal elements are just sums of squares:

$$ss_1 = (-1)^2 + 1^2 + 0^2 = 2$$

$$ss_2 = (-3)^2 + 0^2 + 3^2 = 18$$

Notice that these deviation sums of squares are the numerators of the variances for the variables, since the variance for a variable is

$$s^2 = \sum_i (x_{ii} - \bar{x})^2 / (n - 1).$$

The sum of deviation cross products (ss_{12}) for the two variables is

$$ss_{12} = ss_{21} = (-1)(-3) + 1\,(0) + (0)\,(3) = 3$$

This is just the numerator for the covariance for the two variables, since the definitional formula for covariance is given by:

$$s_{12} = \frac{\sum_{i=1}^{n} (x_{i1} - \bar{x}_1)(x_{i2} - \bar{x}_2)}{n - 1},$$

where $(x_{i1} - \bar{x}_1)$ is the deviation score for the ith subject on x_1 and $(x_{i2} - \bar{x}_2)$ is the deviation score for the ith subject on x_2.

Finally, the matrix of variances and covariances $\mathbf{S}$ is obtained from $\mathbf{SSCP}$ matrix by multiplying by a constant, namely $1/(n - 1)$:

$$\mathbf{S} = \frac{\mathbf{SSCP}}{n - 1} \qquad \text{variance for variable 1}$$

$$\mathbf{S} = \frac{1}{2}\begin{bmatrix} 2 & 3 \\ 3 & 18 \end{bmatrix} = \begin{bmatrix} 1 & 1.5 \\ 1.5 & 9 \end{bmatrix} \longrightarrow \text{variance for variable 2}$$

covariance

Thus, in obtaining $\mathbf{S}$ we have:

1. Represented the scores on several variables as a matrix
2. Illustrated subtraction of matrices—to get $\mathbf{X}_d$
3. Illustrated the transpose of a matrix—to get $\mathbf{X}'_d$
4. Illustrated multiplication of matrices, i.e., $\mathbf{X}'_d\,\mathbf{X}_d$, to get $\mathbf{SSCP}$.
5. Illustrated multiplication of a matrix by a scalar, i.e., by $1/(n - 1)$, to finally obtain $\mathbf{S}$.

2.4.   DETERMINANT OF A MATRIX

The determinant of a matrix $\mathbf{A}$ is denoted by $|\mathbf{A}|$ and is a unique number associated with each *square* matrix. There are two interrelated reasons why consideration of determinants is quite important for multivariate statistical analysis. First, the determinant of a covariance matrix represents the *generalized* variance for several variables. That is, it characterizes in a single number how much variability is present on a set of variables. Secondly, because the determinant represents variance for a set of variables, it is intimately involved in several multivariate test statistics. For example, in chapter three on regression analysis we use a test statistic called Wilk's Λ which involves a ratio of two determinants. Also, in k group multivariate analysis of variance the following form of Wilk's Λ ($\Lambda = |\mathbf{W}|/|\mathbf{T}|$) is the most widely used test statistic for determining whether several groups differ on a set of variables. The $\mathbf{W}$ and $\mathbf{T}$ matrices are multivariate generalizations of SS_w (sum of squares within) and SS_t (sum of squares total) from univariate ANOVA, and are defined and described in detail in Chapters 4 and 5.

There is a formal definition for finding the determinant of a matrix, but it is complicated and we do not present it. There are other ways of finding the determinant, and a convenient method for smaller matrices (4×4 or less) is the method of cofactors. For a 2×2 matrix the determinant could be evaluated by the method of cofactors; however, it is evaluated more quickly as simply the difference in the products of the diagonal elements.

Example

$$\mathbf{A} = \begin{bmatrix} 4 & 1 \\ 1 & 2 \end{bmatrix} \Rightarrow |\mathbf{A}| = 4 \cdot (2) - 1 \cdot (1) = 7$$

In general, for a 2×2 matrix $\mathbf{A} = \begin{bmatrix} a & b \\ c & d \end{bmatrix}$ then, $|\mathbf{A}| = ad - bc$.

To evaluate the determinant of a 3×3 matrix we need the method of cofactors and the following definition.

Definition: The *minor* of an element a_{ij} is the determinant of the matrix formed by deleting the ith row and the jth column.

Example

Consider the following matrix

$$\mathbf{A} = \begin{matrix} & \overset{a_{12}}{\downarrow} & \overset{a_{13}}{\downarrow} \\ \begin{bmatrix} 1 & 2 & 3 \\ 2 & 2 & 1 \\ 3 & 1 & 4 \end{bmatrix} \end{matrix}$$

The minor of $a_{12} = 2$ is the determinant of the matrix $\begin{bmatrix} 2 & 1 \\ 3 & 4 \end{bmatrix}$ obtained by

deleting the first row and the second column. Therefore, the minor of 2 is

$$\begin{vmatrix} 2 & 1 \\ 3 & 4 \end{vmatrix} = 8 - 3 = 5.$$

The minor of $a_{13} = 3$ is the determinant of the matrix $\begin{bmatrix} 2 & 2 \\ 3 & 1 \end{bmatrix}$ obtained by

deleting the first row and the third column. Thus, the minor of 3 is $\begin{vmatrix} 2 & 2 \\ 3 & 1 \end{vmatrix} =$

$2 - 6 = -4.$

Definition: The cofactor of $a_{ij} = (-1)^{i+j} \times$ minor

Thus, the cofactor of an element will differ at most from its minor by sign. We now evaluate $(-1)^{i+j}$ for the first 3 elements of the above **A** matrix:

$$a_{11} : (-1)^{1+1} = 1$$
$$a_{12} : (-1)^{1+2} = -1$$
$$a_{13} : (-1)^{1+3} = 1$$

Notice that the signs for the elements in the first row alternate, and this pattern continues for all the elements in a 3×3 matrix. Thus, when evaluating the determinant for a 3×3 matrix it will be convenient to write down the pattern of signs and use it, rather than figuring out what $(-1)^{i+j}$ is for each element. That pattern of signs is:

$$\begin{bmatrix} + & - & + \\ - & + & - \\ + & - & + \end{bmatrix}$$

We denote the matrix of cofactors **C** as follows:

$$\mathbf{C} = \begin{bmatrix} c_{11} & c_{12} & c_{13} \\ c_{21} & c_{22} & c_{23} \\ c_{31} & c_{32} & c_{33} \end{bmatrix}$$

Now, *the determinant is obtained by expanding along any row or column of the matrix of cofactors.* Thus, for example, the determinant of **A** would be given by

$$|\mathbf{A}| = a_{11} c_{11} + a_{12} c_{12} + a_{13} c_{13}$$

(expanding along the first row)

or by

$$|\mathbf{A}| = a_{12} c_{12} + a_{22} c_{22} + a_{32} c_{32}$$

(expanding along the second column)

We now find the determinant of **A** by expanding along the first row:

Element	Minor	Cofactor	Element × Cofactor
$a_{11} = 1$	$\begin{vmatrix} 2 & 1 \\ 1 & 4 \end{vmatrix} = 7$	7	7
$a_{12} = 2$	$\begin{vmatrix} 2 & 1 \\ 3 & 4 \end{vmatrix} = 5$	-5	-10
$a_{13} = 3$	$\begin{vmatrix} 2 & 2 \\ 3 & 1 \end{vmatrix} = -4$	-4	-12

Therefore, $|\mathbf{A}| = 7 + (-10) + (-12) = -15$.

For a 4 × 4 matrix the pattern of signs is given by:

$$\begin{array}{cccc} + & - & + & - \\ - & + & - & + \\ + & - & + & - \\ - & + & - & + \end{array}$$

and the determinant is again evaluated by expanding along any row or column. However, in this case the minors are determinants of 3 × 3 matrices, and the procedure becomes quite tedious. Thus, we do not pursue it any further here.

In the example in 2.3 we obtained the following covariance matrix

$$\mathbf{S} = \begin{bmatrix} 1.0 & 1.5 \\ 1.5 & 9.0 \end{bmatrix}$$

We also indicated at the beginning of this section that the determinant of $\mathbf{S}$ can be interpreted as the generalized variance for a set of variables.

Now, the generalized variance for the above two variable example is just $|\mathbf{S}|$ = $1 \cdot (9) - (1.5 \cdot 1.5) = 6.75$. Since for this example there is a covariance, the generalized variance is reduced by this. That is, some of the variance in variable 2 is accounted for by variance in variable 1. On the other hand, if the variables were uncorrelated (covariance = 0), then we would expect the generalized variance to be larger (since none of the variance in variable 2 can be acounted for by variance in variable 1), and this is indeed the case:

$$|\mathbf{S}| = \begin{vmatrix} 1 & 0 \\ 0 & 9 \end{vmatrix} = 9$$

Univariate Notion of Variance

In univariate analysis of variance, the variance of a variable x is given by:

$$s_x^2 = \frac{\sum_{i=1}^{n} (x_i - \bar{x})^2}{n - 1}$$

where n is the number of scores. Variance is thus a measure of dispersion or spread of the scores about the mean. How much the points disperse can be depicted graphically by plotting the points on the number line. Consider the following two sets of scores with the same mean of 5:

1. 4.5,4.5, 4.5, 5,5, 5.5, 5.5, 5.5
2. 0, 0, 2, 4, 5, 6, 8, 10, 10

It is clear that the variance is much greater for set 2, and plotting the points on the number line shows this:

Multivariate Notions of Variance

In MANOVA there are several variables, each of which has a variance. In addition, each pair of variables has a covariance. Thus to represent variance in the multivariate case we must take into account all the variances and covariances. This gives rise to a matrix of these quantities. Consider the simplest case of 2 dependent variables. The population covariance matrix $\sum$ looks like this:

$$\sum = \begin{bmatrix} \sigma_1^2 & \sigma_{12} \\ \sigma_{21} & \sigma_2^2 \end{bmatrix}$$

where σ_1^2 is the population variance for variable 1 and σ_{12} is the population covariance for the two variables.

This population matrix is estimated by a sample covariance matrix (**S**)

$$\hat{\sum} = \mathbf{S} = \begin{bmatrix} s_1^2 & s_{12} \\ s_{12} & s_2^2 \end{bmatrix}$$

where s_1^2 is the sample variance for variable 1, and s_{12} is the covariance for the two variables. Recall that the following relationship holds between the correlation and covariance:

$$r_{12} = \frac{s_{12}}{s_1 s_2}$$

Thus, one multivariate generalization of the univariate notion of variance is to replace the variance for a single variable by the *matrix* of variances and covariances for the set of variables. This multivariate generalization of variance is used to measure within-group variability on p dependent variables for the two-group multivariate analysis of variance test statistic (Hotellings T^2).

The other multivariate generalization of variance is to use the *determinant of the sample covariance matrix* **S**, i.e., $|\mathbf{S}|$ as the measure of spread. This generalization *is called the generalized variance.* As we detail shortly, the determinant of the sample covariance matrix for two variables can be interpreted as the squared area of a parallelogram, whose sides are the standard deviations for the variables. For three variables, the determinant of the covariance matrix (generalized variance) can be interpreted as the squared volume of a parallelotype (the 3 dimensional analogue of the parallelogram).

In summarizing then, *for one variable variance can be interpreted as the spread of the points (scores) on a line, for two variables we can think of variance as squared area in the plane, and for 3 variables we can think of variance as squared volume in 3 space.*

In the following we present a concrete illustration of generalized variance with data.

Example

Consider the following scores on 2 dependent variables for 3 subjects.

Subject	x_1	x_2
1	2	3
2	3	7
3	4	5
Means	3	5

The sample variances for x_1 and x_2 are 1 and 4 respectively, and the covariance is 1, as the reader should confirm. Thus, the covariance matrix **S** is:

$$\mathbf{S} = \begin{bmatrix} 1 & 1 \\ 1 & 4 \end{bmatrix} \Rightarrow |\mathbf{S}| = 3 \text{ generalized variance}$$

Also, the correlation between the variables $r_{12} = \dfrac{1}{1 \cdot 2} = .5$.

Now, it can be shown that the cosine of the angle between the sides of the parallelogram is equal to the correlation between the variables (Bock, 1975, p. 28). Thus, here we have $r_{12} = .5 = \cos \theta$ so that from trigonometry $\theta = 60°$. Therefore, the parallelogram is as follows:

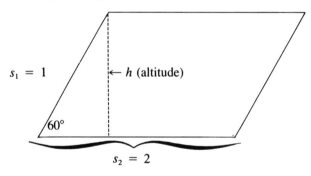

Now,

   Area of Parallelogram = base × altitude

Since

$$\sin 60° = \frac{\text{opposite}}{\text{hypothenuse}} = \frac{h}{1} \Rightarrow h = \sin 60° = \frac{\sqrt{3}}{2}$$

$$\text{Area} = 2 \cdot \frac{\sqrt{3}}{2} = \sqrt{3} \Rightarrow \text{Squared area} = 3 = \text{generalized variance}$$

Notice how generalized variance is affected by the correlation between the variables. If, in the above example the angle had been 30° (indicating a higher correlation), then

Area = $b \cdot h$ = $2 \cdot \frac{1}{2}$ = 1 $\Rightarrow$ generalized variance = 1^2 = 1, instead of 3 as above.

In the limiting case (i.e., where the variables were perfectly correlated), we would have cos θ = 1 $\Rightarrow$ θ = 0°, or no generalized variance since there would be no area.

2.5.   INVERSE OF A MATRIX

The inverse of a square matrix **A** is a matrix $\mathbf{A}^{-1}$ which satisfies the following equation:

$$\mathbf{A}\,\mathbf{A}^{-1} = \mathbf{A}^{-1}\,\mathbf{A} = \mathbf{I}_n$$

where $\mathbf{I}_n$ is the identity matrix of order n. The identity matrix is simply a matrix with 1's on the main diagonal and 0's elsewhere.

$$\mathbf{I}_2 = \begin{bmatrix} 1 & 0 \\ 0 & 1 \end{bmatrix} \quad \mathbf{I}_3 = \begin{bmatrix} 1 & 0 & 0 \\ 0 & 1 & 0 \\ 0 & 0 & 1 \end{bmatrix}$$

Why is finding inverses important in statistical work? Because we do not literally have division with matrices, *inversion for matrices is the analogue of division for numbers*. This is why finding inverses is so important. An analogy with univariate ANOVA may be helpful here. In univariate ANOVA recall that the test statistic $F = MS_b/MS_w = MS_b\,(MS_w)^{-1}$, i.e., a ratio of between to within variability. The analogue of this test statistic in multivariate analysis of variance is $\mathbf{B}\mathbf{W}^{-1}$, where **B** is a matrix which is the multivariate generalization of SS_b (sum of squares between), i.e., it is a measure of how differential the effects of treatments have been on the set of dependent variables. In the multivariate case we also want to "divide" the between-variability by the within-variability, but we don't have division per se. However, multiplying the **B** matrix by $\mathbf{W}^{-1}$ accomplishes this for us, since inversion is the analogue of division. Also, as shown in the next chapter, to obtain the regression coefficients for a multiple regression analysis, it is necessary to find the inverse of a matrix product involving the predictors.

Procedure for Finding the Inverse of a Matrix

1. Replace each element of the matrix **A** by it's minor.
2. Form the matrix of cofactors, attaching the appropriate signs from the pattern of signs.
3. Take the transpose of the matrix of cofactors, forming what is called the adjoint.
4. Divide each element of the adjoint by the determinant of **A**.

For symmetric matrices (with which this text deals almost exclusively), taking the transpose is *not* necessary, and hence when finding the inverse of a symmetric matrix step three is omitted.

We apply this procedure first to the simplest case, i.e., finding the inverse of a 2 × 2 matrix.

Example

$$\mathbf{D} = \begin{bmatrix} 4 & 2 \\ 2 & 6 \end{bmatrix}$$

The minor of 4 is the determinant of the matrix obtained by deleting the first row and the first column. What is left is simply the number 6, and the determinant of a number is that number. Thus we obtain the following matrix of minors:

$$\begin{bmatrix} 6 & 2 \\ 2 & 4 \end{bmatrix}$$

Now the pattern of signs for any 2 × 2 matrix is

$$\begin{bmatrix} + & - \\ - & + \end{bmatrix}$$

Therefore, the matrix of cofactors is

$$\begin{bmatrix} 6 & -2 \\ -2 & 4 \end{bmatrix}$$

The determinant of **D** = 6(4) − 2 (2) = 20.

Finally then, the inverse of **D** is obtained by dividing the matrix of cofactors by the determinant, obtaining

$$\mathbf{D}^{-1} = \begin{bmatrix} \dfrac{6}{20} & \dfrac{-2}{20} \\ \dfrac{-2}{20} & \dfrac{4}{20} \end{bmatrix}$$

To check that $\mathbf{D}^{-1}$ is indeed the inverse of **D**, note that

$$
\underset{\mathbf{D}}{\begin{bmatrix} 4 & 2 \\ 2 & 6 \end{bmatrix}}
\underset{\mathbf{D}^{-1}}{\begin{bmatrix} \dfrac{6}{20} & \dfrac{-2}{20} \\ \dfrac{-2}{20} & \dfrac{4}{20} \end{bmatrix}}
=
\underset{\mathbf{D}^{-1}}{\begin{bmatrix} \dfrac{6}{20} & \dfrac{-2}{20} \\ \dfrac{-2}{20} & \dfrac{4}{20} \end{bmatrix}}
\underset{\mathbf{D}}{\begin{bmatrix} 4 & 2 \\ 2 & 6 \end{bmatrix}}
=
\underset{\mathbf{I}_2}{\begin{bmatrix} 1 & 0 \\ 0 & 1 \end{bmatrix}}
$$

Example

Let us find the inverse for the 3 × 3 **A** matrix that we found the determinant for in the previous section. Since **A** is a symmetric matrix, it is not necessary to find 9 minors, but only 6, since the inverse of a symmetric matrix is symmetric. Thus we just find the minors for the elements on and above the main diagonal.

$$\mathbf{A} = \begin{bmatrix} 1 & 2 & 3 \\ 2 & 2 & 1 \\ 3 & 1 & 4 \end{bmatrix}$$

Recall again that the minor of an element is the determinant of the matrix obtained by deleting the row and column that the element is in.

Element	Matrix	Minor
$a_{11} = 1$	$\begin{bmatrix} 2 & 1 \\ 1 & 4 \end{bmatrix}$	$2\cdot4 - 1\cdot1 = 7$
$a_{12} = 2$	$\begin{bmatrix} 2 & 1 \\ 3 & 4 \end{bmatrix}$	$2\cdot4 - 1\cdot3 = 5$
$a_{13} = 3$	$\begin{bmatrix} 2 & 2 \\ 3 & 1 \end{bmatrix}$	$2\cdot1 - 2\cdot3 = -4$

$a_{22} = 2$ $\begin{bmatrix} 1 & 3 \\ 3 & 4 \end{bmatrix}$ $1 \cdot 4 - 3 \cdot 3 = -5$

$a_{23} = 1$ $\begin{bmatrix} 1 & 2 \\ 3 & 1 \end{bmatrix}$ $1 \cdot 1 - 2 \cdot 3 = -5$

$a_{33} = 4$ $\begin{bmatrix} 1 & 2 \\ 2 & 2 \end{bmatrix}$ $1 \cdot 2 - 2 \cdot 2 = -2$

Therefore, the matrix of minors for **A** is

$$\begin{bmatrix} 7 & 5 & -4 \\ 5 & -5 & -5 \\ -4 & -5 & -2 \end{bmatrix}$$

Recall that the pattern of signs is

$$\begin{matrix} + & - & + \\ - & + & - \\ + & - & + \end{matrix}$$

Thus, attaching the appropriate sign to each element in the matrix of minors and completing step 2 of finding the inverse we obtain:

$$\begin{bmatrix} 7 & -5 & -4 \\ -5 & -5 & 5 \\ -4 & 5 & -2 \end{bmatrix}$$

Now the determinant of **A** was found to be -15. Therefore, to complete the final step in finding the inverse we simply divide the above matrix by -15, and the inverse of **A** is

$$\mathbf{A}^{-1} = \begin{bmatrix} \dfrac{-7}{15} & \dfrac{1}{3} & \dfrac{4}{15} \\[2ex] \dfrac{1}{3} & \dfrac{1}{3} & \dfrac{-1}{3} \\[2ex] \dfrac{4}{15} & \dfrac{-1}{3} & \dfrac{2}{15} \end{bmatrix}$$

Again we can check that this is indeed the inverse by multiplying it by **A** to see if the result is the identity matrix.

Note that for the inverse of a matrix to exist the determinant of the matrix must *not* be equal to 0. This is because in obtaining the inverse each element is divided by the determinant, and division by 0 is not defined. If the determinant of a matrix **B** = 0, we say **B** is *singular*. If $|\mathbf{B}| \neq 0$, we say **B** is nonsingular, and its inverse does exist.

2.6. EIGENVALUES

The eigenvalues (roots) of a $p \times p$ matrix **A** are the solutions to the following determinantal equation: $|\mathbf{A} - \lambda\mathbf{I}| = 0$: **A** will have p roots, some of which may be 0.

Example

$$\mathbf{A} = \begin{bmatrix} 3 & 1 \\ 1 & 2 \end{bmatrix} \Rightarrow \mathbf{A} - \lambda\mathbf{I} = \begin{bmatrix} 3 & 1 \\ 1 & 2 \end{bmatrix} - \begin{bmatrix} \lambda & 0 \\ 0 & \lambda \end{bmatrix} = \begin{bmatrix} 3 - \lambda & 1 \\ 1 & 2 - \lambda \end{bmatrix}$$

Thus we have to solve the following determinantal equation:

$$\begin{vmatrix} 3 - \lambda & 1 \\ 1 & 2 - \lambda \end{vmatrix} = 0 \Rightarrow \lambda^2 - 5\lambda + 5 = 0,$$

an equation of the second degree which has two roots or solutions

Although we have defined eigenvalues abstractly, they are fundamental to the multivariate analysis of variance problem (MANOVA). In MANOVA we are greatly interested in solving the determinantal equation where $\mathbf{BW}^{-1}$ plays the role of **A**.

Consider the following between- and within-matrices:

$$\mathbf{B} = \begin{bmatrix} 5 & 3 \\ 3 & 6 \end{bmatrix} \qquad \mathbf{W} = \begin{bmatrix} 2 & 1 \\ 1 & 3 \end{bmatrix}$$

Find the eigenvalues of $\mathbf{BW}^{-1}$.

$$|\mathbf{W}| = 2 \cdot 3 - 1 \cdot 1 = 5$$

$$\text{Pattern of signs} = \begin{bmatrix} + & - \\ - & + \end{bmatrix}$$

$$\text{Matrix of cofactors} = \begin{bmatrix} 3 & -1 \\ -1 & 2 \end{bmatrix}$$

$$\mathbf{W}^{-1} = \frac{1}{5} \begin{bmatrix} 3 & -1 \\ -1 & 2 \end{bmatrix} = \begin{bmatrix} .6 & -.2 \\ -.2 & .4 \end{bmatrix}$$

Thus,

$$\mathbf{BW}^{-1} = \begin{bmatrix} 5 & 3 \\ 3 & 6 \end{bmatrix} \begin{bmatrix} .6 & -.2 \\ -.2 & .4 \end{bmatrix} = \begin{bmatrix} 2.4 & .2 \\ .6 & 1.8 \end{bmatrix}$$

Now, the eigenvalues of $\mathbf{BW}^{-1}$ are solutions to the following determinantal equation:

$$|\mathbf{B}\,\mathbf{W}^{-1} - \lambda\,\mathbf{I}| = 0$$

$$\mathbf{B}\,\mathbf{W}^{-1} - \lambda\mathbf{I} = \begin{bmatrix} 2.4 & .2 \\ .6 & 1.8 \end{bmatrix} - \begin{bmatrix} \lambda & 0 \\ 0 & \lambda \end{bmatrix}$$

$$|\mathbf{BW}^{-1} - \lambda\mathbf{I}| = \begin{vmatrix} 2.4 - \lambda & .2 \\ .6 & 1.8 - \lambda \end{vmatrix} = 0$$

or $(2.4 - \lambda)(1.8 - \lambda) - .2\,(.6) = 0$

$\lambda^2 - 4.2\,\lambda + 4.2 = 0$

This is an equation of the second degree, a so-called quadratic equation. There is a general formula for solving *any* quadratic equation. If the general equation is given by $a\lambda^2 + b\lambda + c = 0$, then the formula for the two roots is:

$$\lambda_i = \frac{-b \pm \sqrt{b^2 - 4\,ac}}{2a}$$

The coefficients for the above equation are: $a = 1, b = -4.2, c = 4.2$. Plugging into the above formula

$$\lambda_i = \frac{-(-4.2) \pm \sqrt{(-4.2)^2 - 4(1)\cdot(4.2)}}{2(1)}$$

$$\lambda_i = (4.2 \pm .92)/2$$

Thus, the roots or eigenvalues are $\lambda_1 = 2.558$, $\lambda_2 = 1.642$.

The sum of the eigenvalues of a matrix is called the *trace*. If the matrix is $\mathbf{BW}^{-1}$, then the trace will have a very important meaning as it will be one of the multivariate test statistics, and will tell us whether the groups differ significantly on the set of dependent variables.

EXERCISES CHAPTER 2

1. Given:

$$\mathbf{A} = \begin{bmatrix} 2 & 4 & 1 \\ 3 & -2 & 5 \end{bmatrix} \quad \mathbf{B} = \begin{bmatrix} 1 & 2 \\ 2 & 1 \\ 3 & 4 \end{bmatrix} \quad \mathbf{C} = \begin{bmatrix} 1 & 3 & 5 \\ 6 & 2 & 1 \end{bmatrix}$$

$$\mathbf{D} = \begin{bmatrix} 4 & 2 \\ 2 & 6 \end{bmatrix} \quad \mathbf{E} = \begin{bmatrix} 1 & -1 & 2 \\ -1 & 3 & 1 \\ 2 & 1 & 10 \end{bmatrix} \quad \mathbf{X} = \begin{bmatrix} 1 & 2 \\ 3 & 1 \\ 4 & 6 \\ 5 & 7 \end{bmatrix}$$

$$\mathbf{u}' = (1, 3), \ \mathbf{v} = \begin{bmatrix} 2 \\ 7 \end{bmatrix}$$

Find, where meaningful, each of the following:
a) $\mathbf{A} + \mathbf{C}$
b) $\mathbf{A} + \mathbf{B}$
c) $\mathbf{AB}$
d) $\mathbf{AC}$
e) $\mathbf{u}' \mathbf{D} \mathbf{u}$
f) $\mathbf{u}' \mathbf{v}$
g) $(\mathbf{A} + \mathbf{C})'$
h) $3 \mathbf{C}$
i) $|\mathbf{D}|$
j) $\mathbf{D}^{-1}$
k) $|\mathbf{E}|$

l) $\mathbf{E}^{-1}$

m) $\mathbf{u}' \, \mathbf{D}^{-1} \mathbf{u}$

n) $\mathbf{BA}$ (compare this result with [c])

o) $\mathbf{X'X}$

2. In the next chapter on multiple regression we are interested in predicting each person's score on a dependent variable y from a linear combination of their scores on several predictors (x_i's). If there were 3 predictors, then the prediction equations for N subjects would look like this:

$$y_1 = e_1 + b_0 + b_1 \, x_{11} + b_2 \, x_{12} + b_3 \, x_{13}$$

$$y_2 = e_2 + b_0 + b_1 \, x_{21} + b_2 \, x_{22} + b_3 \, x_{23}$$

$$y_3 = e_3 + b_0 + b_1 \, x_{31} + b_2 \, x_{32} + b_3 \, x_{33}$$

$$\vdots \qquad\qquad \vdots \qquad\qquad \vdots$$

$$y_N = e_N + b_0 + b_1 \, x_{N1} + b_2 \, x_{N2} + b_3 \, x_{N3}$$

Note: The e_i's are the portion of y not predicted by the x's, and the b's are the regression coefficient. Express this set of prediction equations as a single matrix equation. Hint: The right hand portion of the equation will be of the form:

vector + matrix times vector

3. Using the approach detailed in section 2.3, find the matrix of variances and covariances for the following data:

x_1	x_2	x_3
4	3	10
5	2	11
8	6	15
9	6	9
10	8	5

4. Consider the following two situations:

a) $s_1 = 10$, $s_2 = 7$, $r_{12} = .80$

b) $s_1 = 9$, $s_2 = 6$, $r_{12} = .20$

For which situation is the generalized variance larger? Does this surprise you?

5. Calculate the determinant for $\mathbf{A} = \begin{bmatrix} 9 & 2 & 1 \\ 2 & 4 & 5 \\ 1 & 5 & 3 \end{bmatrix}$

Could $\mathbf{A}$ be a covariance matrix for a set of variables? Explain.

3 Multiple Regression

3.1   INTRODUCTION

In multiple regression we are interested in predicting a dependent variable from a set of predictors. In a previous course in statistics the reader probably studied simple regression, predicting a dependent variable from a single predictor. An example would be predicting college GPA from high school GPA. Since human behavior is complex and influenced by many factors, such single predictor studies are necessarily limited in their predictive power. For example, in a college GPA study, we are able to predict college GPA better by considering other predictors such as scores on standardized tests (verbal, quantitative), and some noncognitive variables, such as study habits and attitude toward education. That is, we look to other predictors (often test scores) that tap other aspects of criterion behavior.

Consider two other examples of multiple regression studies:

1. Feshbach, Adelman, and Fuller (1977) conducted a study of 850 middle class children. The children were measured in kindergarten on a battery of variables: WPPSI, deHirsch-Jansky Index (assessing various linguistic and perceptual motor skills), the Bender Motor Gestalt, and a Student Rating Scale developed by the authors that measures various cognitive and affective behaviors and skills. These measures were used to predict reading achievement for these same children in grades 1, 2, and 3.

2. Crystal (1988) attempted to predict chief executive officer (CEO) pay for the top 100 of last year's FORTUNE 500 and the 100 top entries form last year's Service 500. He used the following predictors: company size,

64

company performance, company risk, government regulation, tenure, location, directors, ownership, and age. He found that only about 39% of the variance in CEO pay can be accounted for by these factors.

In modeling the relationship between y and the x's, we are assuming a *linear* model is appropriate. Of course, it is possible that a more complex model (curvilinear) may be necessary to predict y accurately. Polynomial regression may be appropriate, or if there is non-linearity in the parameters, then either the SPSSX NONLINEAR program (*SPSSX USER'S GUIDE*, 3rd Ed., 1988, Chapter 36) or the SAS nonlinear program (*SAS/STAT USER'S GUIDE*, Vol 2, 1990, Chapter 29) can be used to fit a model.

This is a long chapter with many sections, not all of which are equally important. The three most fundamental sections are on model selection (3.8), checking assumptions underlying the linear regression model (3.10), and model validation (3.11). The other sections should be thought of as supportive of these. We discuss several ways of selecting a "good" set of predictors, and illustrate these with two computer examples. An important theme throughout this entire book is determining whether the assumptions underlying a given analysis are tenable. This chapter initiates that theme, and we will see that there are various graphical plots available for assessing assumptions underlying the regression model. Another very important theme throughout this book is the mathematical maximization nature of many advanced statistical procedures, and the concomitant possibility of results looking very good on the sample on which they were derived (because of capitalization on chance), but not generalizing to a population. Thus it becomes extremely important to validate the results on an independent sample(s) of data, or at least obtain an estimate of the generalizability of the results. Section 3.11 illustrates both of the aforementioned ways of checking the validity of a given regression model. A final pedagogical point on reading this chapter: Section 3.14 deals with outliers and influential data points. We already indicated in Chapter 1 with several examples the dramatic effect an outlier(s) can have on the results of any statistical analysis. Section 3.14 is rather lengthy, however, and the applied researcher may not want to "plow" through all the details. Recognizing this, I begin that section with a brief overview discussion of statistics for assessing outliers and influential data points, with prescriptive advice on how to flag such cases from computer printout.

We wish to emphasize that our focus in this chapter is on the use of multiple regression for prediction. Another broad, related area is the use of regression for explanation. Cohen and Cohen (1983) and Pedhazur (1982) have excellent, extended discussions of the use of regression for explanation (e.g., causal modeling).

There have been innumerable books written on regression analysis. In my opinion, the books by Cohen & Cohen (1983), Pedhazur (1982), Myers (1990), Weisberg (1985), Belsley, Kuh and Welsch (1980) and Draper and

Smith (1981) are worthy of special attention. The first two books are written for individuals in the social sciences and have very good narrative discussions. The Myers and Weisberg books are excellent in terms of the modern approach to regression analysis, and have especially good treatments of regression diagnostics. The Draper and Smith book is one of the classic texts, generally used for a more mathematical treatment, with most of its examples slanted toward the physical sciences.

We start the chapter with a brief discussion of simple regression, which most readers probably encountered in a previous statistics course.

3.2 SIMPLE REGRESSION

For one predictor the mathematical model is

$$y_i = \beta_0 + \beta_1 x_i + e_i \qquad i = 1, 2, \ldots, n$$

where β_0 and β_1 are parameters to be estimated. The e_i's are the errors of prediction, and are assumed to be independent, with constant variance and normally distributed with a mean of 0. If these assumptions are valid for a given set of data, then the estimated errors $(\hat{e}_i)$ should have similar properties. For example, the $\hat{e}_i$ should be normally distributed, or at least approximately normally distributed. This is considered further in section 3.9. The $\hat{e}_i$ are called the residuals. How do we estimate the parameters? The *least squares* criterion is used, i.e., the sum of the squared estimated errors of prediction is minimized:

$$\hat{e}_1^{\,2} + \hat{e}_2^{\,2} + \ldots\ldots + \hat{e}_n^{\,2} = \sum_{i=1}^{n} \hat{e}_i^{\,2} = \min$$

Now, $\hat{e}_i = y_i - \hat{y}_i$, where y_i is the actual score on the dependent variable and $\hat{y}_i$ is the estimated score for the ith subject.

The scores for each subject (x_i, y_i) define a point in the plane. What the least squares criterion does is find the line which best fits the points. Geometrically this corresponds to minimizing the sum of the squared vertical distances $(\hat{e}_i^{\,2})$ of each subject's score from their estimated y score. This is illustrated in Figure 3.1.

Example 1

To illustrate simple regression we consider a small part of a Sesame Street data base from Glasnapp and Poggio (1985), who present data on many variables, including 12 background variables and 8 achievement variables, for 240 subjects. Sesame Street was developed as a television series aimed mainly at teaching preschool skills to three to five year old children. Data was collected on many achievement variables both before (pretest) and after

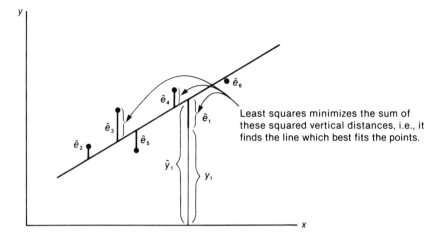

FIG. 3.1   Geometrical Representation of Least Squares Criterion

TABLE 3.1
Control Lines for Simple Regression on SPSSX Regression

TITLE 'SIMPLE REGRESSION ON SESAME DATA'
DATA LIST FREE/PREBODY POSTBODY
LIST
BEGIN DATA

    DATA LINES

END DATA
REGRESSION DESCRIPTIVES = DEFAULT/
    VARIABLES = PREBODY POSTBODY/
    DEPENDENT = POSTBODY/
①   METHOD = ENTER/
②   SCATTERPLOT (POSTBODY,PREBODY)/
③   RESIDUALS = HISTOGRAM(ZRESID)/

① DESCRIPTIVES = DEFAULT subcommand yields the means, standard deviations and the correlation matrix for the variables.

② This SCATTERPLOT subcommand yields the scatterplot for the variables. Note that the variables have been standardized (z scores) and then plotted.

③ This RESIDUALS subcommand yields the histogram of the standardized residuals.

(posttest) viewing of the series. We consider here only one of the achievement variables, knowledge of body parts. In particular, we consider pretest and posttest data on body parts for a sample of 80 children.

The control lines for running the simple regression on SPSSX REGRESSION are given in Table 3.1, along with annotation on how to obtain the scatterplot and plot of the residuals in the same run. Figure 3.2 presents the

```
             Standardized Scatterplot
             Across - PREBODY    Down - POSTBODY
         Out ++-----+-----+-----+-----+-----+-----++
           3 +                                     +    Symbols:
             |                                     |
             |                                     |    Max N
           2 +                                     +
             |              .              .       |.        .       1.0
             |                    . : .. :.        |    :            2.0 ①
           1 +                 .   ..::. : .       +    *            5.0
             |            :.   . ...  *.... ..      |
             |              .:        ..            |
           0 +              . .  :  ... .           +
             |             . .. .                   |
             |           .:: .     ..               |
          -1 +          . ... .  :.      .          +
             |        .                             |
             |           ....      .                |
          -2 +            . .                        +
             |             .                        |
             |         .                            |
          -3 +                                      +
         Out ++-----+-----+-----+-----+-----+-----++
             -3    -2    -1     0     1     2     3 Out
```

Equation Number 1   Dependent Variable..   POSTBODY

 Descriptive Statistics are printed on Page   5

Block Number 1. Method: Enter

Variable(s) Entered on Step Number 1..   PREBODY

		Analysis of Variance		
Multiple R	.58253 ②		DF	Sum of Squares
R Square	.33934			
Mean Square				
Adjusted R Square	.33087	Regression	1	642.02551
642.02551				
Standard Error	4.00314	Residual	78	1249.96199
16.02515				
		F = 40.06361	Signif F = .0000	

------------------ Variables in the Equation ------------------

Variable ③	B	SE B	Beta	T	Sig T
PREBODY	.501970	.079305	.582528	6.330	.0000
(Constant)	14.688877	1.763786		8.328	.0000

①This legend means there is one observation whenever a single dot appears, two observations whenever a : appears, and 5 observations where there is an asterisk (*).

②The multiple correlation here is in fact the simple correlation between postbody and prebody, since there is just one predictor.

③These are the raw coefficients which define the prediction equation: POSTBODY = .50197 PREBODY + 14.6888.

FIG. 3.2   Scatterplot and Selected Printout for Simple Regression

scatterplot, along with some selected printout. The scatterplot shows a fair amount of clustering, reflecting the moderate correlation of .583, about the regression line. Table 3.2 has the histogram of the standardized residuals, which indicates a fair approximation to a normal distribution.

TABLE 3.2
Histogram of Standardized Residuals

Histogram—Standardized Residual

N	Exp N		(* = 1 Cases, . : = Normal Curve)
0	.09	Out	
0	.04	3.00	
0	.06	2.88	
0	.09	2.75	
0	.13	2.63	
0	.18	2.50	
0	.24	2.38	
0	.32	2.25	
0	.42	2.13	
1	.54	2.00	:
1	.69	1.88	:
1	.86	1.75	:
1	1.07	1.63	:
2	1.30	1.50	:*
0	1.55	1.38	.
3	1.83	1.25	*:*
1	2.12	1.13	*.
4	2.42	1.00	*:**
2	2.72	.88	**.
6	3.01	.75	**:***
6	3.28	.63	**:***
4	3.52	.50	***:
5	3.72	.38	***:*
4	3.86	.25	***:
4	3.96	.13	***:
2	3.99	.00	** .
7	3.96	−.13	***:***
1	3.86	−.25	* .
1	3.72	−.38	* .
3	3.52	−.50	***.
3	3.28	−.63	**:
1	3.01	−.75	* .
2	2.72	−.88	**.
2	2.42	−1.00	*:
2	2.12	−1.13	*:
3	1.83	−1.25	*:*
1	1.55	−1.38	*.
0	1.30	−1.50	.
1	1.07	−1.63	:
2	.86	−1.75	:*
1	.69	−1.88	:
1	.54	−2.00	:
1	.42	−2.13	*
1	.32	−2.25	*
0	.24	−2.38	
0	.18	−2.50	
0	.13	−2.63	
0	.09	−2.75	
0	.06	−2.88	
0	.04	−3.00	
0	.09	Out	

3.3 MULTIPLE REGRESSION FOR TWO PREDICTORS — MATRIX FORMULATION

The linear model for two predictors is a simple extension of what we had for one predictor:

$$y_i = \beta_0 + \beta_1 x_1 + \beta_2 x_2 + e_i$$

where β_0 (regression constant), β_1 and β_2 are the parameters to be estimated, and e is error of prediction. We consider a small data set to illustrate the estimation process.

y	x_1	x_2
3	2	1
2	3	5
4	5	3
5	7	6
8	8	7

We model each subject's y score as a linear function of the β's:

$$y_1 = 3 = \boxed{1 \cdot \beta_0 + 2 \cdot \beta_1 + 1 \cdot \beta_2} + e_1$$
$$y_2 = 2 = \boxed{1 \cdot \beta_0 + 3 \cdot \beta_1 + 5 \cdot \beta_2} + e_2$$
$$y_3 = 4 = \boxed{1 \cdot \beta_0 + 5 \cdot \beta_1 + 3 \cdot \beta_2} + e_3$$
$$y_4 = 5 = \boxed{1 \cdot \beta_0 + 7 \cdot \beta_1 + 6 \cdot \beta_2} + e_4$$
$$y_5 = 8 = \boxed{1 \cdot \beta_0 + 8 \cdot \beta_1 + 7 \cdot \beta_2} + e_5$$

This series of equations can be expressed as a single matrix equation:

$$\mathbf{y} = \begin{bmatrix} 3 \\ 2 \\ 4 \\ 5 \\ 8 \end{bmatrix} = \overset{\mathbf{X}}{\begin{bmatrix} 1 & 2 & 1 \\ 1 & 3 & 5 \\ 1 & 5 & 3 \\ 1 & 7 & 6 \\ 1 & 8 & 7 \end{bmatrix}} \overset{\boldsymbol{\beta}}{\begin{bmatrix} \beta_0 \\ \beta_1 \\ \beta_2 \end{bmatrix}} + \overset{\mathbf{e}}{\begin{bmatrix} e_1 \\ e_2 \\ e_3 \\ e_4 \\ e_5 \end{bmatrix}}$$

It is pretty clear that the y scores and the e_i define column vectors, while not so clear is how the boxed-in area can be represented as the product of two matrices, i.e., $\mathbf{X}\boldsymbol{\beta}$.

The first column of 1s is used to obtain the regression constant. The remaining two columns contain the scores for the subjects on the two predictors. Thus, the classic matrix equation for multiple regression is:

$$\mathbf{y} = \mathbf{X}\,\beta + \mathbf{e} \tag{1}$$

Now, it can be shown using the calculus that the least square estimates of the β's are given by:

$$\hat{\beta} = (\mathbf{X}'\,\mathbf{X})^{-1}\,\mathbf{X}'\mathbf{y} \tag{2}$$

Thus, for our data the estimated regression coefficients would be:

$$
\hat{\beta} = \left\{
\underbrace{\begin{bmatrix} 1 & 1 & 1 & 1 & 1 \\ 2 & 3 & 5 & 7 & 8 \\ 1 & 5 & 3 & 6 & 7 \end{bmatrix}}_{\mathbf{X}'}
\underbrace{\begin{bmatrix} 1 & 2 & 1 \\ 1 & 3 & 5 \\ 1 & 5 & 3 \\ 1 & 7 & 6 \\ 1 & 8 & 7 \end{bmatrix}}_{\mathbf{X}}
\right\}^{-1}
\underbrace{\begin{bmatrix} 1 & 1 & 1 & 1 & 1 \\ 2 & 3 & 5 & 7 & 8 \\ 1 & 5 & 3 & 6 & 7 \end{bmatrix}}_{\mathbf{X}'}
\underbrace{\begin{bmatrix} 3 \\ 2 \\ 4 \\ 5 \\ 8 \end{bmatrix}}_{\mathbf{y}}
$$

Let us do this in pieces. First

$$
\mathbf{X}'\mathbf{X} = \begin{bmatrix} 5 & 25 & 22 \\ 25 & 151 & 130 \\ 22 & 130 & 120 \end{bmatrix} \quad \text{and} \quad \mathbf{X}'\mathbf{y} = \begin{bmatrix} 22 \\ 131 \\ 111 \end{bmatrix}
$$

Furthermore, the reader should show that

$$
(\mathbf{X}'\mathbf{X})^{-1} = \frac{1}{1016} \begin{bmatrix} 1220 & -140 & -72 \\ -140 & 116 & -100 \\ -72 & -100 & 130 \end{bmatrix}
$$

where 1016 is the determinant of $\mathbf{X}'\mathbf{X}$. Thus, the estimated regression coefficients are given by

$$
\hat{\beta} = \frac{1}{1016} \begin{bmatrix} 1220 & -140 & -72 \\ -140 & 116 & -100 \\ -72 & -100 & 130 \end{bmatrix} \begin{bmatrix} 22 \\ 131 \\ 111 \end{bmatrix} = \begin{bmatrix} .50 \\ 1 \\ -.25 \end{bmatrix}
$$

Therefore, the regression (prediction) equation is

$$\hat{y}_i = .50 + x_1 - .25\, x_2$$

To illustrate the use of this equation, we find the predicted score for subject 3 and the residual for that subject:

$$\hat{y}_3 = .5 + 5 - .25(3) = 4.75$$

$$\hat{e}_3 = y_3 - \hat{y}_3 = 4 - 4.75 = -.75$$

3.4   MATHEMATICAL MAXIMIZATION NATURE OF LEAST SQUARES REGRESSION

In general then, in multiple regression the *linear combination* of the x's which is maximally correlated with y is sought. Minimizing the sum of squared errors of prediction is equivalent to *maximizing* the correlation between the observed and predicted y scores. This maximized Pearson correlation is called the multiple correlation, i.e., $R = r_{y,\hat{y}_i}$. Nunnally (1978) characterized the procedure as "wringing out the last ounce of predictive power" (obtained from the linear combination of x's, i.e., from regression equation). Since the correlation is maximum for the sample from which it is derived, when the regression equation is applied to an independent sample from the same population (i.e., cross-validated), the predictive power drops off. If the predictive power drops off sharply, then the equation is of limited utility. That is, it has no generalizability, and hence is of limited scientific value. After all, we derive the prediction equation for the purpose of predicting with it on future (other) samples. If the equation does not predict well on other samples, then it is not fulfilling the purpose for which it was designed.

Sample size (n) and the number of predictors (k) are two crucial factors which determine how well a given equation will cross-validate (i.e., generalize). In particular, the n/k ratio is crucial. For small ratios (5:1 or less) the shrinkage in predictive power can be substantial. A study by Guttman (1941) illustrates this point. He had 136 subjects and 84 predictors, and found the multiple correlation on the original sample to be .73. However, when the prediction equation was applied to an independent sample the new correlation was only .04! In other words, the good predictive power on the original sample was due to capitalization on chance, and the prediction equation had no generalizability.

We return to the cross-validation issue in more detail later in this chapter, where we show that *for social science research, about 15 subjects per predictor are needed for a reliable equation*, i.e., for an equation that will cross-validate with little loss in predictive power.

3.5 BREAKDOWN OF SUM OF SQUARES IN REGRESSION AND F TEST FOR MULTIPLE CORRELATION

In analysis of variance we broke down variability about the grand mean into between-and within-variability. In regression analysis variability about the mean is broken down into variability due to regression and variability about the regression. To get at the breakdown, we start with the following identity:

$$y_i - \hat{y}_i = (y_i - \bar{y}) - (\hat{y}_i - \bar{y})$$

Now we square both sides, obtaining

$$(y_i - \hat{y}_i)^2 = [(y_i - \bar{y}) - (\hat{y}_i - \bar{y})]^2$$

Then we sum over the subjects, from 1 to n:

$$\sum_{i=1}^{n} (y_i - \hat{y}_i)^2 = \sum_{i=1}^{n} [(y_i - \bar{y}) - (\hat{y}_i - \bar{y})]^2$$

By algebraic manipulation (see Draper & Smith, 1981, pp. 17–18), this can be rewritten as:

$$\sum (y_i - \bar{y})^2 = \sum (y_i - \hat{y}_i)^2 + \sum (\hat{y}_i - \bar{y})^2 \qquad (3)$$

	sum of squares about mean	=	sum of squares about regression (SS_{res})	+	sum of squares due to regression (SS_{reg})
df:	$n - 1$	=	$(n - k - 1)$	+	k (df = degrees of freedom)

This results in the following analysis of variance table and the F test for determining whether the population multiple correlation is different from 0.

Analysis of Variance Table for Regression

Source	SS	df	MS	F
Regression	SS_{reg}	k	S_{reg}/k	
Residual (error)	SS_{res}	$n - k - 1$	$SS_{res}/(n - k - 1)$	$\dfrac{MS_{reg}}{MS_{res}}$

Recall that since the residual for each subject is $\hat{e}_i = y_i - \hat{y}_i$, the mean square error term can be written as $MS_{res} = \Sigma \hat{e}_i^2/(n - k - 1)$. Now, R^2 (squared multiple correlation) is given by:

$$R^2 = \frac{\text{sum of squares due to regression}}{\text{sum of squares about the mean}} = \frac{\Sigma (\hat{y}_i - \bar{y})^2}{\Sigma (y_i - \bar{y})^2} = \frac{SS_{reg}}{SS_{tot}}$$

Thus, R^2 measures the proportion of total variance on y that is accounted for by the set of predictors. By simple algebra then we can rewrite the F test in terms of R^2 as follows:

$$F = \frac{R^2/k}{(1 - R^2)/(n - k - 1)}, \text{ with } k \text{ and } (n - k - 1) \text{ } df \qquad (4)$$

We feel this test is of limited utility, since it does *not necessarily* imply that the equation will cross-validate well, and this is the crucial issue in regression analysis.

Example 2

An investigator obtains $R^2 = .50$ on a sample of 50 subjects with 10 predictors. Do we reject the null hypothesis that the population multiple correlation $= 0$?

$$F = \frac{.50/10}{(1 - .50)/(50 - 10 - 1)} = 3.9 \text{ with 10 and 39 } df$$

This is significant at .01 level, since the critical value is 2.8.

However, since the n/k ratio is only 5/1, the prediction equation will probably not predict well on other samples and is therefore of questionable utility.

Myers' (1990) response to the question of what constitutes an acceptable value for R^2 is illuminating:

This is a difficult question to answer, and, in truth, what is acceptable depends on the scientific field from which the data where taken. A chemist, charged with doing a linear calibration on a high precision piece of equipment, certainly expects to experience a very high R^2 value (perhaps exceeding .99), while a behavioral scientist, dealing in data reflecting human behavior, may feel fortunate to observe an R^2 as high as .70. An experienced model fitter senses when the value of R^2 is large enough, given the situation confronted. Clearly, some scientific phenomena lend themselves to modeling with considerably more accuracy then others. (p. 37)

His point is that how well one can predict depends on *context*. In the physical sciences, generally quite accurate prediction is possible. In the social sciences, where we are attempting to predict human behavior (which can be influenced by many systematic and some idiosyncratic factors), prediction is much more difficult.

3.6   RELATIONSHIP OF SIMPLE CORRELATIONS TO MULTIPLE CORRELATION

The ideal situation, in terms of obtaining a high R would be to have each of the predictors significantly correlated with the dependent variable and for the predictors to be uncorrelated with each other, so that they measure different constructs and are able to predict different parts of the variance on y. Of course, in practice we will not find this because almost all variables are correlated to some degree. A good situation in practice then would be one in which most of our predictors correlate significantly with y and the predictors have relatively low correlations among themselves. To illustrate the above points further, consider the following three patterns of intercorrelations for three predictors.

		X_1	X_2	X_3			X_1	X_2	X_3			X_1	X_2	X_3
(1)	Y	.20	.10	.30	(2)	Y	.60	.50	.70	(3)	Y	.60	.70	.70.
	X_1		.50	.40		X_1		.20	.30		X_1		.70	.60
	X_2			.60		X_2			.20		X_2			.80

In which of these cases would you expect the multiple correlation to be the largest and the smallest respectively? Here it is quite clear that R will be the smallest for 1 because the highest correlation of any of the predictors with y is .30, whereas for the other two patterns at least one of the predictors has a correlation of .70 with y. Thus, we know that R will be at least .70 for cases 2 and 3, whereas for case 1 we only know that R will be at least .30. Furthermore, there is no chance that R for case 1 might become larger than that for cases 2 and 3, because the intercorrelations among the predictors for 1 are approximately as large or larger than those for the other two cases.

We would expect R to be largest for case 2 because each of the predictors is moderately to strongly tied to y and there are low intercorrelations (i.e., little redundancy) among the predictors, exactly the kind of situation we would hope to find in practice. We would expect R to be greater in case 2 than in case 3, because in case 3 there is considerable redundancy among the predictors. Although the correlations of the predictors with y are slighter higher in case 3 (.60, .70, .70) than in case 2 (.60, .50, .70), the much higher intercorrelations among the predictors for case 3 will severely limit the ability of X_2 and X_3 to predict additional variance beyond that of X_1 (and hence significantly increase R), whereas this will not be true for case 2.

3.7 MULTICOLLINEARITY

When there are moderate to high intercorrelations among the predictors, as is the case when several cognitive measures are used as predictors, the problem is referred to as *multicollinearity*. Multicollinearity poses a real problem for the researcher using multiple regression for three reasons:

1. It severely limits the size of R, because the predictors are going after much of the same variance on y. A study by Dizney and Gromen (1967) illustrates very nicely how multicollinearity among the predictors limits the size of R. They studied how well reading proficiency (x_1) and writing proficiency (x_2) would predict course grade in college German. The following correlation matrix resulted:

	x_1	x_2	y
x_1	1.00	.58	.33
x_2		1.00	.45
y			1.00

Note the multicollinearity for x_1 and x_2 $(r_{x_1 x_2} = .58)$, and also that x_2 has a simple correlation of .45 with y. The multiple correlation R was only .46. Thus, the relatively high correlation between reading and writing severely limited the ability of reading to add hardly anything (only .01) to the prediction of German grade above and beyond that of writing.

2. Multicollinearity makes determining the importance of a given predictor difficult because the effects of the predictors are confounded due to the correlations among them.

3. Multicollinearity increases the variances of the regression coefficients. The greater these variances, the more unstable the prediction equation will be.

The following are two methods for diagnosing multicollinearity:

1.   Examine the simple correlations among the predictors from the correlation matrix. These should be observed, and are easy to understand, but the researcher need be warned that they do not always indicate the extent of multicollinearity. More subtle forms of multicollinearity may exist. One such more subtle form is discussed next.

2.   Examine the variance inflation factors for the predictors.

The quantity $1/(1 - R_j^2)$ is called the jth *variance inflation factor*, where R_j^2 is the squared multiple correlation for predicting the jth predictor from all other predictors.

The variance inflation factor for a predictor indicates whether there is a strong linear association between it and all the remaining predictors. It is distinctly possible for a predictor to have only moderate and/or relatively weak associations with the other predictors in terms of simple correlations, and yet to have a quite high R when regressed on all the other predictors. When is the value for a variance inflation factor large enough to cause concern? Myers (1990) offers the following suggestion: "Though no rule of thumb on numerical values is foolproof, it is generally believed that if any VIF exceeds 10, there is reason for at least some concern; then one should consider variable deletion or an alternative to least squares estimation to combat the problem" (p. 369). The variance inflation factors are easily obtained from SAS REG (cf. Table 3.6).

There are at least three ways of combating multicollinearity. One way is to combine predictors that are highly correlated. For example, if there are three measures relating to a single construct which have intercorrelations of about .80 or larger, then add them to form a single measure.

A second way, if one has initially a fairly large set of predictors, is to consider doing a principal components analysis (a type of factor analysis) to reduce to a much smaller set of predictors. For example, if there are 30 predictors we are undoubtedly not measuring 30 different constructs. A factor analysis will tell us how many main constructs we are actually measuring. The factors become the new predictors, and since the factors are uncorrelated by construction, we eliminate the multicollinearity problem. Principal components analysis is discussed in some detail in Chapter 11. In that chapter we show how to use SAS and SPSSX to do a components analysis on a set of predictors and then pass the factor scores to a regression program.

A third way of combating multicollinearity is to use a technique called ridge regression. This approach is beyond the scope of this text, although Myers (1990) has a nice discussion for those who are interested.

3.8 MODEL SELECTION

There are various methods available for selecting a good set of predictors:

1. **Substantive Knowledge.** As Weisberg (1985) has noted, "The single most important tool in selecting a subset of variables for use in a model is the analyst's knowledge of the substantive area under study . . ." (p. 210). It is important for the investigator to be judicious in his/her selection of predictors. Far too many investigators have abused multiple regression by"throwing everything in the hopper," often merely because the variables are available. Cohen (1990), among many others, has commented on the indiscriminate use of variables; "I have encountered too many studies with prodigious numbers of dependent variables, or with what seemed to me far too many independent variables, or (heaven help us) both."

There are several good reasons for generally preferring to work with a small number of predictors: (a) Principle of scientific parsimony; (b) Reducing the number of predictors improves the n/k ratio, and this helps cross validation prospects; (c) Note the following from Lord and Novick (1968):

> Experience in psychology and in many other fields of application has shown that it is seldom worthwhile to include very many predictor variables in a regression equation, for the incremental validity of new variables, after a certain point, is usually very low. This is true because tests tend to overlap in content and consequently the addition of a fifth or sixth test may add little that is new to the battery and still relevant to the criterion. (p. 274)

2. **Sequential Methods.** These are the forward, stepwise, and backward selection procedures that are very popular with many researchers. All these procedures involve a partialling-out process, that is, they look at the contribution of a predictor with the effects of the other predictors partialled out, or held constant. Many readers may have been exposed in a previous statistics course to the notion of a partial (and maybe a part) correlation, but a review is nevertheless in order.

We consider a procedure that, for a *given ordering* of the predictors, will enable us to determine the unique contribution each predictors is making in accounting for variance on y. This procedure, which uses semipartial correlations, will disentangle the correlations among the predictors.

The partial correlation between variables 1 and 2 with variable 3 partialled from both 1 and 2 is the correlation with variable 3 held constant, as the reader may recall. The formula for the partial correlation is given by

$$r_{12.3} = \frac{r_{12} - r_{13}\, r_{23}}{\sqrt{1 - r_{13}^2}\ \sqrt{1 - r_{23}^2}}$$

We have introduced the partial correlation first for two reasons: (1) the semipartial correlation is a variant of the partial correlation and (2) the partial correlation will be involved in computing more complicated semipartial correlations.

For breaking down R^2 we will want to work with the semipartial, sometimes called part, correlation. The formula for the semipartial correlation is:

$$r_{12.3(s)} = \frac{r_{12} - r_{13}\, r_{23}}{\sqrt{1 - r_{23}^2}}$$

The only difference between this equation and the previous one is that the denominator here doesn't contain the standard deviation of the partialled scores for variable 1.

In multiple correlation we wish to partial the independent variables (the predictors) from one another, but not from the dependent variable. We wish to leave the dependent variable intact, and not partial any variance attributable to the predictors. Let $R^2_{y12 \ldots k}$ denote the squared multiple correlation for the k predictors, where the predictors appear after the dot. Consider the case of one dependent variable and three predictors. It can be shown that:

$$R^2_{y.123} = r_{y1}^2 + r_{y2.1(s)}^2 + r_{y3.12(s)}^2$$

where

$$r_{y2.1(s)} = \frac{r_{y2} - r_{y1}\, r_{21}}{\sqrt{1 - r_{21}^2}} \tag{5}$$

is the semipartial correlation between y and variable 2, with variable 1 partialled only from variable 2, and $r_{y3\ 12(s)}$ is the semipartial correlation between y and variable 3 with variables 1 and 2 partialled only from variable 3:

$$r_{y3.12(s)} = \frac{r_{y3.1(s)} - r_{y2.1(s)}\, r_{23.1}}{\sqrt{1 - r_{23.1}^2}} \tag{6}$$

Thus, through the use of semipartial correlations we disentangle the correlations among the predictors and determine how much *unique* variance on each predictor is related to variance on y.

We now consider two examples to illustrate the meaning of squared semipartial correlations; the first example being a verbal explanation while the second is a graphical representation.

Example 3 — Verbal Explanation of Variance Breakdown

y — freshman college GPA
predictor 1 — high school GPA

predictor 2 — SAT total score
predictor 3 — attitude toward education

$$R^2_{y.123} = r_{y1}^2 + r^2_{y2.1(s)} + r^2_{y3.12(s)}$$

r_{y1}^2 gives the variance in college GPA scores that is predictable from variability on high school GPA scores. That is, because of differences in high school GPA the subject will differ (vary) in college GPA.

$r^2_{y2.1(s)}$ gives the residual variance in SAT scores (i.e., variance *unrelated* to variance on high school GPA) which is related to variance in college GPA.

$r^2_{y3.12(s)}$ gives the residual variance on attitude (i.e., variance *not* related to its correlations with high school GPA and SAT score) which is related to variance on college GPA.

Example 4 — Graphical Representation of Variance Breakdown

This is easiest to see for 2 predictors. Therefore, suppose we have the following: $r_{y1} = .60$, $r_{y2} = .50$ and $r_{12} = .70$. We will use a Venn diagram, where a circle represents variance for a variable, and overlap between two circles indicates amount of variance the two variables share.

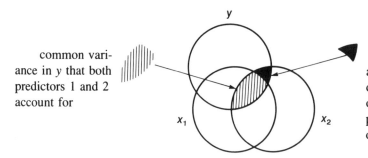

common variance in *y* that both predictors 1 and 2 account for

variance in *y* accounted for by predictor 2 after the effect of predictor 1 has been partialled out—this is only 1.2.

Below we present the semipartial correlation, showing how the 1.2% is arrived at:

$$r_{y2.1(s)} = \frac{r_{y2} - r_{y1}\, r_{21}}{\sqrt{1 - r^2_{21}}} = \frac{.50 - .60(.70)}{\sqrt{1 - .49}} = .11 \Rightarrow r^2_{y2.1(s)} = .012$$

FORWARD—The first predictor that has an opportunity to enter the equation is the one which has the largest simple correlation with *y*. If this predictor is significant, then the predictor with the largest semipartial correlation with *y* is considered, etc. At some stage a given predictor will not make a significant contribution to prediction, and the procedure terminates. It is important to remember that with this procedure, once a variable gets into the equation it stays.

STEPWISE—This is basically a variation on the forward selection procedure. However, at each stage of the procedure, a test is made of the least useful predictor. The importance of each predictor is constantly reassessed. Thus, a predictor that may have been the best entry candidate earlier may now be superfluous.

BACKWARD SELECTION—The steps are as follows: (a) An equation is computed with all the predictors; (b) The partial *F* is calculated for every predictor, treated as though it were the last predictor to enter the regression equation; (c) The smallest partial *F* value, say F_1, is compared to a preselected significance value (F_0), or to an *F* to remove, as in the BMDP2R program. If $F_1 < F_0$, remove that predictor and recompute the equation with the remaining variables. Reenter stage B.

3. **Use of Mallow's** C_p Before we introduce Mallows' C_p, it is important to consider the consequences of underfitting (important variables are left out of the model) and overfitting (having variables in the model that make essentially no contribution or are marginal). Myers (1990, pp 178-180) has an excellent discussion on the impact of underfitting and overfitting, and notes that, "A model that is too simple may suffer from biased coefficients and biased prediction, while an overly complicated model can result in large variances, both in the coefficients and in the prediction."

This measure was introduced by C. L. Mallows (1973) as a criterion for selecting a model. It measures total squared error, and it was recommended by Mallows to choose the model(s) where $C_p \approx p$. For these models the amount of underfitting and/or overfitting is minimized. Mallows' criterion may be written as

$$C_p = p + \frac{(s^2 - \hat{\sigma}^2)(N-p)}{\hat{\sigma}^2} \quad (p = k + 1) \tag{7}$$

where s^2 is the residual variance for the model being evaluated and $\hat{\sigma}^2$ is an estimate of the residual variance that is usually based on the full model.

4. **Use of MAXR Procedure From SAS.** There are *nine* methods of model selection in the SAS REG program (*SAS/STAT USER'S GUIDE, VOLUME 2*, 1990), MAXR being one of them. This procedure produces

several models; the best one variable model, the best two variable model, etc. Here is the description of the procedure from the *SAS/STAT* manual

> The MAXR method begins by finding the one variable model producing the highest R^2. Then another variable, the one that yields the greatest increase in R^2, is added. Once the two variable model is obtained, each of the variables in the model is compared to each variable not in the model. For each comparison, MAXR determines if removing one variable and replacing it with the other variable increases R^2. After comparing all possible switches, MAXR makes the switch that produces the largest increase in R^2. Comparisons begin again, and the process continues until MAXR finds that no switch could increase R^2. . . . Another variable is then added to the model, and the comparing and switching process is repeated to find the best three variable model. (p.1398)

5. **All Possible Regressions.** If you wish to follow this route, then the biomedical program BMDP9R should be considered. The number of possible regressions increases quite sharply as k increases; however, the algorithm used by the program efficiently identifies good subsets while computing only a small fraction of all possible regressions. The manual indicates that computation time for about 25 predictors is comparable to that for stepwise regression. An adjusted R^2 method and Mallows' C_k identify, by default, the 5 best subsets without regard to subset size. This pool of candidate models can then be examined further using regression diagnostics and cross validity criteria to be mentioned below.

Use of one or more of the above methods will often yield a number of models of roughly equal efficacy. As Myers (1990) noted, "The successful model builder will eventually understand that with many data sets, several models can be fit that would be of nearly equal effectiveness. Thus the problem that one deals with is the selection of *one model* from a pool of *candidate models*" (p. 164). One of the problems with the stepwise methods, which are very frequently used, is that they have led many investigators to conclude that they have found *the* best model, when in fact there may be some better models and/or several other models that are about as good. As Huberty notes (1989), "And one or more of these subsets may be more interesting or relevant in a substantive sense" (p. 46).

As mentioned earlier, Mallows' criterion is useful in guarding against both underfitting and overfitting. Three other very important criteria that can be used to select from the candidate pool all relate to the generalizability of the prediction equation, that is, how well will the equation predict on an independent sample(s) of data. The 3 methods of model validation, which are discussed in detail in 3.11, are:

1. Data splitting—Randomly split the data, obtain a prediction equation on one half of the random split and then check it's predictive power (cross validate) on the other sample.
2. Use of the PRESS statistic.
3. Obtain an *estimate* of the average predictive power of the equation on many other samples from the same population, using a formula due to Stein (Herzberg, 1969).

3.9 TWO COMPUTER EXAMPLES

To illustrate the use of several of the aforementioned model selection methods, we consider two computer examples. The first example illustrates the SPSSX REGRESSION program, and uses data from Morrison (1983) on 32 students enrolled in an MBA course. We predict instructor course evaluation from 5 predictors. The second example illustrates SAS REG on quality ratings of 46 research doctorate programs in psychology, where we are attempting to predict quality ratings from factors such as number of program graduates, percentage of graduates that received fellowships or grant support, etc. (Singer & Willett, 1988).

Example 5—SPSSX Regression on Morrison MBA Data

The data for this problem is from Morrison (1983). The dependent variable is instructor course evaluation in an MBA course, with the five predictors being clarity, stimulation, knowledge, interest, and course evaluation. We illustrate two of the sequential procedures, stepwise and backward selection, using the SPSSX REGRESSION program. The control lines for running the analyses, along with the correlation matrix, are given in Table 3.3.

SPSSX REGRESSION has "p values," denoted by PIN and POUT, which govern whether a predictor will enter the equation and whether it will be deleted. The default values are PIN = .05 and POUT = .10. In other words, a predictor must be "significant" at the .05 level to enter, or must not be significant at the .10 level to be deleted.

First, we discuss the stepwise procedure results. Examination of the correlation matrix in Table 3.3 reveals that three of the predictors (CLARITY, STIMUL, and COUEVAL) are strongly related to INSTEVAL (simple correlations of .862, .739, and .738, respectively). Because clarity has the highest correlation, it will enter the equation first. Superficially, it might appear that STIMUL or COUEVAL would enter next; however, we

TABLE 3.3
SPSSX Control Lines for Stepwise and Backward Selection Runs
on the Morrison MBA Data and the Correlation Matrix

TITLE 'MULTIPLE REGRESSION - 5 PREDICTORS'
DATA LIST FREE/INSTEVAL CLARITY STIMUL KNOWLDGE INTEREST
  COUEVAL
LIST
BEGIN DATA

1	1	2	1	1	2	1	2	2	1	1	1	1	1	1	1	1	2	1	1	2	1	1	2
2	1	3	2	2	2	2	2	4	1	1	2	2	3	3	1	1	2	2	3	4	1	2	3
2	2	3	1	3	3	2	2	2	2	2	2	2	2	3	2	1	2	2	2	2	3	3	2
2	2	2	1	1	2	2	2	4	2	2	2	2	3	3	1	1	3	2	3	4	1	1	2
2	3	2	1	1	2	3	4	4	3	2	2	3	4	3	1	1	4	3	4	3	1	2	3
3	4	3	2	2	3	3	3	4	2	3	3	3	3	4	2	3	3	3	4	3	1	1	2
3	4	5	1	1	3	3	3	5	1	2	3	3	4	4	1	2	3	3	4	4	1	1	3
3	3	3	2	1	3	3	3	5	1	1	2	4	5	5	2	3	4	4	4	5	2	3	4

END DATA
① REGRESSION DESCRIPTIVES = DEFAULT/
  VARIABLES = INSTEVAL TO COUEVAL/
② STATISTICS = DEFAULTS HISTORY/
  DEPENDENT = INSTEVAL/
③ METHOD = STEPWISE/
④ CASEWISE = ALL PRED RESID ZRESID LEVER COOK/
⑤ SCATTERPLOT(*RES,*PRE)/

CORRELATION MATRIX

	INSTEVAL	CLARITY	STIMUL	KNOWLDGE	INTEREST	COUEVAL
INSTEVAL	1.000	.862	.739	.282	.435	.738
CLARITY	.862	1.000	.617	.057	.200	.651
STIMUL	.739	.617	1.000	.078	.317	.523
KNOWLEDGE	.282	.057	.078	1.000	.583	.041
INTEREST	.435	.200	.317	.583	1.000	.448
COUEVAL	.738	.651	.523	.041	.448	1.000

① The DESCRIPTIVES = DEFAULT subcommand yields the means, standard deviations and the correlation matrix for the variables.

② The DEFAULTS part of the STATISTICS subcommand yields, among other things, the ANOVA table for each step, R, R^2 and adjusted R^2. The HISTORY part is needed to obtain a summary table, which is very helpful to have.

③ To obtain the backward selection procedure, we would simply put METHOD = BACKWARD/

④ This CASEWISE subcommand yields important regression diagnostics : ZRESID (standardized residuals—for identifying outliers on y), LEVER (hat elements—for identifying outliers on predictors), and COOK (Cook's distance—for identifying influential data points).

⑤ This SCATTERPLOT subcommand yields the plot of the residuals vs the predicted values, which is very useful for determining whether any of the assumptions underlying the linear regression model may be violated.

must take into account how these predictors are correlated with CLARITY, and indeed both have fairly high correlations with CLARITY (.617 and .651 respectively). Thus, they will not account for as much unique variance on INSTEVAL, above and beyond that of CLARITY, as first appeared. On the other hand, INTEREST, which has a considerably lower correlation with INSTEVAL (.44), is only correlated .20 with CLARITY. Thus, the variance on INSTEVAL it accounts for is relatively independent of the variance CLARITY accounted for. And, as seen in Table 3.4, it is INTEREST that enters the regression equation second.

STIMUL is the third and final predictor to enter, since it's p value (.0086) is less than the default value of .05. Finally, the other predictors (KNOWLEDGE and COUEVAL) don't enter since their p values (.0989 and .1288) are greater than .05.

Selected printout from the backward selection procedure appears in Table 3.5. First, all of the predictors are put into the equation. Then, the procedure determines which of the predictors makes the *least* contribution when entered last in the equation. That predictor is INTEREST, and since it's p value is .9097, it is deleted from the equation. None of the other predictors can be further deleted because their p values are much less than .10.

Interestingly, note that two *different* sets of predictors emerge from the two sequential selection procedures. The stepwise procedure yields the set (CLARITY, INTEREST, and STIMUL), while the backward procedure yields (COUEVAL, KNOWLEDGE, STIMUL, and CLARITY). However, CLARITY and STIMUL are common to both sets. On the grounds of parsimony, we might prefer the set (CLARITY, INTEREST, and STIMUL), especially since the adjusted R^2's for the two sets are quite close (.84 and .87).

There are three other things that should be checked out before settling on this as our chosen model:

1. We need to determine if the assumptions of the linear regression model are tenable.
2. We need an estimate of the cross validity power of the equation.
3. We need to check for the existence of outliers and/or influential data points.

Figure 3.4 shows the plot of the residuals versus the predicted values from SPSSX. This plot shows essentially random variation of the points about the horizontal line of 0, indicating no violations of assumptions.

The issues of cross validity power and outliers are considered later in this chapter, and we are applied to this problem in 3.15, after both topics have been covered.

TABLE 3.4

Selected Printout From SPSSX Regression for the Stepwise Regression Run on the Morrison MBA Data

Block Number 1. Method: Stepwise Criteria PIN .0500 POUT .1000
Variable(s) Entered on Step Number 1.. CLARITY ①

Multiple R	.86181
R Square	.74271
Adjusted R Square	.73414
Standard Error	.41123

Analysis of Variance

	DF	Sum of Squares	Mean Square
Regression	1	14.64541	14.64541
Residual	30	5.07334	.16911
F = 86.60220		Signif F = .0000	

----Variables in the Equation----

Variable	B	SE B	Beta	T	Sig T
CLARITY	.635893	.068331	.861809	9.306	.0000
(Constant)	.597929	.207470		2.882	.0072

----Variables not in the Equation----

Variable	Beta In	Partial	Min Toler	T	Sig T
STIMUL	.334997	.519545	.618839	3.274	.0027
KNOWLDGE	.233238	.459070	.996721	2.783	.0094
② INTEREST	.273474	.528237	.959930	3.350	.0023
COUEVAL	.306916	.459298	.576190	2.784	.0093

Variable(s) Entered on Step Number 2.. INTEREST

Multiple R	.90250
R Square	.81451
Adjusted R Square	.80171
Standard Error	.35514

Analysis of Variance

	DF	Sum of Squares	Mean Square
Regression	2	16.06105	8.03052
Residual	29	3.65770	.12613
F = 63.66980		Signif F = .0000	

----Variables in the Equation----

Variable	B	SE B	Beta	T	Sig T
CLARITY	.595501	.060231	.807067	9.887	.0000
INTEREST	.277009	.082684	.273474	3.350	.0023
(Constant)	.253999	.206500		1.230	.2286

----Variables not in the Equation----

Variable	Beta In	Partial	Min Toler	T	Sig T
③ STIMUL	.266309	.470863	.579889	2.824	.0086
KNOWLDGE	.115971	.218095	.631813	1.183	.2469
COUEVAL	.191064	.304529	.471225	1.692	.1018

Variable(s) Entered on Step Number 3.. STIMUL

		Analysis of Variance			
Multiple R	.92500		DF	Sum of Squares	Mean Square
R Square	.85563	Regression	3	16.87200	5.62400
Adjusted R Square	.84016	Residual	28	2.84675	.10167
Standard Error	.31886	F = 55.31646	Signif F = .0000		

------Variables in the Equation------

Variable	B	SE B	Beta	T	Sig T
CLARITY	.482109	.067352	.653390	7.158	.0000
INTEREST	.222672	.076688	.219831	2.904	.0071
STIMUL	⑥ .194742	.068954	.266309	2.824	.0086
(Constant)	.021368	.202874		.105	.9169

------Variables not in the Equation------

Variable	Beta In	Partial	Min Toler	T	Sig T
KNOWLDGE	.147622	.312481	.571790	1.709	.0989
COUEVAL	.160769	.288726	.451476	1.567	.1288 ④

* * * * * * * * * * * * * *

Summary table

	Variable	FCh	SigCh		Variable	BeaIn	Correl
In:	KNOWLDGE	86.602	.000		CLARITY	.8618	.8618
In:	COUEVAL	11.224	.002		INTEREST	.2735	.4350
In:	STIMUL	7.976	.009		STIMUL	.2663	.7394

SQUARED SEMIPARTIAL CORRELATIONS

⑤

Step	MultR	Rsq	AdjRsq	F(Eqn)	SigF	RsqCh
1	.8618	.7427	.7341	86.602	.000	.7427
2	.9025	.8145	.8017	63.670	.000	.0718
3	.9250	.8556	.8402	55.316	.000	.0411

① This predictor enters the equation first, since it has the highest simple correlation with the dependent variable INSTEVAL, i.e., .8618.

② INTEREST has the opportunity to enter the equation next since it has the largest partial correlation (.528) with the dependent variable, and does enter since its p value (.0023) is less than the default entry value of .05.

③ Since STIMUL has the strongest tie to INSTEVAL, after the effects of CLARITY and INTEREST are partialled out, it gets the opportunity to enter the equation next. STIMUL does enter since it's p value (.0086) is less than .05.

④ Since neither of these p values is less than .05, no other predictors can enter, and the procedure terminates.

⑤ This column shows how the variance accounted for on the dependent variable increases as predictors are added to the equation. With just CLARITY in the equation we account for 74.27%; adding INTEREST increases the variance accounted for to 81.45%, and finally with 3 predictors (STIMUL added) we account for 85.56% of the variance on INSTEVAL.

⑥ These are the raw regression coefficients that define the prediction equation, i.e., INSTEVAL = .482 CLARITY + .223 INTEREST + .195 STIMUL + .021 The coefficient of .482 for CLARITY means that for every unit change on CLARITY there is a change of .482 units on INSTEVAL. The coefficient of .223 for INTEREST means that for every unit change on INTEREST there is a change of .223 units on INSTEVAL.

TABLE 3.5
Selected Printout From SPSSX Regression for Backward Selection on the Morrison MBA Data

Equation Number 1.   Dependent Variable..   INSTEVAL
Descriptive Satistics are printed on Page 4
Block Number 1. Method: Enter

Variable(s) Entered on Step Number
1.. COUEVAL
2.. KNOWLDGE
3.. STIMUL
4.. INTEREST
5.. CLARITY

Multiple R	.94568	Analysis of Variance		
R Square	.89432		DF	Sum of Squares	Mean Square
Adjusted R Square	.87399	Regression	5	17.63481	3.52696
Standard Error	.28311	Residual	26	2.08394	.08015
		F = 44.00370	Signif F = .0000		

Block Number 2. Method: Backward   Criterion POUT .1000
Variable(s) Entered on Step Number   6.. INTEREST

Multiple R	.94566	Analysis of Variance		
R Square	.89426		DF	Sum of Squares	Mean Square
Adjusted R Square	.87860	Regression	4	17.63376	4.40844
Standard Error	.27789	Residual	27	2.08499	.07722
		F = 57.08797	Signif F = .0000		

---------------- Variables in the Equation ----------------

Variable	B	SE B	Beta	T	Sig T
COUEVAL	.276256	.093552	.248604	2.953	.0064
KNOWLDGE	.284567	.080892	.220832	3.518	.0016
STIMUL	.198408	.059490	.271322	3.335	.0025
CLARITY	.383548	.067316	.519812	5.698	.0000
(Constant)	-.450027	.222006		-2.027	.0526

---------------- Variables not in the Equation ----------------

Variable	Beta In	Partial	Min Toler	T	Sig T
INTEREST	.010995	.022460	.416440	.115	.9097

End Block Number 2   POUT = .100 Limits reached.

Example 6—SAS REG on Doctoral Programs in Psychology

The data for this example come from a National Academy of Sciences report (1982) that, among other things, provided ratings on the quality of 46 research doctoral programs in psychology. The six variables used to predict quality are:

NFACULTY—number of faculty members in the program as of December 1980
NGRADS—number of program graduates from 1975 through 1980
PCTSUPP—percentage of program graduates from 1975–1979 that received fellowships or training grant support during their graduate education
PCTGRANT—percentage of faculty members holding research grants from the Alcohol, Drug Abuse, and Mental Health Administration, the National Institute of Health or the National Science Foundation at any time during 1978–1980
NARTICLE—number of published articles attributed to program faculty members from 1978–1980
PCTPUB—percentage of faculty with one or more published articles from 1978–1980

Both the stepwise procedure and the MAXR procedure were used on this data to generate several regression models. The control lines for doing this, along with the correlation matrix, are given in Table 3.6.

One very nice feature of SAS REG, which we did not have for SPSSX, is that Mallows' C_p is given for each model. The stepwise procedure terminated after 4 predictors entered. Below is the summary table, exactly as it appears on the printout:

Summary of Stepwise Procedure for Dependent Variable QUALITY

Step	Variable Entered Removed	Partial $R**2$	Model $R**2$	$C(p)$	F	Prob $> F$
1	NARTIC	0.5809	0.5809	55.1185	60.9861	0.0001
2	PCTGRT	0.1668	0.7477	18.4760	28.4156	0.0001
3	PCTSUPP	0.0569	0.8045	7.2970	12.2197	0.0011
4	NFACUL	0.0176	0.8221	5.2161	4.0595	0.0505

This four predictor model appears to be a reasonably good one. First, Mallows[1] C_p is very close to p (recall $p = k + 1$), that is, $5.216 \approx 5$,

TABLE 3.6

SAS Reg Control Lines for Stepwise and MAXR Runs on the National
Academy of Sciences Data and the Correlation Matrix

DATA SINGER;
INPUT QUALITY NFACUL NGRADS PCTSUPP PCTGRT NARTIC PCTPUB;
CARDS;

DATA LINES

① PROC REG SIMPLE CORR;
② MODEL QUALITY = NFACUL NGRADS PCTSUPP PCTGRT NARTIC PCTPUB/
SELECTION = STEPWISE VIF R INFLUENCE;
MODEL QUALITY = NFACUL NGRADS PCTSUPP PCTGRT NARTIC PCTPUB/
SELECTION = MAXR VIF R INFLUENCE;

① SIMPLE is needed to obtain descriptive statistics (means, variances, etc) for all
variables.
CORR is needed to obtain the correlation matrix for the variables.

② In this MODEL statement, the dependent variable goes on the left and all predictors to
the right of the equals.
SELECTION is where we indicate which of the 9 procedures we wish to use. There is a
wide variety of other information we can get printed out. Here we have selected VIF
(variance inflation factors), R (analysis of residuals — standard residuals, hat elements,
Cooks D), and INFLUENCE (influence diagnostics).

Note that there are two separate MODEL statements for the two regression procedures
being requested. Although multiple procedures can be obtained in one run, you *must*
have separate MODEL statement for each procedure.

CORRELATION MATRIX

		NFACUL	NGRADS	PCTSUPP	PCTGRT	NARTIC	PCTPUB	QUALITY
		2	3	4	5	6	7	1
NFACUL	2	1.000						
NGRADS	3	0.692	1.000					
PCTSUPP	4	0.395	0.337	1.000				
PCTGRT	5	0.162	0.071	0.351	1.000			
NARTIC	6	0.755	0.646	0.366	0.436	1.000		
PCTPUB	7	0.205	0.171	0.347	0.490	0.593	1.000	
QUALITY	1	0.622	0.418	0.582	0.700	0.762	0.585	1.000

---

indicating that there is not much bias in the model. Secondly, $R^2 = .8221$,
indicating that we can predict quality quite well from the 4 predictors.
Although this R^2 is *not* adjusted, the adjusted value will not differ much
because we have not selected from a large pool of predictors.

Selected printout from the MAXR procedure run appears in Table 3.7.
From Table 3.7 we can construct the following results:

TABLE 3.7
Selected Printout From the MAXR Run on the National Academy of Sciences Data

Maximum R-square Improvement for Dependent Variable QUALITY

Step 1 Variable NARTIC Entered   R-square = 0.58089673   C(p) = 55.11853652
The above model is the best 1-variable model found.

Step 2 Variable PCTGRT Entered   R-square = 0.74765405   C(p) = 18.47596774
Step 3 Variable NARTIC Removed   R-square = 0.75462892   C(p) = 16.85968570
        Variable NFACUL Entered

The above model is the best 2-variable model found.

Step 4 Variable PCTPUB Entered   R-square = 0.79654184   C(p) = 9.14723035

The above model is the best 3-variable model found.

Step 5 Variable PCTSUPP Entered   R-square = 0.81908649   C(p) = 5.92297432
Step 6 Variable PCTPUB Removed   R-square = 0.82213698   C(p) = 5.21608457
        Variable NARTIC Entered

	DF	Sum of Squares	Mean Square	F	Prob > f
Regression	4	3752.82298869	938.20574717	47.38	0.0001
Error	41	811.89440261	19.80230250		
Total	45	4564.71739130			

Variable	Parameter Estimate	Standard Error	Type II Sum of Squares	F	Prob > F
INTERCEP	9.06132974	1.64472577	601.05272060	30.35	0.0001
NFACUL	0.13329934	0.06615919	80.38802096	4.06	0.0505
PCTSUPP	0.09452909	0.03236602	168.91497705	8.53	0.0057
PCTGRT	0.24644511	0.04414314	617.20528404	31.17	0.0001
NARTIC	0.05455483	0.01954712	154.24691982	7.79	0.0079

The above model is the best 4-variable model found.

91

BEST MODEL	VARIABLE(S)	MALLOWS C_p
for 1 variable	NARTIC	55.118
for 2 variables	PCTGRT, NFACUL	16.859
for 3 variables	PCTPUB, PCTGRT, NFACUL	9.147
for 4 variables	NFACUL, PCTSUPP, PCTGRT, NARTIC	5.216

In this case, the *same* 4 predictor model is selected by the MAXR procedure that was selected by the stepwise procedure.

Caveat on p Values for the "Significance" of Predictors

The p values that are given by SPSSX and SAS for the "significance" of each predictor at each step for stepwise or the forward selection procedures should be treated tenuously, especially if your initial pool of predictors is moderate (15) or large (30). The reason is that the ordinary F distribution is *not* appropriate here, because the largest F is being selected out of all F's available. Thus, the appropriate critical value will be larger (and can be considerably larger) than would be obtained from the ordinary null F distribution. Draper and Smith (1981) note, "Studies have shown, for example, that in some cases where an entry F test was made at the α level, the appropriate probability was $q\alpha$, where there were q entry candidates at that stage" (p. 311). This is saying, for example, that an experimenter may think his or her probability of erroneously including a predictor is .05, when in fact the *actual* probability of erroneously including the predictor is .50 (if there were 10 entry candidates at that point)!

Thus, the F tests are positively biased, and the greater the number of predictors, the larger the bias. Hence, these F tests should be used only as rough guides to the usefulness of the predictors chosen. The acid test is how well the predictors do under cross validation. It can be unwise to use *any* of the stepwise procedures with 20 or 30 predictors and only 100 subjects, since capitalization on chance is great, and the results may well not cross-validate. To find an equation that probably will have generalizability, it is best to carefully select (using substantive knowledge and/or any previous related literature) a small or relatively small set of predictors.

3.10 CHECKING ASSUMPTIONS FOR THE REGRESSION MODEL

Recall that in the linear regression model it is assumed that the errors are independent and follow a normal distribution with constant variance. The normality assumption can be checked through use of the histogram of the standardized or studentized residuals, as we did in Table 3.2 for the simple regression example. The independence assumption implies that the subjects are responding independently of one another. This is an important assumption. We show in Chapter 6, in the context of analysis of variance, that if independence is violated only mildly, then the probability of a type I error will be *several* times greater than the level the experimenter thinks he or she is working at. Thus, instead of rejecting falsely 5% of the time, the experimenter may be rejecting falsely 25 or 30% of the time.

We now consider an example where this assumption was violated. Nold and Freedman (1977) had each of 22 college freshmen write four in-class essays in two 1 hour sessions, separated by a span of several months. In doing a subsequent regression analysis to predict quality of essay response, they used an n of 88. However, the responses for each subject on the 4essays are obviously going to be correlated, so that there are not 88 independent observations, but only 22.

Residual Plots

There are various types of plots that are available for assessing potential problems with the regression model (Draper & Smith, 1981; Weisberg, 1985). One of the most useful graphs the standardized residuals (r_i) versus the predicted values $(\hat{y}_i)$. If the assumptions of the linear regression model are tenable, then the standardized residuals should scatter randomly about a horizontal line defined by $r_i = 0$, as shown in Figure 3.3a. *Any systematic pattern or clustering of the residuals suggests a model violation(s).* Three such systematic patterns are indicated in Figures 3.3b to 3.3d. Figure 3.3b shows a systematic quadratic (second degree equation) clustering of the residuals. For Figure 3.3c the variability of the residuals increases systematically as the predicted values increase, suggesting a violation of the constant variance assumption.

It is important to note that the plots in Figure 3.3 are somewhat idealized, constructed to be clear violations. As Weisberg (1985) states, "Unfortunately, these idealized plots cover up one very important point; in real data sets, the true state of affairs is rarely this clear" (p. 131).

In Figure 3.4 we present residual plots for three real data sets. The first plot is for the Morrison data (the first computer example), and shows essentially random scatter of the residuals, suggesting no violations of assumptions. The remaining two plots are from a study by a statistician who analyzed the salaries of over 260 major league hitters, using predictors such as career batting average, career home runs per time at bat, years in the major leagues, etc. These plots are from Moore and McCabe (1989), and are used with permission. Figure 3.4b, which plots the residuals versus

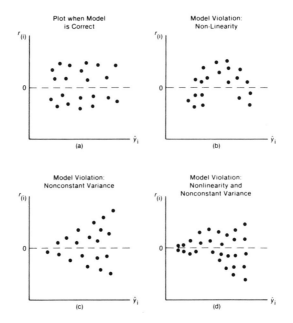

FIG. 3.3   Residual Plots of Studentized Residuals vs Predicted Values

predicted salaries, shows a clear violation of the constant variance assumption. For lower predicted salaries there is little variability about 0, but for the high salaries there is considerable variability of the residuals. The implication of this is that the model will predict lower salaries quite accurately, but not so for the higher salaries.

Figure 3.4c plots the residuals versus number of years in the major

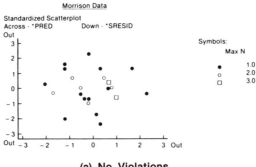

(a) No Violations

FIG. 3.4.   Residual Plots for Three Real Data Sets Showing No Violations, Heterogenous Variance and Curvilinearity

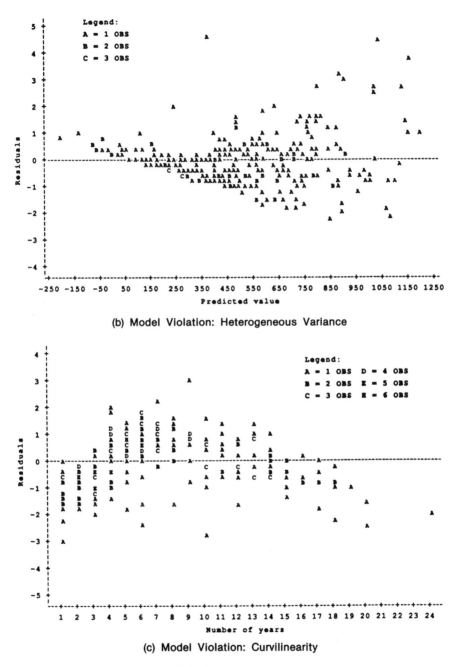

(b) Model Violation: Heterogeneous Variance

(c) Model Violation: Curvilinearity

FIG. 3.4.   (*Continued*)

leagues. This plot shows a clear curvilinear clustering, that is, quadratic. The curved lines encompass the vast majority of points to make this trend even more evident. The implication of this curvilinear trend is that the regression model will tend to overestimate the salaries of players who have been in the major years only a few years or over 15 years, while it will underestimate the salaries of players who have been in the majors about 5 to 9 years.

In concluding this section, note that if nonlinearity or nonconstant variance are found, there are various remedies. For non-linearity, perhaps a polynomial model is needed. Or sometimes a transformation of the data will enable a nonlinear model to be approximated by a linear one. For non-constant variance, weighted least squares is one possibility, or more commonly, a variance stabilizing transformation (such as square root or log) may be used. I refer the reader to Weisberg (1985, Chapter 6) for an excellent discussion of remedies for regression model violations.

3.11 MODEL VALIDATION

We indicated earlier that it was crucial for the researcher to obtain some measure of how well the regression equation will predict on an independent sample(s) of data. That is, it was important to determine whether the equation had generalizability. We discuss here three forms of model validation, two being empirical and the other involving an *estimate* of average predictive power on other samples. First, I give a brief description of each form, and then elaborate on each form of validation.

1. Data splitting. Here the sample is randomly split in half. It does not have to be split evenly, but we use this for illustration. The regression equation is found on the so-called derivation sample (also called the screening sample, or the sample that "gave birth" to the prediction equation by Tukey). This prediction equation is then applied to the other sample (called validation or calibration) to see how well it predicts the y scores there.

2. Compute an adjusted R^2. There are various adjusted R^2 measures, or measures of shrinkage in predictive power, but they do not all estimate the same thing. The one most commonly used, and that which is printed out by all three major statistical packages (BMDP, SAS, and SPSSX) is due to Wherry. It is very important to note here that the Wherry formula estimates how much variance on y would be accounted for if we had derived the prediction equation in the population from which the sample was drawn. The Wherry formula does *not* indicate how well the derived equation will predict on other samples from the same population. A formula due to Stein

(1960) does estimate average cross validation predictive power. As of this writing it is not printed out by any of the three major packages. The formulas due to Wherry and Stein are presented shortly.

   3.   Use the PRESS statistic.   As pointed out by several authors, in many instances one does not have enough data to be randomly splitting it. One can obtain a good measure of *external* predictive power by use of the PRESS statistic. In this approach the y value for *each* subject is set aside and a prediction equation derived on the remaining data. Thus, n prediction equations are derived and n true prediction errors are found. To be very specific, the prediction error for subject 1 is computed from the equation derived on the remaining $(n-1)$ data points, the prediction error for subject 2 is computed from the equation derived on the other $(n-1)$ data points, etc. As Myers (1990) put it, "PRESS is important in that one has information in the form of n validations in which the fitting sample for each is of size $n-1$" (p. 171).

Data Splitting

Recall that the sample is randomly split. The regression equation is found on the derivation sample and then is applied to the other sample (validation) to determine how well it will predict y there. Below we give a hypothetical example, randomly splitting 100 subjects.

Derivation Sample	Validation Sample		
$n = 50$	$n = 50$		
Prediction Equation $\hat{y}_i = 4 + .3x_1 + .7x_2$	y	x_1	x_2
	6	1	.5
	4.5	2	.3
	. . . .		
	7	5	.2

   Now, using the above prediction equation we predict the y scores in the validation sample:

$$\hat{y}_1 = 4 + .3\,(1) + .7\,(.5) = 4.65$$

$$\hat{y}_2 = 4 + .3\,(2) + .7\,(.3) = 4.81$$

. . . .

$$\hat{y}_{50} = 4 + .3\,(5) + .7(.2) = 5.64$$

   The cross-validated R then is the correlation for the following set of scores:

y	$\hat{y}_i$
6	4.65
4.5	4.81
. . . .	
7	5.64

We illustrate the random splitting and cross-validation using the BMDP9R and BMDP6D programs. The 9R program randomly splits the sample (in the TRANSFORM paragraph) and does the regression analysis. The 6D program is used to obtain the cross-validated correlation. In Table 3.8 we present the control lines for randomly splitting and cross validating for a data set having 50 subjects and 5 predictors. The data for this example is given in the appendix of this chapter.

Adjusted R^2

Herzberg (1969) presents a discussion of various formulas that have been used to estimate the amount of shrinkage found in R^2. As mentioned earlier, the one most commonly used, and due to Wherry, is given by

TABLE 3.8
Control Lines for Randomly Splitting the Sample and Cross
Validating the Regression Equation with BMDP9R

```
//   EXEC BIMED, PROG = BMDP9R
//SYSIN DD *
/PROBLEM TITLE IS 'CROSS VALIDATION'.
/INPUT VARIABLES ARE 6. FORMAT IS STREAM.
/VARIABLE ADD IS 1. WEIGHT IS 7.
/REGRESSION DEPENDENT IS 1. INDEPENDENT ARE 2 TO 6. METHOD IS NONE
/PRINT MATRICES = CORR.RESID.
/TRANSFORM TEMP IS RNDU(1232557). X(7) IS TEMP LT. .5.    ①
/SAVE UNIT = 3. NEW.CODE IS RESID.
/END

     DATA

//   EXEC BIMED,PROG = BMDP6D
//SYSIN DD *
/PROBLEM TITLE IS 'PLOT'.
/INPUT UNIT = 3. CODE = RESID.
/VARIABLE GROUPING IS 7.
/GROUP CODES(7) ARE 0,1. NAMES(7) ARE VALID,DERIV.
/PLOT YVAR = 1. XVAR = PREDICTD. GROUP IS VALID. GROUP IS DERIV. STATISTICS.
/END
```

①In the TRANSFORM paragraph we randomly split the sample. A dummy variable taking on the values 0 and 1 is created to label the members of the derivation and validation samples. The fact that we are adding a new variable to the file is indicated by ADD IS 1 in the VARIABLE paragraph. The number in parentheses after the random number routine RNDU is a large positive *odd* integer which is used to start the random number sequence. The random number routine generates numbers on the interval from 0 to 1. Those cases that are associated with random numbers less than .5 are put in the derivation sample, with the remaining cases constituting the validation sample.

$$\hat{\rho}^2 = 1 - \frac{(n - 1)}{(n - k - 1)} (1 - R^2) \tag{8}$$

where $\hat{\rho}$ is the estimate of ρ, the population multiple correlation coefficient. This is the adjusted R^2 printed out by SAS and SPSSX. Draper and Smith (1981) comment on Equation 8: "A related statistic . . . is the so called adjusted r (R_a^2), the idea being that the statistic R_a^2 can be used to compare equations fitted not only to a specific set of data but also to two or more entirely different sets of data. The value of this statistic for the latter purpose is, in our opinion, not high" (p. 92).

Herzberg notes that, "In applications, the population regression function can never be known and one is more interested in how effective the *sample* regression function is in *other* samples. A measure of this effectiveness is r_c, the sample cross validity. For any given regression function r_c will vary from validation sample to validation sample. The average value of r_c will be approximately equal to the correlation, in the *population,* of the sample regression function with the criterion. This correlation is the population cross-validity, ρ_c. Wherry's formula estimates ρ rather than ρ_c." (p.4).

There are two possible models for the predictors: (1) regression—the values of the predictors are fixed, i.e., we study y only for certain values of x, and (2) correlation—the predictors are random variables—this is a much more reasonable model for social science research. Herzberg presents the following formula for estimating ρ_c^2 under the correlation model:

$$\hat{\rho}_c^2 = 1 - \left(\frac{n - 1}{n - k - 1}\right)\left(\frac{n - 2}{n - k - 2}\right)\left(\frac{n + 1}{n}\right)(1 - R^2) \tag{9}$$

where n is sample size and k is the number of predictors. It can be shown that $\rho_c < \rho$.

If you are interested in cross validity predictive power, then the Stein formula (Equation 9) should be used. As an example, suppose $n = 50$, $k = 10$ and $R^2 = .50$. If you used the Wherry formula (Equation 8), then your estimate is

$$\hat{\rho}^2 = 1 - 49/39 \ (.50) = .372,$$

whereas with the proper Stein formula you would obtain

$$\hat{\rho}_c^2 = 1 - (49/39)(48/38)(51/50)(.50) = .191$$

In other words, use of the Wherry formula would give a misleadingly positive impression of the cross validity predictive power of the equation.

Table 3.9 shows how the estimated predictive power drops off using the Stein formula (Equation 9) for small to fairly large subject/variable ratios when $R^2 = .50$.

TABLE 3.9
Estimated Predictive Power Using the Stein Formula for Small to Fairly
Large Subject/Variable Ratios

Subject/Variable Ratio	Stein Estimate $$1 - \left(\frac{n-1}{n-k-1}\right)\left(\frac{n-2}{n-k-2}\right)\left(\frac{n+1}{n}\right)(1-R^2)$$	Comment
Small (5:1) $n=50$, $k=10$ $R^2=.50$ ②	$1 - (49/39)\,(48/38)\,(51/50)\,(.5)$ $= .191$ ①	The estimated amount of shrinkage is great, i.e., on the average we expect the predictive power to be reduced by about 60%.
Moderate (10:1) $n=100$, $k=10$ $R^2=.50$	$1 - (99/98)\,(98/88)\,(101/100)\,(.5)$ $= .374$	The shrinkage is still fairly substantial.
Fairly Large (15:1) $n=150$, $k=10$ $R^2=.50$	$1 - (149/139)\,(148/138)\,(151/150)\,(.5)$ $= .421$	We finally reach a point where the expected amount of shrinkage is fairly small, i.e., about 16%.

①If we were to apply the prediction equation to many other samples from the same population, then on the *average* we would account for 19.1% of the variance on y.

②We have chosen this value to illustrate since the typical R^2 values found in social science are often around .50.

Press Statistic

The PRESS approach is important in that one has n validations, each based on $(n - 1)$ observations. Thus, each validation is based on essentially the entire sample. This is very important when one does not have large n, for in this situation data splitting is really not practical. For example, if $n = 60$ and we have 6 predictors, randomly splitting the sample involves obtaining a prediction equation on only 30 subjects.

Recall that in deriving the prediction (via the least squares approach), the sum of the squared errors is *minimized*. The PRESS residuals, on the other hand, are true prediction errors, since the y value for each subject was not simultaneously used for fit and model assessment. Let us denote the predicted value for subject i, where that subject was *not* used in developing the prediction equation, by $\hat{y}_{(-i)}$. Then the PRESS residual for each subject is given by

$$\hat{e}_{(-i)} = y_i - \hat{y}_{(-i)}$$

and the PRESS sum of squared residuals is given by

$$\text{PRESS} = \Sigma \, \hat{e}_{(-i)}^{2} \qquad\qquad (10)$$

Therefore, one might prefer the model with the smallest PRESS value. The above PRESS value can be used to calculate an R^2-like statistic that more accurately reflects the generalizability of the model. It is given by

$$R^2_{\text{Press}} = 1 - (\text{PRESS})/\Sigma \, (y_i - \bar{y})^2 \qquad\qquad (11)$$

Importantly, the SAS REG program does routinely print out PRESS, although it is called PREDICTED RESID SS (PRESS). Given this value, it is a simple matter to calculate the R^2 PRESS statistic, since $s_y^2 = \Sigma \, (y_i - \bar{y})^2 \, / \, (n - 1)$.

3.12 IMPORTANCE OF THE ORDER OF THE PREDICTORS IN REGRESSION ANALYSIS

The order in which the predictors enter a regression equation can make a great deal of difference with respect to how much variance on y they account for, especially for moderate or highly correlated predictors. Only for uncorrelated predictors (which would rarely occur in practice), does the order not make a difference. We give two examples to illustrate.

Example 7

A dissertation by Crowder (1975) attempted to predict ratings of trainably mentally (TMs) retarded individuals using I.Q. (x_2) and scores from a TEST of Social Inference (TSI). He was especially interested in showing that the TSI had incremental predictive validity. The criterion was the average ratings by two individuals in charge of the TMs. The intercorrelations among the variables were:

$$r_{x_1 x_2} = .59, \, r_{yx_2} = .54, \, r_{yx_1} = .566$$

Now, consider two orderings for the predictors, one where TSI is entered first, and the other ordering where I.Q. is entered first.

First Ordering % of variance		Second Ordering % of variance	
TSI	32.04	I.Q.	29.16
I.Q.	6.52	TSI	9.40

The first ordering conveys an overly optimistic view of the utility of the TSI scale. Since we know that I.Q. will predict ratings it should be entered first in the equation (as a control variable), and then TSI to see what it's incremental validity is, i.e., how much it *adds* to predicting ratings above and beyond what I.Q. does. Because of the moderate correlation between I.Q. and TSI, the amount of variance accounted for by TSI differs considerably when entered first vs. second (32.04 vs. 9.4).

The 9.4% of variance accounted for by TSI when entered second is obtained through the use of the semipartial correlation previously introduced:

$$r_{y1.2(s)} = \frac{.566 - .54(.59)}{\sqrt{1 - .59^2}} = .306 \Rightarrow r^2_{y1.2(s)} = .094$$

Example 8

Consider the following matrix of correlations for a three predictor problem:

	x_1	x_2	x_3
y	.60	.70	.70
x_1		.70	.60
x_2			.80

Notice that the predictors are strongly intercorrelated.

How much variance in y will x_3 account for if entered first? if entered last?

If x_3 is entered first, then it will account for $(.7)^2$ x 100 or 49% of variance on y, a sizable amount.

To determine how much variance x_3 will account for if entered last, we need to compute the following second order semipartial correlation:

$$r_{y3.12(s)} = \frac{r_{y3.1(s)} - r_{y2.1(s)} r_{23.1}}{\sqrt{1 - r_{23.1}^2}}$$

We show the details below for obtaining $r_{y3.12(s)}$.

$$r_{y2.1(s)} = \frac{r_{y2} - r_{y1} r_{21}}{\sqrt{1 - r_{21}^2}} = \frac{.70 - (.6)(.7)}{\sqrt{1 - .49}}$$

$$r_{y2.1(s)} = \frac{.28}{.714} = .392$$

$$r_{y3.1.(s)} = \frac{r_{y3} - r_{y1} r_{31}}{\sqrt{1 - r_{31}^2}} = \frac{.7 - .6(.6)}{\sqrt{1 - .6^2}} = .425$$

$$r_{23.1} = \frac{r_{23} - r_{21} r_{31}}{\sqrt{1 - r_{21}^2} \sqrt{1 - r_{31}^2}} = \frac{.80 - (.7)(.6)}{\sqrt{1 - .49} \sqrt{1 - .36}} = .665$$

$$r_{y3.12(s)} = \frac{.425 - .392(.665)}{\sqrt{1 - .665^2}} = \frac{.164}{.746} = .22$$

$$r^2_{y3.12(s)} = (.22)^2 = .048$$

Thus, when x_3 enters last it accounts for only 4.8% of the variance on y! This is a tremendous drop from the 49% it accounted for when entered first. Because the 3 predictors are so highly correlated, most of the variance on y that x_3 could have accounted for has already been accounted for by x_1 and x_2.

Controlling the Order of Predictors in the Equation

With the forward and stepwise selection procedures, the order of entry of predictors into the regression equation is determined via a mathematical maximization procedure. That is, the first predictor to enter is the one with the largest (maximized) correlation with y, the second to enter is the predictor with the largest semi-partial correlation, etc. However, there are situations where one may not want the mathematics to determine the order of entry of predictors. For example, suppose we have a five predictor problem, with two proven predictors from previous research. The other three predictors are included to see if they have any incremental validity. In this case we would want to enter the two proven predictors in the equation first (as control variables), and then let the remaining three predictors "fight it out" to determine whether any of them add anything significant to predicting y above and beyond the proven predictors.

With SPSSX REGRESSION or SAS REG we can control the order of predictors, and in particular, we can *force* predictors into the equation. In Table 3.10 we illustrate how this is done for SPSSX and SAS for the above five predictor situation.

3.13   OTHER IMPORTANT ISSUES

Preselection of Predictors

An industrial psychologist hears about the predictive power of multiple regression and is excited. He wants to predict success on the job, and gathers data for 20 potential predictors on 70 subjects. He obtains the correlation matrix for the variables, and then picks out 6 predictors which correlate significantly with success on the job and which have low intercorrelations among themselves. The analysis is run, and the R^2 is highly

TABLE 3.10

Controlling the Order of Predictors and Forcing Predictors into the Equation with SPSSX Regression and SAS Reg

---

SPSSX REGRESSION

TITLE 'FORCING X3 AND X4 & USING STEPWISE SELECTION FOR OTHERS'
DATA LIST FREE/Y X1 X2 X3 X4 X5
LIST
BEGIN DATA

    DATA LINES

END DATA
REGRESSION VARIABLES = Y X1 X2 X3 X4 X5/
  DEPENDENT = Y/
① ENTER X3/ENTER X4/STEPWISE/

SAS REG

  DATA FORCEPR;
  INPUT Y X1 X2 X3 X4 X5;
  CARDS;

  DATA LINES

  PROC REG SIMPLE CORR;
② MODEL Y = X3 X4 X1 X2 X5/INCLUDE = 2 SELECTION = STEPWISE;

---

①These two ENTER subcommands will force the predictors in the specific order indicated. Then the STEPWISE subcommand will determine whether any of the remaining predictors (X1, X2 or X5) have semipartial correlations large enough to be "significant." If we wished to force in predictors X1, X3, and X4 and then use STEPWISE, the subcommand is ENTER X1 X3 X4/STEPWISE/

②The INCLUDE = 2 forces the *first 2* predictors listed in the MODEL statement into the prediction equation. Thus, if we wish to force X3 and X4 we must list them first on the MODEL statement.

significant. Furthermore, he is able to explain 52% of the variance on y (more than other investigators have been able to do). Are these results generalizable? Probably not, since what he did involves a *double* capitalization on chance:

1. First, in preselecting the predictors from a larger set, he is capitalizing on chance. Some of these variables would have high correlations with y because of sampling error, and consequently their correlations would tend to be lower in another sample.

2. Secondly, the mathematical maximization involved in obtaining the multiple correlation involves capitalizing on chance.

Preselection of predictors is common among many researchers, who are unaware of the fact that this tends to make their results sample specific. Nunnally (1978) has a nice discussion of the preselection problem, and Wilkinson (1979) has shown the considerable positive bias preselection can have on the test of significance of R^2 in forward selection. The following example from his tables illustrates. The critical value for a 4 predictor problem ($n = 35$) at .05 level is .26, while the appropriate critical value for the *same* n and α level, when preselecting 4 predictors from a set of 20 predictors is .51! Unawareness of the positive bias has led to many results in the literature which are not replicable, for as Wilkinson notes, "A computer assisted search for articles in psychology using stepwise regression from 1969 to 1977 located 71 articles. Out of these articles, 66 forward selections analyses reported as significant by the usual F tests were found. Of these 66 analyses, 19 were *not* significant by [his] Table 1."

It is important to note that both the Wherry and Herzberg formulas do *not* take into account preselection. Hence, the following from Cohen and Cohen (1983) should be seriously considered: "A more realistic estimate of the shrinkage is obtained by substituting for k the *total* number of predictors from which the selection was made." (p. 107) In other words, they are saying if 4 predictors were selected out of 15, use $k = 15$ in the Herzberg formula. While this may be conservative, using 4 will certainly lead to a positive bias. Probably a median value between 4 and 15 would be closer to the mark, although this needs further investigation.

Positive Bias of R^2

A study by Schutz (1977) on California principals and superintendents illustrates how capitalization on chance in multiple regression (if theresearcher is unaware of it) can lead to misleading conclusions. Schutz was interested in validating a "contingency theory of leadership," that is, that success in administering schools calls for different personality styles depending on the social setting of the school. The theory seems plausible, and in what follows we are not criticizing the theory per se, but the empirical validation of it. Schutz's procedure for validating the theory involved establishing a relationship between various personality attributes (24 predictors) and several measures of administrative success in heterogeneous samples with respect to social setting using multiple regression, that is, find the multiple R for each measure of success on 24 predictors. Then he showed that the magnitude of the relationships was greater for subsamples homogeneous with respect to social setting. The problem was that he had nowhere near adequate sample size for a reliable prediction equation. Below we present the total sample sizes and the subsamples homogeneous with respect to social setting:

	Superintendents	*Principals*
Total	$n = 77$	$n = 147$
Subsample(s)	$n = 29$	$n_1 = 35,\ n_2 = 61,\ n_2 = 36$

Indeed, Schutz did find that the R's in the homogeneous subsamples were on the average .34 greater than in the total samples; however, this was an artifact of the multiple regression procedure in this case. As Schutz went from total to his subsamples the number of predictors (k) approached sample size (n). For this situation the multiple correlation increases to 1 *regardless* of whether there is any relationship between y and the set of predictors. And in 3 of 4 of Schutz's subsamples the n/k ratios became dangerously close to 1. In particular it is the case that $E(R^2) = k/(n-1)$, when the population multiple correlation $= 0$ (Morrison, 1976).

To dramatize this, consider subsample 1 for the principals. Then $E(R^2) = 24/34 = .706$, even when there is *no* relationship between y and the set of predictors. The critical value required just for statistical significance of R at .05 is 2.74, which implies $R^2 > .868$, just to be confident that the population multiple correlation is different from 0!

Suppressor Variables

Lord and Novick (1968) state the following two rules of thumb for the selection of predictor variables:

1. Choose variables that correlate highly with the criterion but that have low intercorrelations.
2. To these variables add other variables that have low correlations with the criterion but that have high correlations with the other predictors.

At first blush the second rule of thumb may not seem to make sense, but what they are talking about is suppressor variables. To illustrate specifically why a suppressor variable can help in prediction we consider a hypothetical example.

Example 9

Consider a two predictor problem with the following correlations among the variables: $r_{yx_1} = .60$, $r_{yx_2} = 0$, and $r_{x_1x_2} = .50$.

Note that x_1 by itself accounts for $(.6)^2 \times 100$, or 36% of the variance on y. Now consider entering x_2 into the regression equation first. It will of course account for no variance on y, and it may seem like we have gained nothing. But, if we now enter x_1 into the equation (after x_2), it's predictive power is enhanced. This is because there is irrelevant variance on x_1 (i.e., variance that does not relate to y) which is related to x_2. In this case that irrelevant variance is $(.5)^2 \times 100$ or 25%. When this irrelevant variance is partialled out (or suppressed), the remaining variance on x_1 is more strongly tied to y. Calculation of the semipartial correlation shows this:

$$r_{y1.2(s)} = \frac{r_{yx_1} - r_{yx_2} r_{x_1 x_2}}{\sqrt{1 - r_{x_1 x_2}^2}} = \frac{.60 - 0}{\sqrt{1 - .5^2}} = .693$$

Thus, $r_{y1.2(s)}^2 = .48$, and the predictive power of x_1 has increased from accounting for 36% to accounting for 48% of the variance on y.

3.14 OUTLIERS AND INFLUENTIAL DATA POINTS

Since multiple regression is a mathematical maximization procedure, it can be very sensitive to data points within "split off" or are different from the rest of the points, that is, to outliers. Just 1 or 2 such points can affect the interpretation of results, and it is certainly moot as to whether 1 or 2 points should be permitted to have such a profound influence. Therefore, it is important to be able to detect outliers and influential points. There is a distinction between the two because a point that is an outlier (either on y or for the predictors) will *not necessarily* be influential in affecting the regression equation.

The fact that a simple examination of summary statistics can result in misleading interpretations was illustrated by Anscombe (1973). He presented three data sets that yielded the same summary statistics (i.e., regression coefficients and same $r^2 = .667$). In one case linear regression was perfectly appropriate. In the second case, however, a scatter plot showed that curvilinear regression was appropriate. In the third case, linear regression was appropriate for 10 of 11 points, but the other point was an outlier and possibly should have been excluded from the analysis.

There are two basic approaches that can be used in dealing with outliers and influential points. We consider the approach of having an arsenal of tools for isolating these important points for further study, with the possibility of deleting some or all of the points from the analysis. The other approach is to develop procedures that are relatively insensitive to wild points (i.e., robust regression techniques). (Some pertinent references for robust regression are Hogg, 1979; Huber, 1977; Mosteller & Tukey, 1977). It is important to note that even robust regression may be ineffective when there are outliers in the space of the predictors (Huber, 1977). Thus, even in robust regression there is a need for case analysis. Also, a modification of robust regression, called bounded-influence regression, has been developed by Krasker and Welsch (1979).

Data Editing

Outliers and influential cases can occur because of recording errors. Consequently, researchers should give more consideration to the data editing phase of the data analysis process (i.e., *always* listing the data and examining the list for possible errors). There are many possible sources of error from the initial data collection to the final keypunching. First, some of the data may have been recorded incorrectly. Second, even if recorded correctly, when all of the data are transferred to a single sheet or a few sheets in preparation for keypunching, errors may be made. Finally, even if no errors are made in these first two steps, an error(s) could be made in entering the data into the terminal.

There are various statistics for identifying outliers on y and on the set of predictors, as well as for identifying influential data points. We discuss first, in brief form, a statistic for each, with advice on how to interpret that statistic. Equations for the statistics are given latter in the section, along with a more extensive and somewhat technical discussion for those who are interested.

Measuring Outliers on y

For finding subjects whose predicted scores are quite different from their actual y scores (i.e., they do not fit the model well), the *standardized residuals* (r_i) can be used. If the model is correct, then they have a normal distribution with a mean of 0 and a standard deviation of 1. Thus, about 95% of the r_i should lie within two standard deviations of the mean and about 99% within three standard deviations. Therefore, any standardized residual greater than about 3 in absolute value is unusual and should be carefully examined.

Measuring Outliers on Set of Predictors

The *hat elements* (h_{ii}) can be used here. It can be shown that the hat elements lie between 0 and 1, and that the average hat element is p/n, where $p = k + 1$. Because of this, Hoaglin and Welsch (1978) suggest that $2p/n$ may be considered large. However, this can lead to more points then we really would want to examine, and the reader should consider using $3p/n$. For example, with 6 predictors and 100 subjects, any hat element (also called leverage) greater than $3(7)/100 = .21$ should be carefully examined. This is a very simple and useful rule of thumb for quickly identifying subjects who are very different from the rest of the sample on the set of predictors.

Measuring Influential Data Points

An influential data point is one that when deleted produces a substantial change in at least one of the regression coefficients. That is, the prediction equations with and without the influential point are quite different. *Cook's distance* (1977) is very useful for identifying influential points. It measures the *combined* influence of the case being an outlier on *y* and on the set of predictors. Cook and Weisberg (1982) have indicated that a Cook's distance > *1 would generally be considered large*. This provides a "red flag," when examining computer printout, for identifying influential points.

All of the above diagnostic measures are easily obtained from SPSSX REGRESSION (cf. Table 3.3) or SAS REG (cf. Table 3.6).

Measuring Outliers on *y*

The raw residuals, $\hat{e}_i = y_i - \hat{y}_i$, in linear regression are assumed to be independent, to have a mean of 0, to have constant variance, and to follow a normal distribution. However, because the *n* residuals have only *n-k* degrees of freedom (*k* degrees of freedom were lost in estimating the regression parameters), they can't be independent. If *n* is large relative to *k*, however, then the $\hat{e}_i$ are essentially independent. Also, the residuals have different variances. It can be shown (cf. Draper & Smith, 1981, p. 144) that the variance for the *i*th residual is given by:

$$s_{e_i}^2 = \hat{\sigma}^2 (1 - h_{ii})$$

(12)

where $\hat{\sigma}^2$ is the estimate of variance not predictable from the regression (MS_{res}), and h_{ii} is the *i*th diagonal element of the hat matrix $X(X'X)^{-1}X'$. Recall that X is the score matrix for the predictors. The h_{ii} play a key role in determining the predicted values for the subjects. Recall that

$$\hat{\beta} = (X'X)^{-1}X'y \text{ and } \hat{y} = X\hat{\beta}$$

Therefore, $\hat{y} = X(X'X)^{-1}X'y$, by simple substitution. Thus, the predicted values for *y* are obtained by postmultipling the hat matrix by the column vector of observed scores on *y*.

Since the predicted values ($\hat{y}_i$) and the residuals are related by $\hat{e}_i = y_i - \hat{y}_i$, it should not be surprising in view of the above that the variability of the $\hat{e}_i$ would be affected by the h_{ii}.

Since the residuals have different variances, we need to standardize to meaningfully compare them. This is completely analogous to what is done in comparing raw scores from distributions with different variances and different means. There, one means of standardizing was to convert to *z* scores, using $z_i = (x_i - x)/s$. Here we also subtract off the mean (which is 0 and hence has no effect) and then divide by the standard deviation. The standard deviation is the square root of Equation 12. Therefore,

$$r_i = \frac{\hat{e}_i - 0}{\hat{\sigma}\sqrt{1 - h_{ii}}} = \frac{\hat{e}_i}{\hat{\sigma}\sqrt{1 - h_{ii}}}$$

(13)

Because the r_i are assumed to have a normal distribution with a mean of 0 (if the model is correct), then about 99% of the r_i should lie within 3 standard deviations of the mean.

Weisberg (1980) has given the following t statistic for testing an outlier on y for significance:

$$t_i = r_i \sqrt{\frac{n - p' - 1}{n - p' - r_i^2}} \tag{14}$$

where r_i is the standardized residual, n is sample size, k' is the number of parameters (including the regression constant), and df $= n - k' - 1$. Although t_i is not given on the printout from BMDP, or SPSSX, r_i is given and therefore t_i is found by plugging into Equation 13.

Assessing the significance of the case with the largest value of t_i is equivalent to performing n significance tests, one for each of the n cases. To control the resulting inflated Type I error rate, the somewhat conservative Bonferroni inequality is used, doing each test at the α/n level of significance. Table 3.11 gives the critical values (Weisberg, 1980) for various n and k', which keeps overall $\alpha = .05$.

Example 10

Consider a regression analysis with 4 predictors on 50 subjects; the largest $r_i = 2.8$. Is this a statistically significant deviation (overall $\alpha = .05$) according to the Weisberg test?

$$t_i = r_i \sqrt{\frac{n - k' - 1}{n - k' - r_i^2}}$$

$$= 2.8 \sqrt{\frac{50 - 5 - 1}{50 - 5 - 7.84}}$$

$$= 2.8(1.088) = 3.047.$$

Because the critical value is 3.53, this is not a significant deviation.

Measuring Outliers on the Predictors

The h_{ii}'s are one measure of the extent to which the ith observation is an outlier for the predictors. The h_{ii}'s are important because they can play a key role in determining the predicted values for the subjects. Recall that

$$\hat{\beta} = (X'X)^{-1}X'y \text{ and } \hat{y} = X\hat{\beta}$$

Therefore, $\hat{y} = X(X'X)^{-1}X'y$ by simple substitution.

Thus, the predicted values for y are obtained by postmultiplying the hat matrix by the column vector of observed scores on y. It can be shown that the h_{ii}'s lie between 0 and 1, and that the average value for $h_{ii} = k/n$. From Equation 12 it may be seen that when h_{ii} is large (i.e., near 1), then the variance for the ith residual is near 0. This means that $y_i \approx \hat{y}_i$. In other words, an observation may fit the linear model well and yet be an influential data point. This second diagnostic, then, is "flagging" observations that need to be examined carefully because they may have an unusually large influence on the regression coefficients.

What is a significant value for the h_{ii}? Hoaglin and Welsch (1978) suggest that $2p/n$ may be considered large. Belsey et al. (1980, pp. 67–68) show that when the set of predictors is multivariate normal, then $(n - p)\,[h_{ii} - 1/n]/(1 - h_{ii})(p - 1)$ is distributed as F with $(p - 1)$ and $(n - p)$ degrees of freedom.

Rather than computing the above F and comparing against a critical value, Hoaglin and Welsch suggest $2p/n$ as rough guide for a large h_{ii}.

An important point to remember concerning the hat elements is that the points they identify will not necessarily be influential in affecting the regression coefficients.

Mahalanobis' distance for case $i(D_i^2)$ indicates how far the case is from the centroid of all cases for the predictor variables. A large distance indicates an observation that is an outlier for the predictors. The Mahalanobis distance can be written in terms of the covariance matrix $\mathbf{S}$ as

$$D_i^2 = (\mathbf{x}_i - \bar{\mathbf{x}})'\mathbf{S}^{-1}(\mathbf{x}_i - \bar{\mathbf{x}}), \tag{15}$$

where $\mathbf{x}_i$ is the vector of the data for case i and $\bar{\mathbf{x}}$ is the vector of means (centroid) for the predictors.

For a better understanding of D_i^2, consider two small data sets. The first set has two predictors. In Table 3.12, the data is presented, as well as the D_i^2 and the descriptive statistics (including $\mathbf{S}$). The D_i^2 for Cases 6 and 10 are large because the score for Case 6 on x_i (150) was deviant, whereas for Case 10 the score on x_2 (97) was very deviant. The graphical split-off of Cases 6 and 10 is quite vivid and is displayed in Figure 1.2.

In the previous example, because the numbers of predictors and subjects were few, it would have been fairly easy to spot the outliers even without the Mahalanobis distance. However, in practical problems with 200 or 300 subjects and 10 predictors, outliers are not always easy to spot and can occur in more subtle ways. For example, a case may have a large distance because there are moderate to fairly large differences on many of the predictors. The second small data set with 4 predictors and $N = 15$ in Table 3.12 illustrates this latter point. The D_i^2 for case 13 is quite large (7.97) even

TABLE 3.11
Critical Values for Weisberg Outlier Test with Overall $\alpha = .05$

$k' = k + 1$

n	1	2	3	4	5	6	7	8	9	10	11	12	13	14	15	20	25	30
6	4.85	6.23	10.89	76.39														
7	4.38	5.07	6.58	11.77	89.12													
8	4.12	4.53	5.26	6.90	12.59	101.9												
9	3.95	4.22	4.66	5.44	7.18	13.36	114.6											
10	3.83	4.03	4.32	4.77	5.60	7.45	14.09	127.3										
11	3.75	3.90	4.10	4.40	4.88	5.75	7.70	14.78	140.1									
12	3.69	3.81	3.96	4.17	4.49	4.98	5.89	7.94	15.44	152.8								
13	3.65	3.74	3.86	4.02	4.24	4.56	5.08	6.02	8.16	16.08	165.5							
14	3.61	3.69	3.79	3.91	4.07	4.30	4.63	5.16	6.14	8.37	16.69	178.2						
15	3.58	3.65	3.73	3.83	3.95	4.12	4.36	4.70	5.25	6.25	8.58	17.28	191.0					
16	3.56	3.62	3.68	3.77	3.87	4.00	4.17	4.41	4.76	5.33	6.36	8.77	17.85	203.7				
17	3.54	3.59	3.65	3.72	3.80	3.90	4.04	4.21	4.46	4.82	5.40	6.47	8.95	18.40	216.4			
18	3.53	3.57	3.62	3.68	3.75	3.83	3.94	4.08	4.26	4.51	4.88	5.47	6.47	9.13	18.93			
19	3.52	3.56	3.60	3.65	3.71	3.78	3.86	3.97	4.11	4.30	4.55	4.93	5.54	6.67	9.30			
20	3.51	3.54	3.58	3.62	3.67	3.73	3.81	3.89	4.00	4.15	4.33	4.59	4.98	5.60	6.76			
21	3.50	3.53	3.57	3.60	3.65	3.70	3.76	3.83	3.92	4.03	4.18	4.37	4.64	5.03	5.67			
22	3.50	3.52	3.55	3.59	3.63	3.67	3.72	3.78	3.86	3.95	4.06	4.21	4.40	4.68	5.08	280.1		
23	3.49	3.52	3.54	3.57	3.61	3.65	3.69	3.75	3.81	3.88	3.98	4.09	4.24	4.44	4.71	21.41		
24	3.49	3.51	3.53	3.56	3.59	3.63	3.67	3.71	3.77	3.83	3.91	4.00	4.12	4.27	4.47	10.07		
25	3.48	3.50	3.53	3.55	3.58	3.61	3.65	3.69	3.73	3.79	3.85	3.93	4.02	4.14	4.30	7.17		
26	3.48	3.50	3.52	3.54	3.57	3.60	3.63	3.66	3.70	3.75	3.81	3.87	3.95	4.05	4.17	5.95		
27	3.48	3.50	3.52	3.54	3.56	3.58	3.61	3.65	3.68	3.72	3.77	3.83	3.89	3.97	4.07	5.29	353.80	
28	3.48	3.50	3.51	3.53	3.55	3.58	3.60	3.63	3.66	3.70	3.74	3.79	3.84	3.91	3.99	4.88	23.63	
29	3.48	3.49	3.51	3.53	3.55	3.57	3.59	3.62	3.64	3.68	3.71	3.76	3.81	3.86	3.93	4.61	10.74	
30	3.48	3.49	3.51	3.52	3.54	3.56	3.58	3.60	3.63	3.66	3.69	3.73	3.77	3.82	3.88	4.42	7.53	
31	3.48	3.49	3.50	3.52	3.54	3.55	3.57	3.59	3.62	3.64	3.67	3.71	3.74	3.79	3.84	4.28	6.18	
32	3.48	3.49	3.50	3.52	3.53	3.55	3.57	3.59	3.61	3.63	3.66	3.69	3.72	3.76	3.80	4.17	5.47	407.4

33	3.48	3.49	3.50	3.52	3.53	3.54	3.56	3.58	3.60	3.62	3.64	3.67	3.70	3.74	3.77	4.08	5.03	25.66
34	3.48	3.49	3.50	3.51	3.53	3.54	3.56	3.57	3.59	3.61	3.63	3.66	3.68	3.71	3.75	4.01	4.74	11.34
35	3.48	3.49	3.50	3.51	3.52	3.54	3.55	3.47	3.58	3.60	3.62	3.64	3.57	3.70	3.73	3.96	4.53	7.84
36	3.48	3.49	3.50	3.51	3.52	3.54	3.55	3.56	3.58	3.60	3.61	3.63	3.66	3.68	3.71	3.91	4.37	6.39
37	3.48	3.49	3.50	3.51	3.52	3.53	3.55	3.56	3.57	3.59	3.61	3.62	3.65	3.67	3.69	3.87	4.26	5.62
38	3.49	3.49	3.50	3.51	3.52	3.53	3.54	3.56	3.58	3.60	3.62	3.60	3.66	3.68	3.84	4.16	5.16	
39	3.49	3.49	3.50	3.51	3.52	3.53	3.54	3.55	3.57	3.58	3.59	3.61	3.63	3.65	3.67	3.81	4.09	4.84
40	3.49	3.49	3.50	3.51	3.52	3.53	3.54	3.55	3.56	3.59	3.60	3.62	3.64	3.66	3.79	4.03	4.62	
50	3.51	3.51	3.51	3.52	3.53	3.55	3.54	3.54	3.55	3.56	3.57	3.57	3.58	3.59	3.60	3.66	3.75	3.88
60	3.53	3.53	3.53	3.54	3.54	3.54	3.55	3.55	3.56	3.56	3.57	3.57	3.58	3.58	3.59	3.62	3.67	3.73
70	3.55	3.55	3.55	3.55	3.56	3.56	3.56	3.56	3.57	3.57	3.57	3.58	3.58	3.59	3.59	3.61	3.64	
80	3.57	3.57	3.57	3.57	3.58	3.57	3.58	3.58	3.58	3.57	3.59	3.59	3.58	3.59	3.60	3.61	3.63	3.66
90	3.58	3.59	3.59	3.59	3.59	3.58	3.58	3.60	3.60	3.58	3.59	3.60	3.59	3.60	3.61	3.62	3.63	3.65
100	3.60	3.60	3.60	3.60	3.61	3.61	3.61	3.61	3.61	3.61	3.61	3.62	3.60	3.61	3.61	3.63	3.64	3.65
200	3.73	3.73	3.73	3.73	3.73	3.73	3.73	3.73	3.73	3.73	3.73	3.73	3.73	3.73	3.74	3.74	3.74	3.74
300	3.81	3.81	3.81	3.81	3.81	3.81	3.81	3.81	3.81	3.81	3.82	3.82	3.82	3.82	3.82	3.82	3.82	3.82
400	3.87	3.87	3.87	3.87	3.87	3.87	3.87	3.88	3.88	3.88	3.88	3.88	3.88	3.88	3.88	3.88	3.88	3.88
500	3.92	3.92	3.92	3.92	3.92	3.92	3.92	3.92	3.92	3.92	3.92	3.92	3.92	3.92	3.92	3.92	3.92	3.92

TABLE 3.12
Raw Data and Mahalanobis Distances for Two Small Data Sets

Case	Y	X_1	X_2	X_3	X_4	D_i^2
1	476	111	68	17	81	0.30
2	457	92	46	28	67	1.55
3	.540	90	50	19	83	1.47
4	551	107	59	25	71	0.01
5	575	98	50	13	92	0.76
6	698	150	66	20	90	5.48
7	545	118	54	11	101	0.47
8	574	110	51	26	82	0.38
9	645	117	59	18	87	0.23
10	556	94	97	12	69	7.24
11	634	130	57	16	97	
12	637	118	51	19	78	
13	390	91	44	14	64	
14	562	118	61	20	103	
15	560	109	66	13	88	
Summary statistics						
M	561.70000	108.70000	60.00000			
SD	70.74846	17.73289	14.84737			

$$S = \begin{bmatrix} 314.455 & 19.483 \\ 19.483 & 220.444 \end{bmatrix}$$

Note: Boxed-in entries are the first data set and corresponding D_i^2. The 10 case numbers having the largest D_i^2 for a four-predictor data set are: 10, 10.859; 13, 7.977; 6, 7.223; 2, 5.048; 14, 4.874; 7, 3.514; 5, 3.177; 3, 2.616; 8, 2.561; 4, 2.404.

①Calculation of D_i^2 for Case 6:

$$D_6^2 = (41.3, 6) \begin{bmatrix} 314.455 & 19.483 \\ 19.483 & 220.440 \end{bmatrix}^{-1} \begin{pmatrix} 41.3 \\ 6 \end{pmatrix}$$

$$S^{-1} = \begin{bmatrix} .00320 & -.00029 \\ -.00029 & .00456 \end{bmatrix} \rightarrow D_6^2 = 5.484$$

though the scores for that subject do not split off in a striking fashion for any of the predictors. Rather, it is a cumulative effect that produces the separation.

How large must D_i^2 be before one can say that case i is significantly separated from the rest of the data at the .05 level of significance? If it is tenable that the predictors came from a multivariate normal population, then the critical values (Barnett & Lewis, 1978) are given in Table 3.13 for 2 through 5 predictors. An easily implemented graphical test for multivariate normality is available (Johnson & Wichern, 1982). The test involves plotting ordered Mahalanobis distances against chi-square percentile points. The D_i^2 can be obtained from the BMDP9R program.

Table 3.13
Critical Values for an Outlier on the Predictors as Judged by
Mahalanobis D^2

	Number of Predictors							
	$k = 2$		$k = 3$		$k = 4$		$k = 5$	
n	5%	1%	5%	1%	5%	1%	5%	1%
5	3.17	3.19						
6	4.00	4.11	4.14	4.16				
7	4.71	4.95	5.01	5.10	5.12	5.14		
8	5.32	5.70	5.77	5.97	6.01	6.09	6.11	6.12
9	5.85	6.37	6.43	6.76	6.80	6.97	7.01	7.08
10	6.32	6.97	7.01	7.47	7.50	7.79	7.82	7.98
12	7.10	8.00	7.99	8.70	8.67	9.20	9.19	9.57
14	7.74	8.84	8.78	9.71	9.61	10.37	10.29	10.90
16	8.27	9.54	9.44	10.56	10.39	11.36	11.20	12.02
18	8.73	10.15	10.00	11.28	11.06	12.20	11.96	12.98
20	9.13	10.67	10.49	11.91	11.63	12.93	12.62	13.81
25	9.94	11.73	11.48	13.18	12.78	14.40	13.94	15.47
30	10.58	12.54	12.24	14.14	13.67	15.51	14.95	16.73
35	11.10	13.20	12.85	14.92	14.37	16.40	15.75	17.73
40	11.53	13.74	13.36	15.56	14.96	17.13	16.41	18.55
45	11.90	14.20	13.80	16.10	15.46	17.74	16.97	19.24
50	12.23	14.60	14.18	16.56	15.89	18.27	17.45	19.83
100	14.22	16.95	16.45	19.26	18.43	21.30	20.26	23.17
200	15.99	18.94	18.42	21.47	20.59	23.72	22.59	25.82
500	18.12	21.22	20.75	23.95	23.06	26.37	25.21	28.62

Referring back to the example with 2 predictors and $n = 10$, if we assume multivariate normality, then Case 6 ($D_i^2 = 5.48$) is not significantly separated from the rest of the data at .05 level because the critical value equals 6.32. In contrast, Case 10 is significantly separated.

(Weisberg, 1980, p. 104) has shown that if n is even moderately large (50 or more), then D_i^2 is approximately proportional to h_{ii}:

$$D_i^2 \approx (n - 1)h_{ii} \tag{16}$$

Thus, with large n, either measure may be used. Also, because we have previously indicated what would correspond roughly to a significant h_{ii} value, from Equation 16 we can immediately determine the corresponding significant D_i^2 value. For example, if $k = 7$ and $n = 50$, then a large $h_{ii} = .42$ and the corresponding large $D_i^2 = 20.58$. If $k = 20$ and $n = 200$, then a large $h_{ii} = 2k/n = .20$ and the corresponding large $D_i^2 = 39.90$.

Measures for Influential Data Points

Cook's Distance

Cook's distance (CD) is a measure of the change in the regression coefficients that would occur if this case was omitted, thus revealing which cases are most influential in affecting the regression equation. It is affected by both the case being an outlier on y and on the set of predictors. Cook's distance is given by

$$CD_i = (\hat{\beta} - \hat{\beta}_{(-i)})'\mathbf{X}'\mathbf{X}(\hat{\beta} - \hat{\beta}_{(-i)})/(k + 1) MS_{res} \qquad (17)$$

where $\hat{\beta}_{(-i)}$ is the vector of estimated regression coefficients with the ith data point deleted, k is the number of predictors, and MS_{res} is the residual (error) variance for the full data set.

Removing the ith data point should keep $\hat{\beta}_{(-i)}$ close to $\hat{\beta}$ unless the ith observation is an outlier. Cook and Weisberg (1982, p. 118) indicate that *a $CD_i > 1$ would generally be considered large.* Cook's distance can be written in an alternative revealing form:

$$CD_i = \frac{1}{(k + 1)} r_i^2 \frac{h_{ii}}{1 - h_{ii}}, \qquad (18)$$

where r_i is the standardized residual and h_{ii} is the hat element. Thus, *Cook's distance measures the joint (combined) influence of the case being an outlier on y and on the set of predictors.* A case may be influential because it is a significant outlier only on y, for example,

$$k = 5, n = 40, r_i = 4, h_{ii} = .3 \rightarrow CD_i > 1,$$

or because it is a significant outlier only on the set of predictors, for example,

$$k = 5, n = 40, r_i = 2, h_{ii} = .7 \rightarrow CD_i > 1.$$

Note, however, that a case may not be a significant outlier on either y or on the set of predictors, but may still be influential, as in the following

$$k = 3, n = 20, h_{ii} = 4, r_i = 2.5 \rightarrow CD_i > 1.$$

DFFITS

This statistic (Belsley, Kuh, & Welsch, 1980) indicates how much the ith fitted value $(\hat{y}_i)$ will change if the ith observation is deleted. It is given by

$$(\text{DFFITS})_i = \frac{\hat{y}_i - \hat{y}_{i-1}}{s_{-i}\overline{h_{ii}}} \qquad (19)$$

The numerator simply expresses the difference between the fitted values, with the ith point in and with it deleted. The denominator provides a measure of variability since $s^2_y = \sigma^2 h_{ii}$. Therefore, *DEFITS indicates the number of estimated standard errors that the fitted value changes when the ith point is deleted.*

DFBETAS

These are very useful in dictating how much *each* regression coefficient will change if the ith observation is deleted. They are given by

$$(\text{DFBETAS})_{j,i} = \frac{b_j - b_{j,-i}}{s_{-i}\ c_{jj}} \qquad (20)$$

Each of the *DFBETAS therefore indicates the number of standard errors the coefficient changes when the ith point is deleted.* The DFBETAS are available on both SAS and SPSSX. Any DFBETA with a value $> |2|$ indicates a sizable change, and should be investigated. Thus, while Cook's D is a *composite* measure of influence, the DFBETAS indicates which specific coefficients are being most affected.

It was mentioned earlier that a data point which is an outlier either on y or on the set of predictors will not *necessarily* be an influential point. Figure 3.5 illustrates how this can happen. In this simplified example with just one predictor, both points A and B are outliers on x. Point B is influential, and to accomodate it the least squares regression line will be pulled downward toward the point. However, Point A is not influential because this point closely follows the trend of the rest of the data.

Summary

In summarizing then, use of the Weisberg test (with standardized residuals) will detect y outliers, and the hat elements or the Mahalanobis distances will detect outliers on the predictors. Such outliers will not necessarily be influential points. To determine which outliers are influential, find those whose Cook distances are > 1. Those points that are flagged as influential by Cook's distance need to be examined carefully to determine whether they should be deleted from the analysis. If there is a reason to believe that these cases arise from a process different from that for the rest of the data, then the cases should be deleted. For example, the

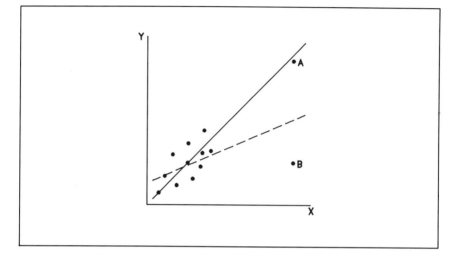

FIG. 3.5   Examples of Two Outliers on the Predictors: One Influential and the Other Not Influential

failure of a measuring instrument, a power failure, or the occurrence of an unusual event (perhaps inexplicable) would be instances of a different process.

If a point is a significant outlier on y, but it's Cook distance is < 1, there is no real need to delete the point since it does not have a large effect on the regression analysis. However, one should still be interested in studying such points further to understand why they did not fit the model. After all, the purpose of any study is to understand the data. In particular, one wants to ascertain if there are any communalities among the S's corresponding to such outliers, suggesting that perhaps these subjects come from a different population. For an excellent, readable, and extended discussion of outliers, influential points, identification of and remedies for, see Weisberg (1980, chapters 5 and 6).

In concluding this summary the following from Belsley, Kuh, and Welsch (1980) is appropriate:

> A word of warning is in order here, for it is obvious that there is room for misuse of the above procedures. High-influence data points could conceivably be removed solely to effect a desired change in a particular estimated coefficient, its *t* value, or some other regression output. While this danger exists, it is an unavoidable consequence of a procedure that successfully highlights such points . . . the benefits obtained from information on influential points far outweigh any potential danger. (pp. 15–16)

Example 11

We now consider the data in Table 3.12 with four predictors ($n = 15$). This data was run on SPSSX REGRESSION, which compactly and conveniently presents all the outlier information on a single page. The regression with all four predictors is significant at the .05 level ($F = 3.94$, $p < .0358$). However, we wish to focus our attention on the outlier analysis, a summary of which is given in Table 3.15. Examination of the studentized residuals shows no significant outliers on y. To determine whether there are any significant outliers on the set of predictors, we examine the Mahalanobis distances. Case 10 is an outlier on the x's since the critical value from Table 3.12 is 10, while case 13 is not significant. Cook's distances reveal that both cases 10 and 13 are influential data points, since the distances are > 1. Note that case 13 is an influential point even though it is *not* a significant outlier on either y or on the set of predictors. We indicated that this is possible, and indeed it has occurred here. This is the

TABLE 3.14
Selected Output for Sample Problem on Outliers
and Influential Points

OUTLIERS—STANDARDIZED RESIDUAL		OUTLIERS—STUDENTIZED RESIDUAL	
CASE #	*ZRESID	CASE #	*SRESID
1	− 1.60229	13	− 1.73853
12	1.23548	1	− 1.69609
9	1.04904	12	1.39104
13	− 1.04818	14	− 1.26662
5	1.00288	5	1.19324
14	− .96888	10	1.15951
3	.80693	9	1.09324
7	− .74268	3	.93397
2	− .54545	7	− .89911
10	.46043	2	− .72075

OUTLIER—STUDENTIZED DELETED (PRESS) RESIDUAL		OUTLIERS—MAHALANOBIS' DISTANCE	
CASE #	*SDRESID	CASE #	*MAHAL
13	− 1.97449	10	10.85912
1	− 1.90647	13	7.97770
12	1.46946	6	7.22347
14	− 1.31142	2	5.04841
5	1.22237	14	4.87493
10	1.18236	7	3.51446
9	1.10529	5	3.17728
3	.92741	3	2.61511
7	− .88969	8	2.56197
2	− .70224	4	2.40401

OUTLIERS—COOK'S DISTANCE			OUTLIERS—LEVERAGE	
CASE #	*COOK D	SIG F	CASE #	*LEVER
10	1.43639	.2922	10	.77565
13	1.05851	.4370	13	.56984
14	.22751	.9420	6	.51596
5	.11837	.9853	2	.36060
12	.10359	.9891	14	.34821
2	.07751	.9943	7	.25103
7	.07528	.9947	5	.22695
1	.06934	.9956	3	.18686
3	.05925	.9970	8	.18300
9	.02057	.9998	4	.17172

TABLE 3.15
Selected Output for Sample Problem on Outliers
and Influential Points

BEGINNING BLOCK NUMBER 1. METHOD: ENTER

VARIABLES(S) ENTERED ON STEP NUMBER 1··   X4
2··   X2
3··   X3
4··   X1

		ANALYSIS OF VARIANCE			
MULTIPLE R	.78212				
R SQUARE	.61171		DF	SUM OF SQUARES	MEAN SQUARE
ADJUSTED R SQUARE	.45639	REGRESSION	4	52231.50225	13057.87556
STANDARD ERROR	57.57994	RESIDUAL	10	33154.49775	3315.44977

F = 3.93849   SIGNIF F = .0358

----------VARIABLES IN THE EQUATION----------

VARIABLE	B	SE B	BETA	T	SIG T
X4	1.48832	1.78548	.23194	.834	.4240
X2	1.27014	1.34394	.21016	.945	.3669
X3	2.01747	3.55943	.13440	.567	.5833
X1	2.80343	1.26554	.58644	2.215	.0511
(CONSTANT)	15.85866	180.29777		.088	.9316

FOR BLOCK NUMBER 1 ALL REQUESTED VARIABLES ENTERED.

REGRESSION COEFFICIENTS WITH CASE 10 DELETED		REGRESSION COEFFICIENTS WITH CASE 13 DELETED	
VARIABLE	B	VARIABLE	B
X4	2.07788	X4	− 1.33883
X2	− 1.48076	X2	− .70800
X3	2.75130	X1	3.41539
X1	3.52924	X3	− 3.45596
(CONSTANT)	23.36214	(CONSTANT)	410.45740

more subtle type of influential points which Cook's distance brings to our attention.

In Table 3.14 we have presented the regression coefficients that resulted when cases 10 and 13 were deleted. There is a fairly dramatic shift in the coefficients in each case. For Case 10 the dramatic shift occurs for x_2, where the coefficient changes from 1.27 (for all data points) to − 1.48 (with case 10 deleted). This is a shift of just over 2 standard errors (standard error for x_2 on printout is 1.34). For case 13 the coefficients change in sign for 3 of the 4 predictors (x_4, x_2, and x_3).

3.15   FURTHER DISCUSSION OF THE TWO COMPUTER EXAMPLES

Morrison Data

Recall that for the Morrison data the stepwise procedure yielded the more parsimonious model involving 3 predictors: CLARITY, INTEREST, and

STIMUL. If we were interested in an estimate of the predictive power in the population, then the Wherry estimate given by Equation 8 is appropriate. This is given under STEP NUMBER 3 on the SPSSX printout in Table 3.6 as ADJUSTED R SQUARE .84016. Here the estimate is used in a descriptive sense; to describe the relationship in the population. However, if we are interested in the cross validity predictive power, then the Stein estimate (Equation 9) should be used. The Stein adjusted R^2 in this case is

$$\rho_c^2 = 1 - (31/28)(30/27)(33/32)(1 - .856) = .82$$

This estimates that if we were to cross validate the prediction equation on many other samples from the same population, then *on the average* we would account for about 82% of the variance on the dependent variable. In this instance the estimated dropoff in predictive power is very little from the maximized value of 85.56%. The reason is that the association between the dependent variable and the set of predictors is *very* strong. Thus, we can have confidence in the future predictive power of the equation.

It is also important to examine the regression diagnostics to check for any outliers and/or influential data points. Table 3.16 presents the appropriate statistics, as discussed in 3.16, for identifying outliers on the dependent variable (standardized residuals), outliers on the set of predictors (hat elements), and influential data points (Cook's distance).

First, we would expect only about 5% of the standardized residuals to be > |2| if the linear model is appropriate. From Table 3.16 we see that 2 of the ZRESID are > |2|, and we would expect about 32(.05) = 1.6, so nothing seems to be awry here. Next, we check for outliers on the set of predictors. The rough "critical value" here is $3p/n = 3(4)/32 = .375$. Since there are no values under LEVER in Table 3.16 exceeding this value, we have no outliers on the set of predictors. Finally, and perhaps most importantly, we check for the existence of influential data points using Cook's *D*. Recall that Cook (1982) has suggested if $D > 1$, then the point is influential. All the COOK *D*'s in Table 3.16 are far less than 1, so we have no influential data points.

In summary then, the linear regression model is quite appropriate for the Morrison data. The estimated cross validity power is excellent, and there are no outliers or influential data points.

National Academy of Sciences Data

Recall that both the stepwise procedure and the MAXR procedure yielded the same "best" 4-predictor set: NFACUL, PCTSUPP, PCTGRT, AND NARTIC. The maximized $R^2 = .8221$, indicating that 82.21% of the variance in quality can be accounted for by these 4 predictors in *this* sample. Now we obtain two measures of the cross validity power of the equation. First, from the SAS REG printout, we have PREDICTED RESID SS

TABLE 3.16

Regression Diagnostics (Standardized Residuals, Hat Elements and Cook's Distance) for Morrison MBA Data

Casewise Plot of Standardized Residual

*: Selected   M: Missing

Plot axis (standardized residual) ranges from −3.0 through 0.0 to 3.0.

Case #	① PRED	② RESID	③ ZRESID	④ LEVER	⑤ COOK D
1	1.1156	-.1156	-.3627	.1021	.0058
2	1.5977	-.5977	-1.8746	.0541	.0896
3	.9209	.0791	.2481	.1541	.0043
4	1.1156	-.1156	-.3627	.1021	.0058
5	1.5330	.4670	1.4645	.1349	.1281
6	1.9872	.0128	.0401	.1218	.0001
7	2.2746	-.2746	-.8612	.0279	.0124
8	2.6920	-.6920	-2.1703	.0180	.0641
9	2.2378	-.2378	-.7459	.1381	.0341
10	1.8204	.1796	.5632	.0708	.0100
11	1.7925	.2075	.6508	.0412	.0089
12	2.0431	-.0431	-.1351	.2032	.0018
13	1.5977	.4023	1.2616	.0541	.0406
14	2.2099	-.2099	-.6583	.0863	.0164
15	2.2746	-.2746	-.8612	.0279	.0124
16	2.4693	-.4693	-1.4719	.0541	.0553
17	2.0799	-.0799	-.2504	.0953	.0026
18	3.1741	-.1741	-.5461	.0389	.0060
19	2.7567	.2433	.7630	.1039	.0263
20	2.9794	.0206	.0647	.0933	.0002
21	2.9147	.0853	.2676	.0976	.0030
22	2.9147	.0853	.2676	.0976	.0030
23	2.7567	.2433	.7630	.1039	.0263
24	3.1462	-.1462	-.4585	.1408	.0132
25	2.8868	.1132	.3552	.1116	.0061
26	3.1741	-.1741	-.5461	.0389	.0060
27	2.9514	.0486	.1523	.0756	.0008
28	2.2746	.7254	2.2750	.0279	.0865
29	2.6641	.3359	1.0535	.1738	.0900
30	4.0736	-.0736	-.2310	.1860	.0047
31	3.5915	.4085	1.2810	.1309	.0948
Case #	*PRED	*RESID	*ZRESID	*LEVER	*COOK D

① These are the predicted values

② These are the raw residuals, that is, $\hat{e}_i = y_i - \hat{y}_i$. Thus, for the first subject we have $\hat{e}_1 = 1 - 1.1156 = -.1156$.

③ These are the standardized residuals.

④ The hat elements—they have been called leverage elements elsewhere; hence the abbreviation LEVER.

⑤ Cook's distance—useful for identifying influential data points. Cook suggests if $D > 1$, then the point generally would be considered influential

(PRESS) = 1350.33. Furthermore, the variance for QUALITY is 101.438, so that $\Sigma (Y_i - Y)^2 = 4564.71$. From these numbers we can compute

$$R^2{}_{\text{Press}} = 1 - (1350.33)/4564.71 = .7042$$

This is a good measure of the external predictive power of the equation, where we have n validations, each based on $(n-1)$ observations.

The Stein *estimate* of how much variance on the average we would account for if the equation were applied to many other samples is

$$\rho_c{}^2 = 1 - (45/41)(44/40)(47/46)(1-.822) = .7804$$

Now we turn to the regression diagnostics from SAS REG, which are presented in Table 3.17. In terms of the standardized residuals for y, there are two that stand out (-3.0154 and 2.5276 for observations 25 and 44). These are for the University of Michigan and Virginia Polytech. In terms of outliers on the set of predictors, using $2p/n = 2(5)/46 = .217$, there are outliers for observation 15 (University of Georgia), observation 25 (University of Michigan again) and observation 30 (Northeastern).

Using the criterion of Cook $D > 1$, there is one influential data point, observation 25 (University of Michigan). Recall that whether a point will be influential is a *joint* function of being an outlier on y and on the set of predictors. In this case, the University of Michigan definitely doesn't fit the model and it differs dramatically from the other psychology departments on the set of predictors. A check of the DFBETAS reveals that it is very different in terms of number of faculty (DFBETA $= -2.7653$), and a scan of the raw data show the number of faculty at 111, while the average number of faculty members for all the departments is only 29.5. The question needs to be raised as to whether the University of Michigan is "counting" faculty members in a different way from the rest of the schools. For example, are they including part time and adjunct faculty, and if so, is the number of these quite large?

For comparison purposes, the analysis was also run with the University of Michigan deleted. Interestingly, the same 4 predictors emerge from the stepwise procedure, although the results are better in some ways. For example, Mallows' C_k is now 4.5248, whereas for the full data set is was 5.216. Also, the PRESS residual sum of squares is now only 899.92, whereas for the full data set it was 1350.33.

3.16   SAMPLE SIZE DETERMINATION FOR A RELIABLE PREDICTION EQUATION

The reader may recall that in power analysis one is interested in determining a priori how many subjects are needed per group to have, say, power = .80

TABLE 3.17

Regression Diagnostics (Standardized Residuals, Hat Elements and Cook's Distance) for National Academy of Science Data

Obs	Student Residual	$-2-1-0\ 1\ 2$	Cook's D	Rstudent	Hat Diag H
1	− 0.708	*	0.007	− 0.7039	0.0684
2	− 0.078		0.000	− 0.0769	0.1064
3	0.403		0.003	0.3992	0.0807
4	0.424		0.009	0.4193	0.1951
5	0.800	*	0.012	0.7968	0.0870
6	− 1.447	**	0.034	− 1.4677	0.0742
7	1.085	**	0.038	1.0874	0.1386
8	− 0.300		0.002	− 0.2968	0.1057
9	− 0.460		0.010	− 0.4556	0.18765
10	1.694	* ***	0.48	1.7346	0.0765
11	− 0.694	*	0.004	− 0.6892	0.0433
12	− 0.870	*	0.016	− 0.8670	0.0956
13	− 0.732		0.007	− 0.7276	0.0652
14	0.359	*	0.003	0.3556	0.0885
15	− 0.942	**	0.054	− 0.9403	0.2328
16	1.282		0.063	1.2927	0.1613
17	0.424		0.001	0.4200	0.0297
18	0.227		0.001	0.2241	0.1196
19	0.877	*	0.007	0.8747	0.0464
20	0.643	*	0.004	0.6382	0.0456
21	− 0.417		0.002	− 0.4127	0.0429
22	0.193		0.001	0.1907	0.0696
23	0.490		0.002	0.4856	0.0460
24	0.357		0.001	0.3533	0.0503
25	− 2.756	*****	2.292	− 3.0154	0.6014
26	− 1.370	**	0.068	− 1.3855	0.1533
27	− 0.799	*	0.017	− 0.7958	0.1186
28	0.165		0.000	0.1629	0.0573
29	0.995	*	0.018	0.9954	0.0844
30	− 1.786	***	0.241	− 1.8374	0.2737
31	− 1.171	**	0.018	− 1.1762	0.0613
32	− 0.994	*	0.017	− 0.9938	0.0796
33	1.394	**	0.037	1.4105	0.0859
34	1.568	***	0.051	1.5978	0.0937
35	− 0.622	*	0.006	− 0.6169	0.0714
36	0.282		0.002	0.2791	0.1066
37	− 0.831	*	0.009	− 0.8277	0.0643
38	1.516	***	0.039	1.5411	0.0789
39	1.492	**	0.081	1.5151	0.1539
40	0.314		0.001	0.3108	0.0638
41	− 0.977	*	0.016	− 0.9766	0.0793
42	− 0.581	*	0.006	− 0.5766	0.0847
43	0.059		0.000	0.0584	0.0877
44	2.376	****	0.164	2.5276	0.1265
45	− 0.508	*	0.003	− 0.5031	0.0592
46	− 1.505	***	0.085	− 1.5292	0.1583

at the .05 level. Thus, planning is done ahead of time to ensure that one has a good chance of detecting an effect of a given magnitude. Now, in multiple regression the focus is different and the concern, or at least one very important concern, is development of a prediction equation that has generalizability. A study by Park and Dudycha (1974) provides several tables that, given certain input parameters, enable one to determine how many subjects will be needed for a reliable prediction equation. They considered from 3 to 25 random variable predictors, and found that with about 15 subjects per predictor the amount of shrinkage is small ($< .05$) with high probability (.90), if the squared population multiple correlation (ρ^2) is .50. In Table 3.18 we present selected results from the Park and Dudycha study for 3, 4, 8, and 15 predictors.

To use Table 3.18 we need an estimate of ρ^2, that is, the squared *population* multiple correlation. Unless an investigator has a good estimate from a previous study that used similar subjects and predictors, we feel taking $\rho^2 = .50$ is a reasonable guess for social science research. In the physical sciences, estimates $> .75$ are quite reasonable. If we set $\rho^2 = .50$ and want the loss in predictive power to be less than .05 with probability $= .90$, then the required sample sizes are as follows:

		Number of Predictors		
$\rho^2 = .50$ $\epsilon = .05$	3	4	8	15
n	50	66	124	214
n/k ratio	16.7	16.7	15.5	14.3

The n/k ratios in all 4 cases are around 15/1.

We had indicated earlier that *generally* about 15 subjects per predictor are needed for a reliable regression equation in the social sciences, that is, an equation that will cross validate well. There are three converging lines of evidence that support this conclusion:

1. The Stein formula for estimated shrinkage (Table 3.10)
2. My own experience
3. The results just presented from the Park and Dudycha study.

However, the Park and Dudycha study (cf. Table 3.18) clearly shows that *the magnitude of* ρ (population multiple correlation) strongly affects how many subjects will be needed for a reliable regression equation. For example, if $\rho^2 = .75$, then for 3 predictors only 28 subjects are needed, whereas 50 subjects were needed for the same case when $\rho^2 = .50$.

Also, from the Stein formula (Table 3.9), you will see if you plug in .40 for R^2 that more than 15 subjects per predictor will be needed to keep the shrinkage fairly small, while if you insert .70 for R^2, significantly less than 15 will be needed.

TABLE 3.18

Sample Size such that the Difference Between the Squared Multiple Correlation and Squared Cross Validated Correlation is Arbitrarily Small with Given Probability

Three Predictors

ρ^2	ϵ	γ .99	.95	.90	.80	.60	.40
.05	.01	858	554	421	290	158	81
	.03	269	166	123	79	39	18
.10	.01	825	535	410	285	160	88
	.03	271	174	133	91	50	27
	.05	159	100	75	51	27	14
.25	.01	693	451	347	243	139	79
	.03	232	151	117	81	48	27
	.05	140	91	71	50	29	17
	.10	70	46	36	25	15	7
	.20	34	22	17	12	8	6
.50	.01	464	304	234	165	96	55
	.03	157	104	80	57	34	21
	.05	96	64	50	36	22	14
	.10	50	34	27	20	13	9
	.20	27	19	15	12	9	7
.75	.01	235	155	120	85	50	30
	.03	85	55	43	31	20	13
	.05	51	35	28	21	14	10
	.10	28	20	16	13	9	7
	.20	16	12	10	9	7	6
.98	.01	23	17	14	11	9	7
	.03	11	9	8	7	6	6
	.05	9	7	7	6	6	5
	.10	7	6	6	6	5	5
	.20	6	6	5	5	5	5

Four Predictors

ρ^2	ϵ	γ .99	.95	.90	.80	.60	.40
.05	.01	1041	707	559	406	245	144
	.03	312	201	152	103	54	27
.10	.01	1006	691	550	405	253	155
	.03	326	220	173	125	74	43
	.05	186	123	95	67	38	22
.25	.01	853	587	470	348	221	140
	.03	283	195	156	116	73	46
	.05	168	117	93	69	43	28
	.10	84	58	46	34	20	14
	.20	38	26	20	15	10	7
.50	.01	573	396	317	236	152	97
	.03	193	134	108	81	53	35
	.05	117	82	66	50	33	23
	.10	60	43	35	27	19	13
	.20	32	23	19	15	11	9
.75	.01	290	201	162	121	78	52
	.03	100	70	57	44	30	21
	.05	62	44	37	28	20	15
	.10	34	25	21	17	13	11
	.20	19	15	13	11	9	7
.98	.01	29	22	19	15	12	10
	.03	14	11	10	9	8	7
	.05	10	9	8	8	7	7
	.10	8	8	7	7	7	6
	.20	7	7	7	6	6	6

Eight Predictors

ρ²	ε	γ .99	.95	.90	.80	.60	.40
.05	.01	1640	1226	1031	821	585	418
	.03	447	313	251	187	116	71
.10	.01	1616	1220	1036	837	611	450
	.03	503	373	311	246	172	121
	.05	281	202	166	128	85	55
.25	.01	1376	1047	893	727	538	404
	.03	453	344	292	237	174	129
	.05	267	202	171	138	101	74
	.10	128	95	80	63	45	33
	.20	52	37	30	24	17	12
.50	.01	927	707	605	494	368	279
	.03	312	238	204	167	125	96
	.05	188	144	124	103	77	59
	.10	96	74	64	53	40	31
	.20	49	38	33	28	22	18
.75	.01	470	360	308	253	190	150
	.03	162	125	108	90	69	54
	.05	100	78	68	57	44	35
	.10	54	43	38	32	26	22
	.20	31	25	23	20	17	15
.98	.01	47	38	34	29	24	21
	.03	22	19	18	16	15	14
	.05	17	16	15	14	13	12
	.10	14	13	12	12	11	11
	.20	12	11	11	11	11	10

Fifteen Predictors

ρ²	ε	γ .99	.95	.90	.80	.60	.40
.05	.01	2523	2007	1760	1486	1161	918
	.03	640	474	398	316	222	156
.10	.01	2519	2029	1794	1532	1220	987
	.03	762	600	524	438	337	263
	.05	403	309	265	216	159	119
.25	.01	2163	1754	1557	1339	1079	884
	.03	705	569	504	431	345	280
	.05	413	331	292	249	198	159
	.10	191	151	132	111	87	69
	.20	76	58	49	40	30	24
.50	.01	1461	1188	1057	911	738	608
	.03	489	399	355	306	249	205
	.05	295	261	214	185	151	125
	.10	149	122	109	94	77	64
	.20	75	62	55	48	40	34
.75	.01	741	605	539	466	380	315
	.03	255	210	188	164	135	113
	.05	158	131	118	103	86	73
	.10	85	72	65	58	49	43
	.20	49	42	39	35	31	28
.98	.01	75	64	59	53	46	41
	.03	36	33	31	29	27	25
	.05	28	26	25	24	23	22
	.10	23	21	21	20	20	19
	.20	20	19	19	19	18	18

*Entries in the body of the table are the sample size such that $P(\rho^2 - \rho_c^2 < \epsilon) = \gamma$ where ρ is population multiple correlation, ϵ is some tolerance and γ is the probability.

3.17   COMPARING REGRESSION EQUATIONS ACROSS GROUPS

There are situations where we might be interested in whether the nature of the predictive relationship is different for subgroups. For example, can we assume the same equation for males as for females, or for blacks as for whites? Another example that came across my desk recently involved two groups of subjects who responded in a somewhat different way: (a) About half the subjects had a face to face interview; (b) The remaining subjects filled out a mail questionnaire. The student wished to determine whether the prediction equation was the same for the two groups. If it was, then she would pool the data; otherwise, the results would need to be discussed for each group.

The biomedical program BMDP1R tests whether the prediction equation is the same for several groups. To illustrate it's use we modify an example presented in the BMDP manual (Vol. 2, 1988). The example uses data from the Berkeley Guidance Study, which monitored a group of girls and boys born in Berkeley, California between 1928 and 1929. The complete data for this example appear in Weisberg (1980, pp 52–53). We will predict fatness (FAT) at age 18 from weight at age 9 (WGT9), height at age 9 (HGT9) and a measure of strength at age 9 (STREN9). In our example we assume the data is inline, that is, part of the command file, in contrast to the BMDP example, which considers accessing the data from a file. The control lines are given in Table 3.19. They will yield a separate prediction equation for each sex, and also a test of whether the prediction equations are equal for boys and girls.

The portion of the printout testing equality of the equations is presented below:

ANALYSIS OF VARIANCE OF REGRESSION COEFFICIENTS OVER GROUPS
(REDUCTION OF RESIDUALS DUE TO GROUPING)

	SUM OF SQUARES	DF	MEAN SQUARE	F RATIO	P (TAIL)
REGRESSION OVER GROUPS	26.239	4	6.560	6.443	.00029
RESIDUAL WITHIN GROUPS	50.908	50	1.018		

The above p value indicates that the equations are significantly different well beyond the .01 level.

3.18   OTHER TYPES OF REGRESSION ANALYSIS

Least squares regression is only one (although the most prevalent) way of conducting a regression analysis. The least squares estimator has two

TABLE 3.19
BMDP1R Control Lines for Testing the Equality of the Prediction Equations
for Boys and Girls

PROBLEM TITLE IS 'TESTING EQUALITY OF EQUATIONS './
INPUT VARIABLES = 5. FORMAT IS FREE./
VARIABLE NAMES ARE SEX,WGT9,HGT9,STREN9,FAT.
GROUPING = SEX./GROUP CODES(SEX) = 0,1.
NAMES(SEX) = FEMALE,MALE./REGRESS DEPENDENT = FAT.
INDEP = WGT9,HGT9,STREN9./
END/

DATA LINES

---

desirable statistical properties, i.e., it is an unbiased, minimum variance estimator. Mathematically, unbiased means that $E(\hat{\beta}) = \beta$, the expected value of the vector of estimated regression coefficients is the vector of population regression coefficients. To elaborate on this a bit, unbiased means that the estimate of the population coefficients will not be consistently high or low, but will "bounce around" the population values. And, if we were to average the estimates from many repeated samplings, the averages would be very close to the population values.

The minimum variance notion can be misleading. It does not mean that the variance of the coefficients for the least squares estimator is small per se, but that *among the class* of unbiased estimators β has the minimum variance. The fact that the variance of β can be quite large led Hoerl and Kenard (1970a, 1970b) to consider a biased estimator of β which has considerably less variance, and the development of their ridge regression technique. Ridge regression is available on the BMDP package. Although ridge regression has been strongly endorsed by some, it has also been criticized (Draper & Smith, 1981; Morris, 1982; Smith & Campbell, 1980). Morris, for example, found that ridge regression never cross-validated better than other types of regression (least squares, equal weighting of predictors, reduced rank) for a set of data situations.

Another class of estimators are the James-Stein (1961) estimators. Regarding the utility of these, the following from Weisberg (1980) is relevant, "the improvement over least squares will be very small whenever the parameter β is well estimated, i.e., collinearity is not a problem and β is not too close to **O**."

Since, as we have indicated earlier, least square regression can be quite sensitive to outliers, some researchers prefer regression techniques that are relatively insensitive to outliers, i.e., robust regression techniques. Since the early 1970s the literature on these techniques has grown considerably (Hogg, 1979; Huber, 1977; Mosteller & Tukey, 1977). Although these techniques have merit, we feel that use of least squares, along with the appropriate identification of outliers and influential points, is a quite adequate procedure.

3.19 MULTIVARIATE REGRESSION

In multivariate regression we are interested in predicting several dependent variables from a set of predictors. The dependent variables might bedifferentiated aspects of some variable. For example, Finn (1974) broke Grade Point Average (GPA) up into GPA required and GPA elective, and considered predicting these two dependent variables from high school GPA, a general knowledge test score, and attitude toward education. Or, one might measure "success as a professor" by considering various aspects of success such as: rank (assistant, associate, full), rating of institution working at, salary, rating by experts in the field and number of articles published. These would constitute the multiple dependent variables.

Mathematical Model

In multiple regression (one dependent variable), the model was

$$y = X\beta + e,$$

where y was the vector of scores for the subjects on the dependent variable, X was the matrix with the scores for the subjects on the predictors, and e was the vectors of errors and β was vector of regression coefficients.

In multivariate regression the y, β, and e vectors become matrices, which we denote by Y, B, and E:

$$Y = XB + E$$

$$
\overset{\mathbf{Y}}{
\begin{bmatrix}
y_{11} & y_{12} & \cdots & y_{1p} \\
y_{21} & y_{22} & \cdots & y_{2p} \\
\cdots & \cdots & \cdots & \\
y_{n1} & y_{n2} & & y_{np}
\end{bmatrix}}
=
\overset{\mathbf{X}}{
\begin{bmatrix}
1 & x_{12} & \cdots & x_{1k} \\
1 & x_{22} & \cdots & x_{2k} \\
\cdots & \cdots & \cdots & \\
1 & x_{n2} & & x_{nk}
\end{bmatrix}}
\overset{\mathbf{B}}{
\begin{bmatrix}
b_{01} & b_{02} & \cdots & b_{1p} \\
b_{11} & b_{12} & \cdots & b_{1p} \\
\cdots & \cdots & \cdots & \\
b_{k1} & b_{k2} & \cdots & b_{kp}
\end{bmatrix}}
+
\overset{\mathbf{E}}{
\begin{bmatrix}
e_{11} & e_{12} & \cdots & e_{1p} \\
e_{21} & e_{22} & \cdots & e_{2p} \\
\cdots & \cdots & \cdots & \\
e_{n1} & e_{n2} & \cdots & e_{np}
\end{bmatrix}}
$$

The first column of Y gives the scores for the subjects on the first dependent variable, the second column the scores on the second dependent variable, etc. The first column of B gives the set of regression coefficients for the first dependent variable, the second column the regression coefficients for the second dependent variable, etc.

Example 12

As an example of multivariate regression, we consider part of a data set from Timm (1975). The dependent variables are Peabody Picture Vocabulary Test score and score on the Ravin Progressive Matrices Test. The predictors were scores from different types of paired associate learning tasks, called "named still (ns)," "named action (na)," and "sentence still (ss)." The control lines for running the analysis on SPSSX MANOVA are given in Table 3.20, along with annotation. In understanding the annotation the reader should refer back to Table 1.4, where we indicated some of the basic elements of the SPSSX control language.

Selected output from the multivariate regression analysis run is given in Table 3.21. The multivariate test determines whether there is a significant relationship between the two *sets* of variables, i.e., the two dependent variables and the three predictors. At this point, the reader should focus on Wilk's Λ, the most commonly used multivariate test statistic. We have more to say about the other multivariate tests in Chapter 5. Wilk's Λ here is given by:

$$\Lambda = \frac{|SS_{\text{resid}}|}{|SS_{\text{tot}}|} = \frac{|SS_{\text{resid}}|}{|SS_{\text{reg}} + SS_{\text{resid}}|}, \ 0 \le \Lambda \le 1$$

Recall from the matrix algebra chapter that the determinant of a matrix served as a multivariate generalization for the variance of a set of variables. Thus, $|SS_{\text{resid}}|$ indicates the amount of variability for the set of 2 dependent variables that is not accounted for by regression, and $|SS_{\text{tot}}|$ gives the total variability for the 2 dependent variables about their means. The sampling distribution of Wilk's Λ is quite complicated, however, there is an excellent F approximation (due to Rao), which is what appears in Table 3.21. Note that the multivariate $F = 4.82$, $p < .000$, which indicates a significant relationship between the dependent variables and the 3 predictors beyond the .01 level.

The univariate F's are the tests for the significance of the regression of each dependent variable separately. They indicate that PEVOCAB is significantly related to the set of predictors at the .05 level ($F = 9.501$, $p < .000$), while RAVIN is not significantly related at the .05 level ($F = 2.652$, $p < .065$). Thus, the overall multivariate significance is primarily attributable to PEVO-CAB's relationship with the three predictors.

It is important for the reader to realize that although the multivariate tests take into account the correlations among the dependent variables, the regression equations that appear in Table 3.21 are those that would be obtained if each dependent variable were regressed *separately* on the set of predictors. That is, in deriving the prediction equations, the correlations among the dependent variables are ignored, or not taken into account.

TABLE 3.20
Control Lines for Multivariate Regression Analysis of Timm Data —
Two Dependent Variables and Three Predictors

    TITLE 'MULT. REGRESS. — 2 DEP. VARS AND 3 PREDS'
① DATA LIST FREE/PEVOCAB RAVIN NS NA SS
② LIST
③ BEGIN DATA

48	8	6	12	16	76	13	14	30	27
40	13	21	16	16	52	9	5	17	8
63	15	11	26	17	82	14	21	34	25
71	21	20	23	18	68	8	10	19	14
74	11	7	16	13	70	15	21	26	25
70	15	15	35	24	61	11	7	15	14
54	12	13	27	21	55	13	12	20	17
54	10	20	26	22	40	14	5	14	8
66	13	21	35	27	54	10	6	14	16
64	14	19	27	26	47	16	15	18	10
48	16	9	14	18	52	14	20	26	26
74	19	14	23	23	57	12	4	11	8
57	10	16	15	17	80	11	18	28	21
78	13	19	34	23	70	16	9	23	11
47	14	7	12	8	94	19	28	32	32
63	11	5	25	14	76	16	18	29	21
59	11	10	23	24	55	8	14	19	12
74	14	10	18	18	71	17	23	31	26
54	14	6	15	14					

    END DATA
④ MANOVA PEVOCAB RAVIN WITH NS NA SS/
      PRINT = CELLINFO(MEANS,COR)/

---

  ① The variables are separated by blanks; they could also have been separated by commas.
  ② This LIST command is to get a listing of the data.
  ③ The data is preceded by the BEGIN DATA command and followed by the END DATA command.
  ④ The predictors follow the keyword WITH in the MANOVA command.

TABLE 3.21

Multivariate and Univariate Tests of Significance and Regression Coefficients for Timm Data

EFFECT .. WITHIN CELLS REGRESSION

MULTIVARIATE TESTS OF SIGNIFICANCE (S = 2, M = 0, N = 15)

TEST NAME	VALUE	APPROX. F	HYPOTH. DF	ERROR DF	SIG. OF F
PILLAIS	.57254	4.41203	6.00	66.00	.001
HOTELLINGS	1.00976	5.21709	6.00	62.00	.000
WILKS	.47428	4.82197	6.00	64.00	.000
ROYS	.47371				

This test indicates there is a significant (at α = .05) regression of the set of 2 dependent variables on the three predictors.

UNIVARIATE F-TESTS WITH (3.33) D. F.

VARIABLE	SQ. MUL. R.	MUL. R	ADJ. R-SQ.	F	SIG. OF F
PEVOCAB	.46345	.68077	.41467	① 9.50121	.000
RAVIN	.19429	.44078	.12104	2.65250	.065

These results show there is a significant regression for PEVOCAB, but RAVIN is not significantly related to the three predictors at .05, since .065 > .05.

DEPENDENT VARIABLE .. PEVOCAB

COVARIATE		B	BETA	STD. ERR.	T-VALUE	SIG. OF T.
NS		-.2056372599	-.1043054487	.40797	-.50405	.618
NA	②	1.01272293634	.5856100072	.37685	2.68737	.011
SS		.3977340740	.2022598804	.47010	.84606	.404

DEPENDENT VARIABLE .. RAVIN

COVARIATE	B	BETA	STD. ERR.	T-VALUE	SIG. OF T
NS	.2026184278	.4159658338	.12352	1.64038	.110
NA	.0302663367	.0708355423	.11410	.26527	.792
SS	-.0174928333	-.0360039904	.14233	-.12290	.903

① Using Equation 4, $F = \dfrac{R^2/k}{(1 - R^2)/(n - k - 1)} = \dfrac{.46345/3}{.53655/(37 - 3 - 1)} = 9.501$

② These are the raw regression coefficients for predicting PEVOCAB from the 3 predictors, excluding the regression constant.

133

We indicated earlier in this chapter that an R^2 value around .50 occurs quite often with educational and psychological data, and this is precisely what has occurred here with the PEVOCAB variable (R^2 = .463). Also, we can be fairly confident that the prediction equation for PEVOCAB will cross-validate, since the n/k ratio is = 12.33, which is close to the ratio we indicated is necessary.

3.20 SUMMARY OF IMPORTANT POINTS

1. A particularly good situation for multiple regression is where each of the predictors is correlated with y and the predictors have low intercorrelations, for then each of the predictors is accounting for a relatively distinct part of the variance on y.

2. Moderate to high correlations among the predictors (multicollinearity) creates three problems: it (a) severely limits the size of R, (b) makes determining the importance of given predictor difficult, and (c) increases the variance of regression coefficients, making for an unstable prediction equation. There are at least three ways of combating this problem. One way is to combine into a single measure a set of predictors that are highly correlated. A second way is to consider the use of principal components analysis (a type of "factor analysis") to reduce the number of predictors. Since the components are uncorrelated, we have eliminated multicollinearity. A third way is through the use of ridge regression. This technique is beyond the scope of this book.

3. Preselecting a small set of predictors by examining a correlation matrix from a large initial set, or by using one of the stepwise procedures (forward, stepwise, backward) to select a small set, is likely to produce an equation that is sample specific. If one insists on doing this, and I do not recommend it, then the onus is on the investigator to demonstrate that the equation has adequate predictive power beyond the derivation sample.

4. Mallow's C_p was presented as a measure that minimizes the effect of underfitting (important predictors left out of the model) and overfitting (having predictors in the model that make essentially no contribution or are marginal). This will be the case if one chooses models for which $C_p \approx p$.

5. With many data sets, more than one model will provide a good fit to the data. Thus, one deals with selecting a model from a *pool* of candidate models.

6. There are various graphical plots for assessing how well the model fits the assumptions underlying linear regression. One of the most useful graphs the standardized residuals (y axis) versus the predicted values (x axis). If the assumptions are tenable, then one should observe roughly a random

scattering. Any *systematic clustering* of the residuals indicates a model violation(s).

7. It is crucial to validate the model(s) by either randomly splitting the sample and cross validating, or using the PRESS statistic, or by obtaining the Stein estimate of the *average* predictive power of the equation on other samples from the same population. Studies in the literature that have not cross validated should be checked with the Stein estimate to assess the generalizability of the prediction equation(s) presented.

8. Results from the Park and Dudycha study indicate that the magnitude of the *population* multiple correlation strongly affects how many subjects will be needed for a reliable prediction equation. If your estimate of the squared population value is .50, then about 15 subjects per predictor are needed. On the other hand, if your estimate of the squared population value is substantially *larger* than .50, then far less than 15 subjects per predictor will be needed.

9. Influential data points, that is points that strongly affect the prediction equation, can be identified by seeing which cases have Cook distances > 1. These points need to be examined very carefully. If such a point is due to a recording error, then one would simply correct it and redo the analysis. Or if it is found that the influential point is due to an instrumentation error or that the process that generated the data for that subject was different, then it is legitimate to drop the case from the analysis. If, however, none of these appears to be the case, then one should *not* drop the case, but perhaps report the results of several analyses; one analysis with all the data and an additional analysis(ses) with the influential point(s) deleted.

REGRESSION EXERCISES – CHAPTER 3

1. Consider this set of data:

x	y
2	3
3	6
4	8
6	4
7	10
8	14
9	8
10	12
11	14
12	12
13	16

a) Run this data on SPSSX, obtaining the case analysis.

b) Do you see any pattern in the plot of the standardized residuals? What does this suggest?

c) Plot the points, sketch in the regression equation, and indicate the raw residuals by vertical lines.

2. Consider the following small set of data:

PREDX	DEP
0	1
1	4
2	6
3	8
4	9
5	10
6	10
7	8
8	7
9	6
10	5

a) Run this data set on SPSSX, forcing the predictor in the equation and obtaining the casewise analysis.

b) Do you see any pattern in the plot of the standardized residuals? What does this suggest?

c) Plot the points. What type of relationship exists between PREDX and DEP?

3. Consider the following correlation matrix:

	y	x_1	x_2
y	1.00	.60	.50
x_1	.60	1.00	.80
x_2	.50	.80	1.00

a) How much variance on y will x_1 account for if entered first?

b) How much variance on y will x_1 account for if entered second?

c) What, if anything, do the above results have to do with the multicollinearity problem?

4. A medical school admissions official has two proven predictors (x_1 and x_2) of success in medical school. He has two other predictors under consideration (x_3 and x_4), of which he wishes to choose just one which will add the most (beyond what x_1 and x_2 already predict) to predicting success. Below is the matrix of intercorrelations he has gathered on a sample of 100 medical students:

	x_1	x_2	x_3	x_4
y	.60	.55	.60	.46
x_1		.70	.60	.20
x_2			.80	.30
x_3				.60

a) What procedure would he use to determine which predictor has the greater incremental validity? Do *not* go into any numerical details, just indicate the general procedure. Also, what is your educated guess as to which predictor (x_3 or x_4) will probably have the greater incremental validity.

b) Suppose the investigator has found his third predictor, runs the regression and finds $R = .76$. Apply the Herzberg formula (use $k = 3$), and tell exactly what the resulting number represents.

5. In a study from a major journal (Bradley, Caldwell, and Elardo, 1977) the investigators were interested in predicting I.Q. of 3-year-old children from four measures of socioeconomic status and six environmental process variables (as assessed by a HOME inventory instrument). Their total sample size was 105. They were also interested in determining whether the prediction varied depending on sex and on race. The following is from their PROCEDURE section:

> To examine the relations among SES, environmental process, and IQ data, three multiple correlation analyses were performed on each of five samples: total group, males, females, whites, and blacks. First, four SES variables (maternal education, paternal education, occupation of head of household, and father absence) plus six environmental process variables (the six HOME inventory subscales) were used as a set of predictor variables with IQ as the criterion variable. Third, the six environmental process variables were used as the predictor set with IQ as the criterion variable.

Below is the table they present with the 15 multiple correlations:

Multiple Correlations Between Measures
of Environmental Quality and IQ

Measure	Males (n = 57)	Females (n = 48)	Whites (n = 37)	Black (n = 68)	Total (N = 105)
Status variables (A)	.555	.636	.582	.346	.556
HOME inventory (B)	.647	.790	.622	.576	.742
A and B	.682	.825	.683	.614	.765

a) The authors state that all of the above multiple correlations are statistically significant (.05 level) except for .346 obtained for Blacks with Status variables. Show that .346 is not significant at .05 level.

b) For Males, does the addition of the Home inventory variables to the prediction equation significantly increase (use .05 level) predictive power beyond that of the Status variables?

The following F statistic is appropriate for determining whether a set B significantly adds to the prediction beyond what set A contributes:

$$F = \frac{(R^2_{y \cdot AB} - R^2_{y \cdot A})/k_b}{(1 - R^2_{y \cdot AB})/(n - k_A - k_B - 1)}, \ k_B + (n - k_A - k_B - 1) \ df$$

Where k_A and k_B represent the number of predictors in sets A and B respectively.

6. Consider the following RESULTS section from a study by Sharp (1981):

The regression was performed to determine the extent to which a linear combination of two or more of the five predictor variables could account for the variance in the dependent variable (posttest). Three steps in the multiple regression were completed before the contributions of additional predictor variables were deemed insignificant ($p > .05$). In Step #1, the pretest variable was selected as the predictor variable that explained the greatest amount of variance in posttest scores. The R^2 value using this single variable was .25. The next predictor variable chosen (Step #2) in conjunction with pretest, was interest in participating in the CTP. The R^2 value using these two variables was .36. The final variable (Step #3), which significantly improved the prediction of posttest scores, was the treatment — viewing the model videotape (Tape). The multiple regression equation, with all three significant predictor variables entered, yielded an R^2 of .44. The other two predictor variables, interest and relevance, were not entered into the regression equation as both failed to meet the statistical significance criterion.

Correlations Among Criterion and Predictor Variables

	Posttest	Pretest	Tape	Campus Teaching Program	Interest	Relevancy
Posttest	1.0					
Pretest	.50*	1.0				
Tape	.27	−.02	1.0			
Campus Teaching Program	.35*	.06	−.07	1.0		
Interest	−.02	.14	.07	−.06	1.0	
Relevance	−.06	−.02	.07	.05	.31	1.0

Note: $N = 37$, *$p < .05$

a) Which specific predictor selection procedure were the authors using?

b) They give the R^2 for the first predictor as .25. How did they arrive at this figure?

c) The R^2 for the first two predictors was .36, an increase of .11 over the R^2 for just the first predicter. Using the appropriate correlations in the Table show how the value of .11 is obtained.

d) Is there evidence of multicollinearity among the predictors? Explain.

e) Do you think the author's regression equation would cross-validate well? Explain.

7. Plante and Goldfarb (1984) predicted social adjustment from Cattell's 16 personality factors. There were 114 subjects, consisting of students and employees from two large manufacturing companies. They state in their RESULTS section:

Stepwise multiple regression was performed. . . . The index of social adjustment significantly correlated with 6 of the primary factors of the 16 PF. . . . Multiple regression analysis resulted in a multiple correlation of $R = .41$ accounting for 17% of the variance with these 6 factors. The multiple R obtained while utilizing all 16 factors was $R = .57$, thus accounting for 32% of the variance.

a) Would you have much faith in the reliability of either of the above regression equations?

b) Apply the Stein formula for random predictors (Equation 9) to the 16 variable equation to estimate how much variance on the average we could expect to account for if the equation were cross validated on many other random samples.

8. Consider again the Sesame Street data set analyzed in 3.2 where we predicted knowledge of body parts (postbody) after viewing the series from previous knowledge of body parts (prebody). Now we add another predictor, amount of time the children viewed the Sesame Street series (scaled from 1 to 4, with 4 meaning more viewing time), to see if postbody can be predicted better from prebody and viewing.

a) Run the multiple regression on SPSSX REGRESSION, using the stepwise procedure. Are both predictors "significant"?

b) How much variance on postbody is accounted for by the significant predictor(s)?

c) Write out the prediction equation.

d) Would you be confident of the generalizability of the equation? Explain.

e) Are there any standardized or studentized residuals > 2?

f) Are there any standardized residuals that would be significant at overall $\alpha = .05$, i.e., using the Bonferroni inequality?

g) Are there any significant (α = .05) outliers for the predictors according to Mahalanobis distance?

h) Using Cook's distance, are there any influential data points?

9. An investigator has 15 variables on a file. Denote them by X1, X2, X3, ..., X15. Assume that there are spaces between all variables, so that free format can be used to read the data. The investigator wishes to predict X4. First, however, he obtains the correlation matrix among the predictors. He finds that variables 7 and 8 are very highly correlated and decides to combine those as a single predictor. He also finds that the correlations among variables 2, 5, and 10 are quite high, so he will combine those and use as a single predictor. He will also use variables 1, 3, 11, 12, 13, and 14 as individual predictors. Show the single set of control lines for doing both a stepwise and backward selection, obtaining the casewise statistics and scatterplot of residuals vs predicted values for both analyses.

10. A different investigator has 8 variables on a data file, with no spaces between the variables, so that fixed format will be needed to read the data. The data looks as follows:

2534674823178659
3645738234267583
        etc

The first two variables are single digit integers, the next three variables are two digit integers, the 6th variable is GPA (where you will need to deal with an implied decimal point), the 7th variable is a three digit integer and the 8th variable is a two digit integer. The 8th variable is the dependent variable. She wishes to force in variables 1 and 2, and then determine whether variables 3 through 5 (as a block) have any incremental validity. Show the complete SPSSX REGRESSION control lines.

11. A statistician, Al Phalevel, wishes to know the sample size he will need in a multiple regression study. He has 4 predictors and can tolerate at most a .10 dropoff in predictive power. But he wants this to be the case with .95 probability. From previous related research he estimates that the squared population multiple correlation will be .62. How many subjects will he need?

12. Recall that the Nold and Freedman (1977) study had each of 22 college freshmen write 4 essays, and used a stepwise regression analysis to predict quality of essay response. It was already mentioned in the chapter that the n of 88 used in the study is incorrect, since there are only 22 independent responses. Now let us concentrate on a different aspect of the study. They had 17 predictors, and found 5 of them to be "significant," accounting for

42.3% of the variance in quality. Using a median value between 5 and 17 and the proper sample size of 22, apply the Stein formula to estimate the cross validity predictive power of the equation. What do you conclude?

13. It was mentioned in the chapter that $E(R^2) = k/(n-1)$, when there is *no* relationship between the dependent variable and set of predictors in the population. It is very important to be aware of the above extreme positive bias in the sample multiple correlation when the number of predictors is close or fairly close to sample size in interpreting results from the literature. Comment on the following situation:

a) A team of medical researchers had 32 subjects measured on 28 predictors, which were used to predict three criterion variables. If they obtain squared multiple correlations of .83, .91 and .72 respectively, should we be impressed? What value for squared multiple correlation would be expected, even if there is no relationship? Suppose they used a stepwise procedure for one of the criterion measures and found 6 significant predictors which accounted for 74% of the variance. Apply the Stein formula, using a median value between 6 and 28, to estimate how much variance we would expect to account for on other samples. This example, only slightly modified, is taken from a paper by researchers at a major university that was submitted for publication (for which the author was one of the reviewers).

14. A regression analysis was run on the Sesame St ($n = 240$) data set, predicting postbody from the following 5 pretest measures: prebody, prelet, preform, prenumb and prerelat. The control lines for doing a stepwise regression, obtaining a histogram of the residuals, obtaining 10 largest values for the standardized residuals, the hat elements and Cook's distance, and for obtaining a plot of the standardized residuals versus the predicted y values are given below:

```
title  'mult reg for sesame data'
data list free/id site sex age viewcat setting viewenc
   prebody prelet preform prenumb prerelat preclasf postbody
   postlet postform postnumb postrel postclas peabody
begin data
data lines
end data
regression descriptives=default/
   variables=prebody to prerelat postbody/
   statistics=defaults history/
   dependent=postbody/
   method=stepwise/
   residuals=histogram(zresid) outliers(zresid,sresid,lever,cook)/
   scatterplot size(large) (*res,*pre)/
```

The SPSSX printout, which follows, is labeled 1 through 6 in the upper right hand corner of each page. Answer the following questions:

a) Why did PREBODY enter the prediction equation first?

b) Why did PREFORM enter the prediction equation second?

c) Write the prediction equation, rounding off to 3 decimals.

d) Is multicollinearity present? Explain.

e) Compute the Stein estimate and indicate in words exactly what it represents.

f) On page 3, show by using the appropriate correlations from the correlation matrix how the RSQCH = .0219 is obtained.

g) Refer to the standardized residuals on page 4. Is the number of these greater than $|2|$ about what you would expect if the model is appropriate? Why, or why not?

h) Are there any outliers on the set of predictors?

i) Are there any influential data points? Explain.

j) From examination of the residual plot (page 6), does it appear there may be some model violation(s)? Why, or why not?

k) From the histogram of standardized residuals on page 5, does it appear that the normality assumption is reasonable?

**** M U L T I P L E   R E G R E S S I O N ****

Listwise Deletion of Missing Data

	Mean	Std Dev	Label
PREBODY	21.400	6.391	
PRELET	15.938	8.536	
PREFORM	9.921	3.737	
PRENUMB	20.896	10.685	
PRERELAT	9.938	3.074	
POSTBODY	25.263	5.412	

N of Cases =   240

Correlation:

	PREBODY	PRELET	PREFORM	PRENUMB	PRERELAT	POSTBODY
PREBODY	1.000	.453	.680	.698	.623	.650
PRELET	.453	1.000	.506	.717	.471	.371
PREFORM	.680	.506	1.000	.673	.596	.551
PRENUMB	.698	.717	.673	1.000	.718	.527
PRERELAT	.623	.471	.596	.718	1.000	.449
POSTBODY	.650	.371	.551	.527	.449	1.000

①

21-Feb-92   mult. reg. - sesame data - 5 predictors
15:35:18   Univ of Cinti Computer Center on UCBEH::   VMS V5.4   ②

* * * * M U L T I P L E   R E G R E S S I O N * * * *

Equation Number 1   Dependent Variable.. POSTBODY

  Descriptive Statistics are printed on Page 2

Block Number 1. Method: Stepwise   Criteria PIN .0500   POUT .1000

Variable(s) Entered on Step Number 1..   PREBODY

Multiple R   .65043
R Square   .42306
Adjusted R Square   .42063
Standard Error   4.11947

Analysis of Variance

	DF	Sum of Squares	Mean Square
Regression	1	2961.60243	2961.60243
Residual	238	4038.86007	16.97000

F = 174.51988   Signif F = .0000

------- Variables in the Equation -------

Variable	B	SE B	Beta	T	Sig T
PREBODY	.550811	.041695	.650429	13.211	.0000
(Constant)	13.475137	.931046		14.473	.0000

------- Variables not in the Equation -------

Variable	Beta In	Partial	Min Toler	T	Sig T
PRELET	.095809	.112454	.794829	1.742	.0828
PREFORM	.201781	.194811	.537772	3.058	.0025
PRENUMB	.142743	.134575	.512807	2.091	.0376
PRERELAT	.072468	.074644	.612120	1.152	.2503

* *

Variable(s) Entered on Step Number 2..   PREFORM

Multiple R   .66705
R Square   .44495
Adjusted R Square   .44027
Standard Error   4.04906

Analysis of Variance

	DF	Sum of Squares	Mean Square
Regression	2	3114.88288	1557.44144
Residual	237	3885.57962	16.39485

F = 94.99577   Signif F = .0000

------- Variables in the Equation -------

Variable	B	SE B	Beta	T	Sig T
PREBODY	.434637	.055885	.513243	7.777	.0000
PREFORM	.292236	.095575	.201781	3.058	.0025
(Constant)	13.062051	.925051		14.120	.0000

------- Variables not in the Equation -------

Variable	Beta In	Partial	Min Toler	T	Sig T
PRELET	.050220	.057284	.488618	.881	.3790
PRENUMB	.075274	.066962	.432255	1.031	.3036
PRERELAT	.017172	.017200	.464300	.264	.7918

③

* * * *   M U L T I P L E   R E G R E S S I O N   * * * *

Equation Number 1   Dependent Variable..   POSTBODY

End Block Number   1   PIN =   .050 Limits reached.

* *

Summary table

Step	MultR	Rsq	AdjRsq	F(Eqn)	SigF	RsqCh	FCh	SigCh		Variable	BetaIn	Correl
1	.6504	.4231	.4206	174.520	.000	.4231	174.520	.000	In:	PREBODY	.6504	.6504
2	.6670	.4450	.4403	94.996	.000	.0219	9.349	.002	In:	PREFORM	.2018	.5507

* *

Residuals Statistics:

	Min	Max	Mean	Std Dev	N
*PRED	16.2543	32.5229	25.2625	3.6101	240
*ZPRED	-2.4952	2.0111	.0000	1.0000	240
*SEPRED	.2629	.9162	.4362	.1213	240
*ADJPRED	16.1999	32.5682	25.2669	3.6077	240
*RESID	-12.3732	12.7074	.0000	4.0321	240
*ZRESID	-3.0558	3.1384	.0000	.9958	240
*SRESID	-3.0681	3.1762	-.0005	1.0023	240
*DRESID	-12.4732	13.0154	-.0044	4.0852	240
*SDRESID	-3.1243	3.2392	-.0014	1.0078	240
*MAHAL	.0115	11.2410	1.9917	1.7309	240
*COOK D	.0000	.0815	.0044	.0092	240
*LEVER	.0000	.0470	.0083	.0072	240

Total Cases =   240

21-Feb-92   mult. reg. - sesame data - 5 predictors
15:35:20   Univ of Cinti Computer Center on UCBEH::   VMS V5.4

Outliers - Standardized Residual

Case #	*ZRESID
219	3.13837
139	-3.05583
125	-2.87264
155	-2.75661
39	-2.62930
147	2.49143
210	-2.34537
40	-2.30544
135	2.20274
36	2.10772

Outliers - Cook's Distance

Case #	*COOK D	Sig F
219	.08150	.9700
125	.07825	.9717
39	.04206	.9885
38	.03198	.9923
40	.02535	.9945
139	.02534	.9945
147	.02490	.9947
177	.02300	.9953
140	.02157	.9957
13	.02027	.9961

Outliers - Studentized Residual

Case #	*SRESID
219	3.17617
139	-3.06815
125	-2.91213
155	-2.76660
39	-2.65277
147	2.50621
210	-2.35352
40	-2.32164
135	2.20997
36	2.12003

Outliers - Leverage

Case #	*LEVER
140	.04703
32	.03595
23	.03042
114	.02778
167	.02610
52	.02595
233	.02543
8	.02470
236	.02346
161	.02306

④

⑤

Histogram - Standardized Residual

```
N  Exp N      (* = 1 Cases,   . : = Normal Curve)
1   .26  Out  *
0   .13 3.00
0   .19 2.88
0   .27 2.75
0   .38 2.63
1   .53 2.50  :
0   .72 2.38  :
1   .95 2.25  .:
1  1.25 2.13  .:
0  1.62 2.00  .
1  2.07 1.88  *.
3  2.59 1.75  **:
1  3.20 1.63  .
2  3.89 1.50  **
6  4.65 1.38  *****:.*
3  5.48 1.25  ***
8  6.36 1.13  *****:.**
4  7.26 1.00  ****
13 8.16  .88  ********:****
13 9.03  .75  ********:***
14 9.84  .63  ********:****
11 10.56 .50  ********:
24 11.15 .38  **********:***********
17 11.59 .25  ********:*****
5  11.87 .13  ******
13 11.96 .00  ********:**
11 11.87 -.13 ********:*
8  11.59 -.25 ********
11 11.15 -.38 ********
8  10.56 -.50 ********
8  9.84 -.63  *****
5  9.03 -.75  *****
5  8.16 -.88  *****
11 7.26 -1.00 ********:****
6  6.36 -1.13 ******
4  5.48 -1.25 ****:
5  4.65 -1.38 ****:
4  3.89 -1.50 ***:.
1  3.20 -1.63 *.
2  2.59 -1.75 **:
3  2.07 -1.88 *.
4  1.62 -2.00 *:.**
2  1.25 -2.13 *:*
1   .95 -2.25 .:
1   .72 -2.38 .:
0   .53 -2.50 .
1   .38 -2.63 *
1   .27 -2.75 *
1   .19 -2.88 *
1   .13 -3.00 *
0   .26  Out
```

147

⑥

148

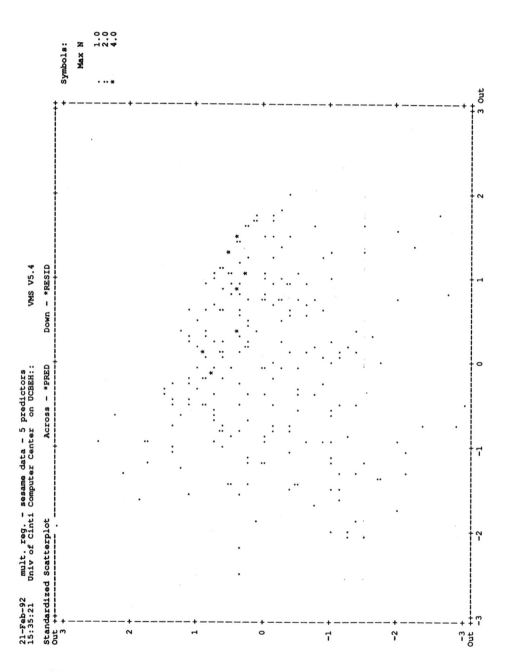

21-Feb-92   mult. reg. - sesame data - 5 predictors
15:35:21   Univ of Cinti Computer Center on UCBEH::   VMS V5.4

Standardized Scatterplot
Out ++--------------------   Across - *PRED   Down - *RESID

Symbols:

Max N

. 1.0
: 2.0
* 4.0

15. As was mentioned in the chapter, occasionally a categorical variable(s) may be used as a predictor. Remember that if there are k categories, then $(k\text{-}1)$ dummy variables are needed. Consider again the Sesame St data. A stratified 25% random sample of that data was selected for *just the first three sites.* Since SITE has three categories, two dummy variables are needed to code it. A single dummy variable (0 for male and 1 for female) was used to code sex. These variables, along with PREBODY, PRELET, PREFORM, PRENUMB and PRERELAT were used to predict POST-BODY. The data is presented below.

X1	X2	SEX	PREBODY	PRELET	PREFORM	PRENUMB	PRERELAT	POSTBODY
1.00	.00	.00	16.00	23.00	12.00	40.00	14.00	18.00
1.00	.00	1.00	29.00	26.00	10.00	33.00	14.00	27.00
1.00	.00	.00	27.00	44.00	18.00	42.00	15.00	32.00
1.00	.00	1.00	25.00	48.00	14.00	38.00	16.00	26.00
1.00	.00	.00	25.00	15.00	13.00	16.00	10.00	25.00
1.00	.00	.00	19.00	19.00	8.00	23.00	14.00	28.00
1.00	.00	.00	11.00	6.00	8.00	16.00	8.00	22.00
1.00	.00	.00	24.00	4.00	11.00	25.00	11.00	21.00
1.00	.00	1.00	11.00	12.00	9.00	5.00	5.00	12.00
1.00	.00	1.00	13.00	10.00	7.00	8.00	5.00	26.00
1.00	.00	1.00	26.00	15.00	11.00	22.00	10.00	24.00
1.00	.00	.00	13.00	11.00	6.00	15.00	10.00	15.00
1.00	.00	.00	16.00	15.00	6.00	13.00	11.00	19.00
.00	1.00	.00	28.00	13.00	10.00	29.00	11.00	30.00
.00	1.00	.00	28.00	19.00	14.00	37.00	13.00	32.00
.00	1.00	.00	30.00	14.00	17.00	37.00	13.00	28.00
.00	1.00	.00	31.00	30.00	15.00	47.00	15.00	23.00
.00	1.00	1.00	31.00	13.00	18.00	39.00	15.00	31.00
.00	1.00	1.00	31.00	19.00	14.00	36.00	13.00	32.00
.00	1.00	1.00	32.00	46.00	15.00	48.00	13.00	32.00
.00	1.00	1.00	32.00	22.00	15.00	32.00	11.00	31.00
.00	1.00	.00	31.00	14.00	16.00	29.00	11.00	32.00
.00	1.00	1.00	17.00	10.00	5.00	11.00	8.00	18.00
.00	1.00	1.00	21.00	23.00	14.00	27.00	13.00	31.00
.00	1.00	1.00	24.00	15.00	12.00	30.00	14.00	31.00
.00	1.00	.00	21.00	22.00	12.00	25.00	12.00	29.00
.00	1.00	1.00	32.00	8.00	13.00	23.00	11.00	29.00
.00	1.00	.00	32.00	16.00	14.00	30.00	11.00	25.00
.00	.00	1.00	20.00	11.00	5.00	25.00	9.00	26.00
.00	.00	.00	22.00	19.00	11.00	35.00	10.00	23.00
.00	.00	1.00	16.00	14.00	9.00	10.00	11.00	22.00
.00	.00	1.00	31.00	19.00	11.00	27.00	11.00	31.00
.00	.00	.00	18.00	13.00	9.00	24.00	10.00	25.00
.00	.00	1.00	21.00	12.00	12.00	17.00	9.00	23.00
.00	.00	1.00	29.00	18.00	12.00	22.00	11.00	30.00
.00	.00	1.00	17.00	15.00	5.00	11.00	10.00	32.00
.00	.00	.00	22.00	13.00	10.00	20.00	11.00	22.00
.00	.00	1.00	28.00	10.00	10.00	22.00	12.00	28.00
.00	.00	.00	14.00	7.00	9.00	15.00	9.00	18.00
.00	.00	.00	6.00	13.00	2.00	8.00	7.00	18.00
.00	.00	.00	10.00	12.00	4.00	9.00	10.00	13.00
.00	.00	1.00	23.00	10.00	9.00	9.00	7.00	21.00
.00	.00	.00	11.00	7.00	4.00	14.00	3.00	11.00
1.00	.00	1.00	23.00	12.00	8.00	9.00	5.00	29.00
1.00	.00	.00	16.00	13.00	10.00	10.00	9.00	7.00

Number of cases read: 45   Number of cases listed: 45

a) Use SAS REG to obtain a stepwise analysis. What model is selected?

b) Run the MAXR procedure on SAS REG. Of the models generated, which model(s) appear to give the "best" fit?

16.a) Use BMDP9R to run all possible regressions on the Morrison MBA data.

b) Although a long list of regression models appears on the output, with the R squared, adjusted R squared and Mallow's C for each model, the *five best* models are indicated by printing the regression coefficients and associated t statistics. And the best model, that is, having the smallest Mallow's value, is printed at the end.

How does this "best" model compare with the one selected by the stepwise and backward procedures in the chapter?

17.a) Use BMDP9R to run all possible regressions on the National Academy of Sciences data.

b) What are the five best models?

c) What is the best model, and how does it compare to the one selected by the stepwise and MAXR procedures in the chapter?

4 Two Group Multivariate Analysis of Variance

4.1 INTRODUCTION

In this chapter we consider the statistical analysis of two groups of subjects on several dependent variables simultaneously, focusing on cases where the variables are correlated and share a common conceptual meaning. That is, the dependent variables considered together make sense as a group. For example, they may be different dimensions of self concept (physical, social, emotional, academic), teacher effectiveness, speaker credibility, or reading (blending, syllabication, comprehension, etc.). We consider the multivariate tests along with their univariate counterparts and show that the multivariate two-group test (Hotelling's T^2) is a natural generalization of the univariate t test. We initially present the traditional analysis of variance approach for the two-group multivariate problem, and then later present and compare a regression analysis of the same data. In the next chapter studies with more than two groups are considered, where multivariate tests are employed that are generalizations of Fisher's F found in a univariate one way ANOVA. The last part of the chapter (Sections 4.9–4.13). presents a fairly extensive discussion of power, including introduction of a multivariate effect size measure and the use of SPSSX MANOVA for estimating power.

There are two reasons one should be interested in using more than one dependent variable when comparing two treatments:

1. Any treatment "worth it's salt" will affect the subjects in more than one way; hence the need for several criterion measures.

2. Through the use of several criterion measures we can obtain a more complete and detailed description of the phenomenon under investigation, whether it is reading achievement, math achievement, self concept, physiological stress, or teacher effectiveness or counselor effectiveness.

If we were comparing two methods of teaching second-grade reading, we would obtain a more detailed and informative breakdown of the differential effects of the methods if reading achievement were split into its subcomponents: syllabication, blending, sound discrimination, vocabulary, comprehension, and reading rate. Comparing the two methods only on total reading achievement might yield no significant difference; however, the methods may be making a difference. The differences may be confined to only the more basic elements of blending and syllabication. Similarly, if two methods of teaching sixth-grade mathematics were being compared, it would be more informative to compare them on various levels of mathematics achievement (computations, concepts, and applications).

4.2 FOUR STATISTICAL REASONS FOR PREFERRING A MULTIVARIATE ANALYSIS

1. The use of fragmented univariate tests leads to a greatly inflated overall type I error rate, i.e., the probability of at least one false rejection. Consider a two-group problem with 10 dependent variables. What is the probability of one or more spurious results, if we do 10 t tests, each at the .05 level of significance? If we assume the tests are independent as an approximation (since the tests are not independent), then the probability of *no* type I errors is:

$$\underbrace{(.95)(.95) \ldots \ldots (.95)}_{10 \text{ times}} \approx .60$$

since the probability of not making a type I error for each test is .95, and with the independence assumption we can multiply probabilities. Therefore, the probability of at least one false rejection is $1 - .60 = .40$, which is unacceptably high. Thus, with the univariate approach not only does overall α become too high, but we can't even accurately estimate it!

2. The univariate tests ignore important information, i.e., the correlations among the variables. The multivariate test incorporates the correlations (via the covariance matrix) right into the test statistic, as is shown in the next section.

3. Although the groups may not be significantly different on any of the variables individually, *jointly* the set of variables may reliably differentiate the groups. That is, small differences on several of the variables may combine to produce a reliable overall difference. Thus, the multivariate test will be more powerful in this case.

4. It is sometimes argued that the groups should be compared on total test score first to see if there is a difference. If so, then compare the groups further on subtest scores to locate the sources responsible for the global difference. On the other hand, if there is no total test score difference, then stop. This procedure could definitely be misleading. Suppose, for example, that the total test scores were not significantly different, but that on subtest 1 group 1 was quite superior, on subtest 2 group 1 was somewhat superior, on subtest 3 there was no difference, and on subtest 4 group 2 was quite superior. Then it would be clear why the univariate analysis of total test score found nothing: because of a cancelling out effect. But the two groups do differ substantially on 2 of the 4 subtests, and to some extent on a third. A multivariate analysis of the subtests would reflect these differences and would show a signficant difference.

Many investigators, especially when they first hear about multivariate analysis of variance (MANOVA), will lump all the dependent variables in a single analysis. This is not necessarily a good idea. If several of the variables have been included without any strong rationale (empirical and/or theoretical), then small or negligible differences on these variables may obscure a real difference(s) on some of the other variables. That is, the multivariate test statistic detects mainly error in the system (i.e., in the set of variables), and therefore declares no reliable overall difference. In a situation such as this what is called for are two separate multivariate analyses, one multivariate analysis for the variables for which there is solid support and a separate multivariate analysis for the variables which are being tested on a heuristic basis.

4.3 THE MULTIVARIATE TEST STATISTIC AS A GENERALIZATION OF UNIVARIATE t

For the univariate t test the null hypothesis is:

H_0: $\mu_1 = \mu_2$ (population means are equal)

In the multivariate case the null hypothesis is:

$$H_0 : \begin{pmatrix} \mu_{11} \\ \mu_{21} \\ \vdots \\ \mu_{p1} \end{pmatrix} = \begin{pmatrix} \mu_{12} \\ \mu_{22} \\ \vdots \\ \mu_{p2} \end{pmatrix} \text{ (population mean vectors are equal)}$$

Saying that the vectors are equal implies that the groups are equal on all p dependent variables. The first part of the subscript refers to the variable and the second part to the group. Thus, μ_{21} refers to the population mean for variable 2 in group 1.

Now, for the univariate t test the reader should recall that there are 3 assumptions involved: (1) independence of the observations, (2) normality, and (3) equality of the population variances (homogeneity of variance). In testing the multivariate null hypothesis the corresponding assumptions are: (1) independence of the observations, (2) multivariate normality on the dependent variables in each population, and (3) equality of the covariance matrices. The latter two multivariate assumptions are much more stringent than the corresponding univariate assumptions. For example, saying that two covariance matrices are equal for 4 variables implies that the variances are equal for each of the variables *and* that the 6 covariances for each of the groups are equal. Consequences of violating the multivariate assumptions are discussed in detail in Chapter 6.

We now show how the multivariate test statistic arises naturally from the univariate t by replacing scalars (numbers) by vectors and matrices. The univariate t is given by:

$$t = \frac{\bar{y}_1 - \bar{y}_2}{\sqrt{\dfrac{(n_1 - 1) s_1^2 + (n_2 - 1) s_2^2}{n_1 + n_2 - 2} \left(\dfrac{1}{n_1} + \dfrac{1}{n_2}\right)}} \tag{1}$$

where s_1^2 and s_2^2 are the sample variances for groups 1 and 2 respectively. The quantity under the radical, excluding the sum of the reciprocals, is the pooled estimate of the assumed common within population variance, call it s^2. Now, replacing that quantity by s^2 and squaring both sides, we obtain:

$$t^2 = \frac{(\bar{y}_1 - \bar{y}_2)^2}{s^2 \left(\dfrac{1}{n_1} + \dfrac{1}{n_2}\right)}$$

$$= (\bar{y}_1 - \bar{y}_2) \left[s^2 \left(\frac{1}{n_1} + \frac{1}{n_2}\right)\right]^{-1} (\bar{y}_1 - \bar{y}_2)$$

$$= (\bar{y}_1 - \bar{y}_2) \left[s^2 \left(\frac{n_1 + n_2}{n_1 n_2}\right)\right]^{-1} (\bar{y}_1 - \bar{y}_2)$$

$$t^2 = \frac{n_1 n_2}{n_1 + n_2} (\bar{y}_1 - \bar{y}_2) (s^2)^{-1} (\bar{y}_1 - \bar{y}_2)$$

Hotelling's T^2 is obtained by replacing the means on each variable by the vectors of means in each group, and by replacing the univariate measure of within variability s^2 by it's multivariate generalization $\mathbf{S}$ (the estimate of the assumed common population covariance matrix). Thus we obtain:

$$T^2 = \frac{n_1 n_2}{n_1 + n_2} (\bar{\mathbf{y}}_1 - \bar{\mathbf{y}}_2)' \, \mathbf{S}^{-1} \, (\bar{\mathbf{y}}_1 - \bar{\mathbf{y}}_2) \tag{2}$$

Recall that the matrix analogue of division is inversion: thus $(s^2)^{-1}$ is replaced by the inverse of $\mathbf{S}$.

Hotelling (1931) showed that the following transformation of T^2 yields an exact F distribution:

$$F = \frac{n_1 + n_2 - p - 1}{(n_1 + n_2 - 2)\, p} \, T^2 \tag{3}$$

with p and $(N - p - 1)$ degrees of freedom, where p is the number of dependent variables and $N = n_1 + n_2$, i.e., total number of subjects.

We can rewrite T^2 as:

$$T^2 = k\, \mathbf{d}' \mathbf{S}^{-1} \, \mathbf{d}$$

where k is a constant involving the group sizes, $\mathbf{d}$ is the vector of mean differences and $\mathbf{S}$ is the covariance matrix. Thus, what we have reflected in T^2 is a comparison of between-variability (given by the $\mathbf{d}$ vectors) to within-variability (given by $\mathbf{S}$). This is perhaps not obvious, since we are not literally dividing between by within as in the univariate case (i.e., $F = MS_h / MS_w$). However, recall again that inversion is the matrix analogue of division, so that multiplying by $\mathbf{S}^{-1}$ is in effect "dividing" by the multivariate measure of within variability.

4.4 NUMERICAL CALCULATIONS FOR A TWO-GROUP PROBLEM

We now consider a small example to illustrate the calculations associated with Hotelling's T^2. The fictitious data shown below represent scores on two measures of counselor effectiveness, client satisfaction (SA) and client self acceptance (CSA). Six subjects were originally randomly assigned to counselors who used either Rogerian or Adlerian methods, however, three in the Rogerian group were unable to continue for reasons unrelated to the treatment.

Rogerian		Adlerian	
SA	CSA	SA	CSA
1	3	4	6
3	7	6	8
2	2	6	8
$\bar{y}_{11} = 2$	$\bar{y}_{21} = 4$	5	10
		5	10
		4	6
		$\bar{y}_{12} = 5$	$\bar{y}_{22} = 8$

Recall again that the first part of the subscript denotes the variable and the second part the group, i.e., y_{12} is the mean for variable 1 in group 2.

In words, our multivariate null hypothesis is "There is no difference between the Rogerian and Adlerian groups when they are compared simultaneously on client satisfaction and client self acceptance." Let client satisfaction be variable 1 and client self acceptance be variable 2. Then the multivariate null hypothesis in symbols is:

$$H_0 : \begin{pmatrix} \mu_{11} \\ \mu_{21} \end{pmatrix} = \begin{pmatrix} \mu_{12} \\ \mu_{22} \end{pmatrix}$$

That is, we wish to determine whether it is tenable that the population means are equal for variable 1 ($\mu_{11} = \mu_{12}$) and that the population means for variable 2 are equal ($\mu_{21} = \mu_{22}$). To test the multivariate null hypothesis we need to calculate F in Equation 3. But to obtain this we first need T^2, and the tedious part of calculating T^2 is in obtaining $\mathbf{S}$, which is our pooled estimate of within-group variability on the set of two variables, i.e., our estimate of error. Before we begin calculating $\mathbf{S}$ it will be helpful to go back to the univariate t test (Equation 1) and recall how the estimate of error variance was obtained there. The estimate of the assumed common within population variance (σ^2) (i.e., error variance) is given by

$$s^2 = \frac{(n_1 - 1) s_1^2 + (n_2 - 1) s_2^2}{n_1 + n_2 - 2} = \frac{ss_{g_1} + ss_{g_2}}{n_1 + n_2 - 2} \tag{4}$$

(cf. Equation 1)   (from the definition of variance)

where ss_{g1} and ss_{g2} are the within sums of squares for groups 1 and 2. In the multivariate case (i.e., in obtaining $\mathbf{S}$) we replace the univariate measures of within-group variability (ss_{g1} and ss_{g2}) by their matrix multivariate generalizations, which we call W_1 and W_2.

W_1 will be our estimate of within variability on the two dependent variables in group 1. Since we have two variables, there is variability on each, which we denote by ss_1 and ss_2, and covariability, which we denote by ss_{12}. Thus, the matrix $\mathbf{W}_1$ will look as follows:

TABLE 4.1
Estimation of Error Term for t Test and Hotelling's T^2

	t test (univariate)	T^2 (multivariate)
Assumption	Within group population variances are equal, i.e., $\sigma_1^2 = \sigma_2^2$ Call the common value σ^2	Within group population covariance matrices are equal $\Sigma_1 = \Sigma_2$ Call the common value Σ
		To estimate these assumed common population values we employ the three steps indicated below:
Calculate the within group measures of variability.	ss_{g1} and ss_{g2}	W_1 and W_2
Pool the above estimates	$ss_{g1} + ss_{g2}$	$W_1 + W_2$
Divide by the degrees of freedom	$\dfrac{ss_{g1} + ss_{g2}}{n_1 + n_2 - 2} = \hat{\sigma}^2$	$\dfrac{W_1 + W_2}{n_1 + n_2 - 2} = \hat{\Sigma} = S$

The rationale for pooling is that if we are measuring the same variability in each group (which is the assumption), then we obtain a better estimate of this variability by combining our estimates.

$$W_1 = \begin{bmatrix} ss_1 & ss_{12} \\ ss_{21} & ss_2 \end{bmatrix}$$

Similarly, W_2 will be our estimate of within variability (error) on variables in group 2. After W_1 and W_2 have been calculated, we will pool them (i.e., add them) and divide by the degrees of freedom, as was done in the univariate case (cf. Equation 4), to obtain our multivariate error term, the covariance matrix S. Table 4.1 shows schematically the procedure for obtaining the pooled error terms for both the univariate t test and for Hotelling's T^2.

Calculation of the Multivariate Error Term S

First we calculate W_1, the estimate of within variability for group 1.

Now, ss_1 and ss_2 are just the sum of the squared deviations about the means for variables 1 and 2 respectively. Thus,

$$ss_1 = \sum_{i=1}^{3} (y_{1(i)} - \bar{y}_{11})^2 = (1 - 2)^2 + (3 - 2)^2 + (2 - 2)^2 = 2$$

($y_{1(i)}$ denotes the score for the ith subject on variable 1)

and

$$ss_2 = \sum_{i=1}^{3} (y_{2(i)} - \bar{y}_{21})^2 = (3 - 4)^2 + (7 - 4)^2 + (2 - 4)^2 = 14$$

Finally, ss_{12} is just the sum of deviation cross products:

$$ss_{12} = \sum_{i=1}^{3} (y_{1(i)} - 2)(y_{2(i)} - 4)$$

$$= (1 - 2)(3 - 4) + (3 - 2)(7 - 4) + (2 - 2)(2 - 4) = 4$$

Therefore, the within SSCP matrix for group 1 is

$$\mathbf{W}_1 = \begin{bmatrix} 2 & 4 \\ 4 & 14 \end{bmatrix}$$

Similarly, as we leave for the reader to show, the within matrix for group 2 is

$$\mathbf{W}_2 = \begin{bmatrix} 4 & 4 \\ 4 & 16 \end{bmatrix}$$

Thus, the multivariate error term (i.e., the pooled within covariance matrix) is calculated as:

$$\mathbf{S} = \frac{\mathbf{W}_1 + \mathbf{W}_2}{n_1 + n_2 - 2} = \frac{\begin{bmatrix} 2 & 4 \\ 4 & 14 \end{bmatrix} + \begin{bmatrix} 4 & 4 \\ 4 & 16 \end{bmatrix}}{7} = \begin{bmatrix} 6/7 & 8/7 \\ 8/7 & 30/7 \end{bmatrix}$$

Note that 6/7 is just the sample variance for variable 1, 30/7 is the sample variance for variable 2, and 8/7 is the sample covariance.

Calculation of the Multivariate Test Statistic

To obtain Hotelling's T^2 we need the inverse of S as follows:

$$\mathbf{S}^{-1} = \begin{bmatrix} 1.811 & -.483 \\ -.483 & .362 \end{bmatrix}$$

From Equation 2 then, Hotelling's T^2 is

$$T^2 = \frac{n_1 n_2}{n_1 + n_2} (\bar{y}_1 - \bar{y}_2)' \, \mathbf{S}^{-1} \, (\bar{y}_1 - \bar{y}_2)$$

$$T^2 = \frac{3(6)}{3 + 6} (2 - 5, 4 - 8) \begin{bmatrix} 1.811 & -.483 \\ -.483 & .362 \end{bmatrix} \begin{pmatrix} 2 - 5 \\ 4 - 8 \end{pmatrix}$$

$$T^2 = (-6, -8) \begin{pmatrix} -3.501 \\ .001 \end{pmatrix} = 21$$

The exact F transformation of T^2 is then

$$F = \frac{n_1 + n_2 - p - 1}{(n_1 + n_2 - 2) p} T^2 = \frac{9 - 2 - 1}{7 (2)} (21) = 9,$$

where F has 2 and 6 degrees of freedom (cf. Equation 3).

If we were testing the multivariate null hypothesis at the .05 level, then we would reject (since the critical value = 5.14) and conclude that the two groups differ on the set of two variables.

After finding that the groups differ, we would now like to determine which of the variables are contributing to the overall difference, i.e., a post hoc procedure is needed. This is similar to the procedure followed in a one way ANOVA, where first an overall F test is done. If F is significant, then a post hoc technique (such as Scheffe's or Tukey's) is used to determine which specific groups differed, and thus contributed to the overall difference. Here, instead of groups, we wish to know which variables contributed to the overall multivariate significance.

Now, multivariate significance implies there is a linear combination of the dependent variables (the discriminant function) that is significantly separating the groups. We defer extensive discussion of discriminant analysis to chapter 7. Harris (1985, p. 9) argues vigorously for focusing on such linear combinations. "Multivariate statistics can be of considerable value in suggesting new, emergent variables of this sort that may not have been anticipated-but the researcher must be prepared to think in terms of such combinations . . ." While we agree that discriminant analysis can be of value, there are at least 3 factors that can mitigate it's usefulness in many instances:

1) There is no guarantee that the linear combination (the discriminant function) will be a meaningful variate, i.e., that it will make substantive or conceptual sense.

2) Sample size must be considerably larger than many investigators realize in order for the results of a discriminant analysis to be reliable. More details on this later.

3) The investigator may be more interested in what specific variables contributed to treatment differences, rather than on some combination of them.

4.5   THREE POST HOC PROCEDURES

We now consider three possible post hoc approaches. One approach is to use the Roy-Bose simultaneous confidence intervals. These are a generalization of the Scheffe' intervals, and are illustrated in Morrison (1976) and in Johnson and Wichern (1982). The intervals are nice in that we can not only determine whether a pair of means is different, but in addition can obtain a range of values within which the population mean differences probably lie. Unfortunately, however, the procedure is extremely conservative (Hummel & Sligo, 1971), and this will hurt power (sensitivity for detecting differences).

As Bock (1975, p. 422) has noted, "Their [Roy-Bose intervals] use at the conventional 90% confidence level will lead the investigator to overlook many differences that should be interpreted and defeat the purposes of an exploratory comparative study." What Bock says applies with particularly great force to a very large number of studies in social science research where the group and/or effect sizes are small or moderate. In these studies power will be poor or not adequate to begin with. To be more specific, consider the power table from Cohen (1977, p. 36) for a two-tailed t test at the .05 level of significance. For group sizes ≤ 20 and small or medium effect sizes through .60 standard deviations, which is a quite common class of situations, the *largest* power is .45! The use of the Roy-Bose intervals will dilute the power even further to extremely low levels.

A second, less conservative post hoc procedure is to follow a significant multivariate result by univariate t's, but to do each t test at the α/p level of significance. Then we are assured by the Bonferroni inequality that the overall type I error rate for the set of t tests will be less than α. This is a good procedure, if the number of dependent variables is small (say ≤ 7). Thus, if there were 4 variables and we wished to take at most a 10% chance of one or more false rejections, this can be assured by setting $\alpha = 10/4 = .025$ for each t test. Recall that the Bonferroni inequality simply says that the overall α level for a set of tests is less than or equal to the sum of the α levels for each test.

The third post hoc procedure we consider is following a significant multivariate test at the .05 level by univariate tests, each at the .05 level. The results of a Monte Carlo study by Hummel and Sligo (1971) indicate that, if the multivariate null hypothesis is true, then this procedure keeps the overall α level under control for the set of t tests (cf. Table 4.2). This procedure has greater power for detecting differences than the two previous approaches, and this is an important consideration when small or moderate sample sizes are involved. Timm (1975) has noted that if the multivariate null hypothesis is only partially true (e.g., for only 3 of 5 variables there are no differences in the population means), and the multivariate null hypothesis is likely to be rejected, then the Hummel and Sligo results are not directly applicable. He suggested use of the second approach we mentioned. While this approach will guard against spurious results, power will be severely attentuated if the number of dependent variables is even moderately large. For example, if $p = 15$ and we wish to set overall $\alpha = .05$, then each univariate test must be done at the $.05/15 = .0033$ level of significance! There are two things that can be done to improve power and yet provide reasonably good protection against type I errors. First, there are several reasons (which we detail in Chapter 5) for *generally* preferring to work with a relatively small number of dependent variables (say ≤ 10). Secondly, in many cases it may be possible to divide the dependent variables up into 2 or 3 of the following categories: (1) those variables likely to show a difference, (2) those variables (based on past research) that may show a difference, and (3) those variables that are being tested on a heuristic basis.

As an example, suppose we conduct a study, limiting the number of variables to 8. There is fairly solid evidence from the literature that 3 of the variables should show a difference, while the other 5 are being tested on a heuristic basis. In this situation, as indicated in 4.2, two multivariate tests should be done. If the multivariate test is significant for the fairly solid variables, then we would test each of the individual variables at the .05 level. Here we are not as concerned about type I error in the followup phase, since there is prior reason to believe they will be significant. A separate multivariate test is done for the 5 heuristic variables. If this is significant, then we would employ the Timm approach, but set overall α somewhat higher for better power (especially if sample size is small or moderate). For example, set overall $\alpha = .15$, and thus test each variable for significance at the $.15/5 = .03$ level of significance.

4.6 SAS AND SPSSX CONTROL LINES FOR SAMPLE PROBLEM AND SELECTED PRINTOUT

Table 4.3 presents the complete SAS and SPSSX control lines for running the two-group sample MANOVA problem. Table 4.4 gives selected printout from the SAS and SPSSX runs. Note that both SAS and SPSSX give all four multivariate test statistics, although in different orders. Recall also from earlier in the chapter that for two groups they are equivalent, and therefore the multivariate F is the same for all four. I prefer the arrange-

TABLE 4.2
Experimentwise Error Rates for Analyzing Multivariate Data with
only Univariate Tests and with a Multivariate Test followed by
Univariate Tests*

Sample Size	Number of Variables	Univariate Tests Only Proportion of variance in common			
		.10	.30	.50	.70
10	3	.145	.112	.114	.077
10	6	.267	.190	.178	.111
10	9	.348	.247	.209	.129
30	3	.115	.119	.117	.085
30	6	.225	.200	.176	.115
30	9	.296	.263	.223	.140
50	3	.138	.124	.102	.083
50	6	.230	.190	.160	.115
50	9	.324	.258	.208	.146
	Multivariate Test Followed by Univariate Tests				
10	3	.044	.029	.035	.022
10	6	.046	.029	.030	.017
10	9	.050	.026	.025	.018
30	3	.037	.044	.029	.025
30	6	.037	.037	.032	.021
30	9	.042	.042	.030	.021
50	3	.038	.041	.033	.028
50	6	.037	.039	.028	.027
50	9	.036	.038	.026	.020

*Nominal $\alpha = .05$.

ment of the multivariate and univariate results given by SPSSX (the lower half of Table 4.4). The multivariate tests are presented first, followed by the univariate tests. The multivariate tests show significance at the .05 level, since .016 < .05. The univariate F's show that both variables are contributing at the .05 level to the overall multivariate significance, since the p values (.003 and .029) are less than .05. These F's are equivalent to squared t values. Recall that for two groups $F = t^2$.

Although both variables are contributing to the multivariate significance, it needs to be emphasized that *because the univariate F's ignore how a given variable is correlated with the others in the set, they do not give an indication of the relative importance of that variable to group differentiation.* A technique for determining the relative importance of each variable to group separation is discriminant analysis; discussed in Chapter 7. To obtain reliable results with discriminant analysis, however, a large subject to variable ratio is needed, that is, about 20 subjects per variable are required.

TABLE 4.3
SAS GLM and SPSSX MANOVA Control Lines for Two-Group MANOVA
Sample Problem

SAS GLM	SPSSX MANOVA
TITLE 'MANOVA';	TITLE 'MANOVA'
DATA TWOGP;	DATA LIST FREE/GP Y1 Y2
INPUT GP Y1 Y2 @@;	LIST
CARDS;	BEGIN DATA
1 1 3 1 3 7 1 2 2	⑤ 1 1 3 1 3 7 1 2 2
2 4 6 2 6 8 2 6 8	2 4 6 2 6 8 2 6 8
2 5 10 2 5 10 2 4 6	2 5 10 2 5 10 2 4 6
① PROC GLM;	END DATA
② CLASS GP;	⑥ MANOVA Y1 Y2 BY GP(1,2)/
③ MODEL Y1 Y2 = GP;	⑦ PRINT = CELLINFO (MEANS)/
④ MANOVA H = GP/PRINTE PRINTH;	

①The GENERAL LINEAR MODELS procedure is called. This is a very powerful and general procedure which does univariate and multivariate analysis of variance and covariance, etc.

②The CLASS statement tell SAS which variable is the grouping variable.

③In the MODEL statement the dependent variables are put on the left hand side and the grouping variable(s) on the right side.

④It is necessary to identify the effect to be used as the hypothesis matrix, which here by default is GP. After the slash a wide variety of optional output is available. We have selected PRINTE (prints the error SSCP matrix) and PRINTH (prints the matrix associated with the effect), which here is group.

⑤The first number for each triplet is the group identification with the remaining two numbers the scores on the dependent variables.

⑥The general form for the MANOVA command is

MANOVA   list of   BY   list of   WITH   list of
              dep. vars   factors   covariates

Since we have no covariates here, the WITH part is dropped.

⑦This PRINT subcommand yields descriptive statistics for the groups, that is, means and standard deviations.

4.7 MULTIVARIATE SIGNIFICANCE BUT NO UNIVARIATE SIGNIFICANCE

If the multivariate null hypothesis is rejected, then *generally* at least one of the univariate t's will be significant, as in our previous example. This will not always be the case. It is possible to reject the multivariate null hypothesis and yet for none of the univariate t's to be significant. As Timm (1975, p. 166) has pointed out. "Furthermore, rejection of the multivariate test does not guarantee that there exists at least one significant univariate F ratio. For a given set of data, the significant comparison may involve some linear combination of the variables." This is analogous to what happens occasionally in univariate analysis of variance. The overall F is significant, but when say the Tukey procedure is used to determine which pairs of groups are significantly different none are found. Again, all the significant

TABLE 4.4
Selected Output From SAS GLM and SPSSX MANOVA For Two-Group
MANOVA Sample Problem

SAS GLM OUTPUT

E = Error SSS & CP Matrix

	Y1	Y2
Y1	6	8
Y2	8	30

In 4.4, under CALCULATING THE MULIVARIATE ERROR TERM, we computed the W_1 and W_2 matrices (the within sums of squares and cross products matrices), and then pooled or aded them in getting to the covariance marix S. What SAS is outputting here is the $W_1 + W_2$ matrix.

General Linear Models Procedure
Multivariate Analysis of Variance

H = Type III SS&CP Matrix for GP

	Y1	Y2
Y1	$\boxed{18}$	24
Y2	24	$\boxed{32}$

Note that the diagonal elements of this hypothesis SSCP matrix are just the hypothesis mean squares for the univariate F tests.

Manova Test Criteria and Exact F Statistics for the Hypothesis of no Overall GP Effect
H = Type III SS&CP Matrix for GP   E = Error SS&CP Matrix
S=1   M=0   N=2

Statistic	Value	F	Num DF	Den DF	Pr > F
Wilks' Lambda	0.25000000	9.0000	2	6	0.0156
Pillai's Trace	0.75000000	9.0000	2	6	0.0156
Hotelling-Lawley Trace	3.00000000	9.0000	2	6	0.0156
Roy's Greateset Root	3.00000000	9.0000	2	6	0.0156

SPSSX MANOVA OUTPUT

EFFECT .. GP
Multivariate Tests of Significance (S = 1, M = 0, N = 2)

Test Name	Value	Exact F	Hypoth. DF	Error DF	Sig. of F
Pillais	.75000	9.00000	2.00	6.00	.016
Hotelling	3.00000	9.00000	2.00	6.00	.016
Wilks	.25000	9.00000	2.00	6.00	.016
Roys	.75000				

Note .. F statistics are exact.

EFFECT .. GP (Cont.)
Univariate F-tests with (1, 7) D. F.

Variable	Hypoth. SS	Error SS	Hypoth. MS	Error MS	F	Sig. of F
Y1	18.00000	6.00000	18.00000	.85714	21.00000	.003
Y2	32.00000	30.00000	32.00000	4.28571	7.46667	.029

F guarantees is that there is at least one comparison among the group means that is significant at or beyond the same α level: The particular comparison may be a complex one, and may or may not be a meaningful one.

One way of seeing that there will be no necessary relationship between multivariate significance and univariate significance is to observe that the tests make use of different information. For example, the multivariate test takes into account the correlations among the variables whereas the univariate don't. Also, the multivariate test considers the differences on all variables jointly, while the univariate tests consider the difference on each variable separately.

We now consider a specific example, explaining in a couple of ways why multivariate significance was obtained but univariate significance was not.

Example

Kerlinger and Pedhazur (1973) present a three-group, two dependent variable example where the MANOVA test is significant at the .001 level, yet neither univariate test is significant, even at the .05 level. To explain this geometrically they plot the scores for the variables in the plane (cf. Figure 4.1), along with the means for the groups in the plane (the problem con-

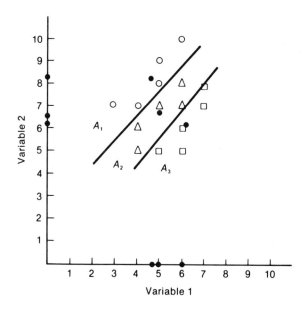

Data for Above Plot

	A_1		A_2		A_3	
1	2	1	2	1	2
3	7	4	5	5	5
4	7	4	6	6	5
5	8	5	7	6	6
5	9	6	7	7	7
6	10	6	8	7	8

FIGURE 1   Graphical Plot of Scores for Three-Group Case with Multivariate Significance but no Univariate Significance.

sidered as two-dimensional, i.e., multivariate). The separation of the means for the groups along each axis (i.e., when the problem is considered as two unidimensional or univariate analyses) is also given in Figure 4.1. Note that the separation of the groups in the plane is clearly greater than the separation along either axis, and in fact yielded multivariate significance. Thus, the smaller unreliable differences on each of the variables combined to produce a cumulative reliable overall difference when the variables are considered jointly.

We wish to dig a bit more deeply into this example, for there are two factors present which make it a near optimal situation for the multivariate test. First, treatments affected the dependent variables in different ways, i.e., the across-groups association between the variables was weak, so each variable was adding something relatively unique to group differentiation. This is analogous to having low intercorrelations among the predictors in a multiple regression situation. Each predictor is then adding something relatively unique to prediction of y. The pattern of means for the problem is presented below:

	Gp 1	Gp 2	Gp 3
Dep. 1	4.6	5.0	6.2
Dep. 2	8.2	6.6	6.2

The second factor that contributed to a particularly sensitive multivariate test is that the variables had a very strong *within* group correlation. (.88). This is important, because it produced a smaller generalized error term against which multivariate significance was judged. The error term in MANOVA which corresponds to MS_w in ANOVA is $|\mathbf{W}|$. That is, $|\mathbf{W}|$ is a measure of how much the subjects scores vary within groups on the set of variables.

Consider the following two $\mathbf{W}$ matrices (the first matrix is from the above example) whose off diagonal elements differ because the correlation between the variables in the first case is .88 while in the other case it is .33.

$$\mathbf{W}_1 = \begin{bmatrix} 12.0 & 13.2 \\ 13.2 & 18.8 \end{bmatrix} \quad \mathbf{W}_2 = \begin{bmatrix} 12.0 & 5.0 \\ 5.0 & 18.8 \end{bmatrix}$$

The multivariate error term in the first situation is $|\mathbf{W}_1| = 12$ (18.8) $- 13.2^2 = 51.36$, while for $\mathbf{W}_2$ the error term is 200.6, i.e., almost four times greater! Thus, the size of the correlation can make a considerable difference in the magnitude of the multivariate error term. If the correlation is weak, then most of the error on the second variable cannot be accounted for by error on the first, and all that additional error becomes part of the multivariate error. On the other hand, when the correlation is strong the second variable adds little additional error, and therefore the multivariate error term is much smaller.

Summarizing then, in the Kerlinger and Pedhazur example it was the *combination* of weak across group association (meaning each variable was making a relatively unique contribution to group differentiation) coupled with a strong within group correlation (producing a small multivariate error term) that yielded an excellent situation for the multivariate test.

4.8 MULTIVARIATE REGRESSION ANALYSIS FOR THE SAMPLE PROBLEM

This section is presented to show that ANOVA and MANOVA are special cases of regression analysis, i.e., of the so-called general linear model. Cohen's (1968) seminal article was primarily responsible for bringing the general linear model to the attention of social science researchers. The regression approach to MANOVA is accomplished by dummy coding group membership. This amounts, for the two-group problem, to coding the subjects in group 1 by some numerical value, say 1, and the subjects in group 2 by another numerical value, say 0. Thus, the data for our sample problem would look like this:

y_1	y_2	x	
1	3	1	
3	7	1	Group 1
2	2	1	
4	6	0	
4	6	0	
5	10	0	
5	10	0	Group 2
6	8	0	
6	8	0	

In a typical regression problem, as considered in the previous chapters, the predictor(s) have been continuous variables. Here, for MANOVA the predictor is a categorical or nominal variable, and is used to determine how much of the variance in the dependent variables is accounted for by group membership. It should be noted that values other than 1 and 0 could have been used as the dummy codes without affecting the results. For example, the subjects in group 1 could have been coded as 1's and the subjects in group 2 as 2's. All that is necessary is to distinguish between the subjects in the two groups by two different values.

The setup of the two-group MANOVA as a multivariate regression may seem somewhat strange since there are two dependent variables and only one predictor. In the previous chapters there has been either one dependent variable and several predictors, or several dependent variables and several predictors. However, the examination of the association is done in the same way. Recall, that Wilk's Λ was the statistic for determining whether there is a significant association between the dependent variables and the predictor(s):

$$\Lambda = \frac{|S_e|}{|S_e + S_r|}$$

where S_e is the error SSCP matrix, i.e., the sum of square and cross-products not due to regression (or the residual), and S_r is the regression SSCP matrix, i.e., an index of how much variability in the dependent variables is due to regression. In this case variability due to regression is variability in the dependent variables due to group membership, since the predictor is group membership.

Part of the output from SPSSX for the two-group MANOVA, set up and ran as a regression, is presented in Table 4.5. The error matrix S_e is called adjusted within cells sum of squares and cross products, and the regression SSCP matrix is called adjusted hypothesis sum of squares and cross products. Using these matrices, we can form Wilk's Λ (and see how the value of .25 is obtained):

$$\Lambda = \frac{|S_e|}{|S_e + S_r|} = \frac{\begin{vmatrix} 6 & 8 \\ 8 & 30 \end{vmatrix}}{\left| \begin{bmatrix} 6 & 8 \\ 8 & 30 \end{bmatrix} + \begin{bmatrix} 18 & 24 \\ 24 & 32 \end{bmatrix} \right|}$$

$$\Lambda = \frac{\begin{vmatrix} 6 & 8 \\ 8 & 30 \end{vmatrix}}{\begin{vmatrix} 24 & 32 \\ 32 & 62 \end{vmatrix}} = \frac{116}{464} = .25$$

Note first that the multivariate F's are *identical* for Table 4.4 and Table 4.5; thus, significant separation of the group mean vectors is equivalent to

TABLE 4.5

Selected Output from SPSSX for Regression Analysis on Two-Group MANOVA with Group Membership as Predictor

EFFECT .. WITHIN CELL REGRESSION

ADJUSTED WITHIN CELLS SUM-OF-SQUARES AND CROSS-PRODUCTS

	Y1	Y2
Y1	6.0000	
Y2	8.0000	30.00000

ADJUSTED HYPOTHESIS SUM-OF-SQUARES AND CROSS-PRODUCTS

	Y1	Y2
Y1	18.00000	
Y2	24.00000	32.00000

MULTIVARIATE TESTS OF SIGNIFICANCE (S = 1, M = 0, N = 2)

TEST NAME	VALUE	APPROX. F.	HYPOTH. DF	ERROR DF	SIG. OF F
PILLAIS	.75000	9.00000	2.00	6.00	.016
HOTELLINGS	3.00000	9.00000	2.00	6.00	.016
WILKS	.25000	9.00000	2.00	6.00	.016
ROYS	.75000				

UNIVARIATE F-TESTS WITH (1,7) D.F.

VARIABLE	SQ. MUL. R	MUL. R	ADJ. R-SQ.	HYPOTH. MS	ERROR MS	F	SIG. OF F
Y1	.75000	.86603	.71429	18.00000	.85714	21.00000	.003
Y2	.51613	.71842	.44700	32.00000	4.28571	7.46667	.029

significant association between group membership (dummy coded) and the set of dependent variables.

The univariate F's are also the same for both analyses, although it may not be clear to the reader why this is so.

In traditional ANOVA, the total sum of squares (ss_t) is partitioned as:

$$ss_t = ss_b + ss_w$$

while in regression analysis the total sum of squares is partitioned as follows:

$$ss_t = ss_{reg} + ss_{resid}$$

The corresponding F ratios, for determining whether there is significant group separation and for determining whether there is a significant regression are:

$$f = \frac{ss_b/df_b}{ss_w/df_w} \text{ and } F = \frac{ss_{reg}/df_{reg}}{ss_{resid}/df_{resid}}$$

To see that these F ratios are equivalent, note that since the predictor variable is group membership, ss_{reg} is just the amount of variability between groups or ss_b, while ss_{resid} is just the amount of variability not accounted for by group membership, or the variability of the scores within each group (i.e., ss_w).

The regression output from SPSSX also gives some information *not* on the traditional MANOVA output, ie., the squared multiple R's for each dependent variable. Since in this case there is just one predictor, these multiple R's are just squared Pearson correlations. In particular, they are squared pt-biserial correlations since one of the variables is dichotomous (dummy coded group membership). The relationship between the pt biserial correlation and the F statistic is given by:

$$r_{pb} = \sqrt{\frac{F}{F + df_w}} \text{ (Welkowitz, Ewen, & Cohen, 1982)}$$

$$r_{pb}^2 = \frac{F}{F + df_w}$$

Thus, for dependent variable 1, we have

$$r_{pb}^2 = \frac{21}{21 + 7} = .75$$

This squared correlation has a very meaningful and important interpretation. It tells us that 75% of the variance in the dependent variable is accounted for by group membership. Thus, we not only have a statistically significant relationship, as indicated by the *F* ratio, but in addition the relationship is very strong. It should be recalled that it is important to have a measure of strength of relationship *along* with a test of significance, as significance resulting from large sample size might indicate a very weak relationship, and therefore one that may be of little practical significance.

Various textbook authors have recommended measures of association or strength of relationship measures (Cohen & Cohen, 1975; Hays, 1981; Kerlinger & Pedhazur, 1973; Kirk, 1982). We also feel that they can be useful, but they also have limitations.

For example, simply because a strength of relationship indicates that say only 10% of variance is accounted for does not *necessarily* imply that the result has no practical significance, as O'Grady (1982) has indicated in an excellent review on measures of association. There are several factors that affect such measures. One very important factor is context, i.e., 10% of variance accounted for in certain research areas may indeed be practically significant.

A good example illustrating this point is provided by Rosenthal and Rosnow (1984). They consider the comparison of a treatment and control group where the dependent variable is dichotomous, whether the subjects survive or die. The following table is presented:

	Treatment Outcome		
	Alive	Dead	
Treatment	66	34	100
Control	34	66	100
	100	100	

Since both variables are dichotomous, the phi coefficient (a special case of the Pearson correlation for two dichotomous variables, Glass and Hopkins, 1984) measures the relationship between them

$$\phi = \frac{34^2 - 66^2}{\sqrt{100\ (100)(100)(100)}} = -.32 \Rightarrow \phi^2 = .10$$

Thus, even though the treatment-control distinction accounts for "only" 10% of the variance in the outcome, it increases the survival rate from 34% to 66%, far from trivial! The same type of interpretation would hold if we considered some less dramatic type of outcome like improvement vs. no improvement, where treatment was a type of psychotherapy. Also, the interpretation is *not* confined to a dichotomous outcome measure. Another factor to consider is the design of the study. As O'Grady (1982) notes.

"Thus, true experiments will frequently produce smaller measures of explained variance than will correlational studies. At the least this implies that consideration should be given to whether an investigation involves a true experiment or a correlational approach in deciding whether an effect is weak or strong." Another point to keep in mind is that since most behaviors have multiple causes, it will be difficult in these cases to account for a large percent of variance with just a single cause (say treatments). Still another factor is the homogeneity of the population sampled. Since measures of association are correlational type measures, the more homogeneous the population the smaller the correlation will tend to be, and therefore the smaller the percent of variance accounted for can potentially be (this is the restriction of range phenomenon).

Finally, we focus on a topic that is generally neglected in texts on MANOVA, i.e., estimation of power. We start at a basic level, reviewing what power is, factors affecting power, and reasons why estimation of power is important. Then the notion of effect size for the univariate t test is given, followed by the multivariate effect size concept for Hotelling's T^2.

4.9   POWER ANALYSIS[1]

Type I error, or the level of significance (α), is familiar to all readers. This is the probability of rejecting the null hypothesis when it is true, i.e., saying the groups differ when in fact they don't. The α level set by the experimenter is a subjective decision, but is usually set at .05 or .01 by most researchers to minimize the probability of making this kind of error. There is however another type of error that one can make in conducting a statistical test, and this is called a type II error. Type II error, denoted by β, is the probability of accepting H_0 when it is false, i.e., saying the groups don't differ when they do. Now, not only can either of these errors occur, but in addition they are inversely related. Thus, as we control on type I error, type II error increases. This is illustrated below for a two-group problem with 15 subjects per group:

α	β	$1 - \beta$
.10	.37	.63
.05	.52	.48
.01	.78	.22

Notice that as we control on α more severely (from .10 to .01), type II error increases fairly sharply (from .37 to .78). Therefore, the problem for

[1]Much of the material in this section is identical to that presented in 1.2; however, it was felt worth repeating in this more extensive discussion of power.

the experimental planner is achieving an appropriate balance between the two types of errors. While we do not intend to minimize the seriousness of making a type I error, we hope to convince the reader that much more attention should be paid to type II error. Now, the quantity in the last column is the *power* of a statistical test, and is the probability of rejecting the null hypothesis when it is false. Thus, power is the probability of making a correct decision. In the above example if we are willing to take a 10% chance of rejecting H_0 falsely, then we have a 63% chance of finding a difference of a specified magnitude in the population (more specifics on this shortly). On the other hand, if we insist on only a 1% chance of rejecting H_0 falsely, then we have only about 2 chances out of 10 of finding the difference. This example with small sample size suggests that in this case it might be prudent to abandon the traditional α levels of .01 or .05 to a more liberal α level to improve power sharply. Of course, one does not get something for nothing. We are taking a greater risk of rejecting falsely, but that increased risk is *more than balanced* by the increase in power.

There are two types of power estimation, a priori and post hoc, and very good reasons why each of them should be considered seriously. If a researcher is going to invest a great amount of time and money in carrying out a study, then he or she would certainly want to have a 70% or 80% chance (i.e., power of .70 or .80) of finding a difference if one is there. Thus, the a priori estimation of power will alert the researcher to how many subjects per group will be needed for adequate power. Later on we consider an example of how this is done in the multivariate case.

The post hoc estimation of power is important in terms of how one interprets the results of completed studies. Researchers not sufficiently sensitive to power may interpret nonsignificant results from studies as demonstrating that treatments made no difference. In fact, it may be that treatments did make a difference but that the researchers had poor power for detecting the difference. The poor power may result from small sample size and/or effect size. The following example shows how important an awareness of power can be. Cronbach and Snow had written a report on aptitude-treatment interaction research, not being fully cognizant of power. By the publication of their text, *Aptitudes and Instructional Methods* (1977) on the same topic, they acknowledged the importance of power, stating in the preface. "[We] . . . became aware of the critical relevance of statistical power, and consequently changed our interpretations of individual studies and sometimes of whole bodies of literature." Why would they change their interpretation of a whole body of literature? Because, prior to being sensitive to power when they found most studies in a given body of literature had nonsignificant results, they concluded no effect existed. However, after being sensitized to power they took into account the sample sizes in the studies, and also the magnitude of the effects. If the sample sizes were small in most of the studies with nonsignificant results, then lack of significance is due to poor power. Or, in other words, several low power studies that report nonsignificant results of the same character *are* evidence for an effect.

The power of a statistical test is dependent on three factors:

1. The α level set by the experienter
2. Sample size
3. Effect size—How much of a difference the treatments make, or the extent to which the groups differ in the population on the dependent variable(s).

For the univariate independent samples *t* test, Cohen (1977) has defined the population effect size as $d = (\mu_1 - \mu_2)/\sigma$, where σ is the assumed common population standard deviation. Thus, effect size simply indicates how many standard deviation units the group means are separated by.

Power is *heavily* dependent on sample size. Consider a two-tailed test at the .05 level for the *t* test for independent samples. Suppose we have an effect size of .5 standard deviations. The table below shows how power changes dramatically as sample size increases.

n (subjects per group)	power
10	.18
20	.33
50	.70
100	.94

As the above example suggests, when sample size is large (say 100 or more subjects per group) power is not an issue. It is when one is conducting a study where the group sizes are small (n ≤ 20), or when one is evaluating a completed study that had small group size, that it is imperative to be very sensitive to the possibility of poor power (or equivalently, a type II error).

We have indicated that power is also influenced by effect size. For the *t* test, Cohen (1977) has suggested as a rough rule of thumb that an effect size around .20 is small, an effect size around .50 is medium, and an effect size > .80 is large. The difference in the mean I.Q.'s between Ph.D's and the typical college freshmen is an example of a large effect size (about .8 of a standard deviation).

Cohen and many others have noted that *small and medium effect sizes are very common in social science research.* Light and Pillimer (1984) comment on the fact that most evaluations find small effects in reviews of the literature on programs of various types (social, educational, etc.): "Review after review confirms it and drives it home. Its importance comes from having managers understand that they should not expect large, positive findings to emerge routinely from a single study of a new program" (pp. 153–154). Results from Becker (1987) of effect sizes for three sets of studies (on teacher expectancy, desegregation, and gender influenceability) showed only 3 large effect sizes out of 40. Also, Light, Singer, and Willett (1990) note that, "Meta-analyses often reveal a sobering fact: effect sizes are not nearly as large as we all might hope" (p. 195). To illustrate, they present average effect sizes from six meta analyses in different areas, which yielded .13, .25, .27, .38, .43, and .49; all in the small to medium range.

4.10 WAYS OF IMPROVING POWER

Given how poor power generally is with less than 20 subjects per group, the following 4 methods of improving power should be seriously considered:

1. Adopt a more lenient α level, perhaps $\alpha = .10$ or $\alpha = .15$.
2. Use one-tailed tests where the literature supports a directional hypothesis. This option is not available for the multivariate tests since they are inherently two-tailed.
3. Consider ways of reducing within-group variability, so that one has a more sensitive design. One way is through sample selection; more homogeneous subjects tend to vary less on the dependent variable(s). For example, use just males, rather than males and females, or use only 6 and 7 year old children rather than 6 through 9 year old children. A second way is through the use of factorial designs, which we consider in Chapter 8. A third way of reducing within-group variability is through the use of analysis of covariance, which we consider in Chapter 9. Covariates which have low correlations with each other are particularly helpful since then each is removing a somewhat different part of the within-group (error) variance. A fourth means is through the use of repeated measures designs. These designs are particularly helpful since all individual differences due to the average response of subjects is removed from the error term, and individual differences are the main reason for within group variability.
4. Make sure there is a strong linkage between the treatments and the dependent variable(s), and that the treatments extend over a long enough period of time to produce a large or at least fairly large effect size.

Using these methods *in combination* can make a considerable difference in effective power. To illustrate we consider a two-group situation with 18 subjects per group and one dependent variable. Suppose a two tailed test was done at the .05 level, and that the effect size was

$$\hat{d} = (\bar{x}_1 - \bar{x}_2)/s = (8 - 4)/10 = .40,$$

where s is pooled within standard deviation. Then, from Cohen (1977, p. 36), power = .21, which is very poor.

Now, suppose that through the use of two good covariates we are able to reduce pooled within variability (s^2) by 60%, from 100 (as above) to 40. This is a definite realistic possibility in practice. Then our new estimated effect size would be $\hat{d} \approx 4/\sqrt{40} = .61$. Suppose in addition that a one tail test was really appropriate, and that we also take a somewhat greater risk of a type I error, i.e., $\alpha = .10$. Then, our new estimated power changes dramatically to .69 (Cohen, 1977, p. 32)!

It needs to be emphasized, before leaving this section, that how far one "pushes" the power issue depends on the *consequences* of making a type I error. We give three examples to illustrate. First, suppose that in a medical study examining the safety of a drug we have the following null and alternative hypotheses:

H_0: The drug is unsafe
H_1: The drug is safe

Here making a type I error (rejecting H_0 when true) is concluding that the drug is safe when in fact it is unsafe. This is a situation where we would want type I error to be very small, because making a type I error could harm or possibly kill some people.

As a second example, suppose we are comparing two teaching methods, where method A is several times more expensive than method B to implement. If we conclude that method A is more effective (when in fact it is not), this will be a very costly mistake for a school district.

Finally, a classical example of the relative consequences of type I and type II errors may be taken from our judicial system, under which a defendant is innocent until proven guilty. Thus, we could formulate the following null and alternative hypotheses:

H_0: The defendant is innocent
H_1: The defendant is guilty

If we make a type I error we conclude that the defendant is guilty when he is innocent, while a type II error is concluding the defendant is innocent when he is guilty. Most would probably agree that the type I error is by far the more serious here, and thus we would want type I error to be very small.

4.11   POWER ESTIMATION ON SPSSX MANOVA

Starting with Release 2.2 (1988), power estimates for a wide variety of statistical tests can be obtained using the SPSSX MANOVA program with the POWER subcommand. To quote from the *SPSSX USER'S GUIDE*

(3rd Edition), "The POWER subcommand requests observed power values based on fixed-effect assumptions for all univariate and multivariate F and T tests" (p. 601). Power can be obtained for any α level between 0 and 1, with .05 being the default value. If we wish power at the .05 level, we simply insert POWER/, or if we wish power at the .10 level, then the subcommand is POWER $= F(.10)/$. You will also want an effect size measure to go along with the power values, and these are obtained by putting SIGNIF (EFSIZE) in the PRINT subcommand. The effect size measure for the univariate F's is partial eta squared, which is given by

$$\eta_p^2 = (df \cdot F)/(df_h \cdot F + df_e)$$

where df_h denotes degrees of freedom for hypothesis and df_e denotes degrees of freedom for error (Cohen, 1973). The justification for the use of this measure, according to the *SPSSX USERS GUIDE* (1988), is that, "partial eta squared is an overestimate of the actual effect size. However, it is a consistent measure of effect size and is applicable to all F and t tests" (p. 602). Actually partial η^2 and η^2 differ by very little when total sample size is about 50 or more. In terms of interpreting the partial eta squares for the univariate tests, Cohen (1977) characterizes $\eta^2 = .01$ as small, $\eta^2 = .06$ as medium, and $\eta^2 = .14$ as a large effect size.

We obtained power at the .05 level for the multivariate and univariate tests, and the effect size measures for the sample problem (Table 4.3) by inserting the following subcommands after the MANOVA statement:
PRINT $=$ CELLINFO(MEANS) SIGNIF(EFSIZE)/
POWER/
The results are presented in Table 4.6, along with annotation.

4.12 MULTIVARIATE ESTIMATION OF POWER

Stevens (1980) has discussed estimation of power in MANOVA at some length, and in what follows we borrow heavily from his work. Below we present the univariate and multivariate measures of effect size for the two-group problem. Recall, that the univariate measure was presented earlier.

Measures of Effect Size

Univariate	*Multivariate*
$d = \dfrac{\mu_1 - \mu_2}{\sigma}$	$D^2 = (\mu_1 - \mu_2)'\Sigma^{-1}(\mu_1 - \mu_2)$
$\hat{d} = \dfrac{\bar{y}_1 - \bar{y}_2}{s}$	$\hat{D}^2 = (\bar{y}_1 - \bar{y}_2)' \, S^{-1} \, (\bar{y}_1 - \bar{y}_2)$

TABLE 4.6

SPSSX MANOVA Run on Sample Problem Obtaining Power and Multivariate and Univariate Effect Size Measure

EFFECT .. GP
Multivariate Tests of Significance (S = 1, M = 0, N = 2)

Test Name	Value	Exact F	Hypoth. DF	Error DF	Sig. of F
Pillais	.75000	9.00000	2.00	6.00	.016
Hotelling	3.00000	9.00000	2.00	6.00	.016
Wilks	.25000	9.00000	2.00	6.00	.016
Roys	.75000				

Note .. F statistics are exact.

Multivariate Effect Size and Observed Power at .0500 Level

Test Name	① Effect Size	Noncent.	Power
(All)	.75000	18.00000	.83

EFFECT .. GP (Cont.)
Univariate F-tests with (1, 7) D. F.

Variable	Hypoth. MS	Error MS	F	Sig. of F	ETA Square
Y1	18.00000	.85714	21.00000	.003	② .75000
Y2	32.00000	4.28571	7.46667	.029	.51613

Variable	Noncent.	Power
Y1	21.00000	.97346
Y2	7.46667	.65066

① We prefer the two group multivariate effect size measure introduced in the chapter, that is, Mahalanobis D^2. To obtain it we first need to multiply Hotelling's by degrees of freedom for error $N - k = 9 - 2 = 7$. This yields 3(7) = 21. then, we obtain $D^2 = (n_1 + n_2)/n_1 n_2 \ T^2 = (9/18) 21 = 10.5$. This is a huge multivariate effect size. Without at least a very large effect size we would not have found significance.

② These are the partial η^2 for the individual variables. Recall that the formula is: partial $\eta^2 = df_h \ F / (df_h \cdot F + df_e)$. Thus partial η^2 for Y1 is $1 \cdot 21 / (1 \cdot 21 + 7) = .75$, while for Y2 we have $1 \cdot 7.46667 / (1 \cdot 7.46667 + 7) = .51613$.

The first row gives the population values, and the second row the estimated effect sizes. Notice that the multivariate measure $\hat{D}^2$ is Hotelling's T^2 without the sample sizes (cf. Equation 2), i.e., it is a measure of separation of the groups that is *independent* of sample size. D^2 is called in the literature Mahalanobis distance. Note also that the multivariate measure $\hat{D}^2$ *is a natural squared generalization of the univariate measure* d, *where the means have been replaced by mean vectors and* s *(standard deviation) has been replaced by its squared multivariate generalization of within variability, the sample covariance matrix* S.

Table 4.7 from Stevens (1980) provides power values for two-group MANOVA for 2 through 7 variables, with group size varying from small (15) to large (100), and with effect size varying from small ($D^2 = .25$) to very large ($D^2 = 2.25$). Earlier, we had indicated that small and/or moderate group and effect sizes produce inadequate power for the univariate t test. Inspection of Table 4.7 shows that a similar situation exists for MANOVA. The following from Stevens (1980, p. 731) provides a summary of the results in Table 4.7:

> For values of $D^2 \leq .64$ and $n \leq 25, \ldots$ power is generally poor ($< .45$) and never really adequate (i.e., $> .70$) for $\alpha = .05$. Adequate power (at $\alpha = .10$) for two through seven variables at a moderate overall effect size of .64 would require about 30 subjects per group. When the overall effect size is large ($D \geq 1$), then 15 or more subjects per group is sufficient to yield power values $\geq .60$ for two through seven variables at $\alpha = .10$ (p. 731).

Post Hoc Estimation of Power

Suppose you wish to evaluate the power of a two-group MANOVA that was completed in a journal in your content area. Here SPSSX MANOVA is not going to help. However, Table 4.7 can be used, assuming the number of dependent variables in the study is between 2 and 7. Actually, with a slight amount of extrapolation, the table will yield a reasonable approximation for 8 or 9 variables. For example, for $D^2 = .64$, 5 variables and $n = 25$, power = .42 at the .05 level. For the same situation, but with 7 variables, power = .38. Therefore, a reasonable estimate for power for 9 variables is about .34.

Now, to use Table 4.7, the value of D^2 is needed, and this almost certainly will not be reported. Very probably then, a couple of steps will be required to obtain D^2. The investigator(s) will probably report the multivariate F. From this one obtains T^2 using equation 3. Finally, D^2 is obtained using equation 2. Since the right hand side of equation 2 without the sample sizes is D^2, it follows that $T^2 = [n_1 n_2/(n_1 + n_2)] D^2$, or $D^2 = [(n_1 + n_2)/n_1 n_2] T^2$.

We now consider two examples to illustrate how to use Table 4.7 to estimate power for studies in the literature when (a) the number of dependent variables is not explicitly given in Table 4.7, and (b) the group sizes are not equal.

Example 1

Consider a two-group study in the literature with 25 subjects per group that used 4 dependent variables and reports a multivariate $F = 2.81$. What is the estimated power at the .05 level? First, we convert F to corresponding T^2 value:

$$F = [(N - p - 1)/(N - 2) p] T^2 \text{ or } T^2 = (N - 2) p F/(N - p - 1)$$

TABLE 4.7
Power of Hotelling's T^2 at α = .05 and .10 for Small Through Large
Overall Effect and Group Sizes

No. of Variables	n*	.25	D^2** .64	1	2.25
2	15	26 (32)	44 (60)	65 (77)	95***
2	25	33 (47)	66 (80)	86	97
2	50	60 (77)	95	1	1
2	100	90	1	1	1
3	15	23 (29)	37 (55)	58 (72)	91
3	25	28 (41)	58 (74)	80	95
3	50	54 (65)	93 (98)	1	1
3	100	86	1	1	1
5	15	21 (25)	32 (47)	42 (66)	83
5	25	26 (35)	42 (68)	72	96
5	50	44 (59)	88	1	1
5	100	78	1	1	1
7	15	18 (22)	27 (42)	37 (59)	77
7	25	22 (31)	38 (62)	64 (81)	94
7	50	40 (52)	82	97	1
7	100	72	1	1	1

Note—Power values at α = .10 are in parentheses.
*Equal group sizes are assumed.
**$D^2 = (\mu_1 - \mu_2)'\Sigma^{-1}(\mu_1 - \mu_2)$
***Decimal points have been omitted. Thus, 95 means a power of .95. Also, a value of 1 means the power is approximately equal to 1.

Thus, $T^2 = 48(4)\, 2.81/45 = 11.99$. Now, since $D^2 = (NT^2)/n_1 n_2$, we have $D^2 = 50\,(11.99)/625 = .96$. This is a large multivariate effect size. Table 4.7 does not have power for 4 variables, but we can interpolate between 3 and 5 variables. Using $D^2 = 1$ in the table we find that:

No. of Variables	n	$D^2 = 1$
3	25	.80
5	25	.72

Thus, a good approximation to power is .76, which is adequate power. Here, as in univariate analysis, with a large effect size, not many subjects are needed per group to have adequate power.

Example 2

Now consider an article in the literature which is a two-group MANOVA with five dependent variables, having 22 subjects in one group and 32 in the other group. The investigators obtain a multivariate $F = 1.61$, which is not significant at the .05 level (critical value $= 2.42$). Calculate power at the .05 level and comment on the size of the multivariate effect measure. Here the number of dependent variables (5) is given in the table, but the group sizes are unequal. Following Cohen (1977), we use the harmonic mean as the n with which to enter the table. The harmonic mean for two groups is $\tilde{n} = 2n_1n_2/(n_1+n_2)$. Thus, for this case we have $\tilde{n} = 2(22)\ (32)/54 = 26.07$. Now, to get D^2 we first obtain T^2 : $T^2 = (N-2)p\ F/(N-p-1) = 52(5)1.61/48 = 8.72$. Now, $D^2 = N\ T^2/n_1n_2 = 54(8.72)/22(32) = .67$. Using $n = 25$ and $D^2 = .64$ to enter Table 4.7, we see that power $= .42$. Actually power is slightly greater than .42 since $n=26$ and $D^2 = .67$, but it would still not reach even .50. Thus, power is definitely inadequate here, but yet there is a solid medium multivariate effect size that may be of practical significance.

A Priori Estimation of Sample Size

Suppose that from a pilot study or from a previous study that used the same kind of subjects, an investigator had obtained the following pooled within-group covariance matrix for three variables:

$$S = \begin{bmatrix} 16 & 6 & 1.6 \\ 6 & 9 & .9 \\ 1.6 & .9 & 1 \end{bmatrix}$$

Recall that the elements on the main diagonal of S are the variances for the variables, i.e., 16 is the variance for variable 1, etc.

To complete the estimate of D^2 the difference in the mean vectors must be estimated. This amounts to estimating the mean difference expected for each variable. Suppose that on the basis of previous literature, the investigator hypothesizes that the mean differences on variables 1 and 2 will be 2 and 1.5. Thus, they will correspond to moderate effect sizes of .5 standard derivations. Why? The investigator further expects the mean difference on variable 3 will be .2, i.e., .2 of a standard deviation, or a small effect size. How many subjects per group are required, at $\alpha = .10$, for detecting this set of differences if power $= .70$ is desired?

To answer this question we first need to estimate D^2:

$$\hat{D}^2 = (2, 1.5, .2) \begin{bmatrix} .0917 & -.0511 & -.1008 \\ -.0511 & .1505 & -.0538 \\ -.1008 & -.0538 & 1.2100 \end{bmatrix} \begin{pmatrix} 2.0 \\ 1.5 \\ .2 \end{pmatrix} = .3347$$

The middle matrix is the inverse of S. Since moderate and small univariate effect sizes produced this $\hat{D}^2$ value of .3347, such a numerical value for D^2 would probably occur fairly frequently in social science research. To determine the n required for power $= .70$ we enter Table 4.7 for 3 variables and use the values in parentheses. For $n = 50$ and 3 variables, note that power $= .65$ for $D^2 = .25$ and power $= .98$ for $D^2 = .64$. Therefore, we have

$$\text{Power}(D^2 = .33) = \text{Power}(D^2 = .25) + [.08/.39] (.33) = .72$$

4.13 SUMMARY

In this chapter we have considered the statistical analysis of two groups on several dependent variables simultaneously. Among the reasons for preferring a MANOVA over separate univariate analyses were (a) MANOVA takes into account important information, i.e., the intercorrelations among the variables, (b) MANOVA keeps the overall α level under control, and (c) MANOVA has greater sensitivity for detecting differences in certain situations. It was shown how the multivariate test (Hotelling's T^2) arises naturally from the univariate t by replacing the means with mean vectors and by replacing the pooled within-variance by the covariance matrix. An example indicated the numerical details associated with calculating T^2.

Three post hoc procedures, for determining which of the variables contributed to the overall multivariate significance, were considered. The Roy-Bose simultaneous confidence interval approach was rejected because it is extremely conservative, and hence has poor power for detecting differences. The approach of testing each variable at the α/p level of significance was considered a good procedure if the number of variables is small.

An example where multivariate significance was obtained but not univariate significance was considered in detail. Examination showed that the example was a near optimal situation for the multivariate test since the treatments affected the dependent variables in different ways (thus each variable was making a relatively unique contribution to group differentiation), while the dependent variables were strongly correlated within groups (providing a small multivariate error term).

Group membership for the sample problem was dummy coded, and it was run as a regression analysis. This yielded the same multivariate and univariate results as when the problem was run as a traditional MANOVA. This was done to show that MANOVA is a special case of regression analysis, i.e., of the general linear model. It was noted that the regression output also provided useful strength of relationship measures for each variable (R^2's). However, the reader was warned against concluding that a result is of little practical significance simply because the R^2 value is small (say .10). Several reasons were given for this; one of the most important being context. Thus, 10% variance accounted for in some research areas may indeed be practically significant.

Power analysis was considered in some detail. It was noted that small and medium effect sizes are *very common* in social science research. Mahalanobis D^2 was presented as the multivariate effect size measure, with the following guidelines for interpretation: $D^2 = .25$ small effect, $D^2 = .50$ medium effect, and $D^2 > 1$ large effect. Power estimation on SPSSX MANOVA was illustrated. A couple of examples were given to show how to estimate multivariate power (using a table from Stevens, 1980), for studies in the literature, where only the multivariate F statistic is given.

EXERCISES – CHAPTER 4

1. Which of the following are multivariate studies, i.e., involve several correlated dependent variables?

a) An investigator classifies high school freshmen by sex, socioeconomic status, and teaching method, and then compares them on total test score on the Lankton algebra test.

b) A treatment and control group are compared on measures of reading speed and reading comprehension.

c) An investigator is predicting success on the job from high school gpa and a battery of personality variables.

d) An investigator has administered a 50-item scale to 200 college freshmen and he wished to determine whether a smaller number of underlying constructs account for most of the variance in the subjects responses to the items.

e) The same middle and upper class children have been measured in grades 6, 7, and 8 on reading comprehension, math ability, and science ability. The researcher wishes to determine whether there are social class differences on these variables and if the differences change over time.

2. An investigator has a 50-item scale. He wishes to compare two groups of subjects on the scale. He has heard about MANOVA, and realizes that the items will be correlated. Therefore, he decided to do such an analysis. The scale is administered to 45 subjects, and the analysis is run on SPSSX. However, he finds that the analysis is aborted. Why? What might the investigator consider doing before running the analysis?

3. Suppose you come across a journal article where the investigators have a three-way design and five correlated dependent variables. They report the results in five tables, having done a univariate analysis on each of the five

variables. They find four significant results at the .05 level. Would you be impressed with these results? Why, or why not? Would you have more confidence if the significant results had been hypothesized a priori? What else could they have done that would have given you more confidence in their significant results?

4. Consider the following data for a two-group two-dependent variable problem:

T_1		T_2	
y_1	y_2	y_1	y_2
1	9	4	8
2	3	5	6
3	4	6	7
5	4		
2	5		

a) Compute W, i.e., the pooled within-SSCP matrix
b) Find the pooled within covariance matrix, and indicate what each of the elements in the matrix represents.
c) Find Hotelling's T^2.
d) What is the multivariate null hypothesis in symbolic form?
e) Test the null hypothesis at the .05 level. What is your decision?

5. The following are the means, standard deviations, and pooled within-group correlation matrix from a study by Crocker and Benson (1976).

Group		Achievement without penalty	Achievement with penalty	Guess	Risk
Norm Referenced	$\bar{x}=$	6.375	6.821	5.526	2.885
Instructions	$sd=$	2.496	1.774	3.242	2.528
($n = 78$)					
Criterion Referenced	$\bar{x}=$	5.821	5.670	5.525	2.756
Instructions	$sd=$	2.577	2.519	3.500	2.801
($n = 78$)					

Correlation Matrix

	Achievement without penalty	Achievement with penalty	Guess	Risk
Achievement without penalty	1	.45	.20	.015
Achievement with penalty		1	.16	.20
Guess			1	.51
Risk				1

Run the two-group MANOVA on SPSSX. If the multivariate F is significant, then which of the variables are contributing to this overall difference?

6. Suppose we have two groups, with 30 subjects in each group. The means for the two criterion measures in group 1 are 10 and 9, while the means in group 2 are 9 and 9.5. The pooled within sample variances are 9 and 4 for variables 1 and 2, while the pooled within correlation is .70.

a) Show that each of the univariate t's is not significant at .05 (2-tailed test), but that the multivariate test is significant at .05.

b) Now change the pooled within correlation to .20 and determine whether the multivariate test is still significant at .05. Explain.

7. Consider the following set of data for two groups of subjects on two dependent variables:

Group 1		Group 2	
y_1	y_2	y_1	y_2
3	9	8	13
5	15	4	9
5	15	4	7
4	13	2	7
1	8	9	15

a) Analyze this data using the traditional MANOVA approach. Does anything interesting happen?

b) Use the regression approach (i.e., dummy coding of group membership) to analyze the data and compare the results.

8. An investigator ran a two-group MANOVA with 3 dependent variables on SPSSX. There were 12 subjects in group 1 and 26 subjects in group 2. The following selected output gives the results for the multivariate tests (remember that for 2 groups they are equivalent). Note that the multivariate F is significant at the .05 level. Estimate what power the investigator had at the .05 level for finding a significant difference.

EFFECT . . TREATS
MULTIVARIATE TESTS OF SIGNIFICANCE (S = 1, M = 1/2, N = 16)

TEST NAME	VALUE	APPROX. F	HYPOTH. DF	ERROR DF	SIG. DF
PILLAIS	.33083	5.60300	3.00	34.00	.000
HOTELLINGS	.49438	5.60300	3.00	34.00	.000
WILKS	.66917	5.60300	3.00	34.00	.000
ROYS	.33083				

Hint: One would think that the value for "Hotellings" could be used directly in conjunction with Equation 2. However, the value for Hotellings must first be multiplied by $(N - k)$, where N is total number of subjects and k is the number of groups.

9. An investigator has an estimate of $D^2 = .61$ from a previous study that used the same 4 dependent variables on a similar group of subjects. How many subjects per group are needed to have power $= .70$ at $\alpha = .10$?

10. A two-group MANOVA having 5 dependent variables is run on BMDP3D. There are 30 subjects per group, Mahalanobis $D^2 = .48$ on the printout, and multivariate significance is not found at the .05 level. What power did the investigator have?

11. From a pilot study; a researcher has the following pooled within covariance matrix for two variables

$$\mathbf{S} = \begin{bmatrix} 8.6 & 10.4 \\ 10.4 & 21.3 \end{bmatrix}$$

From previous research a moderate effect size of .5 standard deviations on variable 1 and a small effect size of ⅓ standard deviations on variable 2 are anticipated. For the researcher's main study, how many subjects per group are needed for power $= .70$ at the .05 level? At the .10 level?

12. Ambrose (1985) compared elementary school children who received instruction on the clarinet via programmed instruction (experimental group) vs those who received instruction via traditional classroom instruction on the following six performance aspects: interpretation (interp), tone, rhythm, intonation (inton), tempo, and articulation (artic). The data, representing the average of two judges ratings, is listed below, with GPID $= 1$ referring to the experimental group and GPID $= 2$ referring to the control group:

a) Run the two-group MANOVA on these data using SAS GLM. Is the multivariate null hypothesis rejected at the .05 level?

b) What is the value of Mahalanobis D^2? How would you characterize the magnitude of this effect size? Given this, is it surprising that the null hypothesis was rejected?

c) Setting overall $\alpha = .05$ and using the Bonferroni inequality approach, which of the individual variables are significant, and hence contributing to the overall multivariate significance.

GP	INT	TONE	RHY	INTON	TEM	ARTIC
1	4.2	4.1	3.2	4.2	2.8	3.5
1	4.1	4.1	3.7	3.9	3.1	3.2
1	4.9	4.7	4.7	5.0	2.9	4.5
1	4.4	4.1	4.1	3.5	2.8	4.0
1	3.7	2.0	2.4	3.4	2.8	2.3
1	3.9	3.2	2.7	3.1	2.7	3.6
1	3.8	3.5	3.4	4.0	2.7	3.2
1	4.2	4.1	4.1	4.2	3.7	2.8
1	3.6	3.8	4.2	3.4	4.2	3.0
1	2.6	3.2	1.9	3.5	3.7	3.1
1	3.0	2.5	2.9	3.2	3.3	3.1
1	2.9	3.3	3.5	3.1	3.6	3.4
2	2.1	1.8	1.7	1.7	2.8	1.5
2	4.8	4.0	3.5	1.8	3.1	2.2
2	4.2	2.9	4.0	1.8	3.1	2.2
2	3.7	1.9	1.7	1.6	3.1	1.6
2	3.7	2.1	2.2	3.1	2.8	1.7
2	3.8	2.1	3.0	3.3	3.0	1.7
2	2.1	2.0	2.2	1.8	2.6	1.5
2	2.2	1.9	2.2	3.4	4.2	2.7
2	3.3	3.6	2.3	4.3	4.0	3.8
2	2.6	1.5	1.3	2.5	3.5	1.9
2	2.5	1.7	1.7	2.8	3.3	3.1

5 K Group MANOVA: A Priori and Post Hoc Procedures

5.1. INTRODUCTION

In this chapter we consider the case where more than two groups of subjects are being compared on several dependent variables simultaneously. We first show how the MANOVA can be done within the regression model by dummy coding group membership for a small sample problem and using it as a nominal predictor. In doing this we build upon the multivariate regression analysis of two-group MANOVA which was presented in the last chapter. Then we consider the traditional analysis of variance for MANOVA, introducing the most familiar multivariate test statistic Wilk's Λ. Three post hoc procedures, for determining which groups and which variables are contributing to overall multivariate significance, are discussed. The first two employ Hotelling T^2's, to locate which pairs of groups differ significantly on the set of variables. The first post hoc procedure then uses univariate t's to determine which of the variables are contributing to the significant pairwise differences that are found, while the second procedure uses the Tukey simultaneous confidence interval approach to identify the variables. As a third procedure, we consider the Roy-Bose multivariate simultaneous confidence intervals.

Next we consider a different approach to the k group problem, that of using planned comparisons rather than an omnibus F test. Hays (1981) has an excellent discussion of this approach for univariate ANOVA. Our discussion of multivariate planned comparisons is extensive and is made quite concrete through the use of several examples, including two studies from the literature. The setup of multivariate contrasts on SPSSX MANOVA is illustrated and some printout is discussed.

We then consider the important problem of a priori determination of sample size for 3, 4, 5, and 6 group MANOVA for the number of dependent variables ranging from 2 to 15, using extensive tables developed by Lauter (1978). Finally, the chapter concludes with a discussion of some considerations which mitigate generally against the use of a large number of criterion variables in MANOVA.

5.2. MULTIVARIATE REGRESSION ANALYSIS FOR A SAMPLE PROBLEM

In the previous chapter we indicated how analysis of variance can be incorporated within the regression model by dummy coding group membership and using it as a nominal predictor. For the two group case just one dummy variable (predictor) was needed, which took on the value 1 for subjects in group 1 and was 0 for the subjects in the other group. For our three group example we need two dummy variables (predictors) to identify group membership. The first dummy variable (x_1) is 1 for all subjects in group 1 and 0 for all other subjects. The other dummy variable (x_2) is one for all subjects in group 2 and 0 for all other subjects. A third dummy variable is *not* needed since the subjects in group 3 are identified by 0's on x_1 and x_2, i.e., not in group 1 or group 2. Therefore, by default, those subjects must be in group 3. In general, for k groups, the number of dummy variables needed is $(k - 1)$, corresponding to the between degrees of freedom.

The data for our two-dependent variable, three-group problem is presented below:

Dep. 1	Dep. 2	x_1	x_2	
2	3	1	0	
3	4	1	0	Group 1
5	4	1	0	
2	5	1	0	
4	8	0	1	
5	6	0	1	Group 2
6	7	0	1	
7	6	0	0	
8	7	0	0	
10	8	0	0	Group 3
9	5	0	0	
7	6	0	0	

Thus, cast in a regression mold, we are relating two sets of variables, the two dependent variables and the two predictors (dummy variables). The regression analysis will then determine how much of the variance on the dependent variables is accounted for by the predictors, i.e., by group membership.

In Table 5.1 we present the control lines for running the sample problem as a multivariate regression on SPSSX MANOVA, and the lines for running the

TABLE 5.1
SPSSX MANOVA Control Lines for Running Sample Problem as
Multivariate Regression and as MANOVA

```
       TITLE' THREE GROUP MANOVA RUN AS MULTIVARIATE REGRESSION '
       DATA LIST FREE/ DEP1 DEP2 X1 X2
       LIST
       BEGIN DATA
①      2 3 1 0
       3 4 1 0
       5 4 1 0
       2 5 1 0
       4 8 0 1
       5 6 0 1
       6 7 0 1
       7 6 0 0
       8 7 0 0
       10 8 0 0
       9 5 0 0
       7 6 0 0
       END DATA
         MANOVA DEP1 DEP2 WITH X1 X2/


       TITLE ' MANOVA RUN ON SAMPLE PROBLEM '
       DATA LIST FREE/ DEP1 DEP2 GPS
       LIST
       BEGIN DATA
②      2 3 1
       3 4 1
       5 4 1
       2 5 1
       4 8 2
       5 6 2
       6 7 2
       7 6 3
       8 7 3
       10 8 3
       9 5 3
       7 6 3
       END DATA
       MANOVA DEP1 DEP2 BY GPS(1,3)/
         PRINT = CELLINFO (MEANS,COV,COR) HOMOGENEITY (COCHRAN,BOXM)/
```

①The last two columns of data are for the dummy variables $X1$ and $X2$, which identify group membership (cf the data display in Section 5.2).

②The last column of data identifies group membership—again compare the data display in 5.2.

problem as a traditional MANOVA. The reader may verify by running both analyses that the multivariate F's for the regression analysis are identical to those obtained from the MANOVA run.

5.3.   TRADITIONAL MULTIVARIATE ANALYSIS OF VARIANCE

In the k group MANOVA case we are comparing the groups on p dependent variables simultaneously. For the univariate case, the null hypothesis is:

H_0: $\mu_1 = \mu_2 = \ldots = \mu_k$ (population means are equal)

while for MANOVA the null hypothesis is

H_0: $\mathbf{\mu}_1 = \mathbf{\mu}_2 = \ldots = \mathbf{\mu}_k$ (population mean vectors are equal)

For univariate analysis of variance the F statistic ($F = MS_b/MS_w$) is used for testing the tenability of H_0. What statistic do we use for testing the multivariate null hypothesis? There is no single answer, as several test statistics are available (Olson, 1974). The one which is most widely known is Wilk's Λ, where Λ is given by:

$$\Lambda = \frac{|\mathbf{W}|}{|\mathbf{T}|} = \frac{|\mathbf{W}|}{|\mathbf{B} + \mathbf{W}|}, \quad 0 \leq \Lambda \leq 1$$

$|\mathbf{W}|$ and $|\mathbf{T}|$ are the determinants of the within and total sum of squares and cross-products matrices. $\mathbf{W}$ has already been defined for the two-group case, where the observations in each group are deviated about the individual group means. Thus $\mathbf{W}$ is a measure of within-group variability and is a multivariate generalization of the univariate sum of squares within (SS_w). In $\mathbf{T}$ the observations in each group are deviated about the *grand* mean for each variable. $\mathbf{B}$ is the between sum of squares and cross-products matrix, and is the multivariate generalization of the univariate sum of squares between (SS_b). Thus, $\mathbf{B}$ is a measure of how differential the effect of treatments has been on a set of dependent variables. We define the elements of $\mathbf{B}$ shortly. We need matrices to define within, between, and total variability in the multivariate case since there is variability on each variable (these variabilities will appear on the main diagonals of the $\mathbf{W}$, $\mathbf{B}$, and $\mathbf{T}$ matrices) as well as covariability for each pair of variables (these will be the off diagonal elements of the matrices).

Since Wilk's Λ is defined in terms of the determinants of $\mathbf{W}$ and $\mathbf{T}$, it is important to recall from the matrix algebra chapter (Chapter 2) that the determinant of a covariance matrix is called the *generalized variance* for a set of variables. Now, since $\mathbf{W}$ and $\mathbf{T}$ only differ from their corresponding covariance matrices by a scalar we can think of $|\mathbf{W}|$ and $|\mathbf{T}|$ in the same basic way. Thus, the determinant neatly characterizes within and total variability in terms of *single* numbers. It may also be helpful for the reader to recall that geometrically the generalized variance for two variables is the square of the area of a parallelogram whose sides are the standard deviations for the variables, and that for three variables the generalized variance is the square of the volume of a three dimensional parallelogram whose sides are the standard deviations for the variables. Although it is not clear why the generalized variance is square of the area of a parallelogram, the important fact here is the area interpretation of variance for two variables.

For one variable variance indicates how much scatter there is about the mean on a line, i.e., in one dimension. For two variables the scores for each subject on the variables defines a point in the plane, and thus generalized variance indicates how much the points (subjects) scatter in the plane, i.e., in two dimensions. For three variables the scores for the subjects define points in three space, hence generalized variance shows how much the subjects scatter (vary) in three dimensions. An excellent, extended discussion of generalized variance for the more mathematically inclined is provided in Johnson and Wichern (1982, pp. 103–112).

For univariate ANOVA the reader may recall that

$$SS_t = SS_b + SS_w,$$

where SS_t is the total sum of squares.

For MANOVA the corresponding matrix analogue holds

$$T = \mathbf{B} + \mathbf{W}$$

Total SSCP = Between SSCP + Within SSCP

Matrix   Matrix   Matrix

Notice that Wilk's Λ is an inverse criterion, i.e., the smaller the value of Λ the more evidence for treatment effects (between group association). If there were no treatment effect, then $\mathbf{B} = \mathbf{0}$ and $\Lambda = \dfrac{|\mathbf{W}|}{|\mathbf{0} + \mathbf{W}|} = 1$, whereas if $\mathbf{B}$ were very large relative to $\mathbf{W}$ then Λ would approach 0.

The sampling distribution of Λ is very complicated, and generally an approximation is necessary. Two approximations are available: (1) Bartlett's χ^2 and (2) Rao's F. Bartlett's χ^2 is given by:

$$\chi^2 = -[(N - 1) - .5 (p + k)] \ln \Lambda, \qquad p (k - 1) \, df$$

where N is total sample size, p is the number of dependent variables, and k is the number of groups. Bartlett's χ^2 is a good approximation for moderate to large sample sizes. For smaller sample size, Rao's F is a better approximation (Lohnes, 1961), although generally the two statistics will lead to the same decision on H_0. The multivariate F given on SPSSX and on BMDP is the Rao F. The formula for Rao's F is complicated and is presented later. We point out, now, however, that the degrees of freedom for error with Rao's F can be *non-integer*, so that the reader should not be alarmed if this happens on the computer printout.

As alluded to above, there are certain values of p and k for which a function of Λ is exactly distributed as an F ratio (for example, $k = 2$ or 3 and any p; see Tatsuoka, 1971, p. 89).

5.4. MULTIVARIATE ANALYSIS OF VARIANCE FOR SAMPLE DATA

We now consider the MANOVA of the data given earlier. For convenience, we present the data again below, with the means for the subjects on the two dependent variables in each group:

T_1		T_2		T_3	
y_1	y_2	y_1	y_2	y_1	y_2
2	3	4	8	7	6
3	4	5	6	8	7
5	4	6	7	10	8
2	5	$\bar{y}_{12} = 5$	$\bar{y}_{22} = 7$	9	5
$\bar{y}_{11} = 3$	$\bar{y}_{21} = 4$			7	6
				$\bar{y}_{13} = 8.2$	$\bar{y}_{23} = 6.4$

We wish to test the multivariate null hypothesis with the χ^2 approximation for Wilk's Λ. Recall that $\Lambda = |\mathbf{W}|/|\mathbf{T}|$, so that $\mathbf{W}$ and $\mathbf{T}$ are needed. $\mathbf{W}$ is the pooled estimate of within variability on the set of variables, i.e., our multivariate error term.

Calculation of W

Calculation of $\mathbf{W}$ proceeds in exactly the same way as we obtained $\mathbf{W}$ for Hotelling's T^2 in the two-group MANOVA case in Chapter 4. That is, we determine how much the subjects scores vary on the dependent variables within *each* group, and then pool (add) these together. Symbolically, then

$$\mathbf{W} = \mathbf{W}_1 + \mathbf{W}_2 + \mathbf{W}_3$$

where $\mathbf{W}_1$, $\mathbf{W}_2$, and $\mathbf{W}_3$ are the within sums of squares and cross-products matrices for groups 1, 2, and 3. As in the two-group chapter, we denote the elements of $\mathbf{W}_1$ by ss_1 and ss_2 (measuring the variability on the variables within group 1) and ss_{12} (measuring the covariability of the variables in group 1).

$$\mathbf{W}_1 = \begin{bmatrix} ss_1 & ss_{12} \\ ss_{21} & ss_2 \end{bmatrix}$$

Then, we have

$$ss_1 = \sum_{j=1}^{4} (y_{1(j)} - \bar{y}_{11})^2$$
$$= (2 - 3)^2 + (3 - 3)^2 + (5 - 3)^2 + (2 - 3)^2 = 6$$

$$\text{SS}_2 = \sum_{j=1}^{4} (y_{2(j)} - \bar{y}_{21})^2$$

$$= (3 - 4)^2 + (4 - 4)^2 + (4 - 4)^2 + (5 - 4)^2 = 2$$

$$ss_{12} = ss_{21} = \sum_{j=1}^{4} (y_{1(j)} - \bar{y}_{11})(y_{2(j)} - \bar{y}_{21})$$

$$= (2 - 3)(3 - 4) + (3 - 3)(4 - 4) + (5 - 3)(4 - 4)$$
$$+ (2 - 3)(5 - 4) = 0$$

Thus, the matrix which measures within variability on the two variables in group 1 is given by:

$$\mathbf{W}_1 = \begin{bmatrix} 6 & 0 \\ 0 & 2 \end{bmatrix}$$

In exactly the same way the within SCCP matrices for groups 2 and 3 can be shown to be:

$$\mathbf{W}_2 = \begin{bmatrix} 2 & -1 \\ -1 & 2 \end{bmatrix} \qquad \mathbf{W}_3 = \begin{bmatrix} 6.8 & 2.6 \\ 2.6 & 5.2 \end{bmatrix}$$

Therefore, the pooled estimate of within variability on the set of variables is given by

$$\mathbf{W} = \mathbf{W}_1 + \mathbf{W}_2 + \mathbf{W}_3 = \begin{bmatrix} 14.8 & 1.6 \\ 1.6 & 9.2 \end{bmatrix}$$

Calculation of T

Recall, from earlier in this chapter, that $\mathbf{T} = \mathbf{B} + \mathbf{W}$. We will find the $\mathbf{B}$ (between) matrix, and then obtain the elements of $\mathbf{T}$ by adding the elements of $\mathbf{B}$ to the elements of $\mathbf{W}$.

The diagonal elements of $\mathbf{B}$ are defined as follows:

$$b_{ii} = \sum_{j=1}^{k} n_j (\bar{y}_{ij} - \bar{\bar{y}}_i)^2,$$

where n_j is the number of subjects in group j, $\bar{y}_{ij}$ is the mean for variable i in group j, and $\bar{\bar{y}}_i$ is the grand mean for variable i. Notice that for any particular variable, say variable 1, b_{11} is simply the sum of squares between for a univariate analysis of variance on that variable.

The off diagonal elements of **B** are defined as follows:

$$b_{mi} = b_{im} = \sum_{j=1}^{k} n_j \, (\bar{y}_{ij} - \bar{\bar{y}}_i)(\bar{y}_{mj} - \bar{\bar{y}}_m)$$

To find the elements of **B** we need the grand means on the two variables. These are obtained by simply adding up all the scores on each variable and then dividing by the total number of scores. Thus, $\bar{\bar{y}}_1 = 68/12 = 5.67$, and $\bar{\bar{y}}_2 = 69/12 = 5.75$

Now we find the elements of the **B** (between) matrix:

$$b_{11} = \sum_{j=1}^{3} n_j \, (\bar{y}_{1j} - \bar{\bar{y}}_1)^2, \text{ where } \bar{y}_{1j} \text{ is the mean of variable 1 in group } j.$$

$$= 4(3 - 5.67)^2 + 3(5 - 5.67)^2 + 5(8.2 - 5.67)^2 = 61.87$$

$$b_{22} = \sum_{j=1}^{3} n_j \, (\bar{y}_{2j} - \bar{\bar{y}}_2)^2$$

$$= 4(4 - 5.75)^2 + 3(7 - 5.75)^2 + 5(6.4 - 5.75)^2 = 19.05$$

$$b_{12} = b_{21} = \sum_{j=1}^{3} n_j \, (\bar{y}_{1j} - \bar{\bar{y}}_1)(\bar{y}_{2j} - \bar{\bar{y}}_2)$$

$$= 4(3 - 5.67)(4 - 5.75) + 3(5 - 5.67)(7 - 5.75) + 5(8.2 - 5.67)(6.4 - 5.75) = 24.4$$

Therefore, the **B** matrix is

$$\mathbf{B} = \begin{bmatrix} 61.87 & 24.40 \\ 24.40 & 19.05 \end{bmatrix}$$

and the diagonal elements 61.87 and 19.05 represent the between sum of squares that would be obtained if separate univariate analyses had been done on variables 1 and 2.

Since $\mathbf{T} = \mathbf{B} + \mathbf{W}$, we have

$$\mathbf{T} = \begin{bmatrix} 61.87 & 24.40 \\ 24.40 & 19.05 \end{bmatrix} + \begin{bmatrix} 14.80 & 1.6 \\ 1.6 & 9.2 \end{bmatrix} = \begin{bmatrix} 76.72 & 26.00 \\ 26.00 & 28.25 \end{bmatrix}$$

Calculation of Wilks Λ and the Chi-Square Approximation

Now we can obtain Wilk's Λ:

$$\Lambda = \frac{|\mathbf{W}|}{|\mathbf{T}|} = \frac{\begin{vmatrix} 14.8 & 1.6 \\ 1.6 & 9.2 \end{vmatrix}}{\begin{vmatrix} 76.72 & 26 \\ 26 & 28.25 \end{vmatrix}} = \frac{14.8(9.2) - 1.6^2}{76.72(28.25) - 26^2} = .0897$$

Finally, we can compute the chi-square test statistic:

$$\chi^2 = -[(N - 1) - .5(p + k)] \ln \Lambda, \text{ with } p(k - 1) \; df$$

$$\chi^2 = -[(12 - 1) - .5(2 + 3)] \ln (.0897)$$

$$\chi^2 = -8.5 (-2.4116) = 20.4987, \text{ with } 2(3 - 1) = 4 \; df$$

The multivariate null hypothesis here is:

$$\begin{pmatrix} \mu_{11} \\ \mu_{21} \end{pmatrix} = \begin{pmatrix} \mu_{12} \\ \mu_{22} \end{pmatrix} = \begin{pmatrix} \mu_{13} \\ \mu_{23} \end{pmatrix}$$

i.e., that the population means in the three groups on variable 1 are equal, and similarily that the population means on variable 2 are equal. Since the critical value at .05 is 9.49, we reject the multivariate null hypothesis and conclude that the three groups differ overall on the set of two variables. Table 5.2 gives the multivariate F's and the univariate F's from the SPSSX MANOVA run on the sample problem and presents the formula for Rao's F approximation and also relates some of the output from the univariate F's to the $\mathbf{B}$ and $\mathbf{W}$ matrices that we computed. After overall multivariate significance one would like to know which groups and which variables were responsible for the overall association, i.e., a more detailed breakdown. This is considered next.

5.5.   POST HOC PROCEDURES

Since pairwise differences are easy to interpret and often the most meaningful, we concentrate on procedures for locating significant pairwise differences, both multivariate and univariate. We consider three procedures, from least to most conservative, in terms of protecting against type I error.

Procedure 1—Hotelling T^2's and Univariate t Tests

Follow a significant overall multivariate result by all pairwise multivariate tests (T^2's) to determine which pairs of groups differ significantly on the set of variables. Then use univariate t tests, each at the .05 level, to determine which of

TABLE 5.2
Multivariate F's and Univariate F's for Sample Problem from SPSSX
MANOVA

EFFECT .. GPID

MULTIVARIATE TESTS OF SIGNIFICANCE (S = 2, M = −½, N = 3)

TEST NAME	VALUE	APPROX. F	HYPOTH. DF	ERROR DF	SIG. OF F
PILLAIS	1.30178	8.38990	4.00	18.00	.001
HOTELLINGS	5.78518	10.12581	4.00	14.00	.000
WILKS	.08967	9.35751	4.00	16.00	.000
ROYS	.83034				

$$\frac{1 - \Lambda^{1/s}}{\Lambda^{1/s}} \frac{ms - p(k-1)/2 + 1}{p(k-1)}, \text{ where } m = N - 1 - (p+k)/2 \text{ and}$$

$$s = \sqrt{\frac{p^2(k-1)^2 - 4}{p^2 + (k-1)^2 - 5}},$$

is approximately distributed as F with $p(k-1)$ and $ms - p(k-1)/2 + 1$ degrees of freedom. Here Wilk's $\Lambda = .08967$, $p = 2$, $k = 3$ and $N = 12$. Thus, we have $m = 12 - 1 - (2 + 3)/2 = 8.5$ and

$$s = \sqrt{\{4(3 - 1)^2 - 4\}/\{4 + (2)^2 - 5\}} = \sqrt{12/3} = 2,$$

and

$$F = \frac{1 - \sqrt{.08967}}{\sqrt{.08967}} \frac{8.5(2) - 2(2)/2 + 1}{2(3 - 1)} = \frac{1 - .29945}{.29945} \cdot \frac{16}{4} = 9.357,$$

as given on printout above. The pair of degrees of freedom is $p(k-1) = 2(3-1) = 4$ and $ms - p(k-1)/2 + 1 = 8.5(2) - 2(3-1)/2 + 1 = 16$.

UNIVARIATE F-TESTS WITH (2,9) D. F.

VARIABLE	HYPOTH. SS	ERROR SS	HYPOTH. MS	ERROR MS	F	SIG. OF F.
Y1	① 61.86667	② 14.80000	30.93333	1.64444	18.81081	.001
Y2	19.05000	9.20000	9.52500	1.02222	9.31793	.006

①These are the diagonal elements of the **B** (between) matrix we computed in the example:

$$\mathbf{B} = \begin{bmatrix} 61.87 & 24.40 \\ 24.40 & 19.05 \end{bmatrix}$$

②Recall that the pooled within matrix computed in the example was

$$\mathbf{W} = \begin{bmatrix} 14.8 & 1.6 \\ 1.6 & 9.2 \end{bmatrix}$$

and these are the diagonal elements of **W**. The univariate F ratios are formed from the elements on the main diagonals of **B** and **W**. Dividing the elements of **B** by hypothesis degrees of freedom gives the hypothesis mean squares, while dividing the elements of **W** by error degrees of freedom gives the error mean squares. Then, dividing hypothesis mean squares by error mean squares yields the F ratios. Thus, for $Y1$ we have

$$F = \frac{30.933}{1.644} = 18.81$$

the individual variables are contributing to the significant multivariate pairwise differences. To keep the overall α for the set of pairwise multivariate tests under some control (and still maintain reasonable power) we may want to set overall $\alpha = .15$. Thus, for 4 groups there will be 6 Hotelling T^2's, and we would do each T^2 at the $.15/6 = .025$ level of significance. This procedure has fairly good control on type I error for the first two parts, and not as good control for the last part (i.e., identifying the significant individual variables). It has the best power of the three procedures we discuss, and as long as we recognize that the individual variables identified must be treated somewhat tenuously, it has merit.

Procedure 2—Hotelling T^2's and Tukey Confidence Intervals

Once again we follow a significant overall multivariate result by all pairwise multivariate tests, but then we apply the Tukey simultaneous confidence interval technique to determine which of the individual variables are contributing to each pairwise significant multivariate result. This procedure affords us better protection against type I errors, especially if we set the experimentwise error rate (EER) for each variable that we are applying the Tukey to such that the overall α is *at maximum* .15. Thus, depending on how large a risk of spurious results (within the .15) we can tolerate, we may set EER at .05 for each variable in a 3 variable problem, at .025 for each variable in a 6 variable problem, variable, or at .01 for each variable in an 8 variable study. As we shall see in an example shortly, the 90%, 95%, and 99% confidence intervals, corresponding to EER's of .10, .05, and .01, are easily obtained from the SAS GLM program.

Procedure 3—Roy-Bose Simultaneous Confidence Intervals

In exploratory research in univariate ANOVA after the null hypothesis has been rejected, one wishes to determine where the differences lie with some post hoc procedure. One of the more popular post hoc procedures is the Scheffe', with which a wide variety of comparisons can be made. For example, all pairwise comparisons as well as complex comparisons such as $\mu_1 - (\mu_2 + \mu_3)/2$ or $(\mu_1 + \mu_2) - (\mu_3 + \mu_4)$ can be tested. The Scheffe' allows one to examine *any* complex comparison, as long as the sum of the coefficients for the means is 0. All these comparisons can be made with the assurance that overall type I error is controlled (i.e., the probability of one or more type I errors) at a level set by the experimenter. Importantly, however, the price one pays for being allowed to do all this data snooping is loss of power for detecting differences. This is due to the basic principle that as one type of error (in this case Type I) is controlled, the other type (type II here) increases and therefore power decreases, since power = 1 − type II error. Glass and Hopkins (1984, p. 382) note, "The

Scheffe' method is the most widely presented MC (multiple comparison) method in textbooks of statistical methods; ironically it is rarely the MC method of choice for the questions of interest in terms of power efficiency."

The Roy-Bose intervals are the multivariate generalization of the Scheffe' univariate intervals. After the multivariate null hypothesis has been rejected, the Roy-Bose intervals can be used to examine all pairwise group comparisons as well as all complex comparisons for *each* dependent variable. In addition to all these comparisons, one can examine pairwise and complex comparisons on various linear combinations of the variables (such as the difference of two variables). Thus, *the Roy-Bose approach controls on overall α for an enormous number of comparisons. To do so power has to suffer, and it suffers considerably, especially for small or moderate sized samples.* Hummel and Sligo (1971) found the Roy-Bose procedure to be extremely conservative, and recommended generally against it's use. We agree. In many studies the sample sizes are small or relatively small *and* the effect sizes are small. In these circumstances power will be far from adequate to begin with, and the use of Roy-Bose intervals will further sharply diminish the researchers chances of finding any differences. In addition, there is the question of why one would want to examine all or most of the comparisons allowed by the Roy-Bose procedure. As Bird commented (1975, p. 344), "a completely unrestricted analysis of multivariate data, however, would be extremely unusual."

Example—Illustrating Post Hoc Procedures 1 and 2

We illustrate first the use of post hoc procedure 1 on social psychological data collected by Novince (1977). She was interested in improving the social skills of college females and reducing their anxiety in heterosexual encounters. There were three groups in her study: control group, behavioral reharal, and a behavioral rehearsal + cognitive restructuring group. We consider the analysis on the following set of dependent variables: (1) anxiety—physiological anxiety in a series of heterosexual encounters, (2) measure of social skills in social interactions, (3) appropriateness, and (4) assertiveness. The raw data for this problem is given in the Appendix of this chapter.

The control lines for obtaining the overall multivariate test on SPSSX MANOVA and all pairwise multivariate tests (using the SPSSX DISCRIMINANT program), along with selected printout, is given in Table 5.3. That printout indicates that groups 1 and 2 and groups 2 and 3 differ in a multivariate sense. Therefore, the SPSSX T-TEST procedure was used to determine which of the individual variables contributed to the multivariate significance in each case. The results of the t tests are presented in Table 5.4, and indicate that all of the variables contribute to each multivariate significance at the .01 level of significance.

TABLE 5.3
SPSSX MANOVA and Discriminant Control Lines on Novince Data for
Locating Multivariate Group Differences

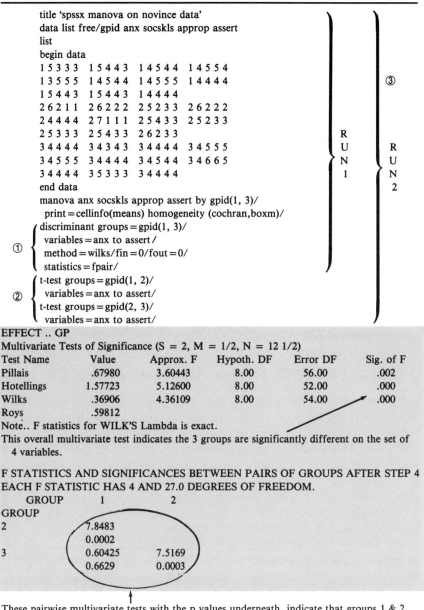

```
         title 'spssx manova on novince data'
         data list free/gpid anx socskls approp assert
         list
         begin data
         1 5 3 3 3   1 5 4 4 3   1 4 5 4 4   1 4 5 5 4
         1 3 5 5 5   1 4 5 4 4   1 4 5 5 5   1 4 4 4 4
         1 5 4 4 3   1 5 4 4 3   1 4 4 4 4
         2 6 2 1 1   2 6 2 2 2   2 5 2 3 3   2 6 2 2 2
         2 4 4 4 4   2 7 1 1 1   2 5 4 3 3   2 5 2 3 3
         2 5 3 3 3   2 5 4 3 3   2 6 2 3 3
         3 4 4 4 4   3 4 3 4 3   3 4 4 4 4   3 4 5 5 5
         3 4 5 5 5   3 4 4 4 4   3 4 5 4 4   3 4 6 6 5
         3 4 4 4 4   3 5 3 3 3   3 4 4 4 4
         end data
         manova anx socskls approp assert by gpid(1, 3)/
           print = cellinfo(means) homogeneity (cochran,boxm)/
   ⎧     discriminant groups = gpid(1, 3)/
   ⎪       variables = anx to assert /
 ① ⎨       method = wilks/fin = 0/fout = 0/
   ⎩       statistics = fpair/
   ⎧     t-test groups = gpid(1, 2)/
 ② ⎨       variables = anx to assert/
   ⎪     t-test groups = gpid(2, 3)/
   ⎩       variables = anx to assert/
```

EFFECT .. GP
Multivariate Tests of Significance (S = 2, M = 1/2, N = 12 1/2)

Test Name	Value	Approx. F	Hypoth. DF	Error DF	Sig. of F
Pillais	.67980	3.60443	8.00	56.00	.002
Hotellings	1.57723	5.12600	8.00	52.00	.000
Wilks	.36906	4.36109	8.00	54.00	.000
Roys	.59812				

Note.. F statistics for WILK'S Lambda is exact.
This overall multivariate test indicates the 3 groups are significantly different on the set of
4 variables.

F STATISTICS AND SIGNIFICANCES BETWEEN PAIRS OF GROUPS AFTER STEP 4
EACH F STATISTIC HAS 4 AND 27.0 DEGREES OF FREEDOM.

	GROUP 1	2
GROUP		
2	7.8483	
	0.0002	
3	0.60425	7.5169
	0.6629	0.0003

These pairwise multivariate tests, with the p values underneath, indicate that groups 1 & 2,
and groups 2 & 3 are significantly different at the .05 level.

① This is set of control lines needed to obtained the pairwise multivariate tests. FIN = 0
AND FOUT = 0 are necessary if one wishes all the dependent variables in the analysis.

② This set of control lines yields the univariate t tests for those pairs of groups (1 and 2, 2
and 3) that were different on the multivariate tests.

③ Actually two separate runs would be required. The first run is to determine whether there
is an overall difference, and if so, which pairs of groups are different (in multivariate sense). The
second run is to obtain the univariate t's, to determine which of the variables are
contributing to each pairwise multivariate significance.

TABLE 5.4

Univariate *t* Tests for Each of the Significant Multivariate Pairs for the Novince Data

t-tests for independent samples of GPID
GROUP 1 – GPID EQ 1.00
GROUP 2 – GPID EQ 2.00

Variable	Number of cases	Mean	Standard Deviation	Standard Error	F Value	2-tail Prob.	Pooled Variance estimate		
							t Value	Degrees of Freedom	2-tail Prob.
ANX									
GROUP 1	11	4.2727	.647	.195	1.61	.465	– 3.75	20	.001
GROUP 2	11	5.4545	.820	.247					
SOCSKLS									
GROUP 1	11	4.3636	.674	.203	2.36	.192	4.88	20	.000
GROUP 2	11	2.5455	1.036	.312					
APPROP									
GROUP 1	11	4.1818	.603	.182	2.40	.184	4.88	20	.000
GROUP 2	11	2.5455	.934	.282					
ASSERT									
GROUP 1	11	3.8182	.751	.226	1.55	.502	3.52	20	.002
GROUP 2	11	2.5455	.934	.282					

(*Continued*)

TABLE 5.4 *(Continued)*

t-tests for independent samples of GPID

GROUP 1 – GPID EQ 2.00
GROUP 2 – GPID EQ 3.00

Variable	Number of cases	Mean	Standard Deviation	Standard Error	Test for Variances F Value	Test for Variances 2-tail Prob.	Pooled Variance estimate* t Value	Pooled Variance estimate* Degrees of Freedom	Pooled Variance estimate* 2-tail Prob.
ANX									
GROUP 1	11	5.4545	.820	.247	7.40	.004	5.18	20	.000
GROUP 2	11	4.0909	.302	.091					
SOCSKLS									
GROUP 1	11	2.5455	1.036	.312	1.31	.677	−4.17	20	.000
GROUP 2	11	4.2727	.905	.273					
APPROP									
GROUP 1	11	2.5455	.934	.282	1.41	.596	−4.69	20	.000
GROUP 2	11	4.2727	.786	.237					
ASSERT									
GROUP 1	11	2.5455	.934	.282	1.78	.378	−4.39	20	.000
GROUP 2	11	4.0909	.701	.211					

*SPSSX also prints a SEPARATE VARIANCE ESTIMATE *t* test. It should be used when group sizes are sharply unequal *and* a statistical test indicates the population variances are different.

5.6. THE TUKEY PROCEDURE

The Tukey procedure (Glass & Hopkins, 1984, p. 370) enables us to examine *all* pairwise group differences on a variable with experimentwise error rate held in check. The studentized range statistic (which we denote by q) is used in the procedure, and the critical values for it are in Table D of the statistical tables in the Appendix of this volume. If there are k groups and the total sample size is N, then any two means are declared significantly different at the .05 level if the following inequality holds:

$$|\bar{y}_i - \bar{y}_j| > q_{.05;k,N-k} \sqrt{\frac{MS_w}{n}}$$

where MS_w is the error term for a one-way ANOVA, and n is the common group size.

Equivalently, and somewhat more informative, we can determine whether the population means for groups i and j (μ_i and μ_j) differ if the following confidence interval does *not* include 0:

$$\bar{y}_i - \bar{y}_j \pm q_{.05;k,N-k} \sqrt{\frac{MS_w}{n}}$$

i.e.,

$$\bar{y}_i - \bar{y}_j - q_{.05;k,N-k} \sqrt{\frac{MS_w}{n}} < \mu_i - \mu_j < \bar{y}_i - \bar{y}_j + q_{.05;k,N-k} \sqrt{\frac{MS_w}{n}}$$

If the confidence interval includes 0, we conclude the population means are not significantly different. Why? Because if the interval includes 0 that means 0 is a likely value for $\mu_i - \mu_j$, which is to say it is likely that $\mu_i = \mu_j$.

Example

To illustrate numerically the Tukey procedure we consider obtaining the confidence interval for the anxiety (ANX) variable from the Novince study in Table 5.3. In particular we obtain the 95% confidence interval for groups 1 and 2. The mean difference, not given in Table 5.5, is -1.18. Recall that the common group size in this study is $n = 11$. MS_w, denoted by MSE in Table 5.5, is .39394 for ANX. Finally, from Table D the critical value for the studentized range statistic is $q_{.05;3,30} = 3.49$. Thus, the confidence interval is given by

$$-1.18 - 3.49 \sqrt{\frac{.39394}{11}} < \mu_1 - \mu_2 < -1.18 + 3.49 \sqrt{\frac{.39394}{11}}$$

$$-1.84 < \mu_1 - \mu_2 < -.52$$

Since this interval does not cover 0, we conclude that the population means for the anxiety variable in groups 1 and 2 are significantly different. Why is the confidence interval approach more informative, as indicated earlier, then simply testing whether the means are different? Because the confidence interval not only tells us whether the means differ, but it also gives us a range of values within which the mean difference probably lies. This tells us the precision with which we have captured the mean difference, and can be used in judging the practical significance of a result. In the above example the mean difference could be anywhere in the range from -1.84 to $-.52$. If the investigator had decided on some grounds that a difference of at least 1 had to be established for practical significance, then the statistical significance found would not be sufficient.

The Tukey procedure assumes that the variances are homogeneous and it also assumes equal group sizes. If the group sizes are unequal, even very sharply unequal, then various studies (e.g., Dunnett, 1980; Kesselman, Murray, & Rogan, 1976) indicate that the procedure is still appropriate provided that n is replaced by the harmonic mean for each pair of groups *and* provided that the variances are homogeneous. Thus, for groups i and j with sample sizes n_i and n_j, we replace n by $\dfrac{2}{\dfrac{1}{n_i} + \dfrac{1}{n_j}}$. The studies cited above showed that under the conditions given the type I error rate for the Tukey procedure is kept very close to the nominal α, and always less than nominal α (within .01 for $\alpha = .05$ from the Dunnett study).

We indicated earlier that the Tukey procedure can be easily implemented using the SAS GLM procedure. Below are the SAS GLM control lines for applying the Tukey procedure to each of the four dependent variables from the Novince data.

```
data novince;
input gpid anx socskls approp assert @@;
cards;
1 5 3 3 3     1 5 4 4 3     1 4 5 4 4     1 4 5 5 4
1 3 5 5 5     1 4 5 4 4     1 4 5 5 5     1 4 4 4 4
1 5 4 4 3     1 5 4 4 3     1 4 4 4 4
2 6 2 1 1     2 6 2 2 2     2 5 2 3 3     2 6 2 2 2
2 4 4 4 4     2 7 1 1 1     2 5 4 3 3     2 5 2 3 3
2 5 3 3 3     2 5 4 3 3     2 6 2 3 3
3 4 4 4 4     3 4 3 4 3     3 4 4 4 4     3 4 5 5 5
3 4 5 5 5     3 4 4 4 4     3 4 5 4 4     3 4 6 6 5
3 4 4 4 4     3 5 3 3 3     3 4 4 4 4
proc print;
proc glm;
class gpid;
model anx socskls approp assert=gpid/alpha=.05;
means gpid/tukey;
```

Selected printout from the run is presented in Tables 5.5 and 5.6.

TABLE 5.5
Tukey Procedure Printout From SAS GLM for Novince Data

The SAS System

General Linear Models Procedure

Tukey's Studentized Range (HSD) Test for variable: ANX

Note: This test controls the type I experimentwise error rate, but generally has a higher type II error rate than REGWQ.

Alpha = 0.05 df = 30 MSE = 0.393939
Critical Value of Studentized Range = 3.486
Minimum Significant Difference = 0.6598

Means with the same letter are not significantly different.

Tukey Grouping	Mean	N	GPID
A	5.4545	11	2
B	4.2727	11	1
B	4.0909	11	3

Tukey's Studentized Range (HSD) Test for variable: SOCSKLS

Note: This test controls the type I experimentwise error rate, but generally has a higher type II error rate than REGWQ.

Alpha = 0.05 df = 30 MSE = 0.781818
Critical Value of Studentized Range = 3.486
Minimum Significant Difference = 0.9295

Means with the same letter are not significantly different.

Tukey Grouping	Mean	N	GPID
A	4.3636	11	1
A	4.2727	11	3
B	3.5455	11	2

TABLE 5.6
Tukey Printout From SAS GLM for Novince Data (cont.)

Tukey's Studentized Range (HSD) Test for variable: APPROP

Note: This test controls the type I experimentwise error rate, but generally has a higher type II error rate than REGWQ.

Alpha = 0.05 df = 30 MSE = 0.618182
Critical Value of Studentized Range = 3.486
Minimum Significant Difference = 0.8265

Means with the same letter are not significantly different.

Tukey Grouping	Mean	N	GPID
A	4.2727	11	3
A			
B	4.1818	11	1
B	2.5455	11	2

Tukey's Studentized Range (HSD) Test for variable: ASSERT

Note: This test controls the type I experimentwise error rate, but generally has a higher type II error rate than REGWQ.

Alpha = 0.05 df = 30 MSE = 0.642424
Critical Value of Studentized Range = 3.486
Minimum Significant Difference = 0.8425

Means with the same letter are not significantly different.

Tukey Grouping	Mean	N	GPID
A	4.0909	11	3
A			
A	3.8182	11	1
B	2.5455	11	2

5.7. PLANNED COMPARISONS

One approach to the analysis of data is to first demonstrate overall significance, and then follow this up to assess the subsources of variation (i.e., which particular groups and/or variables) were primarily responsible for the overall significance. One such procedure using pairwise T^2's has been presented. This approach is appropriate in exploratory studies where the investigator first has to establish that an effect exists. However, in many instances there is more of an empirical and/or theoretical base and the investigator is conducting a confirmatory study. Here the existence of an effect may be taken for granted, and the investigator has specific questions he wishes to ask of the data. Thus, rather than examining all 10 pairwise comparisons for a five-group problem, there may be only 3 or 4 comparisons (which may or may not be paired comparisons) of interest. It is important to use planned comparisons when the situation justifies them, since performing a small number of statistical tests cuts down on the probability of spurious results (type I errors), which can result much more readily when a large number of tests are done.

Hays (1981) has shown in univariate ANOVA that the test is more powerful when the comparison is planned. This would carry over to MANOVA. This is a very important factor weighing in favor of planned comparisons. Many studies in educational research have only 10 to 20 subjects per group. With these sample sizes, power is generally going to be poor unless the treatment effect is large (Cohen, 1977). *If we plan a small or moderate number of contrasts that we wish to test, then power can be improved considerably, while control on overall α can be maintained through the use of the Bonferroni Inequality.* Recall this inequality states that if k hypotheses, k planned comparisons here, are tested separately with type I error rates of $\alpha_1, \alpha_2, \ldots , \alpha_k$, then

$$\text{Overall } \alpha \leq \alpha_1 + \alpha_2 + \ldots + \alpha_k,$$

where overall α is the probability of one or more type I errors when all the hypotheses are true. Therefore, if 3 planned comparisons were tested each at $\alpha = .01$, then the probability of one or more spurious results can be no greater than .03 for the *set* of 3 tests.

Let us now consider two situations where planned comparisons would be appropriate:

1. Suppose an investigator wishes to determine whether each of two drugs produces a differential effect on three measures of task performance over a placebo. Then if we denote the placebo as group 2, the following set of planned comparisons would answer the investigator's questions:

$$\psi_1 = \mu_1 - \mu_2 \text{ and } \psi_2 = \mu_2 - \mu_3$$

2.   Secondly, consider the following four-group schematic design:

	Groups		
control	T_1 & T_2 combined	T_1	T_2
μ_1	μ_2	μ_3	μ_4

(T_1 and T_2 represent two treatments)

As outlined this could represent the format for a variety of studies (e.g., if T_1 and T_2 were two methods of teaching reading, or if T_1 and T_2 were two counseling approaches). Then the three most relevant questions the investigator wishes to answer are given by the following planned and so called Helmert contrasts:

1.   Do the treatments as a set make a difference?

$$\psi_1 = \mu_1 - \frac{\mu_2 + \mu_3 + \mu_4}{3}$$

2.   Is the combination of treatments more effective than either treatment alone?

$$\psi_2 = \mu_2 - \frac{\mu_3 + \mu_4}{2}$$

3.   Is one treatment more effective than the other treatment?

$$\psi_3 = \mu_3 - \mu_4$$

Assuming equal n per group, the above two situations represent dependent vs. independent planned comparisons. Two comparisons among means are *independent* if the sum of the products of the coefficients is 0. We represent the contrasts for situation 1 as follows:

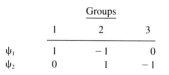

	Groups		
	1	2	3
ψ_1	1	-1	0
ψ_2	0	1	-1

These contrasts are dependent since the sum of products of the coefficients $\neq 0$ as shown below:

sum of products $= 1\,(0) + (-1)(1) + 0\,(-1) = -1$

Now consider the contrasts from situation 2:

	Groups			
	1	2	3	4
ψ_1	1	$-\frac{1}{3}$	$-\frac{1}{3}$	$-\frac{1}{3}$
ψ_2	0	1	$-\frac{1}{2}$	$-\frac{1}{2}$
ψ_3	0	0	1	-1

Below we show that these contrasts are pairwise independent by demonstrating that the sum of the products of the coefficients in each case $= 0$:

$$\psi_1 \text{ and } \psi_2 : 1(0) + (-\tfrac{1}{3})(1) + (-\tfrac{1}{3})(-\tfrac{1}{2}) + (-\tfrac{1}{3})(-\tfrac{1}{2}) = 0$$

$$\psi_1 \text{ and } \psi_3 : 1(0) + (-\tfrac{1}{3})(0) + (-\tfrac{1}{3})(1) + (-\tfrac{1}{3})(-1) = 0$$

$$\psi_2 \text{ and } \psi_3 : 0(0) + 1(0) + (-\tfrac{1}{2})(1) + (-\tfrac{1}{2})(-1) = 0$$

Now consider two general contrasts for k groups:

$$\psi_1 = c_{11}\mu_1 + c_{12}\mu_2 + \ldots\ldots + c_{1k}\mu_k$$

$$\psi_2 = c_{21}\mu_1 + c_{22}\mu_2 + \ldots\ldots + c_{2k}\mu_k$$

The first part of the c subscript refers to the contrast number and the second part to the group. The condition for independence in symbols then is:

$$c_{11}c_{21} + c_{12}c_{22} + \ldots\ldots + c_{1k}c_{2k} = \sum_{j=1}^{k} c_{1j}c_{2j} = 0$$

If the sample sizes are not equal, then the condition for independence is more complicated and becomes:

$$\frac{c_{11}c_{21}}{n_1} + \frac{c_{12}c_{22}}{n_2} + \ldots\ldots + \frac{c_{1k}c_{2k}}{n_k} = 0$$

It is very desirable, both statistically and substantively, to have orthogonal multivariate planned comparisons. Since the comparisons are uncorrelated, we obtain a nice additive partitioning of the total between group association (Stevens, 1972). The reader may recall that in univariate ANOVA the between sum of squares is split into additive portions by a set of orthogonal planned comparisons (see Hays, 1981, chapter 14). Exactly the same type of thing is accomplished in the multivariate case, however, now the between matrix is split into additive portions, which yield nonoverlapping pieces of information. Since the orthogonal comparisons are uncorrelated, the interpretation is clear and straightforward.

Although it is desirable to have orthogonal comparisons, the set to impose depends on the questions which are of primary interest to the investigator. The first example we gave of planned comparisons was not orthogonal, but corresponded to the important questions the investigator wanted answered. The interpretation of correlated contrasts requires some care, however, and we consider these in more detail later on in this chapter.

5.8. TEST STATISTICS FOR PLANNED COMPARISONS

Univariate Case

The reader may have been exposed to planned comparisons for a single dependent variable, i.e., the univariate case. For k groups, with population means μ_1, μ_2, . . . , μ_k, a constrast among the population means is given by

$$\psi = c_1\mu_1 + c_2\mu_2 + \ldots + c_k\mu_k$$

where the sum of the coefficients (c_i) must equal 0.

This contrast is estimated by replacing the population means by the sample means, yielding

$$\hat{\psi} = c_1\bar{x}_1 + c_2\bar{x}_2 + \ldots + c_k\bar{x}_k$$

To test whether a given contrast is significantly different from 0, i.e., to test

$$H_0 : \psi = 0 \qquad \text{vs. } H_1 : \psi \neq 0$$

we need an expression for the standard error of a constrast. It can be shown that the variance for a contrast is given by

$$\hat{\sigma}_{\hat{\psi}}^2 = MS_w \cdot \sum_{i=1}^{k} \frac{c_i^2}{n_i} \tag{1}$$

where MS_w is the error term from all the groups (the denominator of the F test) and n_i are the group sizes. Thus, the standard error of a contrast is simply the square root of (1) and the following t statistic can be used to determine whether a contrast is significantly different from 0:

$$t = \frac{\hat{\psi}}{\sqrt{MS_w \cdot \sum_{i=1}^{k} \frac{c_i^2}{n_i}}}$$

SPSSX MANOVA reports the univariate results for contrasts as F values. Recall, that since $F = t^2$, the following F test with 1 and $N - k$ degrees of freedom is equivalent to a two-tailed t test at the same level of significance:

$$F = \frac{\hat{\psi}^2}{MS_w \cdot \sum_{i=1}^{k} \frac{c_i^2}{n_i}}$$

If we rewrite the above as

$$F = \frac{\hat{\psi}^2 \Big/ \sum_{i=1}^{k} \frac{c_i^2}{n_i}}{MS_w} \qquad (2)$$

we can think of the numerator of (2) as the sum of squares for a contrast, and this will appear as hypothesis sum of squares (HYPOTH. SS specifically) on the SPSSX printout. MS_w will appear under the heading ERROR MS.

Let us consider a special case of Equation 2. Suppose the group sizes are equal and we are making a simple paired comparison. Then the coefficient for one mean will be 1 and the coefficient for the other mean will be -1, and $\Sigma c_i^2 = 2$. Then the above F statistic can be written as

$$F = \frac{n\hat{\psi}^2/2}{MS_w} = \frac{n}{2} \, \hat{\psi} \, (MS_w)^{-1} \, \hat{\psi} \qquad (3)$$

We have rewritten the test statistic in the form on the extreme right because we will be able to relate it more easily to the multivariate test statistic for a two-group planned comparison.

Multivariate Case

All contrasts, whether univariate or multivariate, can be thought of as fundamentally "two-group" comparisons. We are literally comparing two groups, or we are comparing one set of means vs another set of means. In the multivariate case this means that Hotelling's T^2 will be appropriate for testing the multivariate contrasts for significance.

We now have a contrast among the population mean vectors $\mu_1, \mu_2, \ldots, \mu_k$, given by

$$\psi = c_1\mu_1 + c_2\mu_2 + \ldots + c_k\mu_k$$

This contrast is estimated by replacing the population mean vectors by the sample mean vectors:

$$\hat{\psi} = c_1\bar{x}_1 + c_2\bar{x}_2 + \ldots + c_k\bar{x}_k$$

We wish to test that the contrast among the population mean vectors is the null vector:

$$H_0 : \psi = 0$$

Our estimate of error is **S**, the estimate of the assumed common within group population covariance matrix Σ, and the general test statistic is

$$T^2 = \left(\sum_{i=1}^{k} \frac{c_i^2}{n_i} \right)^{-1} \hat{\psi}'S^{-1}\hat{\psi} \qquad (4)$$

where, as in the univariate case, the n_i refer to the group sizes. Suppose we wish to contrast group 1 against the average of groups 2 and 3. If the group sizes are 20, 15, and 12, then the term in parenthesis would be evaluated as [1^2/ 20 + $(-.5)^2$/15 + $(-.5)^2$/12]. Complete evaluation of a multivarate contrast is given in Table 5.10. Note that the first part of Equation 4, involving the summation, is exactly the same as in the univariate case (cf. Equation 2). Now, however, there are matrices instead of scalars. For example, the univariate error term MS_w has been replaced by the matrix **S**.

Again, as in the two-group MANOVA chapter, we have an exact F transformation of T^2, which is given by

$$F = \frac{(n_e - p + 1)}{n_e \; p} \; T^2, \text{ with } p \text{ and } (n_e - p + 1) \text{ degrees of freedom} \quad (5)$$

In Equation 5, $n_e = N - k$, i.e., the degrees of freedom for estimating the pooled within covariance matrix. Note that for $k = 2$, (5) reduces to Equation 3 in Chapter 4.

For equal n per group and a simple paired comparison, observe that (4) can be written as

$$T^2 = \frac{n}{2} \, \hat{\psi}' \mathbf{S}^{-1} \hat{\psi} \quad (6)$$

Note the analogy with the univariate case in Equation 3, except that now we have matrices instead of scalars. The estimated contrast has been replaced by the estimated mean vector contrast ($\hat{\psi}$) and the univariate error term (MS_w) has been replaced by the corresponding multivariate error term **S**.

5.9. MULTIVARIATE PLANNED COMPARISONS ON SPSSX MANOVA

SPSSX MANOVA is set up very nicely for running multivariate planned comparisons. The following type of contrasts are automatically generated by the program: Helmert (which we have discussed), Simple, Repeated (comparing adjacent levels of a factor), Deviation, and Polynomial. Thus, if we wish Helmert contrasts, it is not necessary to set up the coefficients, the program does this automatically. All we need do is give the following CONTRAST SUBCOMMAND:

CONTRAST(FACTORNAME) = HELMERT/

We remind the reader that all subcommands are indented at least one column and begin with a keyword (in this case CONTRAST) followed by an equals sign, then the specifications, and are terminated by a slash.

An example of where Helmert contrasts are very meaningful has already been given. Simple contrasts involve comparing each group against the last group. A situation where this set of contrasts would make sense is if we were mainly interested in comparing each of several treatment groups against a control group (labeled as the last group). Repeated contrasts might be of considerable interest in a repeated measures design where a single group of subjects is measured at say 5 points in time (a longitudinal study). We might be particularily interested in differences at adjacent points in time. For example, a group of elementary school children is measured on a standardized achievement test in grades 1, 3, 5, 7, and 8. We wish to know the extent of change from grade 1 to 3, from grade 3 to 5, from grade 5 to 7, and from grade 7 to 8. The coefficients for the contrasts would be as follows:

		Grade		
1	3	5	7	8
1	-1	0	0	0
0	1	-1	0	0
0	0	1	-1	0
0	0	0	1	-1

Polynomial contrasts are useful in trend analysis, i.e., where we wish to determine whether there is a linear, quadratic, cubic, etc. trend in the data. Again, these contrasts can be of great interest in repeated measures designs in growth curve analysis, where we wish to model the mathematical form of the growth. To reconsider the previous example, some investigators may be more interested in whether the growth in some basic skills areas like reading and mathematics is linear (proportional) during the elementary years, or perhaps curvilinear. For example, maybe growth is linear for a while and then somewhat levels off, suggesting an overall curvilinear trend.

If none of the above automatically generated contrasts answer the research questions, then one can set up their own contrasts using SPECIAL as the code name. Special contrasts are "tailor made" comparisons for the group comparisons suggested by your hypotheses. In setting these up, however, remember that for k groups there are only $(k - 1)$ between degrees of freedom, so that only $(k - 1)$ non-redundant contrasts can be run. The coefficients for the contrasts are enclosed in parentheses after special:

CONTRAST(FACTORNAME) = SPECIAL(1, 1, . . . , 1 coefficients for contrasts)/

There *must* first be as many 1's as there are groups (see SPSSX User's Guide, 1988, p. 590). We give an example illustrating special contrasts shortly.

Example 1—Helmert contrasts

An investigator has a three-group, two-dependent variable problem with 5 subjects per group. The first is a control group, and the remaining two groups are treatment groups. The Helmert contrasts test each level (group) against the average of the remaining levels. In this case the two single degree of freedom Helmert contrasts, corresponding to the two between degrees of freedom, are very meaningful. The first tests whether the control group differs from the average of the treatment groups on the set of variables. The second Helmert contrast tests whether the treatments are differentially effective. In Table 5.7 we present the control lines, along with the data as part of the command file, for running

TABLE 5.7
SPSSX MANOVA Control Lines for Multivariate Helmert
Contrasts

```
TITLE ' MULTIVARIATE HELMERT CONTRASTS '
DATA LIST FREE/GPS Y1 Y2
LIST
BEGIN DATA
1 5 6   1 6 7   1 6 7
1 4 5   1 5 4
2 2 2   2 3 3   2 4 4
2 3 2   2 2 1
3 4 3   3 6 7   3 3 3
3 5 5   3 5 5
END DATA
MANOVA Y1 Y2 BY GPS(1,3)/
   CONTRAST(GPS) = HELMERT/
① PARTITION(GPS)/
② DESIGN = GPS(1),GPS(2)/
   PRINT = CELLINFO(MEANS,COV,COR)/
```

---

①In general, for k groups, the between degrees of freedom could be partitioned in various ways. If we wish all single degree of freedom contrasts, as here, then we could put PARTITION(GPS) = (1,1)/. Or, this can be abbreviated to PARTITION(GPS)/.

②This DESIGN subcommand specifies the effects we are testing for significance, in this case the two single degree of freedom multivariate contrasts. The numbers in parentheses refer to the part of the partition. Thus, GPS(1) refers to the first part of the partition (the first Helmert contrast) and GPS(2) refers to the second part of the partition, i.e., the second Helmert contrast.

the contrasts. Recall that when the data is part of the command file it is preceded by the BEGIN DATA command and the data is followed by the END DATA command.

The means, standard deviations and pooled within covariance matrix S are presented in Table 5.8. In Table 5.8 we also calculate S^{-1} which will serve as the error term for the multivariate contrasts (cf. Equation 4). Table 5.9 presents the output for the multivariate and univariate Helmert contrasts comparing the treatment groups against the control group. The multivariate contrast is significant at the .05 level ($F = 4.303, p < .042$), indicating that something is better than

TABLE 5.8
Means, Standard Deviations and Pooled Within Covariance Matrix
for Helmert Contrast Example

CELL MEANS AND STANDARD DEVIATIONS

VARIABLE ... Y1

FACTOR	CODE	MEAN	STD. DEV.
GPS	1	5.20000	.83666
GPS	2	2.80000	.83666
GPS	3	4.60000	1.14018
FOR ENTIRE SAMPLE		4.20000	1.37321

VARIABLE .. Y2

FACTOR	CODE	MEAN	STD. DEV.
GPS	1	5.80000	1.30384
GPS	2	2.40000	1.14018
GPS	3	4.60000	1.67332
FOR ENTIRE SAMPLE		4.26667	1.94447

POOLED WITHIN-CELLS VARIANCE-COVARIANCE MATRIX

	Y1	Y2
Y1	.90000	
Y2	1.15000	1.93333

DETERMINANT OF POOLED VARIANCE-COVARIANCE MATRIX .... .41750

To compute the multivariate test statistic for the contrasts we need the inverse of this covariance matrix S; compare Equation 4.

The procedure for finding the inverse of a matrix was given in section 2.5. We obtain the matrix of cofactors and then divide by the determinant. Thus, here we have

$$S^{-1} = \frac{1}{.4175}\begin{bmatrix} 1.933 & -1.15 \\ -1.15 & .9 \end{bmatrix} = \begin{bmatrix} 4.631 & -2.755 \\ -2.755 & 2.156 \end{bmatrix}$$

TABLE 5.9
Multivariate and Univariate Tests for Helmert Contrast Comparing the Control Group Against the Two Treatment Groups

EFFECT .. GPID(1)

MULTIVARIATE TESTS OF SIGNIFICANCE (S = 1, M = 0, N = 4 1/2)

TEST NAME	VALUE	APPROX. F	HYPOTH. DF	ERROR DF	SIG. OF F
PILLAIS	.43897	4.30339	2.00	11.00	.042
HOTELLINGS	.78244	4.30339	2.00	11.00	.042 ①
WILKS	.56103	4.30339	2.00	11.00	.042
ROYS	.43897				

UNIVARIATE F-TESTS WITH (1,12) D. F.

VARIABLE	HYPOTH. SS	ERROR SS	HYPOTH. MS	ERROR MS	F	SIG. OF F
Y1	7.50000	10.80000	7.50000	.90000	8.33333	.014
Y2	17.63333	23.20000	17.63333	1.93333	9.12069	.011

The univariate contrast for $Y1$ is given by $\Psi_1 = \mu_1 - (\mu_2 + \mu_3)/2$.

Using the boxed in means of Table 5.8, we obtain the following estimate for the contrast: $\hat{\Psi}_1 = 5.2 - (2.8 + 4.6)/2 = 1.5$.

Recall from Equation 2 that the hypothesis sum of squares is given by $\Psi^2/\sum_{i=1}^{k} \dfrac{c_i^2}{n_i}$. For equal group sizes, as here, this becomes $n\Psi^2/\sum_{i=1}^{k} c_i^2$. Thus,

$$\text{HYPOTH } SS = \frac{5(1.5)^2}{1^2 + (-.5)^2 + (-.5)^2} = 7.5.$$

The error term for the contrast is MS_w appears under ERROR MS and is .900. Thus, the F ratio for $Y1$ is 7.5/.90 = 8.333. Notice that both variables are significant at the .05 level.

---

① This indicates that the multivariate contrast $\Psi_1 = \mu_1 - (\mu_2 + \mu_3)/2$ is significant at the .05 level (since .042 < .05). That is, the control group differs significantly from the average of the two treatment groups on the set of two variables.

TABLE 5.10
Multivariate and Univariate Tests for Helmert Contrast Comparing the Two Treatment Groups

EFFECT .. GPID(2)

MULTIVARIATE TESTS OF SIGNIFICANCE (S = 1, M = 0, N = 4 1/2)

TEST NAME	VALUE	APPROX. F	HYPOTH. DF	ERROR DF	SIG. OF F
PILLAIS	.43003	4.14970	2.00	11.00	.045
HOTELLINGS	.75449	4.14970	2.00	11.00	① .045
WILKS	.56997	4.14970	2.00	11.00	.045
ROYS	.43003				

Recall from Table 5.8 that the inverse of pooled within covariance matrix is

$$S^{-1} = \begin{bmatrix} 4.631 & -2.755 \\ -2.755 & 2.156 \end{bmatrix}$$

Since this is a simple contrast with equal n, we can use Equation 6:

$$T^2 = \frac{n}{2}\hat{\psi}'S^{-1}\hat{\psi} = \frac{n}{2}(\bar{x}_2 - \bar{x}_3)'S^{-1}(\bar{x}_2 - \bar{x}_3) = \frac{5}{2}\left[\begin{pmatrix} 2.8 \\ 2.4 \end{pmatrix} - \begin{pmatrix} 4.6 \\ 4.6 \end{pmatrix}\right]'\begin{bmatrix} 4.631 & -2.755 \\ -2.755 & 2.156 \end{bmatrix}\begin{pmatrix} -1.8 \\ -2.2 \end{pmatrix} = 9.0535$$

To obtain the value of HOTELLING given on printout above we simply divide by error df, i.e., 9.0535/12 = .75446. To obtain the F we use Equation 5:

$$F = \frac{(n_e - p + 1)}{n_e p}T^2 = \frac{(12 - 2 + 1)}{12(2)}(9.0535) = 4.1495,$$

with degrees of freedom $p = 2$ and $(n_e - p + 1) = 11$ as given above.

UNIVARIATE F-TESTS WITH (1,12) D. F.

VARIABLE	HYPOTH. SS	ERROR SS	HYPOTH. MS	ERROR MS	F	SIG. OF F
Y1	8.10000	10.80000	8.10000	.90000	9.00000	.011
Y2	12.10000	23.20000	12.10000	1.93333	6.25862	② .028

① This multivariate test indicates that treatment groups do differ significantly at the .05 level (since .045 < .05) on the *set* of two variables.
② These results indicate that both univariate contrasts are significant at .05 level, i.e., both variables are contributing to overall multivariate significance.

217

nothing. Note also that the F's for all the multivariate tests are the *same*, since this is a single degree of freedom comparison and thus effectively a two-group comparison. The univariate results show that each of the two variables is significant at .05, and are thus contributing to overall multivariate significance. We also show in Table 5.9 how the hypothesis sum of squares is obtained for the first univariate Helmert contrast (i.e., for $Y1$).

In Table 5.10 we present the multivariate and univariate Helmert contrasts comparing the two treatment groups. As the annotation indicates, both the multivariate and univariate contrasts are significant at the .05 level. Thus, the treatment groups differ on the set of variables and both variables are contributing to multivariate significance. In Table 5.10 we also show in detail how the F value for the multivariate Helmert contrast is arrived at.

Example 2—Special Contrasts

We indicated earlier that researchers can set up their own contrasts on MANOVA. We now illustrate this for a four-group, five-dependent variable example. There are two control groups, one of which is a Hawthorne control, and two treatment groups. Three very meaningful contrasts are indicated schematically below:

	T_1 (control)	T_2 (Hawthorne)	T_3	T_4
ψ_1	−.5	−.5	.5	.5
ψ_2	0	1	−.5	−.5
ψ_3	0	0	1	−1

TABLE 5.11
SPSSX MANOVA Control Lines for Special Multivariate Contrasts

```
TITLE ' SPECIAL MULTIVARIATE CONTRASTS '
DATA LIST FREE/GPS 1 Y1 3-4 Y2 6-7(1) Y3 9-11(2)
    Y4 13-15 Y5 17-18
LIST
BEGIN DATA
1 28 13 476 215 74
. . . . . .
4 24 31 668 355 56
END DATA
MANOVA Y1 TO Y5 BY GPS(1,4)/
    CONTRAST(GPS)=SPECIAL(1 1 1 1  −.5  −.5 .5 .5
    0 1 −.5 −.5 0 0 1  −1)/
    PARTITION(GPS)/
    DESIGN = GPS(1),GPS(2),GPS(3)/
    PRINT = CELLINFO(MEAN,COV,COR)/
```

The control lines for running these contrasts on SPSSX MANOVA are presented in Table 5.11. (In this case I have just put in some data schematically and have used column input, simply to illustrate it). As indicated earlier, note that the first 4 numbers in the CONTRAST subcommand are 1's, corresponding to the number of groups. The next 4 numbers define the first contrast, where we are comparing the control groups against the treatment groups. The following 4 numbers define the second contrast, and the last 4 numbers define the third contrast.

5.10. CORRELATED CONTRASTS

The Helmert contrasts we considered in Example 1 are, for equal n, uncorrelated. This is important in terms of clarity of interpretation since significance on one Helmert contrast implies nothing about significance on a different Helmert contrast. For correlated contrasts this is not true. To determine the unique contribution a given contrast is making we need to partial out its correlations with the other contrasts. We will illustrate how this is done on MANOVA.

Correlated contrasts can arise in two ways: (1) the sum of products of the coefficients $\neq 0$ for the contrasts, and (2) the sum of products of coefficients $= 0$, but the group sizes are not equal.

Example 3—Correlated Contrasts

We consider an example with 4 groups and 2 dependent variables. The contrasts are indicated schematically below, with the group sizes in parentheses:

	T_1 & T_2 (12) combined	Hawthorne (14) control	T_1 (11)	T_2 (8)
ψ_1	0	1	-1	0
ψ_2	0	1	$-.5$	$-.5$
ψ_3	1	0	0	-1

Notice that ψ_1 and ψ_2 as well as ψ_2 and ψ_3 are correlated since the sum of products of coefficients in each case $\neq 0$. However, ψ_1 and ψ_3 are also correlated since group sizes are unequal. The data for this problem are given below.

GP 1		GP 2		GP 3		GP 4	
y1	y2	y1	y2	y1	y2	y1	y2
18	5	18	9	17	5	13	3
13	6	20	5	22	7	9	3
20	4	17	10	22	5	9	3
22	8	24	4	13	9	15	5
21	9	19	4	13	5	13	4
19	0	18	4	11	5	12	4
12	6	15	7	12	6	13	5
10	5	16	7	23	3	12	3
15	4	16	5	17	7		
15	5	14	3	18	7		
14	0	18	2	13	3		
12	6	14	4				
		19	6				
		23	2				

1. We used the default method (UNIQUE SUM OF SQUARES—as of Release 2.1). This gives the unique contribution of the contrast to between variation, i.e., each contrast is adjusted for its correlations with the other contrasts.

2. We used the SEQUENTIAL sum of squares option. This is obtained by putting the following subcommand right after the MANOVA statement:

METHOD = SSTYPE(SEQUENTIAL)/

With this option each contrast is adjusted *only* for all contrasts to the *left* of it in the DESIGN subcommand. Thus, if our DESIGN subcommand is

DESIGN = GPS(1),GPS(2),GPS(3)/

then the last contrast (denoted by GPS(3) is adjusted for all other contrasts, and the value of the multivariate test statistics for GPS(3) will be the *same* as we obtained for the default method (unique sum of squares). However, the value of the test statistics for GPS(2) and GPS(1) will differ from those obtained using unique sum of squares, since GPS(2) is only adjusted for GPS(1) and GPS(1) is not adjusted for either of the other two contrasts.

The multivariate test statistics for the contrasts using the unique decomposition are presented in Table 5.12, while the statistics for the hierarchical decomposition are given in Table 5.13. As explained earlier, the results for ψ_3 are identical for both approaches, and indicate significance at the .05 level ($F = 3.499, p < .04$). That is, the combination of treatments differs from T_2 alone. The results for the other two contrasts, however, are quite different for the two approaches. The unique breakdown indicates that ψ_2 is significant at .05 (treatments differ from Hawthorne control) and ψ_1 is not significant (T_1 is not different from Hawthorne control). The results in Table 5.12 for the hierarchical approach yield exactly the opposite conclusion! Obviously the conclusions one draws in this study would depend on which approach was used to test the contrasts for significance. We would express a preference in general for the unique approach.

TABLE 5.12

Multivariate Tests for Unique Contribution of Each Correlated Contrast to Between Variation*

EFFECT .. GPS(3)

MULTIVARIATE TESTS OF SIGNIFICANCE (S = 1, M = 0, N = 19)

TEST NAME	VALUE	APPROX. F	HYPOTH. DF	ERROR DF	SIG. OF F
PILLAIS	.14891	3.49930	2.00	40.00	.040
HOTELLINGS	.17496	3.49930	2.00	40.00	.040
WILKS	.85109	3.49930	2.00	40.00	.040
ROYS	.14891				

EFFECT .. GPS(2)

MULTIVARIATE TESTS OF SIGNIFICANCE (S = 1, M = 0, N = 19)

TEST NAME	VALUE	APPROX. F	HYPOTH. DF	ERROR DF	SIG. OF F
PILLAIS	.18228	4.45832	2.00	40.00	.018
HOTELLINGS	.22292	4.45832	2.00	40.00	.018
WILKS	.81772	4.45832	2.00	40.00	.018
ROYS	.18228				

EFFECT .. GPS(1)

MULTIVARIATE TESTS OF SIGNIFICANCE (S = 1, M = 0, N = 19)

TEST NAME	VALUE	APPROX. F	HYPOTH. DF	ERROR DF	SIG. OF F
PILLAIS	.03233	.66813	2.00	40.00	.518
HOTELLINGS	.03341	.66813	2.00	40.00	.518
WILKS	.96767	.66813	2.00	40.00	.518
ROYS	.03233				

*Each contrast is adjusted for it's correlations with the other contrasts.

TABLE 5.13
Multivariate Tests of Correlated Contrasts for Hierarchical Option of SPSSX MANOVA*

EFFECT .. GPS(3)

MULTIVARIATE TESTS OF SIGNIFICANCE (S = 1, M = 0, N = 19)

TEST NAME	VALUE	APPROX. F	HYPOTH. DF	ERROR DF	SIG. OF F
PILLAIS	.14891	3.49930	2.00	40.00	.040
HOTELLINGS	.17496	3.49930	2.00	40.00	.040
WILKS	.85109	3.49930	2.00	40.00	.040
ROYS	.14891				

EFFECT .. GPS(2)

MULTIVARIATE TESTS OF SIGNIFICANCE (S = 1, M = 0, N = 19)

TEST NAME	VALUE	APPROX. F	HYPOTH. DF	ERROR DF	SIG. OF F
PILLAIS	.10542	2.35677	2.00	40.00	.108
HOTELLINGS	.11784	2.35677	2.00	40.00	.108
WILKS	.89458	2.35677	2.00	40.00	.108
ROYS	.10542				

EFFECT .. GPS(1)

MULTIVARIATE TESTS OF SIGNIFICANTS (S = 1, M = 0, N = 19)

TEST NAME	VALUE	APPROX. F	HYPOTH. DF	ERROR DF	SIG. OF F
PILLAIS	.13641	3.15905	2.00	40.00	.053
HOTELLINGS	.15795	3.15905	2.00	40.00	.053
WILKS	.86359	3.15905	2.00	40.00	.053
ROYS	.13641				

*Each contrast is adjusted *only* for all contrasts to left of it in the DESIGN subcommand.

It should be noted that the unique contribution of each contrast can be obtained using the heirarchical approach; however, in this case three DESIGN subcommands would be required, with each of the contrasts ordered last in one of the subcommands:

DESIGN = GPS(1),GPS(2),GPS(3)/

DESIGN = GPS(2),GPS(3),GPS(1)/

DESIGN = GPS(3),GPS(1),GPS(2)/

All three orderings can be done in a single run.

5.11.   STUDIES USING MULTIVARIATE PLANNED COMPARISONS

Clifford (1972) was interested in the effect of competition as a motivational technique in the classroom. The subjects were primarily white, average I.Q., fifth graders, with about half of each sex. A two week vocabulary learning task was given under three conditions:

1. Control—a noncompetitive atmosphere in which no score comparisons among classmates were made.
2. Reward Treatment—comparisons among relatively homogeneous subjects were made and accentuated by the rewarding of candy to high scoring subjects.
3. Game Treatment—again comparisons were made among relatively homogeneous subjects and accentuated in a followup game activity. Here high scoring subjects received an advantage in a game which was played immediately after the vocabulary task was scored.

The three dependent variables were performance, interest, and retention. The retention measure was given two weeks after the completion of treatments. Clifford had the following two planned comparisons:

1. Competition is more effective than noncompetition. Thus, she was testing the following contrast for significance:

$$\psi_1 = \frac{\mu_2 + \mu_3}{2} - \mu_1$$

2. Game competition is as effective as reward with respect to performance on the dependent variables. Thus, she was predicting the following contrast would *not* be significant:

$$\psi_2 = \mu_2 - \mu_3$$

Clifford's results are presented in Table 5.14.

As predicted, competition was more effective than noncompetition for the set of three dependent variables. Estimation of the univariate results in Table 5.14 shows that the multivariate significance is primarily due to a significant difference

TABLE 5.14
Means and Multivariate and Univariate Results for Two Planned
Comparisons in Clifford Study

	df	MS	F	p
1st Planned Comparison (Control vs. Reward and Game.)				
Multivariate Test	3/61		10.04	.0001
Univariate Tests				
Performance	1/63	.54	.64	.43
Interest	1/63	4.70	29.24	.0001
Retention	1/63	4.01	.18	.67
2nd Planned Comparison (Reward vs. Game)				
Multivariate Test	3/61		.84	.47
Univariate Tests				
Performance	1/63	.002	.003	.96
Interest	1/63	.37	2.32	.13
Retention	1/63	1.47	.07	.80

	Means for the Groups		
	Control	Reward	Games
Variable			
Performance	5.72	5.92	5.90
Interest	2.41	2.63	2.57
Retention	30.85	31.55	31.19

on the interest variable. Clifford's second prediction was also confirmed, i.e., there was no difference in the relative effectiveness of reward vs. game treatments ($F = .84$, $p < .47$).

A second study involving multivariate planned comparisons was conducted by Stevens (1972). He was interested in studying the relationship between parent's educational level and eight personality characteristics of their National Merit scholar children. Part of the analysis involved the following set of orthogonal comparisons (75 subjects per group):

1. Group 1 (parents' education eight grade or less) vs. group 2 (parents' both high school graduates).
2. Groups 1 and 2 (no college) vs. groups 3 and 4 (college for both parents).
3. Group 3 (both parents attended college) vs. group 4 (both parents at least one college degree).

This set of comparisons corresponds to a very meaningful set of questions: Which differences in degree of education produce differential effects on the children's personality characteristics?

Another set of orthogonal contrasts that could have been of interest in this study looks like this schematically:

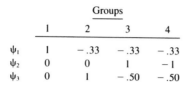

	Groups			
	1	2	3	4
ψ_1	1	−.33	−.33	−.33
ψ_2	0	0	1	−1
ψ_3	0	1	−.50	−.50

This would have resulted in a different meaningful, additive breakdown of the between association. However, one set of orthogonal contrasts does not have an empirical superiority over another (after all, they both additively partition the between association). In terms of choosing one set over the other, it is a matter of which set best answers the experimenter's research hypotheses.

5.12.   STEPDOWN ANALYSIS

We have just finished discussing one type of focused inquiry, planned comparisons, in which specific questions were asked of the data. Another type of directed inquiry in the MANOVA context, but which focuses on the dependent variables rather than the groups, is stepdown analysis. Here, based on previous research and/or theory, we are able to a priori order the dependent variables, and test in that specific order for group discrimination. As an example, let the independent variable be three teaching methods and the dependent variables be the three subtest scores on a common achievement test covering the three lowest levels in Bloom's taxonomy: knowledge, comprehension, and application. An assumption of the taxonomy is that learning at a lower level is a necessary but not sufficient condition for learning at a higher level. Because of this, there is a theoretical rationale for ordering the dependent variables in the above specified way and to test first whether the methods have had a differential effect on knowledge: Then, if so, whether the methods differentially affect comprehension, with knowledge held constant (used as a covariate) etc. Since stepdown analysis is just a series of analyses of covariance, we defer a complete discussion of it to Chapter 10, i.e., until we have covered analysis of covariance in Chapter 9.

5.13.   OTHER MULTIVARIATE TEST STATISTICS

In addition to Wilk's Λ, there are three other multivariate test statistics that are in use and are printed out on the packages:

1. Roy's largest root (eigenvalue) of $\mathbf{BW}^{-1}$
2. The Hotelling-Lawley trace, i.e., the sum of the eigenvalues of $\mathbf{BW}^{-1}$.
3. The Pillai-Bartlett trace, i.e., the sum of the eigenvalues of $\mathbf{B\ T}^{-1}$.

Notice that the Roy and Hotelling-Lawley multivariate statistics are natural generalizations of the univariate F statistic. In univariate ANOVA the test statistic is $F = MS_b/MS_w$, i.e., a measure of between- to within-association. The multivariate analogue of this is $\mathbf{BW}^{-1}$, which is a "ratio" of between- to within-association. With matrices there is no division, so we don't literally divide the between by the within as in the univariate case, however, the matrix analogue of division is inversion.

Since Wilk's Λ can be expressed as a product of eigenvalues of $\mathbf{WT}^{-1}$, *we see that all four of the multivariate test statistics are some function of an eigenvalue(s) (sum, product). Thus, eigenvalues are fundamental to the multivariate problem.* We show in Chapter 7 on discriminant analysis that there are quantities corresponding to the eigenvalues (the discriminant functions) which are linear combinations of the dependent variables and which characterize major differences among the groups.

The reader might well ask at this point, "Which of these four multivariate test statistics should be used in practice?" This is a somewhat complicated question which for full understanding requires a knowledge of discriminant analysis and of the robustness of the four statistics to the assumptions in MANOVA. Nevertheless, the following will provide guidelines for the researcher. In terms of robustness with respect to type I error for the homogeneity of covariance matrices assumption, Stevens (1979) found that *any* of the following three can be used: Pillai-Bartlett trace, Hotelling-Lawley trace, or Wilk's Λ. For subgroup variance differences likely to be encountered in social science research, these three are equally quite robust, provided the group sizes are equal or approximately equal ($\frac{\text{largest}}{\text{smallest}} < 1.5$). In terms of power, no one of the four statistics is always most powerful; which depends on how the null hypothesis is false. Importantly, however, Olson (1973) found that *power differences among the four multivariate test statistics are generally quite small* ($< .06$). So as a general rule, it won't make that much of a difference which of the statistics is used. But, if the differences among the groups are concentrated on the first discriminant function, which does occur quite often in practice (Bock, 1975, p. 154), then Roy's statistic technically would be preferred since it is most powerful. However, Roy's statistic should only be used in this case if there is evidence to suggest that the homogeneity of covariance matrices assumption is tenable. Finally, when the differences among the groups involves two or more discriminant functions, the Pillai-Bartlett trace is most powerful, although it's power advantage tends to be slight.

5.14. HOW MANY DEPENDENT VARIABLES FOR A MANOVA?

Of course, there is no simple answer to this question. However, the following considerations mitigate *generally* against the use of a large number of criterion variables:

1. If a large number of dependent variables are included without any strong rationale (empirical and/or theoretical), then small or negligible differences on most of them may obscure a real difference(s) on a few of them. That is, the multivariate test detects mainly error in the system, i.e., in the set of variables, and therefore declares no reliable overall difference.

2. The power of the multivariate tests generally declines as the number of dependent variables is increased (DasGupta & Perlman, 1973).

3. The reliability of variables can be a problem in behavioral science work. Thus, given a large number of criterion variables, it probably will be wise to combine (usually add) highly similar response measures, particularly when the basic measurements tend individually to be quite unreliable (Pruzek, 1971). As Pruzek states,

> . . . one should always consider the possibility that his variables include errors of measurement which may attentuate F ratios and generally confound interpretations of experimental effects. Especially when there are several dependent variables whose reliabilities and mutual intercorrelations vary widely, inferences based on fallible data may be quite misleading. (p. 187)

4. Based on his Monte Carlo results, Olson had some comments on the design of multivariate experiments which are worth remembering: For example, one generally will not do worse by making the dimensionality p smaller, insofar as it is under experimenter control. Variates should not be thoughtlessly included in an analysis just because the data are available. Besides aiding robustness, a small value of p is apt to facilitate interpretation. (p. 906)

5. Given a large number of variables, one should always consider the possibility that there are a much smaller number of underlying constructs which will account for most of the variance on the original set of variables. Thus, the use of principal components analysis as a preliminary data reduction scheme before the use of MANOVA should be contemplated.

5.15. POWER ANALYSIS—A PRIORI DETERMINATION OF SAMPLE SIZE

There have been several studies that have dealt with power in MANOVA (e.g., Ito, 1962; Pillai & Jayachandian, 1967; Olson, 1974; Laüter, 1978). Olson examined power for small and moderate sample size, but expressed the non-centrality parameter (which measures the extent of deviation from the null hypothesis) in terms of eigenvalues. Also, there were many gaps in his tables; no power values for 4, 5, 7, 8, and 9 variables or for 4 or 5 groups. The Laüter study is much more comprehensive, giving sample size tables for a very wide range of situations:

1. for α = .05 or .01
2. for 2, 3, 4, 5, 6, 8, 10, 15, 20, 30, 50 and 100 variables
3. for 2, 3, 4, 5, 6, 8 and 10 groups
4. for power = 70, .80, .90 and .95

His tables are specifically for the Hotelling-Lawley trace criterion, and this might seem to limit their utility. However, as Morrison (1967) has noted for large sample size, and as Olson (1974) showed for small and moderate sample size, the power differences among the four main multivariate test statistics are generally quite small. Thus, the sample size requirements for Wilk's Λ, the Pillaz-Bartlett trace and Roy's largest root will be very similar to those for the Hotelling-Lawley trace for the vast majority of situations.

Laüter's tables are set up in terms of a certain *minimum* deviation from the multivariate null hypothesis, which can be expressed in the following three forms:

There exists a variable i such that $\frac{1}{\sigma^2} \sum_{j=1}^{J} (\mu_{ij} - \mu_{i.}) \geq q^2$, where $\mu_{i.}$ is the total mean and σ^2 is variance.

There exists a variate i such that $1/\sigma_i |\mu_{ij_1} - \mu_{ij_2}| \geq d$, for two groups j_1 and j_2.

There exists a variate i such that for *all* pairs of groups 1 and m we have $1/\sigma_i |\mu_{il} - \mu_{im}| \geq c$.

In Table E at the end of this volume we present selected situations and power values which it is felt would be of most value to social science researchers: for 2, 3, 4, 5, 6, 8, 10, and 15 variables, with 3, 4, 5, and 6 groups, and for power = .70, .80 and .90. We have also characterized the four different minimum deviation patterns as very large, large, moderate, and small effect sizes. Although the characterizations may be somewhat rough, they are reasonable in the following senses. They agree with Cohen's definitions of large, medium and small effect sizes for one variable (Laüter included the univariatecase in his tables), and with Stevens (1980) definitions of large, medium and small effect sizes for the two group MANOVA case.

It is important to note that there could be several ways, other than that specified by Laüter, in which a large, moderate, or small multivariate effect size could occur. But the essential point is how many subjects will be needed for a given effect size, regardless of the combination of differences on the variables that produced the specific effect size. Thus, the tables do have broad applicability. We will consider shortly a few specific examples of the use of the tables, but first we present a compact table which should be of great interest to applied researchers:

		Groups			
		3	4	5	6
EFFECT SIZE	very large	12–16	14–18	15–19	16–21
	large	25–32	28–36	31–40	33–44
	medium	42–54	48–62	54–70	58–76
	small	92–120	105–140	120–155	130–170

This table gives the range of sample sizes needed per group for adequate power (.70) at $\alpha = .05$ when there are three to six variables.

Thus, if we expect a large effect size and have 4 groups, 28 subjects per group are needed for power $= .70$ with three variables, while 36 subjects per group are required if there were 6 dependent variables.

Now we consider two examples to illustrate the use of the Lauter sample size tables in the appendix.

Example 1

An investigator has a 4-group MANOVA with 5 dependent variables. He wishes power $= .80$ at $\alpha = .05$. From previous research and his knowledge of the nature of the treatments, he anticipates a moderate effect size. How many subjects per group will he need? Reference to Table E (for 4 groups) indicates that 70 subjects per group are required.

Example 2

A team of researchers has a 5 group, 7 dependent variable MANOVA. They wish power $= .70$ at $\alpha = .05$. From previous research they anticipate a large effect size. How many subjects per group are needed? Interpolating in Table E (for 5 groups) between 6 and 8 variables, we see that 43 subjects per group are needed, or a total of 215 subjects.

5.16.   SUMMARY

Cohen's (1968) seminal article showed social science researchers that univariate ANOVA could be considered as a special case of regression, by dummy coding group membership. In this chapter we have pointed out that MANOVA can also be considered as a special case of regression analysis, except that for MANOVA it is multivariate regression since there are several dependent variables being predicted from the dummy variables. That is, separation of the mean vectors is equivalent to demonstrating that the dummy variables (predictors) significantly predict the scores on the dependent variables.

For exploratory research, three post hoc procedures were given for determining which of the groups and/or variables are responsible for an overall difference. One procedure used Hotelling T^2's to determine the significant pairwise multivariate differences, and then univariate t's to determine which of the variables are contributing to the significant pairwise multivariate differences. The second procedure also used Hotelling T^2's, but then used the Tukey intervals to determine which variables were contributing to the significant pairwise multivariate differences. The third post hoc procedure, the Roy-Bose multivariate confidence interval approach (the generalization of the univariate Scheffe' intervals) was discussed and rejected. It was rejected because the power for detecting differences with this approach is quite poor, especially for small or moderate sample size.

For confirmatory research, planned comparisons were discussed. The setup of multivariate contrasts on SPSSX MANOVA was illustrated. Although uncorrelated contrasts are very desirable because of ease of interpretation and the nice additive partitioning they yield, it was noted that often the important questions an investigator has will yield correlated contrasts. The use of SPSSX MANOVA to obtain the unique contribution of each correlated contrast was illustrated.

It was noted that the Roy and Hotelling-Lawley statistics are natural generalizations of the univariate F ratio. In terms of which of the four multivariate test statistics to use in practice, two criteria can be used: robustness and power. Wilk's Λ, the Pillai-Bartlett trace, and Hotelling-Lawley statistics are equally robust (for equal or approximately equal group sizes) with respect to the homogeneity of covariance matrices assumption, and therefore anyone of them can be used. The power differences among the four statistics are in general quite small ($< .06$), so that there is no strong basis for preferring anyone of them over the others on power considerations.

The important problem, in terms of experimental planning, of a priori determination of sample size was considered for 3-, 4-, 5- and 6-group MANOVA for the number of dependent variables ranging from 2 to 15.

APPENDIX

NOVINCE (1977) DATA FOR MULTIVARIATE ANALYSIS OF VARIANCE PRESENTED IN TABLES 5.3 & 5.4

DATA

Behavioral Rehearsal

ANX	SOCSKLS	APPROP	ASSERT
5.	3.	3.	3.
5.	4.	4.	3.
4.	5.	4.	4.
4.	5.	5.	4.
3.	5.	5.	5.
4.	5.	4.	4.
4.	5.	5.	5.
4.	4.	4.	4.
5.	4.	4.	3.
5.	4.	4.	3.
4.	4.	4.	4.

Control Group

ANX	SOCSKLS	APPROP	ASSERT
6.	2.	1.	1.
6.	2.	2.	2.
5.	2.	3.	3.
6.	2.	2.	2.
4.	4.	4.	4.
7.	1.	1.	1.
5.	4.	3.	3.
5.	2.	3.	3.
5.	3.	3.	3.
5.	4.	3.	3.
6.	2.	3.	3.

Behavioral Rehearsal + Cognitive Restructuring

ANX	SOCSKLS	APPROP	ASSERT
4.	4.	4.	4.
4.	3.	4.	3.
4.	4.	4.	4.
4.	5.	5.	5.
4.	5.	5.	5.
4.	4.	4.	4.
4.	5.	4.	4.
4.	6.	6.	5.
4.	4.	4.	4.
5.	3.	3.	3.
4.	4.	4.	4.

EXERCISES—CHAPTER 5

1. Consider the following data for a three group, three dependent variable problem:

	Gp 1			Gp 2			Gp 3	
y_1	y_2	y_3	y_1	y_2	y_3	y_1	y_2	y_3
2.0	2.5	2.5	1.5	3.5	2.5	1.0	2.0	1.0
1.5	2.0	1.5	1.0	4.5	2.5	1.0	2.0	1.5
2.0	3.0	2.5	3.0	3.0	3.0	1.5	1.0	1.0
2.5	4.0	3.0	4.5	4.5	4.5	2.0	2.5	2.0
1.0	2.0	1.0	1.5	4.5	3.5	2.0	3.0	2.5
1.5	3.5	2.5	2.5	4.0	3.0	2.5	3.0	2.5
4.0	3.0	3.0	3.0	4.0	3.5	2.0	2.5	2.5
3.0	4.0	3.5	4.0	5.0	5.0	1.0	1.0	1.0
3.5	3.5	3.5				1.0	1.5	1.5
1.0	1.0	1.0				2.0	3.5	2.5
1.0	2.5	2.0						

Run the one-way MANOVA on SPSSX.

a) What is the multivariate null hypothesis? Do you reject it at $\alpha = .05$?

b) If you reject in part (a), then which pairs of groups are significantly different in a multivariate sense at the .05 level?

c) For the significant pairs, which of the individual variables are contributing (at .01 level) to the multivariate signficiance?

2. Consider the following data from Wilkinson (1975):

Group A			Group B			Group C		
5	6	4	2	2	7	4	3	4
6	7	5	3	3	5	6	7	5
6	7	3	4	4	6	3	3	5
4	5	5	3	2	4	5	5	5
5	4	2	2	1	4	5	5	4

a) Run a one-way MANOVA on SPSSX. Do the various multivariate test statistics agree in a decision on H_0?

b) Below are the multivariate (Roy-Bose) and univariate (Scheffe') 95% simultaneous confidence intervals for the 3 variables for the 3 paired comparisons.

Contrast	Variable	Multivariate Intervals	Univariate Intervals
A–B	1	$-.1 \leq 2.4 \leq 4.9$	$.7 \leq 2.4 \leq 4.1$
	2	$-.3 \leq 3.4 \leq 7.1$	$.9 \leq 3.4 \leq 5.6$
	3	$-4.4 \leq -1.4 \leq 1.6$	$-3.4 \leq -1.4 \leq .6$
A–C	1	$-1.9 \leq .6 \leq 3.1$	$-1.1 \leq .6 \leq 2.3$
	2	$-2.5 \leq 1.2 \leq 4.9$	$-1.3 \leq 1.2 \leq 3.7$
	3	$-3.8 \leq -.8 \leq 2.2$	$-2.8 \leq -.8 \leq 1.2$
B–C	1	$-4.3 \leq -1.8 \leq .7$	$-3.5 \leq -1.8 \leq -.1$
	2	$-5.9 \leq -2.2 \leq 1.5$	$-4.7 \leq -2.2 \leq .3$
	3	$-2.4 \leq .6 \leq 3.6$	$-1.4 \leq .6 \leq 2.6$

Note: Estimates of the contrasts are given at the center of the inequalities.

Comment on the multivariate intervals relative to the decision reached by the test statistics on H_0. Why is the situation different for the univariate intervals?

3.   Skilbeck et al. (1984) examined differences among black, Hispanic and white applicants for outpatient therapy, using symptoms reported on the Symptom Checklist 90-revised. They report the following results, having done 12 univariate ANOVAS.

SCL 90-R Ethnicity Main Effects

	Group					
	Black $N = 48$	Hispanic $N = 60$	White $N = 57$			
Dimension	$\bar{x}$	$\bar{x}$	$\bar{x}$	F	df	Significance
Somatization	53.7	53.2	53.7	.03	2,141	ns
Obsessive-Compulsive	48.7	53.9	52.2	2.75	2,141	ns
Interpersonal Sensitivity	47.3	51.3	52.9	4.84	2,141	$p < .01$
Depression	47.5	53.5	53.9	5.44	2,141	$p < .01$
Anxiety	48.5	52.9	52.2	1.86	2,141	ns
Hostility	48.1	54.6	52.4	3.82	2,141	$p < .03$
Phobic Anxiety	49.8	54.2	51.8	2.08	2,141	ns
Paranoid Ideation	51.4	54.7	54.0	1.38	2,141	ns
Psychoticism	52.4	54.6	54.2	.37	2,141	ns
Global Severity Index	49.7	54.4	54.0	2.55	2,141	ns
Positive Symptom Distress Index	49.3	55.8	53.2	3.39	2,141	$p < .04$
Positive Symptom Total	50.2	52.9	54.4	1.96	2,141	ns

a) Could we be confident that these results would replicate? Explain.
b) Check the article to see if the authors a priori hypothesized differences on the specific variables for which significance was found.
c) What would have been a better method of analysis?

4.   A researcher is testing the efficacy of 4 drugs in inhibiting undesirable responses in mental patients. Drugs A and B are similar in composition, whereas drugs C and D are distinctly different in composition than A and B, although similar in their basic ingredients. He takes 100 patients and randomly assigns them to 5 gps: gp 1—control, gp 2—drug A, gp 3—drug B, gp 4—drug C, and gp 5—drug D. The following would be 4 very relevant planned comparisons to test:

		Control	Drug A	Drug B	Drug C	Drug D
	1	1	−.25	−.25	−.25	−.25
Contrasts	2	0	1	1	−1	−1
	3	0	1	−1	0	0
	4	0	0	0	1	−1

a) Show that these contrasts are orthogonal.

Now, consider the following set of contrasts, which might also be of interest in the above study:

		Control	Drug A	Drug B	Drug C	Drug D
	1	1	−.25	−.25	−.25	−.25
Contrasts	2	1	−.50	−.50	0	0
	3	1	0	0	−.5	−.5
	4	0	1	1	−1	−1

b) Show that these contrasts are not orthogonal.

c) Since neither of the above 2 sets of contrasts are one of the standard sets that come out of SPSSX MANOVA, it would be necessary to use the special contrast feature to test each set. Show the control lines for doing this for each set. Assume 4 criterion measures.

5.   Consider the following three-group MANOVA with two dependent variables. Run the MANOVA on SPSSX. Is it significant at the .05 level? Examine the univariate F's at the .05 level. Are any of them significant? How would you explain this situation?

Gp 1		Gp 2		Gp 3	
y_1	y_2	y_1	y_2	y_1	y_2
3	7	4	5	5	5
4	7	4	6	6	5
5	8	5	7	6	6
5	9	6	7	7	7
6	10	6	8	7	8

6.   Consider the following data from a two-group MANOVA with five dependent variables. Run the MANOVA. Is it significant at the .05 level? Examine the

univariate F's at the .01 level? Are any of them significant? How would you explain this situation?

		Variables		
1.0000	7.0000	10.0000	10.0000	17.0000
1.0000	6.0000	7.0000	6.0000	14.0000
5.0000	3.0000	13.0000	12.0000	20.0000
7.0000	3.0000	5.0000	6.0000	18.0000
1.0000	1.0000	7.0000	6.0000	18.0006
10.0000	13.0000	15.0000	17.0000	10.0000
12.0000	13.0000	18.0000	12.0000	13.0000
9.0000	13.0000	18.0000	14.0000	10.0000
10.0000	10.0000	18.0000	13.0000	8.0000
6.0000	6.0000	11.0000	13.0000	16.0000

Gp 1 corresponds to the first five rows, Gp 2 to the last five rows.

7. Show that the within sums of squares and cross products matrices (SSCP) for the sample problem at the beginning of the chapter are

$$\mathbf{W}_2 = \begin{bmatrix} 2 & -1 \\ -1 & 2 \end{bmatrix} \text{ and } \mathbf{W}_3 = \begin{bmatrix} 6.8 & 2.6 \\ 2.6 & 5.2 \end{bmatrix}$$

8. We have a five-group MANOVA and wish to show through dummy coding of group membership that a multivariate regression analysis will yield the same multivariate F's. Fill in the table below schematically to indicate what the coding would be

		x_1	x_2	x_3	x_4
Group 1	s_1				
	s_{n_1}				
Group 2	s_1				
	s_{n_2}				
Group 3	$\mathbf{s}_1$				
	$\mathbf{s}_{n_3}$				
Group 4	s_1				
	s_{n_4}				
Group 5	s_1				
	s_{n_5}				

9. An extremely important assumption underlying both univariate and multivariate ANOVA is independence of the observations. If this assumption is violated, even to a small degree, it causes the actual α to be several times greater than the level of significance, as you will see in the next chapter. If one suspects dependent observations, as would be the case in studies involving teaching methods, then one might consider using the classroom mean as the unit of analysis. If there are several classes for each method or condition, then you want the software package to compute the means for your dependent variables from the raw data for each method. In a recent dissertation there were a total of 64 classes and about 1200 subjects, with 10 variables. Fortunately, SPSSX has a procedure called AGGRE-GATE (*SPSSX USER'S GUIDE,* 1988, Chapter 18) which computes the mean across a group of cases and produces a new file containing one case for each group.

To illustrate AGGREGATE in a somewhat simpler, but similar context, suppose we are comparing three teaching methods and have 6 classes for method 1, 7 for method 2, and 5 for method 3. There are two dependent variables (denote them by ACH1, ACH2). The AGGREGATE control lines would be:

```
TITLE 'COMBINING SCORES IN CLASSES AND USING GP MEANS'
DATA LIST FREE/METHOD CLASS ACH1 ACH2
BEGIN DATA
      data lines
END DATA
AGGREGATE OUTFILE = */
  BREAK = METHOD CLASS/
  COUNT = N/
  AVACH1  AVACH2 = MEAN(ACH1,ACH2)/
LIST
MANOVA AVACH1,AVACH2 BY METHOD(1,3)/
  PRINT = CELLINFO(MEANS)/
```

The MANOVA indicated above will be done on the classroom means for the 2 variables. That is, there will be 6 observations for method 1, 7 observations for method 2, and 5 for method 3.

a) Read Chapter 18 in the *SPSSX USER'S GUIDE 1988*) and explain the above control language, especially starting with AGGREGATE and ending with AVACH1 AVACH2 = MEAN(ACH1,ACH2)/.

b) Create a small set of data, using 5 or less observations per class, and run the above program to show that it works. Note that the printout states, "A new (aggregated) active file has replaced the existing active file."

6 Assumptions in MANOVA

6.1 INTRODUCTION

The reader may recall that one of the assumptions in analysis of variance is normality; that is, the scores for the subjects in each group are normally distributed. Why should we be interested in studying assumptions in ANOVA and MANOVA? Because in ANOVA and MANOVA, we set up a mathematical model based on these assumptions, and all mathematical models are approximations to reality. Therefore, violations of the assumptions are inevitable. The salient question becomes, How radically must a given assumption be violated before it has a serious effect on Type I and Type II error rates? Thus, we may set our $\alpha = .05$ and think we are rejecting falsely 5% of the time, but if a given assumption is violated, may be rejecting falsely 10%, or if another assumption is violated, may be rejecting falsely 40% of the time. For these kinds of situations, we would certainly want to be able to detect such violations and take some corrective action, but all violations of assumptions are not serious, and hence it is crucial to know *which* assumptions to be particularly concerned about, and under what conditions.

In this chapter, I consider in detail what effect violating assumptions has on Type I error and power. There has been a very substantial amount of research on violations of assumptions in ANOVA and a fair amount of research for MANOVA on which to base our conclusions. First, I remind the reader of some basic terminology that is needed in order to discuss the results of simulation (i.e., Monte Carlo) studies, whether univariate or multivariate. The nominal α (level of significance) is the α level set by the experimenter, and is the percent of time one is rejecting falsely when *all* assumptions are met. The *actual* α is the percent of time one is rejecting falsely if one or more of the assumptions is violated. We say the *F* statistic is *robust* when the actual α is very close to the level of significance (nominal α). For example, the actual αs for some very skewed (non-normal) populations were only .055 or .06, very minor deviations from the level of significance of .05.

6.2   ANOVA AND MANOVA ASSUMPTIONS

The three assumptions for univariate ANOVA are:

1. The observations are independent.
   (violation very serious)
2. The observations are normally distributed on the dependent variable in each group.
   (robust with respect to Type I error)
   (skewness has very little effect on power, while platykurtosis attenuates power)
3. The population variances for the groups are equal, often referred to as the *homogeneity of variance* assumption.
   (conditionally robust — robust if group sizes are equal or approximately equal — largest/smallest < 1.5)

The assumptions for MANOVA are as follows:

1. The observations are independent.
   (violation very serious)
2. The observations on the dependent variables follow a multivariate normal distribution in each group.
   (robust with respect to Type I error)
   (no studies on effect of skewness on power, but platykurtosis attenuates power)
3. The population covariance matrices for the *p* dependent variables are equal.
   (conditionally robust — robust if the group sizes are equal or approximately equal — largest/smallest < 1.5)

6.3   INDEPENDENCE ASSUMPTION

Note that independence of observations is an assumption for both ANOVA and MANOVA. I have listed this assumption first and as emphasizing it for three reasons:

1. A violation of this assumption is *very* serious.
2. Dependent observations do occur fairly often in social science research.
3. Many statistics books do not mention this assumption, and in some cases where they do, misleading statements are made (e.g., that dependent observations occur only infrequently, that random assignment of subjects to groups will eliminate the problem, or that this assumption is usually satisfied by using a random sample).

Now let us consider several situations in social science research where dependence among the observations will be present. Cooperative learning has become very popular since the early 1980s. In this method, students work in small groups, interacting with each other and helping each other learn the lesson. In fact, the evaluation of the success of the group is dependent on the individual success of its members. Many studies have compared cooperative learning versus individualistic learning. A review of such studies in the "best" journals since 1980 found that about 80% of the analyses were done incorrectly (Hykle, Stevens, & Markle, 1993). That is, the investigators used the subject as the unit of analysis, when the very nature of cooperative learning implies dependence of the subjects' scores within each group.

Teaching methods studies constitute another broad class of situations where dependence of observations is undoubtedly present. For example, a few troublemakers in a classroom would have a detrimental effect on the achievement of many children in the classroom. Thus, their posttest achievement would be at least partially dependent on the disruptive classroom atmosphere. On the other hand, even with a good classroom atmosphere, dependence is introduced, for the achievement of many of the children will be enhanced by the positive learning situation. Therefore, in either case (positive or negative classroom atmosphere), the achievement of each child is not independent of the other children in the classroom.

Another situation I came across in which dependence among the observations was present involved a study comparing the achievement of students working in pairs at microcomputers versus students working in groups of three. Here, if Bill and John are working at the same microcomputer, then obviously Bill's achievement is partially influenced by John. The proper unit of analysis in this study is the *mean* achievement for each pair or triplet of students, as it is plausible to assume that the achievement of students working one micro is independent of that of students working at others.

Glass and Hopkins (1984) made the following statement concerning situations where independence may or may not be tenable, "Whenever the treatment is individually administered, observations are independent. But where treatments involve interaction among persons, such as discussion method or group counseling, the observations may influence each other" (p. 353).

Effect of Correlated Observations

I indicated earlier that a violation of the independence of observations assumption is very serious. I now elaborate on this assertion. Just a *small* amount of dependence among the observations causes the actual α to be several times greater than the level of significance. Dependence among the observations is measured by the intraclass correlation R, where:

$$R = (MS_b - MS_w/(MS_b + (n - 1)MS_y)$$

M_b and MS_w are the numerator and denominator of the F statistic and n is the number of subjects in each group.

Table 6.1, from Scariano and Davenport (1987), shows precisely how dramatic an effect dependence has on Type I error. For example, for the three-group case with 10 subjects per group and moderate dependence (intraclass correlation = .30) the actual α is .5379! Also, for three groups with 30 subjects per group and small dependence (intraclass correlation = .10) the actual α is .4917, almost 10 times the level of significance! Notice, also, from the table that for a fixed value of the intraclass correlation, the situation does not improve with larger sample size, but gets far worse.

TABLE 6.1
Actual Type I Error Rates for Correlated Observations
in a One-Way ANOVA

no. gps	gp size	\multicolumn{9}{c}{intraclass correlation}								
		.00	.01	.10	.30	.50	.70	.90	.95	.99
2	3	.0500	.0522	.0740	.1402	.2374	.3819	.6275	.7339	.8800
	10	.0500	.0606	.1654	.3729	.5344	.6752	.8282	.8809	.9475
	30	.0500	.0848	.3402	.5928	.7205	.8131	.9036	.9335	.9708
	100	.0500	.1658	.5716	.7662	.8446	.8976	.9477	.9640	.9842
3	3	.0500	.0529	.0837	.1866	.3430	.5585	.8367	.9163	.9829
	10	.0500	.0641	.2227	.5379	.7397	.8718	.9639	.9826	.9966
	30	.0500	.0985	.4917	.7999	.9049	.9573	.9886	.9946	.9990
	100	.0500	.2236	.7791	.9333	.9705	.9872	.9966	.9984	.9997
5	3	.0500	.0540	.0997	.2684	.5149	.7808	.9704	.9923	.9997
	10	.0500	.0692	.3151	.7446	.9175	.9798	.9984	.9996	1.0000
	30	.0500	.1192	.6908	.9506	.9888	.9977	.9998	1.0000	1.0000
	100	.0500	.3147	.9397	.9945	.9989	.9998	1.0000	1.0000	1.0000
10	3	.0500	.0560	.1323	.4396	.7837	.9664	.9997	1.0000	1.0000
	10	.0500	.0783	.4945	.9439	.9957	.9998	1.0000	1.0000	1.0000
	30	.0500	.1594	.9119	.9986	1.0000	1.0000	1.0000	1.0000	1.0000
	100	.0500	.4892	.9978	1.0000	1.0000	1.0000	1.0000	1.0000	1.0000

6.4 WHAT SHOULD BE DONE WITH CORRELATED OBSERVATIONS?

Given the results in Table 6.1 for a positive intraclass correlation, one route investigators should seriously consider if they suspect that the nature of their study will lead to correlated observations is to test at a more stringent level of significance. For the three- and five-group cases in Table 6.1 with 10 observations per group and intraclass correlation $= .10$, the error rates are 5 to 6 times greater than the assumed level of significance of .05. Thus, for this type of situation, it would be wise to test at $\alpha = .01$, realizing that the actual error rate will be about .05 or somewhat greater. For the three- and five-group cases in Table 6.1 with 30 observations per group and intraclass correlation $= .10$, the error rates are about 10 times greater than .05. Here, it would be advisable to either test at .01, realizing that the actual α will be about .10 or test at an even more stringent α level.

If several small groups (counseling, social interaction, etc.) are involved in each treatment, and there are clear reasons to suspect that observations will be correlated within the groups but uncorrelated across groups, then consider using the *group mean* as the unit of analysis. Of course, this will reduce the effective sample size considerably; however, this will not cause as drastic a drop in power as some have feared. The reason is that the means are much more stable than individual observations and, hence, the within-group variability will be far less.

Table 6.2, from Barcikowski (1981), shows that if the effect size is medium or large, then the number of groups needed per treatment for power .80 doesn't have to be that large. For example, at $\alpha = .10$, intraclass correlation $= .10$, and medium effect size, 10 groups (of 10 subjects each) are needed per treatment. For power .70 (which I consider adequate) at $\alpha = .15$, one probably could get by with about six groups of 10 per treatment. This is a rough estimate, because it involves double extrapolation.

Before we leave the topic of correlated observations, I wish to mention an interesting paper by Kenny and Judd (1986), who discussed how noninde-pendent observations can arise because of several factors, grouping being one of them. The following quote from their paper is important to keep in mind for applied researchers:

Throughout this article we have treated nonindependence as a statistical nuisance, to be avoided because of the bias it introduces. . . . There are, however, many occasions when nonindependence is the substantive problem that we are trying to understand in psychological research. For instance, in developmental psychology, a frequently asked question concerns the development of social interaction. Developmental researchers study the content and rate of vocalization from infants for cues about the onset of interaction.

TABLE 6.2
Number of Groups per Treatment Necessary for Power > .80 in a Two
Treatment Level Design

		Intraclass Correlation					
		.10			.20		
Effect Size		.20	.50	.80	.20	.50	.80[a]
α level	Number per group						
	10	73	13	6	107	18	8
	15	62	11	5	97	17	8
	20	56	10	5	92	16	7
.05	25	53	10	5	89	16	7
	30	51	9	5	87	15	7
	35	49	9	5	86	15	7
	40	48	9	5	85	15	7
	10	57	10	5	83	14	7
	15	48	9	4	76	13	6
	20	44	8	4	72	13	6
.10	25	41	8	4	69	12	6
	30	39	7	4	68	12	6
	35	38	7	4	67	12	5
	40	37	7	4	66	12	5

[a].20—small effect size
.50—medium effect size
.80—large effect size

Social interaction implies nonindependence between the vocalizations of interacting individuals. To study interaction developmentally, then, we should be interested in nonindependence not solely as a statistical problem, but also a substantive focus in itself. . . . In social psychology, one of the fundamental questions concerns how individual behavior is modified by group contexts. (p. 431)

6.5 NORMALITY ASSUMPTION

Recall that the second assumption for ANOVA is that the observations are normally distributed in each group. What are the consequences of violating this assumption? An excellent review regarding violations of assumptions in ANOVA was done by Glass, Peckham, and Sanders (1972), and provides the answer. They found that skewness has only a slight effect (generally only a few hundredths) on level of significance or power. The effects of kurtosis on level of significance, although greater, also tend to be slight.

The reader may be puzzled as to how this can be. The basic reason is the *Central Limit Theorem*, which states that the sum of independent observations having any distribution whatsoever approaches a normal distribution as the number of observations increases. To be somewhat more specific, Bock (1975) noted, "even for distributions which depart markedly from normality, sums of 50 or more observations approximate to normality. For moderately non- normal distributions the approximation is good with as few as 10 to 20 observations" (p. 111). Because the sums of independent observations approach normality rapidly, so do the means, and the sampling distribution of F is based on means. Thus, the sampling distribution of F is only slightly affected, and therefore the critical values when sampling from normal and non-normal distributions will not differ by much.

With respect to power, a platykurtic distribution (a flattened distribution relative to the normal distribution) does attenuate power.

6.6 MULTIVARIATE NORMALITY

The multivariate normality assumption is a much more stringent assumption than the corresponding assumption of normality on a single variable in ANOVA. Although it is difficult to completely characterize multivariate normality, *normality on each of the variables separately is a necessary, but not sufficient, condition for multivariate normality to hold.* That is, each of the individual variables must be normally distributed for the variables to follow a multivariate normal distribution. Two other properties of a multivariate normal distribution are: (a) any linear combination of the variables are normally distributed, and (b) all subsets of the set of variables have multivariate normal distributions. This latter property implies, among other things, that all pairs of variables must be bivariate normal. Bivariate normality, for correlated variables, implies that the scatterplots for each pair of variables will be elliptical; the higher the correlation, the thinner the ellipse. Thus, as a partial check on multivariate normality, one could obtain the scatterplots for pairs of variables from SPSSX or SAS and see if they are approximately elliptical.

Effect of Nonmultivariate Normality on Type I Error and Power

Results from various studies that considered up to 10 variables and small or moderate sample sizes (Everitt, 1979; Hopkins & Clay, 1963; Mardia, 1971; Olson, 1973) indicate that *deviation from multivariate normality has only a small effect on Type I error.* In almost all cases in these studies, the actual α was within .02 of the level of significance for levels of .05 and .10.

Olson found, however, that platykurtosis does have an effect on power, and the severity of the effect increases as platykurtosis spreads from one to all groups. For example, in one specific instance, power was close to 1 under no violation. With kurtosis present in just one group, the power dropped to about .90. When kurtosis was present in all three groups, the power dropped substantially, to .55.

The reader should note that what has been found in MANOVA is consistent with what had been found in univariate ANOVA, in which the F statistic was robust with respect to Type I error against non-normality, making it plausible that this robustness might extend to the multivariate case; this, indeed, is what has been found. Incidentally, there is a multivariate extension of the Central Limit Theorem, which also makes the multivariate results not entirely surprising. Second, Olson's result, that platykurtosis has a substantial effect on power, should not be surprising, given that platykurtosis had been shown in univariate ANOVA to have a substantial effect on power for small ns (Glass et al., 1972).

With respect to skewness, again the Glass et al. (1972) review indicates that distortions of power values are rarely greater than a few hundredths for univariate ANOVA, even with considerably skewed distributions. Thus, it could well be the case that multivariate skewness also has a negligible effect on power, although I have not located any studies bearing on this issue.

Assessing Multivariate Normality

Unfortunately, as was true in 1986, a statistical test for multivariate normality is still not available on SAS, SPSSX, or BMDP. There are empirical and graphical techniques for checking multivariate normality (Gnanedesikan, 1977, pp. 168–175), but they tend to be difficult to implement unless some special-purpose software is used. I included a graphical test for multivariate normality in the first two editions of this text, but have decided not to do so in this edition. One of my reasons is that you can get a pretty good idea as to whether multivariate normality is roughly plausible by seeing whether the marginal distributions are normal and by checking bivariate normality.

6.7   ASSESSING UNIVARIATE NORMALITY

There are three reasons that assessing univariate normality is of interest:

1. We may not have a large enough n to feel comfortable doing the graphical test for multivariate normality.

2. As Gnanadesikan (1977) has stated, "In practice, except for rare or pathological examples, the presence of joint (multivariate) normality is likely to be detected quite often by methods directed at studying the

marginal (univariate) normality of the observations on each variable (p. 168)." Johnson and Wichern (1988) made essentially the same point: "Moreover, for most practical work, one-dimensional and two-dimensional investigations are ordinarily sufficient. Fortunately, pathological data sets that are normal in lower dimensional representations but nonnormal in higher dimensions are not frequently encountered in practice (p. 153)."

3. Because the Box test for the homogeneity of covariance matrices assumption is quite sensitive to non-normality, we wish to detect non-normality on the individual variables and transform to normality to bring the joint distribution much closer to multivariate normality so that the Box test is not unduly affected. With respect to transformations, Fig. 6.1 should be quite helpful.

There are many tests, graphical and nongraphical, for assessing univariate normality. One of the most popular graphical tests is the normal probability plot, where the observations are arranged in increasing order of magnitude and then plotted against expected normal distribution values. The plot should resemble a straight line if normality is tenable. These plots are available on SAS and SPSSX. One could also examine the histogram (or stem and leaf plot) of the variable in each group. This gives some indication of whether normality might be violated. However, with small or moderate sample sizes, it is difficult to tell whether the non-normality is real or apparent, because of considerable sampling error. Therefore, I prefer a nongraphical test.

Among the nongraphical tests are the chi-square goodness of fit, Kolmogorov–Smirnov, the Shapiro–Wilk test, and the use of skewness and kurtosis coefficients. The chi-square test suffers from the defect of depending on the number of intervals used for the grouping, whereas the Kolmogorov–Smirnov test was shown not to be as powerful as the Shapiro–Wilk test or the combination of using the skewness and kurtosis coefficients in an extensive Monte Carlo study by Wilk, Shapiro, and Chen (1968). These investigators studied 44 different distributions, with sample sizes ranging from 10 to 50, and found that the combination of skewness and kurtosis coefficients and the Shapiro–Wilk test were the most powerful in detecting departures from normality. They also found that extreme non-normality can be detected with sample sizes of less than 20 by using sensitive procedures (like the two just mentioned). This is important, because for many practical problems, the group sizes are quite small.

On power considerations then, we use the Shapiro–Wilk statistic. This is easily obtained with the EXAMINE procedure in SPSSX. This procedure also yields the skewness and kurtosis coefficients, along with their standard errors. All of this information is useful in determining whether there is a significant departure from normality, and whether skewness or kurtosis is primarily responsible.

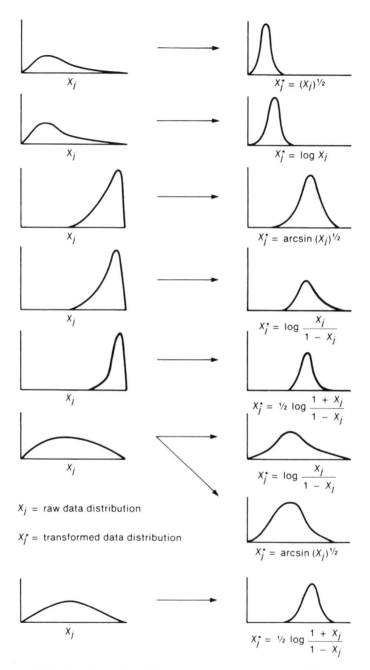

X_j = raw data distribution

X_j^* = transformed data distribution

FIG. 6.1. Distributional Transformations (from Rummel, 1970).

Example 1

Our example comes from a study on the cost of transporting milk from farms to dairy plants. From a survey, cost data on $X1$ - fuel, $X2$ - repair, and $X3$ - capital (all measures on a per mile basis) were obtained for two types of trucks, gasoline and diesel. Thus, we have a two-group MANOVA, with three dependent variables. First, we ran this data through the SPSSX DESCRIPTIVES program. The complete lines for doing so are presented in Table 6.3. This was done to obtain the z scores for the variables *within each group*. Converting to z scores makes it much easier to identify potential outliers. Any variables with z values substantially greater than 2 (in absolute value) need to be examined carefully. Three such observations are marked with an arrow in Table 3.

Next, the data was run through the SPSSX EXAMINE procedure to obtain, among other things, the Shapiro–Wilk statistical test for normality for each variable in each group. The complete lines for doing this are presented in Table 6.4. These are the results for the three variables in each group:

	STATISTIC	SIGNIFICANCE
VARIABLE X1		
GROUP 1		
SHAPIRO-WILK	.8411	.0100
GROUP 2		
SHAPIRO-WILK	.9625	.5105
VARIABLE X2		
GROUP1		
SHAPIRO-WILK	.9578	.3045
GROUP 2		
SHAPIRO-WILK	.9620	.4995
VARIABLE X3		
GROUP 1		
SHAPIRO-WILK	.9653	.4244
GROUP 2		
SHAPIRO-WILK	.9686	.6392

If we were testing for normality in each case at the .05 level, then only variable $X1$ deviates from normality in just Group 1. This would not have much of an effect on power, and hence we would not be concerned. We would have been concerned if we had found deviation from normality on two or more variables, and this deviation was due to platykurtosis, and would then have applied the last transformation in Fig. 6.1: $.05 \log (1 + X)/(1 - X)$.

TABLE 6.3

Control Lines for SPSSX Descriptives and Z Scores for Three Variables
in Two-Group MANOVA

TITLE 'Z SCORES FOR TWO GROUP MANOVA'
DATA LIST FREE/GP X1 X2 X3
BEGIN DATA
  DATA LINES
SELECT IF (GP = 1)
DESCRIPTIVES VARIABLES = X1 X2 X3/
①   SAVE/
LIST

To obtain the z scores for Group 2, a separate run was made, replacing SELECT IF
(GP = 1) with SELECT IF (GP = 2).

① This SAVE subcommand is needed to obtain the z scores for all variables specified on the
DESCRIPTIVES variable list. The new variable names are created by prefixing the letter z to
the original variable name.

	Group 1 (Gasoline trucks)			Group 2 (Diesel trucks)		
$Z \times 1$	$Z \times 2$	$Z \times 3$	$Z \times 1$	$Z \times 2$	$Z \times 3$
.87996	1.03078	.43881	− .76876	.29459	− 1.32610
− 1.04823	− 1.29221	− 1.51743	− 1.28585	− 1.10773	− .14901
− ..47915	− 1.61451	.04274	.08348	− 1.46372	− 1.01573
− 1.66317	− .55687	− .48445	.02602	.77842	− 1.78289
− .21233	− .73116	.28895	1.28523	− 1.29655	1.62687
.42345	− .55687	.07753	− .24210	.38506	− 1.04940
.26711	.68460	.27021	− 1.74070	− .36822	.12183
.22959	1.47007	− .03754	.59578	− .15974	− .53259
→ 3.52108	1.66584	− 1.68871	− .45755	− 1.53846	− .65704
.09618	− .11997	.17120	− .19422	− 1.12150	.39122
− .98153	− .55210	− .39079	− .16071	1.39600	2.49065
− .48332	− 1.07017	− .12318	.72026	.19429	− .17097
− .41036	− .72638	.15514	− .48628	.48930	.36486
− .23109	− .46854	− .52995	− .75440	− .12237	− .10509
− .01013	1.46769	1.28446	− .86931	− .89335	− .26175
− .41245	− 1.31847	− .93672	→ 2.77425	.42047	.13501
− .42496	− .49241	.68234	.87826	− .99759	− .49746
− .69595	− 1.29221	.70642	− .27083	1.18162	.65767
.02530	− .09132	.55923	.15529	1.35469	− 1.-0019
− .77307	1.41039	.64755	.36596	2.11585	1.50828
→ 2.90614	2.22689	1.95349	− 1.42470	.48340	.18625
.15246	.03044	− .64502	.84953	.27886	.44392
.98211	1.25520	2.14082	.92135	− .30331	.72063
.51726	.63685	1.33531			
− .39577	− .70489	1.98293			
− .67510	− .86485	− 1.42645			
− .52501	.83024	− .73868			
.10452	.12355	− 1.07052			
− .56879	− 1.42113	− .89925			
− .83353	− .03880	− .76812			
.30880	.74190	− 1.25250			
− .83561	.41482	− .38008			
.75906	.78965	.92854			
− .63341	.25486	− .02684			
.05657	− .82188	.62881			
1.06340	− .29903	− 1.37828			

TABLE 6.4
Control Lines for EXAMINE Procedure on Two-Group MANOVA

TITLE ' TWO GROUP MANOVA - 3 DEPENDENT VARIABLES '
DATA LIST FREE/GP X1 X21 X3
LIST
BEGIN DATA
1 16.44 12.43 11.23   1 7.19 2.70 3.92   1 9.92 1.35 9.75
1 4.24 5.78 7.78   1 11.20 5.05 10.67   1 14.25 5.78 9.88
1 13.50 10.98 10.60   1 13.32 14.27 9.45   1 29.11 15.09 3.28
1 12.68 7.61 10.23   1 7.51 5.80 8.13   1 9.90 3.63 9.13
1 10.25 5.07 10.17   1 11.11 6.15 7.61   1 12.17 14.26 14.39
1 10.24 2.59 6.09   1 10.18 6.05 12.14   1 8.88 2.70 12.23
1 12.34 7.73 11.68   1 8.51 14.02 12.01   1 26.16 17.44 16.89
1 12.95 8.24 7.18   1 16.93 13.37 17.59   1 14.70 10.78 14.58
1 10.32 5.16 17.00   1 8.98 4.49 4.26   1 9.70 11.59 6.83
1 12.72 8.63 5.59   1 9.49 2.16 6.23   1 8.22 7.95 6.72
1 13.70 11.22 4.91   1 8.21 9.85 8.17   1 15.86 11.42 13.06
1 9.18 9.18 9.49   1 12.49 4.67 11.94   1 17.32 6.86 4.44
2 8.50 12.26 9.11   2 7.42 5.13 17.15   2 10.28 3.32 11.23
2 10.16 14.72 5.99   2 12.79 4.17 29.28   2 9.60 12.72 11.00
2 9.70 5.06 20.84   2 9.77 17.86 35.18   2 11.61 11.75 17.00
2 9.09 13.25 20.66   2 8.53 10.14 17.45   2 8.29 6.22 16.38
2 15.90 12.90 19.09   2 11.94 5.69 14.77   2 9.54 16.77 22.66
2 10.43 17.65 10.66   2 10.87 21.52 28.47   2 7.13 13.22 19.44
2 11.88 12.18 21.20   2 12.03 9.22 23.09
END DATA
① EXAMINE VARIABLES = X1 X2 X3 BY GP/
②   PLOT = STEMLEAF NPPLOT/

---

① The BY keyword will yield variety of descriptive statistics for each group: mean, median, skewness, kurtosis, etc.

② STEMLEAF will yield a stem and leaf plot for each variable in each group. NPPLOT yields normal probability plots, as well as the Shapiro–Wilks and Kolmogorov–Smirnov statistical tests for normality for each variable in each group.

6.8 HOMOGENEITY OF VARIANCE ASSUMPTION

Recall that the third assumption for ANOVA is that of equal population variances. Glass, Peckham, and Sanders' (1972) review indicates that the F statistic is robust against heterogeneous variances when the group sizes are equal. I would extend this a bit further. As long as the group sizes are approximately equal (largest/smallest 1.5), F is robust. On the other hand, when the group sizes are sharply unequal *and* the population variances are different, then if the large sample variances are associated with the small group sizes, the F statistic is *liberal*. A statistic's being liberal means we are rejecting falsely too often; that is, actual α > level of significance. Thus, the experimenter may think he or she is rejecting falsely 5% of the time, but the true rejection rate (actual α) may be 11%. When the large variances are associated with the large group sizes, then the F statistic is *conservative*. This means actual α < level of significance. Many researchers would not consider this serious, but note that the smaller α will cause a decrease in power, and in many studies, one can ill afford to have the power further attenuated.

It is important to note that many of the frequently used tests for homogeneity of variance, such as Bartlett's, Cochran's, and Hartley's F_{max}, are quite sensitive to non-normality. That is, with these tests one may reject and erroneously conclude that the population variances are different when, in fact, the rejection was due to non-normality in the underlying populations. Fortunately, Leven has a test that is more robust against non-normality. This test is available in the EXAMINE procedure in SPSSX. The test statistic is formed by deviating the scores for the subjects in each group from the group mean, and then taking the absolute values. Thus, $z_{ij} = |x_{ij} - \bar{x}_j|$, where $\bar{x}_j$ representsthe mean for the jth group. An ANOVA is then done on the $\bar{z}_{ij}$s. Although the Levene test is somewhatmore robust, an extensive Monte Carlo study by Conover, Johnson and Johnson (1981) showed that if considerable skewness is present, a modification of the Levene test is necessary for it to remain robust. The mean for each group is replaced by the median, and an ANOVA is done on the deviation scores from the group medians. This modification produces a more robust test with good power. It is surprising (and disappointing) that none of the major packages have incorporated this version of the Levene test into their systems.

6.9   HOMOGENEITY OF THE COVARIANCE MATRICES

The assumption of equal (homogeneous) covariance matrices is a very restrictive one. Recall from the matrix algebra chapter (Chapter 2) that two matrices are equal only if all corresponding elements are equal. Let us consider a two-group problem with five dependent variables. All corresponding elements in the two matrices being equal implies, first, that the corresponding diagonal elements are equal. This means that the five population variances in Group 1 are equal to their counterparts in Group 2. But all nondiagonal elements must also be equal for the matrices to be equal, and this implies that all covariances are equal. Because for five variables there are 10 covariances, this means that the 10 covariances in Group 1 are equal to their counterpart covariances in Group 2. Thus, for only five variables, the equal covariance matrices assumption requires that 15 elements of Group 1 be equal to their counterparts in Group 2.

For eight variables, the assumption implies that the eight population variances in Group 1 are equal to their counterparts in Group 2 *and* that the 28 corresponding covariances for the two groups are equal. The restrictiveness of the assumption becomes more strikingly apparent when we realize that the corresponding assumption for the univariate *t* test is that the variances on only *one* variable be equal.

Hence, it is very unlikely that the equal covariance matrices assumption would ever literally be satisfied in practice. The relevant question is, Will the very plausible violations of this assumption that occur in practice have much of an effect on power?

Effect of Heterogeneous Covariance Matrices on Type I Error and Power

Three major Monte Carlo studies have examined the effect of unequal covariance matrices on error rates: Holloway and Dunn (1967) and Hakstian, Roed, and Linn (1979) for the two- group case, and Olson (1974) for the k-group case. Holloway and Dunn considered both equal and unequal group sizes, and modeled moderate to extreme heterogeneity. A representative sampling of their results, presented in Table 6.5, shows that *equal ns keep the actual α very close to the level of significance (within a few percentage points) for all but the extreme cases.* Sharply unequal group sizes for moderate inequality, with the larger variability in the small group produces a liberal test. As a matter of fact, the test can become very liberal (cf. three variables, $N_1 = 35$, $N_2 = 15$, actual $\alpha = .175$). Larger variability in the group with the large size produces a conservative test.

Hakstian et al. modeled heterogeneity that was milder and, I believe, somewhat more representative of what is encountered in practice, than that considered in the Holloway and Dunn study. They also considered more disparate group sizes (up to a ratio of 5 to 1) for the 2-, 6-, and 10-variable cases. The following three heterogeneity conditions were examined:

1. The population variances for the variables in Population 2 are only 1.44 times as great as those for the variables in Population 1.
2. The Population 2 variances and covariances are 2.25 times as great as those for all variables in Population 1.
3. The Population 2 variances and covariances are 2.25 times as great as those for Population 1 for only *half* the variables.

TABLE 6.5
Effect of Heterogeneous Covariance Matrices on Type I Error for
Hotelling's T^2 (Data from Holloway & Dunn, 1967)   ①

Number of Variables	Number of Observations per Group			Degree of Heterogeneity	
	N_1	N_2 ②	③	$D = 3$ (Moderate)	$D = 10$ (Very Large)
3	15	35		.015	0
3	20	30		.03	.02
3	25	25		.055	.07
3	30	20		.09	.15
3	35	15		.175	.28
7	15	35		.01	0
7	20	30		.03	.02
7	25	25		.06	.08
7	30	20		.13	.27
7	35	15		.24	.40
10	15	35		.01	0
10	20	30		.03	.03
10	25	25		.08	.12
10	30	20		.17	.33
10	35	15		.31	.40

①Nominal α = .05.
②Group 2 is more variable.
③D = 3 means that the population variances for all variables in Group 2 are 3 times as large as the population variances for those variables in Group 1.

The results in Table 6.6 for the six-variable case are representative of what Hakstian et al. found. Their results are consistent with the Holloway and Dunn findings, but they extend them in two ways. First, even for milder heterogeneity, sharply unequal group sizes can produce sizable distortions in the Type I error rate (cf. 24:12, Heterogeneity 2 (negative): actual α = .127 vs. level of significance = .05). Second, *severely unequal group sizes can produce sizable distortions in Type I error rates, even for very mild heterogeneity* (cf. 30:6, Heterogeneity 1 (negative): actual α = .117 vs. level of significance = .05).

Olson (1974) considered only equal ns and warned, on the basis of the Holloway and Dunn results and some preliminary findings of his own, that researchers would be well advised to strain to attain equal group sizes in the k-group case. The results of Olson's study should be interpreted with care, because he modeled primarily *extreme* heterogeneity (i.e., cases where the population variances of all variables in one group were 36 times as great as the variances of those variables in all the other groups).

TABLE 6.6
Effect of Heterogeneous Covariance Matrices with Six Variables on Type I
Error for Hotelling's T^2 (Data from Hakstian, Roed, & Lind, 1979)

$N_1{:}N_2$①	Nominal α	Heterog. 1		Heterog. 2		Heterog. 3	
		②POS.	NEG.	POS.	NEG.	POS.	NEG.③
18:18	.01		.006		.011		.012
	.05		.048		.057		.064
	.10		.099		.109		.114
24:12	.01	.007	.020	.005	.043	.006	.018
	.05	.035	.088	.021	.127	.028	.076
	.10	.068	.155	.051	.214	.072	.158
30:6	.01	.004	.036	.000	.103	.003	.046
	.05	.018	.117	.004	.249	.022	.145
	.10	.045	.202	.012	.358	.046	.231

①Ratio of the group sizes.
②Condition in which group with larger generalized variance has larger group size.
③Condition in which group with larger generalized variance has smaller group size.

Testing Homogeneity of Covariance Matrices: The Box Test

Box (1949) has developed a test, which is a generalization of the Bartlett univariate homogeneity of variance test, for determining whether the covariance matrices are equal. The test uses the *generalized variances,* that is, the determinants of the within-covariance matrices. It is very sensitive to non- normality. Thus, one may reject with the Box test because of a lack of multivariate normality, not because the covariance matrices are unequal. Therefore, before employing the Box test, it is important to see whether the multivariate normality assumption is reasonable. As suggested earlier in this chapter, a check of marginal normality for the individual variables is probably sufficient (using the Shapiro–Wilk test). Where there is a departure from normality, find transformations (see Fig. 6.1).

Box has given a χ^2 approximation and an F approximation for his test statistic, both of which appear on the SPSSX MANOVA output, as an upcoming example in this section shows. To decide which of these one should pay more attention to, the following rule is helpful: When all group sizes are 20 and the number of dependent variables is 6, the χ^2 approximation is fine. Otherwise, the F approximation is more accurate and should be used.

Example 2

To illustrate the use of SPSSX MANOVA for assessing homogeneity of the covariance matrices, I consider, again, the data from Example 1. Recall that this involved two types of trucks (gasoline and diesel), with measurements on three variables: $X1$ - fuel, $X2$ - repair, and $X3$ - capital. The raw data are provided in Table 6.4. Recall that there were 36 gasoline trucks and 23 diesel trucks, so we have sharply unequal group sizes. Thus, a significant Box test here will produce biased multivariate statistics that we need to worry about.

The complete control lines for running the MANOVA, along with getting the Box test and some selected printout, are presented in Table 6.7. It is in the PRINT subcommand that we obtain the multivariate (Box test) and univariate tests of homogeneity of variance. Note, in Table 6.7 (center), that the Box test is significant well beyond the .01 level ($F = 5.088$, $p = .000$, approximately). We wish to determine whether the multivariate test statistics will be liberal or conservative. To do this, we examine the determinants of the covariance matrices (they are called variance–covariance matrices on the printout). Remember that the determinant of the covariance matrix is the generalized variance; that is, it is the multivariate measure of within-group variability for a set of variables. In this case, the larger generalized variance (the determinant of the covariance matrix) is in Group 2, which has the smaller group size. The effect of this is to produce positively biased (liberal) multivariate test statistics. Also, although this is not presented in Table 6.7, the group effect is quite significant ($F = 16.375$, $p = .000$, approximately). It is possible, however, that this significant group effect may be mainly due to the positive bias present.

To see whether this is the case, we look for variance stabilizing transformations that, hopefully, will make the Box test not significant, and then check to see whether the group effect is still significant. Note, in Table 6.7, that the Cochran tests indicate there are significant variance differences for $X1$ and $X3$.

The EXAMINE procedure was also run, and indicated that the following new variables will have approximately equal variances: $NEWX1 = X1^{**}$ (-1.678) and $NEWX3 = X3^{**}$ (.395). When these new variables, along with $X2$, were run in a MANOVA (see Table 6.8), the Box test was *not* significant at the .05 level ($F = 1.79$, $p = .097$), but the group effect was still significant well beyond the .01 level ($F = 13.785$, $p = .000$ approximately).

We now consider two variations of this result. In the first, a violation would not be of concern. If the Box test had been significant and the larger generalized variance was with the larger group size, then the multivariate statistics would be conservative. In that case, we would not be concerned, for we would have found significance at an even more stringent level had the assumption been satisfied.

A second variation on the example results that would have been of concern is if the large generalized variance was with the large group size and

TABLE 6.7
SPSSX MANOVA and EXAMINE Control Lines for Milk Data and Selected
Printout

TITLE ' MILK DATA - 2 GROUP MANOVA '
DATA LIST FREE/GP X1 X2 X3
LIST
BEGIN DATA

     DATA LINES

END DATA
MANOVA X1 X2 X3 BY GP(1,2)/
  PRINT = CELLINFO(MEANS) HOMOGENEITY(BOXM,COCHRAN)/
EXAMINE VARIABLES = X1 X2 X3 BY GP(1,2)/
  ①PLOT = SPREADLEVEL/

①This SPREADLEVEL statement yields what power transformation of the variable will
  give approximately equal variances. It will also give Levene's test, based on the original
  data, if no transformation is specified and on the transformed data if a transformation is
  done.

Cell Number . . 1
Determinant of Variance-Covariance matrix = 3172.91372
LOG(Determinant) =   8.06241

Cell Number . . 2
Determinant of Variance-Covariance matrix = 4860.00584
LOG(Determinant) =   8.48879

Determinant of pooled Variance-Covariance matrix
  6619.45043
LOG(Determinant) =   8.79777

Multivariate test for Homogeneity of Dispersion matrices
Box M =   32.53507
F WITH (6,14625) DF =   5.08849, p = .000 (Approx.)
Chi-Square with 6 DF =   30.54428, p = .000 (Approx.)

Univariate Homogeneity of Variance Tests
Variable . . X1

		Levene Statistic	
Cochrans C(29,2) =	.84065, p = .000		
Bartlett-Box F(1,8463) =	14.94860, p = .000	5.0708	Significance .0282

Variable . . X2
Cochrans C(29,2) =   .59571, p = .302
  Bartlett-Box F(1,8463) =   1.01993, p = .313
  Variable . . X3
  Cochrans C(29,2) =   .76965, p = .002
  Bartlett-Box F(1,8463) =   9.97794, p = .002

Table 6.8
SPSSX MANOVA and Examine Control Lines for Milk Data Using Two
Transformed Variables and Selected Printout

TITLE ' MILK DATA - VARIABLES X1 AND X3 TRANSFORMED '
DATA LIST FREE/GP X1 X2 X3
LIST
BEGIN DATA

    DATA LINES

END DATA
COMPUTE NEWX1 = X1**(-1.678)
COMPUTE NEWX3 = X3**.395
MANOVA NEWX1 X2 NEWX3 by GP(1,2)/
   PRINT = CELLINFO(MEANS) HOMOGENEITY(BOXM,COCHRAN)/
EXAMINE VARIABLES = NEWX1 X2 NEWX3 BY GP/
  PLOT = SPREADLEVEL/

Multivariate test for Homogeneity of Dispersion matrices

Boxs M =   11.44292
F WITH (6,14625) DF =   1.78967,   P = .097 (Approx.)
Chi-Square with 6 DF =   10.74274,   P = .097 (Approx.)

EFFECT . . GP
Multivariate Tests of Significance (S = 1, M = 1.2, N = 26 1/2)

Test Name	Value	Exact F	Hypoth. DF	Error DF	Sig. of F
Pillais	.42920	13.78512	3.00	55.00	.000
Hotellings	.75192	13.78512	3.00	55.00	.000
Wilks	.57080	13.78512	3.00	55.00	.000
Roys	.42920				

Note . . F statistics are exact.

Univariate Homogeneity of Variance Tests

Variable . . NEWX1
  Cochrans C(29,2) =   .76043, p = .003
  Bartlett-Box F (1,8463) =   7.77032, p = .005

Dependent Variable: NEWX1

Test of homogeneity of variance		df1	df2	Significance
Levene Statistic	1.0079	1	57	.3196

Dependent variable: NEWX3

Test of homogeneity of variance		df1	df2	Significance
Levene Statistics	.4510	1	57	.5046

This printout from the EXAMINE procedure shows that the homogeneity of
variance assumption is tenable for both transformed variables. We would
expect this, because the transformations produce approximately equal
sample variances.

---

the group effect was *not* significant. Then, it wouldn't be clear whether the reason we did not find significance was because of the conservativeness of the test statistic. In this case, we could simply test at a more liberal level, once again realizing that the effective alpha level will probably be around .05. Or, we could again seek variance stabilizing transformations.

With respect to transformations, there are two possible approaches. If there is a known relationship between the means and variances, then the following two transformations are helpful. The square root transformation, where the original scores are replaced by $\sqrt{y_{ij}}$ will stabilize the variances if the mans and variances are proportional for each group. This can happen when the data are in the form of frequency counts. If the scores are proportions, then the means and variances are related as follows: $\sigma_i^2 = \mu_i(1 - \mu_i)$. This is true because, with proportions, we have a binomial variable, and for a binominal variable the variance is this function of its mean. The arc sine transformation, where the original scores are replaced by arc sin $\sqrt{y_{ij}}$ will also stabilize the variances in this case.

If the relationship between the means and the variances is not known, then one can let the data decide on an appropriate transformation (as in the previous example).

We now consider an example that illustrates the first approach, that of using a *known* relationship between the means and variances to stabilize the variances.

Example 3

	Group 1			Group 2				Group 3			
Y1	Y2	Y1	Y2	Y1	Y2	Y1	Y2	Y1	Y2	Y1	Y2
.30	5	3.5	4.0	5	4	9	5	14	5	18	8
1.1	4	4.3	7.0	5	4	11	6	9	10	21	2
5.1	8	1.9	7.0	12	6	5	3	20	2	12	2
1.9	6	2.7	4.0	8	3	10	4	16	6	15	4
4.3	4	5.9	7.0	13	4	7	2	23	9	12	5
MEANS	$Y1 = 3.1$		$Y2 = 5.6$	$Y1 = 8.5$		$Y2 = 4$		$Y1 = 16$		$Y2 = 5.3$	
VARIANCES	3.31		2.49	8.94		1.78		20		8.68	

Notice that for Y1, as the means increase (from Group 1 to Group 3) the variances also increase. Also, the ratio of variance to mean is approximately the same for the three groups: $3.31/3.1 = 1.068$, $8.94/8.5 = 1.052$, and $20/16 = 1.25$. Further, the variances for Y2 differ by a fair amount. Thus, it is likely here that the homogeneity of covariance matrices assumption is not tenable. Indeed, when the MANOVA was run on SPSSX, the Box test was significant at the .05 level ($F = 2.947$, p .007), and the Cochran univariate tests for both variables were also significant at the .05 level (Y1: Cochran $= .62$; Y2: Cochran $= .67$).

Because the means and variances for *Y1* are approximately proportional, as mentioned earlier, a square root transformation will stabilize the variances. The control lines for running SPSSX MANOVA, with the square root transformation on *Y1*, are given in Table 6.9, along with selected printout. A few comments on the control lines: It is in the COMPUTE command that we do the transformation, calling the transformed variable *RTY1*. We then use the transformed variable *RTY1*, along with *Y2*, in the

6.9
SPSSX Control Lines for Three Group MANOVA with Unequal Variances
(Illustrating Square Root Transformation)

```
TITLE 'THREE GROUP MANOVA—TRANSFORMATION ON Y1'
DATA LIST FREE/GPID,Y1,Y2
BEGIN DATA

      DATA

END DATA
COMPUTE RTY1=SQRT(Y1)
LIST
MANOVA RTY1 Y2 BY GPID(1,3)/
  PRINT=CELLINFO(MEANS,COV,COR) HOMOGENEITY(COCHRAN,BOXM)/
```

CELL MEANS AND STANDARD DEVIATIONS
VARIABLE ... RTY 1

FACTOR	CODE	MEAN	STD.DEV.
GPID	1	1.67019	.58732
GPID	2	2.87309	.52210
GPID	3	3.96360	.56750
FOR ENTIRE SAMPLE		2.83563	1.09507

VARIABLE .. Y2

FACTOR	CODE	MEAN	STD.DEV.
GPID	1	5.60000	1.57762
GPID	2	4.00000	1.33333
GPID	3	5.30000	2.94581
FOR ENTIRE SAMPLE		4.96667	2.12511

UNIVARIATE HOMOGENEITY OF VARIANCE TESTS

VARIABLE .. RTY1
    COCHRANS C(9.3) =   .36712
    BARTLETT—BOX F(2.1640) =   .06176   p = .940

VARIABLE .. Y2
    COCHRANS C(9.3.) =   .67039
    BARTLETT—BOX F(2.1640) =   3.17413.   p = .042
BOXS M =   12.47224
F WITH (6.18158) DF =   1.85561   p = .064 (APPROX.)
CHI SQUARE WITH 6 DF =   11.13777   p = .064 (APPROX.)

MANOVA command for the analysis. Note the stabilizing effect of the square root transformation on $Y1$; the standard deviations are now approximately equal (.587, .522, and .567). Also, Box's test is no longer significant ($F = 1.86$, p .084).

6.10   GENERAL PROCEDURE FOR ASSESSING VIOLATIONS IN MANOVA

We have considered each of the assumptions in MANOVA in some detail individually. I now tie together these pieces of information into an overall strategy for assessing assumptions in a practical problem.

1. Check to determine whether it is reasonable to assume the subjects are responding independently; a violation of this assumption is very serious. Logically, from the context in which the subjects are receiving treatments, one should be able to make a judgment. Empirically, the intraclass correlation can be used (for a single variable) to assess whether this assumption is tenable.

There are at least four types of analyses that are appropriate for correlated observations. If several groups are involved for each treatment condition, then consider using the group mean as the unit of analysis. Another method, which is probably preferable to using the group mean, is to do a hierarchical linear model analysis. The power of these models is that they are statistically correct for situations in which individual scores are not independent observations, and one doesn't waste the information about individuals (which occurs when group or class is the unit of analysis). An in-depth explanation of these models can be found in *Hierarchical Linear Models* (Bryk & Raudenbush, 1992).

Two other methods that are appropriate were developed and validated by Myers, Dicecco, and Lorch (1981). They are presented in the textbook, *Research Design and Statistical Analysis* by Myers and Well (1991). They were shown to have approximately correct Type I error rates and similar power (see Exercise 9).

2. Check to see whether multivriate normality is reasonable. In this regard, checking the marginal (univariate) normality for each variable should be adequate. The EXAMINE procedure from SPSSX is very helpful here. If departure from normality is found, consider transforming the variable(s). Figure 6.1 can be helpful here. The following comment from Johnson and Wichern (1988) should be kept in mind: "Deviations from normality are often due to one or more unusual observations (outliers)" (p. 163). Thus, once again, we see the importance of screening the data initially, converting to z scores, and checking for outliers.

3. Apply Box's test to check the assumption of homogeneity of the covariance matrices. If normality has been achieved in Step 2 on all or most of the variables, then Box's test should be a fairly clean test of variance differences. If the Box test is not significant, then all is fine.

4. If the Box test is significant with equal ns, then, although the Type I error rate will be only slightly affected, power will be attenuated to some extent. Hence, look for transformations on the variables that are causing the covariance matrices to differ.

5. If the Box test is significant with sharply unequal ns for two groups, then compare the determinants of S_1 and S_2 (the generalized variances for the two groups). If the larger generalized variance is with the smaller group size, then T^2 will be liberal. If the larger generalized variance is with the larger group size, then T^2 will be conservative.

6. For the k-group case, if the Box test is significant, examine the $|S_i|$ for the groups. If the generalized variances are largest for the groups with the smaller sample sizes, then the multivariate statistics will be liberal. If the generalized variances are largest for the groups with the larger group sizes, then the statistics will be conservative.

It is possible for the k-group case that neither of these two conditions hold. For example, for three groups, it could happen that the two groups with the smallest and the largest sample sizes have large generalized variances, and the remaining group has a variance somewhat smaller. In this case, however, the effect of heterogeneity should not be serious, because coexisting the liberal and conservative tendencies should cancel each other out somewhat.

Finally, because there are several test statistics in the k-group MANOVA case, the relative robustness of them in the presence of violations of assumptions could be a criterion for preferring one over the others. In this regard, Olson (1976) argued in favor of the Pillai–Bartlett trace, because of its presumed greater robustness against heterogeneous covariances matrices. For variance differences *likely to occur in practice,* however, Stevens (1979) found that the Pillai–Bartlett trace, Wilks's λ, and the Hotelling–Lawley trace are essentially equally robust.

7 Discriminant Analysis

7.1. INTRODUCTION

Discriminant analysis is used for two purposes: (1) describing major differences among the groups in MANOVA, and (2) classifying subjects into groups on the basis of a battery of measurements. Since this text is heavily focused on multivariate tests of group differences, more space is devoted in this chapter to what is called by some descriptive discriminant analysis. We also discuss the use of discriminant analysis for classifying subjects, limiting our attention to the two-group case. The SPSSX package is used for the descriptive discriminant example, and SAS DISCRIM is used for the classification problem. We also illustrate how to use BMDP7M for randomly splitting the sample and cross-validating the classification function.

An excellent, current, and very thorough book on discriminant analysis is by Huberty (1994). He distinguishes between predictive and descriptive discriminant analysis. In predictive discriminant analysis the focus is on classifying subjects into one of several groups, whereas in descriptive discriminant analysis the focus is on revealing major differences among the groups. The major differences are revealed through the discriminant functions. One nice feature of the book is that Huberty describes several "exemplary applications" for each type of discriminant analysis, along with numerous additional applications in chapters 12 and 18. Another nice feature is that there are 5 special purpose programs, along with 4 real data sets, on a 3.5 inch diskette that is included in the text.

7.2. DESCRIPTIVE DISCRIMINANT ANALYSIS

Discriminant analysis is used here to break down the total between association in MANOVA into *additive* pieces, through the use of uncorrelated linear combinations of the original variables (these are the discriminant functions). An additive breakdown is obtained because the discriminant functions are derived to be uncorrelated.

Discriminant analysis has two very nice features: (1) parsimony of description, and (2) clarity of interpretation. It can be quite parsimonious in that in comparing 5 groups on say 10 variables, we may find that the groups differ mainly on only two major dimensions, i.e., the discriminant functions. It has a clarity of interpretation in the sense that separation of the groups along one function is unrelated to separation along a different function. This is all fine, *provided* we can meaningfully name the discriminant functions and that there is adequate sample size so that the results are generalizable.

Recall that in multiple regression we found the linear combination of the predictors that was maximally correlated with the dependent variable. Here in discriminant analysis linear combinations are again used to distinguish the groups. Continuing through the text, it becomes clear that linear combinations are central to many forms of multivariate analysis.

An example of the use of discriminant analysis, which is discussed in complete detail later in this chapter, involved National Merit scholars who were classified in terms of their parents education, from eighth grade or less up to one or more college degrees, yielding four groups. The dependent variables were eight Vocational Personality variables (realistic, conventional, enterprising, sociability, etc.). The major personality differences among the scholars were revealed in one linear combination of variables (the first discriminant function), and showed that the two groups of scholars whose parents had more education were less conventional and more enterprising than the scholars whose parents had less education.

Before we begin a detailed discussion of discriminant analysis, it is important to note that discriminant analysis is a *mathematical maximization* procedure. What is being maximized is made clear shortly. The important thing to keep in mind is that anytime this type of procedure is employed there is a tremendous opportunity for capitalization on chance, especially if the number of subjects is *not large* relative to the number of variables. That is, the results found on one sample may well not replicate on another independent sample. Multiple regression, it will be recalled, was another example of a mathematical maximization procedure. Since discriminant analysis is formally equivalent to multiple regression for two groups (Stevens, 1972), we might expect a similar problem with replicability of results. And indeed, as we see later, this is the case.

If the dependent variables are denoted by $y_1, y_2, \ldots, y_p$, then in discriminant analysis the row vector of coefficients $\mathbf{a}_1'$ is sought which maximizes $\mathbf{a}_1'\mathbf{B}\,\mathbf{a}_1/\mathbf{a}_1'\mathbf{W}\,\mathbf{a}_1$, where $\mathbf{B}$ and $\mathbf{W}$ are the between and the within sum of squares and cross-products matrices. The linear combination of the dependent variables involving the elements of $\mathbf{a}_1'$ as coefficients is the best discriminant function, in that it provides for maximum separation on the groups. Note that both the numerator and denominator in the above quotient are both scalars (numbers). Thus, the procedure finds the linear combination of the dependent variables which maximizes between to within association. The above quotient corresponds to the largest eigenvalue (ϕ_1) of the $\mathbf{BW}^{-1}$ matrix. The next best discriminant, corresponding to the second largest eigenvalue of $\mathbf{BW}^{-1}$, call it ϕ_2, involves the elements of $\mathbf{a}_2'$ in the following ratio: $\mathbf{a}_2'\mathbf{Ba}_2/\mathbf{a}_2'\mathbf{Wa}_2$, as coefficients. This function is derived to be *uncorrelated* with the first discriminant function. It is the next best discriminator among the groups, in terms of separating on them. The third discriminant function would be a linear combination of the dependent variables, derived to be uncorrelated from both the first and second functions, which provides the next maximum amount of separation, etc. The ith discriminant function (z_i) then is given by $z_i = \mathbf{a}_i'\mathbf{y}$, where $\mathbf{y}$ is the column vector of dependent variables.

If k is the number of groups and p is the number of dependent variables, then the number of possible discriminant functions is the minimum of p and $(k - 1)$. Thus, if there were 4 groups and 10 dependent variables, there would be 3 discriminant functions. For 2 groups, no matter how many dependent variables, there will only be one discriminant function. Finally, in obtaining the discriminant functions the coefficients (the a_i) are scaled so that $\mathbf{a}_i'\,\mathbf{a}_i = 1$ for each discriminant function (the so called unit norm condition). This is done so that there is a unique solution for each discriminant function.

7.3. SIGNIFICANCE TESTS

First, it can be shown that Wilk's Λ may be expressed as the following function of eigenvalues (ϕ_i) of $\mathbf{BW}^{-1}$ (Tatsuoka, 1971, p. 164):

$$\Lambda = \frac{1}{1 + \phi_1} \frac{1}{1 + \phi_2} \cdots \frac{1}{1 + \phi_r},$$

where r is the number of possible discriminant functions.

Now, Bartlett showed that the following V statistic can be used for testing the significance of Λ:

$$V = [N - 1 - (p + k)/2] \cdot \sum_{i=1}^{r} \ln(1 + \phi_i),$$

where V is approximately distributed as a χ^2 with $p(k - 1)$ degrees of freedom.

The test procedure for determining how many of the discriminant functions are significant is a residual procedure. First, all of the eigenvalues (roots) are tested together, using the above V statistic. If this is significant, then the largest root (corresponding to the first discriminant function) is removed and a test made of the remaining roots (the first residual) to determine if this is significant. If the first residual (V_1) is not significant, then we conclude that only the first discriminant function is significant. If the first residual is significant, then we examine the second residual, i.e., the V statistic with the largest two roots removed. If the second residual is not significant, then we conclude that only the first two discriminant functions are significant, etc. In general then, when the residual after removing the first s roots is not significant, we conclude that only the first s discriminant functions are significant.

We illustrate this residual test procedure below, also giving the degrees of freedom for each test, for the case of four possible discriminant functions. The constant term, i.e., the term in brackets, is denoted by C for the sake of conciseness.

Residual Test Procedure For Four Possible Discriminant Functions

Name	Test Statistic	df
V	$C \sum_{i=1}^{4} \ln (1 + \phi_i)$	$p(k - 1)$
V_1	$C[\ln (1 + \phi_2) + \ln (1 + \phi_3) + \ln (1 + \phi_4)]$	$(p - 1)(k - 2)$
V_2	$C[\ln (1 + \phi_3) + \ln (1 + \phi_4)]$	$(p - 2)(k - 3)$
V_3	$C[\ln (1 + \phi_4)]$	$(p - 3)(k - 4)$

The general formula for the degrees of freedom for the rth residual is $(p - r)(k - (r + 1))$.

7.4. INTERPRETING THE DISCRIMINANT FUNCTIONS

There are two methods that are in use for interpreting the discriminant functions:

1. Examine the standardized coefficients—these are obtained by multiplying the raw coefficient for each variable by the standard deviation for that variable.
2. Examine the discriminant function—variable correlations, i.e., the correlations between each discriminant function and each of the original variables.

For both of these methods it is the largest (in absolute value) coefficients or correlations that are used for interpretation. It should be noted that the above two methods can give different results, i.e., some variables may have low coefficients and high correlations while other variables may have high coefficients and low correlations. This raises the question of which to use.

Meredith (1964), Porebski (1966) and Darlington, Weinberg, and Walberg (1973) have argued in favor of using the discriminant function—variable correlations for two reasons: (1) the assumed greater stability of the correlations in small- or medium-sized samples, especially when there are high or fairly high intercorrelations among the variables, and (2) the correlations give a direct indication of which variables are most closely aligned with the unobserved trait which the canonical variate (discriminant function) represents. On the other hand, the coefficients are partial coefficients, with the effects of the other variables removed.

Incidentally, the use of discriminant function–variable correlations for interpretation is parallel to what is done in factor analysis, where factor–variable correlations (the so called factor loadings) are used to interpret the factors.

Two Monte Carlo studies (Barcikowski & Stevens, 1975; Huberty, 1975) indicate that unless sample size is large, relative to the number of variables, both the standardized coefficients and the correlations are very unstable. That is, the results obtained in one sample (e.g., interpreting the first discriminant function using variables 3 and 5) will very likely not hold up in another sample from the same population. *The clear implication of both studies is that unless the N (total sample size)/ p (number of variables) ratio is quite large, say 20 to 1, one should be very cautious in interpreting the results.* This is saying, for example, that if there are 10 variables in a discriminant analysis, at least 200 subjects are needed for the investigator to have confidence that the variables he selects as most important in interpreting the discriminant function would again show up as most important in another sample.

Now, given that one has enough subjects to have confidence in the reliability of the index he chooses to use, which should be used? It seems that the following suggestion of Tatsuoka (1973), is very reasonable, "Both approaches are useful, provided we keep their different objectives in mind" (p. 280). That is, use the correlations for substantive interpretation of the discriminant functions, but use the coefficients to determine which of the variables are redundant given that others are in the set. This approach is illustrated in an example later in the chapter.

7.5. GRAPHING THE GROUPS IN THE DISCRIMINANT PLANE

If there are 2 or more significant discriminant functions, then a useful device for determining directional differences among the groups is to graph them in the discriminant plane. The horizontal direction corresponds to the first discriminant function and thus lateral separation among the groups indicates how much they have been distinguished on this function. The vertical dimension corresponds to the second discriminant function and thus vertical separation tells us which groups are being distinguished in a way unrelated to the way they were separated on the first discriminant function (since the discriminant functions are uncorrelated). Since the functions are uncorrelated, it is quite possible for two groups to differ very little on the first discriminant function and yet show a large separation on the second function.

Since each of the discriminant functions is a linear combination of the original variables, the question arises as to how we determine the mean coordinates of the groups on these linear combinations. Fortunately the answer is quite simple since it can be shown that the mean for a linear combination is equal to the linear combination of the means on the original variables. That is,

$$\bar{z}_1 = a_{11}\bar{x}_1 + a_{12}\bar{x}_2 + \cdots + a_{1p}\bar{x}_p,$$

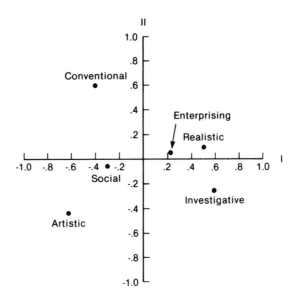

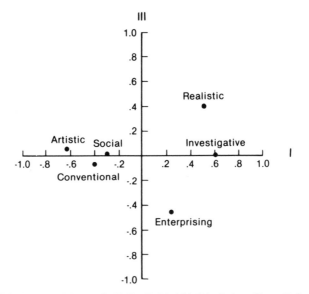

FIG. 7.1. Position of Groups for Holland's Model in Discriminant Planes Defined by Functions 1 & 2 and by Functions 1 & 3

where z_1 is the discriminant function and the x_i are the original variables.

The matrix equation for obtaining the coordinates of the groups on the discriminant functions is given by:

$$Z = \bar{X} \, V,$$

where $\bar{X}$ is the matrix of means for the original variables in the various groups and V is a matrix whose *columns* are the raw coefficients for the discriminant functions (the first column for the first function, etc.). To make this more concrete we consider the case of three groups and four variables. Then the matrix equation becomes:

$$_3Z_2 = {}_3\bar{X}_4 \, {}_4V_2$$

The specific elements of the matrices would be as follows:

$$
\begin{bmatrix}
z_{11} & z_{12} \\
z_{21} & z_{22} \\
z_{31} & z_{32}
\end{bmatrix}
=
\begin{bmatrix}
\bar{x}_{11} & \bar{x}_{12} & \bar{x}_{13} & \bar{x}_{14} \\
\bar{x}_{21} & \bar{x}_{22} & \bar{x}_{23} & \bar{x}_{24} \\
\bar{x}_{31} & \bar{x}_{32} & \bar{x}_{33} & \bar{x}_{34}
\end{bmatrix}
\begin{bmatrix}
a_{11} & a_{12} \\
a_{21} & a_{22} \\
a_{31} & a_{32} \\
a_{41} & a_{42}
\end{bmatrix}
$$

In the above equation $\bar{x}_{11}$ gives the mean for variable 1 in group 1, $\bar{x}_{12}$ the mean for variable 2 in group 1, etc. The first row of Z gives the "x" and "y" coordinates of group 1 on the two discriminant functions, the second row gives the location of group 2 in the discriminant plane, etc.

The location of the groups on the discriminant functions appears in all 3 examples from the literature that we present in this chapter. For plots of the groups in the plane, see the Smart study later in this chapter, and specifically Figure 7.1.

Example 1

The data for the example was extracted from the National Merit file (Stevens, 1972). The classification variable was the educational level of both parents of the National Merit scholars. Four groups were formed: (1) those students for whom at least one of their parents had an eighth grade education or less ($n = 90$), (2) those students both of whose parents were high school graduates ($n = 104$), (3) those students both of whose parents had gone to college, with at most one graduating ($n = 115$), and (4) those students both of whose parents had at least one college degree ($n = 75$). The dependent variables, or those we are attempting to predict from the above grouping, were a subset of the Vocational Personality Inventory (VPI): realistic, intellectual, social, conventional, enterprising, artistic, status and aggression.

In Table 7.1 we present the SPSSX control lines necessary to run the DISCRIMINANT program, along with some descriptive statistics, i.e., the means and the correlation matrix for the VPI variables. Many of the correlations are

TABLE 7.1
Control Lines and Selected Output from SPSSX for Discriminant Analysis

```
TITLE 'DISCRIMINANT ANALYSIS ON NATIONAL MERIT DATA— 4 GPS— N = 384 '.
DATA LIST FREE/ EDUC REAL INTELL SOCIAL CONVEN ENTERP ARTIS STATUS AGGRESS
LIST
BEGIN DATA

   DATA

END DATA
DISCRIMINANT GROUPS = EDUC(1,4)/
   VARIABLES = REAL TO AGGRESS/          ①

OUTPUT
```

POOLED WITHIN-GROUPS CORRELATION MATRIX

	REAL	INTELL	SOCIAL	CONVEN	ENTERP	ARTIS	STATUS	AGGRESS
REAL	1.00000							
INTELL	0.44541	1.00000						
SOCIAL	0.04860	0.24193	1.00000					
CONVEN	0.32733	0.06629	0.23716	1.00000				
ENTERP	0.35377	0.10396	0.35573	0.54567	1.00000			
ARTIS	.04639	0.23030	0.48143	0.13472	0.37977	1.00000		
STATUS	−0.32954	0.06541	0.38498	0.14731	0.28262	0.40873	1.00000	
AGGRESS	0.32066	0.31931	0.49830	0.32698	0.58887	0.50353	0.43702	1.00000

GROUP MEANS

EDUC	REAL	INTELL	SOCIAL	CONVEN	ENTERP	ARTIS	STATUS	AGGRESS
1	2.35556	4.88889	5.73333	2.64444	2.63333	4.45556	8.67778	5.20000
2	2.01923	4.78846	5.42308	2.32692	2.89423	4.06731	8.41346	5.06731
3	1.96522	5.12174	5.25217	1.91304	3.63478	5.20000	8.92174	5.19130
4	1.44000	4.53333	5.10667	1.29333	2.84000	5.08000	9.08000	4.61333
TOTAL	1.96875	4.86198	5.38261	2.07552	3.04427	4.69531	8.80469	5.04688

① The GROUPS and VARIABLES subcommands are the only subcommands required for running a standard discriminant analysis. There are various other options available, such as a varimax rotation to increase interpretability, and several different types of stepwise discriminant analysis.

TABLE 7.2
Tests of Significance for Discriminant Functions, Discriminant Function—Variable Correlations and Standardized Coefficients

CANONICAL DISCRIMINANT FUNCTIONS

$$73.64\% = \frac{\text{EIGENVALUE}}{\text{SUM OF EIGENVALUES}} \times 100 = \frac{.1097}{.1489} \times 100$$

FUNCTION	EIGENVALUE OF BW^{-1}	PERCENT OF VARIANCE	CUMULATIVE PERCENT	CANONICAL CORRELATION	:	AFTER FUNCTION	WILKS' LAMBDA	CHI-SQUARED	D.F.	SIGNIFICANCE
1*	0.10970	73.64	73.64	0.3144148	:	0	0.8666342	53.876	24	0.0004
2*	0.02871	19.27	92.91	0.1670684	:	1	0.9619271	14.634	14	0.4036
3*	0.01056	7.09	100.00	0.1022387	:	2	0.9895472	3.9614	6	0.4819

*MARKS THE 3 CANONICAL DISCRIMINANT FUNCTION(S) TO BE USED IN THE REMAINING ANALYSIS

RESIDUAL TEST PROCEDURE

Let ϕ_1, ϕ_2, etc denote the eigenvalues of BW^{-1}.

$$\chi^2 = [(N - 1) - (p + k)/2]\sum ln(1 + \phi_i)$$

$$\chi^2 = [(384 - 1) - (8 + 4)/2][ln(1 + .11) + ln(1 + .029) + ln(1 + .0106)];$$
$$\chi^2 = 377(.1429) = 53.88, \, df = p(k - 1) = 8(3) = 24$$

FIRST RESIDUAL: $\chi_1^2 = 377 \, [ln(1.029) + ln(1.0106)] = 14.64, \, df = (p - 1)(k - 2) = 14$

SECOND RESIDUAL: $\chi_2^2 = 377 \, ln(1.0106) = 3.97, \, df = (p - 2)(k - 3) = 6$

STANDARDIZED CANONICAL DISCRIMINANT FUNCTION COEFFICIENTS

	FUNC 1	FUNC 2	FUNC 3
REAL	0.33567	0.92803	0.55970
INTELL	-0.24881	-0.42593	0.18729
SOCIAL	0.36854	0.01669	-0.21222
CONVEN	0.79971	-0.19960	0.33530
ENTERP	-1.07691	-0.66618	0.39790
ARTIS	-0.32335	0.41416	0.20551
STATUS	-0.05005	1.13509	0.38153
AGGRESS	0.41918	-0.55000	-0.27073

POOLED WITHIN-GROUPS CORRELATION BETWEEN CANONICAL DISCRIMINANT FUNCTIONS AND DISCRIMINATING VARIABLES VARIABLES ARE ORDERED BY THE FUNCTION WITH LARGEST CORRELATION AND THE MAGNITUDE OF THAT CORRELATION.

	FUNC 1	FUNC 2	FUNC 3
STATUS	-0.17058	0.519084*	0.25516
ENTERP	-0.30649	-0.33095	0.74936
CONVEN	0.47878	-0.24059	0.69316
REAL	0.25946	-0.09310	0.68032
AGGRESS	0.07366	-0.13305	0.47697
INTELL	-0.01297	-0.09701	0.43467
ARTIS	-0.29829	0.27428	0.38834
SOCIAL	0.16516	0.03674	0.19227

CANONICAL DISCRIMINANT FUNCTIONS EVALUATED AT GROUP MEANS (GROUP CENTROIDS)

GROUP	FUNC 1	FUNC 2	FUNC 3
1	0.39158	-0.27492	0.00687
2	0.09873	-0.04190	-0.29200
3	-0.18324	0.27619	0.11148
4	-0.32583	-0.03558	0.22572

in the moderate range (.30 to .58) and clearly significant, indicating that a multivariate analysis is dictated.

At the top of Table 7.2 is the residual test procedure involving Bartlett's Chi-Square tests, to determine the number of significant discriminant functions. Note that there are min $(k - 1, p)$ = min $(3,8)$ = 3 possible discriminant functions. The first line has all 3 eigenvalues (corresponding to the 3 discriminant functions) lumped together, yielding a significant χ^2 at the .0004 level. This tells us there is significant overall association. Now, the largest eigenvalue of $\mathbf{BW}^{-1}$ (i.e., the first discriminant function) is removed, and we test whether the residual, the last two discriminant functions, constitute significant association. The χ^2 for this first residual is not significant ($\chi^2 = 14.63, p < .40$) at the .05 level. The "After Function" column simply means after the first discriminant function has been removed. The third line, testing whether the third discriminant function is significant by itself has a 2 in the "After Function" column. This means, "Is the χ^2 significant after the first *two* discriminant functions have been removed?" To summarize then, only the first discriminant function is significant. The details of obtaining the χ^2, using the eigenvalues of $\mathbf{BW}^{-1}$, which appear in the upper left hand corner of the printout, are given in Table 7.2.

The eigenvalues of $\mathbf{BW}^{-1}$ are .1097, .0287, and .0106. Because the eigenvalues additively partition the total association, since the discriminant functions are uncorrelated, the "Percent of Variance" is simply the given eigenvalue divided by the sum of the eigenvalues. Thus, for the first discriminant function we have:

$$\text{Percent of Variance} = \frac{.1097}{.1097 + .0287 + .0106} \times 100 = 73.64\%$$

The reader should recall from Chapter 5, when we discussed "Other Multivariate Test Statistics," that the sum of the eigenvalues of $\mathbf{BW}^{-1}$ is one of the global multivariate test statistics, i.e., the Hotelling-Lawley trace. Therefore, the sum of the eigenvalues of $\mathbf{BW}^{-1}$ *is* a measure of the total association.

Since the group sizes are sharply unequal ($115/75 > 1.5$), it is important to check the homogeneity of covariance matrices assumption. The Box test for doing so is part of the printout, although we have not presented it. Fortunately, the Box test is not significant ($F = 1.18, p < .09$) at the .05 level.

The means of the groups on the first discriminant function (Table 7.2) show that it separates those children whose parents have had exposure to college (groups 3 and 4) from children whose parents have not gone to college (groups 1 and 2).

For interpreting the first discriminant function, as mentioned earlier, we use both the standardized coefficients and the discriminant function–variable correlations. We use the correlations for substantive interpretation, i.e., to name the underlying construct which the discriminant function represents. The procedure has empirically clustered the variables. Our task is to determine what the variables that correlate highly with the discriminant function have in common, and thus name the function.

The discriminant function–varible correlations are given in Table 7.2. Examining these for the first discriminant function, we see that it is primarily the conventional variable (correlation = .479) that defines the function, with the enterprising and artistic variables secondarily involved (correlations of − .306 and − .298 respectively). Since the correlations are negative for these variables, this means that the groups that scored higher on the enterprising and artistic variables scored lower on the first discriminant function, i.e., those merit scholars whose parents had a college education.

Now, examining the standardized coefficients to determine which of the variables are redundant given others in the set, we see that the conventional and enterprising variables are *not* redundant (coefficients of .80 and − 1.08 respectively), but that the artistic variable is redundant since it's coefficient is only − .32. Thus, combining the information from the coefficients and the discriminant function–variable correlations, we can say that the first discriminant function is characterizable as a conventional–enterprising continuum. Note, from the group centroid means, that it is the merit scholars whose parents have a college education that tend to be less conventional and more enterprising.

Finally, we can have confidence in the reliability of the results from this study since the subject/variable ratio is very large, i.e., about 50 to 1.

7.6. ROTATION OF THE DISCRIMINANT FUNCTIONS

In factor analysis rotation of the factors often facilitates interpretation. The discriminant functions can also be rotated (varimax) to help interpret them. This is easily accomplished with the SPSSX Discrim program by requesting 13 for "Options." Of course, one should only rotate statistically significant discriminant functions to ensure that the rotated functions are still significant. Also, in rotating, the maximizing property is lost, i.e., the first rotated function will no longer *necessarily* account for the maximum amount of between association. The amount of between association that the rotated functions account for tends to be more evenly distributed. The SPSSX package does print out how much of the canonical variance each rotated factor accounts for.

Up to this point, we have used all the variables in forming the discriminant functions. There is a procedure, called stepwise discriminant analysis, for selecting the best set of discriminators, just as one would select the "best" set of predictors in a regression analysis. It is to this procedure that we turn next.

7.7.   STEPWISE DISCRIMINANT ANALYSIS

A popular procedure with both the SPSSX and BMDP packages is stepwise discriminant analysis. In this procedure the first variable to enter is the one which maximizes separation among the groups. The next variable to enter is the one which adds the most to further separating the groups, etc. It should be obvious that this procedure capitalizes on chance in the same way stepwise regression analysis does, where the first predictor to enter is the one which has the maximum correlation with the dependent variable, the second predictor to enter the one which adds the next largest amount to prediction, etc.

The F's to enter and the corresponding significance tests in stepwise discriminant analysis must be interpreted with caution, especially if the subject/variable ratio is small (say ≤ 5). The Wilk's Λ for the "best" set of discriminators is positively biased, and this bias can lead to the following problem (Rencher & Larson, 1980):

> Inclusion of too many variables in the subset. If the significance level shown on a computer output is used as an informal stopping rule, some variables will likely be included which do not contribute to the separation of the groups. A subset chosen with significance levels as guidelines will not likely be stable, i.e., a different subset would emerge from a repetition of the study. (p. 350)

The BMDP manual (1979) warns of the positive bias of the F tests in stepwise regression (p. 403), but does not repeat the warning for stepwise discriminant analysis.

Hawkins (1976) has suggested that a variable be entered only if it is significant at the $\alpha/(k - p)$ level, where α is the desired level of significance, p is the number of variables already included and $(k - p)$ is the number of variables available for inclusion. Although this probably is a good idea if N/p ratio is small, it probably is conservative if $N/p > 10$.

7.8.   TWO OTHER STUDIES THAT USED
DISCRIMINANT ANALYSIS

McNeil & Karr Study

The first study (McNeil & Karr, 1972) involves four cultural systems of varying degrees of modernization in Sierra Leone. From least to most modernized, these systems were (1) village, (2) modernized village, (3) tribal urban, and (4) Creole urban. There were 20 subjects in each group (10 boys and 10 girls in each case). These groups were compared on the nine subtests of the Illinois Test of Psycholinguistic Abilities (ITPA).

The results of the discriminant analysis, along with the group centroids (the means of the groups on the discriminant functions) are presented in Table 7.3. McNeil and Karr tested each eigenvalue *separately* and found the first two discriminant functions significant at the .01 level. This procedure, at the present state of knowledge, is a questionable practice. Employing the residual test procedure, we still find the first discriminant function significant at the .01 level, but the second function ($\chi^2 = 25$, with 16 *df*) is only significant at the .10 level. Thus, the evidence for the second discriminant function is weaker, and it would be wise to have this result replicated in another sample before placing a great amount of confidence in it. A second reason for treating this result somewhat skeptically is that the order of the groups on the second discriminant function was *not* as hypothesized.

The correlations between the discriminant functions and the original variables are also given in Table 7.3. These correlations show that the first discriminant function is interpretable as an auditory-vocal construct (since those variables dominate the function). The groups were ordered along this dimension as hypothesized, with the least modernized having the lowest score and the most modernized the highest score. The second discriminant function seems to be interpretable as primarily a motor encoding variable since the correlation of that variable with the discriminant function is quite strong. Furthermore the correlations of the function with the other variables are considerably lower (the next largest being $-.41$).

TABLE 7.3
Discriminant Function–Variable Correlations and Group Centroids for
McNeil-Karr Study

| Variables | Functions | | |
	1	*2*	*3*
Auditory-vocal automatic	.94	$-.08$	.12
Visual decoding	.25	.20	$-.21$
Motor encoding	.37	.77	$-.19$
Auditory-vocal association	.87	.06	$-.00$
Visual motor sequencing	.07	$-.01$	.51
Vocal encoding	.57	.37	.34
Auditory vocal sequencing	.33	$-.41$	$-.35$
Visual-motor association	.30	.35	.32
Auditory decoding	.27	.09	$-.08$

Group Centroids

| Groups | Discriminant Functions | | |
	1	*2*	*3*
Village	8.92	1.71	-3.02
Modernized village	10.81	5.98	-3.46
Tribal urban	12.27	5.47	-2.44
Creole urban	20.21	3.46	-3.09

The one reservation we have about interpreting the discriminant functions as indicated is that the subject/variable ratio is not large, i.e., it is 80/9 or about 9 to 1. We had indicated earlier that unless the ratio was at least 20 to 1 the stability of the results was questionable. Therefore, either replication of these results on another sample or on a combined sample of about 200 or more subjects is essential.

Smart Study

A study by Smart (1976) provides a nice illustration of the use of discriminant analysis to help validate Holland's (1966) theory of vocational choice/personality. Holland's theory assumes that (a) vocational choice is an expression of personality and (b) most people can be classified as one of six primary personality types: realistic, investigative, artistic, social, enterprising, and conventional. Realistic types, for example, tend to be pragmatic, asocial, and possess strong mechanical and technical competencies, while social types tend to be idealistic, sociable, and possess strong interpersonal skills.

Holland's theory further states that there are six related model environments. That is, for each personality type, there is a logically related environment that is characterized in terms of the atmosphere created by the people who dominate it. For example, realistic environments are dominated by realistic personality types and are characterized primarily by the tendencies and competencies these people possess.

Now, Holland and his associates have developed a hexagonal model that defines the psychological resemblances among the six personality types and the environments. The types and environments are arranged in the following clockwise order: realistic, investigative, artistic, social, enterprising, and conventional. The closer any two environments are on the hexagonal arrangement, the stronger they are related. This means, for example, that since realistic and conventional are next to each other they should be much more similar than realistic and social which are the furthest possible distance apart on an hexagonal arrangement.

In validating Holland's theory, Smart nationally sampled 939 academic department chairmen from 32 public universities. The departments could be classified in one of the six Holland environments. We give a sampling here: realistic—civil and mechanical engineering, industrial arts, and vocational education; investigative—biology, chemistry, psychology, mathematics; artistic—classics, music, english; social—counseling, history, sociology, and elementary education; enterprising—government, marketing, and prelaw; conventional—accounting, business education, and finance.

A questionnaire containing 27 duties typically performed by department chairmen was given to all chairmen, and the responses were factor analyzed (principal components with varimax rotation). The six factors that emerged were the dependent variables for the study, and were named: (1) faculty development, (2) external coordination, (3) graduate program, (4) internal administration, (5) instructional, and (6) program management. The independent variable was environments. The overall multivariate $F = 9.65$ was significant at the .001 level. Thus, the department chairmen did devote significantly different amounts of time to the above six categories of their professional duties. A discriminant analysis breakdown of the overall association showed that there were three significant discriminant functions ($p < .001$, $p < .001$ and $p < .02$ respectively). The standardized coefficients, discussed earlier as one of the devices for interpreting such functions, are given in Table 7.4.

Using the italicized weights, Smart gave the following names to the functions: discriminant function 1—curriculum management, discriminant function 2—internal orientation, and discriminant function 3—faculty orientation. The positions of the groups on the discriminant planes defined by functions 1 and 2, and by functions 1 and 3 are given in Figure 7.1. The clustering of the groups in Figure 7.1 is reasonably consistent with Holland's hexagonal model.

In Figure 7.2 we present the hexagonal model, showing how all three discriminant functions empirically confirm different similarities and disparities which should exist, according to the theory. For example, the realistic and investigative groups should be very similar, and the closeness of these groups appears on discriminant function 1. On the other hand, the conventional and artistic groups should be very dissimilar and this is revealed by their vertical separation on discriminant function 2. Also, the realistic and enterprising groups should be somewhat dissimilar and this appears as a fairly sizable separation (vertical) on discriminant function 3 in Figure 7.2.

In concluding our discussion of Smart's study, there are two important points to be made:

1.   The issue raised earlier about the lack of stability of the coefficients is *not* a problem in this study. Smart had 932 subjects and only six dependent variables, so that his subject/variable ratio was very large.

TABLE 7.4
Standardized Coefficients for Smart Study

Variables	Function 1	Function 2	Function 3
Faculty development	.22	−.20	−.62
External coordination	−.14	.56	.34
Graduate program	.36	.45	.17
Internal administration	.17	−.58	.69
Instructional	−.82	.15	.06
Program management	−.46	−.35	−.09

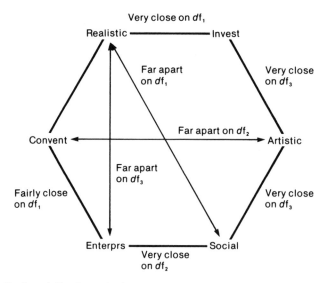

df_1, df_2 and df_3 refer to the first, second and third discriminant functions respectively

FIG. 7.2. Empirical Fit of the Groups as Determined by the Three Discriminant Functions to Holland's Hexagonal Model.

2. Smart did not use the discriminant function-variable correlations in combination with the coefficients to interpret the discriminant functions, as it was unnecessary to do so. Smart's dependent variables were principal components, which are uncorrelated, and for uncorrelated variables the interpretation from the 2 approaches is identical, since the coefficients and correlations are equal (Thorndike, 1976).

7.9.   THE CLASSIFICATION PROBLEM

The classification problem involves classifying subjects (entities in general) into the one of several groups which they most closely resemble on the basis of a set of measurements. We say that a subject most closely resembles group i if the vector of scores for that subject is closest to the vector of means (centroid) for group i. Geometrically, the subject is closest in a distance sense (Mahalanobis distance) to the centroid for that group. Recall that in Chapter 3 (on multiple regression) we used the Mahalanobis distance to measure outliers on the set of predictors, and that the distance for subject i is given as:

$$D_i^2 = (\mathbf{x}_i - \bar{\mathbf{x}})'\mathbf{S}^{-1}(\mathbf{x}_i - \bar{\mathbf{x}}),$$

where $\mathbf{x}_i$ is the vector of scores for subject i, $\bar{\mathbf{x}}$ is the vector of means, and $\mathbf{S}$ is the covariance matrix. It may helpful to review the section on Mahalanobis distance in Chapter 3, and in particular a worked out example of calculating it in Table 3.12 (p. 114).

Our discussion of classification is brief, and focuses on the two-group problem. For a thorough discussion see Johnson and Wichern (1988), and for a good, recent review of discriminant analysis see Huberty (1984).

Let us now consider several examples from different content areas where classifying subjects into groups is of practical interest:

1. A bank wants a reliable means, on the basis of a set of variables, to identify low risk vs. high risk credit customers.
2. A reading diagnostic specialist wishes a means of identifying in kindergarten those children who are likely to encounter reading difficulties in the early elementary grades from those not likely to have difficulty.
3. A special educator wants to classify handicapped children as either learning disabled, emotionally disturbed, or mentally retarded.
4. A Dean of a law school wants a means of identifying those likely to succeed in law school from those not likely to succeed.
5. A vocational guidance counselor, on the basis of a battery of interest variables, wishes to classify high school students into occupational groups (artists, lawyers, scientists, accountants, etc.) whose interests are similar.
6. A clinical psychologist or psychiatrist wishes to classify mental patients into one of several psychotic groups (schizophrenic, manic-depressive, catatonic, etc.).

The Two Group Situation

Let $\mathbf{x}' = (x_1, x_2, \ldots, x_p)$ denote the vector of measurements on the basis of which we wish to classify a subject into one of two groups, G_1 or G_2. Fisher's (1936) idea was to transform the multivariate problem into a univariate one, in the sense of finding the linear combination of the x's (a single composite variable) which will maximally discriminant the groups. This is, of course, the single discriminant function. It is assumed that the two populations are multivariate normal and have the same covariance matrix. Let $\mathbf{z} = a_1 x_1 + a_2 x_2 + \ldots + a_p x_p$ denote the discriminant function, where $\mathbf{a}' = (a_1, a_2, \ldots, a_p)$ is the vector of coefficients. Let $\bar{\mathbf{x}}_1$ and $\bar{\mathbf{x}}_2$ denote the vectors of means for the subjects on the p variables in groups 1 and 2. The location of group 1 on the discriminant function is then given by $\bar{y}_1 = \mathbf{a}'\bar{\mathbf{x}}_1$ and the location of group 2 by $\bar{y}_2 = \mathbf{a}'\bar{\mathbf{x}}_2$. The midpoint between the two groups on the discriminant function is then given by $m = (\bar{y}_1 + \bar{y}_2)/2$.

If we let z_i denote the score for the ith subject on the discriminant function, then the *decision rule* is as follows:

If $z_i \geq m$, then classify subject in group 1

If $z_i < m$, then classify subject in group 2

As we see in a following example, BMDP7M (stepwise discriminant analysis program) prints out the scores on the discriminant function for each subject and the means for the groups on the discriminant function (so that we can easily determine the midpoint *m*). Thus, applying the above decision rule, we are easily able to determine why the program classified a subject in a given group. In the above decision rule, we assume the group which has the higher mean is designated as group 1.

This midpoint rule makes intuitive sense, and is easiest to see for the single variable case. Suppose there two normal distributions with equal variances and means 55 (group 1) and 45. The midpoint is 50. If we consider classifying a subject with a score of 52, it makes sense to put him (her) in group 1. Why? Because the score puts the subject much closer to what is typical for group 1 (i.e., only 3 points away from the mean), whereas this score is nowhere near as typical for a subject from group 2 (7 points from the mean). On the other hand, a subject with a score of 48.5 is more appropriately placed in group 2 since his(her) score is closer to what is typical for group 2 (3.5 points from the mean) than what is typical for group 1 (6.5 points from the mean).

In Figure 7.3 we illustrate the percentages of subjects that would be misclassified in the univariate case and when using discriminant scores.

Example 2

We consider again the Pope (1980) data used in Chapter 6. Children in kindergarten were measured with various instruments to determine whether they could be classified as low risk or high risk with respect to having reading problems later on in school. The variables we considered here are word identification (WI), word comprehension (WC), and passage comprehension (PC). The group sizes are sharply unequal and the homogeneity of covariance matrices assumption here was not tenable at the .05 level, so that a quadratic rule may be more appropriate. But we are just using this example for illustrative purposes.

In Table 7.5 are the control lines for obtaining the classification results on SAS DISCRIM using the ordinary discriminant function. The hit rate, i.e., the number of correct classifications, is quite good, especially since 11 of the 12 high risk subjects have been correctly classified.

In Table 7.6 are given the means for the groups on the discriminant function (.46 for lowrisk and -1.01 for high risk), along with the scores for the subjects on the discriminant function (these are listed under CAN.V—an abbreviation for canonical variate). The histogram for the discriminant scores shows that we have a fairly good separation, although there are several (9) mis-classifications of low risk subjects being classified as high risk.

Assessing the Accuracy of the Maximized Hit Rates

The classification procedure is set up to maximize the hit rates, i.e., the number of correct classifications. This is analogous to the maximization procedure in multiple regression, where the regression equation was designed to maximize predictive power. We saw how misleading the prediction on the derivation sample

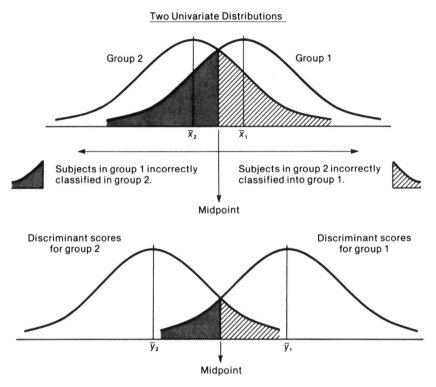

Two Univariate Distributions

Group 2   Group 1

$\bar{x}_2$ $\bar{x}_1$

Subjects in group 1 incorrectly   Subjects in group 2 incorrectly
classified in group 2.   classified into group 1.

Midpoint

Discriminant scores   Discriminant scores
for group 2   for group 1

$\bar{y}_2$ $\bar{y}_1$

Midpoint

For this multivariate problem we have indicated much greater separation for the
groups than in the univariate example above. The amounts of incorrect classifications are indicated by the shaded and lined areas as in univariate example.

$\bar{y}_1$ and $\bar{y}_2$ are the means for the 2 groups on the discriminant function.

FIG. 7.3. Two Univariate Distributions and Two Discriminant Score Distributions
with Incorrectly Classified Cases Indicated.

could be. There is the same need here to obtain a more realistic estimate of the
hit rate through use of an "external" classification analysis. That is, an analysis
is needed in which the data to be classified is *not* used in constructing the
classification function. There are two ways of accomplishing this:

1. We can use the *jackknife* procedure of Lachenbruch (1967). Here,
each subject is classified based on a classification statistic derived from the
remaining $(n - 1)$ subjects. This is the procedure of choice for small or
moderate sample sizes, and is obtained by specifying CROSSLIST as an
option in the SAS DISCRIM program (cf Table 7.7). The jackknifed
probabilities and classification results for the Pope data are given in Table
7.7. The probabilities are different from that obtained with the discriminant
function (Table 7.5), but for this data set the classification results are
identical.

TABLE 7.5

SAS DISCRIM Control Lines and Group Probabilities for Lowrisk and Highrisk Subjects

```
data pope;
input gprisk wi wc pc @@;
cards;
1 5.8 9.7 8.9   1 10.6 10.9 11   1 8.6 7.2 8.7
1 4.8 4.6 6.2   1 8.3 10.6 7.8   1 4.6 3.3 4.7
1 4.8 3.7 6.4   1 6.7 6.0 7.2   1 7.1 8.4 8.4
1 6.2 3.0 4.3   1 4.2 5.3 4.2   1 6.9 9.7 7.2
1 5.6 4.1 4.3   1 4.8 3.8 5.3   1 2.9 3.7 4.2
1 6.1 7.1 8.1   1 12.5 11.2 8.9   1 5.2 9.3 6.2
1 5.7 10.3 5.5   1 6.0 5.7 5.4   1 5.2 7.7 6.9
1 7.2 5.8 6.7   1 8.1 7.1 8.1   1 3.3 3.0 4.9
1 7.6 7.7 6.2   1 7.7 9.7 8.9
2 2.4 2.1 2.4   2 3.5 1.8 3.9   2 6.7 3.6 5.9
2 5.3 3.3 6.1   2 5.2 4.1 6.4   2 3.2 2.7 4.0
2 4.5 4.9 5.7   2 3.9 4.7 4.7   2 4.0 3.6 2.9
2 5.7 5.5 6.2   2 2.4 2.9 3.2   2 2.7 2.6 4.1
proc discrim data = pope testdata = pope testlist;
class gprisk;
var wi wc pc;
```

Obs	From GPRISK	CLASSIFIED into GPRISK	Posterior Probability of Membership in GPRISK: 1	2
1	1	1	0.9317	0.0683
2	1	1	0.9840	0.0160
3	1	1	0.8600	0.1400
4	1	2*	0.4365	0.5635
5	1	1	0.9615	0.0385
6	1	2*	0.2511	0.7489
7	1	2*	0.3446	0.6554
8	1	1	0.6880	0.3120
9	1	1	0.8930	0.1070
10	1	2*	0.2557	0.7443
11	1	2*	0.4269	0.5731
12	1	1	0.9260	0.0740
13	1	2*	0.3446	0.6554
14	1	2*	0.3207	0.6793
15	1	2*	0.2295	0.7705
16	1	1	0.7929	0.2071
17	1	1	0.9856	0.0144
18	1	1	0.8775	0.1225
19	1	1	0.9169	0.0831
20	1	1	0.5756	0.4244
21	1	1	0.7906	0.2094
22	1	1	0.6675	0.3325
23	1	1	0.8343	0.1657
24	1	2*	0.2008	0.7992

(continued)

TABLE 7.5 *(Continued)*

Obs	From GPRISK	CLASSIFIED into GPRISK	Posterior Probability of Membership in GPRISK: 1	2
25	1	1	0.8262	0.1738
26	1	1	0.9465	0.0535
27	2	2	0.0936	0.9064
28	2	2	0.1143	0.8857
29	2	2	0.3778	0.6222
30	2	2	0.3098	0.6902
31	2	2	0.4005	0.5995
32	2	2	0.1598	0.8402
33	2	2	0.4432	0.5568
34	2	2	0.3676	0.6324
35	2	2	0.2161	0.7839
36	2	1*	0.5703	0.4297
37	2	2	0.1432	0.8568
38	2	2	0.1468	0.8532

*Misclassified observation

Number of Observations and Percent into GPRISK:

From GPRISK			1	2	Total	
						We have 9 low risk subjects
1	lowrisk		17	9	26	misclassified as highrisk.
			65.38	34.62	100.00	
						There is only 1 highrisk
2	highrisk		1	11	12	subject misclassified as lowrisk.
			8.33	91.67	100.00	

2.   If the sample size is large, then we can randomly split the sample and cross validate. That is, we compute the classification function on one sample and then check it's hit rate on the other random sample. This provides a good check on the external validity of the classification function. BMDP7M is set up nicely to do this cross validation and we show the control lines in a later example.

Using Prior Probabilities

Ordinarily we would assume that any given subject has a priori an equal probability of being in any of the groups to which we wish to classify. And the packages have equal prior probabilities as the default option. Different a priori group probabilities can have a substantial effect on the classification function, as we will show shortly. The pertinent question is, "How often are we justified in using unequal a priori probabilities for group membership?" If indeed, based on content knowledge, one can be confident that the different sample sizes result *because* of differences in population sizes, then prior probabilities are justified. However, several researchers have urged caution in using anything but equal priors (Lindeman, Merenda, & Gold, 1980; Tatsuoka, 1971).

TABLE 7.6
Means for Groups on Discriminant Function, Scores for Cases on Discriminant Function & Histogram for Discriminant Scores

GROUP	MEAN COORDINATES		SYMBOL FOR CASES	SYMEDL FOR MEAN
LOW RISK	① 0.46	0.00	L	1
HIGH RISK	-1.01	0.00	H	2

GROUP CASE	LOWRISK CAN.V	CASE	② CAN.V	CASE	CAN.V
1	1.50	11	-0.47	21	0.63
2	2.53	12	1.44	22	0.20
3	0.96	13	-0.71	23	0.83
4	-0.44	14	-0.78	24	-1.21
5	1.91	15	-1.09	25	0.79
6	-1.01	16	0.64	26	1.68
7	-0.71	17	2.60		
8	0.27	18	1.07		
9	1.17	19	1.36		
10	-1.00	20	-0.06		

GROUP HIGHRISK

CASE	CAN.V	CASE	CAN.V
27	-1.81	37	-1.49
28	-1.66	38	-1.47
29	-0.81		
30	-0.82		
31	-0.55		
32	-1.40		
33	-0.43		
34	-0.64		
35	-1.15		
36	-0.08		

Histogram for Discriminant Function Scores

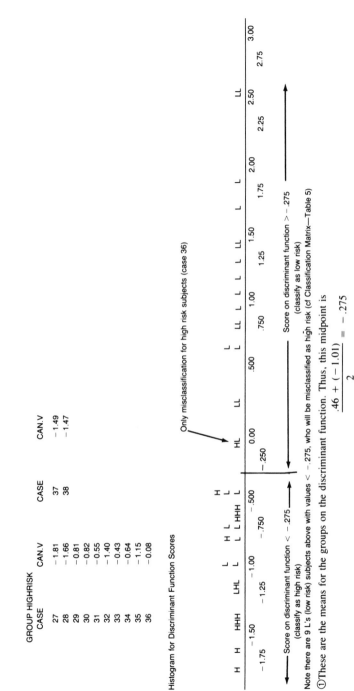

Only misclassification for high risk subjects (case 36)

← Score on discriminant function < -.275
(classify as high risk)

Score on discriminant function > -.275 →
(classify as low risk)

Note there are 9 L's (low risk) subjects above with values < -.275, who will be misclassified as high risk (cf Classification Matrix—Table 5)

①These are the means for the groups on the discriminant function. Thus, this midpoint is

$$\frac{.46 + (-1.01)}{2} = -.275$$

②The scores listed under CAN.V (for canonical variate) these are the scores for the subjects on the discriminant function.

TABLE 7.7
SAS DISCRIM Control Lines and Selected Printout for Classifying the Pope Data with the Jackknife Procedure

```
data pope;
input gprisk wi wc pc @@;
cards;
1 5.8 9.7 8.9   1 10.6 10.9 11   1 8.6 7.2 8.7
1 4.8 4.6 6.2   1 8.3 10.6 7.8   1 4.6 3.3 4.7
1 4.8 3.7 6.4   1 6.7 6.0 7.2    1 7.1 8.4 8.4
1 6.2 3.0 4.3   1 4.2 5.3 4.2    1 6.9 9.7 7.2
1 5.6 4.1 4.3   1 4.8 3.8 5.3    1 2.9 3.7 4.2
1 6.1 7.1 8.1   1 12.5 11.2 8.9  1 5.2 9.3 6.2
1 5.7 10.3 5.5  1 6.0 5.7 5.4    1 5.2 7.7 6.9
1 7.2 5.8 6.7   1 8.1 7.1 8.1    1 3.3 3.0 4.9
1 7.6 7.7 6.2   1 7.7 9.7 8.9
2 2.4 2.1 2.4   2 3.5 1.8 3.9    2 6.7 3.6 5.9
2 5.3 3.3 6.1   2 5.2 4.1 6.4    2 3.2 2.7 4.0
2 4.5 4.9 5.7   2 3.9 4.7 4.7    2 4.0 3.6 2.9
2 5.7 5.5 6.2   2 2.4 2.9 3.2    2 2.7 2.6 4.1
proc discrim data=pope testdata=pope crosslist;
class gprisk;
var wi wc pc;
```

When the CROSSLIST option is listed, the program prints the cross validation classification results for each observation. Listing this option invokes the jackknife procedure (see SAS/STAT USER'S GUIDE, VOL. 1 (p. 688).

Cross-validation Results using Linear Discriminant Fucntion

Generalized Squared Distance Function:

$$D_j^2(X) = X - \overline{X}_{(X)j})' \text{ COV}(X) (X - \overline{X}_{(X)j})$$

Posterior Probability of Membership in each GPRISK:

$$\Pr(j|X) = \exp(-.5\ D_j^2\ (X)) / \underset{k}{\text{SUM}} \exp(-.5\ D_k^2(X))$$

Obs	GPRSK	into GPRISK	1	2
1	1	1	0.9315	0.0685
2	1	1	0.9893	0.0107
3	1	1	0.8474	0.1526
4	1	2*	0.4106	0.5894
5	1	1	0.9634	0.0366
6	1	2*	0.2232	0.7768
7	1	2*	0.2843	0.7157
8	1	1	0.6752	0.3248
9	1	1	0.8873	0.1127
10	1	2*	0.1508	0.8492
11	1	2*	0.3842	0.6158
12	1	1	0.9234	0.0766
13	1	2*	0.2860	0.7140

(continued)

284

TABLE 7.7 (Continued)

Obs	GPRSK	into GPRISK	1	2
14	1	2*	0.3004	0.6996
15	1	2*	0.1857	0.8143
16	1	1	0.7729	0.2271
17	1	1	0.9955	0.0045
18	1	1	0.8639	0.1361
19	1	1	0.9118	0.0882
20	1	1	0.5605	0.4395
21	1	1	0.7740	0.2260
22	1	1	0.6501	0.3499
23	1	1	0.8230	0.1770
24	1	2*	0.1562	0.8438
25	1	1	0.8113	0.1887
26	1	1	0.9462	0.0538
27	2	2	0.1082	0.8918
28	2	2	0.1225	0.8775
29	2	2	0.4710	0.5290
30	2	2	0.3572	0.6428
31	2	2	0.4485	0.5515
32	2	2	0.1679	0.8321
33	2	2	0.4639	0.5361
34	2	2	0.3878	0.6122
35	2	2	0.2762	0.7238
36	2	1*	0.5927	0.4073
37	2	2	0.1607	0.8393
38	2	2	0.1591	0.8409

*Misclassified observation

To use prior probability in the SAS DISCRIM program is easy (see SAS/STAT User's Guide, Vol. 1, p. 694).

Example 3—National Merit Data

We consider a second example to illustrate randomly splitting the sample and cross validating the classification function with BMDP7M.. We use part of the data from the National Merit scholars example used earlier in this chapter. The national merit scholars whose parents had an eighth grade education or less are compared against the scholars both of whose parents had at least one college degree on the conventional, enterprising, and artistic variables. The control lines for running the analysis are given in Table 7.8, along with considerable annotation. The data is given in the back of the book. The classification matrix, giving the number of hits in the derivation sample and the validation sample, is also presented in Table 7.8.

7.10.   LINEAR VS. QUADRATIC CLASSIFICATION RULE

There is a more complicated quadratic classification rule available. However, the following comments should be kept in mind before using it. Johnson and

TABLE 7.8

Randomly Splitting the Grades and College Groups of National Merit
Data and Cross Validating the Classification Function

```
/PROBLEM TITLE IS 'MERIT SCHOLARS-GRADES VS COLLEGE—CROSS VALD CLASSIFICATION FUNCTION'.
/INPUT VARIABLES = 4. FORMAT IS STREAM.
/VARIABLE NAMES ARE GPID,CONVEN,ENTERP,ARTISTIC.GROUPING IS GPID.
/TRANSFORM IF(RNDU(1235783) LE. 5) THEN GPID = GPID + 2.
/GROUP CODE(S) ARE 1 TO 4. NAMES(1) ARE GRAD,COLL,NEWGRAD,NEWCOLL. USE = 1 TO 2.
/ DISCRIM LEVELS ARE 0,1,1,1. FORCE = 1.
/END
```

It is the TRANSFORM paragraph that we split the cases in each of the
grades and college groups into two random subgroups. The random number
routine (RNDU) which generates numbers on the interval from 0 to 1 is
accessed. If the number generated is < .5, then the case in GRAD becomes
a member of a validation sample for GRAD. That is, this case goes in group 3
(NEWGRAD), since it's GPID = GPID + 2 = 1 + 2 = 3. If the number
generated for a case in GRAD is > .5, then the group identification for that
case remains as 1, and this case is a member of the derivation sample for
GRAD. The same type of thing is done in splitting the COLL cases into
derivation and validation subsamples. The USE = 1 to 2. in the GROUP
paragraph indicates that *only* the cases in groups 1 and 2 will be used in
deriving the classification function, which will then be tested on groups 3
and 4 (the validation subsamples).

CLASSIFICATION MATRIX

GROUP	PERCENT CORRECT	NUMBER OF CASES CLASSIFIED INTO GROUP-	
		GRAD	COLL
GRADE	62.5	30	18
COLL	68.8	10	22
NEWGRAD	0.0	24	18
NEWCOLL	0.0	17	26
TOTAL	65.0	81	84

The number of hit drops from 65% for the derivaticn sample (52 of 80) to 58.8%
for the validation sample (50 of 85). While this may not seem like a large
drop, it is large enough to cause the number of hits in validation sample to
dip to the chance level. To show this we employ the Huberty one-tailed z
statistic:

$$z = \frac{(o - e)\sqrt{N}}{\sqrt{e(N - e)}} = \frac{(50 - 42.5)\sqrt{85}}{\sqrt{42.5\,(85 - 42.5)}} = 1.62$$

which is not significant at the .05 level, since the critical value = 1.64. (o is
total number of hits and e is number of hits expected by chance.)

Wichern (1982) indicate, "The quadratic . . . rules are appropriate if normality appears to hold but the assumption of equal covariance matrices is seriously violated. However, the assumption of normality seems to be more critical for quadratic rules than linear rules" (p. 504). And Huberty (1984) states, "The stability of results yielded by a linear rule is greater than results yielded by a quadratic rule when small samples are used and when the normality condition is not met" (p. 165).

7.11. CHARACTERISTICS OF A GOOD CLASSIFICATION PROCEDURE

One obvious characteristic of a good classification procedure is that the hit rate be high, i.e., we should have mainly correct classifications. But another important consideration, sometimes lost sight of, is the cost of misclassification (financial or otherwise). The cost of misclassifying a subject from group A in group B may be greater than misclassifying a subject from group B in group A. We give three examples to illustrate:

1. A medical researcher wishes classify subjects as low risk or high risk in terms of developing cancer on the basis of family history, personal health habits, and environmental factors. Here, saying a subject is low risk when in fact he is high risk is more serious than classifying a subject as high risk when he is low risk.
2. A bank wishes to classify low and high risk credit customers. Certainly, for the bank, misclassifying high risk customers as low risk is going to be more costly than misclassifying low risk as high risk customers.
3. This example was illustrated previously, i.e., of identifying low risk vs. high risk kindergarten children, with respect to possible reading problems in the early elementary grades. Once again, misclassifying a high risk child as low risk is more serious than misclassifying a low risk child as high risk. In the former case, the child who needs help (intervention) doesn't receive it.

The Multivariate Normality Assumption

Recall that linear discriminant analysis is based on the assumption of multivariate normality, and that quadratic rules are also sensitive to a violation of this assumption. Thus, in situations where multivariate normality is particularly suspect, for example when using some discrete dichotomous variables, an alternative classification procedure is desirable. Logistic regression (Press & Wilson, 1978) is a good choice here; it is available on SPSSX (in the Loglinear procedure) and in the BMDP package.

7.12.   SUMMARY OF MAJOR POINTS

1.   Discriminant analysis is used for two purposes: (a) for describing major differences among groups, and (b) for classifying subjects into groups on the basis of a battery of measurements.

2.   The major differences among the groups are revealed through the use of uncorrelated linear combinations of the original variables, i.e., the discriminant functions. Since the discriminant functions are uncorrelated, they yield an additive partitioning of the between association.

3.   Use the discriminant function-variable correlations to name the discriminant functions and the standardized coefficients to determine which of the variables are redundant.

4.   About 20 subjects per variable are needed for reliable results, i.e., to have confidence that the variables selected for interpreting the discriminant functions would again show up in an independent sample from the same population.

5.   Stepwise discriminant analysis should be used with caution.

6.   For the classification problem, it is assumed that the two populations are multivariate normal and have the same covariance matrix.

7.   The hit rate is the number of correct classifications, and is an optimistic value, since we are using a mathematical maximization procedure. To obtain a more realistic estimate of how good the classification function is use the jackknife procedure for small or moderate samples, and randomly split the sample and cross validate with large samples. The use of BMDP7M for cross validation was illustrated.

8.   If the covariance matrices are unequal, then a quadratic classification procedure should be considered.

9.   There is evidence that linear classification is more reliable when small samples are used and normality does not hold.

10.   The cost of misclassifying must be considered in judging the worth of a classification rule. Of procedures A and B, with the same overall hit rate, A would be considered better if it resulted in less "costly" misclassifications.

EXERCISES FOR CHAPTER 7—DISCRIMINANT ANALYSIS

1.   Run a discriminant analysis on the data from Exercise 1 in Chapter 5 using the DISCRIMINANT program.

a) How many discriminant functions are there?
b) Which of the discriminant functions are significant at the .05 level?
c) Show how the chi-square values for the residual test procedure are obtained, using the eigenvalues on the printout.

Run a discriminant analysis on this data again, but this time using SPSSX MANOVA. Use the following PRINT subcommand:

PRINT = ERROR(SSCP) SIGNIF(HYPOTH) DISCRIM(RAW)/

ERROR(SSCP) is used to obtain the error sums of square and cross products matrix, i.e., the **W** matrix. SIGNIF(HYPOTH) is used to obtain the hypothesis SSCP, i.e., the **B** matrix here, while DISCRIM(RAW) is used to obtain the raw discriminant function coefficients.

d) Recall that $\mathbf{a}'$ was used to denote the vector of raw discriminant coefficients. By plugging the coefficients into $\mathbf{a}'\mathbf{B}\mathbf{a}/\mathbf{a}'\mathbf{W}\mathbf{a}$ show that the value is equal to the largest eigenvalue of $\mathbf{B}\mathbf{W}^{-1}$ given on the printout.

2.   Plot the groups for the McNeil-Karr study (Table 7.3) in the discriminant plane. Which groups show the largest visual separation.

3.   (a) Given the results of the Smart study, which of the 4 multivariate test statistics do you think would be most powerful?

b) From the results of the Stevens study, which of the 4 multivariate test statistics would be most powerful?

4.   Press and Wilson (1978) examined population change data for the 50 states. The percent change in population from the 1960 census to the 1970 census for each state was coded as 0 or 1, according to whether the change was below or above the median change for all states. This is the grouping variable. The following demographic variables are to be used to explain the population changes: (1) per capita income (in $1,000), (2) percent birth rate, (3) presence or absence of a coastline and (4) percent death rate.

a) Run the discriminant analysis, forcing in all predictors, to see how well the states can be classified (as below or above the median). What is the hit rate?

b) Run the jackknife classification. Does the hit rate drop off appreciably?

Data for Exercise 4

State	Population change	Income	Births	Coast	Deaths
Arkansas	0	2.878	1.8	0	1.1
Colorado	1	3.855	1.9	0	.8
Delaware	1	4.524	1.9	1	.9
Georgia	1	3.354	2.1	1	.9
Idaho	0	3.290	1.9	0	.8
Iowa	0	3.751	1.7	0	1.0
Mississippi	0	2.626	2.2	1	1.0
New Jersey	1	4.701	1.6	1	.9
Vermont	1	3.468	1.8	0	1.0
Washington	1	4.053	1.8	1	.9

(*Continued*)

Data for Exercise 4 (*Continued*)

State	Population change	Income	Births	Coast	Deaths
Kentucky	0	3.112	1.9	0	1.0
Louisiana	1	3.090	2.7	1	1.3
Minnesota	1	3.859	1.8	0	.9
New Hampshire	1	3.737	1.7	1	1.0
North Dakota	0	3.086	1.9	0	.9
Ohio	0	4.020	1.9	0	1.0
Oklahoma	0	3.387	1.7	0	1.0
Rhode Island	0	3.959	1.7	1	1.0
South Carolina	0	2.990	2.0	1	.9
West Virginia	0	3.061	1.7	0	1.2
Connecticut	1	4.917	1.6	1	.8
Maine	0	3.302	1.8	1	1.1
Maryland	1	4.309	1.5	1	.8
Massachusetts	0	4.340	1.7	1	1.0
Michigan	1	4.180	1.9	0	.9
Missouri	0	3.781	1.8	0	1.1
Oregon	1	3.719	1.7	1	.9
Pennsylvania	0	3.971	1.6	1	1.1
Texas	1	3.606	2.0	1	.8
Utah	1	3.227	2.6	0	.7
Alabama	0	2.948	2.0	1	1.0
Alaska	1	4.644	2.5	1	1.0
Arizona	1	3.665	2.1	0	.9
California	1	4.493	1.8	1	.8
Florida	1	3.738	1.7	1	1.1
Nevada	1	4.563	1.8	0	.8
New York	0	4.712	1.7	1	1.0
South Dakota	0	3.123	1.7	0	2.4
Wisconsin	1	3.812	1.7	0	.9
Wyoming	0	3.815	1.9	0	.9
Hawaii	1	4.623	2.2	1	.5
Illinois	0	4.507	1.8	0	1.0
Indiana	1	.3.772	1.9	0	.9
Kansas	0	3.853	1.6	0	1.0
Montana	0	3.500	1.8	0	.9
Nebraska	0	3.789	1.8	0	1.1
New Mexico	0	3.077	2.2	0	.7
North Carolina	1	3.252	1.9	1	.9
Tennessee	0	3.119	1.9	0	1.0
Virginia	1	3.712	1.8	1	.8

8 Factorial Analysis of Variance

8.1. INTRODUCTION

In this chapter we consider the effect of two or more independent or classification variables (e.g., sex, social class, treatments) on a set of dependent variables. Four schematic two-way designs, where just the classification variables are shown are given below:

	Treatments		
	1	2	3
Male			
Female			

	Teaching Methods		
	1	2	3
Urban			
Suburban			
Rural			

	Drugs			
	1	2	3	4
Schizop.				
Depressives				

	Stimulus Complexity		
Intell.	Easy	Aver.	Hard
Average			
Super.			

We indicate what the advantages of a factorial design are over a one-way design. We also remind the reader what an interaction means, and distinguish between the two types of interaction (ordinal and disordinal). The univariate, equal cell size (balanced design) situation is discussed first. Then we tackle the much more difficult disproportional (non-orthogonal or unbalanced) case. Three different ways of handling the unequal n case are considered, it is indicated why we feel one of these methods is generally superior. We then discuss a multivariate factorial design, and finally the interpretation of a three-way interaction. The control lines for running the various analyses is given, and selected printout from both SPSSX MANOVA and from BMDP4V are discussed.

8.2.   ADVANTAGES OF A TWO-WAY DESIGN

1.   A two-way design enables us to examine the *joint* effect of the independent variables on the dependent variable(s). We cannot get this information by running two separate one-way analyses, one for each of the independent variables. If one of the independent variables is treatments and the other some individual difference characteristic (sex, I.Q., locus of control, age, etc.), then a significant interaction tells us that the superiority of one treatment over another is *moderated* by the individual difference characteristic. (An interaction means that the effect one independent variable has on a dependent variable is not the same for all levels of the other independent variable). This moderating effect can take two forms:

a) The degree of superiority changes, but one subgroup always does better than another. To illustrate this, consider the following ability by teaching methods design:

	Methods of Teaching		
	T_1	T_2	T_3
High Ability	85	80	76
Low Ability	60	63	68

The superiority of the high ability students changes from 25 for T_1 to only 8 for T_3, but high ability students always do better than low ability students. Since the order of superiority is maintained, this is called an *ordinal* interaction.

b) The superiority reverses, i.e., one treatment is best with one group, but another treatment is better for a different group. A study by Daniels and Stevens (1976) provides an illustration of this more dramatic type of interaction, called a disordinal interaction. On a group of college undergraduates, they considered two types of instruction: (1) a traditional, teacher controlled (lecture) type and (2) a contract for grade plan. The subjects were classified as internally or externally controlled, using Rotter's scale. An internal orientation means that those subjects perceive positive events occur as a consequence of their actions (i.e., they are in control), while external subjects feel that positive and/or negative events occur more because of powerful others, or due to chance or fate. The design and the means for the subjects on an achievement posttest in psychology are given below:

		Instruction	
		Contract for Grade	Teacher Controlled
Locus of control	Internal	50.52	38.01
	External	36.33	46.22

The moderator variable in this case is locus of control, and it has a substantial effect on the efficacy of an instructional method. When the subject's locus of control is matched to the teaching method (internals with contract for grade and externals with teacher controlled) they do quite well in terms of achievement; where there is a mismatch achievement suffers.

This study also illustrates how a one-way design can lead to quite misleading results. Suppose Daniels and Stevens had just considered the two methods, ignoring locus of control. The means for achievement for the contract for grade plan and for teacher controlled are 43.42 and 42.11, nowhere near significance. The conclusion would have been that teaching methods don't make a difference. The factorial study shows, however, that methods definitely do make a difference, a quite positive difference if subject locus of control is matched to teaching methods, and an undesirable effect if there is a mismatch.

The general area of matching treatments to individual difference characteristics of subjects is an interesting and important one, and is called *aptitude-treatment interaction* research. A thorough and critical analysis of many studies in this area is covered in the excellent text *Aptitudes and Instructional Methods* by Cronbach and Snow (1977).

2. A second advantage of factorial designs is that they can lead to more powerful tests by reducing error (within cell) variance. If performance on the dependent variable is related to the individual difference characteristic (the blocking variable), then the reduction can be substantial. We consider a hypothetical sex × treatment design to illustrate

	T_1		T_2	
Males	18, 19, 21 20, 22	(2.5)	17, 16, 16 18, 15	(1.3)
Females	11, 12, 11 13, 14	(1.7)	9, 9, 11 8, 7	(2.2)

Notice that *within* each cell there is very little variability. The within cell variances quantify this, and are given in parentheses. The pooled within cell error term for the factorial analysis is quite small, i.e., 1.925. On the other hand, if this had been considered as a two-group design, the variability is considerably greater, as evidenced by the within *group* (treatment) variances for T_1 and T_2 of 18.766 and 17.6, and a pooled error term for the t test of 18.18.

8.3.   UNIVARIATE FACTORIAL ANALYSIS

Equal Cell *n* (Orthogonal) Case

When there are an equal number of subjects in each cell in a factorial design, then the sum of squares for the different effects (main and interactions) are uncorrelated (orthogonal). This is important in terms of interpreting results, since significance for one effect implies nothing about significance on another. This helps for a clean and clear interpretation of results. It puts us in the same nice situation we had with uncorrelated planned comparisons, which we discussed in Chapter 5.

Overall and Spiegel (1969), in a classic paper on analyzing factorial designs, discuss three basic methods of analysis:

Method 1: Adjust each effect for all other effects in the design to obtain it's unique contribution (regression approach).

Method 2: Estimate the main effects ignoring the interaction, but estimate the interaction effect adjusting for the main effects (experimental method).

Method 3: Based on theory and/or previous research, establish an ordering for the effects, and then adjust each effect only for those effects preceding it in the ordering (hierarchical approach).

For equal cell size designs all three of the above methods yield the same results, i.e., the same F tests. Therefore, it will not make any difference, in terms of the conclusions a researcher draws, as to which of these methods is used on one of the packages. *For unequal cell sizes, however, these methods can yield quite different results,* and this is what we consider shortly. First, however, we consider an example with equal cell size to show two things: (1) that the methods do indeed yield the same results, and (2) to demonstrate, using dummy coding for the effects, that the effects are uncorrelated.

Example—Two Way Equal Cell n

Consider the following 2 × 3 factorial data set:

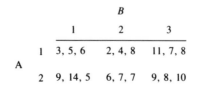

In Table 8.1 we give the control lines for running the analysis on SPSSX MANOVA. In the MANOVA command we indicate the factors after the keyword

BY, with the beginning level for each factor first in parentheses and then the last level for the factor. The DESIGN subcommand lists the effects we wish to test for significance. In this case the program *assumes* a full factorial model by default, and therefore it is not necessary to list the effects.

Method 3, the hierarchical approach, means that a given effect is adjusted for all effects to its left in the ordering. The effects here would go in in the following order: FACA, FACB, FACA BY FACB. Thus, the A main effect is not adjusted for anything. The B main effect is adjusted for the A main effect, and the interaction is adjusted for both main effects.

We also ran this problem using Method 1, the default method starting with Release 2.1, to obtain the unique contribution of each effect, adjusting for all other effects. Note, however, that the F ratios for both methods are identical (cf. Table 8.1). Why? Because the effects are uncorrelated for equal cell size, and therefore no adjustment takes place. Thus, the F for an effect "adjusted" is the same as an effect unadjusted.

To show that the effects are indeed uncorrelated we have dummy coded the effects in Table 8.2 and ran the problem as a regression analysis. The coding scheme is explained there. Predictor A1 represents the A main effect, predictors B1 and B2 represent the B main effect, and predictors A1B1 and A1B2 represent the interaction. We are using all these predictors to explain variation on y. Note that the correlations between predictors representing *different* effects are all 0. This means that those effects are accounting for distinct parts of the variation on y, or that we have an orthogonal partitioning of the y variation.

In Table 8.3 we present the stepwise regression results for the example with the effects entered as the predictors. There we explain how the sum of squares obtained for each effect is exactly the same as was obtained when the problem was run as a traditional ANOVA in Table 8.1.

Example—Two Way Disproportional Cell Size

The data for our disproportional cell size example is given in Table 8.4, along with the dummy coding for the effects, and the correlation matrix for the effects. Here there definitely are correlations among the effects. For example, the correlations between A1 (representing the A main effect) and B1 and B2 (representing the B main effect) are $-.163$ and $-.275$. This contrasts with the equal cell n case where the correlations among the effects were all 0 (Table 8.2). Thus, for disproportional cell sizes the sources of variation are confounded (mixed together). To determine how much unique variation on y a given effect accounts for we must adjust or partial out how much of that variation is explainable because of the effect's correlations with the other effects in the design. Recall that in Chapter 5 the same procedure was employed to determine the unique amount of between variation a given planned comparison accounts for out of a set of correlated planned comparisons.

TABLE 8.1

Control Lines for Two-Way Univariate ANOVA on SPSSX with Sequential and Unique Sum of Square F Ratios

```
TITLE 'TWO WAY UNIVARIATE EQUAL N'
DATA LIST FREE/FACA FACB DEP
LIST
BEGIN DATA
1.00    1.00     3.00
1.00    1.00     5.00
1.00    1.00     6.00
1.00    2.00     2.00
1.00    2.00     4.00
1.00    2.00     8.00
1.00    3.00    11.00
1.00    3.00     7.00
1.00    3.00     8.00
2.00    1.00     9.00
2.00    1.00    14.00
2.00    1.00     5.00
2.00    2.00     6.00
2.00    2.00     7.00
2.00    2.00     7.00
2.00    3.00     9.00
2.00    3.00     8.00
2.00    3.00    10.00
END DATA
MANOVA DEP BY FACA(1,2) FACB(1,3)/
    DESIGN/
```

TESTS OF SIGNIFICANCE FOR DEP USING SEQUENTIAL SUMS OF SQUARES

SOURCE OF VARIATION	SUM OF SQUARES	DF	MEAN SQUARE	F	SIG. OF F
WITHIN CELLS	75.33333	12	6.27778		
CONSTANT	924.50000	1	924.50000	147.26549	.000
FACA	24.50000	1	24.50000	3.90265	.072
FACB	30.33333	2	15.16667	2.41593	.131
FACA BY FACB	14.333333	2	7.16667	1.14159	.352

TESTS OF SIGNIFICANCE FOR DEP USING UNIQUE SUM OF SQUARES

SOURCE OF VARIATION	SUM OF SQUARES	DF	MEAN SQUARE	F	SIG. OF F
WITHIN CELLS	75.33333	12	6.27778		
CONSTANT	924.50000	1	924.50000	147.26549	.000
FACA	24.50000	1	24.50000	3.90265	.072
FACB	30.33333	2	15.16667	2.41593	.131
FACA BY FACB	14.33333	2	7.16667	1.14159	.352

TABLE 8.2

Regression Analysis of Two-Way Equal n ANOVA with Effects
Dummy Coded & Correlation Matrix for the Effects

```
/PROBLEM TITLE IS 'EFFECTS DUMMY CODED FOR 2 WAY—EQUAL N—FOR REGRESSION'.
/INPUT VARIABLES ARE 6. FORMAT IS STREAM.
/VARIABLE NAMES ARE A1,B1,B2,A1B1,AIB2,Y,
/PRINT CORR. DATA.
/REGRESS DEPENDENT IS Y. LEVELS ARE 1,2,2,3,3.
 FORCE = 3.
/END
```

Y	AI ①	B1	B2	A1B1	AIB2
3.000	1.000	1.000	0.0000	1.000	0.0000
5.000	1.000	1.000	0.0000	1.000	0.0000
6.000	1.000	1.000	0.0000	1.000	0.0000
2.000	1.000	0.0000	1.000	0.0000	1.000
4.000	1.000	0.0000	1.000	0.0000	1.000
8.000	1.000	0.0000	1.000	0.0000	1.000
11.00	1.000	− 1.000	− 1.000	− 1.000	− 1.000
7.000	1.000	− 1.000	− 1.000	− 1.000	− 1.000
8.000	1.000	− 1.000	− 1.000	− 1.000	− 1.000
9.000	− 1.000	1.000	0.0000	− 1.000	0.0000
14.00	− 1.000	1.000	0.0000	− 1.000	0.0000
5.000	− 1.000	1.000	0.0000	− 1.000	0.0000
6.000	− 1.000	0.0000	1.000	0.0000	− 1.000
7.000	− 1.000	0.0000	1.000	0.0000	− 1.000
7.000	− 1.000	0.0000	1.000	0.0000	− 1.000
9.000	− 1.000	− 1.000	− 1.000	1.000	1.000
8.000	− 1.000	− 1.000	− 1.000	1.000	1.000
10.00	− 1.000	− 1.000	− 1.000	1.000	1.000

CORRELATION MATRIX

	A MAIN EFFECT	B MAIN EFFECT		AB INTERACTION		
	A1	B1	B2	A1B1	A2B2	Y
A1	1.0000					
B1	0.0000	1.0000				
B2	0.0000	0.5000	1.0000			
A1B1 ②	0.0000	− 0.0000	0.0000	1.0000		
A1B2	0.0000	− 0.0000	− 0.0000	0.5000	1.0000	
Y	− 0.4118	− 0.2642	− 0.4563	− 0.3122	− 0.1201	1.0000

①The S's in the first level of B are coded a 1's on the first dummy variable (A1 here), with the S's for all other levels of B, except the last, coded as 0's. THe S's inthe last level of B are coded as − 1's. Similarly, the S's on the second level of B are coded as 1's on the second dummy variable (B2 here), with the S's for all other levels of B, except the last, coded as 0's. Again, the S's in the last level of B are coded as − 1.'s. To obtain the elements for the interaction dummy variables, ie., A1B1 and A1B2, multiply the corresponding elements of the dummy variables comprising the interaction variable. Thus, to obtain the elements of A1B1 multiply the elements of A1 by the elements of B1.

②Note that the correlations between variables representing *different* effects are all 0. The only non-zero correlations are for the two variables that jointly represent the B main effect (B1 and B2), and for the two variables (A1B1 and A1B2) that jointly represent the AB interaction effect.

TABLE 8.3
Stepwise Regression Results for Two-Way Equal n ANOVA with the
Effects Entered as the Predictors

STEP NO. 1		A1			
VARIABLE ENTERED					
ANALYSIS OF VARIANCE		SUM OF SQUARES	DF	MEAN SQUARE	F RATIO
REGRESSION		24.499954	1	24.49995	3.27
RESIDUAL		120.00003	16	7.500002	
STEP NO.	2	B2			
VARIABLE ENTERED					
ANALYSIS OF VARIANCE		SUM OF SQUARES	DF	MEAN SQUARE	F RATIO
REGRESSION		54.583191	2	27.29160	4.55
RESIDUAL		89.916794	15	8.994452	
STEP NO.	3				
VARIABLE ENTERED		B1			
ANALYSIS OF VARIANCE		SUM OF SQUARES	DF	MEAN SQUARE	F RATIO
REGRESSION		54.833206	3	18.27773	2.85
RESIDUAL		89.666779	14	6.404770	
STEP NO.	4				
VARIABLE ENTERED		AIB1			
ANALYSIS OF VARIANCE		SUM OF SQUARES	DF	MEAN SQUARE	F RATIO
REGRESSION		68.916504	4	17.22913	2.98
RESIDUAL		75.683481	13	5.814114	
STEP NO.	5				
VARIABLE ENTERED		A1B2			
ANALYSIS OF VARIANCE		SUM OF SQUARES	DF	MEAN SQUARE	F RATIO
REGRESSION		69.166489	5	13.83330	2.20
RESIDUAL		75.333496	12	6.277791	

Note that the sum of squares (*SS*) for regression for A1, representing the A main effect, is the same as the *SS* for FACA in Table 8.1. Also, the *additional SS* for B1 and B2, representing the B main effect, is $54.833 - 24.5 = 30.333$, the same as SS for FACB in Table 8.1. Finally, the additional SS for A1B1 and A1B2, representing the AB interaction, is $69.166 - 54.833 = 14.333$, the same as SS for FACA by FACB in Table 8.1

TABLE 8.4
Control Lines for Two-Way Disproportional Cell n ANOVA on SPSSX with the Sequential and Unique Sum of Squares F Ratios

```
TITLE 'TWO WAY UNIVARIATE ANOVA UNEQUAL N'
DATA LIST FREE/ FACA FACB DEF
LIST
BEGIN DATA
1.00          1.00          3.00
1.00          1.00          5.00
1.00          1.00          6.00
1.00          2.00          2.00
1.00          2.00          4.00
1.00          2.00          8.00
1.00          3.00          11.00
1.00          3.00          7.00
1.00          3.00          8.00
1.00          3.00          6.00
1.00          3.00          9.00
2.00          1.00          9.00
2.00          1.00          14.00
2.00          1.00          5.00
2.00          1.00          11.00
2.00          2.00          6.00
2.00          2.00          7.00
2.00          2.00          7.00
2.00          2.00          8.00
2.00          2.00          10.00
2.00          2.00          5.00
2.00          2.00          6.00
2.00          3.00          9.00
2.00          3.00          8.00
2.00          3.00          10.00
END DATA
MANOVA DEP BY FACA(1,2) FACB(1,3)/
```
① `METHOD = SSTYPE (SEQUENTIAL)/`
② `DESIGN/`

TESTS FOR SIGNIFICANCE FOR DEP USING UNIQUE SUMS OF SQUARES

SOURCE OF VARIATION	SUM OF SQUARES	F		SIG. OF F
WITHIN CELLS	98.88333			
CONSTANT	1176.15503	225.99305		.000
FACA	42.38523	8.14414	③	.010
FACB	30.35239	2.91604		.079
FACA BY FACB	16.77800	1.61191		.226

TESTS OF SIGNIFICANCE FOR DEP USING SEQUENTIAL SUMS OF SQUARES

SOURCE OF VARIATION	SUM OF SQUARES	F		SIG. OF F
WITHIN CELLS	98.8333			
CONSTANT	1354.24000	260.21129		.000
FACA	23.22104	4.46182	③	.048
FACB	38.87763	3.73508		.043
FACA BY FACB	16.77800	1.61191		.226

① To obtain the sequential sum of squares for each effect.

② By default a full factorial design is assumed by the program; thus it is not necessary to list each effect.

③ Note that the F ratios for the interation effect are the same, however, the F ratios for the main effects are quite different.

TABLE 8.5
Dummy Coding of the Effects for the Disproportional Cell n ANOVA and Correlation Matrix for the Effects

	DESIGN B		
A	3, 5, 6	2, 4, 8	11, 7, 8, 6, 9
	9, 14, 5, 11	6, 7, 7, 8, 10, 5, 6	9, 8, 10

A1	B1	B2	A1B1	A1B2	Y
1.00	1.00	.00	1.00	.00	3.00
1.00	1.00	.00	1.00	.00	5.00
1.00	1.00	.00	1.00	.00	6.00
1.00	.00	1.00	.00	1.00	2.00
1.00	.00	1.00	.00	1.00	4.00
1.00	.00	1.00	.00	1.00	8.00
1.00	− 1.00	− 1.00	− 1.00	− 1.00	11.00
1.00	− 1.00	− 1.00	− 1.00	− 1.00	7.00
1.00	− 1.00	− 1.00	− 1.00	− 1.00	8.00
1.00	− 1.00	− 1.00	− 1.00	− 1.00	6.00
1.00	− 1.00	− 1.00	− 1.00	− 1.00	9.00
− 1.00	1.00	.00	− 1.00	.00	9.00
− 1.00	1.00	.00	− 1.00	.00	14.00
− 1.00	1.00	.00	− 1.00	.00	5.00
− 1.00	1.00	.00	− 1.00	.00	11.00
− 1.00	.00	1.00	.00	− 1.00	6.00
− 1.00	.00	1.00	.00	− 1.00	7.00
− 1.00	.00	1.00	.00	− 1.00	7.00
− 1.00	.00	1.00	.00	− 1.00	8.00
− 1.00	.00	1.00	.00	− 1.00	10.00
− 1.00	.00	1.00	.00	− 1.00	5.00
− 1.00	.00	1.00	.00	− 1.00	6.00
− 1.00	− 1.00	− 1.00	1.00	1.00	9.00
− 1.00	− 1.00	− 1.00	1.00	1.00	8.00
− 1.00	− 1.00	− 1.00	1.00	1.00	10.00

	FOR A MAIN EFFECT	FOR B MAIN EFFECT		FOR AB INTERACTION EFFECT		
CORRELATION:						
	AI	B1	B2	A1B1	A1B2	Y
A1	1.000	−.163	−.275	−.072	.063	−.361
B1	−.163	1.000	.495	.059	.112	−.148
B2	−.275	.495	1.000	.139	−.088	−.350
A1B1	−0.72	0.59	1.39	1.000	.458	−332
A1B2	.063	.112	−.088	.468	1.000	−.089
Y	−.361	−.148	−.350	−.332	−.089	1.000

The correlations between variables representing different effects are boxed in. Contrast with the situation for equal cell size, as presented in Table 8.2.

In Table 8.5 we present the control lines for running the disproportional cell size example, along with Method 1 (unique sum of squares) results and Method 3 (hierarchical or called sequential on the printout) results. The F ratios for the interaction effect are the same, but the F ratios for the main effects are quite different. For example, if we had used the default option (Method 3) we would have declared a significant B main effect at the .05 level, but with Method 1 (unique decomposition) the B main effect is not significant at the .05 level. Therefore, with unequal n designs the method used can clearly make a difference in terms of the conclusions reached in the study. This raises the question of which of the three methods should be used for disproportional cell size factorial designs.

Which Method Should be Used?

Overall and Spiegel (1969) recommended Method 2 as generally being most appropriate. We do not agree, feeling that Method 2 would rarely be the method of choice, since it estimates the main effects ignoring the interaction. Carlson and Timm's comment (1974) is appropriate here: "We find it hard to believe that a researcher would consciously design a factorial experiment and then ignore the factorial nature of the data in testing the main effects" (p. 156).

We feel that Method 1, where we are obtaining the unique contribution of each effect, is generally more appropriate. This is what Carlson and Timm (1974) recommend, and what Myers (1979) recommends for experimental studies (random assignment involved), or as he put it, "whenever variations in cell frequencies can reasonably be assumed due to chance."

Where an a priori ordering of the effects can be established (Overall and Spiegel, 1969, give a nice psychiatric example), Method 3 makes sense. This is analogous to establishing an a priori ordering of the predictors in multiple regression. Pedhazur (1982) gives the following example. There is a 2 × 2 design in which one of the classification variables is race (black and white) and the other classification variable is education (high school and college). The dependent variable is income. In this case one can argue that race affects one's level of education, but obviously not vice versa. Thus, it makes sense to enter race first to determine it's effect on income, then to enter education to determine how much it adds in predicting income. Finally, the race × education interaction is entered.

8.4. FACTORIAL MULTIVARIATE ANALYSIS OF VARIANCE

Here we are considering the effect of two or more independent variables on a set of dependent variables. To illustrate factorial MANOVA we use an example from Barcikowski (1983). Sixth grade students were classified as being of high,

TABLE 8.6
Control Lines for Factorial MANOVA on SPSSX Using Unique Sum
of Squares Decomposition

```
TITLE 'TWO WAY DISPROP CELL SIZE MANOVA'
DATA LIST FREE/ APTITUDE METHOD ATTIT ACHIEV
LIST
BEGIN DATA
```

1.00	1.00	15.00	11.0
1.00	1.00	9.00	7.00
1.00	2.00	19.00	11.00
1.00	2.00	12.00	9.00
1.00	2.00	12.00	6.00
1.00	3.00	14.00	13.00
1.00	3.00	9.00	9.00
1.00	3.00	14.00	15.00
1.00	4.00	19.00	14.00
1.00	4.00	7.00	8.00
1.00	4.00	6.00	6.00
1.00	5.00	14.00	16.00
1.00	5.00	14.00	8.00
1.00	5.00	18.00	16.00
2.00	1.00	18.00	13.00
2.00	1.00	8.00	11.00
2.00	1.00	6.00	6.00
2.00	2.00	25.00	24.00
2.00	2.00	24.00	23.00
2.00	2.00	26.00	19.00
2.00	3.00	29.00	23.00
2.00	3.00	28.00	26.00
2.00	4.00	11.00	14.00
2.00	4.00	14.00	10.00
2.00	4.00	8.00	7.00
2.00	5.00	18.00	17.00
2.00	5.00	11.00	13.00
3.00	1.00	11.00	9.00
3.00	1.00	16.00	15.00
3.00	2.00	13.00	11.00
3.00	2.00	10.00	11.00
3.00	3.00	17.00	10.00
3.00	3.00	7.00	9.00
3.00	3.00	7.00	9.00
3.00	4.00	15.00	9.00
3.00	4.00	13.00	13.00
3.00	4.00	7.00	7.00
3.00	5.00	17.00	12.00
3.00	5.00	13.00	15.00
3.00	5.00	9.00	12.00

```
END DATA
MANOVA ATTIT ACHIEV BY APTITUDE(1,3) METHOD(1,5)/
   PRINT = CELLINFO(MEANS,COV,COR)/
   DESIGN = APTITUDE, METHOD,APTITUDE BY METHOD/
```

average, or low aptitude, and then within each of these aptitudes were randomly assigned to one of 5 methods of teaching social studies. The dependent variables were measures of attitude and achievement. The data below resulted:

	Method of Instruction				
	1	2	3	4	5
	15, 11	19, 11	14, 13	19, 14	14, 16
High	9, 7	12, 9	9, 9	7, 8	14, 8
	12, 6	14, 15	6, 6	18, 16
Average	18, 13	25, 24	29, 23	11, 14	18, 17
	8, 11	24, 23	28, 26	14, 10	11, 13
	6, 6	26, 19		8, 7
Low	11, 9	13, 11	17, 10	15, 9	17, 12
	16, 15	10, 11	7, 9	13, 13	13, 15
			7, 9	7, 7	9, 12

Of the 45 subjects who started the study, 5 were lost for various reasons. This resulted in a disproportional factorial design. To obtain the unique contribution of each effect, the unique sum of squares decomposition was run on SPSSX MANOVA. The control lines for doing so are given in Table 8.6. The results of the multivariate and univariate tests of the effects are presented in Table 8.7. All of the multivariate effects are significant at the .05 level. We use the F's associated with Wilks to illustrate (aptitude by method: $F = 2.19$, $p < .018$; method: $F = 2.46$, $p < .025$, and aptitude: $F = 5.92$, $p < .001$). Since the interaction is significant, we focus our interpretation on it. The univariate tests for this effect on attitude and achievement are also both significant at the .05 level. Use of simple effects revealed that it was the attitude and achievement of the average aptitude subjects under methods 2 and 3 that were responsible for the interaction.

8.5.   WEIGHTING OF THE CELL MEANS

In experimental studies that wind up with unequal cell sizes, it is reasonable to assume equal population sizes, and equal cell weighting is appropriate in estimating the grand mean. However, when sampling from intact groups (sex, age, race, SES, religions) in nonexperimental studies, the populations may well differ in size, and the sizes of the samples may reflect the different population sizes. In such cases equally weighting the subgroup means will not provide an unbiased estimate of the combined (grand) mean, whereas weighting the means will produce an unbiased estimate. *The BMDP4V program is specifically set up to provide either equal or unequal weighting of the cell means.* There are situations where one may wish to use both weighted and unweighted cell means in a single factorial design, i.e., in a semi-experimental design. In such designs one of the

TABLE 8.7

Results of Multivariate and Univariate Tests for Main Effects and Interaction for Factorial MANOVA Example

EFFECT .. APTITUDE BY METHOD

MULTIVARIATE TESTS OF SIGNIFICANCE (S = 2, M = 2 1/2, N = 11)

TEST NAME	VALUE	APPROX. F	HYPOTH. F	ERROR DF	SIG. OF F
PILLAIS	.75744	1.90496	16.00	50.00	.042
HOTELLINGS	1.72683	2.48232	16.00	46.00	.008
WILKS	.33341	2.19557	16.00	48.00	.018
ROYS	.60802				

UNIVARIATE F-TESTS WITH (8,25) D. F.

VARIABLE	HYPOTH. SS	ERROR SS	HYPOTH. MS	ERROR MS	F	SIG. OF F
ATT IT	503.32072	460.66667	62.91509	18.42667	3.41436	.009
ACHIEV	343.11228	237.16667	42.8904	9.485667	4.52098	.002

EFFECT .. METHOD

MULTIVARIATE TESTS OF SIGNIFICANCE (S = 2, M = 1/2, N = 11)

TEST NAME	VALUE	APPROX. F	HYPOTH. DF	ERROR DF	SIG. OF F
PILLAIS	.53430	2.27837	8.00	50.00	.037
HOTELLINGS	.91570	2.63264	8.00	46.00	.018
WILKS	.50269	2.46254	8.00	48.00	.025
ROYS	.45256				

(Continued)

TABLE 8.7 (Continued)

UNIVARIATE F-TESTS WITH (4,25) D. F.

VARIABLE	HYPOTH. SS	ERROR SS	HYPOTH. MS	ERRORS MS	F	SIG. OF F
ATTIT	237.90643	460.66667	59.47661	18.42667	3.22775	.029
ACHIEV	189.88095	237.16667	47.47024	9.48667	5.00389	.004

EFFECT .. APTITUDE

MULTIVARIATE TESTS OF SIGNIFICANCE (S = 2, M = $-1/2$, N = 11)

TEST NAME	VALUE	APPROX. F	HYPOTH. DF	ERROR DF	SIG. OF F
PILLAIS	.57396	5.03102	4.00	50.00	.002
HOTELLINGS	1.17920	6.78038	4.00	46.00	.000
WILKS	.44855	6.91734	4.00	48.00	.001
ROYS	.53161				

UNIVARIATE F-TESTS WITH (2,25) D. F.

VARIABLE	HYPOTH. SS	ERROR SS	HYPOTH. MS	ERROR MS	F	SIG. OF F
ATTIT	256.50817	460.66667	128.25408	18.42667	6.96024	.004
ACHIEV	267.55842	237.16667	133. 7921	9.48667	14.10181	.000

TABLE 8.8
BMDP4V Control Lines for Factorial MANOVA with Multivariate and Univariate Tests for Effects

```
/PROBLEM TITLE IS ' 3 × 5 FACTORIAL MANOVA—APTITUDE × METHOD
/INPUT VARIABLES = 4. FORMAT IS STREAM.
/VARIABLE NAMES ARE APTITUDE,METHOD.
/BETWEEN FACTORS ARE APTITUDE,METHOD.
 CODES(1) ARE 1 TO 3.
 NAMES(1) ARE HIGH,AVER,LOW.
 CODES(2) ARE 1 TO 5.
 NAMES(2) ARE M1,M2,M3,M4,M5.
/WEIGHTS BETWEEN ARE EQUAL.
 /END
 DATA.
 /END.
/ANALYSIS PROC = FACTORIAL
```

EFFECT	VARIATE	STATISTIC		F	DF		P
A: APTITUDE							
	ALL						
		① LRATIO =	0.448555	5.92	4.	48.00	
		TRACE =	1.17920				
		TZSG = 29.4799					
		CHISQ =	3.60		15.344		0.0006
		MXROOT =	0.531611				0.0005
	ATTITUDE					0.0005	
		SS =	256.508	6.96	2.	25	0.0040
		MS =	128.254				
	ACHIEV		②				
		SS =	267.558	14.10	2.	25	0.0001
		MS = 133.779					
M: METHOD							
	ALL						
		LRATIO =	0.502691	2.46	8.	48.00	0.0254
		TRACE =	0.915701				
		TZSQ =	22.8925				
		CHISQ =	10.08		21.081		0.0215
		MXROOT =	0.452558				0.0287
	ATTITUDE						0.0289
		SS =	237.906				
		MS =	59.4766	3.23	4.	25	
	ACHIEV						
		SS =	189.881	5.00	4.	25	0.0042
		MS =	47.4702				
AM							
	ALL						
		LRATIO =	0.333408	2.20	16.	48.00	0.0184
		TRACE =	1.72683				
		TZSQ =	43.1708				
		CHISQ =	13.03		26.978		0.0111
		MXROOT = 0.608021					0.0454
	ATTITUDE						
		SS =	503.321	3.41	8.	25	.0087
		MS =	62.9151				
	ACHIEV						
		SS =	343.112	4.52	8.	25	0.0017
		MS = 42.8890					
ERROR							
	ATTITUDE						
		SS =	460.66667				
		MS =	18.426667				
	ACHIEV						
		SS =	237.16667				
		MS = 9.4866667					

①LRATIO—Wilk's Λ, TRACE—Hotellings, MXROOT—Roy's (largest root)
②These are the univariate tests for the dependent variables.

factors is an attribute factor (sex, SES, race, etc.) and the other factor is treatments. Suppose for a given situation it is reasonable to assume there are twice as many middle SES in a population as lower SES, and that two treatments are involved. Forty lower SES are sampled and randomly assigned to treatments, and 80 middle SES are selected and assigned to treatments. Schematically then, the setup of the weighted and unweighted means is:

		T_1	T_2	Unweighted Means
SES	Lower	$n_{11} = 20$	$n_{12} = 20$	$(\mu_{11} + \mu_{12})/2$
	Middle	$n_{21} = 40$	$n_{22} = 40$	$(\mu_{21} + \mu_{22})/2$
Weighted Means		$\dfrac{n_{11}\mu_{11} + n_{21}\mu_{21}}{n_{11} + n_{21}}$	$\dfrac{n_{12}\mu_{12} + n_{22}\mu_{22}}{n_{12} + n_{22}}$	

We illustrate the set up of the BMDP4V program for cell mean weighting with the previous aptitude by methods example. The control lines for equal cell mean weighting are given in Table 8.8. Notice that the weighting is requested in the following paragraph:

/WEIGHTS BETWEEN ARE EQUAL.

If we wished to use weighted means for the test of treatment main effect, and unweighted means for the test of the aptitude main effect, as in the above example, then we would make an additional run requesting weighted cell means:

/WEIGHTS BETWEEN ARE SIZES.

Then we would use the test from the weighted cell mean run for the treatment main effect, and use the test from the unweighted cell mean run for the aptitude main effect.

8.6. THREE-WAY MANOVA

This section is included to show how to set up the control lines for running a three-way MANOVA, and to indicate a procedure for interpreting a three way interaction. We take the previous aptitude by method example and add sex as an additional factor. Then assuming we will use the same two dependent variables, the *only* change that is required in the control lines presented in Table 8.6 is that the MANOVA command becomes:

MANOVA ATTIT ACHIEV BY APTITUDE(1,3) METHOD(1,5) SEX(1,2)

We wish to focus our attention on the interpretation of a three-way interaction, if it were significant in such a design. First, what does a significant three-way interaction mean for a single variable? If the 3 factors are denoted by A, B, and C, then *a significant ABC interaction implies that the two-way interaction profiles for the different levels of the third factor are different.* A nonsignificant three-way interaction means that the two-way profiles are the same, i.e., the differences can be attributed to sampling error.

Example

Consider a sex (A) by treatments (B) by race (C) design. Suppose that the two way design (collapsed on race) looked like this:

	Treatments	
	1	2
Males	60	50
Females	40	42

This profile reveals a significant sex main effect and a significant ordinal interaction. But it does not tell the whole story. Let us examine the profiles for blacks and whites separately (we assume equal n per cell):

	Whites				Blacks	
	T_1	T_2			T_1	T_2
M	65	50	M		55	50
F	40	47	F		40	37

We see that for whites there clearly is an ordinal interaction, whereas for blacks there is no interaction effect. The two profiles are distinctly different. The point is, race further moderates the sex by treatments interaction.

In the context of aptitude-treatment interaction (ATI) research, Cronbach (1975) had an interesting way of characterizing higher order interactions:

> When ATI's are present, a general statement about a treatment effect is misleading because the effect will come or go depending on the kind of person treated . . . An ATI result can be taken as a general conclusion only if it is not in turn moderated by further variables. If Aptitude × Treatment × Sex interact, for example, then the Aptitude × Treatment effect does not tell the story. Once we attend to interactions, we enter a hall of mirrors that extends to infinity. (p. 119)

Thus, to examine the nature of a significant three-way multivariate interaction, one might first determine which of the individual variables are significant (by examining the univariate F's). Then look at the two-way profiles to see how they differ for those variables that are significant.

EXERCISES—CHAPTER 8

1.) Consider the following 2 × 4 equal cell size MANOVA data set (2 dependent variables):

B

6, 10	13, 16	9, 11	21, 19
7, 8	11, 15	8, 8	18, 15
9, 9	17, 18	14, 9	16, 13
11, 8	10, 12	4, 12	11, 10
7, 6	11, 13	10, 8	9, 8
10, 5	14, 10	11, 13	8, 15

A

a) Run the factorial MANOVA on SPSSX using the default option.
b) Which of the multivariate tests for the 3 different effects is(are) significant at the .05 level?
c) For the effect(s) which show multivariate significance, which of the individual variables (at .025 level) are contributing to the multivariate significance?
d) Run the above data on SPSSX using METHOD= SSTYPE (SEQUENTIAL). Are the results different? Explain.

2.) An investigator has the following 2 × 4 MANOVA data set for 2 dependent variables:

B

6, 10	13, 16	9, 11	21, 19
7, 8	11, 15	8, 8	18, 15
	17, 18	14, 9	16, 13
		13, 11	
11, 8	10, 12	14, 12	11, 10
7, 6	11, 13	10, 8	9, 8
10, 5	14, 10	11, 13	8, 15
6, 12			17, 12
9, 7			13, 14
11, 14			

A

2.) a) Run the factorial MANOVA on SPSSX.

b) Which of the multivariate tests for the 3 effects is(are) significant at the .05 level?

c) For the effect(s) that show multivariate significance, which of the individual variables is(are) contributing to the multivariate significance at the .025 level?

d) Is the homogeneity of the covariance matrices assumption for the cells tenable at the .05 level?

e) **Run the factorial MANOVA on the data set using sequential sum of squares option of SPSSX.**
Are the F ratios different? Explain.

f) Dummy code group (cell) membership and run as a regression analysis, in the process obtaining the correlations among the effects, as illustrated in Tables 9.2 and 9.5.

3.) Consider the following hypothetical data for a sex × age × treatment factorial MANOVA on two personality measures:

TREATMENTS

	AGE	1		2	3
MALES	14	8,19	5,18	2,23	6,16
		9,16	7,25	3,27	9,12
		4,20	4,17	8,20	13,24
		3,21			5,20
	17	9,22		4,30	5,15
		11,15		7,25	5,16
		8,14		8,28	9,23
				13,23	8,27
FEMALES	14	10,17		8,26	3,21
		12,18		2,29	7,17
		8,14		10,23	4,15
		7,22		7,17	9,22
					12,23
	17	9,13	5,19	5,14	10,14
		6,18	8,15	11,13	15,18
		12,20	11,1	4,21	9,19
				8,18	

a)   Run the three way MANOVA on SPSSX.

b)   Which of the multivariate effects are significant at the .025 level? What is the overall α for the set of multivariate tests?

c)   Is the homogeneity of covariance matrices assumption tenable at the .05 level?

d)   For the multivariate effects that are significant, which of the individual variables are significant at the .01 level? Interpret the results.

9 Analysis of Covariance

9.1 INTRODUCTION

Analysis of covariance is a statistical technique that combines regression analysis and analysis of variance. It can be helpful in nonrandomized studies in drawing more accurate conclusions. However, precautions have to be taken, or analysis of covariance (ANCOVA) can be misleading in some cases. In this chapter we indicate what the purposes of covariance are, when it is most effective, when the interpretation of results from covariance is "cleanest," and when covariance should not be used. We start with the simplest case, one dependent variable and one covariate, with which many readers may be somewhat familiar. Then we consider one dependent variable and several covariates, where our previous study of multiple regression is helpful. Finally, multivariate analysis of covariance is considered, where there are several dependent variables and several covariates. We show how to run a multivariate analysis of covariance on SPSSX and on SAS and explain the proper order of interpretation of the printout. An extension of the Tukey post hoc procedure, the Bryant-Paulson, is also illustrated.

Examples of Univariate and Multivariate Analysis of Covariance

What is a covariate? A potential covariate is any variable that is significantly correlated with the dependent variable. That is, we assume a *linear* relationship between the covariate (x) and the dependent variable (y).

313

Consider now two typical univariate ANCOVAs with one covariate. In a two-group pretest-posttest design, then the pretest is often used as a covariate, since how the subjects score before treatments is generally correlated with how they score after treatments. Or, suppose three groups are compared on some measure of achievement. In this situation I.Q. is often used as a covariate, since I.Q. is usually at least moderately correlated with achievement.

The reader should recall that the null hypothesis being tested in ANCOVA is that the adjusted population means are equal. Since a linear relationship is assumed between the covariate and the dependent variable, the means are adjusted in a linear fashion. We consider this in detail shortly in this chapter. Thus, in interpreting printout, for either univariate or multivariate analysis of covariance (MANCOVA), it is the adjusted means that need to be examined. It is important to note that SPSSX and SAS do not automatically provide the adjusted means; they must be requested.

Now consider two situations where MANCOVA would be appropriate. A counselor wishes to examine the effect of two different counseling approaches on several personality variables. The subjects are pretested on these variables and then posttested two months later. The pretest scores are the covariates and the posttest scores are the dependent variables. Secondly, a teacher educator wishes to determine the relative efficacy of two different methods of teaching 12th grade mathematics. He uses three subtest scores of achievement on a posttest as the dependent variables. A plausible set of covariates here would be grade in math 11, an I.Q. measure, and say, attitude toward education. The null hypothesis that is tested in MANCOVA is that the adjusted population mean vectors are equal. Recall that the null hypothesis for MANOVA was that the population mean vectors are equal.

Before we proceed further, there are four excellent references for further study of covariance: an elementary introduction (Huck, Cormier, & Bounds, 1974), two good classic review articles (Cochran, 1957, Elashoff, 1969), and especially a very comprehensive and thorough text by Huitema (1980).

9.2   PURPOSES OF COVARIANCE

ANCOVA is linked to the following two basic objectives in experimental design:

1. elimination of systematic bias
2. reduction of within group or error variance

The best way of dealing with systematic bias (e.g., intact groups that differ systematically on several variables) is through random assignment of subjects to groups, thus equating the groups on all variables within sampling error. If random assignment is not possible, however, then covariance can be helpful in reducing bias.

Within group variability, which is primarily due to individual differences among the subjects, can be dealt with in several ways: sample selection (subjects who are more homogeneous will vary less on the criterion measure), factorial designs (blocking), repeated measures analysis, and analysis of covariance. Precisely how covariance reduces error is considered soon. Since analysis of covariance is linked to both of the basic objectives of experimental design, it certainly is a useful tool if properly used and interpreted.

In an experimental study (random assignment of subjects to groups) the main purpose of covariance is to reduce error variance, since there will be no systematic bias. However, if only a small number of subjects (say ≤ 10) can be assigned to each group, then chance differences are more possible and covariance is useful in adjusting the posttest means for the chance differences.

In a nonexperimental study the main purpose of covariance is to adjust the posttest means for initial differences among the groups which are very likely with intact groups. It should be emphasized, however, that even the use of several covariates does *not* equate intact groups, i.e., does not eliminate bias. Nevertheless, the use of 2 or 3 appropriate covariates can make for a much fairer comparison.

We now give two examples to illustrate how initial differences (systematic bias) on a key variable between treatment groups can confound the interpretation of results. Suppose an experimental psychologist wished to determine the effect of 3 methods of extinction on some kind of learned response. There are 3 intact groups to which the methods are applied, and it is found that the average number of trials to extinguish the response is least for method 2. Now, it may be that method 2 is more effective, or it may be that the subjects in method 2 didn't have the response as thoroughly ingrained as the subjects in the other two groups. In the latter case, the response would be easier to extinguish, and it wouldn't be clear whether it was the method that made the difference or the fact that the response was easier to extinguish that made method 2 look better. The effects of the two are confounded or mixed together. What is needed here is a measure of degree of learning at the start of the extinction trials (covariate). Then, if there are initial differences between the groups, the posttest means will be adjusted to take this into account. That is, covariance will adjust the posttest means to what they would be if all groups had started out *equally* on the covariate.

As another example, suppose we are comparing the effect of 4 stress situations on blood pressure, and find that situation 3 was significantly more stressful than the other 3 situations. However, we note that the blood pressure of the subjects in group 3 under minimal stress is greater than for subjects in the other groups. Then as in the previous example, it isn't clear that situation 3 is necessarily most stressful. We need to determine whether the blood pressure for group 3 would still be higher if the means for all 4 groups were adjusted, assuming equal average blood pressure initially.

9.3   ADJUSTMENT OF POSTTEST MEANS AND REDUCTION OF ERROR VARIANCE

As mentioned earlier, analysis of covariance adjusts the posttest means to what they would be if all groups started out equally on the covariate; at the grand mean. In this section we derive the general equation for linearly adjusting the posttest means for one covariate. Before we do that, however, it is important to discuss one of the assumptions underlying the analysis of covariance. That assumption for one covariate requires *equal population regression slopes* for all groups. Consider a three group situation, with 15 subjects per group. Suppose that the scatterplots for the 3 groups looked as given below.

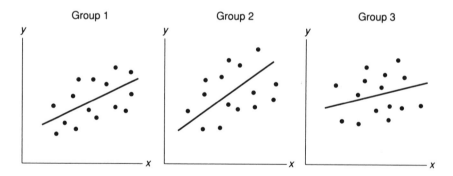

Recall from beginning statistics that the x and y scores for each subject determine a point in the plane. Requiring that the slopes be equal is equivalent to saying that the nature of the linear relationship is the *same* for all groups, or that the rate of change in y as a function of x is the same for all groups. For the above scatterplots the slopes are different, with the slope being the largest for group 2 and smallest for group 3. But the issue is whether the *population* slopes are different, and whether the sample slopes differ sufficiently to conclude that the population values are different. With small sample sizes as in the above scatterplots, it is dangerous to rely on visual inspection to determine whether the population values are equal, because of considerable sampling error. Fortunately there is a statistic for this, and later we indicate how to obtain it on SPSSX and SAS. In deriving the equation for the adjusted means we are going to assume the slopes are equal. What if the slopes are not equal? Then ANCOVA is *not* appropriate, and we indicate alternatives later on in the chapter.

The details of obtaining the adjusted mean for the *i*th group (i.e., any group) are given in Figure 9.1. The general equation follows from the definition for the slope of a straight line and some basic algebra.

In Figure 9.2 we show the adjusted means geometrically for a hypothetical 3 group data set. A positive correlation is assumed between the covariate and the dependent variable, so that a higher mean on x implies a higher mean on y. Note that since group 1 scored below the grand mean on the covariate, its mean is adjusted upward. On the other hand, since the mean for group 3 on the covariate is *above* the grand mean, covariance estimates that it would have scored lower on y if its mean on the covariate was lower (at grand mean), and therefore the mean for group 3 is adjusted downward.

Reduction of Error Variance

Consider a teaching methods study where the dependent variable is chemistry achievement and the covariate is I.Q. Then, within each teaching method there will be considerable variability on chemistry achievement due to individual differences among the students in terms of ability, background, attitude, etc. A sizable portion of this within-variability, however, is due to differences in I.Q. That is, chemistry achievement scores differ partly because the students differ in I.Q. If we can statistically remove this part of the within-variability, a smaller error term results, and hence a more powerful test. We denote the correlation between I.Q. and chemistry achievement by r_{xy}. Recall that the square of a correlation can be interpreted as "variance accounted for." Thus, for example, if $r_{xy} = .71$, then $(.71)^2 = .50$ or 50% of the within variability on chemistry achievement can be accounted for by variability on I.Q.

We denote the within-variability on chemistry achievement by MS_w, i.e., the usual error term for ANOVA. Now, symbolically the part of MS_w that is accounted for by I.Q. is $MS_w \, r_{xy}^2$. Thus, the within-variability that is left, after the portion due to the covariate is removed, is

$$MS_w - MS_w \, r_{xy}^2 = MS_w \, (1 - r_{xy}^2),$$

and this becomes our new error term for analysis of covariance, which we denote by MS_w^*. Technically, there is an additional factor involved, i.e.,

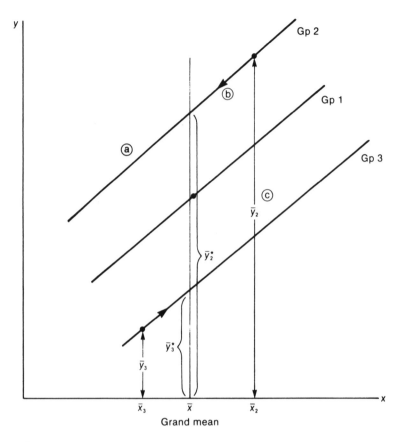

(a) positive correlation assumed between x and y

(b) The arrows on the regression lines indicate that the adjusted
means can be obtained by sliding the mean up (down) the
regression line until it hits the line for the grand mean.

(c) $\bar{y}_2$ is actual mean for Gp 2 and $\bar{y}_2^*$ represents the adjusted mean.

FIG. 9.1.   Regression lines and adjusted means for three-group Analysis of Covariance

$$MS_w{}^* = MS_w\,(1 - r_{xy}{}^2)\,\{1 + 1/(f_e - 2)\} \tag{2}$$

where f_e is error degrees of freedom. However, the effect of this additional
factor is slight as long as $N \geq 50$.

To show how much of a difference a covariate can make in increasing the
sensitivity of an experiment, we consider a hypothetical study. An investigator runs a one-way ANOVA (3 groups and 20 subjects per group), and

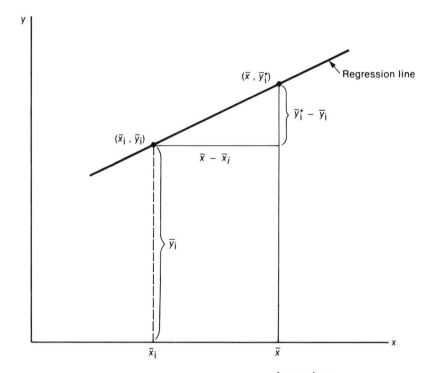

$$\text{Slope of Straight Line} = b = \frac{\text{change in } y}{\text{change in } x}$$

$$b = \frac{\bar{y}_i^* - \bar{y}_i}{\bar{x} - \bar{x}_i}$$

$$b(\bar{x} - \bar{x}_i) = \bar{y}_i^* - \bar{y}_i$$
$$\bar{y}_i^* = \bar{y}_i + b\,(\bar{x} - \bar{x}_i)$$
$$\bar{y}_i^* = \bar{y}_i - b\,(\bar{x}_i - \bar{x}) \qquad (1)$$

FIG. 9.2. Deriving the general equation for the adjusted means in covariance

obtains $F = 200/100 = 2$, which is not significant, since the critical value at .05 is 3.18. He had pretested the subjects, but didn't use the pretest as a covariate since the groups didn't differ significantly on the pretest. (even though the correlation between pretest and posttest was .71). This is a common mistake made by some researchers who are unaware of the other purpose of covariance, that of reducing error variance. The analysis is redone by another investigator using ANCOVA. Using the equation that we just derived for the new error term for ANCOVA he finds:

$$MS_w^* \approx 100 \, (1 - (.71)^2) = 50$$

Thus, the error term for ANCOVA is only half as large as the error term for ANOVA. It is also necessary to obtain a new MS_b for ANCOVA, call it MS_b^*. Since the formula for MS_b^* is complicated, we do not pursue it. Let us assume the investigator obtains the following F ratio for covariance analysis:

$$F^* = 190/\, 50 = 3.8$$

This is significant at the .05 level. Therefore, the use of covariance can make the difference between not finding significance and finding significance. Finally, we wish to note that MS_b^* can be smaller or larger than MS_b, although in a randomized study the expected values of the two are equal.

9.4   CHOICE OF COVARIATES

In general, any variables which theoretically should correlate with the dependent variable, or variables which have been shown to correlate on similar types of subjects, should be considered as possible covariates. The ideal is to chose as covariates variables which of course are significantly correlated with the dependent variable *and* which have low correlations among themselves. If two covariates are highly correlated (say .80), then they are removing much of the *same* error variance from y; x_2 will not have much incremental validity. On the other hand, if two covariates (x_1 and x_2) have a low correlation (say .20), then they are removing relatively distinct pieces of the error variance from y, and we will obtain a much greater total error reduction. This is illustrated below graphically using Venn diagrams, where the circle represents error variance on y.

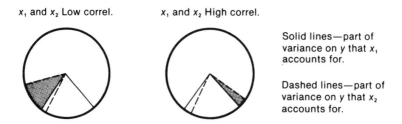

x_1 and x_2 Low correl. x_1 and x_2 High correl.

Solid lines—part of variance on y that x_1 accounts for.

Dashed lines—part of variance on y that x_2 accounts for.

The shaded portion in each case represents the incremental validity of x_2, ie., the part of error variance on y it removes that x_1 did not.

If the dependent variable is achievement in some content area, then one should always consider the possibility of at least 3 covariates:

1. a measure of ability in that specific content area
2. a measure of general ability (I.Q. measure)
3. one or two relevant noncognitive measures (e.g., attitude toward education, study habits, etc.)

An example of the above was given earlier, where we considered the effect of two different teaching methods on 12th grade mathematics achievement. We indicated that a plausible set of covariates would be grade in math 11 (a previous measure of ability in mathematics), an I.Q. measure, and attitude toward education (a noncognitive measure).

In studies with small or relatively small group sizes, it is particularly imperative to consider the use of 2 or 3 covariates. Why? Because for small or medium effect sizes, which are *very common* in social science research, power will be poor for small group size. Thus, one should attempt to reduce the error variance as much as possible to obtain a more sensitive (powerful) test.

Huitema (1980, p. 161) has recommended limiting the number of covariates to the extent that the ratio

$$\frac{C + (J - 1)}{N} < .10, \tag{3}$$

where C is the number of covariates, J is the number of groups, and N is total sample size. Thus, if we had a 3-group problem with a total of 60 subjects, then $(C + 2)/60 < .10$ or $C < 4$. We should use less than 4 covariates. If the above ratio is $> .10$, then the estimates of the adjusted means are likely to be unstable. That is, if the study were cross-validated, it could be expected that the equation used to estimate the adjusted means in the original study will yield very different estimates for another sample from the same population.

Importance of Covariate Being Measured Before Treatments

To avoid confounding (mixing together) of the treatment effect with a change on the covariate, one should use only pretest or other information gathered before treatments begin as covariates. If a covariate is used which is measured after treatments and that variable was affected by treatments, then the change on the covariate may be correlated with change on the dependent variable. Thus, when the covariate adjustment is made, you will remove part of the treatment effect.

9.5 ASSUMPTIONS IN ANALYSIS OF COVARIANCE

Analysis of covariance rests on the same assumptions as analysis of variance plus three additional assumptions regarding the regression part of the covariance analysis. That is, ANCOVA also assumes:

1. a linear relationship between the dependent variable and the covariate(s).*
2. homogeneity of the regression slopes (for one covariate), i.e., that the slope of the regression line is the same in each group. For two covariates the assumption is parallelism of the regression planes, and for more than two covariates the assumption is homogeneity of the regression hyperplanes.
3. the covariate is measured without error.

Since covariance partly rests on the same assumptions as ANOVA, any violations that are serious in ANOVA (like the independence assumption) are also serious in ANCOVA. Violation of *all 3* of the remaining assumptions of covariance are also serious. For example, if the relationship between the covariate and the dependent variable is curvilinear, then the adjustment of the means will be improper. In this case, two possible courses of action are

1. Seek a transformation of the data which is linear.

This is possible if the relationship between the covariate and the dependent variable is monotonic

2. Fit a polynomial ANCOVA model to the data.

There is always measurement error for the variables that are typically used as covariates in social science research. And measurement error causes problems in both randomized and non-randomized designs, but is more serious in non-randomized designs. As Huitema (1980) notes, "In the case of randomized designs, . . . the power of the ANCOVA is reduced relative

---

*Nonlinear analysis of covariance is possible (cf. Huitema, Chapter 9, 1980), but is rarely done.

to what it would be if no error were present, but treatment effects are not biased. With other designs the effects of measurement error in x (covariate) are likely to be serious" (p. 299).

When measurement error is present on the covariate, then treatment effects can be seriously biased in non-randomized designs. In Fig. 9.3 we illustrate the effect measurement error can have when comparing two *different* populations with analysis of covariance. In the hypothetical example, with no measurement error we would conclude group 1 is superior to group 2, whereas with considerable measurement error the opposite conclusion is drawn: This example shows that if the covariate means are not equal, then the difference between the adjusted means is partly a function of the reliability of the covariate. Now, this problem would not be of particular concern if we had a very reliable covariate like I.Q. or other cognitive variables from a good standardized test. If, on the other hand, the covariate is a noncognitive variable, or a variable derived from a nonstandardized instrument (which might well be of questionable reliability), then concern would definitely be justified.

A violation of the homogeneity of regression slopes can also yield misleading results if covariance is used. To illustrate this, we present in

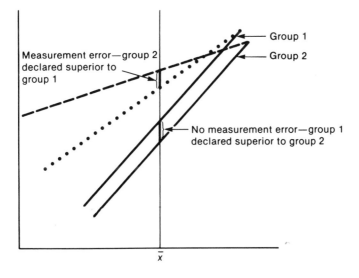

—— Regression lines for the groups with no measurement error
• • • Regression line for group 1 with considerable measurement error
— — Regression line for group 2 with considerable measurement error

FIG. 9.3.   Effect of Measurement Error on Covariance Results When Comparing Subjects from Two Different Populations.

Figure 9.4 the situation where the assumption is met and two situations where the assumption is violated. Notice that with homogeneous slopes the estimated superiority of group 1 at the grand mean is an accurate estimate of group 1's superiority for all levels of the covariate, since the lines are parallel. On the other hand, for Case 1 of heterogeneous slopes, the superiority of group 1 (as estimated by covariance) is *not* an accurate estimate of group 1's superiority for other values of the covariate. For $x = a$, group 1 is only slightly better than group 2, while for $x = b$, the superiority of group 1 is seriously underestimated by covariance. The point is *when the slopes are unequal there is a covariate by treatment interaction.* That is, how much better group 1 is depends on which value of the covariate we specify.

For Case 2 of heterogeneous slopes, use of covariance would be totally misleading. Covariance estimates no difference between the groups, while for $x = c$, group 2 is quite superior to group 1. For $x = d$, group 1 is superior to group 2. We will indicate, later in the chapter, in detail how the assumption of equal slopes is tested on SPSSX.

9.6   USE OF ANCOVA WITH INTACT GROUPS

It should be noted that some researchers (Anderson, 1963; Lord, 1969) have argued strongly against using analysis of covariance with intact groups. Although we do not take this position, it is important that the reader be aware of the several limitations and/or possible dangers when using ANCOVA with intact groups. First, even the use of several covariates will *not* equate intact groups, and one should never be deluded into thinking it can. The groups may still differ on some unknown important variable(s). Also, note that equating groups on one variable may result in accentuating their differences on other variables.

Secondly, recall that ANCOVA adjusts the posttest means to what they would be if all the groups had started out equal on the covariate(s). You then need to consider whether groups that are equal on the covariate would ever exist in the real world. Elashoff (1969) gives the following example. Teaching methods A and B are being compared. The class using A is composed of high ability students, whereas the class using B is composed of low ability students. A covariance analysis can be done on the posttest achievement scores holding ability constant, as if A and B had been used on classes of equal and average ability. But, as Elashoff notes, "It may make no sense to think about comparing methods A and B for students of average ability, perhaps each has been designed specifically for the ability level it was used with, or neither method will, in the future, be used for students of average ability" (p. 387).

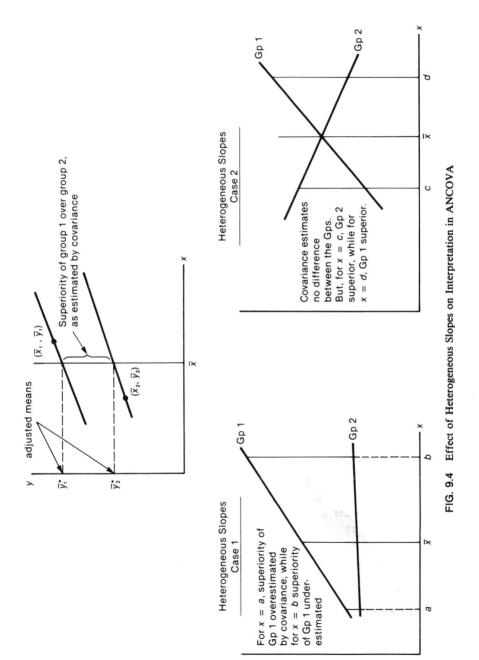

FIG. 9.4 Effect of Heterogeneous Slopes on Interpretation in ANCOVA

Third, the assumptions of linearity and homogeneity of regression slopes need to be satisfied for ANCOVA to be appropriate.

A fourth issue that can confound the interpretation of results is differential growth of subjects in intact or self selected groups on some dependent variable. If the natural growth is much greater in one group (treatment) than for the control group and covariance finds a significance difference, after adjusting for any pretest differences, then it isn't clear whether the difference is due to treatment, differential growth, or part of each. Bryk and Weisberg (1977) discuss this issue in detail and propose an alternative approach for such growth models.

A fifth problem is that of measurement error. Of course this same problem is present in randomized studies. But there the effect is merely to attenuate power. In non-randomized studies measurement error can seriously bias the treatment effect. Reichardt (1979), in an extended discussion on measurement error in ANCOVA, states,

> Measurement error in the pretest can therefore produce spurious treatment effects when none exist. But it can also result in a finding of no intercept difference when a true treatment effect exists, or it can produce an estimate of the treatment effect which is in the opposite direction of the true effect. (p. 164)

It is no wonder then that Pedhazur (1982, p. 524), in discussing the effect of measurement error when comparing intact groups, says,

> The purpose of the discussion here was only to alert you to the problem in the hope that you will reach two obvious conclusions: (1) that efforts should be directed to construct measures of the covariates that have very high reliabilities and (2) that ignoring the problem, as is unfortunately done in most applications of ANCOVA, will not make it disappear. (p. 524)

Porter (1967) has developed a procedure to correct ANCOVA for measurement error, and an example illustrating that procedure is given in Huitema (1980, pp. 315–316). This is beyond the scope of the present text.

Given all of the above problems, the reader may well wonder whether we should abandon the use of covariance when comparing intact groups. But, other statistical methods for analyzing this kind of data (such as matched samples, gain score ANOVA) suffer from many of the same problems, such as seriously biased treatment effects. The fact is that inferring cause-effect from intact groups is treacherous, regardless of the type of statistical analysis. Therefore, the task is to do the best we can and exercise considerable caution, or as Pedhazur (1982) put it, "But the conduct of such research, indeed all scientific research, requires sound theoretical thinking, constant vigilance, and a thorough understanding of the potential and limitations of the methods being used" (p. 525).

9.7 ALTERNATIVE ANALYSES FOR PRETEST-POSTTEST DESIGNS

When comparing two or more groups with pretest and posttest data, the following three other modes of analysis are possible:

1. An ANOVA is done on the difference or gain scores (posttest-pretest).
2. A two way repeated measures (this is covered in Chapter 13) ANOVA is done. This is called a one between (the grouping variable) and one within (pretest-posttest part) factor ANOVA.
3. An ANOVA is done on residual scores. That is, the dependent variable is regressed on the covariate. Predicted scores are then subtracted from observed dependent scores, yielding residual scores ($\hat{e}_i$). An ordinary one-way ANOVA is then preformed on these residual scores. Although some individuals feel this approach is equivalent to ANCOVA, Maxwell, Delaney, & Manheimer (1985) have shown the two methods are not the same and that analysis on residuals should be avoided.

The first two methods are used quite frequently, with ANOVA on residuals being done only occasionally. Huck and McLean (1975) and Jennings (1988) have compared the first two methods mentioned above, along with the use of ANCOVA for the pretest-posttest control group design, and conclude that ANCOVA is the preferred method of analysis. Several comments from the Huck and McLean article are worth mentioning. First, they note that with the repeated measures approach it is the *interaction F* that is indicating whether the treatments had a differential effect, and not the treatment main effect. We consider two patterns of means to illustrate.

	Situation 1			*Situation 2*	
	Pretest	Posttest		Pretest	Posttest
Treat.	70	80	Treat	65	80
Control	60	70	Control	60	68

In situation 1 the treatment main effect would probably be significant, because there is a difference of 10 in the row means. However, the difference of 10 on the posttest just transferred from an initial difference of 10 on the pretest. There is not a differential change in the treatment and control groups here. On the other hand, in situation 2 even though the treatment group scored higher on the pretest, it increased 15 points from pre to post while the control group increased just 8 points. That is, there was a *differential* change in performance in the two groups. But, recall from Chapter 4 that one way of thinking of an interaction effect is as a "difference in the differences." This is exactly what we have in situation 2, hence a significant interaction effect.

Secondly, Huck and McLean (1975) note that the interaction F from the repeated measures ANOVA is *identical* to the F ratio one would obtain from an ANOVA on the gain (difference) scores. Finally, whenever the regression coefficient is not equal to 1 (generally the case), the error term for ANCOVA will be smaller than for the gain score analysis and hence the ANCOVA will be a more sensitive or powerful analysis.

Although not discussed in the Huck and McLean paper, we would like to add a measurement caution against the use of gain scores. It is fairly well known measurement fact that the reliability of gain (difference) scores is generally not good. To be more specific, *as the correlation between the pretest and posttest scores approaches the reliability of the test, the reliability of the difference scores goes to 0.* The following table from Thorndike and Hagen (1977) quantifies things:

	Average reliability of two tests					
	.50	.60	.70	.80	.90	.95
Correlation between tests						
.00	.50	.60	.70	.80	.90	.95
.40	.17	.33	.50	.67	.83	.92
.50	.00	.20	.40	.60	.80	.90
.60		.00	.25	.50	.75	.88
.70			.00	.33	.67	.83
.80				.00	.50	.75
.90					.00	.50
.95						.00

If our dependent variable is some noncognitive measure, or a variable derived from a nonstandardized test (which could well be of questionable reliability), then a reliability of about .60 or so is a definite possibility. In this case, if the correlation between pretest and posttest is .50 (a realistic possibility), the reliability of the difference scores is only .20! On the other hand, the above table also shows that if our measure is quite reliable (say

.90), then the difference scores will be reliable for moderate pre-post correlations. For example, for reliability = .90 and pre-post correlation = .50, the reliability of the differences scores is .80.

9.8   ERROR REDUCTION AND ADJUSTMENT OF POSTTEST MEANS FOR SEVERAL COVARIATES

What is the rationale for using several covariates? First, the use of several covariates will result in greater error reduction than can be obtained with just one covariate. The error reduction will be substantially greater if the covariates have relatively low intercorrelations amongst themselves (say < .40). Secondly, with several covariates we can make a better adjustment for initial differences between intact groups.

For one covariate the amount of error reduction was governed primarily by the magnitude of the correlation between the covariate and the dependent variable (cf. Equation 2). For several covariates the amount of error reduction is determined by the magnitude of the multiple correlation between the dependent variable and the set of covariates (predictors). This is why we indicated earlier it is desirable to have covariates with low intercorrelations amongst themselves, for then the multiple correlation will be larger, and we will achieve greater error reduction. Also, since R^2 has a variance accounted for interpretation, we can speak of the percentage of *within* variability on the dependent variable that is accounted for by the set of covariates.

Recall that the equation for the adjusted posttest mean for one covariate was given by:

$$\bar{y}_i^* = \bar{y}_i - b(\bar{x}_i - \bar{x}),$$

where b is the estimated common regression slope.

With several covariates $(x_1, x_2, \ldots, x_k)$ we are simply regressing y on the set of x's, and the adjusted equation becomes an extension of the above:

$$\bar{y}_j^* = \bar{y}_j - b_1 (\bar{x}_{1j} - \bar{x}_1) - b_2 (\bar{x}_{2j} - \bar{x}_2) - \ldots - b_k (\bar{x}_{kj} - \bar{x}_k), \quad (4)$$

where the b_i are the regression coefficients, $\bar{x}_{1j}$ is the mean for the covariate 1 in group j, $\bar{x}_{2j}$ is the mean for covariate 2 in group j, etc. and the $\bar{x}_i$ are the grand means for the covariates. We will illustrate the use of this equation on a sample MANCOVA problem.

9.9   MANCOVA — SEVERAL DEPENDENT VARIABLES AND SEVERAL COVARIATES

In MANCOVA we are assuming there is a significant relationship between the set of dependent variables and the set of covariates, or that there is a significant regression of the y's on the x's. This is tested through the use of Wilk's Λ. We are also assuming, for more than two covariates, homogeneity of the regression hyperplanes. The null hypothesis that is being tested in MANCOVA is that the adjusted population mean vectors are equal:

$$H_0 : \boldsymbol{\mu}_{1_{adj}} = \boldsymbol{\mu}_{2_{adj}} = \boldsymbol{\mu}_{3_{adj}} = \ldots = \boldsymbol{\mu}_{J_{adj}}$$

In testing the null hypothesis in MANCOVA adjusted W and T matrices are needed; we denote these by $\mathbf{W}^*$ and $\mathbf{T}^*$. In MANOVA recall that the null hypothesis was tested using Wilk's Λ. Thus, we have:

	MANOVA	MANCOVA
Test Statistic	$\Lambda = \dfrac{|\mathbf{W}|}{|\mathbf{T}|}$	$\Lambda^* = \dfrac{|\mathbf{W}^*|}{|\mathbf{T}^*|}$

The calculation of $\mathbf{W}^*$ and $\mathbf{T}^*$ involves considerable matrix algebra, which we wish to avoid. For the reader who is interested in the details, however, Finn (1974) has a nice worked out example.

In examining the printout from the statistical packages it is important to *first* make two checks to determine whether covariance is appropriate:

1. Check to see that there is a significant relationship between the dependent variables and the covariates.
2. Check to determine that the homogeneity of the regression hyperplanes is satisfied.

If either of these is not satisfied, then covariance is not appropriate. In particular, if (2) is not met, then one should consider using the Johnson-Neyman technique, which determines a region of nonsignificance, i.e., a set of x values for which the groups do not differ, and hence for values of x outside this region one group is superior to the other. The Johnson-Neyman technique is excellently described in Huitema (1980), where he shows specifically how to calculate the region of nonsignificance for one covariate, the effect of measurement error on the procedure, and other issues. For further extended discussion on the Johnson-Neyman technique see Rogosa (1977, 1980).

Incidentally, if the homogeneity of regression slopes is rejected for several groups, it does not automatically follow that the slopes for all groups differ. In this case one might follow up the overall test with additional homogeneity tests on all combinations of pairs of slopes. Often, the slopes will be homogeneous for many of the groups. In this case one can apply ANCOVA to the groups that have homogeneous slopes, and apply the Johnson-Neyman technique to the groups with heterogeneous slopes. Unfortunately, at present, none of the three major statistical packages (BMDP, SPSSX, SAS) has the Johnson-Neyman technique.

9.10 TESTING THE ASSUMPTION OF HOMOGENEOUS REGRESSION HYPERPLANES ON SPSSX

Neither SPSSX or SAS automatically provide the test of the homogeneity of the regression hyperplanes. Recall that for one covariate, this is the assumption of equal regression slopes in the groups, and that for two covariates it is the assumption of parallel regression planes. In order to setup the control lines to test this assumption, it is necessary to understand what a violation of the assumption means. As we indicated earlier (and displayed in Figure 9.4), a violation means there is a covariate by treatment interaction. Evidence that the assumption is met means the interaction is not significant.

Thus, what is done on SPSSX is to set up an effect involving the interaction (for one covariate), and then testing whether this effect is significant. If the effect is significant, this means the assumption is *not* tenable. This is one of those cases where we don't want significance, for then the assumption is tenable and covariance is appropriate.

If there is more than one covariate, then there is an interaction effect for each covariate. We lump the effects together and then test whether the combined interactions are significant. Before we give two examples, we note that BY is the keyword used by SPSSX to denote an interaction and + is used to lump effects together.

Example 1 — Two Dependent Variables and One Covariate

We call the grouping variable TREATS, and denote the dependent variables by $Y1$ and $Y2$, and the covariate by $X1$. Then the control lines are

```
ANALYSIS = Y1,Y2/
DESIGN = X1,TREATS,X1 BY TREATS/
```

Example 2 — Three Dependent Variables and Two Covariates

We denote the dependent variables by $Y1$, $Y2$, and $Y3$ and the covariates by $X1$ and $X2$. Then the control lines are

```
ANALYSIS = Y1,Y2,Y3/
DESIGN = X1 + X2,TREATS,X1 BY TREATS + X2 BY TREATS/
```

These two control lines will be imbedded among many others in running a multivariate MANCOVA on SPSSX, as the reader will see in the computer examples we consider next. With the above two examples, and the computer examples, the reader should be able to generalize the set up of the control lines for testing homogeneity of regression hyperplanes for any combination of dependent variables and covariates.

9.11   TWO COMPUTER EXAMPLES

We now consider two examples to illustrate (1) how to setup the control lines to run a multivariate analysis of covariance on both SPSSX MANOVA and on SAS GLM, and (2) how to interpret the output, including that which checks whether covariance is appropriate. The first example uses artificial data and is simpler, having just two dependent variables and one covariate, while the second example uses data from an actual study and is more complex, involving 4 dependent variables and 4 covariates.

Example 3: MANCOVA on SAS GLM

This example has two groups, with 15 subjects in group 1 and 14 subjects in group 2. There are two dependent variables, denoted by POSTCOMP and POSTHIOR in the SAS GLM control lines and on the printout, and one covariate (denoted by PRECOMP). The control lines for running the MANCOVA analysis are given in Table 9.1, along with annotation.

Table 9.2 presents the two multivariate tests for determining whether MANCOVA is appropriate, that is, whether there is a significant relationship between the two dependent variables and the covariate, and whether there is no covariate by group interaction effect. The multivariate test at the top of Table 9.2 indicates there is a significant relationship ($F = 21.4623$, $p < .0001$). Also, the multivariate test in the middle of the table shows there is *not* a covariate by group interaction effect ($F = 1.9048$, $p < .1707$). Therefore, multivariate analysis of covariance is appropriate. In Figure 9.5 we present the scatter plots for POSTCOMP, along with the slopes and the regression lines for each group.

The multivariate null hypothesis tested in covariance is that the adjusted population mean vectors are equal, that is,

$$H_0 : \begin{pmatrix} \overset{*}{\mu}_{11} \\ \overset{*}{\mu}_{21} \end{pmatrix} = \begin{pmatrix} \overset{*}{\mu}_{12} \\ \overset{*}{\mu}_{22} \end{pmatrix}$$

The multivariate test at the bottom of Table 9.2 shows that we reject the multivariate null hypothesis at the .05 level, and hence we conclude that the groups differ on the *set* of two adjusted means. The univariate ANCOVA followup F's in Table 9.3 ($F = 5.26$ for POSTCOMP, $p < .03$ and $F = 9.84$ for POSTHIOR, $p < .004$) show that both variables are contrib-

TABLE 9.1
SAS GLM Control Lines for Two Group MANCOVA: Two Dependent Variables and One Covariate

---

TITLE ' MULTIVARIATE ANALYSIS OF COVARIANCE ';
DATA COMP;
INPUT GPID PRECOMP POSTCOMP POSTHIOR @@;
CARDS;
1 15 17 3   1 10 6 3   1 13 13 1   1 14 14 8
1 12 12 3   1 10 9 9   1 12 12 3   1 8 9 12
1 12 15 3   1 8 10 8   1 12 13 1   1 7 11 10
1 12 16 1   1 9 12 2
2 9 9 3   2 13 19 5   2 13 16 11   2 6 7 18
2 10 11 15   2 6 9 9   2 16 20 8   2 9 15 6
2 10 8 9   2 8 10 3   2 13 16 12   2 12 17 20
2 11 18 12   2 14 18 16
PROC PRINT;
PROC REG;

①   MODEL POSTCOMP POSTHIOR = PRECOMP;
     MTEST;

     PROC GLM;
     CLASSES GPID;
②   MODEL POSTCOMP POSTHIOR = PRECOMP GPID PRECOMP*GPID;
     MANOVA H = PRECOMP*GPID;

     PROC GLM;
     CLASSES GPID;
③   MODEL POSTCOMP POSTHIOR = PRECOMP GPID;
     MANOVA H = GPID;
④   LSMEANS GPID/PDIFF;

---

① PROC REG is used to examine the relationship between the two dependent variables and the covariate. The MTEST is needed to obtain the multivariate test.

② Here GLM is used along with the MANOVA statement to obtain the multivariate test of no overall PRECOMP BY GPID interaction effect.

③ GLM is used again, along with the MANOVA statement, to test whether the adjusted population mean vectors are equal.

④ This statement is needed to obtain the adjusted means.

uting to the overall multivariate significance. The adjusted means for the variables are also given in Table 9.3.

Can we have confidence in the reliability of the adjusted means? From Huitema's inequality we need $C + (J-1)/N < .10$. Since here $J = 2$ and $N = 29$, we obtain $(C + 1)/29 < .10$ or $C < 1.9$. Thus, we should use less than two covariates for reliable results, and we have used just one covariate.

Example 4: MANCOVA on SPSSX MANOVA

Next we consider a social psychological study by Novince (1977) which examined the effect of behavioral rehearsal, and behavioral rehearsal plus cognitive restructuring (combination treatment) on reducing anxiety and facilitating social skills for female college freshmen. There was also a control group (group 2), with 11 subjects in each group. The subjects were pretested and posttested on 4 measures, thus the pretests were the covariates.

TABLE 9.2
Multivariate Tests for Significant Regression, for Covariate by Treatment Interaction and for Group Difference

Multivariate Test:
Multivariate Statistics and Exact F Statistics
S = 1   M = 0   N = 12

Statistic	Value	F	Num DF	Den DF	Pr > F
Wilks' Lambda	0.37722383	21.4623	2	26	0.0001
Pillar's Trace	0.62277617	21.4623	2	26	0.0001
Hotelling-Lawley Trace	1.65094597	21.4623	2	26	0.0001
Roy's Greatest Root	1.65094597	21.4623	2	26	0.0001

Manova Test Criteria and Exact F Statistics for the Hypothesis of no Overall PRECOMP*GPID Effect
H = Type III SS&CP Matrix for PRECOMP*GPID   E = Error SS&CP Matrix
S = 1   M = 0   N = 11

Statistic	Value	F	Num DF	Den DF	Pr > F
Wilks' Lambda	0.86301048	1.9048	2	24	0.1707
Pillar's Trace	0.13698952	1.9048	2	24	0.1707
Hotelling-Lawley Trace	0.15873448	1.9048	2	24	0.1707
Roy's Greatest Root	0.15873448	1.9048	2	24	0.1707

Manova Test Criteria and Exact F Statistics for the Hypothesis of no Overall GPID Effect
H = Type III SS&CP Matrix for GPID   E = Error SS&CP Matrix
S = 1   M = 0   N = 11.5

Statistic	Value	F	Num DF	Den DF	Pr > F
Wilks' Lambda	0.64891393	6.7628	2	25	0.0045
Pillar's Trace	0.35108107	6.7628	2	25	0.0045
Hotelling-Lawley Trace	0.54102455	6.7628	2	25	0.0045
Roy's Greatest Root	0.54102455	6.7628	2	25	0.0045.

In Table 9.4 we present the control lines for running the MANCOVA, along with annotation explaining what the various subcommands are doing. The least obvious part of the setup is obtaining the test for the homogeneity of the regression hyperplanes. Tables 9.5, 9.6 and 9.7 present selected output from the MANCOVA run on SPSSX. Table 9.5 contains descriptive information, i.e., means on the covariates (pretests) and on the dependent variables (posttests). Table 9.6 contains output for determining whether covariance is appropriate for this data. First, in Table 9.6 is the multivariate test for significant association between the dependent variables and the covariates (or significant regression of y's on x's). The multivariate $F = 4.807$ (corresponding to Wilk's Λ), which is significant beyond the .001 level. Now we make the second check to determine whether covariance is appropriate, i.e., is the assumption of homogenous regression hyperplanes tenable. The multivariate test for this assumption is under

"EFFECT . . . PREAVOID BY TREATS +. . . . + PRESR BY TREATS"

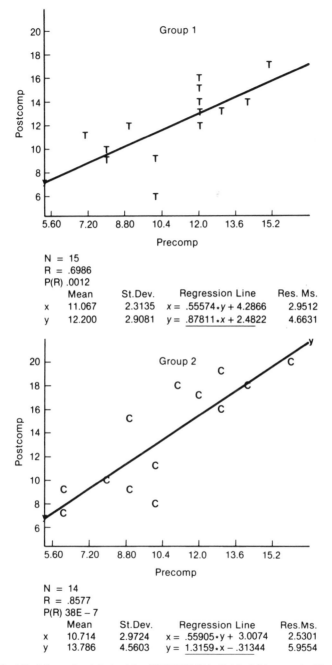

N = 15
R = .6986
P(R) .0012

	Mean	St.Dev.	Regression Line	Res. Ms.
x	11.067	2.3135	$x = .55574 \cdot y + 4.2866$	2.9512
y	12.200	2.9081	$y = \underline{.87811 \cdot x + 2.4822}$	4.6631

N = 14
R = .8577
P(R) 38E − 7

	Mean	St.Dev.	Regression Line	Res.Ms.
x	10.714	2.9724	$x = .55905 \cdot y + 3.0074$	2.5301
y	13.786	4.5603	$y = \underline{1.3159 \cdot x − .31344}$	5.9554

The fact that the univariate test for POSTCOMP in Table 9.2 is not significant ($F = 1.645$, $p < .211$) means that the differences in slopes here (.878 and 1.316) are simply due to sampling error, i.e., the homogeneity of slopes assumption is tenable for this variable.

FIG. 9.5. Scatter Plots and Regression Lines for Postcomp vs Covariate in Two Groups

335

TABLE 9.3
Univariate Tests for Group Differences and Adjusted Means

Source	DF	Type I SS	Mean Square	F Value	Pr > F
PRECOMP	1	237.68956787	237.68956787	43.90	0.000
GPID	1	28.49860091	28.49860091	5.26	0.0301

Source	DF	Type III SS	Mean Square	F Value	Pr > F
PRECOMP	1	17.66221238	17.66221238	0.82	0.3732
GPID	1	28.4986091	28.49860091	5.26	0.0301

Source	DF	Type I SS	Mean Square	F Value	Pr > F
PRECOMP	1	17.66221238	17.66221238	0.82	0.3732
GPID	1	211.59023436	211.59023436	9.84	0.0042

Source	DF	Type I SS	Mean Square	F Value	Pr > F
PRECOMP	1	10.20072260	10.20072260	0.47	0.4972
GPID	1	211.59023436	211.59023436	9.84	0.0042

General Linear Models Procedure
Least Squares Means

GPID	POSTCOMP LSMEAN	Pr > |T| H0: LSMEAN1 = LSMEAN2
1	12.0055476	0.0301
2	13.9940562	

GPID	POSTHIOR LSMEAN	Pr > |T| H0: LSMEAN1 = LSMEAN2
1	5.0394385	0.0042
2	10.4577444	

Since the multivariate $F = .644$ (corresponding to Wilk's Λ), the assumption is quite tenable. Recall that a violation of this assumption implies a covariate by treatment interaction, and that is why we lump together the covariate by treatment interaction effects for each covariate. We then test to see whether this effect is significant.

The main result for the multivariate analysis of covariance, i.e., the multivariate test to determine whether the adjusted population mean vectors are significantly different, is at the top of Table 9.7. The multivariate $F = 5.902$ (corresponding to Wilk's Λ) is significant beyond the .001 level. The univariate analyses of covariance at the bottom of Table 9.7 indicate that all of the variables are contributing to the overall multivariate significance at $\alpha = .05$.

Some other comments on the output in Tables 9.5 through 9.7. We already indicated there is a significant relationship between the set of dependent variables and the set of covariates. The univariate F's in Table 9.6 indicate additionally that the regression of each dependent variable on the set of covariates is also significant at the .05 level. Also, the "SQ. MUL. R" are the squared multiple correlations for each dependent variable regressed *separately* on the 4 covariates. Thus, the first squared multiple

TABLE 9.4

SPSSX MANOVA Control Lines for Example 4: Four Dependent
Variables and Four Covariates

```
        TITLE 'MANCOVA NOVINCE DATA SELF REPORT VARIABES '.
        DATA LIST FREE/ TREATS AVOID NEGEVAL, SOCINT,SRINV,PREAVOID,
           PRENEG,PRESOCI,PRESR
        LIST
        BEGIN DATA

①      DATA LINES

        END DATA
        MANOVA  AVOID,NEGEVAL,SOCINT,SRINV,PREAVOID,PRENEG,PRESOCI,
           PRESR  BY  TREATS(1,3)/
②      ANALYSIS = AVOID,NEGEVAL,SOCINT,SRINV WITH PREAVOID,PRENEG,
        PRESOCI,PRESR/
        PRINT = PMEANS/
        DESIGN/
      ⎡ANALYSIS = AVOID,NEGEVAL,SOCINT,SRINV/
③    ⎨DESIGN = PREAVOID + PREGNEG + PRESOCI + PRESR,TREATS,PREAVOID BY TREATS +
      ⎩PRENEG BY TREATS + PRESOCI BY TREATS + PRESR BY TREATS/
④      ANALYSIS = PREAVOID,PRENEG,PRESOCI,PRESR/
```

①The data is given in the Appendix at the end of this chapter.

②Recall that the keyword WITH precedes the covariates in SPSSX.

③These ANALYSIS and DESIGN subcommands are required for testing the homogeneity of the regression hyperplanes . The third effect in the DESIGN subcommand, i.e., PREAVOID BY TREATS + PRENEG BY TREATS + PRESOCI BY TREATS + PRESR BY TREATS, is testing whether the assumption of homogeneity of the regression hyperplanes is tenable. Recall that a violation of this assumption implies a covariate by treatment interaction. The keyword BY denotes an interaction and + is used for lumping effects together. We lump the 4 covariate by treatment interactions together here since we wish to know whether the covariates as a set violate the assumption.

④This subcommand is used for testing whether the groups differ on the set of covariates. Output from this analysis is needed in applying the Bryant-Paulson post hoc procedure for locating significant pairwise differences (cf. Table 9.8). For example, in a randomized study with several covariates, this analysis will yield the Hotelling-Lawley trace (called Hotelling's on the SPSSX output).

correlation for AVOID of .7326 indicates that above 73% of within group variability on AVOID is accounted for by the 4 covariates.

Recall that the equation for the adjusted mean for a variable when several covariates are involved is obtained through multiple regression and is given by

$$\bar{y}_j^* = \bar{y}_j - b_1 (\bar{x}_{1j} - \bar{x}_1) - b_2 (\bar{x}_{2j} - \bar{x}_2) - \ldots - b_k (\bar{x}_{kj} - \bar{x}_k)$$

To illustrate the application of this equation, we show how the adjusted mean on AVOID in group 1 of 120.637 is obtained. To obtain the adjusted mean the means for all 4 covariates in group 1 are required; these are given in the bottom half of Table 9.5. We also need the grand means for the covariates (x_j), which are obtained by simply taking the average (since the group sizes are equal) of the means for each variable over the groups. Thus, the grand mean for PREAVOID is

$$(104 + 103.273 + 113.636)/3 = 106.97$$

ADJUSTED AND ESTIMATED MEANS

VARIABLE .. AVOID

FACTOR	CODE	OBS. MEAN	ADJ. MEAN
TREATS	1	116.98090	120.63733
TREATS	2	105.90909	110.17788
TREATS	3	132.27273	124.27570

VARIABLE .. NEGEVAL

FACTOR	CODE	OBS. MEAN	ADJ. MEAN
TREATS	1	108.81818	112.37373
TREATS	2	94.36364	97.37026
TREATS	3	131.00000	124.43783

VARIABLE .. SRINV

FACTOR	CODE	OBS. MEAN	ADJ. MEAN
TREATS	1	150.18182	147.98037
TREATS	2	164.81818	161.24915
TREATS	3	127.45455	133.22502

VARIABLE .. SOCINT

FACTOR	CODE	OBS. MEAN	ADJ. MEAN
TREATS	1	102.36364	103.08738
TREATS	2	73.72727	76.11871
TREATS	3	111.27273	108.15755

VARIABLE .. PREVOID

FACTOR	CODE	OBS. MEAN
TREATS	1	104.00000
TREATS	2	103.27273
TREATS	3	113.63635

VARIABLE .. PRENEG

FACTOR	CODE	OBS. MEAN
TREATS	1	93.90909
TREATS	2	95.00000
TREATS	3	109.18182

VARIABLE .. PRESR

FACTOR	CODE	OBS. MEAN
TREATS	1	165.63636
TREATS	2	167.90909
TREATS	3	150.18182

VARIABLE .. PRESOCI

FACTOR	CODE	OBS.MEAN
TREATS	1	79.18182
TREATS	2	73.81818
TREATS	3	80.54545

TABLE 9.6
Multivariate Tests for Relationship between Dependent Variables and Covariates and Test for Parallelism of Regression Hyperplanes

EFFECT .. WITHIN CELLS REGRESSION

MULTIVARIATE TESTS OF SIGNIFICANCE (S = 4, M = −1/2, N = 10 1/2)

TEST NAME	VALUE	APPROX. F	HYPOTH. DF	ERROR DF	SIG. OF F
PILLAIS	1.40810	3.53124	16.00	104.00	.000
HOTELLINGS	4.19499	5.63702	16.00	86.00	.000
WILKS	.10599	4.80699 ①	16.00	70.90	.000
ROYS	.75381				

UNIVARIATE F-TESTS WITH (4,26) D. F.

VARIABLE	SQ. MUL. R	MUL. R	ADJ. R-SQ.	HYPOTH. MS	ERROR MS	F	SIG. OF F
AVOID	.73261	.85592	.69147	1538.84966	86.40774	17.80916	.000
NEGEVAL	.31079 ②	.55748	.20476	649.97439	225.16478	2.93107	.040
SOCINT	.49984	.70699	.42289	682.64351	105.090981	6.49581	.001
SRINV	.34026	.58332	.23876	905.43502	270.08692	3.35238	.024

EFFECT .. PREAVOID BY TREATS + PRENEG BY TREATS + PRESOCI BY TREATS + PRESR BY TREATS

MULTIVARIATE TESTS OF SIGNIFICANCE (S = 4, M = 1 1/2, N = 6 1/2)

TEST NAME	VALUE	APPROX. F	HYPOTH. DF	ERROR DF	SIG. OF F
PILLAIS	.91410	.66649	32.00	72.00	.897
HOTELLINGS	1.45615	.61431	32.00	54.00	.929
WILKS	.31997	.64392 ③	32.00	56.91	.910
ROYS	.42725				

① This multivariate test indicates that there is a significant relationship between the set of dependent and the set of covariates at the .05 level.
② These are for the multiple regression of each dependent variable separately on the set of 4 covariates. The .7326 for AVOID indicates that 73.26% of the within variability on this variable is accounted for by 4 covariates.
③ This indicates that the assumption of homogeneity of the regression hyperplanes is quite tenable here at the .05 level, since $F = .644$, $p < .910$.

339

TABLE 9.7
The Multivariate and Univariate Covariance Results and Regression Coefficients for the Avoidance Variable

EFFECT .. TREATS

MULTIVARIATE TESTS OF SIGNIFICANCE (S = 2, M = 1/2, N = 10 1/2)

TEST NAME	VALUE	APPROX. F	HYPOTH. DF	ERROR DF	SIG. OF F
PILLAIS	.84045	4.34886	8.00	48.00	.001
HOTELLINGS	2.76168	7.59463	8.00	44.00	.000
WILKS	.24352	① 5.90209	8.00	46.00	.000
ROYS	.72456				

UNIVARIATE F-TESTS WITH (2,26) D. F.

VARIABLE	HYPOTH. SS	ERROR SS	HYPOTH. MS	ERROR MS	F	SIG. OF F
AVOID	1047.45440	2246.60137	523.72720	86.40774	6.0611	.007
NEGEVAL	3433.94023	5854.28426	1716.90712	225.16478	7.62539	.002
SOCINT	5926.54223	2732.33503	2963.27112	105.08981	28.19751	.000
SRINV	3598.22806	7022.25991	1799.11403	270.08692	6.66124	.005

② (braces grouping the F column values)

REGRESSION ANALYSIS FOR WITHIN CELLS ERROR TEAM (CONT.)

DEPENDENT VARIABLE .. AVOID

COVARIATE	B	BETA	STD. ERR	T-VALUE	SIG. OF T
PREAVOID	.5732142081	.6324648697	.10787	5.31371	.000
PRENEG	③ .2425192713	.2316063103	.12117	2.00224	.056
PRESOCI	.0041195162	.0042867469	.11024	.03737	.970
PRESR	-.1611494246	-2.088419383	.08515	-1.89245	.070

①This is the main result, indicating that the adjusted population mean vectors are significantly different at the .05 level ($F = 5.902$, $p < .000$). That is, the groups differ on the set of posttest means, after appropriate adjustments have been made for initial differences.

②These are the F's that would result if a separate analysis of covariance was done on each dependent variable. The probabilities indicate that all variables are significant at the .05 level; thus, all of the variables are contributing to the overall multivariate significance.

③These are the regression coefficients that are used in obtaining the adjusted means for AVOID.

Finally, we need the regression coefficients (b_i) for regressing AVOID on the 4 covariates. These are boxed in on Table 9.7. Therefore, the adjusted mean for AVOID in group 1 is given by:

$$\bar{y}_1^* = 116.91 - .5732 (104 - 106.97) - .2425 (93.91 - 99.36)$$

$$- .0041 (79.18 - 77.85) + .1612 (165.64 - 161.24) = 120.637$$

The one concern we have about this study involves the stability of the adjusted means, since sample size $(N = 33)$ does not justify using 4 covariates (cf. Equation 3).

9.12 BRYANT-PAULSON SIMULTANEOUS TEST PROCEDURE

Since the covariate(s) used in social science research are essentially always random, it is important that this information be incorporated into any post hoc procedure following ANCOVA. This is *not* the case for the Tukey procedure, and hence it is not appropriate as a followup technique following ANCOVA. The Bryant-Paulson (1976) procedure was derived under the assumption that the covariate is a random variable and hence is appropriate in ANCOVA. It is a generalization of the Tukey technique. Which particular Bryant-Paulson (BP) statistic we use to determine whether a pair of means are significantly different depends on whether the study is a randomized or non-randomized design and on how many covariates there are (one or several). In Table 9.8 we have the test statistic for each of the 4 cases. Note that if the group sizes are unequal, then the harmonic mean is employed.

We now illustrate use of the Bryant-Paulson procedure on the computer example. Since this was a randomized study with four covariates, the appropriate statistic from Table 9.8 is

$$BP = \frac{\bar{Y}_i^* - \bar{Y}_j^*}{\sqrt{MS_w^* \left[1 + \frac{1}{(J-1)} \, TR(\mathbf{B}_x \, \mathbf{W}_x^{-1})\right]/n}}$$

Is there a significant difference between the adjusted means on avoidance for groups 1 and 2 at the .95 simultaneous level?

Table 9.6 under ERROR MS

Table 9.5(top)

HOTELLING-LAWLEY trace for set of covariates

$$BP = \frac{120.64 - 110.18}{\sqrt{86.41 [1 + 1/2(.307)]/11}}$$

$$BP = \frac{10.46}{\sqrt{86.41(1.15)/11}} = 3.49$$

TABLE 9.8
Bryant-Paulson Statistics for Detecting Significant Pairwise Differences in Covariance Analysis for One and for Several Covariates ①

One Covariate	*Many Covariates* ②

RANDOMIZED STUDY

$$\frac{\bar{Y}_i^* - \bar{Y}_j^*}{\sqrt{MW_w^*[1 + MS_{B_x}/SS_{w_x}]/n}}$$

$$\frac{\bar{Y}_i^* - \bar{Y}_j^*}{\sqrt{MS_w^*[1 + \dfrac{1}{(J - 1)} TR(\mathbf{B}_x \mathbf{W}_x^{-1})]/n}}$$

WHERE

$\bar{Y}_i^*$ IS THE ADJUSTED MEAN FOR GROUP i

MS_{B_x} IS THE MEAN BETWEEN SQUARE ON THE CO-VARIATE

SS_{W_x} IS THE SUM OF SQUARES WITHIN ON THE CO-VARIATE

MS_w^* IS THE ERROR TERM FOR COVARIANCE

n IS THE COMMON GROUP SIZE. IF UNEQUAL n, USE THE HARMONIC MEAN.

$\mathbf{B}_x$ IS THE BETWEEN SSCP MATRIX

$\mathbf{W}_x$ IS THE WITHIN SSCP MATRIX

$TR (\mathbf{B}_x \mathbf{W}_x^{-1})$ IS THE HOTELLING-LAWLEY TRACE.

THIS IS GIVEN ON THE SPSS MANOVA PRINTOUT.

NON-RANDOMIZED STUDY

$$\frac{\bar{Y}_i^* - \bar{Y}_j^*}{\sqrt{MS_w^*(2/n + [(\bar{X}_i - \bar{X}_j)^2/SS_{w_x}])/2}}$$

$$(\bar{Y}_i^* - \bar{Y}_j^*) / \sqrt{\frac{MS_w^*[(2/n) + \mathbf{d}' \mathbf{W}_x^{-1}\mathbf{d}]}{2}}$$

WHERE $\bar{X}_i$ IS THE MEAN FOR THE COVARIATE IN GROUP i. NOTE THAT THE ERROR TERM MUST BE COMPUTED *SEPARATELY* FOR EACH PAIRWISE COMPARISON.

$\mathbf{d}'$ IS THE ROW VECTOR OF DIFFERENCES BETWEEN THE ith and jth GROUPS ON THE COVARIATES.

① The Bryant-Paulson statistics were derived under the assumption that the covariates are random variables, which is almost always the case in practice.
② Degrees of freedom for error is $N - J - C$, where C is the number of covariates.

We have not presented the Hotelling-Lawley trace as part of the selected output for the second computer example. It is the part of the output related to the last ANALYSIS subcommand in Table 4 comparing the groups on the set of covariates. Now, having computed the value of the test statistic, we need the critical value. The critical values are given in Table G in the back of this volume. Table G is entered at $\alpha = .05$, with $df_e = N - J - C = 33 - 3 - 4 = 26$, and for 4 covariates. The table only extends to 3 covariates, but the value of 3 will be a good approximation. The critical value for $df = 24$ with 3 covariates is 3.76, and the critical value for $df = 30$ is 3.67. Interpolating, we find the critical value $= 3.73$. Since the value of the BP statistic is 3.49, there is not a significant difference.

9.13 SUMMARY OF MAJOR POINTS

1. In analysis of covariance a linear relationship is assumed between the dependent variable(s) and the covariate(s).

2. Analysis of covariance is directly related to the two basic objectives in experimental design of (a) eliminating systematic bias and (b) reduction of error variance. While ANCOVA does not eliminate bias, it can reduce bias. This can be helpful in non-experimental studies comparing intact groups. The bias is reduced by adjusting the posttest means to what they would be if all groups had started out equally on the covariate(s), that is, at the grand mean(s). There is disagreement among statisticians about the use of AN-COVA with intact groups, and several precautions were mentioned in 9.6.

3. The main reason for using ANCOVA in an experimental study (random assignment of subjects to groups) is to reduce error variance, yielding a more powerful test. When using several covariates, greater error reduction will occur when the covariates have low intercorrelations amongst themselves.

4. Limit the number of covariates (C) so that

$$\frac{C + (J-1)}{N} < .10,$$

where J is the number of groups and N is total sample size, so that stable estimates of the adjusted means are obtained.

5. In examining printout from the statistical packages, first make two checks to determine whether covariance is appropriate: (a) check that there is a significant relationship between the dependent variables and the covariates, and (b) check that the homogeneity of the regression hyperplanes assumption is tenable. If either of these is not satisfied, then covariance is not appropriate. In particular, if (b) is not satisfied, then the Johnson-Neyman technique should be used.

6. Measurement error on the covariate causes loss of power in randomized designs, and can lead to seriously biased treatment effects in non-randomized designs. Thus, if one has a covariate of low or questionable reliability, then true score ANCOVA should be contemplated.

7. Use the Bryant-Paulson procedure for determining where there are significant pairwise differences. This technique assumes the covariates are random variables, almost always the case in social science research, and with it one can maintain the overall alpha level at .05 or .01.

EXERCISES FOR ANCOVA – CHAPTER 9

1. Scandura (1984) examined the effects of a leadership training treatment on employee work outcomes of job satisfaction (HOPPOCKA), leadership relations (LMXA), performance ratings (ERSA), and actual performance – quantity (QUANAFT) and quality of work (QUALAFT). Thus, there were 5 dependent variables. The names in parentheses are the names used for the variables that appear on selected printout we present here. Since previous research had indicated that the characteristics of the work performed – motivating potential (MPS), work load (OL1), and job problems (DTT) – are related to these work outcomes, these three variables were used as covariates. Of 100 subjects, 35 were randomly assigned to the leadership treatment condition and 65 to the control group. During the 26 weeks of the study, 11 subjects dropped out, about an equal number from each group. Scandura ran the two-group multivariate analysis of covariance on SPSSX.

    a) Show the control lines for running the MANCOVA on SPSSX such that the adjusted means and the test for homogeneity of the regression hyperplanes are also obtained. Assume free format for the variables.

    b) On pages 360–362 we present selected printout from Scandura's run. From the printout determine whether analysis of covariance is appropriate.

    c) If covariance is appropriate, then determine whether the multivariate test is significant at the .05 level.

    d) If the multivariate test is significant, then which of the individual variables, at the .01 level, are contributing to the multivariate significance?

    e) What are the adjusted means for the significant variable(s) found in (d)? Did the treatment group do better than the control (assume higher is better)?

2. Consider the following data from a two-group MANCOVA with two dependent variables (Y1 and Y2) and one covariate (X):

GPS	X	Y1	Y2
1.00	12.00	13.00	3.00
1.00	10.00	6.00	5.00
1.00	11.00	17.00	2.00
1.00	14.00	14.00	8.00
1.00	13.00	12.00	6.00
1.00	10.00	6.00	8.00
1.00	8.00	12.00	3.00
1.00	8.00	6.00	12.00
1.00	12.00	12.00	7.00
1.00	10.00	12.00	8.00
1.00	12.00	13.00	2.00
1.00	7.00	14.00	10.00

GPS	X	Y1	Y2
1.00	12.00	16.00	1.00
1.00	9.00	9.00	2.00
1.00	12.00	14.00	10.00
2.00	9.00	7.00	3.00
2.00	16.00	13.00	5.00
2.00	11.00	14.00	5.00
2.00	8.00	13.00	18.00
2.00	10.00	11.00	12.00
2.00	7.00	15.00	9.00
2.00	16.00	17.00	4.00
2.00	9.00	9.00	6.00
2.00	10.00	8.00	4.00
2.00	8.00	10.00	1.00
2.00	16.00	16.00	3.00
2.00	12.00	12.00	17.00
2.00	15.00	14.00	4.00
2.00	12.00	18.00	11.00

Run the MANCOVA on SAS GLM. Is MANCOVA appropriate? Explain. If it is appropriate, then are the adjusted mean vectors significantly different at the .05 level?

3. Consider a three-group study (randomized) with 24 subjects per group. The correlation between the covariate and the dependent variable is .25, which is statistically significant at the .05 level. Is covariance going to be very useful in this study? Explain.

4. For the Novince example, determine whether there are any significant differences on SOCINT at the .95 simultaneous confidence level using the Bryant Paulson procedure.

5. Suppose we were comparing two different teaching methods and that the covariate was I.Q. The homogeneity of regression slopes is tested and rejected, implying a covariate by treatment interaction. Relate this to what we would have found had we blocked on I.Q. and run a factorial design (I.Q. by methods) on achievement.

6. As part of a study by Benton et al. (1984), three tasks were employed to ascertain differences between good and poor undergraduate writers on recall and manipulation of information: an ordered letters task, an iconic memory task and a letter reordering task. In the following table are means and standard deviations for the percentage of correct letters recalled on the three dependent variables. There were 15 subjects in each group.

	Good writers		Poor writers	
Task	M	SD	M	SD
Ordered letters	57.79	12.96	49.71	21.79
Iconic memory	49.78	14.59	45.63	13.09
Letter reordering	71.00	4.80	63.18	7.03

The following is from their results section (p. 824):

The data were then analyzed via a multivariate analysis of covariance using the background variables (English usage ACT subtest, composite ACT, and grade point average) as covariates, writing ability as the independent variable, and task scores (correct recall in the ordered letters task, correct recall in the iconic memory task, and correct recall in the letter reordering task) as the dependent variables. The global test was significant, $F(3, 23) = 5.43$, $p < .001$. To control for experimentwise Type I error rate at .05, each of the three univariate analyses was conducted at a per comparison rate of .017. No significant difference was observed between groups on the ordered letters task, univariate $F(1, 25) = 1.92$, $p > .10$. Similarly, no significant difference was observed between groups on the iconic memory task, univariate $F < 1$.

However, good writers obtained significantly higher scores on the letter reordering task than the poor writers, univariate $F(1, 25) = 15.02$, $p < .001$.

a) From what is said above, can we be confident that covariance is appropriate here?

b) The "global" multivariate test referred to above is not identified as to whether it is Wilk's Λ, Roy's largest root, etc. Would it make a difference as to which multivariate test was employed in this case?

c) Benton et al. talk about controlling the experimentwise error rate at .05 by conducting each test at the .017 level of significance. Which post hoc procedure that we discussed in Chapter 4 are they employing here?

d) Are there a sufficient number of subjects for us to have confidence in the reliability of the adjusted means?

Novince Data for Multivariate Analysis of Covariance Example (Table 9.4)

TREATS	AVOID	NEGEVAL	SOCINT	SRINV	PREAVOID	PRENEG	PRESOCI	PRESR
1.00	91.00	81.00	108.00	157.00	70.00	102.00	61.00	184.00
1.00	107.00	132.00	88.00	150.00	121.00	71.00	66.00	165.00
1.00	121.00	97.00	90.00	151.00	89.00	76.00	67.00	154.00
1.00	86.00	88.00	119.00	154.00	80.00	85.00	102.00	208.00
1.00	137.00	119.00	114.00	135.00	123.00	117.00	106.00	130.00
1.00	138.00	132.00	110.00	165.00	112.00	106.00	95.00	180.00
1.00	133.00	116.00	102.00	124.00	126.00	97.00	52.00	139.00
1.00	127.00	101.00	105.00	163.00	121.00	85.00	94.00	180.00
1.00	114.00	138.00	86.00	168.00	80.00	105.00	70.00	176.00
1.00	118.00	121.00	108.00	136.00	101.00	113.00	80.00	142.00
1.00	114.00	72.00	96.00	149.00	112.00	76.00	78.00	164.00
2.00	107.00	88.00	64.00	135.00	116.00	97.00	91.00	164.00
2.00	76.00	95.00	68.00	157.00	77.00	64.00	73.00	142.00
2.00	116.00	87.00	84.00	165.00	111.00	86.00	79.00	198.00
2.00	126.00	112.00	93.00	155.00	121.00	106.00	71.00	153.00
2.00	104.00	107.00	62.00	181.00	105.00	113.00	68.00	172.00
2.00	96.00	84.00	56.00	193.00	97.00	92.00	62.00	164.00
2.00	127.00	88.00	82.00	153.00	132.00	104.00	70.00	170.00
2.00	99.00	101.00	66.00	146.00	98.00	81.00	66.00	166.00
2.00	94.00	87.00	54.00	196.00	85.00	96.00	58.00	178.00
2.00	92.00	80.00	84.00	177.00	82.00	88.00	77.00	198.00
2.00	128.00	109.00	98.00	155.00	112.00	118.00	97.00	142.00
3.00	121.00	134.00	111.00	112.00	96.00	96.00	85.00	162.00
3.00	140.00	130.00	104.00	102.00	120.00	110.00	58.00	146.00
3.00	148.00	123.00	116.00	123.00	130.00	111.00	111.00	125.00
3.00	147.00	155.00	137.00	111.00	145.00	118.00	91.00	175.00
3.00	139.00	124.00	116.00	129.00	122.00	105.00	95.00	155.00
3.00	121.00	123.00	107.00	148.00	119.00	122.00	97.00	149.00
3.00	141.00	155.00	124.00	108.00	104.00	139.00	81.00	134.00
3.00	143.00	131.00	122.00	141.00	121.00	108.00	93.00	127.00
3.00	120.00	123.00	88.00	148.00	80.00	77.00	44.00	157.00
3.00	140.00	140.00	107.00	108.00	121.00	121.00	82.00	124.00
3.00	95.00	103.00	92.00	172.00	92.00	94.00	49.00	198.00

EFFECT .. WITHIN CELLS REGRESSION

MULTIVARIATE TESTS OF
SIGNIFICANCE (S = 3, M =
1/2, N = 36)

TEST NAME	VALUE	APPROX. F	HYPOTH. DF	ERROR DF	SIG. OF F
PILLAIS	.32175	1.82605	15.00	228.00	.032
HOTELLINGS	.29799	1.92804	15.00	218.00	.022
WILKS	.69999	1.88208	15.00	204.68	.027
ROYS	.23303				

UNIVARIATE F-TESTS WITH (3,78) D.F.

VARIABLE	SQ. MUL. R	MUL. R	ADJ. R-SQ.	HYPOTH. MS	ERROR MS	F	SIG. OF F
HOPPOCKA	.05146	.22684	.01497	16.04757	11.37763	1.41045	.246
LNXA	.07412	.27225	.03851	33.51239	16.10126	2.08135	.109
ERSA	.13167	.36287	.09827	156.04864	39.58010	3.94260	.011
QUANAFT	.05930	.24351	.02312	.01169	.00713	1.63889	.187
QUALAFT	.14992	.38719	.11722	.00975	.00213	4.58530	.005

REGRESSION ANALYSIS FOR WITHIN CELLS ERROR TEAM

EFFECT .. MPS BY TRIMT2 + OLI BY TRIMT2 + DTT BY TRIMT2

MULTIVARIATE TESTS OF SIGNIFICANCE (S = 3, M = 1/2, N = 34 1/2)

TEST NAME	VALUE	APPROX. F	HYPOTH. DF	ERROR DF	SIG. OF F
PILLAIS	.18417	.95491	15.00	219.00	.504
HOTELLINGS	.20597	.95662	15.00	209.00	.503
WILKS	.82318	.95619	15.00	196.40	.503
ROYS	.13308				

UNIVARIATE F-TESTS WITH (3,75) D. F.

VARIABLE	HYPOTH. SS	ERROR SS	HYPOTH. MS	ERROR MS	F	SIG. OF F
HOPPOCKA	22.41809	865.03704	7.47270	11.53383	.64789	.587
LMXA	21.18137	1234.71668	7.06046	16.46289	.42887	.733
ERSA	249.38711	2837.86037	83.12904	37.83814	2.19696	.095
QUANAFT	.00503	.55127	.00168	.00735	.22812	.877
QUALAFT	.00263	.16315	.00088	.00218	.40343	.751

EFFECT .. TRTMT2

MULTIVARIATE TESTS OF SIGNIFICANCE (S = 1, M = 1 1/2, N = 34 1/2)

TEST NAME	VALUE	APPROX. F	HYPOTH. DF	ERROR DF	SIG. OF F
PILLAIS	.15824	2.66941	5.00	71.00	.029
HOTELLINGS	.18799	2.66941	5.00	71.00	.029
WILKS	.84176	2.66941	5.00	71.00	.029
ROYS	.15824				

UNIVARIATE F-TESTS WITH (1,75) D. F.

VARIABLE	HYPOTH. SS	ERROR SS	F	SIG. OF F
HOPPOCKA	32.81297	865.03704	2.84493	.096
LMXA	.20963	1234.71668	.01273	.910
ERSA	87.59018	2837.86037	2.31486	.132
QUANAFT	.80222	.55127	11.18658	.001
QUALAFT	.00254	.16315	1.16651	.284

ADJUSTED AND ESTIMATED MEANS VARIABLE .. HOPPOCKA

FACTOR	CODE	OBS. MEAN	ADJ. MEAN
TRTMT2	LMX TREA	19.23077	19.31360
TRTMT2	CONTROL	17.98246	17.94467

ADJUSTED AND ESTIMATED MEANS (CONT.)

VARIABLE .. LMXA

FACTOR	CODE	OBS. MEAN	ADJ. MEAN
TRTMT2	LMX TREA	19.03846	19.23177
TRTMT2	CONTROL	19.21053	19.12235

ADJUSTED AND ESTIMATED MEAN (CONT.)

VARIABLE .. ERSA

FACTOR	CODE	OBS. MEAN	ADJ. MEAN
TRMTMT2	LMX TREA	34.34615	34.76489
TRTMT2	CONTROL	32.71930	32.52830

ADJUSTED AND ESTIMATED MEANS (CONT.)

VARIABLE .. QUANAFT

FACTOR	CODE	OBS. MEAN	ADJ. MEAN
TRTMT2	LMX TREA	.38846	.39188
TRMTMT2	CONTROL	.32491	.32335

ADJUSTED AND ESTIMATED MEANS (CONT.)

VARIABL E.. QUALAFT

FACTOR	CODE	OBS. MEAN	ADJ. MEAN
TRTMT2	LMX TREA	.05577	.05330
TRTMT2	CONTROL	.06421	.06534

10 Stepdown Analysis

10.1 INTRODUCTION

In this chapter we consider a type of analysis that is similar to stepwise regression analysis (Chapter 3). The stepdown analysis is similar in that in both analyses we are interested in how much a variable "adds." In regression analysis the question is, "How much does a predictor add to predicting the dependent variable above and beyond the previous predictors in the regression equation?" The corresponding question in stepdown analysis is, "How much does a given dependent variable add to discriminating the groups, above and beyond the previous dependent variables for a given a priori ordering?" *Since the stepdown analysis requires an a priori ordering of the dependent variables, there must be some theoretical rationale or empirical evidence to dictate a given ordering.* If there is such a rationale, then the stepdown analysis determines whether the groups differ on the first dependent variable in the ordering. The stepdown F for the first variable is the same as the univariate F. For the second dependent variable in the ordering, the analysis determines whether the groups differ on this variable with the first dependent variable used as a covariate in adjusting the effects for variable 2. The stepdown F for the third dependent variable in the ordering indicates whether the groups differ on this variable after its' effects have been adjusted for variables 1 and 2, i.e., with variables 1 and 2 used as covariates, etc. Since the stepdown analysis is just a series of analyses of covariance, the reader should examine section 9.2 on purposes of covariance before going any farther in this chapter.

10.2 FOUR APPROPRIATE SITUATIONS FOR STEPDOWN ANALYSIS

To make the foregoing discussion more concrete we consider an example. Let the independent variable be three different teaching methods, and the three dependent variables be the three subtest scores on a common achievement test covering the three lowest levels in Bloom's taxonomy, i.e., knowledge, comprehension, and application. An assumption of the taxonomy is that learning at a lower level is a necessary but not sufficient condition for learning at a higher level. Because of this, there is a theoretical rationale for ordering the variables as given above. The analysis will determine whether methods are differentially affecting learning at the most basic level, i.e., knowledge. At this point the analysis is the same as doing a univariate ANOVA on the single dependent variable knowledge. Next, the stepdown analysis will indicate whether the effect has extended itself to the next higher level, i.e., comprehension, with the differences at the knowledge level eliminated. The stepdown F for comprehension is *identical* to what one would obtain if a univariate analysis of covariance was done with comprehension as the dependent variable and knowledge as the covariate. Finally, the analysis will show whether methods have had a significant effect on application, with the differences at the two lower levels eliminated. The stepdown F for the analysis variable is the *same one* that would be obtained if a univariate analysis of covariance was done with analysis as the dependent variable and knowledge and comprehension as the covariates. Thus, the stepdown analysis not only gives an indication of how comprehensive the effect of the independent variable is, but also details which aspects of a grossly defined variable (such as achievement) have been differentially affected.

A second example is provided by Kohlberg's theory of moral development. Kohlberg describes six stages of moral development, ranging from premoral to the formulation of self accepted moral principles, and argues that attainment of a higher stage should depend on attainment of the preceding stages. Let us assume that tests are available for determining which stage a given individual has attained. Suppose we were interested in determining the extent to which lower, middle, and upper class adults differ with respect to moral development. With Kohlberg's hierarchial theory we have a rationale for ordering from premoral as the first dependent variable on up to self-accepted principles as the last dependent variable in the ordering. The stepdown analysis will then tell us whether the social classes differ on premoral level of development, then whether the social classes differ on the next level of moral development with the differences at the premoral level eliminated, etc. In other words, the analysis will tell us where there are differences among the classes with respect to moral development and how far up the ladder of moral development those differences extend.

As a third example where the stepdown analysis would be particularly appropriate, suppose an investigator wishes to determine whether some conceptually newer measures (among a set of dependent variables) are adding anything beyond what the older, more proven variables contribute, in relation to some independent variable. The above case provides an empirical rationale for ordering the newer measures last, in order for them to demonstrate their incremental importance to the effect under investigation. Thus, in the previous example, the stepdown F for the first new conceptual measure in the ordering would indicate the importance of that variable, with the effects of the more proven variables eliminated. The utility of this approach in terms of providing evidence on variables which are redundant is clear.

A fourth instance in which the stepdown F's are particularly valuable is in the analysis of repeated measures designs, where time provides a natural logical ordering for the measures.

10.3 CONTROLLING ON OVERALL TYPE I ERROR

The stepdown analysis can control very effectively and in a precise way against type I error. To show how Type I error can be controlled for the stepdown analysis, it is necessary to note that *if H_0 is true (i.e., the population mean vectors are equal), then the stepdown F's are statistically independent* (Roy & Bargmann, 1958). How then is the overall α level set for the stepdown Fs for a set of p variables? Each variable is assigned an α level, the ith variable being assigned α_i. Thus, $(1 - \alpha_1)$ is the probability of no type I error for variable 1, $(1 - \alpha_2)$ is the probability of no type I error for variable 2, etc. Now, since the tests are statistically independent, these probabilities can be multiplied. Therefore, the probability of *no* type I errors for *all* p tests is $(1 - \alpha_1) \cdot (1 - \alpha_2)$ $\ldots (1 - \alpha_p)$. Using the symbol π, which denotes "product of," this expression can be written more concisely as $\overset{p}{\underset{i=1}{\pi}} (1 - \alpha_i)$. Finally, our overall α level is:

$$\text{overall } \alpha = 1 - \prod_{i=1}^{p} (1 - \alpha_i),$$

This is the probability of *at least one* stepdown F exceeding its critical value when H_0 is true.

Since we have one exact estimate of the probability of overall type I error, when employing the stepdown Fs it is unnecessary to perform the overall multivariate significance test. We may adopt the rule that the multivariate null hypothesis will be rejected if at least one of the stepdown F's is significant.

Recall that one of the primary reasons for the multivariate test with correlated dependent variables was the difficulty of accurately estimating overall type I error. As Bock and Haggard noted (1968), "Because all variables have been obtained from the same subjects, they are correlated in some arbitrary and unknown manner, and the separate F tests are not statistically independent. No exact probability that at least one of them will exceed some critical value on the null hypothesis can be calculated" (p. 102).

10.4 STEPDOWN F'S FOR TWO GROUPS

To obtain the stepdown F's for the two-group case the pooled within variance matrix S must be factored. That is, the the square root or Cholesky factor of S must be found. What this means is that S is expressed as a product of a lower triangular matrix (all 0's above the main diagonal) and an upper triangular matrix (all 0's below the main diagonal). For 3 variables, it would look as follows:

$$
\overset{\mathbf{S}}{\begin{bmatrix} s_1^2 & s_{12} & s_{13} \\ s_{21} & s_2^2 & s_{23} \\ s_{31} & s_{32} & s_3^2 \end{bmatrix}} = \overset{\mathbf{R}}{\begin{bmatrix} t_{11} & 0 & 0 \\ t_{21} & t_{22} & 0 \\ t_{31} & t_{32} & t_{33} \end{bmatrix}} \overset{\mathbf{R'}}{\begin{bmatrix} t_{11} & t_{12} & t_{13} \\ 0 & t_{22} & t_{23} \\ 0 & 0 & t_{33} \end{bmatrix}}
$$

Now, for two groups the stepdown analysis yields a nice *additive breakdown* of Hotelling's T^2. The first term in the sum (which is an F ratio) gives the contribution of variable 1 to group discrimination, the second term (which is the stepdown F for the second variable in the ordering) the contribution of variable 2 to group discrimination, etc. To at least partially show how this additive breakdown is achieved, recall that Hotelling's T^2 can be written as:

$$T^2 = n_1 n_2/(n_1 + n_2) \, \mathbf{d}' \, \mathbf{S}^{-1} \, \mathbf{d}, \text{ where}$$

$\mathbf{d}$ is the vector of mean differences on the variables for the two groups. Since factoring the covariance matrix S means writing it as $\mathbf{S} = \mathbf{R} \mathbf{R}'$, it can be shown that T^2 may then be re-written as

$$T^2 = n_1 n_2/(n_1 + n_2) \, (\mathbf{R}^{-1} \, \mathbf{d})' \, (\mathbf{R}^{-1}\mathbf{d})$$

But $\underset{(p \times p)}{\mathbf{R}^{-1}} \underset{(p \times 1)}{\mathbf{d}}$ is just a column vector and the transpose of this column vector is a row vector which we denote by $\mathbf{w}' = (w_1, w_2, \ldots, w_p)$. Thus, $T^2 = n_1 n_2/(n_1 + n_2) \, \mathbf{w}' \, \mathbf{w}$. But $\mathbf{w}' \, \mathbf{w} = w_1^2 + w_2^2 + \ldots w_p^2$.

Therefore, we get the following additive breakdown of T^2:

$$T^2 = \frac{n_1 n_2}{n_1 + n_2} w_1^2 + \frac{n_1 n_2}{n_1 + n_2} w_2^2 + \ldots + \frac{n_1 n_2}{n_1 + n_2} w_p^2$$

$$T^2 = \quad F_1 \quad + \quad F_2 \quad + \ldots + \quad F_p$$

| univariate F for first variable in the ordering | stepdown F for second variable in ordering | stepdown F for last variable in the ordering |

We now consider an example to illustrate numerically the breakdown of T^2. In this example we just give the factors R and R' of S without showing the details, as most of our readers are probably not interested in the details. Those who are interested, however, can find the details in Finn (1974).

Example

Suppose there are two groups of subjects ($n_1 = 50$ and $n_2 = 43$) measured on 3 variables. The vector of differences on the means (**d**) and the pooled within covariance matrix **S** are as follows:

$$\mathbf{d'} = (3.7, 2.1, 2.3), \quad \mathbf{S} = \begin{bmatrix} 38.10 & 14.59 & 1.63 \\ 14.59 & 31.26 & 2.05 \\ 1.63 & 2.05 & 16.72 \end{bmatrix}$$

$$\mathbf{S} = \begin{bmatrix} 6.173 & 0 & 0 \\ 2.634 & 5.067 & 0 \\ .264 & .282 & 4.071 \end{bmatrix} \begin{bmatrix} 6.173 & 2.364 & .264 \\ 0 & 5.067 & .282 \\ 0 & 0 & 4.071 \end{bmatrix}$$

Now, to obtain the additive breakdown for T^2 we need $\mathbf{R}^{-1}\mathbf{d}$. This is:

$$\mathbf{R}^{-1}\mathbf{d} = \begin{bmatrix} .162 & 0 & 0 \\ -.076 & .197 & 0 \\ -.005 & -.014 & .25 \end{bmatrix} \begin{bmatrix} 3.7 \\ 2.1 \\ 2.3 \end{bmatrix} = \begin{bmatrix} .60 \\ .133 \\ .527 \end{bmatrix} = \mathbf{w}$$

We have not shown the details but $\mathbf{R}^{-1}$ is the inverse of $\mathbf{R}$. The reader may check this by multiplying the two matrices. The product is indeed the identity matrix (within rounding error). Thus,

$$T^2 = \frac{50\,(43)}{93}\,(.60,\ .133,\ .527)\begin{pmatrix}.60\\.133\\.527\end{pmatrix}$$

$$T^2 = 25.904\,(.36 + .018 + .278)$$

$$T^2 = \underset{\substack{\text{contribution of vari-}\\ \text{able 1}}}{9.325} + \underset{\substack{\text{contribution of vari-}\\ \text{able 2 with effects}\\ \text{of variable 1}\\ \text{removed}}}{.466} + \underset{\substack{\text{contribution of variable 3 to}\\ \text{group discrimination } above\\ and\ beyond \text{ what the first 2}\\ \text{variables contribute}}}{7.201}$$

Each of the above numbers is just the value for the stepdown F (F^*) for the corresponding variable. Now, suppose we had set the probability of a type I error at .05 for the first variable and at .025 for the other two variables. Then, the probability of at least one type I error is $1 - (1 - .05)(1 - .025)(1 - .025) = 1 - .903 = .097$. Thus there is about a 10% chance of falsely concluding that at least one of the variables contributes to group discrimination, when in fact it does not. What is our decision for each of the variables?

F_1^* = 9.325, (crit. val = 3.95) reject and conclude variable 1 signif-
.05; 1, 91   icantly contributes to group discrimination

F_2^* = .466 < 1, so this can't be significant
.025; 1, 90

F_3^* = 7.201, (crit. val = 5.22) reject and conclude variable 3 makes
.025; 1, 89   a significant contribution to group discrimination above and
            beyond what first 2 criterion variables do.

Notice that the degrees of freedom for error decreases by one for each successive stepdown F, just as we lose one degree of freedom for each covariate used in analysis of covariance. The general formula for degrees of freedom for error (df_{w*}) for the ith stepdown F then is $df_{w*} = df_w - (i - 1)$, where $df_w = N - k$, i.e., ordinary formula for df in a one-way univariate analysis of variance. Thus df_{w*} for the 3rd variable above is $df_{w*} = 91 - (3 - 1) = 89$.

10.5 COMPARISON OF INTERPRETATION OF STEPDOWN F'S VS. UNIVARIATE F'S

To illustrate the difference in interpretation when using univariate F's following a significant multivariate F vs. the use of stepdown F's, we consider an example. A different set of four variables which Novince (1977) analyzed in her study are presented in Table 10.1, along with the control lines for obtaining the stepdown *F*'s on SPSSX MANOVA.

The control lines are of exactly the same form as were used in obtaining a one-way MANOVA in Chapter 5. The only difference is that the last line

TABLE 10.1
Control Lines and Data for Stepdown Analysis on SPSSX MANOVA
for Novince Data

```
TITLE 'STEPDOWN ANALYSIS ON NOVINCE DATA'
DATA LIST FREE/ TREATS JRANX JRNEGEVA JRGLOA JRSOCSKL
LIST
BEGIN DATA
1 2 2.5 2.5 3.5   1 1.5 2 1.5 4.5   1 2 3 2.5 3.5
1 2.5 4 3 3.5   1 1 2 1 5   1 1.5 3.5 2.5 4
1 4 3 3 4   1 3 4 3.5 4   1 3.5 3.5 3.5 2.5
1 1 1 1 4   1 1 2.5 2 4.5
2 1.5 3.5 2.5 4   2 1 4.5 2.5 4.5   2 3 3 3 4
2 4.5 4.5 4.5 3.5   2 1.5 4.5 3.5 3.5   2 2.5 4 3 4
2 3 4 3.5 3   2 4 5 5 1   2 3.5 3 3.5 3.5
2 1.5 1.5 1.5 4.5   2 3 4 3.5 3
3 1 2 1 4   3 1 2 1.5 4.5   3 1.5 1 1 3.5
3 2 2.5 2 4   3 2 3 2.5 4.5   3 2.5 3 2.5 4
3 2 2.5 2.5 4   3 1 1 1 5   3 1 1.5 1.5 5
3 1.5 1.5 1.5 5   3 2 3.5 2.5 4
END DATA
MANOVA JRANX TO JRSOCSKL BY TREATS(1,3)/
   PRINT=CELLINFO(MEANS) SIGNIF(STEPDOWN)/
```

NOTE: The last part of the PRINT subcommand is required to obtain the stepdown Fs.

TABLE 10.2
Multivariate Tests, Univariate F's and Stepdown F's for Novince Data

EFFECT .. TREATS

MULTIVARIATE TESTS OF SIGNIFICANCE (S = 2, M = 1/2, N = 12 1/2)

TEST NAME	VALUE	APPROX. F	HYPOTH. DF	ERROR DF	SIG. OF F
PILLAIS	.42619	1.89561	8.00	56.00	.079
HOTELLINGS	.69664	2.26408	8.00	52.00	.037
WILKS	.58362	2.08566	8.00	54.00	.053
ROYS	.40178				

UNIVARIATE F-TESTS WITH (2,30) D. F.

VARIABLE	HYPOTH. SS	ERROR SS	HYPOTH. MS	ERROR MS	F	SIG. OF F
JRANX	6.01515	26.86364	3.00758	.89545	3.35871	.048
JRNEGEVA	14.86364	25.36364	7.43182	.84545	8.79032	.001
JRGLOA	12.56061	21.40909	6.28030	.71364	8.80042	.001
JRSOCSKL	3.68182	16.54545	1.84091	.55152	3.33791	.049

ROY-BARGMAN STEPDOWN F - TESTS

VARIABLE	HYPOTH. MS	ERROR MS	STEP-DOWN F	HYPOTH. DF	ERROR DF	SIG. OF F
JRANX	3.00758	.89545	3.35871	2	30	.048
JRNEGEVA	2.99776	.66964	4.47666	2	29	.020
JRGLOA	.05601	.06520	.85899	2	28	.434
JRSOCSKL	.03462	.32567	.10631	2	27	.900

SIGNIF(STEPDOWN)/ is included to obtain the stepdown F's. In Table 10.2 we present the multivariate tests, along with the univariate F's and the stepdown F's. Even though, as mentioned earlier in this chapter, it is *not* necessary to examine the multivariate tests when using stepdown F's, it was done here for illustrative purposes. This is one of those somewhat infrequent situations where the multivariate tests would not agree in a decision at the .05 level. In this case 96% of between variation was concentrated in the first discriminant function, in which case the Pillai trace is known to be least powerful (Olson, 1976).

Using the univariate F's for interpretation, we would conclude that each of the variables is significant at the .05 level, since all the exact probabilities are $< .05$. That is, when each variable is considered separately, not taking into account how it is correlated with the others, it significantly separates the groups.

However, if we were able to establish a logical ordering of the criterion measures and thus use the stepdown F's, then it is clear that *only the first two* variables make a significant contribution (assuming the nominal levels had been set at .05 for the first variable and .025 for the other 3 variables). Variables 3 and 4 are redundant, i.e., given 1 and 2, they do not make a significant contribution to group discrimination above and beyond what the first 2 variables do.

10.6 STEPDOWN F'S FOR k GROUPS-EFFECT OF WITHIN AND BETWEEN CORRELATIONS

For more than two groups two matrices must be factored, and obtaining the stepdown F's becomes more complicated (Finn, 1974). We will not worry about the details, but instead concentrate on two factors (the within and between correlations), which will determine how much a step-down F for a given variable will differ from the univariate F for that variable.

The within group correlation for variables x and y can be thought of as the weighted average of the individual group correlations. (This is not exactly technically correct, but will yield a value quite close to the actual value and it is easier to understand conceptually.) Consider the data from Exercise 1 in Chapter 5, and in particular variables y_1 and y_2. Suppose we computed r_{y1y2} for subjects in group 1 only, then r_{y1y2} for subjects in group 2 only, and finally r_{r1y2} for subjects in group 3 only. These correlations are .637, .201, and .754 respectively, as the reader should check.

$$r_{y1y2(w)} = \frac{n_1 \cdot r_{(1)} + n_2 \cdot r_{(2)} + n_3 \cdot r_{(3)}}{N}$$

$$= \frac{11(.637) + 8(.201) + 10(.754)}{29} = .56$$

In this case we have taken the weighted average, since the groups sizes were unequal. Now, the actual within (error) correlation is .61, which is quite close to the .56 we obtained.

How does one obtain the between correlation for x and y? The formula for $r_{xy(B)}$ is identical in form to the formula used for obtaining the simple Pearson correlation between two variables. That formula is:

$$r = \frac{\sum_i (x_i - \bar{x})(y_i - \bar{y})}{\sqrt{\sum_i (x_i - \bar{x})^2 \sum_i (y_i - \bar{y})^2)}}$$

The formula for $r_{xy(B)}$ is obtained by replacing x_i and y_i by $\bar{x}_i$ and $\bar{y}_i$ (group means) and by replacing $\bar{x}$ and $\bar{y}$ by the grand means of $\bar{\bar{x}}$ and $\bar{\bar{y}}$. Also, for the between correlation the summation is over *groups*, not individuals. The formula is:

$$r_{xy(B)} = \frac{\sum (\bar{x}_i - \bar{\bar{x}})(\bar{y}_i - \bar{\bar{y}})}{\sqrt{\sum (\bar{x}_i - \bar{\bar{x}})^2 \sum (\bar{y}_i - \bar{\bar{y}})^2}}$$

Now that we have introduced the within and between correlations, and keeping in mind that stepdown analysis is just a series of analyses of covariance, the following from Bock and Haggard (1968, p. 129) is important:

The results of an analysis of covariance depend on the extent to which the correlation of the concomitant and the dependent variables is concentrated in the errors (i.e., within group correlation) or in the effects of the experimental conditions (between correlation). If the concomitant variable is correlated appreciably with the errors, but little or not at all with the effects, the analysis of covariance increases the power of the statistical tests to detect differences. . . . If the concomitant variable is correlated with the experimental effects as much or more than with the errors, the analysis of covariance will show that the effect observed in the dependent variable can be largely accounted for by the concomitant variable (covariate). (p. 129)

Thus, the stepdown F's can differ considerably from the univariate F's and in *either* direction. If a given dependent variable in the ordering is correlated more within groups with the previous variables in the ordering than between groups, then the stepdown F for that variable will be larger than the univariate F, since more within-variability will be removed from the variable by the covariates (i.e., previous dependent variables) than between-groups variability. If, on the other hand, the dependent variable is correlated strongly between groups with the previous dependent variables in the ordering, then we would expect its stepdown F to be considerably smaller than the univariate F. In this case the mean sum of squares between for the variable is markedly reduced, i.e., its effect in discriminating the groups is strongly tied to the previous dependent variables or can be accounted for by them.

Specific illustrations of each of the above situations are provided by two examples from Morrison (1967, p. 127 and p. 154, #3). Our focus is on the first two dependent variables in the ordering for each problem. For the first problem those variables were called information and similarities, while for the second problem they were simply called variable A and variable B. For each pair of variables, the correlation was high (.762 and .657). In the first case, however, the correlation was concentrated in the experimental condition (between correlation), while in the second it was concentrated in the errors (within-group correlation). A comparison of the univariate and stepdown F's shows this very clearly: For similarities (2nd variable in ordering) the univariate $F = 12.04$, while the stepdown $F = 1.37$. Thus, most of the between-association for the similarities variable can be accounted for by its high correlation with the first variable in the ordering, i.e., information. On the other hand, for the other situation the univariate $F = 6.4$ for variable B (2nd variable in ordering), while the stepdown $F = 24.03$! The reason for this striking result is that variable B and variable A (first variable in ordering) are highly correlated *within* groups, and thus most of the error variance for variable B can be accounted for by variance on variable A. Thus, the error variance for B in the stepdown F is much smaller than the error variance for B in the univariate F. The much smaller error coupled with the fact that A and B had a lower correlation across the groups resulted in a much larger stepdown F for B.

10.7 SUMMARY

One could routinely always printout the stepdown F's. This can be dangerous however to users who may try to interpret these when not appropriate. In those cases (probably most cases) where a logical ordering can't be established, one should either not attempt to interpret the stepdown F's or do so very cautiously.

Some investigators may try several different orderings of the dependent variables in order to gather additional information. Although this may prove useful for future studies, it should be kept in mind that the different orderings are *not* independent. Although for a single ordering the overall α can be exactly estimated, for several orderings the probability of spurious results is unknown.

It is important to distinguish between the stepdown analysis, where a single a priori ordering of the dependent variables enables one to exactly estimate the probability of at least one false rejection, and so called stepwise procedures (as previously described in the multiple regression chapter) or as in the *BMDP7M* and *SPSSX* outputs discussed in the k group MANOVA chapter. In these latter stepwise procedures the variable which is the best discriminator among the groups is entered first, then the procedure finds the next best discriminator, etc. In such a procedure, especially with small or moderate sample sizes, there is a substantial hazard of capitalization on chance. That is, the variables which happen to have the highest correlations with the criterion (in multiple regression) or happen to be the best discriminators in the *particular* sample are those that are chosen. Very often, however, in another independent sample (from the population) some or many of the same variables may not be the best.

Thus, the stepdown analysis approach possesses two distinct advantages over such stepwise procedures: (1) It rests on a solid theoretical and/or empirical foundation—necessary to order the variables,and (2) the probability of one or more false rejections can be exactly estimated—statistically very desirable. The stepwise procedure, on the other hand, is likely to produce results that will not replicate and are therefore of dubious scientific value.

11

EXPLORATORY AND CONFIRMATORY FACTOR ANALYSIS

11.1 INTRODUCTION

Consider the following two common classes of research situations:

1. Exploratory regression analysis: An experimenter has gathered a moderate to large number of predictors (say 15 to 40) to predict some dependent variable.
2. Scale development: An investigator has assembled a set of items (say 20 to 50) designed to measure some construct (e.g., attitude toward education, anxiety, sociability). Here we will think of the items as the variables.

In both of these situations the number of simple correlations among the variables is very large, and it is quite difficult to summarize by inspection precisely what the pattern of correlations represents. For example, with 30 variables that are 435 simple correlations! Some means is needed for determining if there are a small number of underlying constructs which might account for the main sources of variation in such a complex set of correlations.

Furthermore, if there are 30 variables (whether predictors or items), we are undoubtedly not measuring 30 different constructs; hence, it makes sense to find some variable reduction scheme that will indicate how the variables cluster or hang together. Now, if sample size is not large enough (how large N needs to be is discussed in 11.7), then we need to resort to a logical clustering (grouping) based on theoretical and/or substantive grounds. On the other hand, with adequate sample size an empirical approach is preferable. Two basic empirical approaches are (1) principal components analysis and (2) factor analysis. In both approaches linear combinations of the original variables (the factors) are derived, and often a small number of these account for most of the variation or the pattern of correlations. In factor analysis a mathematical model is set up, and the factors can only be estimated, whereas in components analysis we are simply transforming the original variables into the new set of linear combinations (the principal components).

Both methods often yield similar results. We prefer to discuss principal components for several reasons:

1. It is a psychometrically sound procedure.
2. It is simpler mathematically, relatively speaking, than factor analysis. And a main theme in this text is to keep the mathematics as simple as possible.
3. The factor indeterminacy issue associated with common factor analysis (Steiger, 1979) is a troublesome feature.
4. A thorough discussion of factor analysis would require hundreds of pages, and there are other good sources on the subject (Gorsuch, 1983).

Recall that for discriminant analysis uncorrelated linear combinations of the original variables were used to additively partition the association between the classification variable and the set of dependent variables. Here we will be again using uncorrelated linear combinations of the original variables (the principal components), but this time to additively partition the variance for a set of variables.

In this chapter we consider in some detail two fundamentally different approaches to factor analysis. The first approach, just discussed, is called exploratory factor analysis. Here the researcher is attempting to determine how many factors are present, whether the factors are correlated or not, and wishes to name the factors. The other approach, called confirmatory factor analysis, rests on a solid theoretical and/or empirical base. Here, the researchers "knows" how many factors there are and whether the factors should be correlated or not. Also, the researcher generally forces items to load only on a specific factor and wishes to "confirm" his hypothesized factor structure with data. There is an overall statistical test for doing so. First, however, we turn to the exploratory mode.

EXPLORATORY FACTOR ANALYSIS

11.2 THE NATURE OF PRINCIPAL COMPONENTS

If we have a single group of subjects measured on a set of variables, then principal components partitions the total variance (i.e., the sum of the variances for the original variables) by first finding the linear combination of the variables which accounts for the maximum account of variance:

$$y_1 = a_{11}x_1 + a_{12}x_2 + \ldots + a_{1p}x_p$$

y_1 is called the first principal component, and if the coefficients are scaled such that $\mathbf{a}_1'\mathbf{a}_1 = 1$, [where $\mathbf{a}_1' = (a_{11}, a_{12}, \ldots, a_{1p})$] then the variance of y_1 is equal to the *largest* eigenvalue of the sample covariance matrix (Morrison, 1967, p. 224). The coefficients of the principal component are the elements of the eigenvector corresponding to the largest eigenvalue.

Then the procedure finds a second linear combination, *uncorrelated* with the first component, such that it accounts for the next largest amount of variance (after the variance attributable to the first component has been removed) in the system. This second component y_2 is

$$y_2 = a_{21} x_1 + a_{22} x_2 + \ldots a_{2p} x_p$$

and the coefficients are scaled so that $\mathbf{a_2}' \mathbf{a_2} = 1$, as for the first component. The fact that the two components are constructed to be uncorrelated means that the Pearson correlation between y_1 and y_2 is 0. The coefficients of the second component are simply the elements of the eigenvector associated with the second largest eigenvalue of the covariance matrix, and the sample variance of y_2 is equal to the second largest eigenvalue.

The third principal component is constructed to be uncorrelated with the first two, and accounts for the third largest amount of variance in the system, etc. Principal components analysis is therefore still another example of a mathematical maximation procedure, where each successive component accounts for the maximum amount of the variance that is left.

Thus, through the use of principal components a set of correlated variables is transformed into a set of uncorrelated variables (the components). The hope is that a much smaller number of these components will account for most of the variance in the original set of variables, and of course that we can meaningfully interpret the components. By most of the variance we mean about 75% or more, and often this can be accomplished with five or less components.

The components are interpreted by using the component-variable correlations (called *factor loadings*) which are largest in absolute magnitude. For example, if the first component loaded high and positive on variables 1, 3, 5, and 6, then we would interpret that component by attempting to determine what those four variables have in common. The component procedure has empirically clustered the four variables, and the job of the psychologist is to give a name to the construct that underlies variability and thus identify the component substantively.

In the above example we assumed that the loadings were all in the same direction (all positive). Of course, it is possible to have a mixture of high positive and negative loadings on a particular component. In this case we have what is called a *bipolar* factor. For example, in components analyses of I.Q. tests, the second component may be a bipolar factor contrasting verbal abilities against spatial-perceptual abilities.

Social science researchers would be used to extracting components from a correlation matrix. The reason for this standardization is that scales for tests used in educational, sociological, and psychological research are usually arbitrary. If, however, the scales are reasonably commensurable, performing a components analysis on the *covariance* matrix is preferable for statistical reasons. (Morrison, 1967, p. 222). The components obtained from the correlation and covariance matrices are, in general, *not* the same. The option of doing the components analysis on either the correlation or covariance matrix is available on SAS and SPSSX.

A precaution that researchers contemplating a components analysis with a small sample size (certainly any n around 100) should take, especially if most of the elements in the sample correlation matrix are small, is to apply Bartlett's sphericity test (Cooley & Lohnes, 1971, p. 103). This procedure tests the null hypothesis that the variables in the *population* correlation matrix are uncorrelated. If one fails to reject with this test, then there is no reason to do the components analysis since the variables are already uncorrelated. The sphericity test is available on both the SAS and SPSSX packages.

11.3 THREE USES FOR COMPONENTS AS A VARIABLE REDUCING SCHEME

We now consider three cases in which the use of components as a variable reducing scheme can be very valuable.

1. The first use has already been mentioned, and that is to determine empirically how many dimensions (underlying constructs) account for most of the variance on an instrument (scale). The original variables in this case are the items on the scale.

2. In a multiple regression context, if the number of predictors is large relative to the number of subjects, then we may wish to use principal components on the predictors to reduce markedly the number of predictors. If so, then the N/variable ratio increases considerably and the possibility of the regression equation holding up under cross-validation is much better (cf. Herzberg, 1969). We show later in the chapter (example 3) how to do this on SAS and SPSSX.

The use of principal components on the predictors is also one way of attacking the multicollinearity problem (correlated predictors). Furthermore, since the new predictors (i.e., the components) are uncorrelated, the order in which they enter the regression equation makes no difference in terms of how much variance in the dependent variable they will account for.

3. In the chapter on k group MANOVA we indicated several reasons (reliability consideration, robustness, etc.) which generally mitigate against the use of a large number of criterion variables. Therefore, if there is initially a large number of potential criterion variables, it probably would be wise to perform a principal components analysis on them in an attempt to work with a smaller set of new criterion variables. We show later in the chapter (in Example 4) how to do this for SAS and SPSSX. It must be

recognized, however, that the components are *artificial* variables and are not necessarily going to be interpretable. Nevertheless, there are techniques for improving their interpretability, and we discuss these later.

11.4 CRITERIA FOR DECIDING ON HOW MANY COMPONENTS TO RETAIN

There are four methods that can be used in deciding how many components to retain:

1. Probably the most widely used criterion is that of Kaiser (1960): Retain only those components whose eigenvalues are greater than 1. Unless something else is specified, this is the rule that is used by SPSSX, but not by SAS. Although generally using this rule will result in retention of only the most important factors, blind use could lead to retaining factors which may have no practical significance (in terms of % of variance accounted for).

Studies by Cattell and Jaspers (1967), Browne (1968), and Linn (1968) have evaluated the accuracy of the eigenvalue > 1 criterion. In all three studies the authors determined how often the criterion would identify the correct number of factors from matrices with a known number of factors. The number of variables in the studies ranged from 10 to 40. Generally the criterion was accurate to fairly accurate, with gross overestimation occurring only with a large number of variables (40) *and* low communalities. (around .40). The criterion is more accurate when the number of variables is small (10 to 15) or moderate (20 to 30) and the communalities are high (> .70). The communality of a variable is the amount of variance on a variable accounted for by the set of factors. We see how it is computed later in this chapter.

2. A graphical method called the *scree test* has been proposed by Cattell (1966). In this method the magnitude of the eigenvalues (vertical axis) are plotted against their ordinal numbers (whether it was the first eigenvalue, the second, etc.). Generally what happens is that the magnitude of successive eigenvalues drops off sharply (steep descent) and then tends to level off. The recommendation is to retain all eigenvalues (and hence components) in the sharp descent *before* the first one on the line where they start to level off. In one of our examples we illustrate this test. This method will generally retain components which account for large or fairly large and distinct amounts of variances (e.g., 31%, 20%, 13%, and 9%). Here, however, blind use might lead to not retaining factors which, although they account for a smaller amount of variance, might be practically significant. For example, if the first eigenvalue at the break point accounted for 8.3%

of variance and then the next three eigenvalues accounted for 7.1%, 6%, and 5.2%, then 5% or more might well be considered significant in some contexts, and retaining the first and dropping the next three seems somewhat arbitrary. The scree plot is available on SPSSX (in FACTOR program) and in the SAS package. Several studies have investigated the accuracy of the scree test. Tucker, Koopman, and Linn (1969) found it gave the correct number of factors in 12 of 18 cases. Linn (1968) found it to yield the correct number of factors in 7 of 10 cases, while Cattell and Jaspers (1967) found it to be correct in 6 of 8 cases.

A more recent, extensive study on the number of factors problem (Hakstian, Rogers, & Cattell, 1982) adds some additional information. They note that for $N > 250$ and a mean communality $\geq .60$, either the Kaiser or Scree rules will yield an accurate estimate for the number of true factors. They add that such an estimate will be just that much more credible if the Q/P ratio is $< .30$ (P is the number of variables and Q is the number of factors). With mean communality .30 or $Q/P > .3$, the Kaiser rule is less accurate and the Scree rule much less accurate.

3. There is a statistical significance test for the number of factors to retain which was developed by Lawley (1940). However, as with all statistical tests, it is influenced by sample size, and large sample size may lead to the retention of too many factors.

4. Retain as many factors as will account for a specified amount of total variance. Generally one would want to account for at least 70% of the total variance, although in some cases the investigator may not be satisfied unless 80 to 85% of the variance is accounted for. This method could lead to the retention of factors which are essentially variable specific, i.e., load highly on only a single variable.

So what criterion should be used in deciding how many factors to retain? *Since the Kaiser criterion has been shown to be quite accurate when the number of variables is < 30 and the communalities are > .70, or when $N > 250$ and the mean communality is $\geq .60$, we would use it under these circumstances.* For other situations use of the scree test with an $N > 200$ will probably not lead us too far astray, provided that most of the communalities are reasonably large.

In all of the above we have assumed that we will retain only so many components, which will hopefully account for a sizable amount of the total variance, and simply discard the rest of the information, i.e., not worry about the 20 or 30% of the variance that is not accounted for. However, it seems to us that in some cases the following suggestion of Morrison (1967) has merit, "Frequently it is better to summarize the complex in terms of the first components with large and markedly distinct variances and include as highly specific and unique variates those responses which are generally independent in the system. Such unique responses could probably be represented by high loadings in the later components but only in the presence of considerable noise from the other unrelated variates" (p. 228).

In other words, if we did a components analysis on say 20 variables and only the first 4 components accounted for large and distinct amounts of variance, then we should summarize the complex of 20 variables in terms of the 4 components *and* those particular variables which had high correlations (loadings) with the latter components. In this way more of the total information in the complex is retained although some parsimony is sacrificed.

11.5 INCREASING INTERPRETABILITY OF FACTORS BY ROTATION

Although the principal components are fine for summarizing most of the variance in a large set of variables with a small number of components, often the components are not easily interpretable. The components are artificial variates designed to maximize variance accounted for, not designed for interpretability. There are two major classes of rotations that are available:

1. orthogonal (rigid) rotations—here the new factors are still uncorrelated, as where the original components.
2. oblique rotations—here the new factors will be correlated

Orthogonal Rotations

We discuss two such rotations:

1. Quartimax—Here the idea is to clean up the variables. That is, the rotation is done so that each variable loads mainly on one factor. Then that variable can be considered to be a relatively pure measure of the factor. The problem with this approach is that most of the variables tend to load on a single factor (producing the so called "g" factor in analyses of IQ tests), making interpretation of the factor difficult.
2. Varimax—Kaiser (1960) took a different tact. He designed a rotation to clean up the factors. That is, with his rotation each factor tends to load high on a smaller number of variables and low or very low on the other variables. This will generally make interpretation of the resulting factors easier. The Varimax rotation is the default option in SPSSX.

It should be mentioned that when the Varimax rotation is done the *maximum variance property* of the original components is destroyed. The rotation essentially reallocates the loadings. Thus, the first rotated factor will no longer *necessarily* account for the maximum amount of variance. The amount of variance accounted for by each rotated factor has to be recalculated. You will see this on the printout from SAS and SPSSX. Even though this is true, and somewhat unfortunate, it is more important to be able to interpret the factors.

Oblique Rotations

Numerous oblique rotations have been proposed, for example, oblimax, quartimin, maxplane, orthoblique (Harris–Kaiser), promax, oblimin. Promax and orthoblique are available on SAS, while oblimin is available on SPSSX.

Many have argued that correlated factors are much more reasonable to assume in most cases (Cliff, 1987; Pedhazur & Schmelkin, 1991; *SAS STAT USER'S GUIDE,* Vol 1, p. 776, 1990), and therefore oblique rotations are quite reasonable. The following from Pedhazur and Schmelkin (1991) is interesting:

> From the perspective of construct validation, the decision whether to rotate factors orthogonally or obliquely reflect's one's conception regarding the structure of the construct under consideration. It boils down to the question: Are aspects of a postulated multidimensional construct intercorrelated? The answer to this question is relegated to the status of an assumption when an orthogonal rotation is employed. . . . The preferred course of action is, in our opinion, to rotate both orthogonally and obliquely. When, on the basis of the latter, it is concluded that the correlations among the factors are negligible, the interpretation of the simpler orthogonal solution becomes tenable. (p. 615)

It has also been argued that there is no such thing as a "best" oblique rotation. The following from the *SAS STAT USER'S GUIDE* (Vol 1, p. 776, 1990) strongly expresses this view:

> You cannot say that any rotation is better than any other rotation from a statistical point of view; all rotations are equally good statistically. Therefore, the choice among different rotations must be based on nonstatistical grounds. . . . If two rotations give rise to different interpretations, those two interpretations must not be regarded as conflicting. Rather, they are two different ways of looking at the same thing, two different points of view in the common factor space.

In the two computer examples we simply did the components analysis and a Varimax rotation, that is, an orthogonal rotation. The solutions obtained may or may not be the most reasonable ones. We also did an oblique rotation (promax) on the Personality Research Form using SAS. Interestingly, the correlations among the factors were very small (all < .10 in absolute value), suggesting that the original orthogonal solution is quite reasonable. We leave it to the reader to run an oblique rotation (oblimin) on the California Psychological Inventory using SPSSX, and to compare the orthogonal and oblique solutions.

The reader needs to be aware that when an oblique solution is more reasonable, interpretation of the factors becomes more complicated. Two matrices need to be examined:

1. Factor pattern matrix—the elements here are analogous to standardized regression coefficients from a multiple regression analysis. That is, a given element indicates the importance of that variable to the factor with the influence of the other variables partialled out.
2. factor structure matrix—the elements here are the simple correlations of the variables with the factors, that is, they are the factor loadings.

For orthogonal factors the above two matrices are the same.

11.6   WHAT LOADINGS SHOULD BE USED FOR INTERPRETATION?

Recall that a loading is simply the Pearson correlation between the variable and the factor (linear combination of the variables). Now, certainly any loading which is going to be used to interpret a factor should be statistically significant at a minimum. The formula for the standard error of a correlation coefficient is given in elementary statistics books as $1/\sqrt{N-1}$ and one might think it could be used to determine which loadings are significant. But in components analysis (where we are maximizing again) and in rotating there is considerable opportunity for capitalization on chance. This is especially true for small or moderate sample sizes, or even for fairly large sample size (200 or 300) if the number of variables being factored is large (say 40 or 50). Because of this capitalization on chance, the formula for the standard error of correlation can *seriously underestimate* the actual amount of error in the factor loadings.

A study by Cliff and Hamburger (1967) showed that the standard errors of factor loadings for orthogonally rotated solutions in all cases were considerably greater (150 to 200% in most cases) than the standard error for an ordinary correlation. Thus, a rough check as to whether a loading is statistically significant can be obtained by *doubling* the standard error, i.e., doubling the critical value required for significance for an ordinary correlation. This kind of statistical check is most crucial when sample size is small or small relative to the number of variables being factor analyzed. When sample size is quite large (say 1,000), or large relative to the number of variables ($N = 500$ for 20 variables), then significance is ensured. It may be that doubling the standard error in general is too conservative since for the case where a statistical check is more crucial ($N = 100$), the errors were generally less than one and a half times greater. However, since Cliff and Hamburger (1967, p. 438) suggest that the sampling error might be greater in situations that aren't as clean as the one they analyzed, it probably is advisable to be conservative until more evidence becomes available.

Given the Cliff and Hamburger results, we feel it is time that investigators stopped blindly using the rule of interpreting factors with loadings greater than $|.30|$, and take sample size into account. Also, since in checking to determine which loadings are significant many statistical tests will be done, it is advisable to set the α level more stringently for each test. This is done in order to control on overall α, i.e., the probability of at least one false rejection. We would recommend testing each loading for significance at $\alpha = .01$ (two-tailed test). To aid the reader in this task we present in Table 11.1 the critical values for a simple correlation at $\alpha = .01$ (two-tailed test) for sample size ranging from 50 to 1,000. Remember that the critical values in Table 11.1 should be doubled, and it is the doubled value that is used as the critical value for testing the significance of a loading. To illustrate the use of Table 11.1, suppose a factor analysis had been run with 140 subjects. Then only loadings $> 2(.217) = .434$ in absolute value would be declared statistically significant. If sample size in this example had been 160, then interpolation between 140 and 180 will give a very good approximation to the critical value.

Once one is confident that the loadings being used for interpretation are significant (because of a significance test or because of large sample size), then the question becomes which loadings are large enough to be practically

TABLE 11.1
Critical Values for a Correlation Coefficient at $\alpha = .01$ for a Two-Tailed Test

n	C. V.	n	C. V.	n	C. V.
50	.361	180	.192	400	.129
80	.286	200	.182	600	.105
100	.256	250	.163	800	.091
140	.217	300	.149	1000	.081

significant. For example, a loading of .20 could well be significant with large sample size, but this indicates only 4% shared variance between the variable and the factor. It would seem that one would want in general a variable to share *at least* 15% of its variance with the construct (factor) it is going to be used to help name. This means only using loadings which are about .40 or greater for interpretation purposes. To interpret what the variables with high loadings have in common, i.e., to name the factor (construct), a substantive specialist is needed.

11.7 SAMPLE SIZE AND RELIABLE FACTORS

A variety of rules have been suggested in terms of the sample size required for reliable factors. Many of the popular rules suggest that sample size be determined as a function of the number of variables being analyzed, ranging anywhere from two subjects per variable to 20 subjects per variable. And indeed, in the previous edition of this text, I suggested 5 subjects per variable as the minimum needed. However, a recent Monte Carlo study by Guadagnoli and Velicer (1988) indicates, contrary to the popular rules, that the most important factors are component saturation (the absolute magnitude of the loadings) and absolute sample size. Also, number of variables per component is somewhat important. Their recommendations for the applied researcher were as follows:

1. Components with four or more loadings above .60 in absolute value are reliable, regardless of sample size.
2. Components with about 10 or more low (.40) loadings are reliable as long as sample size is greater than about 150.
3. Components with only a few low loadings should not be interpreted unless sample size is at least 300.

An additional reasonable conclusion to draw from their study is that any component with at least 3 loadings above .80 will be reliable.

These results are nice in establishing at least some empirical basis, rather than "seat of the pants" judgement, for assessing what components we can have confidence in. However, as with any study, they only cover a certain set of situations. For example, what if we run across a component that has two loadings above .60 and six loadings of at least .40; is this a reliable component? My guess is that it probably would be, but at this time we don't have a strict empirical basis for saying so.

The third recommendation of Guadagnoli and Velicer, that components with only a few low loadings being interpreted tenuously, doesn't seem that important to me. The reason is that a factor defined by only a few loadings is not much of a factor; as a matter of fact we are as close as we can get to the factor being variable specific.

11.8   FOUR COMPUTER EXAMPLES

We now consider four examples to illustrate the use of components analysis and the varimax rotation in practice. The first two involve popular personality scales: the California Psychological Inventory and the Personality Research Form. Example 1 shows how to input a correlation matrix using the SPSSX FACTOR program, while example 2 illustrates correlation matrix input for the SAS FACTOR program. Example 3 shows how to do a components analysis on a set of predictors and then pass the new predictors (the factor scores) to a regression program for both SAS and SPSSX. Example 4 illustrates a components analysis and varimax rotation on a set of dependent variables and then passing the factor scores to a MANOVA program for both SAS and SPSSX.

Example 1—California Psychological Inventory on SPSSX

The first example is a components analysis of the California Psychological Inventory followed by a varimax rotation. The data was collected on 180 college freshmen (90 males and 90 females) by Smith (1975). He was interested in gathering evidence to support the uniqueness of death anxiety as a construct. Thus, he wanted to determine to what extent death anxiety could be predicted from general anxiety, other personality variables (hence the use of the CPI), and situational variables related to death (recent loss of a love one, recent experiences with a deathly situation, etc.). In this use of multiple regression Smith was hoping for a *small R^2*, i.e., he wanted only a small amount of the variance in death anxiety scores to be accounted for by the other variables.

Table 11.2 presents the SPSSX control lines for the factor analysis, along with annotation explaining what several of the commands mean. The correlation matrix for the CPI variables is given in Table 11.3. Table 11.4 presents part of the printout from SPSSX. The printout indicates that the first component (factor) accounted for 37.1% of the total variance. This is arrived at by dividing the eigenvalue for the first component (6.679), which tells how much variance that component accounts for, by the total variance (which for a correlation matrix is just the sum of the diagonal elements, or 18 here). The second component accounts for 2.935/18 × 100 = 16.3% of the variance, etc.

TABLE 11.2

SPSSX Factor Control Lines for Principal Components Analysis
on the California Psychological Inventory

TITLE 'PRINCIPAL COMPONENTS ON THE CPI'
① MATRIX DATA VARIABLES = DOM CAPSTAT SOCIAL SOCPRES SELFACP
WELLBEG RESPON SOCLIZ SELFCTRL TOLER GOODIMP COMMUNAL
ACHCONF ACHINDEP INTELEFF PSYMIND FLEX FEMIN
BEGIN DATA
1.000
.467 1.000
.681 .600 1.000
.447 .585 .643 1.000
  ETC.
.099 .061 − .069 − .158 − .097 − .038 .275 .159 .215 .032 .091
.139 .071 .033 − .031 − .145 − .344 1.000
END DATA
② FACTOR MATRIX IN (COR = *)/
③ PRINT = CORRELATION DEFAULT/
④ PLOT = EIGEN/
⑤ FORMAT = SORT BLANK(.25)/

---

①The MATRIX DATA command is similar to a DATA LIST command. It can define both inline data that appear between the BEGIN DATA and END DATA commands, and data from an external file.

②To read and write matrices in FACTOR the MATRIX subcommand is used. The keyword IN specifies the file from which the matrix is read (see *SPSSX USER'S GUIDE*, 3rd Ed. 1988, p. 497). The CORR = * means we are reading the correlation matrix from the active file. It is important to note that MATRIX IN reads all the variables in the matrix; it *cannot* read a subset.

③The CORRELATION in the PRINT subcommand yields the correlation matrix for the variables.

④This PLOT subcommand yields the scree plot.

⑤The SORT and BLANK parts of the FORMAT subcommand are very useful for zeroing in on the important or salient loadings for each factor. The blank (.25) here means that all loadings less than .25 in absolute value will not be printed (effectively set equal to 0).

As to how many components to retain, Kaiser's rule of using only those components whose eigenvalues are greater than 1, would indicate that we should retain only the first four components (which is what has been done on the printout; remember Kaiser's rule is the default option for SPSSX). Thus, as the printout indicates, we account for 71.4% of the total variance. Cattell's screen test (cf. Table 11.4) would not agree with the Kaiser rule, since there are only three eigenvalues (associated with the first three factors) before the breaking point, the point where the steep descent stops and the eigenvalues start to level off. However, we interpret four factors, since the number of variables is less than 30 and most of the communalities are either greater than .70 or very close to .70 (15 of 18).

Table 11.5 gives the unrotated loadings and the varimax rotated loadings. From Table 11.1 the critical value for a significant loading is $2(.192) = .384$. Thus, this is an absolute minimum value for us to be

TABLE 11.3
Intercorrelations of the California Psychological Inventory Scales for 180 College Students (90 Male and 90 Female)

Scale	DO	CS	SY	SP	SA	WB	RE	SO	SC	TA	GI	CM	AC	AI	IE	PY	FX	FE
DO	1.000																	
CS	.467	1.000																
SY	.681	.600	1.000															
SP	.447	.585	.643	1.000														
SA	.610	.466	.673	.612	1.000													
WB	.236	.324	.339	.357	.077	1.000												
RE	.401	.346	.344	.081	.056	.518	1.000											
SO	.214	.179	.242	.003	-.029	.517	.632	1.000										
SC	-.062	.105	-.001	-.130	-.352	.619	.476	.544	1.000									
TO	.227	.465	.295	.330	.004	.698	.502	.517	.575	1.000								
GI	.238	.392	.367	.178	.023	.542	.381	.367	.697	.501	1.000							
CM	.189	.146	.227	.159	.117	.336	.380	.384	.084	.192	-.001	1.000						
AC	.401	.374	.479	.296	.154	.676	.567	.589	.633	.588	.610	.307	1.000					
AI	.075	.400	.140	.289	-.027	.513	.369	.280	.464	.720	.359	.175	.465	1.000				
IE	.314	.590	.451	.457	.192	.671	.500	.442	.456	.716	.460	.333	.616	.688	1.000			
PY	.167	.337	.239	.336	.011	.463	.217	.182	.410	.502	.397	-.060	.393	.519	.466	1.000		
FX	.148	.203	-.028	.236	.037	.051	-.155	-.300	-.043	.218	.079	-.149	-.120	.444	.199	.276	1.000	
FE	.099	.061	-.069	-.158	-.097	-.038	.275	.159	.215	.032	.091	.139	.071	.033	-.031	-.145	-.344	1.000

TABLE 11.4
Eigenvalues, Communalities, and Scree Plot for CPI from SPSSX Factor Analysis Program

FINAL STATISTICS:

VARIABLE	COMMUNALITY	FACTOR	① EIGENVALUE	PCT OF VAR	CUM PCT
DO	.66861	1	6.67907	37.1	37.1
CS	.61861	2	2.93494	16.3	53.4
SY	.83160	3	2.11392	11.7	65.2
SP	.72899	4	1.11592	6.2	② 71.4
SA	.80185				
WB	.69772				
RE	.66676				
SO	.69190				
SC	.89418				
TA	③ .77198				
GI	.77148				
CM	.78142				
AC	.74630				
AI	.77480				
IE	.78641				
PY	.58322				
FX	.69176				
FE	.33627				

SCREE PLOT

BREAK POINT

```
6.679 +    •
      I
      I
      I
      I
      I
      I
      I
      I
      I
      I
      I
      I
      I
      I
      I
      I
      I
      I
      I
2.935 +      •
      I
      I
2.114 +        •
      I
      I
      I
      I
1.116 +          •
 .978 +            •
      I
 .571 +                •    •
 .426 +                   •    •
 .211 +                                          •    •    •    •    •
 .000 + ---+---+---+---+---+---+---+---+---+---+---+---+---+---+---+---•---•---•
        1   2   3   4   5   6   7   8   9  10  11  12  13  14  15 16 17 18
```

①The eigenvalue indicates the amount of variance accounted for by each factor.

②Since the Kaiser criterion is the default option, only factors with eigenvalues > 1 are retained. The 4 factors account for 71.4% of the total variance.

③Since 15 of the 18 communalities are either > .70 or very close to .70, the Kaiser criterion will be accurate here in identifying the true number of factors.

376

TABLE 11.5
Unrotated Components Loadings and Varimax Rotated Loadings for California
Psychological Inventory

FACTOR MATRIX:

	FACTOR 1	FACTOR 2	FACTOR 3	FACTOR 4
DO	.50138	.55614	.29246	−.14969
CS	.64991	.43579	−.04968	−.06202
SY	.60979	.60143	.25638	−.17972
SP	.51249	.66550	−.13753	.06743
SA	.27041	.82105	.22488	−.06352
WB	.80595	−.19642	−.04812	.08525
RE	.67774	−.22010	.38890	.08805
SO	.61108	−.37498	.41038	.09723
SC	.60941	−.67660	−.06199	−.24732
TA	.81618	−.19838	−.22772	.12088
GI	.67347	−.20929	−.07448	−.51824
CM	.35560	−.01207	.43937	.67954
AC	.81977	−.15062	.18110	−.13710
AI	.67845	−.17075	−.45206	.28457
IE	.84604	.01749	−.14830	.21982
PY	.57314	−.04265	−.47150	−.17493
FX	.12880	.24623	−.76719	.16110
FE	.06827	−.27146	.49436	−.11630

ROTATED FACTOR MATRIX: ①

	FACTOR 1	FACTOR 2	FACTOR 3	FACTOR 4
DO	.14163	.79400	.12857	.03982
CS	.38642	.66435	−.16224	.04007
SY	.22573	.87857	.09161	.01933
SP	.17176	.74804	−.35729	.11079
SA	−.17010	.87575	−.04815	.06045
WB	.78875	.18571	.00605	.20268
RE	.59787	.21260	.40252	.31952
SO	.60350	.05621	.46943	.32275
SC	.86379	−.25241	.24986	−.14800
TA	.83224	.13884	−.16455	.18166
GI	.73890	.20992	.16605	−.39226
CM	.16277	.14699	.19767	.83322
AC	.75317	.32434	.26281	.06902
AI	.73196	.01485	−.42514	.24097
IE	.73722	.33508	−.19421	.30484
PY	.62886	.14622	−.34842	−.21207
FX	.14590	.05002	−.81464	−.06584
FE	.08839	−.05355	.56781	.05638

Legend: DO - Dominance, CS - Capacity for Status, SY - Sociability, SP - Social Presence, SA - Self Acceptance, WB - Sense of Well Being, RE -Responsibility, SO - Socialization, SC - Self-Control, TA - Tolerance, GI - Good Impression, CM - Communality, AC - Achievement via Conformance, AI - Achievement via Independence, IE - Intellectual Efficiency, PY - Psychological Mindedness, FX - Flexibility, FE - Femininity.

①To omit (blank out) small loading less than a given value (say .4) in SPSSX, use this subcommand:
FORMAT = SORT BLANK (.4)./

TABLE 11.6
SAS Factor Control Lines for Components Analysis and Varimax Rotation
on the Personality Research Form

```
DATA PRF(TYPE=CORR);
TYPE='CORR';
INPUT NAME $ ABASE ACH AGGRESS AUTON CHANGE COGSTR DEF DOMIN
ENDUR EXHIB HARAVOD IMPLUS NUTUR ORDER PLAY;
CARDS;
ABASE      1.0 . . . . . . . . . . . . .
ACH        .01 1.0 . . . . . . . . . . . .
AGGRESS    − .32 − .08 1.0 . . . . . . . . . . .
AUTON      .13 .03 .04 1.0 . . . . . . . . . .
CHANGE     .15 .09 .06 .28 1.0 . . . . . . . . .
COGSTR     − .23 .22 .02 − .17 − .27 1.0 . . . . . . . .
DEF        − .42 .06 .57 .04 − .01 .14 1.0 . . . . . . .
DOMIN      − .22 .37 .25 .08 .17 − .05 .32 1.0 . . . . . .
ENDUR      .01 .65 − .11 .09 .03 .20 .02 .39 1.0 . . . . . .
EXHIB      − .09 .13 .28 − .07 .15 − .24 .10 .52 .08 1.0 . . . . .
HARAVOD    − .22 − .02 − .01 − .28 − .33 .45 .08 − .21 − .08 − .22 1.0 . . . .
IMPLUS     .14 − .16 .30 .16 .33 − .46 .14 .07 − .23 .34 − .31 1.0 . . .
NUTUR      .33 .30 − .23 − .24 .03 − .05 − .19 .16 .20 .22 − .04 .04 1.0 . .
ORDER      − .11 .29 .01 − .13 − .17 .53 .09 .08 .27 − .11 .22 − .35 0.0 1.0 .
PLAY       .05 − .25 .27 − .02 .12 − .31 − .02 .11 − .27 .43 − .26 .48 − .10 − .25 1.0
PROC FACTOR CORR FUZZ=.34 MINEIGEN=1.0 REORDER ROTATE=VARIMAX SCREE;
```

confident that we are dealing with non-chance loadings. The original components are somewhat difficult to interpret, especially the first component, since 14 of the loadings are "significant." Therefore, we focus our interpretation on the rotated factors. The variables that we use in interpretation are boxed in on Table 11.5. The first rotated factor still has significant loadings on 11 variables, although since one of these (.386 for CS) is just barely significant, and is also substantially less than the other significant loadings (the next smallest is .597), we disregard it for interpretation purposes. Among the adjectives that characterize high scores on the other 10 variables, from the CPI manual, are: calm, patient, thorough, non-aggressive, conscientious, cooperative, modest, diligent, and organized. Thus, this first rotated factor appears to be a "conforming, mature, inward tendencies" dimension. That is, it reveals a low profile individual, who is conforming, industrious, thorough and nonaggressive.

The loadings that are significant on the second rotated factor, are also strong loadings (the smallest is .664): .794 for dominance, .664 for capacity for status, .878 for sociability, .748 for social presence and .875 for self acceptance. Adjectives, from the CPI manual, used to characterize high scores on these variables are: aggressive, ambitious, spontaneous, outspoken, self-centered, quick and enterprising. Thus, this factor appears to describe an "aggressive, outward tendencies" dimension. High scores on this dimension reveal a high profile individual who is aggressive, dynamic, and outspoken.

Factor 3 is somewhat dominated by the flexibility variable (loading = −.814), although we also consider the femininity variable for interpretation. Three other variables are also significant (RE, SO and Ai), although barely so. Also, since these variables were much more strongly associated with factor 1, we will not use them for interpretation of this factor. Low scores on flexibility, from the CPI manual, characterize an individual as cautious, guarded, mannerly, and overly deferential to authority. High scores on femininity reflect an individual who is patient, gentle, and as respectful and accepting of others. Factor three thus seems to be measuring a "demure inflexibility in intellectual and social matters."

Factor 4 is dominated by the communality variable, which is characterized in the CPI manual with adjectives like "dependable, tactful, reliable, and sincere."

Before proceeding to another example, there are a few additional points we wish to make. Nunnally (1978, pp. 433–436) has indicated, in an excellent discussion, several ways in which one can be fooled by factor analysis. One point he makes, which we wish to elaborate on, is that of ignoring the simple correlations among the variables after the factors have been derived. That is, not checking the correlations among the variables which have been used to define a factor, to see if there is communality among them in the simple sense. As Nunnally notes, in some cases variables used to define a factor may have simple correlations near 0.

For our example this is not the case. Examination of the simple correlations in Table 11.3 for the 10 variables used to define factor 1 shows that most of the correlations are in the moderate to fairly strong range. Also, the correlations among the 5 variables used to define factor 2 are also in the moderate to fairly strong range.

There is an additional interesting point concerning factor 2. The empirical clustering of the variables coincides almost exactly with the logical clustering of the variables given in the CPI manual. The only difference is that Wellbe is in the logical cluster but not in the empirical cluster (i.e., not on the factor).

Example 2 — Personality Research Form on SAS

We now consider the interpretation of a principal components analysis and varimax rotation on the Personality Research Form for 231 undergraduate males from a study by Golding and Seidman (1974). The control lines for running the analysis on the SAS FACTOR program and the correlation matrix are presented in Table 11.6. It is important to note here that SAS is different from the other two major packages (BMDP and SPSSX) in that (a) a varimax rotation is *not* a default option – the default is no rotation, and (b) the Kaiser criterion (retaining only those factors whose eigenvalues are > 1) is not a default option. In Table 11.6 we have requested the Kaiser criterion be used by specifying MINEIGEN = 1.0, and have requested the varimax rotation by specifying ROTATE = VARIMAX.

To indicate to SAS that we are inputting a correlation matrix, the TYPE = CORR in parentheses after the name for the data set is necessary. The TYPE = 'CORR' on the next line is also required. Note that the name for each variable precedes the correlations for it with all the other variables. Also, note that there are 14 periods for the ABASE variable, 13 periods for the ACH variable, 12 periods for AGGRESS, etc. These periods need to be inserted. Finally, the correlations for each row of the matrix must be on a separate record. Thus, although we may need two lines for the correlations of ORDER with all other variables, once we put the last correlation there (which is a 1) we must start the correlations for the next variable (PLAY) on a *new* line. The same is true for the SPSSX FACTOR program.

The CORR in this statement yields the correlation matrix for the variables. The FUZZ = .34 prints correlations and factor loadings with absolute value less than .34 as missing values. Our purpose in using FUZZ is to think of values < |.34| as chance values, and to treat them as 0. The SCREE is inserted to obtain Cattell's scree test; useful in determining the number of factors to retain.

The first part of the printout appears in Table 11.7, and the output at the top indicates that according to the Kaiser criterion only 4 factors will be retained because there are only 4 eigenvalues > 1. Will the Kaiser criterion accurately identify the true number of factors in this case? To answer this question it is helpful to refer back to the Hakstian et al. (1982) study cited earlier. They note that for $N > 250$ and a mean communality > .60, the Kaiser criterion is accurate. Since the total of the communality estimates in Table 11.7 is given as 9.338987, the mean communality here is $9.338987/15 = .622$. Although N is not > 250, it is close ($N = 231$), and we feel the Kaiser rule will be accurate.

The scree plot in Table 11.7 also supports using four factors, because the break point occurs at the fifth eigenvalue. That is, the eigenvalues level off from the fifth eigenvalue on. To further support the claim of four true factors, note that the Q/P ratio is $4/15 = .267 < .30$, and Hakstian et. al. (1982) indicate that when this is the case the estimate of the number of factors will be just that more credible.

To interpret the four factors, the sorted, rotated loadings in Table 11.8 are very useful. Referring back to Table 11.1, we see that the critical value for a significant loading at the .01 level is $2(.17) = .34$. So, we certainly would not want to pay any attention to loadings less than .34 in absolute

TABLE 11.7
Eigenvalues and Scree Plot From the SAS Factor Program for Personality Research Form

Eigenvalues of the Correlation Matrix: Total = 15   Average = 1

	1	2	3	4	5	6	7	8
Eigenvalue	3.1684	2.4821	2.2464	1.4422	0.8591	0.8326	0.6859	0.6047
Difference	0.6862	0.2358	0.8042	0.5830	0.0266	0.1466	0.0812	0.0636
Proportion	0.2112	0.1655	0.1498	0.0961	0.0573	0.0555	0.0457	0.0403
Cumulative	0.2112	0.3767	0.5265	0.6226	0.6799	0.7354	0.7811	0.8214

	9	10	11	12	13	14	15
Eigenvalue	0.5411	0.4382	0.4060	0.3826	0.3283	0.3108	0.2717
Difference	0.1029	0.0322	0.0234	0.0543	0.0175	0.0391	
Proportion	0.0361	0.0292	0.0271	0.0255	0.0219	0.0207	0.0181
Cumulative	0.8575	0.8867	0.9138	0.9393	0.9612	0.9819	1.0000

4 factors will be retained by the MINEIGEN criterion.

Scree Plot of Eigenvalues

381

value. That is why we have had SAS print those loadings as a period. This helps to sharpen our focus on the salient loadings. The loadings that most strongly characterize the first three factors (and are of the same order of magnitude) are boxed in on Table 11.8. In terms of interpretation, factor 1 represents an "unstructured, free spirit tendency," with the loadings on factor 2 suggesting a "structured, hard driving tendency" construct. Factor 3 appears to represent a "non-demeaning aggressive tendency," while the loadings on factor 4, which are dominated by the very high loading on autonomy, imply a "somewhat fearless tendency to act on one's own."

As mentioned in the first edition of this text, it would help if there were a statistical test, even a rough one, for determining when one loading on a factor is significantly greater than another loading on the same factor. This would then provide a more solid basis for including one variable in the interpretation of a factor and excluding another, assuming we can be confident that both are non-chance loadings. I remain unaware of such a test.

Example 3—Regression Analysis on Factor Scores—SAS and SPSSX

We mentioned earlier in this chapter that one of the uses of components analysis is to reduce the number of predictors in regression analysis. This makes good statistical and conceptual sense for several reasons. First, if there are a fairly large number of initial predictors (say 15), we are undoubtedly not measuring 15 different constructs, and hence it makes sense to determine what the main constructs are that we are measuring. Secondly, this is desirable from the viewpoint of scientific parsimony. Third, if we reduce from 15 initial predictors to, say, 4 new predictors (the components or rotated factors), our N/k ratio increases dramatically and this helps cross-validation prospects considerably. Fourth, our new predictors are uncorrelated, which means we have eliminated multicollinearity, which is a major factor in causing unstable regression equations. Fifth, because the new predictors are uncorrelated, we can talk about the unique contribution of each predictor in accounting for variance on y, that is, there is a unambiguous interpretation of the importance of each predictor.

We illustrate the process of doing the components analysis on the predictors and then passing the factor scores (as the new predictors) for a regression analysis for both SAS and SPSSX using the National Academy of Science data introduced in chapter 3 on multiple regression. Although there is not a compelling need for a factor analysis here because there are just 6 predictors, this example is simply meant to show the process. The new predictors, that is, the retained factors, will then be used to predict quality of the graduate psychology program. The control lines for doing both the factor analysis and the regression analysis for both packages are given in Table 11.9.

Note in the SAS control lines that the output data set from the principal components procedure contains the original variables *and* the factor scores for the first two components. It is this data set that we are accessing in the PROC REG procedure. Similarily, for SPSSX the factor scores for the first two components are saved and *added* to the active file (as they call it), and it is this file that the regression procedure is dealing with.

So that the results are comparable for the SAS and SPSSX runs, a couple of things *must* be done. First, as mentioned in Table 11.9, one must insert STANDARD into the control lines for SAS, so that the components have a variance of 1, as they have by default for SPSSX. Secondly, because SPSSX does a varimax rotation by default while SAS does not, we must insert the subcommand ROTATION = NOROTATE into the SPSSX control lines so that is the principal components scores that are being used by the regression procedure in each case. If one does not insert the NOROTATE subcommand, then the regression analysis will use the *rotated* factors as the predictors.

Example 4—MANOVA on Factor Scores-SAS and SPSSX

In Table 11.10 we illustrate a components analysis on a hypothetical set of 7 variables, and then passing the first 2 components to do a two-group MANOVA on these "new" variables. Because the components are uncorrelated, one might argue for performing just three univariate tests, for in this case an exact estimate of overall α is available from $1 - (1 - .05)^3 = .145$. While an exact estimate is available, the multivariate approach covers a possibility which the univariate approach would miss, that is, the case where there are small nonsignificant differences on each of the variables, but cumulatively (with the multivariate test) there is a significant difference.

Also, if we had done an oblique rotation, and hence were passing correlated factors, then the case for a multivariate analysis is even more compelling since an exact estimate of overall α is not available. Another case where some of the variables would be correlated is if we did a factor analysis and retained three factors and two of the original variables (which were relatively independent of the factors). Then there would be correlations between the original variables retained and between those variables and the factors.

11.9   THE COMMUNALITY ISSUE

In principal components analysis we simply transform the original variables into linear combinations of these variables, and often 3 or 4 of these

TABLE 11.8
Factor Loading and Rotated, Sorted Loadings For Personality Research Form

Factor Pattern

	FACTOR1	FACTOR2	FACTOR3	FACTOR4
IMPLUS	0.76960	·	·	·
PLAY	0.66312	·	·	·
CHANGE	0.46746	·	·	·
HARMAVOD	−0.58060	·	−0.35665	−0.36271
ORDER	−0.60035	·	·	·
COGSTR	−0.73891	·	·	·
DOMIN	·	0.80853	·	·
ACH	·	0.61394	0.48781	·
ENDUR	·	0.57943	0.49114	·
EXHIB	0.48854	0.53279	·	0.44574
ABASE	·	−0.37413	0.62691	·
NUTUR	·	0.54265	0.60007	0.52851
DEF	·	·	−0.56778	·
AGGRESS	·	0.45762	−0.61053	·
AUTON	·	·	·	−0.77911

NOTE: Values less than 0.34 have been printed as '·'.

Variance explained by each factor

FACTOR1	FACTOR2	FACTOR3	FACTOR4
3.168359	2.482114	2.246351	1.442163

Final Community Estimates: Total = 9.338987

AGGRESS 0.670982	AUTON 0.701144	CHANGE 0.448672	COGSTR 0.624114	DEF 0.644643	DOMIN 0.701961
ACH 0.715861	EXHIB 0.724334	HARMAVOD 0.537959	IMPLUS 0.502875	NUTUR 0.659155	ORDER 0.452917	PLAY 0.573546
ABASE 0.567546	ENDUR 0.713278				

384

Rotated Factor Pattern

	FACTOR1	FACTOR2	FACTOR3	FACTOR4
PLAY	0.73149	.	.	.
IMPLUS	0.73013	.	.	.
EXHIB	0.66060	0.47003	.	.
ORDER	−0.53072	.	.	.
COGSTR	−0.66102	.	.	.
ACH	.	0.78676	.	.
ENDUR	.	0.75731	.	.
DOMIN	.	0.71173	0.35986	.
NUTUR	.	0.51149	−0.50100	.
DEF	.	.	0.79311	.
AGGRESS	.	.	0.76624	.
ABASE	.	.	−0.71271	0.83214
AUTON	.	.	.	0.57560
CHANGE	.	.	.	−0.53376
HARMAVOD	−0.44237	.	.	.

Variance explained by each factor

FACTOR1	FACTOR2	FACTOR3	FACTOR4
2.891095	2.405032	2.297653	1.745206

385

TABLE 11.9
SAS and SPSSX Control Lines for Components Analysis on National Academy of Science Data and Then Passing Factor Scores for a Regression Analysis

SAS

DATA REGRESS;
INPUT QUALITY NFACUL NGRADS PCTSUPP PCTGRT NARTIC PCTPUB @@;
CARDS;

DATA IN BACK OF TEXT

① PROC PRINCOMP N=2 STANDARD OUT=FSCORES;
② VAR=NFACUL NGRADS PCTSUPP PCTGRT NARTIC PCTPUB;
PROC REG DATA=FSCORES;
③ MODEL QUALITY=PRIN1 PRIN2;
SELECTION=STEPWISE;
PROC PRINT DATA=FSCORES;

SPSSX

DATA LIST FREE/QUALITY NFACUL NGRADS PCTSUPP PCTGRT NARTIC
PCTPUB
BEGIN DATA

DATA IN BACK OF TEXT

END DATA
④ FACTOR VARIABLES=NFACUL TO PCTPUB/
⑤ ROTATION=NOROTATE/
⑥ SAVE REG (ALL FSCORE)/
LIST
REGRESSION DESCRIPTIVES=DEFAULT/
⑦ VARIABLES=QUALITY FSCORE1 FSCORE2/
DEPENDENT=QUALITY/
METHOD=STEPWISE/

---

① The N=2 specifies the number of components to be computed; here we just want two. STANDARD is necessary for the components to have variance of 1; otherwise the variance will equal the eigenvalue for the component (see *SAS STAT USER'S GUIDE*, Vol 2, p. 1247). The OUT data set (here called FSCORES) contains the original variables and the component scores.

② In this VAR statement we "pick off" just those variables we wish to do the components analysis on, that is, the predictors.

③ The principal component variables are denoted by default as PRIN1, PRIN2, etc.

④ Recall that TO enables one to refer to a consecutive string of variables more concisely.

⑤ By default in SPSSX the VARIMAX rotation would be done, and the factor scores obtained would be those for the rotated factors. Therefore, we specify NOROTATE so that no rotation is done.

⑥ There are three different methods for computing factor scores, but for components analysis they all yield the same scores. Thus, we have used the default method REG (regression method).

⑦ In saving the factor scores we have used the rootname FSCORE; the maximum number of characters for this name is 7. This rootname is then used along with a number to refer to consecutive factor scores. Thus, FSCORE1 for the factor scores on component 1, FSCORE2 for the factor scores on component 2, etc.

Table 11.10

SAS and SPSSX Control Lines for Components Analysis on Set of Dependent Variables and Then Passing Factor Scores for Two-Group MANOVA

SAS

```
DATA MANOVA;
INPUT GP X1 X2 X3 X4 X5 X6 X7;
CARDS;
1 23 4 45 43 34 8 89 1 34 46 54 46 27 6 93
1 31 34 45 43 56 5 78 1 36 8 65 57 56 3 104
1 43 56 67 54 67 78 92 1 23 43 54 76 54 2 112
2 21 32 65 47 65 56 69 2 34 54 32 45 67 65 74
2 31 23 43 45 76 86 61 2 17 23 43 25 46 65 66
PROC PRINCOMP N=2 STANDARD OUT=FSCORES;
VAR X1 X2 X3 X4 X5 X6 X7;
PROC GLM DATA=FSCORES;
MODEL PRIN1 PRIN2=GP;
MANOVA H=GP;
PROC PRINT DATA=FSCORES;
```

SPSSX

```
DATA LIST FREE/GP X1 X2 X3 X4 X5 X6 X7
BEGIN DATA
1 23 4 45 43 34 8 89 1 34 46 54 46 27 6 93
1 31 34 45 43 56 5 78 1 36 8 65 57 56 3 104
1 43 56 67 54 67 78 92 1 23 43 54 76 54 2 112
2 21 32 65 47 65 56 69 2 34 54 32 45 67 65 74
2 31 23 43 45 76 86 61 2 17 23 43 25 46 65 66
END DATA
FACTOR VARIABLES=X1 TO X7/
 ROTATION=NOROTATE/
 SAVE REG (ALL FSCORE)/
LIST
MANOVA FSCORE1 FSCORE2 BY GP(1,2)/
```

---

combinations (i.e., the components) account for most of the total variance. Also, we used 1's in the diagonal of the correlation matrix. Factor analysis per se differs from components analysis in two ways: (1) The hypothetical factors that are derived can only be *estimated* from the original variables, whereas in components analysis, since the components are specific linear combinations, no estimate is involved, and (2) Numbers less than 1, called communalities, are put in the main diagonal of the correlation matrix in factor analysis. A relevant question is "Will different factors emerge if 1's are put in the main diagonal (as in components analysis), then will emerge if communalities (the squared multiple correlation of each variable with all the others is one of the most popular) are placed in the main diagonal?"

The following quotes from five different sources give a pretty good sense of what might be expected in practice. Cliff (1987) notes that, "the choice of common factors or components methods often makes virtually no difference to the conclusions of a study" (p. 349). Guadagnoli and Velicer (1988) cite several studies by Velicer et al. that, "have demonstrated that principal components solutions differ little from the solutions generated from factor analysis methods" (p. 266).

Harman (1967) states, "As a saving grace, there is much evidence in the literature that for all but very small sets of variables, the resulting factorial solutions are little affected by the particular choice of communalities in the principal diagonal of the correlation matrix" (p. 83). Nunnally (1978) notes, "It is very safe to say that if there are as many as 20 variables in the analysis, as there are in nearly all exploratory factor analyses, then it does not matter what one puts in the diagonal spaces" (p. 418). Gorsuch (1983) takes a somewhat more conservative position, "If communalities are reasonably high (e.g., .7 and up), even unities are probably adequate communality estimates in a problem with more than 35 variables" (p. 108). A general, somewhat conservative conclusion from the above is that when the number of variables is moderately large (say > 30), and the analysis contains virtually no variables expected to have low communalities (e.g., .4), then practically any of the factor procedures will lead to the same interpretations. Differences can occur when the number of variables is fairly small (< 20), and some communalities are low.

11.10   A FEW CONCLUDING COMMENTS

We have focused on an internal criterion in evaluating the factor solution, i.e., how interpretable are the factors. However, an important external criterion is the reliability of the solution. If the sample size is large, then one should randomly split the sample to check the consistency (reliability) of the factor solution on both random samples. In checking to determine whether the same factors have appeared in both cases it is not sufficient to just examine the factor loadings. One needs to obtain the correlations between the factor scores for corresponding pairs of factors. If these correlations are high, then one may have confidence of factor stability.

Finally, there is the issue of "factor indeterminancy" when estimating factors as in the common factor model. This refers to the fact that the factors are not uniquely determined. The importance of this for the common factor model has been the subject of much hot debate in the literature. We tend to side with Steiger (1979), who states, "My opinion is that indeterminacy and related problems of the factor model counterbalance the model's theoretical advantages, and that the elevated status of the common factor model (relative to, say, components analysis) is largely undeserved" (p. 157).

CONFIRMATORY FACTOR ANALYSIS

11.11   EXPLORATORY AND CONFIRMATORY FACTOR ANALYSIS

The principal component analyses presented previously in this chapter are a form of what are commonly termed *exploratory factor analyses* (EFAs). The purpose of exploratory analysis is to identify the factor structure or model for a set of variables. This often involves determining how many factors exist, as well as the pattern of the factor loadings. Although most EFA programs allow for the number of factors to be specified in advance, it is not possible in these programs to force variables to load only on certain factors. EFA is generally considered to be more of a theory-generating than a theory-testing procedure. In contrast, *confirmatory factor analysis* (CFA) is generally based on a strong theoretical and/or empirical foundation that allows the researcher to specify an exact factor model in advance. This model usually specifies which variables will load on which factors, as well as such things as which factors are correlated. It is more of a theory-testing procedure than is EFA. Although, in practice, studies may contain aspects of both exploratory and confirmatory analyses, it is useful to distinguish between the two techniques in terms of the situations in which they are commonly used. The following table displays some of the general differences between the two approaches.

EXPLORATORY THEORY GENERATING	CONFIRMATORY THEORY TESTING
Heuristic — weak literature base	Strong theory and/or strong empirical base
Determine the number of factors	Number of factors fixed a priori
Determine whether the factors are correlated or uncorrected	Factors fixed a priori as correlated or uncorrelated
Variables free to load on all factors	Variables fixed to load on a specific factor or factors

Let us consider an example of an EFA. Suppose a researcher is developing a scale to measure self-concept. The researcher does not conceptualize specific self-concept factors in advance, and simply writes a variety of items designed to tap into various aspects of self-concept. An EFA or components analysis of these items may yield three factors that the researcher then identifies as physical (PSC), social (SSC), and academic (ASC) self-concept. The researcher notes that items with large loadings on one of the three factors tend to have very small loadings on the other two, and interprets this as support for the presence of three distinct factors or dimensions underlying self-concept.

A less common variation on this example would be one in which the researcher had hypothesized the three factors a priori and intentionally written items to tap each dimension. Note, however, that in both of these EFA situations, the researcher was *not* able to force items to load on certain factors. Also, there is no overall statistical test to help the researcher determine whether the pattern of loadings confirms the three-factor structure. Both of these are limitations of EFA.

Before we turn to how a CFA would be done in this example, it is important to consider situations in which CFA would be appropriate: that is, situations in which a strong theory and/or empirical base exists.

Strong Theory

The four-factor model of self-concept (Shavelson et al., 1976), which includes general self-concept, academic self-concept, English self-concept, and math self-concept, has a strong theory. This model is presented and tested in Byrne (1994).

Strong Empirical Base

The "big five" factors of personality: extraversion, agreeableness, conscientiousness, neuroticism, and intellect — is an example. Goldberg (1990), among others, has provided some strong empirical evidence for the five-factor trait model of higher order personality. The five-factor model is not without its critics; see, for example, Block (1995). Using English trait adjectives data obtained from three studies, he employed five different EFA techniques, each one rotated orthogonally and obliquely, and found essentially the same five uncorrelated factors of personality in each analysis. A recent confirmatory analysis of these five personality factors by Church and Burke (1994) again found evidence for the five factors, although these authors concluded that some of the factors may be correlated.

The Maslach Burnout Inventory was examined by Byrne (1994), who indicated that considerable empirical evidence exists to suggest the existence of three factors for this instrument. She conducted a confirmatory factor analysis to test this theory.

Karl Jöreskog (1967, 1969; Jöreskog & Lawley, 1968) is generally credited with overcoming the limitations of EFA through his development of CFA. In CFA, researchers can specify the structure of their factor models a priori, according to their theories about how the variables ought to be related to the factors. For example, in the second EFA situation I just presented, the researcher could constrain the ASC items to load on the ASC factor and have loadings of zero on the other two factors; the other loadings could be similarly constrained.

Figure 11.1 gives a pictorial representation of the hypothesized three-factor structure. This type of representation, usually referred to as a *path*

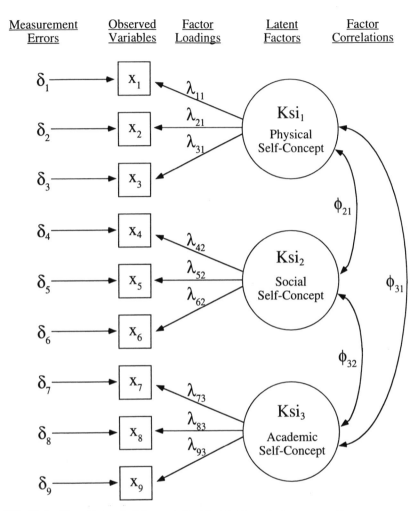

Measurement	Observed	Factor	Latent	Factor
Errors	Variables	Loadings	Factors	Correlations

FIG. 11.1   Three-Factor Self-Concept Model with Three Indicators per Factor

model, is a common way of showing the hypothesized or actual relationships among observed variables and the factors they were designed to measure.

The path model shown in Fig. 11.1 indicates that three factors are hypothesized, as represented by the three circles. The curved arrows connecting the circles indicate that all three factors are hypothesized to be correlated. The items are represented by squares and are connected to the factors by straight arrows, which indicate causal relationships. Recall that the factors can be conceptualized as causing the observed variables.

In CFA, each observed variable has an error term associated with it.

These error terms are similar to the residuals in a regression analysis, in that they are the part of each observed variable that is not explained by the factors. In CFA, however, the error terms contain measurement error due to the lack of reliability of the observed variables, in addition to unexplained or unique variance. The error terms are represented by the symbol δ (delta) in Fig. 11.1, and are referred to here as the *measurement errors.* The straight arrows from the δs to the observed variables indicate that the observed variables are influenced by both measurement error and the factors.

A common form of notation used in CFA path models is that popularized by the LISREL (LInear Structural RELationships) computer program (Jöreskog & Sörbum, 1986, 1988, 1993). Figure 11.1 includes the LISREL symbol for each part of the model. Table 11.11 presents a summary of the notation introduced in this section.

As can be seen in Figure 11.1, observed variables are represented by the symbol X, whereas factors are represented by ξs. The paths from factors to observed variables, or factor loadings, are represented by the symbol λ (lambda). The correlations or covariances among the factors, represented by the curved arrows between each pair of factors, are represented by the symbol Φ (phi). Similarly, covariances among the measurements errors (δs) are contained in the matrix $\Theta\delta$ (theta delta). If the measurement errors are considered to be uncorrelated, the matrix $\Theta\delta$ consists only the variances of the δs, which would be the diagonal elements of the matrix.

We could write equations to specify the relationships of the observed variables to the factors and measurement errors. For X_2, this equation would be written as:

$$X_1 = \lambda_{21}\xi_1 + \delta_2$$

This is similar to the regression equation:

$$Y = \beta_1 X_1 + e_1$$

where β corresponds to λ and e corresponds to δ. One difference between the two equations is that in the regression equation, X and Y are both

TABLE 11.11
LISREL Symbols and Descriptions

Symbol	Name	Description	Cov Matrix	Name	Keyword
ξ	KKsi	Latent variability	Φ	Phi	KS
λ	Lambda	Factor Loading			LX
δ	Delta	Measurement Error	$\Theta\delta$	Theta Delta	TD

observed variables, whereas in the CFA equation, X is an observed variable, but ξ is a latent factor. One implication of this is that we cannot obtain estimates of Λ and δ through typical regression methods. Instead, the correlation or covariance matrix of the observed variables is used as data in finding solutions for elements of the matrices. This matrix is usually symbolized by S for a sample matrix and Σ (sigma) for a population matrix. The relationships between the elements of S or Σ and the elements of Λ, ξ, and δ can be obtained by expressing each side of the equation:

$$X_j = \lambda_{jk}\xi k + {}_j$$

as a covariance matrix. The algebra is not presented here (cf. Bollen, 1989, p. 35), but results in the following equality:

$$\Sigma = \Lambda \Theta \Lambda + \Phi \delta.$$

This shows that the covariances among the X variables (Σ) can be broken down into the CFA matrices Λ, Φ, and $\Theta\delta$. It is this equation that is solved by CFA programs to find values for the elements of Λ, Φ, and $\Theta\delta$.

As the first step in any CFA, the researcher must, therefore, fully specify the structure or form of the matrices Λ, Φ, and $\Theta\delta$ in terms of which elements are to be included. In our example, the Λ matrix would be specified to include only the loadings of the three items designated to measure each factor represented in Fig. 11.1 by the straight arrows from the factors to the variables. The Φ matrix would include all the factor correlations represented by the curved arrows between each pair of factors in Fig. 11.1. Finally, one measurement error for each item would be estimated.

These specifications are based on the researcher's theory about the relationships among the observed variables, latent factors, and measurement errors. This theory may be based on previous empirical research, the current thinking in a particular field, the researcher's own hypotheses about the variables, or any combination of these. It is essential that the researcher be able to base a model on theory, however, because, as we shall see, it is not always possible to distinguish between different models on statistical grounds alone. In many cases, theoretical considerations are the only way one model can be distinguished from another.

In Section 11.12, an example using the LISREL program is presented in order to demonstrate the steps involved in carrying out a CFA. The sections following explain each step in more detail.

11.12 A LISREL EXAMPLE

In this example, the LISREL 8 program is used to analyze data from the common situation in which a researcher wishes to test a hypothesis about the underlying factor structure of a set of observed variables. The researcher usually has several hypotheses about the nature of the matrices Λ, Φ, and $\Theta\delta$. Common hypotheses are that the items load on the appropriate factors, that the factors are correlated in a certain way or are uncorrelated, that the measurement errors are uncorrelated, or, in some cases, that some of these are correlated. These hypotheses can all be tested simultaneously using CFA models.

In our example, the observed variables are 12 items from a measure of test anxiety known as the Reactions to Tests (RTT) scale. The RTT was developed by Sarason (1984) to measure the four hypothesized dimensions of worry, tension, test-irrelevant thinking, and bodily symptoms. For simplicity, only three items from each scale are used. The data are drawn from a study by Benson and Bandalos (1992) in which the items were found to be approximately normally distributed.

The factor structure tested is shown in Figure 11.2. As can be seen from the figure, each of the three items for each scale is hypothesized to load only on the scale it was written to measure. This is accomplished in LISREL by *freeing,* or allowing to load, the appropriate three loadings for each scale and *fixing* (to zero) all others. The four factors are all hypothesized to correlate with one another. This is accomplished by freeing the subdiagonal elements of Φ, which represent the correlations or covariances among the factors.

The diagonal elements of Φ, representing the factor variances, were set to one in order to set scales for the four factors. This is part of the process of *identification,* and is necessary because the factors, as latent variables, have no inherent scale. A common way of assigning them a scale in CFA is to set their variances equal to one. This is similar to standardizing variables by transforming them to z-scores.

Finally, the 12 diagonal elements of $\Theta\delta$, or the measurement error variances, are included in the model. The absence of curved arrows connecting the δs in Fig. 11.2 means that the measurement errors were not hypothesized to be correlated. These hypotheses imply that the diagonal elements of $\Theta\delta$ (the measurement error variances) should be estimated, or freed, whereas the subdiagonal elements (the correlations/covariances among the measurement errors) should be fixed to zero.

The SIMPLIS command lines are given in Table 11.12. These are the simplified commands that are available in the LISREL 8 program, and can be written in either uppercase or lowercase letters. For those who do not have access to the SIMPLIS language of LISREL 8, the LISREL commands are given in Appendix 1 of this chapter.

Tables 11.13, 11.14, and 11.15 show the estimates of the factor loadings, factor correlations, and measurement error variances, respectively. The standard error of each parameter estimate and a t value obtained by dividing the estimate by its standard error are shown below each one.

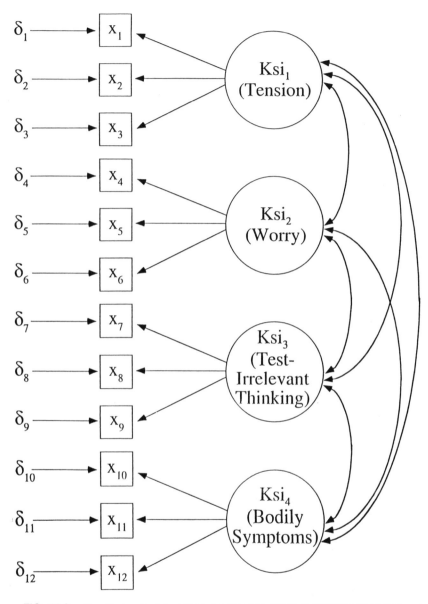

FIG. 11.2. Four-Factor Model of Test Anxiety with Three Indicators per Factor

Values of t greater than $|2.0|$ are commonly taken to be significant. An inspection of the t values for these parameter estimates reveals that all are significant, with the exception of the correlation between the Tension and Test-irrelevant thinking factors, which has a t value of 1.76. There are nounreasonable parameter estimates, such as negative variances or corre-

TABLE 11.12
SIMPLIS Command Lines for Test Anxiety Example

TITLE: FOUR FACTOR STRUCTURE FOR ANXIETY
OBSERVED VARIABLES: TEN1 TEN2 TEN3 WOR1 WOR2 WOR3 IRTHK1
IRTHK2 IRTHK3 BODY1 BODY2 BODY3   ①
COVARIANCE MATRIX:
.7821
.5602 .9299   ②
.5695 .6281 .9751
.1969 .2599 .2362 .6352
.2290 .2835 .3079 .4575 .7943
.2609 .3670 .3575 .4327 .4151 .6783
.0556 .0740 .0981 .2094 .2306 .2503 .6855
.0025 .0279 .0798 .2047 .2270 .2257 .4224 .6952
.0180 .0753 .0744 .1892 .2352 .2008 .4343 .4514 .6065
.1617 .1919 .2893 .1376 .1744 .1845 .0645 .0731 .0921 .4068
.2628 .3047 .4043 .1742 .2066 .2547 .1356 .1336 .1283 .1958 .7015
.2966 .3040 .3919 .1942 .1864 .2402 .1073 .0988 .0599 .2233 .3033
.5786
SAMPLE SIZE: 318
LATENT VARIABLES: TENSION WORRY TIRT BODY   ③
RELATIONSHIPS:
TEN1 TEN2 TEN3 = TENSION   ④
WOR1 WOR2 WOR3 = WORRY
IRTHK1 IRTHK2 IRTHK3 = TIRT
BODY1 BODY2 BODY3 = BODY
END OF PROBLEM

---

①Up to 8 characters can be used to name each observed variable.
②Only the lower half of the covariance matrix need be inserted.
③Names (8 characters or less) are given to the latent variables (factors).
④Here, under relationships, we link the observed variables to the factors.

lations greater than one. All of the parameter estimates appear to be in the expected range of values and to have the expected signs. This is important, because unreasonable values may indicate a problem with the model, such as a lack of identification.

The significance of the factor loadings is of special interest, because they indicate that the items did have significant loadings on the factors they were intended to measure. The lack of a significant correlation between Tension and Test-irrelevant thinking is not surprising; other studies have also found the Test-irrelevant thinking factor to be the most distinct of the four factors. The magnitudes and statistical significance of the remaining factor correlations support the hypothesis that the four factors are distinct, yet related, dimensions of test anxiety.

Our inspection of the parameter values and t statistics indicate support for the hypothesized four-factor structure. However, note that these are tests of *individual* parameters. There are also statistics that test all of the parameters simultaneously. Many such statistics, commonly called *overall*

TABLE 11.13
Factor Loadings, Standard Errors, and *t* Values for Test Anxiety Example

LISREL ESTIMATES (MAXIMUM LIKELIHOOD)

LAMBDA-X (factor loadings)

	Tension	Worry	Tirt	Body
VAR 1	.69①	— ④	—	—
	(.04)②			
	15.59③			
VAR 2	.76	—	—	—
	(.05)			
	16.01			
VAR 3	.84	—	—	—
	(.05)			
	17.70			
VAR 4	—	.64	—	—
		(.04)		
		16.18		
VAR 5	—	.66	—	—
		(.05)		
		14.51		
VAR 6	—	.67	—	—
		(.04)		
		16.30		
VAR 7	—	—	.64	—
			(.04)	
			15.47	
VAR 8	—	—	.67	—
			(.04)	
			16.09	
VAR 9	—	—	.67	—
			(.04)	
			17.69	
VAR 10	—	—	—	.38
				(.04)
				10.51
VAR 11	—	—	—	.54
				(.05)
				11.52
VAR 12	—	—	—	.66
				(.04)
				13.29

① Factor loading.
② Standard error.
③ *t* value.
④ — indicates a factor loading that was constrained to equal zero by the program.

fit indices, have been developed. These are discussed in more detail in Section 11.15. For now, we consider only the chi-square test and the goodness-of-fit index (GFI).

The chi-square statistic in CFA tests the hypothesis that the model fits, or is consistent with, the pattern of covariation among the observed variables.

TABLE 11.14
Factor Correlations, Standard Errors, and *t* Values for Test Anxiety Example

| | PHI (factor correlations) | | | |
	Tension	Worry	Tirt	Body
Tension	1.00①			
Worry	.55②	1.00		
	(.05)③			
	11.01④			
Tirt	.11	.49	1.00	
	(.06)	(.05)		
	1.76	9.28		
Body	.78	.59	.29	1.00
	(.04)	(.05)	(.07)	
	18.73	10.89	4.25	

①Factor variances were set to equal 1.0 in order to give a metric to the factors.
②Factor correlation.
③Standard error.
④*t* value.

TABLE 11.15
Covariance Matrix of Measurement Errors, Standard Errors, and *t* Values for
Test Anxiety Example

THETA-DELTA (covariance matrix of measurement errors)					
VAR 2	VAR 4	VAR 5	VAR 6	VAR 7	VAR 8
.31①	.34	.27	.22	.35	.23
(.03)②	(.04)	(.04)	(.03)	(.04)	
(.03)					
9.60③	9.26	7.46	8.28	9.78	8.15
THETA-DELTA					
VAR 12	VAR 15	VAR 16	VAR 18	VAR 19	VAR 20
.27	.25	.16	.26	.41	.27
(.03)	(.03)	(.02)	(.02)	(.04)	(.03)
9.31	8.66	6.55	10.68	10.10	8.49

Note: Only measurement error variances were estimated, because all measurement error covariances were constrained to equal zero.
①measurement error variance.
①standard error.
③*t* value.

If this hypothesis were rejected, it would mean that the four-factor model is not reasonable, or does not fit with our data. Therefore, contrary to the usual hypothesis-testing procedures, we do *not* want to reject the null hypothesis. Unfortunately, the chi-square statistic used in CFA is very sensitive to sample size, so that, with a large enough sample size, almost any hypothesis will be rejected. This dilemma, which is discussed in more detail in Section 11.15, has led to the development of many other statistics

TABLE 11.16
Goodness-of-fit Statistics for Test Anxiety Example

CHI-SQUARE WITH 48 DEGREES OF FREEDOM = 88.396 (p = 0.000345)
GOODNESS OF FIT INDEX (GFI) = 0.957
ADJUSTED GOODNESS OFF IT INDEX (AGFI) = 0.929
EXPECTED CROSS-VALIDATION INDEX (ECVI) = 0.477
90% CONFIDENCE INTERVAL FOR ECVI = (0.397–0.564)
ECVI FOR SATURATED MODEL = 0.492
INDEPENDENCE AIC = 1634.054
MODEL AIC = −7.604
NORMED FIT INDEX (NFI) = 0.95
NON-NORMED FIT INDEX (NNFI) = 0.967
PARSIMONY NORMED FIT INDEX = 0.691

---

designed to assess overall model fit in some way. One of these is the GFI produced by the LISREL program. This index is roughly analogous to the multiple R^2 value in multiple regression in that it represents the overall amount of the covariation among the observed variables that can be accounted for by the hypothesized model.

Values of the chi-square statistic and GFI obtained for our four-factor model, as well as many other overall fit indices produced by the LISREL 8 program, are presented in Table 11.16.

The chi-square value of 88.396 with 48 degrees of freedom, is significant, with a probability of .0003, indicating that the model does not adequately account for the observed covariation among the variables. However, the GFI exceeds .90, the criterion used by many researchers as an indication of a good fit. It may be that the significant chi-square value is, at least in part, due to the large sample size, rather than to any substantial misspecification of the model. However, it is also possible that the model is misspecified in some fundamental way. For example, one or more of the items may actually have loadings on more than one of the factors, instead of loading on only one, as specified in our model. Before making any decision about the model, we must examine such possibilities. We learn more about how to do this in the following sections, in which model identification, estimation, assessment, and modification are discussed more thoroughly.

11.13 IDENTIFICATION

The topic of identification is complex, and a thorough treatment is beyond the scope of this chapter. The interested reader is encouraged to consult Bollen (1989).

Identification of a CFA model is a prerequisite for obtaining correct estimates of the parameter values. A simple algebraic example can be used to illustrate this concept. Given the equation $x + y = 5$, we cannot obtain *unique* solutions for x and y, because an infinite number of values for x and y will produce solutions (5 and 0, 100 and -95, 2.5 and 2.5, etc.). However, if we impose another constraint on our solution by specifying that $2x = 4$, we can obtain one, and only one, solution: $x = 2$ and $y = 3$. After imposing the additional constraint, we have two unknowns, x and y, and two pieces of information, $x + y = 5$, and $2x = 4$. Note that in the first situation, with two unknowns and only one piece of information, the problem was not that we could not find a solution, but that we could find too many solutions. When this is the case, there is no way of determining which solution is "best" without imposing further constraints. Identification refers, therefore, to whether the parameters of a model can be *uniquely* determined.

Models that have more unknown parameters than pieces of information are called *unidentified* or *underidentified* models, and cannot be solved uniquely. Models with just as many unknowns as pieces of information are referred to as *just identified* models, and can be solved, but cannot be tested statistically. Models with more information than unknowns are called *overidentified* models, or sometimes simply *identified* models, and can be solved uniquely; in addition, as we shall see in Section 11.15, overidentified models can be tested statistically.

As we have seen, one condition for identification is that the number of unknown parameters must be less than or equal to the number of pieces of information. In CFA, the unknown parameters are those elements of Λ, Φ, and $\Theta\delta$ that have not been fixed to zero, and the information available to solve for these are the elements of the covariance matrix for the observed variables. In our test anxiety example, the number of parameters to be estimated would be the 12 factor loadings in Λ, plus the 6 factor correlations in Φ, plus the 12 measurement error variances on the diagonal of $\Theta\delta$, for a total of 30 parameters. The number of unique values in a covariance matrix is equal to $p(p + 1)/2$, where p is the number of observed variables. This number represents the number of covariance elements below the diagonal plus the number of variance elements. Above-diagonal elements are not counted, because they are the same as the below-diagonal elements. For the 12 items in our test anxiety example, the number of elements in the covariance matrix would be $12(13)/2$, or 78. Because the number of pieces of information is greater than the number of parameters to be estimated, we should have enough information to identify our four-factor model.

Bollen (1989) gave several rules that enable researchers to determine the identification status of their models. In general, CFA models should be identified if they have at least three items for each factor. However, there are some situations in which this will not be the case, and applied researchers should be alert for signs of underidentification. These include negative variances, correlations greater than 1.0, and factor loadings or correlations that seem to have the wrong sign or are much smaller or much larger in magnitude than what was expected (for further discussion, see Wothke, 1992).

As we saw in Section 11.12, one more piece of information is necessary in order to assure identification of CFA models: Each factor must have a unit of measurement. Because the factors are unobservable, they have no inherent scale. Instead, they are usually assigned scales in a convenient metric. One common way of doing this is to set the variances of the factors, or the diagonal elements of Φ, equal to one (Bentler, 1992a, p. 22), as we did in the test anxiety example.

Once the identification of a model has been established, estimation of the parameters in Λ, Φ, and $\Theta\delta$ can proceed. The estimation process is the subject of Section 11.14.

11.14   ESTIMATION

Recall that in CFA it is hypothesized that the relationships among the observed variables can be explained by the factors. The researchers' hypotheses about the form of these relationships are represented by the structure of the matrices, Λ, Φ, and $\Theta\delta$. Thus, the relationship between the observed variables and the researchers' hypotheses or model is represented by the equation $\Sigma = \Lambda\Phi\Lambda + \Theta\delta$. Estimation is concerned with finding the values for Λ, gF, and $\Theta\delta$ that will best reproduce the matrix Σ. This is analogous to the situation in multiple regression in which values of β are sought that will reproduce the original y values as closely as possible.

In reality, we do not have the population matrix Σ, but rather the sample matrix S. It is this original matrix that is compared to the matrix reproduced by the estimates of the parameters in Λ, Φ, and $\Theta\delta$, referred to as $\hat{\Sigma}$.

In practice, our model will probably not reproduce S perfectly. The best we can usually do is to find parameter estimates that result in matrix $\hat{\Sigma}$ that is close to S. A function that measures how close $\hat{\Sigma}$ is to S is called a *discrepancy* or *fit function,* and is usually symbolized as $F(S;\hat{\Sigma})$. Many different fit functions are available in CFA programs, but probably the most commonly used is the maximum likelihood function, defined as:

$$F(S;\hat{\Sigma}) = \text{tr}(S\hat{\Sigma}^{-1} + [\ln|\hat{\Sigma}| - \ln|S|] - p$$

where tr stands for the trace of a matrix, defined as the sum of its diagonal elements, and p is the number of variables.

The criterion for finding estimates of the parameters in Λ, Φ, and $\Theta\delta$ is that they result in values of $F(S;\hat{\Sigma})$ that are as small as possible. In maximum likelihood terminology, we are trying to find parameter estimates that will *maximize* the likelihood that the differences between S and $\hat{\Sigma}$ are due to random sampling fluctuations, rather than to some type of model misspecification. Although the maximum likelihood criterion involves maximizing a quantity rather than minimizing one, it is similar in purpose to the least squares criterion in multiple regression, in which the quantity $\Sigma(\bar{y}_i - \hat{y}_i)^2$ is minimized.

Unlike the least squares criterion, however, the criterion used in maximum likelihood estimation of CFA parameters cannot usually be solved algebraically. Instead, computer programs have been developed that use an iterative process for finding the parameter estimates. In an iterative solution, a set of initial values for the parameters of Λ, Φ, and $\Theta\delta$ are used as starting points. The matrix $\hat{\Sigma} = \Lambda\Phi\Lambda + \Theta\delta$ is then calculated based on these values, and is compared to S. If $\hat{\Sigma}$ is not close to S, one or more of the initial values is changed in such a way as to improve the fit, and $\hat{\Sigma}$ is recomputed. This process continues until $\hat{\Sigma}$ is sufficiently close to S, or until no further improvements can be made that are within the constraints of the hypothesized model. The final values obtained are taken as the best estimates of the elements Λ, Φ, and $\Theta\delta$.

The value of the fit function $F(S; \hat{\Sigma})$ that is based on these final values can be used to determine how well the hypothesized model fits the observed matrix S. The topic of assessing model fit is taken up in Section 11.15. Before concluding our discussion about estimation, however, a few words concerning the appropriate sample size are essential. Several studies have focused on the question of how large a sample should be in order to obtain accurate results in maximum likelihood CFA. Most have recommended minimum sample sizes of 200, although smaller sample sizes may be adequate for models with a relatively small number of observed variables or parameters to be estimated (see, e.g., Anderson & Gerbing, 1984, 1985; Boomsma, 1982). For models with many observed variables and/or paths to be estimated, larger sample sizes are needed.

11.15   ASSESSMENT OF MODEL FIT

The appropriate way to assess the fit of CFA models has been a subject of debate since the 1970s. A plethora of fit statistics has been developed and discussed in the literature. In this section, I focus only on the most commonly used fit statistics and present some general guidelines for model assessment. For more detailed information, the reader is directed to the excellent presentations in Bollen (1989), Bollen and Long (1993), and Loehlin (1992). As we saw in Section 11.12, it is useful to divide statistics for assessing the fit of a model, commonly called *fit statistics,* into two categories: those that measure the overall fit of the model and those that are concerned with individual model parameters, such as factor loadings or correlations.

Probably the most well-known measure of overall model fit is the chi-square (χ^2) statistic, which was presented briefly in Section 11.12. This statistic is calculated as

$$(n - 1)F(S; \hat{\Sigma})$$

and is distributed as a chi-square with degrees of freedom equal to the number of unique elements in $S(p(p + 1)/2)$ minus the number of parameters estimated, if certain conditions are met. These conditions include having a large enough sample size and having variables that follow a multivariate normal distribution. Notice that, for a just-identified model, the degrees of freedom are zero, because the number of parameters estimated is equal to the number of unique elements in S. This means that just-identified models cannot be tested. However, recall that just-identified models will *always* reproduce S perfectly; therefore, a test of such a model would be pointless, because we already know the answer.

The chi-square statistic can be used to test the hypothesis that $\Sigma = \hat{\Sigma}$, or that the original population matrix is equal to the matrix reproduced from one's model. Remember that, contrary to the general rule in hypothesis testing, the researcher would *not* want to reject the null hypothesis, as finding $\Sigma \neq \hat{\Sigma}$ would mean that the hypothesized model parameters were unable to reproduce S. Thus, smaller rather than larger chi-square values are indicative of a good fit.

From the chi-square formula we can see that, as n increases, the value of chi-square will increase to the point at which, for a large enough n, even trivial differences between S and $\hat{\Sigma}$ will be found significant. Largely because of this, as early as 1969, Jöreskog recommended that the chi-square statistic be used more as a descriptive index of fit rather than as a statistical test. Accordingly, Jöreskog and Sörbom (1993) have included other fit indices in the LISREL output. The GFI was introduced in Section 11.12. This index is defined there as:

$$GFI = 1 - \frac{F(S; \hat{\Sigma})}{F(S; \hat{\Sigma}(0))}$$

where $F(S; \hat{\Sigma}(0))$ is the value of fit function for a null model in which all parameters are zero. It can be thought of as the amount of the overall variance and covariance in S that can be accounted for by Σ, and is roughly analogous to the multiple R^2 in multiple regression. The adjusted GFI (AGFI) is given as:

$$AGFI = 1 - \frac{k(k + 1)}{2df}(1 - GFI)$$

(Jöreskog & Sörbom, 1993) where k represents the number of variables in the model, and df represents the degrees of freedom. The AGFI adjusts the GFI for degrees of freedom, resulting in lower values for models with more parameters. The rationale behind this adjustment is that models can always be made to reproduce S more closely by adding more parameters to the model. The ultimate example of this is the just identified model, which always reproduces S exactly, because it includes all possible parameters. In our test anxiety example, the value of the GFI and AGFI were .957 and .929, respectively. Here, the AGFI was not substantially lower than the GFI because the number of parameters estimated was not overly large, given the number of pieces of information (covariance elements) that were available to estimate them.

Another measure of overall fit is the difference between the elements of the matrices S and $\hat{\Sigma}$. These differences are called *residuals* and can be obtained as output from CFA computer programs. *Standardized* or *normalized* residuals are residuals that have been standardized to have a mean of zero and a standard deviation of one, making them easier to interpret. Standardized residuals larger than $|2.0|$ are usually considered to indicate a lack of fit.

Bentler and Bonett (1980) introduced a class of fit indices commonly called *comparative fit indices*. These indices compare the fit of the hypothesized model to a baseline or null model, in order to determine the amount by which the fit is improved by using the hypothesized model over the null model. The most commonly used null model is that of completely uncorrelated variables. This would mean that $\hat{\Sigma}$ would be a diagonal matrix containing only the variances of the observed variables.

The normed fit index (NFI; Bentler & Bonett, 1980) can be computed as:

$$(\chi_0^2 - \chi_1^2)\chi_0^2$$

where χ_0^2 and χ_1^2 are the χ^2 values for the null and hypothesized model, respectively. The NFI represents the increment in fit obtained by using the hypothesized model relative to the fit of the null model. Value range from zero to one, with higher values indicative of a greater improvement in fit. Bentler and Bonett's non-normed fit index (NNFI) can be calculated as:

$$(\chi_0^2/df_0 - \chi_1^2/df_1)/\chi_0^2/df_0 - 1)$$

where χ_0^2 and χ_1^2 are as before and df_0 and df_1 are the degrees of freedom for the null and hypothesized models, respectively. This index is referred to as non-normed because it is not constrained to have values between zero and one, as is common for comparative fit indices. The NNFI can be interpreted as the increment in fit per degree of freedom obtained by using the hypothesized model, relative to the best possible fit that could be obtained by using the hypothesized model. As with the NFI, higher values are suggestive of more improvement in fit. Values greater than .9 are usually considered indicative of a good fit (Bentler, 1992b; Byrne, 1989).

Because a better fit can always be obtained by adding more parameters to the model, James, Mulaik, and Brett (1982) suggested a modification of the NFI to adjust for the loss of degrees of freedom associated with such improvements in fit. This parsimony adjustment is obtained by multiplying the NFI by the ratio of degrees of freedom of the hypothesized model to those of the null model. A similar adjustment to the GFI was suggested by Mulaik et al. (1989). The PNFI is defined (Jöreskog & Sörbom, 1993) as:

$$\text{PNFI} = (df_1/df_0)(1 - F_1/F_0)$$

where F_1 and F_0 are the values of the fit function for the hypothesized and null models. The PGFI is given by Jöreskog and Sörbom (1993) as:

$$\text{PGFI} = 2df_1/k(k + 1)) \text{ GFI}$$

where k is the number of variables in the hypothesized model.

For our test anxiety example from Section 11.12, the NFI and NNFI values are .95 and .967, respectively, indicating that the hypothesized model represents a substantial improvement in fit over the null model of uncorrelated variables. However, the value of the PNFI is much lower, at .691, which could be interpreted to mean that some of this improvement in fit has been gained at the expense of parsimony.

Finally, Browne and Cudeck (1989) proposed a single-sample cross-validation index developed to assess the degree to which a set of parameter estimates estimated in one sample would fit if used in another, similar sample. This index is roughly analogous to the adjusted or "shrunken" R^2 value obtained in multiple regression. It is given as the ECVI, or expected cross-validation index, in the LISREL program and is calculated as:

$$\text{ECVI} = \chi^2/(n - 1) + 2(t/(n - 1))$$

(Jöreskog & Sörbom, 1993) where t is the number of parameters estimated. Smaller values are desired, which would indicate a greater likelihood that the model would cross-validate in another sample of the same size. A similar index is reported as part of the output from the LISREL 8, as well as the EQS (Bentler, 1989, 1992a) programs. This is the Akaike (1987) Information Criterion (AIC), calculated as:

$$\text{AIC} = \chi^2 + 2t$$

(Jöreskog & Sörbom, 1993). As with the ECVI, smaller values of the AIC represent a greater likelihood of cross-validation. In a recent study by Bandalos (1993), values of the ECVI and AIC were compared to the values obtained by carrying out an actual two-sample cross-validation procedure in CFA. Although both indices provided very accurate estimates of the actual two-sample cross-validation values, the ECVI was more accurate.

In practices, indices such as the ECVI and AIC are useful primarily for situations in which the researcher is interested in selecting one of a set of competing models hypothesized a priori. In such a situation, the model with the lowest ECVI and/or AIC value would generally be preferred. In our test anxiety example, we have only hypothesized a single model, so values of the ECVI and AIC are presented here only to illustrate how they would appear on the printout. The ECVI has a value of .477, indicating that if the model were to be cross-validated using another, similar sample, the value of the discrepancy function $F(S;\Sigma)$ should be close to .477. The value of the AIC for the hypothesized model is -7.604. Note that the AIC for the hypothesized model in this example is much lower than both the AIC for the independence model and the null model of no correlations among the variables. This is, of course, what we would expect, because the independence model is really the lack of any model and hypothesizes that no correlations exist among the variables.

In addition to the overall fit indices, individual parameter values should be scrutinized closely. Computer programs such as LISREL and EQS provide tests of each parameter estimate, computed by dividing the parameter estimate by its standard error. (Recall that these are referred to as t values in LISREL.) These values can be used to test the hypothesis that the parameter value is significantly different from zero. The actual values of the parameter estimates should also be examined to determine whether any appear to be out of range. Out-of-range parameter values may take the form of negative variances in Φ or $\Theta\delta$, factor correlations above one, parameter estimates that seem much too high or much too low, or parameter estimates that have the opposite sign from what was expected. Models resulting in any of these problems should be studied carefully to determine the cause of the error. One possible reason for problems of this type is that the model is not identified. However, it may also be that the researcher has inadvertently set the model up incorrectly.

It should be clear from the foregoing discussion that the assessment of model fit is not a simple process and that there is no definitive way to assess how well a model fits the data. However, *several criteria have been developed over the years with which most experts are in agreement.* These have been discussed by Bollen and Long (1993) and are summarized here.

1. Hypothesize *at least* one model a priori, based on the best theory available. Often, theoretical knowledge in an area may be ambiguous or contradictory, and more than one model may be tenable. The relative fit of the different models can be compared using such indices as the NFI, NNFI, PNFI, ECVI, and AIC.

2. Do not rely on the chi-square statistic as the only basis for assessing fit. The use of several indices is encouraged.

3. Examine the values of individual parameter estimates, in addition to assessing the overall fit.

4. Assess model fit in the context of prior studies in the area. Less stringent standards may be acceptable in fields in which little research has been done than in areas in which well-developed theory is available.

5. As in any statistical analysis, screen data for outliers and for violations of distributional assumptions. Bollen (1989), in his excellent text on structural equation models, mentions on the very first page the drastic effect outliers can have on covariances. Multivariate normality is one assumption underlying the use of maximum likelihood estimation in CFA.

11.16   MODEL MODIFICATION

It is not uncommon, in practice, to find large discrepancies between S and $\hat{\Sigma}$, indicating that the hypothesized model was unable to accurately reproduce the original covariance matrix. Assuming that the hypothesized model was based on the best available theory, changes based on theoretical considerations may not be feasible. In this situation, the researcher may opt to modify the model in a post hoc fashion, by adding or deleting parameters suggested by the fit statistics obtained. Statistics are available from both the LISREL and EQS programs that suggest possible changes to the model that will improve fit.

Two caveats are in order before we begin our discussion of these statistics. First, as in any post hoc statistical analysis, modifications made on the basis of information derived from a given sample cannot properly be tested on that same sample. This is because the results obtained from any sample data will have been fit to the idiosyncracies of those data, and may not generalize to other samples. For this reason, *post hoc model modifications must be regarded as tentative until they have been replicated on a different sample.* The second point that must be kept in mind is that the modifications suggested by programs such as LISREL and EQS can only tell us what additions or deletions of parameters will result in a better *statistical* fit. These modifications may or may not be defensible from a theoretical point of view. Changes that cannot be justified theoretically should not be made.

Bollen (1989), in discussing modifying models, wrote:

> Researchers with inadequate models have many ways—in fact, too many ways—in which to modify their specification. An incredible number of major or minor alterations are possible, and the analyst needs some procedure to

[handwritten margin note: Key sentence modification indices (Bollen 1989)]

narrow the choices. The empirical means can be helpful, but they can also lead to nonsensical respecifications. Furthermore, empirical means work best in detecting simple alterations and are less helpful when major changes in structure are needed. The potentially richest source of ideas for respecification is the theoretical or substantive knowledge of the researcher. (pp. 296–297)

With these caveats, we can turn our attention to the indices that may be useful in suggesting possible model modifications. One obvious possibility is to delete parameters that are nonsignificant. For example, a parameter estimate may be found for which the reported t value in LISREL is less than $|2.0|$, indicating that the estimated value of that parameter is not significantly different from zero. This was the case with the correlation between the Test-irrelevant thinking and Tension factors from our test anxiety example.

Deleting a parameter from the model will not result in a better fit, but will gain a degree of freedom, resulting in a lower critical value. However, if the same data are used to both obtain and modify the model, this increase in degrees of freedom is not justified. This is because the degree of freedom has already been used to obtain the estimate in the original model. In subsequent analyses on other data sets, however, the researcher could omit the parameter, thus gaining a degree of freedom and obtaining a simpler model. Simpler models are generally preferred over more complex models for reasons of parsimony.

Another type of model modification that might be considered is to add parameters to the model. For example, a variable that had been constrained to load on only one factor might be allowed to have loadings on two factors. The LISREL program provides modification indices (MIs) that estimate the decrease in the chi-square value that would result if a given parameter were to be added to the model. MIs are available for all parameters that were constrained to be zero in the original model. MIs are accompanied by the expected parameter change (EPC) statistics. These represent the estimated value a given parameter would have if it were added to the model. In the EQS program, the Lagrange Multiplier (LM) statistics serve the same function as the MIs serve in LISREL. EQS also provides multivariate LM statistics that take into account the correlations among the parameters.

The MI values for the Λ and $\Theta\delta$ matrices from our test anxiety example are shown in Table 11.17. Because all the factor correlations were estimated as part of the original model, no MIs were computed for the Φ matrix.

As stated in the last line of the table, the maximum modification index is 18.33 for element (3,4) of Lambda-X, which is the loading of Variable 3 on the Bodily symptoms factor. The value of 18.33 means that the chi-square value would decrease by approximately 18.33 if Variable 3 were to be allowed to load on that factor. If this change were to be made, the model

11.17
Modification Indices for Test Anxiety Example

MODIFICATION INDICES FOR LAMBDA-X

	Tension	Worry	Tirt	Body	
VAR 1	— ①	2.29	2.60	5.76	
VAR 2	—	2.41	.06	4.45	
VAR 3	—	.01	1.47	18.33	
VAR 4	9.58	—	.66	8.71	
VAR 5	.17	—	.68	.39	
VAR 6	11.94	—	.00	12.36	
VAR 7	1.19	1.96	—	.92	
VAR 8	.50	.00	—	.01	
VAR 9	.09	1.54	—	.58	
VAR 10	.40	.96	.22	—	
VAR 11	.07	.03	1.77	—	
VAR 12	.12	1.03	2.62	—	

MODIFICATION INDICES FOR THETA-DELTA

	VAR 1	VAR 2	VAR 3	VAR 4	VAR 5	VAR 6
VAR 1	—					
VAR 2	10.58	—				
VAR 3	1.58	4.38	—			
VAR 4	.03	.08	6.55	—		
VAR 5	.02	.41	.43	12.99	—	
VAR 6	.55	5.00	.39	.03	14.16	—
VAR 7	1.02	.18	.00	.15	.47	3.51
VAR 8	1.13	3.27	1.48	.01	.08	.25
VAR 9	.33	3.18	.10	.64	2.15	2.45
VAR 10	5.14	2.83	7.70	.28	1.34	.17
VAR 11	1.13	.31	4.16	1.68	.07	.84
VAR 12	.68	1.99	.27	.79	2.13	.05

MODIFICATION INDICES FOR THETA-DELTA

	VAR 7	VAR 8	VAR 9	VAR 10	VAR 11	VAR 12
VAR 7	—					
VAR 8	2.61	—				
VAR 9	.45	1.20	—			
VAR 10	2.79	.33	3.49	—		
VAR 11	.01	.24	.36	.90	—	
VAR 12	1.00	1.33	7.98	.94	.00	—

MAXIMUM MODIFICATION INDEX IS 18.33 FOR ELEMENT (3, 4) OF LAMBDA-X.

① — indicates that the modification index was not computed because this parameter was estimated as part of the original model.

would have to be re-estimated, and it is likely that the other parameter estimates and their MI values, as well as the chi-square value, would change. This is the reason for the common recommendation that only one modification based on MIs be made to a model at a time. Finally, no model modifications should be made unless they are theoretically defensible. In the current example, Variable 3 is worded, "I have an uneasy feeling before an important test." It is conceivable that the word *uneasy* in this item might have been interpreted by some respondents as referring to a physical symptom, such as an uneasy stomach. In this case, a loading of the item on the bodily symptoms factor might be defensible. It is important to realize, however, that questions like this must be considered carefully by the researcher and should not be made casually.

Section 11.18 provides a discussion of some concerns that have been voiced about current practices in CFA studies. One of these pertains to the use of MIs in making post hoc model modifications; the other has to do with the issue of equivalent or alternative models. Before discussing these issues, however, we consider an example using the EQS program (Bentler, 1989).

11.17   EQS EXAMPLE

Having present an example using the LISREL program, I now discuss one using Bentler's (1989) EQS program. This chapter is not intended as a comprehensive guide to either program, however. The interested reader should consult the program manuals or the excellent references on these two programs by Byrne (1989, 1994).

In this example, the data given in Exercise 7 have been reanalyzed using the EQS program. Although the data presented in Exercise 7 are in the form of a correlation matrix, the inclusion of the standard deviations makes it possible for the program to calculate a covariance matrix, which, you will recall, is preferred for use in CFA. The data consist of 10 communication skills measured on 159 deaf rehabilitation candidates. A two-factor solution was obtained. In this example, the data have been reanalyzed using this two-factor solution as the hypothesized model in order to demonstrate the similarities of, and differences between, the EFA solution presented earlier, and the CFA analysis. I emphasize that the reanalysis cannot be used as a test of the factor structure reported in Section 11. because the same data are being used in both the confirmatory and the exploratory analyses. If our objective were to test the structure described in Section 11., a new set of data would have to be obtained. This analysis is therefore introduced only for the purpose of contrasting the exploratory and confirmatory procedures.

The EQS command lines are presented in Table 11.18.

The factor loadings are shown in Table 11.19, along with their standard errors and *t* values. The measurement error variances are included in a separate matrix labeled Variances of Independent Variables. In order to conserve space, and because our primary interest is in the factor loadings, that matrix is not reproduced here.

Command Lines for EQS CFA of Bolton Data

	/TITLE
	EXAMPLE 2: BOLTON DATA;
①	/SPECS
	CAS = 159; VARS = 10; ME = ML; MA = COV;
	/EQUATIONS
	V1 = 1.000*F2 + E1;
	V2 = 1.000*F2 + E2;
	V3 = 1.000*FI + 1.000*F2 + E3;
	V4 = 1.000*FI + 1.000*F2 + E4;
②	V5 = 1.000*FI + E5;
	V6 = 1.000*F1 + E6;
	V7 = 1.000*F2 + E7;
	V8 = 1.000*F1 + 1.000*F2 + E8;
	V9 = 1.000*FI + E9;
	V10 = 1.000*FI + E10;
	/VARIANCES
③	E1 TO E10 = .500*;
	F1 TO F2 = 1.000;
	/MATRIX
	1.0
	.59 1.0
	.30 .34 1.0
	.16 .24 .62 1.0
	−.02 −.13 .28 .37 1.0
	.00 −.05 .42 .51 .90 1.0
④	.39 .61 .70 .59 .05 .20 1.0
	.17 .29 .57 .88 .30 .46 .60 1.0
	−.04 −.14 .28 .33 .93 .86 .04 .28 1.0
	−.04 −.08 .42 .50 .87 .94 .17 .45 .90 1.0
	/STANDARD DEVIATIONS
	.45 1.06 1.17 1.11 1.50 .144 1.31 1.04 1.49
	1.41
⑤	/LMTEST; /WTEST;
	./END

①ME = ML means that the method of estimation (ME) is maximum likelihood (ML). The type of matrix (MA) to be analyzed is a covariance matrix (COV).

②These lines give the structure for the factor loadings. The astericks designate the loadings that are to be estimated.

③The measurement error variances (E_i) must be given starting values: here, we have used .50. The variances for the factors are fixed at 1.00.

④Only the lower half of the correlation matrix is required, along with the standard deviations, to obtain the covariance matrix.

⑤Here, we request the Lagrange multiplier (LMTEST) and Wald (WTEST) tests. LMTEST is basically equivalent to the modification index given be LISREL; WTEST assesses whether any model parameters could be dropped without significantly worsening the overall fit.

TABLE 11.19
Factor Loadings, Standard Errors, and *t* Values for CFA of Bolton Data

MEASUREMENT EQUATIONS WITH STANDARD ERRORS AND TEST STATISTICS

V1	=V1	=	.302①*F2	+ 1.0000④E1	
			.081②		
			3.711③		
V2	=V2	=	.461*F2	+ 1.000 E2	
			.079		
			5.863		
V3	=V3	=	.349*F1	+ .585*F2	+1.000E3
			.068	.069	
			5.150	8.527	
V4	=V4	=	.428*F1	+ .796*F2	+1.000E4
			.056	.057	
			7.613	14.022	
V5	=V5	=	.934*F1	+ 1.000 E5	
			.060		
			15.560		
V6	=V6	=	.960*F1	+ 1.000 E6	
			.059		
			16.382		
V7	=V7	=	.728*F2	+ 1.000 E7	
			.071		
			10.276		
V8	=V8	=	.371*F1	+ .815*F2	+1.000E8
			.057	.059	
			6.530	13.883	
V9	=V9	=	.930*F1	+ 1.000 E9	
			.060		
			15.464		
V10	=V10	=	.965*F1	+ 1.000 E10	
			.058		
			16.518		

① Factor loading.
② Standard error.
③ *t* value.

An inspection of the *t* values for the factor loadings reveals that all are statistically significant. They also appear to be reasonable, of the expected magnitude, and in the expected direction. The factor loadings differ somewhat from those reported in Section 11., but these differences do not appear to be substantial. Recall that in the original EFA, each variable actually had loadings on both factors, but loadings less than .30 were not reported. In the current analysis, loadings less than .30 were constrained to be zero. This probably accounts for most of the discrepancies between the two sets of factor loadings.

In order to ascertain whether the two-factor model represents a good fit to the data, the fit statistics must be considered. Some of these are presented in Table 11.20.

TABLE 11.20
Goodness-of-Fit Statistics from CFA of Bolton Data

GOODNESS OF FIT SUMMARY

INDEPENDENCE AIC = 1602.04359
       MODEL AIC = 262.60282
CHI-SQUARE =   326.603 BASED ON 32 DEGREES OF FREEDOM
PROBABILITY VALUE FOR THE CHI-SQUARE STATISTIC IS LSES THAN 0.001
BENTLER-BONETT NORMED   FIT INDEX = .807
BENTLER-BONETT NONNORMED FIT INDEX = .748

Overall, the fit statistics do not suggest a good fit to the data. The chi-square value is highly significant, indicating that the model has not adequately reproduced the original covariance matrix. Both the NFI and the NNFI are well below the value of .9 that is often considered as evidence of a good fit. The AIC value of 262.6 for our model is considerably lower than the independence model AIC value of 1602.04, but this indicates only that the hypothesized model represents a considerable improvement over a model in which the variables are hypothesized to be uncorrelated.

The results of the LM and Wald tests are often useful in identifying the sources of model misfit. The LM test is equivalent to the MI in LISREL and represents the amount by which the overall chi-square value should decrease if a parameter were to be added to the model. In contrast, values of the Wald test represent the amount by which the overall chi-square value would increase if a parameter were to be dropped from the model. The LM and Wald tests are, thus, tests of whether parameters should be added to or deleted from the model, respectively. The results of the Wald and LM tests are presented in Table 11.21.

The results of the Wald test indicate that there are no model parameters that could be dropped without significantly worsening overall model fit. This is not surprising, because all of the parameter estimates were found to be highly significant.

The EQS program computes both univariate and multivariate forms of the LM test. The multivariate LM is generally preferred because it takes into account the correlations among the parameters. It may be that two parameters have high values for the univariate LM tests, but that they are highly correlated with one another. In such a case, adding both parameters will not decrease the overall chi-square value much more than adding only one. The multivariate LM tests take the intercorrelations among the parameters into account in computing the estimated decrease in the overall chi-square. This is why some parameters that are included in the univariate LM tests are not included in the multivariate test. For example, the parameter V6,F2 has a univariate value of 15.386, indicating that if Variable 6 were allowed to load on Factor 2, the overall chi-square value would decrease by 15.386. However, note that this decrease in chi-square

TABLE 11.21
Results of Wald and LM Tests from CFA of Bolton Data

WALD TEST (FOR DROPPING PARAMETERS)
NONE OF FREE PARAMETERS IS DROPPED IN THIS PROCESS.

LAGRANGE MULTIPLIER TEST (FOR ADDING PARAMETERS)
ORDERED UNIVARIATE TEST STATISTICS:

NO	PARAMETER	CHI-SQUARE	PROBABILITY	PARAMETER CHANGE
1	V9,F2①	22.643②	.000③	−.159④
2	V6,F2	15.386	.000	.110
3	V5,F2	13.986	.000	−.123
4	V10,F2	10.107	.001	.087
5	V7,F1	5.646	.017	.177
6	V2,F1	3.651	.056	−.145
7	F2,F1	.882	.348	.098
8	V1,F1	.434	.510	−.052
9	F2,F2	.000	1.000	.000
10	F1,F1	.000	1.000	.000

MULTIVARIATE LAGRANGE MULTIPLIER TEST BY SIMULTANEOUS PROCESS
IN STAGE 1

		CUMULATIVE MULTIVARIATE STATISTICS			UNIVARIATE INCREMENT	
STEP	PARAMETER	CHI-SQUARE	D.F.	PROB	CHI-SQUARE	PROB
1	V9,F2	22.643	1	.000	22.643	.000
2	V5,F2	45.826	2	.000	23.183	.000
3	V7,F1	53.946⑤	3	.000	8.119⑥	.004

① V9,F2 represents te loading of Variable 9 on Factor 2.

② Amount by which the overall chi-square value would decrease if the parameter V9,F2 were added to the model.

③ Probability of the associated chi-square value with 1 df.

④ Value that the associated parameter would have if added to the model.

⑤ Total amount by which the overall chi-square value would decrease if the three parameters V9,F2; V5,F2; and V7,F1 were added to the model.

⑥ Amount of the decrease in chi-square that would be accounted for by adding the parameter V7,F1 to the model.

would result only if that were the only parameter added to the model. The fact that the parameter V6,F2 is not included in the multivariate LM test probably indicates that it is so highly correlated with one or more of the other parameters that it would not result in a large decrease if other parameters were also added. The results of the multivariate LM test indicate that the greatest decrease in the overall chi-square value would occur if Variables 9 and 5 were allowed to load on Factor 2, and Variable 7 were allowed to load on Factor 1. Of course, these changes should be made only if they can be supported by theory.

Overall, then, the structure reported for these 10 items in Section 11. cannot be shown to fit the data optimally. Even the addition of the three factor loadings described in the previous paragraph would not result in a nonsignificant chi-square value. It may be that more than two factors are needed, or that the factors should be allowed to correlate. At this point, however, the researcher should carefully consider whether any proposed changes in the model can be justified theoretically.

11.18   SOME CAVEATS REGARDING STRUCTURAL EQUATION MODELING*

Covariance structure modeling (CSM) or structural equation modeling (SEM) techniques, which include CFA, have been used extensively since the 1980s. They have been touted as one of the most important advances in quantitative methodology in many years. One of the advantages of these techniques is that they allow for measurement error to be taken into account, which traditional procedures do not. Although these techniques are very sophisticated mathematically, they can now be implemented easily with the latest releases of programs such as LISREL and EQS. The availability of Windows versions of these programs has made their implementation still easier. Cliff (1983), among others, however, has cautioned researchers that the sophistication of these techniques and the facility with which they can now be applied should not blind researchers to some basic research principles.

One of these principles concerns the issue of capitalization on chance, which is a major theme in this book. MacCallum, Roznowski, and Necowitz (1992) reported a compelling study on this issue. As noted earlier, it is not uncommon, in practice, for researchers to modify their models in a post hoc fashion, based on such indices as the LISREL MIs or the LM and Wald tests given by the EQS program. This process of post hoc model modification is often called a *specification search*. What most researchers appear to be unaware of is that this is a *data driven* process that is very susceptible to capitalization on chance. Because of this, modifications made this way are likely to be very unstable and are unlikely to cross-validate. This is particularly true when sample size is small, the number of modifications is large, and the modifications are not theoretically defensible (MacCallum, 1986). As MacCallum et al. (1992) noted, "Model modification in practice is usually done with no substantive justification and no cross-validation, often involves a substantial number of modifications, and is often based on samples that may be too small for such analyses . . . We consider this to be an unfortunate state of affairs, representing a dangerous and misleading methodological trend" (p. 494).

---

*An excellent edited book is Hoyle (1995), especially chapters 2, 5, and 9.

The MacCallum et al. (1992) study found that there were no searches based on a sequence of four modifications that resulted in the same modified models when sample size was 250 or less. Only when the sample size reached 400 was there *some* consistency. Unfortunately, most studies reported in the literature have sample sizes between 100 and 350.

A recent Monte Carlo study by Hutchinson (1994) is right on target in having investigated the stability of post hoc model modifications for some CFA models. Two population models were created, involving two- and four-factor oblique factor structures. In each model, all factors had four primary indicators (with population loadings varying from .60 to .80) and two secondary population loadings of .40. Four levels of misspecification were imposed on the two models by incorrectly setting certain loadings to zero. I discuss only the first two levels of misspecification here. For model 1, the first level had two secondary loadings incorrectly set to zero, and the second level had one primary and one secondary loading incorrectly set to zero. For the four-factor model, Level 1 misspecification involved incorrectly setting four secondary loadings to zero, and Level 2 had two primary and two secondary loadings incorrectly set to zero.

Sample sizes of 200, 400, 800, and 1,200 were chosen. One hundred samples were generated for each model and sample size combination, for a total of 800 samples. Hutchinson found that, "Conditions with marked declines in values of MIs were also those that exhibited greater modification consistency. . . . When values of MIs seem to gradually decrease, even if still statistically significant, it suggests that there may be a number of specification errors present, but none of substantial size. Errors of this type are more likely to reflect chance characteristics of the data. Consequently, in practice one should probably try to limit modifications to correction of noticeably large specification errors which would be more likely to replicate in other samples" (p. 25).

The following table shows that if the specification errors are relatively minor, a sample size of 400 gives one a good chance (from 64% to 78%) of recovering a known population model. More severe misspecification requires at least 800 subjects to obtain similar results.

Number of Times (out of 100) Population Models Recovered

| | *Level of Misspecification* | | | |
| | *1* | *2* | *1* | *2* |
n	Two-Factor Model		Four-Factor Model	
200	23	26	19	30
400	64	78	64	71
800	94	93	96	99
1,200	94	93	100	100

Another problem encountered in SEM analyses is that researchers too often seem to interpret the finding that their model fits the data as meaning it is the *only* model that can do so. Various individuals (Bollen, 1989, p. 71; Cliff, 1983; Jöreskog, 1993, p. 298) have noted that there are always other models that can fit the data as well, if not better, than the one originally hypothesized. These alternative models represent competing hypotheses that must be ruled out if the originally hypothesized model is to be supported.

In a 1993 paper, MacCallum, Wegener, Uchino, and Fabrigar (1993) discussed this issue in the context of mathematically equivalent models. These are models that cannot be distinguished from the originally hypothesized model on the basis of their goodness of fit. For example, in CFA one model with items that load on more than one factor and another model with items that load on only one factor but have correlated measurement errors may fit equally well in terms of their chi-square values, even though they represent fundamentally different hypotheses. In cases like this, there is no statistical basis for choosing one model over another, and such decisions must be made on the basis of theoretical considerations. MacCallum et al. (1993) catalogued all applications of CSM in three prominent journals (*Journal of Educational Psychology, Journal of Applied Psychology,* and *Journal of Personality and Social Psychology*) for the years 1988 through 1991. For these articles, the median number of equivalent models was quite large:

MacCallum et al. (1993) Survey of Multiple Models

JOURNAL	NO. ARTICLES	% WITH EQUIVALENT MODELS	MEDIAN NO. OF MODELS
Educational Psychology	14	86	16.5
Applied Psychology	19	74	12.0
Personality & Social Psychology	20	100	21.0

They selected one article from each of the three journals and presented an analysis of three of the plausible equivalent models for each case. As MacCallum et al. (1993) noted:

Importantly, the presented equivalent models have theoretical implications that differ substantially from the models preferred by the authors of the published applications. We know of no compelling evidence that would suggest that these equivalent models are theoretically less plausible than the original models. . . . The gravity of this issue for empirical research is increased by the fact that the phenomenon of equivalent models has been virtually ignored in practice. Of the 72 published applications examined by Breckler (1990) and the additional 53 studies considered in this article, only *one* study contained an explicit acknowledgment of the existence of even a

single equivalent model . . . Without adequate consideration of alternative
equivalent models, *support for one model from a class of equivalent models
is suspect at best and potentially groundless and misleading.* (p. 196)

When taken in conjunction with MacCallum et al. (1992), the picture
painted by MacCallum et al. (1993) is a bleak one with regard to the amount
of confidence one is justified in placing in the results of many CSM studies.
What, then, should be done in CSM studies to enhance meaningfulness and
generalizability? First, if post hoc model modifications are to be made,
sample size must be adequate (probably 400 subjects for most studies,
although this will depend on the size of the model). Also, no modifications
should be made without a clear theoretical justification. Any model
obtained as a result of such modifications should be treated *very tentatively*
until the model has been validated on an independent sample of data. This
is the issue of cross-validation, which has been stressed here, and which
several prominent CSM researchers (Breckler, 1990; Browne & Cudeck,
1989; Cudeck & Browne, 1983; Jöreskog, 1993; MacCallum et al., 1992)
have indicated is crucial in CSM research.

The problem of equivalent or alternative models must also be seriously
considered in CSM studies. Although Jöreskog (1993, p. 295) indicated that
the consideration of several *a priori* models is rare in practice, Bollen and
Long (1993), in the same volume, stated that one point of consensus among
CSM researchers is that ". . . it is better to consider several alternative
models than to examine only a single model" (p. 7). Although not all
alternative models will be plausible, those that are should be estimated
along with the originally hypothesized model. The values of such indices as
the AIC, ECVI, PGFI, and PNFI can then be used as a basis for comparing
the fit of the various models.

APPENDIX 1

LISREL command lines for test anxiety example

---

1. TITLE FOUR FACTOR MODEL FOR TEST ANXIETY
2. DA NI=12 NO=316 MA=CM
3. CM FI= TESTANX.COV
4. MO NX=12 NK=4 LX=FU,FI TD=SY,FR PH=SY,FI
5. LK; TENSION WORRY TIRT BODY
6. VA 1.0 PH 1 1 PH 2 2 PH 3 3 PH 4 4
7. FR PH 2 1 PH 3 A PH 4 1 PH 3 2 PH 4 2 PH 4 3
8. FR LX 1 1 LX 2 1 LX 3 1 LX 4 2 LX 5 2 LX 6 2 LX 7 3
9. FR LX 8 3 LX 9 3 LX 10 4 LX 11 4 LX 12 4
9. OU MI

Line 1 is a title line and can contain any title desired. It is best to begin the title line with the word *title* to avoid the inadvertent use of a reserved LISREL keyword. Line 2 is the data line, indicated by the keyword DA. It specifies that the number of input variable (NI) = 12, the number of observations (NO), or sample size, is 316, and the matrix to be analyzed is a covariance matrix (CM). Line 3 tells the program where to look for the data. It begins with the keyword CM for covariance matrix and gives the filename (FI) as tentanx.cov. This file contains the covariance matrix of the 12 variables.

Line 4 is a very important one: It describes the model (MO). In this line, it is specified that there are 12 X variables (NX = 12) and four ξs (NK = 4). It then specifies the structure of Λ, Φ, and $\Theta\delta$. The keywords identifying these matrices are those given in Table 11.11: LX, PH, and TD, respectively. Each of these matrices needs two specifications: one for the form of the matrix and one stating whether its elements are to be free (FR; estimated) or fixed (FI; not estimated). In general, if the majority of the elements in a matrix are to be estimated, it is better to specify the matrix as free. Any individual elements for which estimates are not wanted can then be fixed with a later command, as I show further on. If the majority of the elements in the matrix are to be fixed at zero (not estimated), it is better to specify the matrix as fixed. Elements for which estimates are desired can then be freed with a later command.

The form of a matrix can be full or symmetric. The Λ matrix is specified here to be a full, fixed matrix (LX = FU, FI), whereas Φ and $\Theta\delta$ ar symmetric and fixed (PH = SY, FI; TD = SY, FI).

Line 5 is similar to a variable labels statement in SPSS. It is an optional command that can be used to assign labels to the ξs (LK).

Line 6 specifies that all the variances in Φ (PH 1 1, PH 2 2, PH 3 3, PH 4 4) are to be given values of one (VA 1.0) in order to establish metrics for the factors.

In Line 7, the correlations among the factors (PH 2 1, PH 3 1, PH 3 2, and PH 4 3) are specified to be (FR). Lines 8 and 9 free the three items hypothesized to load on each of the four factors: LX 1 1 LX 2 1, LX 3 1, LX 4 2, LX 5 2, LX 6 2, LX 7 3, LX 8 3, LX 9 3, LX 10 4, LX 11 4, and LX 12 4.

Line 10 requests certain output (OU) to be printed, in addition to the standard output. Here, the MIs have been requested.

11.11 SUMMARY OF MAJOR POINTS

1. Principal components are uncorrelated, linear combinations of the original variables. They therefore provide for an *additive* partitioning of the total variance.

2. When there are a large number of variables, say 30, the number of correlations is 435, and it is very difficult to summarize by inspection precisely what this pattern of correlations represents. Principal components analysis is a means of "boiling down" the main sources of variation in such a complex set of correlations, and often a small number of components will account for most of the variance.

3. Three uses for components analysis as a variable reducing scheme are: (a) determining the number of dimensions underlying a test, (b) reducing the number of predictors, prior to a regression analysis, and (c) reducing the number of dependent variables, prior to a MANOVA.

4. The absolute magnitude and number of loadings are crucial in determining reliable components. Components with at least 4 loadings $> |.60|$, or with at least 3 loadings $> |.80|$ are reliable. Also, components with at least 10 loadings $> |.40|$ are reliable for $N > 150$.

5. The Kaiser rule will accurately determine the number of components to retain when the number of variables < 30 and the communalities are $> .70$, *or* when $N > 250$ and the mean communality $> .60$. For other situations when $N < 200$, a statistical test is advisable. For $N > 200$, use of the scree' test will probably be reasonably accurate, provided most of the communalities are fairly large.

6. I suggest *doubling* the critical value for an ordinary correlation and using that, at the .01 level, to determine whether a loading is significant.

7. For increasing interpretability of factors, there are two basic types of rotations: (a) orthogonal—the rotated factors are still uncorrelated, and (b) oblique—the rotated factors are correlated.

8. When uncorrelated factors are appropriate, the varimax rotation generally is quite useful in improving interpretability. Often, however, oblique or correlated factors are more reasonable to assume. There are many different oblique rotations. No one of them should be considered superior, but rather they represent different ways of looking at the factors in the factor space.

9. With respect to using communality estimates in the main diagonal of the matrix being factor analyzed (rather than 1's), several sources suggest that when the number of variables is greater than 30 and only a few variables have low communalities, then practically any one of the factor procedures leads to the same conclusions. When the number of variables is < 20 and some of the communalities are low, then differences can occur.

10. Complete control lines were given for both SAS and SPSSX for saving factor scores and then passing them to another program for regression analysis and for doing a MANOVA.

EXERCISES – CHAPTER 11

1. The notion of a linear combination of variables and how much variance that linear combination accounts for is fundamental not only in principal components analysis but also in other forms of multivariate analysis such as discriminant analysis and canonical correlation. We indicated in this chapter that the variances for the successive components are equal to eigenvalues of covariance (correlation) matrix. However, the variance for a linear combination is defined more fundamentally in terms of the variances and covariances of the variables which make up the composite. We denote the matrix of variances and covariances for a set of p variables as:

$$S = \begin{bmatrix} s_1^2 & s_{12} & \cdots & s_{1p} \\ s_{21} & s_2^2 & \cdots & s_{2p} \\ \vdots & \vdots & & \vdots \\ s_{p1} & s_{p2} & & s_p^2 \end{bmatrix}$$

The variance of a linear combination is defined as:

$$\text{var}\,(a_{11}\,x_1 + a_{12}\,x_2 + \ldots + a_{1p}\,x_p) = \text{var}\,(a'x) = a'Sa,$$

where $a' = (a_{11}, a_{12}, \ldots, a_{1p})$.

a) Write out what the formula for the variance of a linear combination of 2 and 3 variables will be.

b) The covariance matrix S for a set of 3 variables was:

$$S = \begin{bmatrix} 451.4 & 271.2 & 168.7 \\ & 171.7 & 103.3 \\ \text{symm} & & 66.7 \end{bmatrix}$$

and the first principal component of S was

$$y_1 = .81\,x_1 + .50\,x_2 + .31\,x_3$$

What is the variance of y_1? (Ans. 681.9)

2. Golding and Seidman (1974) measured 231 undergraduate males enrolled in an undergraduate psychology course on the *Strong Vocational Interest Blank for Men,* and obtained the following correlation matrix on the 22 basic interest scales: public speaking, law/politics, business management, sales, merchandising, office practice, military activities, technical supervision, mathematics, science, mechanical, nature, agriculture, adventure, recreational leadership, medical service, social service, religious activities, teaching, music, art, and writing.

	1	2	3	4	5	6	7	8	9	10	11	12	13	14	15	16	17	18	19	20	21	22
1	1.0																					
2	.77	1.0																				
3	53	50	1.0																			
4	54	44	74	1.0																		
5	54	48	91	82	1.0																	
6	30	28	72	63	75	1.0																
7	16	20	28	19	26	31	1.0															
8	36	34	79	56	70	63	38	1.0														
9	−11	−05	08	02	05	20	03	14	1.0													
10	−10	−09	−03	−07	−08	02	15	05	50	10												
11	−02	−07	22	23	21	27	29	37	44	62	1.0											
12	14	−02	04	05	07	−03	23	11	−04	37	31	1.0										
13	09	−01	06	10	09	−03	24	11	−10	08	21	73	1.0									
14	21	18	15	15	14	−01	16	13	13	11	28	12	31	1.0								
15	16	21	22	22	22	23	29	18	03	−07	09	10	32	41	1.0							
16	23	24	09	12	12	05	19	08	08	41	24	33	05	12	10	1.0						
17	38	36	13	21	14	10	07	00	−19	−04	−07	23	09	−01	18	29	1.0					
18	32	17	18	22	17	27	17	13	−01	12	14	33	19	00	19	20	47	1.0				
19	37	23	29	35	28	30	15	20	−03	18	16	36	12	−02	12	22	51	41	1.0			
20	22	04	−01	05	06	−05	−22	−06	01	22	11	31	00	−05	−28	26	27	37	42	1.0		
21	19	−01	−06	04	05	−13	−15	−10	02	22	12	49	17	02	−22	23	26	25	34	73	1.0	
22	49	26	04	16	10	−08	−10	−06	−23	−04	−12	28	09	08	−02	15	42	31	42	57	62	1.0

Run a components analysis on this matrix. Also, do a varimax rotation, and compare the interpretations.

3. In which, if either, of the below cases would it be advisable to apply Bartlett's sphericity test before proceeding with a components analysis?

Case 1

1	.31	.45	.18	.56	.41	.50	
	1	.27	.36	.04	.30	.21	
		1	.63	.16	.41	.25	
			1.	.28	.15	.32	125 subjects
				1	.46	.53	
					1	.39	
						1	

Case 2

1	.29	.18	.04	.11	.15	111 subjects
	1	.07	.40	.12	.03	
		1	.23	.06	.13	
			1	−.08	−.14	
				1	.12	
					1	

The actual sphericity test statistic is:

$$\chi^2 = -(N - 1 - \frac{2p + 5}{6}) \ln |\mathbf{R}|, \text{ with } 1/2\, p\, (p - 1)\ df$$

However, Lawley has shown that a good approximation to this statistic is:

$$\chi^2 = (N - 1 - \frac{2p + 5}{6}) \sum\sum r_{ij}^2,$$

where the sum extends only over the correlations (r_{ij}) above the main diagonal.

Use the Lawley approximation for the above two cases to determine whether you would reject the null hypothesis of uncorrelated variables in the population.

4. Consider the following correlation matrix:

$$\mathbf{R} = \begin{bmatrix} 1 & .6579 & .0034 \\ & 1 & -.0738 \\ & & 1 \end{bmatrix}$$

A principal components analysis on this matrix produced the following factor structure, i.e., component-variable correlations:

	Principal Components		
	1	*2*	*3*
Variables			
1	.906	.112	.408
2	.912	−.005	−.411
3	−.097	.994	−.048

We denote the column of component-variable correlations for the first component by $\mathbf{h}_1$, for the second component by $\mathbf{h}_2$, and for the third component by $\mathbf{h}_3$. Show that the original correlation matrix $\mathbf{R}$ will be reproduced, within rounding error, by $\mathbf{h}_1\mathbf{h}_1' + \mathbf{h}_2\mathbf{h}_2' + \mathbf{h}_3\mathbf{h}_3'$. As you are doing this, observe what part of $\mathbf{R}$ the matrix $\mathbf{h}_1\mathbf{h}_1'$ reproduces, etc.

5. Consider the following principal components solution on 5 variables and the corresponding varimax rotated solution. Only the first two components are given, since the eigenvalues corresponding to the remaining components were very small ($< .3$).

Variables	comp 1	comp 2	Varimax solution factor 1	Varimax solution factor 2
1	.581	.806	.016	.994
2	.767	−.545	.941	−.009
3	.672	.726	.137	.980
4	.932	−.104	.825	.447
5	.791	−.558	.968	−.006

a) Find the percent of variance accounted for by each principal component.

b) Find the percent of variance accounted for by each varimax rotated factor.

c) Compare the variance accounted for by component 1 (2) with variance accounted for by each corresponding rotated factor.

d) Compare the total percent of variance accounted for by the 2 components with the total percent of variance accounted for by the two rotated factors.

6. Consider the following correlation matrix for the 12 variables on the General Aptitude Test Battery (GATB):

NAMES	1.000											
ARITH	.697	1.000										
DIM	.360	.366	1.00									
VOCAB	.637	.580	.528	1.00								
TOOLS	.586	.471	.554	.425	1.00							
MATH	.552	.760	.468	.616	.369	1.000						
SHAPES	.496	.411	.580	.444	.531	.400	1.00					
MARK	.561	.501	.249	.465	.444	.407	.387	1.000				
PLACE	.338	.297	.276	.211	.292	.300	.323	.494	1.00			
TURN	.349	.247	.279	.209	.336	.234	.401	.540	.773	1.00		
ASMBL	.390	.319	.358	.267	.361	.208	.444	.439	.468	.476	1.00	
DASMBL	.354	.325	.234	.283	.267	.311	.428	.422	.453	.482	.676	1.00

a) Run a components analysis and varimax rotation on the SAS FACTOR program.

b) Interpret the components and the varimax rotated factors.

b) Use the oblique rotation PROMAX, and interpret the oblique factors.

c) What are the correlations among the oblique factors?

d) Which factors seem more reasonable to use here?

7. Bolton (1971) measured 159 deaf rehabilitation candidates on 10 communication skills, of which 6 were reception skills in unaided hearing, aided hearing, speech reading, reading, manual signs and fingerspellings. The other four communication skills were expression skills: oral speech, writing, manual signs and fingerspelling. Bolton did what is called a principal axis analysis, which is identical to a components analysis, except that the factors are extracted from a correlation matrix with communality estimates on the main diagonal rather than 1's, as in components analysis. He obtained the following correlation matrix and varimax factor solution:

Correlation Matrix of Communication Variables for 159 Deaf Persons

	C_1	C_2	C_3	C_4	C_5	C_6	C_7	C_8	C_9	C_{10}	M	S
C_1	39										1.10	0.45
C_2	59	55									1.49	1.06
C_3	30	34	61								2.56	1.17
C_4	16	24	62	81							2.63	1.11
C_5	-02	-13	28	37	92						3.30	1.50
C_6	00	-05	42	51	90	94					2.90	1.44
C_7	39	61	70	59	05	20	71				2.14	1.31
C_8	17	29	57	88	30	46	60	78			2.42	1.04
C_9	-04	-14	28	33	93	86	04	28	92		3.25	1.49
C_{10}	-04	-08	42	50	87	94	17	45	90	94	2.89	1.41

Note—The italicized diagonal values are squared multiple correlations.

Varimax Factor Solution for 10 Communication Variables
for 159 Deaf Persons

		I	II
C_1	Hearing (Unaided)		49
C_2	Hearing (Aided)		66
C_3	Speech Reading	32	70
C_4	Reading	45	71
C_5	Manual Signs	94	
C_6	Fingerspelling	94	
C_7	Speech		86
C_8	Writing	38	72
C;9	Manual Signs	94	
C_{10}	Fingerspelling	96	
Percent of Common Variance		53.8	39.3

Note—Factor loadings less than .30 are omitted.

a) Interpret the varimax factors. What does each of them represent?

b) Does the way the variables which defined factor 1 correspond to the way they are correlated. That is, is the empirical clustering of the variables by the principal axis technique consistent with the way those variables "go together" in the original correlation matrix?

8. a) As suggested in the chapter, do the SPSSX oblique rotation OBLIMIN on the California Psychological Inventory.

b) Do the oblique factors seem to be easier to interpret than the uncorrelated, varimax factors?

c) What are the correlations among the oblique factors?

d) Which factors, correlated or uncorrelated, would you prefer here?

9. a) Consider again the factor analysis of the CPI, and in particular, the first two rotated factors presented in Table 11.5. Can we have confidence in the reliability of these factors according to the Monte Carlo results of Guadagnoli and Velicer?

b) Now consider the rotated factor loadings for the SAS run on the Personality Research Form given in Table 11.8. Can we have confidence in the reliability of the 4 rotated factors according to the Guadagnoli and Velicer study? For which factor(s) is the evidence strong, but not totally conclusive?

Velicer also indicates that when the *average* of the 4 largest loadings is $> .60$, or the *average* of the 3 largest loadings is $> .8$ that the factors will be reliable (personal communication, August, 1992).

12 Canonical Correlation

12.1 INTRODUCTION

In Chapter 3, we examined breaking down the association between two sets of variables using multivariate regression analysis. This is the appropriate technique if our interest is in prediction, and if we wish to focus our attention primarily on the individual variables (both predictors and dependent), rather than on linear combinations of the variables. *Canonical correlation* is another means of breaking down the association for two sets of variables, and *is appropriate if the wish is to parsimoniously describe the number and nature of mutually independent relationships existing between the two sets.* This is accomplished through the use of pairs of linear combinations that are uncorrelated. Since the combinations are uncorrelated, we will obtain a very nice additive partitioning of the total between association. Thus, there are several similarities to principal components analysis (discussed in the previous chapter). Both are variable reduction schemes that use uncorrelated linear combinations. In components analysis, generally the first few linear combinations (the components) account for most of the total variance in the original set of variables, while in canonical correlation the fist few pairs of linear combinations (the so-called *canonical variates*) generally account for most of the between association. Also, in interpreting the principal components, we used the correlations between the original variables and the components. In canonical correlation, the correlations between the original variables and the canonical variates will again be used to name the canonical variates.

One could consider doing canonical regression. However, as Darlington et al. (1973) have stated, investigators are generally not interested in predicting linear combinations of the dependent variables.

Let us now consider a couple of situations where canonical correlation would be useful. An investigator wishes to explore the relationship between a set of personality variables (say, as measured by the Cattell 16 PF scale or by the California Psychological Inventory) and a battery of achievement test scores for a group of high school students. The first pair of canonical variates will tell us what type of personality profile (as revealed by the linear combination, and named by determining which of the original variables correlate most highly with this linear combination) is maximally associated with a given profile of achievement (as revealed by the linear combination for the achievement scores). The second pair of canonical variates will yield an uncorrelated personality profile that is associated with a different pattern of achievement, etc.

As a second example, consider the case where a single group of subjects is measured on the *same* set of variables at two different points in time. We wish to investigate the stability of the personality profiles of female college subjects from their freshman to their senior years. Canonical correlation analysis will reveal which dimension of personality is most stable or reliable. This dimension would be named by determining which of the original variables correlate is most highly with the canonical variates corresponding to the largest canonical correlation. Then the analysis will find an uncorrelated dimension of personality that is next most reliable. This dimension is named by determining which of the original variables has the highest correlations with the second pair of canonical variates, etc. This type of *multivariate reliability analysis* using canonical correlation has been in existence for some time. Merenda, Novack, and Bonaventure (1976) did such an analysis on the subtest scores of the California Test of Mental Maturity for a group of elementary school children.

12.2   THE NATURE OF CANONICAL CORRELATION

To focus more specifically on what canonical correlation does, consider the following hypothetical situation. A researcher is interested in the relationship between "job success" and "academic achievement." He has two measures of job success: (1) the amount of money the individual is making, and (2) the status of the individual's position. He has four measures of academic achievement: (1) high school GPA, (2) college GPA, (3) number of degrees, and (4) ranking of the college where the last degree was obtained. We denote the first set of variables by xs and the second set of variables (academic achievement) by ys.

The canonical correlation procedure first finds two linear combinations (one from the job success measures and one from the academic achievement measures) that have the maximum possible Pearson correlation. That is,

$$u_1 = a_{11}x_1 + a_{12}x_2 \text{ and } v_1 = b_{11}y_1 + b_{12}y_2 + b_{13}y_3 + b_{14}y_4$$

are found such that $r_{u_1 v_1}$ is maximum. Note that if this were done with data, the as and bs would be known numerical values, and a single score for each subject on each linear composite could be obtained. These two sets of scores for the subjects are then correlated just as we would perform the calculations for the scores on two individual variables, say x and y. The maximized correlation for the scores on two linear composites $(r_{u_1 v_1})$ is called the *largest canonical correlation,* and we denote it by R_1.

Now, the procedure searchers for a second pair of linear combinations, *uncorrelated* with the first pair, such that the Pearson correlation between this pair is the next largest possible. That is,

$$u_2 = a_{21}x_1 + a_{22}x_2 \text{ and } v_2 = b_{21}y_1 + b_{22}y_2 + b_{23}y_3 + b_{24}y_4$$

are found such that $r_{u_2 v_2}$ is maximum. This correlation, because of the way the procedure is set up, will be less than $r_{u_1 v_1}$. For example, $r_{u_1 v_1}$ might be .73 and $r_{u_2 v_2}$ might be .51. We denote the second largest canonical correlation by R_2.

When we say that this second pair of canonical variates are uncorrelated with the first pair we mean that (1) the canonical variates *within* each set are uncorrelated, i.e., $r_{u_1 u_2} = 0$, and (2) the canonical variates are uncorrelated *across* sets, i.e., $r_{u_1 v_2} = r_{v_1 u_2} = 0$.

For this example, there are just two possible canonical correlations and hence only two pairs of canonical variates. In general, if one has p variables in one set and q in the other set, the number of possible canonical correlations is min $(p,q) = m$ (cf. Tatsuoka, 1971, p. 186, as to the reason why). Therefore, for our example, there are only min $(2,4) = 2$ canonical correlations. To determine how many of the possible canonical correlations indicate statistically significant relationships, a residual test procedure, identical in form to that for discriminant analysis, is used. Thus, canonical correlation is still another example of a mathematical maximization procedure (as were multiple regression and principal components), which partitions the total between association through the use of uncorrelated pairs of linear combinations.

12.3   SIGNIFICANCE TESTS

First, we determine whether there is *any* association between the two sets with the following test statistic:

$$V = - \{(N - 1.5) - (p + q)/2\} \sum_{i=1}^{m} \ln (1 - R_i^2)$$

where N is sample size, and R_i denotes the ith canonical correlation. V is approximately distributed as a χ^2 statistic with pq degrees of freedom. If this overall test is significant, then the largest canonical correlation is removed and the residual is tested for significance. If we denote the term in braces by k, then the first residual test statistic (V_1) is given by:

$$V_1 = -k \cdot \sum_{i=2}^{m} ln\ (1 - R_i^2)$$

V_1 is distributed as a χ^2 with $(p - 1)(q - 1)$ degrees of freedom. If V_1 is not significant, then we conclude that only the largest canonical correlation is significant. If V_1 is significant, then we continue and examine the next residual (which has the two largest roots removed), V_2, where:

$$V_2 = -k \cdot \sum_{i=3}^{m} ln\ (1 - R_i^2)$$

V_2 is distributed as a χ^2 with $(p - 2)(q - 2)$ degrees of freedom. If V_2 is not significant, then we conclude that only the two largest canonical correlations are significant.

If V_2 is significant, we examine the next residual, etc. In general, then, when the residual after removing the first s canonical correlations is not significant, we conclude that only the first s canonical correlations are significant. The degrees of freedom for the ith residual is $(p - i)(q - i)$.

When we introduced canonical correlation, it was indicated that the canonical variates additively partition the association. The reason they do is because the variates are uncorrelated both within and across sets. As an analogy, recall that when the predictors are uncorrelated in multiple regression, we obtain an additive partitioning of the variance on the dependent variable.

The sequential testing procedure has been criticized by Harris (1976). However, a Monte Carlo study by Mendoza, Markos, and Gonter (1978) has refuted Harris' criticism. Mendoza et al. considered the case of a total of 12 variables, 6 variables in each set, and chose six population situations. The situations varied from three strong population canonical correlations (η_i), i.e., .9, .8, and .7, to three weak population canonical correlations (.3, .2, and .1), to a null condition (all population canonical correlations $= 0$). The last condition was inserted to check on the accuracy of their generation procedure. One thousand sample matrices, varying in size from 25 to 100, were generated from each population, and the number of significant canonical correlations declared by Bartlett's test (the one we have described) and three other tests were recorded.

Strong population canonical correlations (.9, .8, and .7) will be detected over 90% of the time with as small a sample size as 50. For a more moderate population, canonical correlation (.50), a sample size of 100 is needed todetect it about 67% of the time. A weak population canonical correlation (.30), which is probably *not* worth detecting because it would be of little practical value, requires a sample size of 200 to be detected about 60% of the time. It is fortunate that the tests are conservative in detecting weaker canonical correlations, given the tenuous nature of trying to accurately interpret the canonical variates associated with smaller canonical correlations (Barcikowski & Stevens, 1975), as we shall see in the next section.

12.4   INTERPRETING THE CANONICAL VARIATES

The two methods in use for interpreting the canonical variates are the same as were used for interpreting the discriminant functions:

1. Examine the standardized coefficients.
2. Examine the canonical variate–variable correlations.

For both of these methods, it is the largest (in absolute value) coefficients or correlations that are used. I now refer the reader back to the corresponding section in the chapter on discriminant analysis, because all of the discussion there is relevant here and will not be repeated.

I do add, however, some detail from the Barcikowski and Stevens (1975) Monte Carlo study on the stability of the coefficients and the correlations, since it was for canonical correlation. They sampled eight correlation matrices from the literature and found that *the number subjects per variable necessary to achieve reliability in determining the most important variables for the two largest canonical correlations was very large, ranging from 42/1 to 68/1. This is a somewhat conservative estimate, and if we were just interpreting the largest canonical correlation, then a ratio of about 20/1 is sufficient for accurate interpretation.* However, it doesn't seem likely, in general, that in practice there will be just one significant canonical correlation. The association between two sets of variables is likely to be more complex than that.

To impress on the reader the danger of misinterpretation if the subject/variable ratio is not large, we consider the *second* largest canonical correlation for a 31-variable example from our study. Suppose we were to interpret the left canonical variate using the canonical variate–variable correlations for 400 subjects. This yields a subject/variable ratio of about 13 to 1, a ratio many readers might feel is large enough. However, the frequency rank table (i.e,. a ranking of how often each variable was ranked from most to least important) that resulted is presented here:

Var.	Total number of times less than third	Rank 1 2 3	Population value
1	76	4 11 9	.43
2	43	34 7 16	.64
3	86	1 4 9	.10
4	74	6 12 8	.16
5	60	19 16 5	.07
6	92	2 4 2	.09
7	78	1 5 16	.34
8	64	11 13 12	.40
9	72	6 13 9	.27
10	55	16 15 14	.62

Variables 2 and 10 are clearly the most important. Yet, with an n of 400, about 50% of the time each of them is *not* identified as being one of the three most important variables for interpreting the canonical variate. Furthermore, Variable 5, which is clearly not an important variable in the population, is identified 40% of the time as one of the three most important variables.

In view of the above reliability results, an investigator considering a canonical analysis on a fairly large number of variables (say 20 in one set and 15 in the other set) should consider doing a components analysis on *each* set to reduce the total number of variables dramatically, and then relate the two sets of components via canonical correlation. This should be done even if the investigator has 300 subjects, for this yields a subject/ variable ratio less than 10 to 1 with the *original* set of variables. The practical implementation of this procedure, as will be seen in 12.7, can be accomplished efficiently and elegantly with the SAS package.

12.5   COMPUTER EXAMPLE USING SAS CANCORR

To illustrate how to run canonical correlation on SAS CANCORR and how to interpret the output, we consider data from a study by Lehrer and Schimoler (1975). This study examined the cognitive skills underlying an inductive problem solving method that has been used to develop critical reasoning skills for educable mentally retarded children. A total of 112 EMR's were given the Cognitive Abilities Test, which consists of four subtests measuring the following skills: oral vocabulary (CAT1), relational concepts (CAT2), multimental concepts (one that doesn't belong) CAT3, and quantitative concepts (CAT4). We relate these skills via canonical correlation to seven subtest scores from the Children's Analysis of Social-

Situations (CASS), a test which is a modification of the Test of Social Inference. The CASS was developed as a means of assessing inductive reasoning processes. For the CASS, the children respond to a sample picture and various pictorial stimuli at various levels: CASS1 — labeling — identification of a relevant object; CASS2 — detail — represents a further elaboration of an object; CASS3 — low-level inference — a guess concerning a picture based on obvious clues; CASS4 — high-level inference; CASS5 — prediction — a statement concerning future outcomes of a situation; CASS6 — low-level generalization — a rule derived from the context of a picture, but which is specific to the situation in that picture; and CASS7 — high-level inference — deriving a rule that extends beyond the specific situation.

In Table 12.1 we present the correlation matrix for the 11 variables, and in Table 12.2 give the control lines from SAS CANCORR for running the canonical correlation analysis, along with the significance tests.

Table 12.3 has the standardized coefficients and canonical variate-variable correlations that we use jointly to interpret the pair of canonical variates corresponding to the only significant canonical correlation. These coefficients and loadings are boxed in on Table 12.3. For the cognitive ability variables (CAT), note that all four variables have uniformly strong loadings, although the loading for CAT1 is extremely high (.953). Using the standardized coefficients, we see that CAT2 through CAT4 are redundant, since their coefficients are considerably lower than that for CAT1. For the CASS variables, the loadings on CASS4 through CASS7 are clearly the strongest and of uniform magnitude. Turning to the coefficients for those variables, we see that CASS4 and CASS5 are redundant, since they clearly have the smallest coefficients. Thus, the only significant linkage between the two sets of variables relates oral vocabulary (CAT1) to the children's ability to generalize in social situations, particularly low-level generaliza-

TABLE 12.1
Correlation Matrix for Cognitive Ability Variables and Inductive
Reasoning Variables

CAT1	1.000										
CAT2	.662	1.000									
CAT3	.661	.697	1.000								
CAT4	.641	.730	.703	1.000							
CASS1	.131	−.112	.033	.040	1.000						
CASS2	.253	.031	.185	.149	.641	1.000					
CASS3	.332	.133	.197	.132	.574	.630	1.000				
CASS4	.381	.304	.304	.382	.312	.509	.583	1.000			
CASS5	.413	.313	.276	.382	.254	.491	.491	.731	1.000		
CASS6	.520	.485	.450	.466	.034	.117	.294	.595	.534	1.000	
CASS7	.434	.392	.380	.390	.065	.100	.203	.328	.355	.508	1.000

TABLE 12.2
SAS CANCORR Control Lines for Canonical Correlation Relating Cognitive
Abilities Subtests to Subtests From Children's Analysis of Social Situations

TITLE 'CANONICAL CORRELATION';
DATA CANCORR(TYPE = CORR);
TYPE = 'CORR';
INPUT NAME $ CAT1 CAT2 CAT3 CAT4 CASS1 CASS2 CASS3 CASS4
CASS5 CASS6 CASS7;
CARDS;
CAT1 1.00 . . . .
CAT2 .662 1.00 . . . .
CAT3 .661 .697 1.00 . . . .
CAT4 .641 .730 .703 1.00 . . . . . .
CASS1 .131 −.112 .033 .040 1.00 . . . . . .
CASS2 .253 .031 .185 .149 .641 1.00 . . . . .
CASS3 .332 .133 .197 .132 .574 .630 1.00 . . . .
CASS4 .381 .304 .304 .382 .312 .509 .583 1.00 . . .
CASS5 .413 .313 .276 .382 .254 .491 .491 .731 1.00 . .
CASS6 .520 .485 .450 .466 .034 .117 .294 .595 .534 1.00 .
CASS7 .434 .392 .380 .390 .065 .100 .203 .328 .355 .508 1.00
PROC CANCORR EDF = 111 CORR;
VAR CAT1 CAT2 CAT3 CAT4;
WITH CASS1 CASS2 CASS3 CASS4 CASS5 CASS6 CASS7;

tion. We now consider a study from the literature that used canonical correlation analysis.

12.6 A STUDY THAT USED CANONICAL CORRELATION: RELATIONSHIP BETWEEN STUDENT NEEDS AND TEACHER RATINGS

A study by Tetenbaum (1975) addressed the issue of the validity of student ratings of teachers. She noted that current instruments generally list several teaching behaviors and ask the student to rate the instructor on each of them. The assumption is made that all students focus on the same teaching behavior, and furthermore that when focusing on the same behavior, students perceive it in the same way. Tetenbaum noted that principles from social perception theory (Warr & Knapper, 1968) make both of these assumptions questionable. She argued that the social psychological needs of the students would influence their ratings, stating, "It was reasoned that in the process of rating a teacher the student focuses on the need-related aspects of the perceptual situation and bases his judgement on those areas of the teacher's performance most relevant to his own needs" (p. 418).

To assess student needs, the *Personality Research Form* was administered *(handwritten margin notes:)* ① Coefficients which determine which VARs are redundant   ② r's used for interpretation or naming of the derived constructs.

TABLE 12.3
Standardized Coefficients and Canonical Variate–Variable Loadings

Standardized Canonical Coefficients for the 'VAR' Variables

	V1	V	V3	V$
CAT1	0.6331	−0.9449	−0.0508	−0.9198
CAT2	0.1660	1.1759	−1.0730	−0.3528
CAT3	0.1387	−0.5642	−0.3944	1.4179
CAT4	0.1849	0.4858	.5341	0.0334

Standardized Canonical Coefficients for the 'WITH' Variables

	W1	W2	W3	W4
CASS1	−0.1513	−0.3613	0.8506	−0.3307
CASS2	0.2444	−0.5973	−0.0118	1.0508
CASS3	0.1144	−0.4815	−1.0841	−0.6960
CASS4	−0.0954	0.6193	0.6808	0.4785
CASS5	0.1416	0.2564	0.4075	−1.1752
CASS6	0.6355	−0.1473	−0.3623	0.3471
CASS7	0.3681	0.0394	0.0008	0.2202

Correlations Between the 'VAR' Variables and Their Canonical Variables

	V1	V2	V3	V4
CAT1	0.9532	−0.2281	−0.0384	−0.1947d
CAT2	0.8168	0.5117	−0.2616	0.0510
CAT3	0.8025	−0.0287	−0.1004	0.5874
CAT4	0.8091	0.3430	0.4418	0.1802

Correlations Between the 'WITH' Variables and Their Canonical Variables

	W1	W2	W3	W4
CASS1	0.1228	−0.7646	0.5245	−0.1798
CASS2	0.3517	−0.7044	0.3548	0.1294
CASS3	0.4570	−0.6136	−0.1126	−0.3752
CASS4	0.6509	0.0345	0.3907	−0.0760
CASS5	0.6796	0.0230	0.3899	−0.4717
CASS6	0.8984	0.1544	−0.0304	0.0231
CASS7	0.7477	0.0778	0.0187	0.0785

to 405 graduate students. The entire scale was not administered because some of the needs were not relevant to an academic setting. The part administered was then factor analyzed and a four-factor solution was obtained. For each factor, the three subscales having the highest loadings (.50) were selected to represent that factor, with the exception of one subscale (dominance), which had a high loading on more than one factor and one subscale (harm avoidance), which was not felt to be relevant to the classroom setting. The final instrument consisted of 12 scales, 3 scales representing each of the four obtained factors: Factor I: Cognitive Structure (CS), Impulsivity (IM), Order (OR); Factor II: Endurance (EN),

Achievement (AC), Understanding (UN); Factor III: Affiliation (AF), Autonomy (AU), Succorance (SU); Factor IV: Aggression (AG), Defendance (DE), Abasement (AB). These factors were named Need for Control, Need for Intellectual Striving, Need for Gregariousness-Defendance, and Need for Ascendancy, respectively.

Student ratings of teachers were obtained on an instrument constructed by Tetenbaum, which consisted of 12 vignettes, each describing a college classroom in which the teacher was engaged in a particular set of behaviors. The particular behaviors were designed to correspond to the four need factors, i.e., within the 12 vignettes there were three replications for each of the four teacher orientations. For example, in three teacher vignettes the orientation was aimed at meeting control needs. In these vignettes, the teachers attempted to control the classroom environment by organizing and structuring all lessons and assignments so that the students would know what was expected of them; by stressing order, neatness, clarity, and logic; and by encouraging deliberation of thought and moderation of emotion.

Tetenbaum hypothesized that specific student needs (e.g., control needs) would be related to teacher orientations that met those needs. The 12 need variables (Set 1) were related to the 12 rating variables (Set 2) via canonical correlation. Three significant canonical correlations were obtained: $R_1 =$ .486, $R_2 = .389$, and $R_3 = .323$ (p .01 in all cases). Tetenbaum chose to use the canonical variate–variable correlations to interpret the variates. These are presented in Table 12.4. Examining the underlined correlations for the

TABLE 12.4
Canonical Variate – Variable Correlations for Tetenbaum Study

		Canonical Variables				
First Pair		*Second Pair*		*Third Pair*		
Needs	*Ratings*	*Needs*	*Ratings*	*Needs*	*Ratings*	
.111	.028	.614	.453	−.018	−.325	⎫
−.099	−.051	−.785	.491	.078	−.397	⎬ Control
.065	.292	.774	.597	−.050	.059	⎭
−.537	−.337	.210	.263	.439	.177	⎫
−.477	−.294	.252	.125	.500	.102	⎬ Intellectual Striving
−.484	−.520	−.005	.154	.452	.497	⎭
−.134	−.233	−.343	−.210	−.354	−.335	⎫
.270	−.141	.016	.114	.657	−.468	⎬ Gregarious
−.271	−.072	−.155	−.175	−.414	−.579	⎭
−.150	.395	.205	.265	.452	.211	⎫
.535	.507	−.254	.034	.421	.361	⎬ Ascendancy
.333	.673	−.312	−.110	.289	.207	⎭

*Correlations > |.3| are underlined.

first pair (i.e., for the largest canonical correlation), we see that it clearly reflects the congruence between the intellectual striving needs and ratings on the corresponding vignettes, as well as the congruence between the ascendancy needs and ratings. The second pair of canonical variates (corresponding to the second largest canonical correlation) reflects the congruence between the control needs and the ratings. Note that the correlation for impulsivity is negative, since a low score on this variable would imply a high rating for a teacher who exhibits order and moderation of emotion.

The interpretation of the third pair of canonical variates is not as clean as it was for the first two pairs. Nevertheless, the correspondence between gregariousness-dependency needs and ratings is revealed, a correspondence that did *not* appear for the first two pairs. However, there are "high" loadings on other needs and ratings as well. The interested reader is referred to Tetenbaum's article for a discussion of why this may have happened.

In summary, then, the correspondence that Tetenbaum hypothesized between student needs and ratings was clearly revealed by canonicalcorrelation. Two of the need–rating correspondences were revealed by the first canonical correlation, a third correspondence (for control needs) was established by the second canonical correlation, and finally the gregariousness need–rating correspondence was revealed by the third canonical correlation.

Through the use of factor analysis, the author in this study was able to reduce the number of variables to 24 and achieve a fairly large subject/variable ratio (about 17/1). Based on our Monte Carlo results, one could interpret the largest canonical correlation with confidence; however, the second and third canonical correlations should be interpreted with some caution.

12.7 USING SAS FOR CANONICAL CORRELATION ON TWO SETS OF FACTOR SCORES

As indicated previously, if there is a large or fairly large number of variables in each of two sets, it is desirable to do a factor analysis on each set of variables for two reasons:

1. To obtain a more parsimonious description of what each set of variables is really measuring.
2. To reduce the total number of variables that will appear in the eventual canonical correlation analysis so that a much larger subject/variable ratio is obtained, making for more reliable results.

The practical implementation of doing the component analyses and then passing the factor scores for a canonical correlation can be accomplished quite efficiently and elegantly with the SAS package. To illustrate, we use the National Academy of Science data from Chapter 3. Those data were based on 46 observations and involved the following seven variables: QUALITY, NFACUL, NGRADS, PCTSUPP, PCTGRT, NARTIC, and PCTPUB. We use SAS to do a components analysis on NFACUL, NGRADS, and PCTSUPP and then do a separate component analysis on PCTGRT, NARTIC, and PCTPUB. Obviously, with such a small number of variables in each set, a factor analysis is really not needed, but this example is for pedagogical purposes only. Then we use the SAS canonical correlation program (CANCORR) to relate the two sets of factor scores. The complete SAS control lines for doing both component analyses and the canonical correlation analysis on the factor scores are given in Table 12.5.

Now, let us consider a more realistic example, that is, where factor analysis is really needed. Suppose an investigator has 15 variables in set X and 20 variables in set Y. She wishes to run a canonical correlation analysis to determine the relationship between the two sets of variables, and has 250 subjects. Recall from section 12.4 that at least 20 subjects per variable are needed for reliable results, and the investigator is not near that ratio. Thus,

TABLE 12.5
SAS Control Lines for a Components Analysis on Each of Two Sets of Variables and Then a Canonical Correlation Analysis on the Two Sets of Factor Scores

```
    DATA NATACAD;
    INPUT QUALITY NFACUL NGRADS PCTSUPP PCTGRT NARTIC PCTPUB;
    CARDS;
    DATA
① ┌ PROC PRINCOMP N=2 OUT=FSCORE1;
   └ VAR NFACUL NGRADS PCTSUPP;
② ┌ PROC PRINCOMP N=3 PREFIX=PCTSET2 OUT=FSCORE2;
   └ VAR PCTGRT NARTIC PCTPUB;
③   PROC PRINT DATA=FSCORE2;
    ┌ PROC CANCORR CORR;
④ │ VAR PRIN1 PRIN2;
    └ WITH PCSET21 PCSET22 PCSET23;
```

① The principal components procedure is called and a components analysis is done on only the 3 variables indicated.

② The components procedure is called again, this time to do a components analysis on the PCTGRT, NARTIC and PCTPUB variables.
To distinguish the names for the components retained for this second analysis, we use the PREFIX option.

③ This statement is to obtain a listing of the data for all the variables, that is, the original variables, the factor scores for the two components for the first analysis and the factor scores for the three components from the second analysis.

④ The canonical correlation procedure is called to determine the relationship between the two components from the first analysis and the three components from the second analysis.

a components analysis is run on each set of variables to achieve a more adequate ratio and to determine more parsimoniously the main constructs involved for each set of variables. The components analysis and varimax rotation is done for each set. On examining the output for the two component analyses, using Kaiser's rule and the scree test in combination, she decides to retain three factors for Set X and four factors for Set Y. In addition, from examination of the output, the investigator finds that the communalities for Variables 2 and 7 are low. That is, these variables are relatively independent of what the three factors are measuring, and thus she decides to retain these original variables for the eventual canonical analysis. Similarly, the communality for Variable 12 in set Y is low, and that variable will also be retained for the canonical analysis.

We denote the variables for Set X by X1, X2, X3, . . , X15 and the variables for Set Y by Y1, Y2, Y3, . . . , Y20. The complete control lines in this case are:

```
DATA REAL;
INPUT X1 X2 X3 X4 X5 X6 X7 X8 X9 X10 X11 X12 X13 X14 X15
Y1 Y2 Y3 Y4 Y5 Y6 Y7 Y8 Y9 Y10 Y11 Y12 Y13 Y14 Y15 Y16 Y17
Y18 Y19 Y20;
CARDS;

    DATA

PROC FACTOR ROTATE=VARIMAX N=3 SCREE OUT=FSCORES1;
VAR X1-X15;
PROC DATASETS;
MODIFY FSCORES1;
RENAME FACTOR1=SET1FAC1 FACTOR2=SET1FAC2 FACTOR 3=SET1FAC3;
PROC FACTOR ROTATE=VARIMAX N=4 SCREE OUT=FSCORES2;
VAR Y1-Y20;
PROC PRINT DATA=FSCORES2;
PROC CANCORR CORR;
VAR SET1FAC1 SET1FAC2 SET1FAC3 X2 X7;
WITH FACTOR1 FACTOR2 FACTOR3 FACTOR4 Y12;
```

12.8   THE REDUNDANCY INDEX OF STEWART AND LOVE

In multiple regression, the squared multiple correlation represents the proportion of criterion variance accounted for by the optimal linear combination of the predictors. In canonical correlation, however, a squared canonical correlation only tells us the amount of variance that the two canonical variates share, and does not necessarily indicate considerable variance overlap between the two sets of variables. The canonical variates are derived to maximize the correlation between them, and thus we can't necessarily expect each canonical variate will extract much variance from its set. For example, the third canonical variable from Set X may be close to a last principle component, and thus extract negligible variance from Set X. That is, it may not be an important factor for Battery X. Stewart and Love (1968) realized that interpreting squared canonical correlations as indicating the amount of informational overlap between two batteries (sets of variables) was not appropriate, and developed their own index of redundancy.

The essence of the Stewart and Love idea is quite simple. First, determine how much variance in Y the first canonical variate (C_1) accounts for. How this is done will be indicated shortly. Then multiply the extracted variance (we denote this by VC_1) by the square of the canonical correlation between C_1 and the corresponding canonical variate (P_1) from Set X. This product then gives the amount of variance in Set Y that is predictable from the first canonical variate for Set X. Next, the amount of variance in Y that the second canonical variate (C_2) for Y accounts for is determined, and is multiplied by the square of the canonical correlation between C_2 and the corresponding canonical variate (P_2) from Set X. This product gives the amount of variance in Set Y predictable from the second canonical variate for Set X. This process is repeated for all possible canonical correlations. Then, the products are added (since the respective pairs of canonical variates are uncorrelated) to determine the redundancy in Set Y, given Set X, which we denote by $R_{Y/X}$. If the square of the ith canonical correlation is denoted by λ_i, then $R_{Y/X}$ is given by:

$$R_{Y/X} = \sum_{i=1}^{h} \lambda_i \, VC_i,$$

where h is the number of possible canonical correlations.

The amount of variance canonical variate i extracts from Set Y is given by:

$$VC_I = \frac{\Sigma \text{ squared canonical variate–variable correlations}}{q \text{ (number of variables in Set } Y)}$$

There is an important point I wish to make concerning the redundancy index. It is equal to the average squared multiple correlation for predicting the variables in one set from the variables in the other set. To illustrate, suppose we had four variables in Set X and three variables in Set Y, and we computed the multiple correlation for each y variable *separately* with the four predictors. Then, if these multiple correlations are squared and the sum of squares divided by 3, this number is equal to $R_{Y/X}$. This fact hints at a problem with the redundancy index, as Cramer and Nicewander (1979) have noted, "Moreover, the redundancy index is not multivariate in the strict sense because it is unaffected by the intercorrelations of the variables being predicted. The redundancy index is only multivariate in the sense that it involves several criterion variables" (p. 43).

This is saying we would obtain the same amount of variance accounted for with the redundancy index for three y variables that are highly correlated a we would for three y variables that have low intercorrelations (other factors being held constant). This is very undesirable in the same sense as it would be undesirable if in a multiple regression context the multiple correlation were unaffected by the magnitude of the intercorrelations among the predictors.

This defect can be eliminated by first orthogonalizing the y variables (e.g., obtaining a set of uncorrelated variables, such as principal components or varimax rotated factors), and then computing the average squared multiple correlation between the uncorrelated y variables and the x variables. In this case we could, of course, compute the redundancy index, but it is unnecessary since it is equal to the average squared multiple correlation.

Cramer and Nicewander recommended using the *average squared canonical correlation* as the measure of variance accounted for. Thus, for example, if there were two canonical correlations, simply square each of them and then divide by 2.

12.9   ROTATION OF CANONICAL VARIATES

In the chapter on principal components, it was stated that often the interpretation of the components can be difficult, and that a rotation (e.g., varimax) can be quite helpful in obtaining factors that tend to load high on only a small number of variables and therefore are considerably easier to interpret. In canonical correlations, the same rotation idea can be employed to increase interpretability. The situation, however, is much more complex, since two sets of factors (the successive pairs of canonical variates) are being simultaneously rotated. Cliff and Krus (1976) have shown mathematically that such a procedure is sound, and the practical implementation of the procedure is possible in Multivariance (Finn, 1978). Cliff and Krus also demonstrate, through an example, how interpretation is made clearer through rotation.

When such a rotation is done, the variance will be spread more evenly across the pairs of canonical variates, i.e., the maximization property is lost. Recall that this is what happened when the components were rotated. But we were willing to sacrifice this property for increased interpretability. Of course, only the canonical variates corresponding to *significant* canonical correlations should be rotated, in order to ensure that the rotated variates still correspond to significant association (Cliff & Krus, 1976).

12.10   OBTAINING MORE RELIABLE CANONICAL VARIATES

In concluding this chapter, I mention five approaches that will increase the probability of accurately interpreting the canonical variates, i.e., the probability that the interpretation made in the given sample will hold up in another sample from the same population. The first two points have already been made, but are repeated as a means of summarizing:

1. Have a very large (1,000 or more) number of subjects, or a large subject/variable ratio.

2. If there is a large or fairly large number of variables in each set, then perform a components analysis on each set. Use only the components (or rotated factors) from each set that account for most of the variance in the canonical correlation analysis. In this way an investigator, rather than doing a canonical analysis on a total of, say, 35 variables with 300 subjects, may be able to account for most of the variance in each of the sets with a total of 10 components, and thus achieve a much more favorable subject/variable ratio (30/1). The components analysis approach is one means of attacking the multicollinearity problem, which makes accurate interpretation difficult.

3. Ensure at least a moderate to large subject/variable ratio by judiciously selecting a priori a small number of variables for each of the two sets that will be related.

4. Another way of dealing with multicollinearity is to use canonical ridge regression. With this approach the coefficients are biased, but their variance will be much less, leading to more accurate interpretation. Monte Carlo studies (Anderson & Carney, 1974; Barcikowski & Stevens, 1978) of the effectiveness of ridge canonical regression show that it can yield more stable canonical variate coefficients and canonical variate–variable correlations. Barcikowski and Stevens examined 11 different correlation matrices that exhibited varying degrees of within and between multicollinearity. They found that, in general, ridge became more effective as the degree of multicollinearity increased. Secondly, ridge canonical regression was particularly effective with small subject/variable ratios. These are precisely the situations where the greater stability is desperately needed.

5. Still another approach to more accurate interpretation of canonical variates has been presented by Weinberg and Darlington (1976), who used biased coefficients of 0 and 1 to form the canonical variates. This approach makes interpretation of the most important variables, those receiving 1s in the canonical variates, relatively easy.

12.11 SUMMARY

Canonical correlation is a parsimonious way of breaking down the association between two sets of variables through the use of linear combinations. In this way, since the combinations are uncorrelated, we can describe the number and nature of independent relationships existing between two sets of variables. That canonical correlation does indeed give a parsimonious description of association can be seen by considering the case of 5 variables in Set X and 10 variables in Set Y. To obtain an overall picture of the association using simple correlations would be very difficult, since we would have to deal with 50 fragmented between correlations. Canonical correlation, on the other hand, consolidates or channels all the association into five uncorrelated "big pieces," i.e., the canonical correlations.

There are two devices available for interpreting the canonical variates: (1) standardized coefficients, and (2) canonical variate–variable correlations. Both of these are quite unreliable unless the n/total number of variables ratio is very large; at least 42/1 if interpreting the largest two canonical correlations, and about 20/1 if interpreting only the largest canonical correlation. The correlations should be used for substantive interpretation of the canonical variates, i.e., for naming the constructs, while the coefficients are used for determining which of the variables are redundant.

Because of the probably unattainably large n required for reliable results (especially if there are a fairly large or large number of variables in each set), several suggestions were given for obtaining reliable results with the n available, or perhaps just a somewhat larger n. The first suggestion involved doing a components analysis and varimax rotation on each set of variables and then relating the components or rotated factors via canonical correlation. An efficient, practical implementation of this procedure, using the SAS package, was illustrated.

Some other means of obtaining more reliable canonical variates were:

1. Selecting a priori a small number of variables from each of the sets, and then relating these. This would be an option to consider if the n was not judged to be large enough to do a reliable components analysis. For example, if there were 20 variables in Set X and 30 variables in Set Y and $n = 120$.
2. The use of canonical ridge regression.
3. The use of the technique developed by Weinberg and Darlington.

A study from the literature that used canonical correlation was discussed in detail.

The redundancy index, for determining the variance overlap between two sets of variables, was considered. It was indicated that this index suffers from the defect of being unaffected by the intercorrelations of the variables being predicted. This is undesirable in the same sense as it would be undesirable if the multiple correlation were unaffected by the intercorrelations of the predictors.

Finally, in evaluating studies from the literature that have used canonical correlation, remember it isn't just the n in a vacuum that is important. The n/total number of variables ratio, along with the degree of multicollinearity, must be examined to determine how much confidence can be placed in the results. Thus, not a great deal of confidence can be placed in the results of a study involving a total of 25 variables (say 10 in Set X and 15 in Set Y) based on 200 subjects. Even if a study had 400 subjects, but did the canonical analysis on a total of 60 variables, it is probably of little scientific value since the results are unlikely to replicate.

EXERCISES

1. Name four features that canonical correlation and principal components analysis have in common.

2. Suppose that a canonical correlation analysis on two sets of variables yielded ... onical correlations. Indicate schematically what the matrix of intercorrelations for the canonical variates would look like.

3. Shin (1971) examined the relationship between creativity and achievement. He used Guilford's battery to obtain the following six creativity scores: ideational fluency, spontaneous flexibility, associational fluency, expressional fluency, and originality and elaboration. The Kropp test was used to obtain the following six achievement variables: knowledge, comprehension, application, analysis, synthesis, and evaluation. Data from 116 eleventh-grade suburban high school students yielded this correlation matrix:

	IDEAFLU	FLEXIB	ASSOCFLU	EXPRFLU	ORIG	ELAB	KNOW	COMPRE	APPLIC	ANAL	SYNTH	EVAL
IDEAFLU	1.000											
FLEXIB	0.710	1.000										
ASSOCFLU	0.120	0.120	1.000									
EXPRFLU	0.340	0.450	0.430	1.000								
ORIG	0.270	0.330	0.240	0.330	1.000							
ELAU	0.210	0.110	0.420	0.460	0.320	1.000						
KNOW	0.130	0.270	0.210	0.390	0.270	0.380	1.000					
COMPRE	0.180	0.240	0.150	0.360	0.330	0.260	0.620	1.000				
APPLIC	0.080	0.140	0.090	0.250	0.130	0.230	0.440	0.660	1.000			
ANAL	0.100	0.160	0.090	0.250	0.120	0.280	0.580	0.660	0.640	1.000		
SYNTH	0.130	0.230	0.420	0.500	0.410	0.470	0.460	0.470	0.370	0.530	1.000	
EVAL	0.080	0.150	0.360	0.280	0.210	0.260	0.300	0.240	0.190	0.290	0.580	1.000

Examine the association between the creativity and achievement variables via canonical correlation, and from the printout answer the following question:

a) How would you characterize the strength of the relationship between the two sets of variables from the simple correlations?

b) How many of the canonical correlations are significant at the .05 level?

c) Use the canonical variable loadings to interpret the canonical variates corresponding to the largest canonical correlation.

d) How large of an n is needed for reliable interpretation of the canonical variates in (c)?

e) Considering all the canonical correlations, what is the value of the redundancy index for the creativity variables given the achievement variables? Express in words what this number tells us.

f) Cramer and Nicewander (1979) have argued that the *average* squared canonical correlation should be used as the measure of association for two sets of variables, stating, "This index has a clear interpretation, being an arithmetic mean, and gives the proportion of variance of the average of the canonical variates of the y variables predictable from the x variables" (p. 53). Obtain the Cramer-Nicewander measure for the present problem, and compare it's magnitude to that obtained for the measure in (e). Explain the reason for the difference, and in particular, the direction of the difference.

4. Shanahan (1984) examined the nature of the reading–writing relationship through canonical correlation analysis. The following measures of writing ability (t unit, vocabulary diversity, episodes, categories, information units, spelling, phonemic accuracy, and visual accuracy) were related to reading measures of vocabulary, word recognition, sentence comprehension, and passage comprehension. Separate canonical correlation analyses were done for 256 second graders and 251 fifth graders.

a) How many canonical correlations will there be for each analysis?

b) Shanahan found that for second graders there were only two significant canonical correlations, and he only interpreted the largest one. Given his sample size, was he wise in doing this?

c) For fifth graders there was only one significant canonical correlation. Given his sample size, can we have confidence in the reliability of the results?

d) Shanahan presents the following canonical variate–variable correlations for the largest canonical correlation for both the second- and fifth-grade samples. If you have an appropriate content background, interpret the results and then compare your interpretation with his.

Canonical Factor Structures for the Grade 2 and Grade 5 Samples:
Correlations of Reading and Writing Variables With Canonical Variables

| | Canonical variable | | | |
| | 2nd Grade | | 5th Grade | |
	Reading	Writing	Reading	Writing
Writing				
t-unit	.32	.41	.19	.25
Vocabulary diversity	.46	.59	.47	.60
Episodes	.25	.32	.20	.26
Categories	.37	.48	.33	.43
Information units	.36	.46	.24	.30
Spelling	.74	.95	.71	.92
Phonemic accuracy	.60	.77	.67	.86
Visual accuracy	.69	.89	.68	.88
Reading				
Comprehension	.81	.63	.79	.61
Cloze	.86	.66	.80	.62
Vocabulary	.65	.51	.89	.69
Phonics	.88	.68	.85	.66

5. Edwards (1984) collected data from 802 full-time nursing faculty in 32 states on House's Leadership Behavior Scale and on Borrevak's Organizational Climate Questionnaire. Factor analysis of the leadership scale yielded these two factors: Participatory/supportive leadership behavior (LBPS) and instrumental leadership behavior (LBI). Factor analysis of the organizational climate questionnaire produced the following three factors: organizational climate-intimacy, disengagement (OCID); organizational climate-consideration (OCC); and organizational climate-production emphasis (OCP). These three organizational climate factors were related via canonical correlation to the above two leadership behavior factors, education (ED) and faculty size (FSIZ). Missing data reduced the sample size for the canonical correlation to .662. The correlation matrix for the variables is:

	OCC	OCID	OCP	LBPS	LBI	ED	FSIZ
OCC	1.000						
OCID	0.129	1.000					
OCP	0.429	0.070	1.000				
LBPS	0.895	0.104	0.402	1.000			
LBI	0.254	0.050	0.627	0.279	1.000		
ED	−0.036	0.021	−0.052	−0.043	−0.038	1.000	
FSIZ	−0.108	0.018	0.154	0.094	0.147	0.072	1.000

a) Run the canonical correlation on SAS CANCORR. How many significant canonical correlations are there at the .01 level?

b) Interpret the canonical variates corresponding to the significant canonical correlations.

c) Is the sample size large enough to have confidence in the reliability of the results?

6. Estabrook (1984) examined the relationship among the 11 subtests on the Wechsler Intelligence Scale for Children-Revised (WISC-R) and the 12 subtests on the Woodcock–Johnson Tests of Cognitive Ability for 152 learning disabled children. He seems to acknowledge sample size as a problem in his study, stating, "The primary limitation of this study is the size of the sample. . . . However, a more conservative criterion of $100(p + q) + 50$ (where p and q refer to the number of variables in each set) has been suggested by Thorndike." Is this really a conservative criterion according to the results of Barcikowski and Stevens (1975)?

13 Repeated Measures Analysis

13.1 INTRODUCTION

Recall that the two basic objectives in experimental design are the elimination of systematic bias and the reduction of error (within group or cell) variance. The main reason for within-group variability is individual differences among the subjects. Thus, even though the subjects receive the same treatment, their scores on the dependent variable can differ considerably because of differences on I.Q., motivation, SES, etc. One statistical way of reducing error variance is through analysis of covariance, which was discussed in Chapter 9. Another way of reducing error variance, which was mentioned earlier, is through blocking on a variable such as I.Q. Here the subjects are first blocked into more homogeneous subgroups, and then randomly assigned to treatments. For example, the subjects may be in blocks with only 9 point I.Q. ranges: 91–100, 101–110, 111–120, 121–130 and 131–140. The subjects within each block may score more similarly on the dependent variable, and the average scores for the subjects between blocks can be fairly large. But all of this variability between blocks is removed from the within-variability, yielding a much more sensitive (powerful) test. *In repeated measures designs,* blocking is carried to it's extreme. That is, *we are blocking on each subject. Thus, variability among the subjects due to individual differences is completely removed from the error term.* This makes these designs much more powerful than completely randomized designs, where different subjects are randomly assigned to the different treatments. Given the emphasis in this text on power, one should seriously consider the use of repeated measures designs where appropriate and practical. And there are many situations where such designs are appropriate. The simplest example of a repeated measures design the reader may have encountered in a beginning statistics course, i.e., the correlated or dependent samples *t* test. Here, the same subjects are pretested and posttested (measured repeatedly) on a dependent variable with an intervening treatment. The subjects are used as their own controls. Another class of repeated measures situations occurs when we are comparing the *same* subjects under several different treatments (drugs, stimulus displays of different complexity, etc.).

Repeated measures is also the natural design to use when the concern is with performance trends over time. For example, Bock (1975) presented an example comparing boys' and girls' performance on vocabulary over grades 8 through 11. Here we are also concerned with the mathematical form of the trend, i.e., whether it is linear, quadratic, cubic, etc.

Another distinct advantage of repeated measures designs, since the same subjects are being used repeatedly, is that far less subjects are required for the study. For example, if three treatments are involved in a completely randomized design, we may require 45 subjects (15 subjects per treatment). With a repeated measures design we would need only 15 subjects. This can be a very important practical advantage in many cases, since numerous subjects are not easy to come by in areas like counseling, school psychology, clinical psychology, and nursing.

In this chapter consideration is given to repeated measures designs of varying complexity. We start with the simplest design; a single group of subjects measured under various treatments (conditions), or at different points in time. Schematically, it would look like this:

	Treatments				
	1	2	3	$\cdots$	k
1					
2					
Subjects $\vdots$					
n					

We then consider a one between and one within design. Many texts use the term "between" and "within" in referring to repeated measures factors. A between variable is simply a grouping or classification variable such as sex, age, social class. A within variable is one on which the subjects have been measured repeatedly (like time). Some authors even refer to repeated measures designs as within designs (Keppel, 1983). An example of a one between and one within design would be:

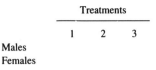

where the same males and females are measured under all three treatments.

Another useful application of repeated measures occurs in combination with a one-way ANOVA design. In a one-way design involving treatments, the subjects are posttested to determine which treatment is best. If we are interested in the lasting or residual effects of treatments, then we need to measure the subjects at least a few more times. Huck, Cormier, and Bounds (1974) present an example in which three teaching methods are compared, but in addition the subjects are again measured 6 weeks and 12 weeks later to determine the residual effect of the methods on achievement. A repeated measures analysis of such data *could* yield a quite different conclusion as to which method might be preferred. Suppose the pattern of means looked as follows:

	POSTTEST	SIX WEEKS	12 WEEKS
METHOD 1	66	64	63
METHOD 2	69	65	59
METHOD 3	62	56	52

Just looking at a one-way ANOVA on posttest scores (if significant) could lead one to conclude that method 2 is best. Examination of the pattern of achievement over time, however, shows that for lasting effect method 1 is to be preferred, because after 12 weeks the achievement for method 1 is superior to method 2 (63 vs 59). What we have here is an example of a method-by-time interaction.

In the above example, teaching method is the between variable and time is the within, or repeated measures factor. The reader should be aware that there are three other names that are used to describe a one between and one within design by some authors: split plot, Lindquist Type I, and two-way ANOVA, with repeated measures on one factor. Our computer example in this chapter involves verbal recall after 1, 2, 3, 4, and 5 days for two treatment groups.

Next we consider a one between and two within repeated measures design, using the following example. Two groups of subjects are administered two types of drugs at each of three doses. The study aims to estimate the relative potency of the drugs in inhibiting a response to a stimulus. Schematically, the design is as follows:

Dose	Drug 1			Drug 2		
	1	2	3	1	2	3
Gp 1						
Gp 2						

Each subject is measured six times, for each dose of each drug. The two within variables are dose and drug.

Then we consider a two between and a one within design from a study comparing the relative efficacy of a behavior modification approach to dieting versus a behavior modification approach + exercise on weight loss for a group of overweight women. The weight loss is measured two, four, and six months after the diets begin. The design is:

GROUP	AGE	WGTLOSS1	WGTLOSS2	WGTLOSS3
CONTROL	20–30 YRS			
CONTROL	30–40 YRS			
BEH. MOD	20–40 YRS			
BEH. MOD.	30–40 YRS			
BEH. MOD + EXER.	20–30 YRS			
BEH. MOD + EXER.	30–40 YRS			

This is a two between design, because we are subdividing the subjects on the basis of both treatment and age, that is, we have two grouping variables.

For each of the above designs we indicate the complete control lines for running both the univariate and multivariate approaches to repeated measures analysis on both SPSSX and SAS, and explain selected printout.

Finally, we consider profile analysis, in which two or more groups of subjects are compared on a battery of tests. The analysis determines whether the profiles for the groups are parallel. If the profiles are parallel, then the analysis will determine whether the profiles are coincident.

Although increased precision and economy of subjects are two distinct advantages of repeated measures designs, such designs also have potentially serious disadvantages, unless care is taken. When several treatments are involved, the order in which treatments are administered might make a difference in the subjects performance. Thus, it is important to *counterbalance* the order of treatments.

For two treatments this would involve randomly assigning half of the subjects to get treatment *A* first, and the other half to get treatment *B* first, which would look like this schematically:

Order of Administration

1	2
A	B
B	A

It is balanced since an equal number of subjects have received each treatment in each position.

For three treatments counterbalancing involves randomly assigning one third of the subjects to each of the following sequences:

Order of Administration
of Treatments

A	B	C
B	C	A
C	A	B

This is balanced since an equal number of subjects have received each treatment in each position. This type of design is called a Latin Square.

Also, it is important to allow sufficient time between treatments to minimize carryover effects, which certainly could occur if treatments were drugs. How much time is necessary is of course a substantive, not a statistical question. A nice discussion of these two problems is found in Keppel (1983) and Myers (1979).

13.2 SINGLE GROUP REPEATED MEASURES

Suppose we wish to study the effect of 4 drugs on reaction time to a series of tasks. Sufficient time is allowed to minimize the effect that one drug may have on the subject's response to the next drug. The following data is from Winer (1971):

S's	Drugs 1	2	3	4	Means	
1	30	28	16	34	27	
2	14	18	10	22	16	
3	24	20	18	30	23	
4	38	34	20	44	34	
5	26	28	14	30	24.5	
	26.4	25.6	15.6	32	24.9	(grand mean)

We will analyze this set of data in three different ways: (1) as a completely randomized design (pretending that there are different subjects for the different drugs), (2) as a univariate repeated measures analysis, and (3) as a multivariate repeated measures analysis. The purpose of including the completely randomized approach is to contrast the error variance that results against the markedly smaller error variance that results in the repeated measures approach. The multivariate approach to repeated measures analysis may be new to our readers, and a specific numerical example will help in understanding how some of the printout on the packages is arrived at.

Completely Randomized Analysis for the Drug Data

This simply involves doing a one-way ANOVA. Thus, we compute the sum of squares between (SS_b) and the sum of squares within (SS_w):

$$SS_b = n \sum_{j=1}^{4} (\bar{y}_j - \bar{y})^2 = 5[(26.4 - 24.9)^2 + (25.6 - 24.9)^2 + (15.6 - 24.9)^2$$
$$+ (32 - 24.9)^2]$$

$$SS_b = 698.2$$
$$SS_w = (30 - 26.4)^2 + (14 - 26.4)^2 + \ldots + (26 - 26.4)^2 + \ldots +$$
$$(34 - 32)^2 + (22 - 32)^2 + \ldots + (30 - 32)^2 = 793.6$$

Thus, $MS_b = 698.2/3 = 232.73$ and $MS_w = 793.6/16 = 49.6$ and our $F = 232.73/49.6 = 4.7$, with 3 and 16 degrees of freedom. This is not significant at the .01 level, since the critical value is 5.29.

Univariate Repeated Measures Analysis for Drug Data

Note from the column of means for the drug of data that the subjects average responses to the 4 drugs differ considerably (ranging from 16 to 34). We quantify this variability through the so called sum of squares for blocks (SS_{bl}), where here we are blocking on the subjects. The error variability that was calculated above is split up into two parts, i.e., $SS_w = SS_{bl} + SS_{res}$, where SS_{res} stands for sum of squares residual. Denote the number of repeated measures by k.

Now we calculate the sum of squares for blocks:

$$SS_{bl} = k \sum_{i=1}^{5} (\bar{y}_i - \bar{y})^2$$

$$= 4[(27 - 24.9)^2 + (16 - 24.9)^2 + \ldots + (24.5 - 24.9)^2]$$

$$SS_{bl} = 680.8$$

Our errors term for the repeated measures analysis is formed from $SS_{res} = SS_w - SS_{b1} = 793.6 - 680.8 = 112.8$. Note that the vast portion of the within variability is due to individual differences (680.8 out of 793.6), and that we have removed all of this from our error term for the repeated measures analysis. Now,

$$MS_{res} = SS_{res}/(n - 1)(k - 1) = 112.8/4(3) = 9.4$$

and $F = MS_b/MS_{res} = 232.73/9.4 = 24.76$, with $(k - 1) = 3$ and $(n - 1)(k - 1) = 12$ degrees of freedom. This is significant well beyond the .01 level, and is approximately 5 times as large as the F obtained under the completely randomized design.

13.3 THE MULTIVARIATE TEST STATISTIC FOR REPEATED MEASURES

Before we consider the multivariate approach, it is instructive to go back to the t test for correlated(dependent) samples. The subjects are pretested and posttested, and difference (d_I) scores are formed:

S's	Pretest	Posttest	d_i
1	7	10	3
2	5	4	−1
3	6	8	2
. . . .			
n	3	7	4

The null hypothesis here is

$H_0 : \mu_1 = \mu_2$ or equivalently that $\mu_1 - \mu_2 = 0$

The t test for determining the tenability of H_0 is

$$t = \frac{\overline{d}}{s_d/\sqrt{n}},$$

where $\overline{d}$ is the average difference score and s_d is the standard deviation for the difference scores. It is important to note that the analysis is done on the difference variable d_i.

In the multivariate case for repeated measures the test statistic for k *repeated measures is formed from the* (k − 1) *difference variables and their variances and covariances.* The transition here from univariate to multivariate parallels that for the two-group independent samples case

Independent Samples

$$t = \frac{(\bar{y}_1 - \bar{y}_2)^2}{s^2(1/n_1 + 1/n_2)}$$

$$t^2 = \frac{n_1 n_2}{n_1 + n_2}(\bar{y}_1 - \bar{y}_2)(s^2)^{-1}(\bar{y}_1 - \bar{y}_2)$$

In obtaining the multivariate statistic we replace the means by mean vectors and the pooled within-variance (s^2) by pooled within-covariance matrix.

$$T^2 = \frac{n_1 n_2}{n_1 + n_2}(\bar{\mathbf{y}}_1 - \bar{\mathbf{y}}_2)' \mathbf{S}^{-1}(\bar{\mathbf{y}}_1 - \bar{\mathbf{y}}_2)$$

S is the pooled within covariance matrix, i.e., the measure of error variability.

Dependent Samples

$$t^2 = \frac{\bar{d}^2}{s_d^2/n}$$

$$t^2 = n\,\bar{d}\,(s_d^2)^{-1}\,\bar{d}$$

To obtain the multivariate statistic we replace the mean difference by a vector of mean differences and the variance of difference scores by the matrix of variances and covariances on the $(k-1)$ created difference variables.

$$T^2 = n\,\mathbf{y}_d'\,\mathbf{S}_d^{-1}\,\mathbf{y}_d$$

$\mathbf{y}_d'$ is the row vector of mean difference on the $(k-1)$ difference variables, i.e. $\mathbf{y}_d' = (\bar{y}_1 - \bar{y}_2, \bar{y}_2 - \bar{y}_3, \ldots, \bar{y}_{k-1} - \bar{y}_k)$ and $\mathbf{S}_d$ is the matrix of variances and covariances on the $(k-1)$ difference variables, i.e., the measure of error variability.

We now calculate the above multivariate test statistic for dependent samples (repeated measures) on the drug data. This should help to clarify the somewhat abstract development thus far.

Multivariate Analysis of the Drug Data

The null hypothesis that we are testing for the drug data is that the drug population means are equal, or in symbols:

$$H_0 : \mu_1 = \mu_2 = \mu_3 = \mu_4$$

But this is equivalent to saying that $\mu_1 - \mu_2 = 0$, $\mu_2 - \mu_3 = 0$ and $\mu_3 - \mu_4 = 0$. (The reader is asked to show this in one of the exercises.) We create 3 difference variables on the adjacent repeated measures ($y_1 - y_2$, $y_2 - y_3$ and $y_3 - y_4$) and test H_0 by determining whether the means on all 3 of these difference variables are simultaneously 0. Below we display the scores on the difference variables:

	$y_1 - y_2$	$y_2 - y_3$	$y_3 - y_4$	
	2	12	−18	
	−4	8	−12	
	4	2	−12	
	4	14	−24	Thus, the row vector of
	−2	14	−16	mean differences here is
Means	.8	10	−16.4	$\mathbf{y}_d' = (.8, 10, -16.4)$
Variances	13.2	26	24.8	

We need to create S_d, the matrix of variances and covariances on the difference variables. We already have the variances, but need to compute the covariances. The calculation for the covariance for the first two difference variables is given below, while calculation of the other two is left as an exercise.

$$S_{y1-y2,y2-y3} = \frac{(2-.8)(12-10)+(-4-.8)(8-10)+\ldots+(-2-.8)(14-10)}{4} = -3$$

Recall that in computing the covariance for two variables the scores for the subjects are simply deviated about the means for the variables. The matrix of variances and covariances is

$$S_d = \begin{array}{c} \begin{array}{ccc} y_1-y_2 & y_2-y_3 & y_3-y_4 \end{array} \\ \left[\begin{array}{ccc} 13.2 & -3 & -8.6 \\ -3 & 26 & -19 \\ -8.6 & -19 & 24.8 \end{array} \right] \end{array}$$

covariance for (y_1-y_2) & (y_3-y_4)

covariance for (y_2-y_3) & (y_3-y_4)

Therefore,

$$T^2 = 5 \underbrace{(.8,\ 10,\ -16.4)}_{y_d'} \overbrace{\left[\begin{array}{ccc} .458 & .384 & .453 \\ .384 & .409 & .446 \\ .453 & .446 & .539 \end{array} \right]}^{S_d^{-1}} \overbrace{\begin{pmatrix} .8 \\ 10 \\ -16.4 \end{pmatrix}}^{y_d}$$

$$T^2 = (-16.114, -14.586, -20.086) \begin{pmatrix} .8 \\ 10 \\ -16.4 \end{pmatrix} = 170.659$$

There is an exact F transformation of T^2, which is

$$F = \frac{n-k+1}{(n-1)(k-1)} T^2, \text{ with } (k-1) \text{ and } (n-k+1) \text{ df}$$

Thus, $F = \dfrac{5-4+1}{4(3)} (170.659) = 28.443$, with 3 and 2 df

This is significant at the .05 level, exceeding the critical value of 19.16. The critical value is very large here, since the error degrees of freedom is extremely small (2). We conclude that the drugs are different in effectiveness.

13.4 ASSUMPTIONS IN REPEATED MEASURES ANALYSIS

The three assumptions for a single-group univariate repeated measures analysis are:

1. independence of the observations
2. multivariate normality
3. sphericity (sometimes called circularity)[1]

The first two assumptions are also required for the multivariate approach, but the sphericity assumption is not necessary. The reader should recall from Chapter 6 that a violation of the independence assumption is very serious in independent samples ANOVA and MANOVA, and it is also serious here. Just as ANOVA and MANOVA are fairly robust against violation of multivariate normality, so that also carries over here.

What is the sphericity condition? Recall that in testing the null hypothesis for the previous numerical example, we transformed from the original 4 repeated measures to 3 new variables, which were then used jointly in the multivariate approach. In general, if there are k repeated measures, then we transform to $(k - 1)$ new variables. There are other choices for the $(k - 1)$ variables, than the adjacent differences used in the drug example, which will yield the *same* multivariate test statistic. This follows from the invariance property of the multivariate statistic (Morrison, 1976, p. 145).

Suppose that the $(k - 1)$ new variates selected are orthogonal (uncorrelated) and are scaled such that the sum of squares of the coefficients for each variate is 1. Then we have what is called an *orthonormal* set of variates. If the transformation matrix is denoted by $\mathbf{C}$ and the population covariance matrix for the original repeated measures by Σ, then the sphericity assumption says that the covariance matrix for the new (transformed) variables is a diagonal matrix, with equal variances on the diagonal:

$$\mathbf{C}' \, \Sigma \, \mathbf{C} = \sigma^2 \mathbf{I} = \quad \begin{array}{c} \\ 1 \\ 2 \\ 3 \\ \\ k-1 \end{array} \begin{array}{cccccc} 1 & 2 & 3 & \cdots & k-1 \\ \left[\begin{array}{ccccc} \sigma^2 & 0 & 0 & & 0 \\ 0 & \sigma^2 & 0 & & 0 \\ 0 & 0 & \sigma^2 & & \\ \multicolumn{5}{c}{\cdots\cdots\cdots\cdots} \\ 0 & 0 & & & \sigma^2 \end{array}\right] \end{array}$$

with header **Transformed Variables**

---

[1] For many years it was thought that a stronger condition, called uniformity (compound symmetry) was necessary. The uniformity condition required that the population variances for all treatments be equal and also that all population covariances are equal. However, Huynh and Feldt (1970) and Rounet and Lepine (1970) showed that sphericity is an exact condition for the F test to be valid. Sphericity only requires that the variances of the differences for *all* pairs of repeated measures be equal.

Saying that the off diagonal elements are 0 means that the covariances for all transformed variables are 0, which implies that the correlations are 0.

Box (1954) showed that if the sphericity assumption is not met, then the F ratio is positively biased (we are rejecting falsely too often). In other words, we may set our α level at .05, but may be rejecting falsely 8% or 10% of the time. The extent to which the covariance matrix deviates from sphericity is reflected in a parameter called ϵ (Greenhouse & Geisser, 1959). We give the formula for $\hat{\epsilon}$ in one of the exercises. If sphericity is met, then $\epsilon = 1$, while for the worst possible violation the value of $\epsilon = 1/(k - 1)$, where k is the number of treatments. To adjust for the positive bias Greenhouse and Geisser suggested altering the degrees of freedom from

$(k - 1)$ and $(k - 1)(n - 1)$ to $[1/(k - 1)]\,(k - 1) = 1$
and $[1/(k - 1)]\,(k - 1)(n - 1) = n - 1$

Doing this makes the test *very* conservative, since adjustment is made for the worst possible case, and we don't recommend it. A more reasonable approach is to estimate ϵ. SPSSX MANOVA and SAS GLM both print out $\hat{\epsilon}$. Then adjust the degrees of freedom from

$(k - 1)$ and $(k - 1)(n - 1)$ to $\hat{\epsilon}\,(k - 1)$ and $\hat{\epsilon}\,(k - 1)(n - 1)$.

Results from Collier, Baker, Mandeville, and Hayes (1967) and Stoloff (1967) show that this approach keeps the actual alpha very close to the level of significance.

Huynh and Feldt (1976) found that even multiplying the degrees of freedom by $\hat{\epsilon}$ is somewhat conservative when the true value of ϵ is above about .70. They recommend using the following for those situations:

$$\bar{\epsilon} = \frac{n(i - 1)\hat{\epsilon} - 2}{(i - 1)[(n - 1) - (i - 1)\hat{\epsilon}]}$$

The above Huynh and Feldt epsilon is printed out by both SPSSX MANOVA and SAS GLM.

The Greenhouse-Geisser estimator tends to *underestimate* ϵ, especially when ϵ is close to 1, while the Huynh-Feldt estimator tends to *overestimate* ϵ (Maxwell & Delaney, 1990). Because of these facts, our recommendation is to use the average of the estimators as the estimate of ϵ. If one wishes to be somewhat conservative, then one could always go with the Greenhouse-Geisser estimate.

There are various tests for sphericity, and in particular the Mauchley test (Kirk, 1982, p. 259) is used in Release 4.0 of SPSSX. However, based on the results of Monte Carlo studies (Keselman, Rogan, Mendoza, & Breen, 1980; Rogan, Keselman, & Mendoza, 1979), we don't recommend using these tests.

The above studies showed that the tests are highly sensitive to departures from multivariate normality and from their respective null hypotheses.

13.5 COMPUTER ANALYSIS OF THE DRUG DATA

We now consider the univariate and multivariate repeated measures analysis of the drug data that was worked out in numerical detail earlier in this chapter. The control lines for both SAS GLM and SPSSX MANOVA are presented in Table 13.1. The means and standard deviations for the variables are given in Table 13.2. For this example we focus on selected printout from SPSSX MANOVA, which is presented in Table 13.3. Annotation is given in Table 13.3, explaining parts of the printout. We just make a few comments here. First, note that the multivariate test is significant at the .05 level ($F = 28.41, p < p < .034$), and that the F value agrees, within rounding error, with the F calculated earlier ($F = 28.25$). The unadjusted univariate test is significant at .05, based on 3 and 12 degrees of freedom. However, the *adjusted* univariate F is also easily significant at .05 ($p < .001$), based on 1.81 and 7.26 df.

We wish to note that the above example is not a good situation for the multivariate approach, because sample size is so small (5 subjects). That is, this is not a favorable situation for the multivariate approach in terms of statistical power. We discuss this further later on in the chapter.

Further Comments on the Transformed Variables

We indicated earlier that the multivariate test statistic for repeated measures is based on the $(k - 1)$ transformed variables, not on the original k variables. SPSSX MANOVA creates a specific set of orthonormalized transformed variables on which the multivariate test statistic is based, although the reader should recall that there are many choices for the $(k - 1)$ transformed variables that will yield the *same* multivariate test value. The specific set of orthonormal transformed variables for the drug data example was discussed in Table 13.3. The "univariate" tests following the multivariate test (cf. Table 13.3) are thus tests on the transformed variables, not on the original repeated measures.

In Releases 2.0 and 2.1 of SPSSX, the original measures (Y1, Y2, Y3, and Y4) for the drug data, prefaced by an asterisk, denoted the transformed variables. This was confusing to many users, and starting with Release 2.2, the transformed variables are denoted by T1, T2, etc. (the T denoting transformed variable). Thus, although not displayed in Table 13.3, it is the following *contrasts on the repeated measures* that are being tested for significance:

TABLE 13.1

SAS and SPSSX Control Lines for Single Group Repeated Measures

SAS(Release 6.0)	SPSSX(Release 4.0)
TITLE 'REPEATED MEASURES';	TITLE 'REPEATED MEASURES'
DATA SINGLE;	DATA LIST FREE/ Y1 Y2 Y3 Y4
① INPUT SUBJ TREAT REAC @@;	LIST
CARDS;	BEGIN DATA
② 1 1 30 1 2 28 1 3 16 1 3 34	30 28 16 34 14 18 10 22
2 1 14 2 2 18 2 3 10 2 3 22	24 20 18 30 38 34 20 44
3 1 24 3 2 20 3 3 18 3 1 30	26 28 14 30
4 1 38 4 2 34 4 3 20 4 2 44	END DATA
5 1 26 5 2 28 5 3 14 5 3 30	MANOVA Y1 Y2 Y3 Y4/
PROC PRINT;	④ WSFACTOR = GP(4)/
PROC GLM;	WSDESIGN = GP/
③ CLASS SUBJ TREAT;	ANALYSIS (REPEATED)/
MODEL REAC = SUBJ TREAT;	⑤ PRINT = TRANSFORM CELLINFO
	(MEANS)
	⑥ SIGNIF (AVERF UNIV GG HF)/

① In order to run the single group repeated measures on SAS we treat it as a two way ANOVA, with subjects and treatments as the grouping variables and reaction as the dependent variable.

② The first two numbers of each block of three gives the cell identification. Thus, the first subject in treatment 1 (1 1) had a reaction score of 30, the second subject in treatment 3 (2 3) had a reaction score of 22, etc.

③ In the CLASS statement we list the classification or grouping variables, which here are subject and treatment.

④ The WSFACTOR (within subject factor) and the WSDESIGN (within subject design) are fundemental to running repeated measures analysis on SPSSX MANOVA. In the WSFACTOR subcommand we specify which are the repeated measures, or within subject, factors, and indicate, in parentheses, the number of levels for each repeated measures factor. The WSDESIGN specifies the design on the measures; here it is simply the treatment effect.

⑤ The TRANSFORM part of the PRINT subcommand prints out in columns the uncorrelated, transformed variables that are created by the program for the multivariate approach.

⑥ The UNIV is necessary to obtain the significance tests for each of the transformed variables created by the program for the multivariate approach to repeated measures. The AVERF yields the *unjusted*, overall univariate test for repeated measures. GG and HF are necessary to obtain the corrected significance levels for the univariate approach.

$$T2 = .70711Y1 - .70711Y4$$

$$T3 = - .40825Y1 + .8165Y2 - .40825Y4$$

$$T4 = - .28868Y1 - .28868Y2 + .86603Y3 - .28868Y4$$

13.6 POST HOC PROCEDURES IN REPEATED MEASURES ANALYSIS

As in a one way independent samples ANOVA, if an overall difference is found, one would almost always want to determine which specific treat-

TABLE 13.2
Means and Standard Deviations for
Single Group Repeated Measures

CELL MEANS AND STANDARD DEVIATIONS

VARIABLE .. Y1		
	MEAN	STD. DEV.
FOR ENTIRE SAMPLE	26.40000	8.76356

VARIABLE .. Y2		
	MEAN	STD. DEV.
FOR ENTIRE SAMPLE	25.60000	6.54217

VARIABLE .. Y3		
	MEAN	STD. DEV.
FOR ENTIRE SAMPLE	15.60000	3.84708

VARIABLE .. Y4		
	MEAN	STD. DEV.
FOR ENTIRE SAMPLE	32.00000	8.00000

ments or conditions differed. This entails a post hoc procedure. There are several reasons for preferring pairwise procedures: (1) they are easily interpreted, (2) they are quite meaningful, and (3) some of these procedures are fairly powerful. The Tukey procedure is appropriate in repeated measures designs, provided that the sphericity assumption is met. Recall that for the drug data the sphericity assumption was met (Table 13.5). We now apply the Tukey procedure, setting overall $\alpha = .05$, i.e., we take at most a 5% chance of one or more false rejections. Some readers may have encountered the Tukey procedure in an intermediate statistics course. The studentized range statistic (which we denote by q) is used in the procedure. If there are k samples and the total sample size is N, then any two means are declared significantly different at the .05 level if the following inequality holds:

$$|\bar{y}_i - \bar{y}_j| > q_{.05;k,N-k} \sqrt{\frac{MS_w}{n}},$$

where MS_w is the error term in a one-way ANOVA, and n is the common group size.

The modification of the Tukey for the one sample repeated measures is

$$|\bar{y}_i - \bar{y}_j| > q_{.05;k,(n-1)(k-1)} \sqrt{\frac{MS_{res}}{n}},$$

where $(n-1)(k-1)$ is the error degrees of freedom (replacing $N-k$, the error df for independent samples ANOVA), and MS_{res} is the error term for repeated measures, replacing MS_w (the error term for ANOVA).

TABLE 13.3
Selected SPSSX MANOVA Printout for the Single Group Repeated Measures
Drug Data

Orthonormalized Transformation Matrix (Transposed)

	T1	T2	T3	T4
Y1	.50000	.70711	−.40825	−.28868
Y2	.50000	.00000	.81650	−.28868
Y3	.5000	.00000	.00000	.86603
Y4	.50000	−.70711	−.40825	−.28868

Order of Variables for Analysis   ①

Variates   Covariates

T2
T3
T4

3 Dependent Variables
0 Covariates

Note: TRANSFORMED variables are in the variates column.
      These TRANSFORMED variables correspond to the
      'GP' WITHIN-SUBJECT effect.

Effect . . GP
Multivariate Tests of Significance (S = 1), M = 1/2, N = 0)

Test Name	Value	Exact F	Hypoth. DF	Error DF	Sig. of F
Pillais	.97707	28.41231	3.00	2.00	.034
Hotellings	42.61846	28.41231	3.00	2.00	.034
Wilks	.02293	28.41231	3.00	2.00	.034
Roys	.97707				

Note: F statistics are exact.

Effect . . . GP (Cont.)
Univariate F-tests with (1,4) D. F.

Variable	Hypoth. SS	Error SS	Hypoth. MS	Error MS	F	Sig. of F
T2	78.40000	5.60000	78.40000	1.40000	56.00000	.002
T3 ②	43.20000	32.80000	43.20000	8.20000	5.26829	.083
T4	576.60000	74.40000	576.60000	18.60000	31.00000	.005

Tests involving 'GP' Within-Subject Effect.

Mauchly sphericity test, W =	.18650
Chi-square approx. =	4.57156 with 5 D. F.
Significance =	.470
Greenhouse-Geisser Epsilon =	.60487
Huynh-Feldt Epsilon =	1.00000
Lower-bound Epsilon =	.33333 ③

AVERAGED Tests of Significance that follow multivariate tests are equivalent to univariate or split-plot or mixed-model approach to repeated measures. Epsilons may be used to adjust d.f. for the AVERAGED results.

(Continued)

TABLE 13.3 *(Continued)*

Tests involving 'GP' Within-Subject Effect.

AVERAGED Tests of Significance for Y using UNIQUE sums of squares

Source of Variation	SS	DF	MS	F	Sig of F
WITHIN CELLS	112.80	12	9.40		
(Greenhouse-Geisser)		7.26			
(Huynh-Feldt)		12.00	④		
(Lower bound)		4.00			
GP	698.20	3	232.73	24.76	.000
(Greenhouse-Geisser)		1.81		24.76	.001
(Huynh-Feldt)		3.00		24.76	.000
(Lower bound)		1.00		24.76	.008

① Columns 2 through 4 are the transformed variates created by the program for the purpose of obtaining the multivariate test. These comparisons may or may not be of interest to the researcher. The second transformed variate (column 2) contrasts drug 1 vs drug 4, while column 3 contrasts drug 2 vs the average of drugs 1 and 4. Finally, transformed variate 4 contrasts drug 3 vs the average of drugs 1, 2 and 4.

② These are the tests of significance for the transformed variates. T2 is significant at .05, indicating that drug 1 is different in effectiveness from drug 4. Also, T4 is significant at .05, indicating that drug 3 is different in effectiveness from the average of the other three drugs.

③ Recall that the minimum value for ϵ is $1/(k-1)$. Since $k=4$ here, the minimum value is $1/3 = .33333$.

④ The degrees of freedom for the adjusted univariate test are given by .60487(3) and .60487(12) or 1.81 and 7.26, i.e., they are obtained by multiplying the original df by the value of the Greenhouse-Geisser epsilon.

Tukey Procedure Applied to the Drug Data

The drug means, from Table 13.2, are

	Drugs		
1	2	3	4
26.4	25.6	15.6	32

If we set overall $\alpha = .05$, then the appropriate studentized range value is $q_{.05\ k,(n-1)(k-1)} = q_{.05,4,12} = 4.20$. The error term for the drug data, from Table 13.3 is 9.40, and the number of subjects is $n = 5$. Thus, two drugs will be declared significantly different if

$$|\bar{y}_i - \bar{y}_j| > 4.20 \sqrt{\frac{9.4}{5}} = 5.76$$

Reference to the means above shows that the following pairs of drugs differ: drugs 1 and 3, drugs 2 and 3, drugs 3 and 4, and drugs 2 and 4.

There are several other pairwise post hoc procedures which Maxwell

(1980) discusses. One can employ the Tukey, but with separate error terms. The Roy-Bose intervals can be used. We recommended against the use of these in Chapter 4 because of their extreme conservativeness, and the same applies here. Still another approach is to use multiple *dependent t* tests, but employing the Bonferroni inequality to keep overall α under control. For example, if there are 5 treatments, then there will be 10 paired comparisons. If we wish overall α to equal .05, then we simply do each dependent *t* test at the .05/10 = .005 level of significance. In general, if there are k treatments, then to keep overall α at .05, do each test at the .05/$[k(k - 1)/2]$ level of significance (since for k treatments there are $k(k - 1)/2$ paired comparisons).

Maxwell (1980), using a Monte Carlo approach, has compared the following five pairwise post hoc procedures in terms of how well they control on overall α when the sphericity assumption is violated:

1. Tukey
2. Roy-Bose
3. Bonferroni (multiple dependent *t* tests)
4. Tukey, with separate error terms on $(n - 1)$ df
5. Tukey, with separate error term on $(n - 1)(k - 1)$ df

Results from Maxwell concerning the effect of violation of sphericity on type I error for 3, 4, and 5 treatments and for sample sizes of 8 and 15 are given in Table 13.4. This table shows, as expected, that the Roy-Bose approach is too conservative. It also shows that *the Bonferroni approach keeps the actual α < nominal α in all cases, even when there is a severe violation of the sphericity assumption.* (e.g., for $k = 3$ the min $\epsilon = .50$, and one of the conditions modeled had $\epsilon = .54$). Because of this Maxwell recommended the Bonferroni approach for post hoc pairwise comparisons in repeated measures analysis if the sphericity assumption is violated. Maxwell also studied the power of the five approaches, and found the Tukey to be most powerful. Also, when $\epsilon > .70$ in Table 13.4 the deviation of actual α from nominal α is less than .02 for the Tukey procedure. This, coupled with the fact that the Tukey tends to be most powerful, would lead us to prefer the Tukey when $\epsilon > .70$. When $\epsilon < .70$, however, then we agree with Maxwell that the Bonferroni approach should be used.

13.7 SHOULD WE USE THE UNIVARIATE OR MULTIVARIATE APPROACH?

In terms of controlling on type I error, there is no real basis for preferring the multivariate approach, because use of the modified test (i.e., multi-

TABLE 13.4
Type I Error Rates for Various Pairwise Multiple Comparison Procedures in Repeated Measures Analysis under Different Violations of Sphericity Assumption

Type I Error Rates for $k=3$

Method of Analysis

n	ϵ	* WSD	SCI	BON	SEP1	SEP2
15	1.00	.041	.026	.039	.046	.058
15	0.86	.043	.026	.036	.045	.058
15	0.74	.051	.025	.033	.040	.054
15	0.54	.073	.021	.033	.040	.045
8	1.00	.046	.035	.050	.065	.089
8	0.86	.048	.030	.042	.052	.082
8	0.74	.054	.028	.038	.050	.076
8	0.54	.078	.026	.036	.044	.064

$$\min \epsilon = 1/(3-1) = .50$$

Type I Error Rates for $k=4$

Method of Analysis

n	ϵ	WSD	SCI	BON	SEP1	SEP2
15	1.00	.045	.019	.043	.056	.080
15	1.00	.044	.020	.044	.056	.083
15	0.53	.081	.014	.030	.042	.064
15	0.49	.087	.018	.036	.050	.073
8	1.00	.045	.010	.048	.070	.128
8	1.00	.048	.013	.048	.072	.126
8	0.53	.084	.011	.042	.061	.104
8	0.49	.095	.011	.032	.054	.108

$$\min \epsilon = 1/(4-1) = .333$$

Type I Error Rates for $k=5$

Method of Analysis

n	ϵ	WSD	SCI	BON	SEP1	SEP2
15	1.000	.050	.007	.040	.065	.109
15	0.831	.061	.009	.044	.066	.108
15	0.752	.067	.008	.042	.060	.106
15	0.522	.081	.010	.038	.058	.092
8	1.000	.048	.003	.044	.071	.172
8	0.831	.058	.004	.044	.074	.162
8	0.752	.060	.002	.042	:072	.156
8	0.522	.076	.003	.044	.066	.137

*WSD - Tukey procedure, SCI—Roy-Bose, BON—Bonferroni, SEP1 - Tukey with separate error term and $(n - 1)df$, SEP 2 - Tukey with separate error term and $(n-1)(k-1)df$.

plying the degrees of freedom by $\hat{\varepsilon}$) yields an "honest" error rate. The choice then involves a question of power. If sphericity holds, then the univariate approach is more powerful. When sphericity is violated, however, then the situation is much more complex. Davidson (1972) has stated, "When small but reliable effects are present with the effects being highly variable . . . the multivariate test is far more powerful than the univariate test" (p. 452). And O'Brien and Kaiser (1985), after mentioning several studies that compared the power of the multivariate and modified univariate tests, state, "Even though a limited number of situations have been investigated, this work found that *no procedure is uniformly more powerful or even usually the most powerful*"(p. 319). Maxwell and Delaney (1990, pp 602–604) present a nice extended discussion concerning the relative power of the univariate and multivariate approaches. They note that, "All other things being equal, the multivariate test is relatively less powerful than the mixed model test (the univariate approach) as *n* decreases. . . . This statement implies that if the multivariate test has a power advantage for a certain pattern of population means and covariances, the magnitude of the advantage tends to decrease for smaller *n* and to increase for larger *n*" (p. 602). "Based on the above statement, they further state, "As a rough rule of thumb, we would suggest that the *multivariate approach should probably not be used if n is less than a + 10* (a is number of levels for repeated measures)" (p. 602, emphasis added). I feel that the above statement should be seriously considered, and would generally not advocate use of the multivariate approach if one has only a handful of observations more than the number of repeated measures, because of power considerations. However, I still tend to agree with Barcikowski and Robey (1984) that, given an exploratory study, *both* the adjusted univariate and multivariate tests be routinely used because they may differ in the treatment effects they will discern. In such a study half, the experimentwise level of significance might be set for each test. Thus, if we wish overall alpha to be .05, do each test at the .025 level of significance.

13.8   SAMPLE SIZE FOR POWER = .80 IN SINGLE SAMPLE CASE

Although the classic text on power analysis by Cohen (1977) has power tables for a variety of situations (*t* tests, correlation, chi square tests, differences between correlations, differences between proportions, one-way and factorial ANOVA, etc.), it does *not* provide tables for repeated measures designs. Some work has been done in this area, although as far as I am aware, it is confined to the single sample case. Barcikowski and Robey (1985) have given power tables for various alpha levels for the single group repeated measures design. Their tables assume a common correlation for the repeated measures, which generally will not be tenable (especially in longitudinal studies); however, a later paper by Green (1990) indicates that use of an estimated *average* correlation (from all the correlations among the repeated measures) is fine. Selected results from their work are presented in Table 13.5, which indicates sample size needed for power = .80 for small, medium, and large effect sizes at alpha = .01, .05, .10, and .20 for two through 7 repeated measures. We give two examples to show how to use the table.

Example 1

An investigator has a three treatment design, that is, each of the subjects is exposed to 3 treatments. He uses $r = .80$ as his estimate of the average correlation of the subjects' responses to the 3 treatments. How many subjects will he need for power = .80 at the .05 level, if he anticipates a medium effect size?

Reference to Table 13.5 with correl = .80, effect size = .35, $k = 3$, and $\alpha = .05$, shows that only 14 subjects are needed.

Example 2

An investigator will be carrying out a longitudinal study, measuring the subjects at 5 points in time. She wishes to detect a large effect size at the .10 level of significance, and estimates that the average correlation among the 5 measures will be about .50. How many subjects will she need?

Reference to Table 13.5 with correl = .50, effect size = .57, $k = 5$, and $\alpha = .10$, shows that 11 subjects are needed.

13.9   MULTIVARIATE MATCHED PAIRS ANALYSIS

It was mentioned in Chapter 4 that often in comparing intact groups the subjects are matched or paired on variables known or suspected to be related to performance on the dependent variable(s). This is done so that if a significant difference is found, the investigator can be more confident it was the treatment(s) that "caused" the difference. In Chapter 4 we gave a univariate example, where kindergarteners were compared against non-kindergarteners on first-grade readiness, after they were matched on I.Q., SES, and number of children in the family.

Now consider a multivariate example, i.e., where there are several dependent variables. Kvet (1982) was interested in determining whether excusing elementary school children from regular classroom instruction for the study of instrumental music affected sixth-grade reading, language, and mathematics achievement. These were the three dependent variables. In-

TABLE 13.5
Sample Sizes Needed for Power = .80 in a Single Group Repeated Measures

AVER CORR.	EFFECT SIZE	NUMBER OF REPEATED MEASURES					
		2	3	4	5	6	7
				$\alpha = .01$			
.30	.12	404	324	273	238	214	195
	.30	68	56	49	44	41	39
	.49	28	24	22	21	21	21
.50	.14	298	239	202	177	159	146
	* .35	51	43	38	35	33	31
	.57	22	19	18	18	18	18
.80	.22	123	100	86	76	69	65
	.56	22	20	19	18	18	18
	.89	11	11	11	12	12	13
				$\alpha = .05$			
.30	.12	268	223	192	170	154	141
	.30	45	39	35	32	30	29
	.49	19	17	16	16	16	16
.50	.14	199	165	142	126	114	106
	.35	34	30	27	25	24	23
	.57	14	14	13	13	13	14
.80	.22	82	69	60	54	50	47
	.56	15	14	13	13	14	14
	.89	8	8	8	9	10	10
				$\alpha = .10$			
.30	.12	209	178	154	137	125	116
	.30	35	31	28	26	25	24
	.49	14	14	13	13	13	13
.50	.14	154	131	114	102	93	87
	.35	26	24	22	20	20	19
	.57	11	11	11	11	11	12
.80	.22	64	55	49	44	41	39
	.56	12	11	11	11	12	12
	.89	6	7	7	8	9	9
				$\alpha = .20$			
.30	.12	149	130	114	103	94	87
	.30	25	23	21	20	19	19
	.49	10	10	10	10	11	11
.50	.14	110	96	85	76	70	65
	.35	19	17	16	16	15	15
	.57	8	8	8	9	9	10
.80	.22	45	40	36	33	31	30
	.56	8	8	9	9	10	10
	.89	4	5	6	7	8	8

*These are small, medium, and large effect sizes, and are obtained from the corresponding effect size measures for independent samples ANOVA (i.e., .10, .25, and .40) by dividing by $\sqrt{1 - \text{correl}}$. Thus, for example, $.14 = .10 / \sqrt{1 - .50}$, and $.57 = .40 / \sqrt{1 - .50}$.

strumental and non-instrumental students from 4 public school districts were used in the study. We consider the analysis from just one of the districts. The instrumental and non-instrumental students were matched on the following variables: sex, race, I.Q., cumulative achievement in fifth grade, elementary school attended, sixth-grade classroom teacher, and instrumental music outside the school.

Table 13.6 shows the control lines for running the analysis on SPSSX

TABLE 13.6
Control Lines for Multivariate Matched Pairs Analysis on SPSSX MANOVA
and Selected Output

```
TITLE 'MULTIVARIATE MATCHED PAIRS – KVET DATA'
DATA LIST FREE/READ1 READ2 LANG1 LANG2 MATH1 MATH2
BEGIN DATA
62  67  72  66  67  35    95  87  99  96  82  82
66  66  96  87  74  63    87  91  87  82  98  85
70  74  69  73  85  63    96  99  96  76  74  61
85  99  99  71  91  60    54  60  69  80  66  71
82  83  69  99  63  66    69  60  87  80  69  71
55  61  52  74  55  67    87  87  88  99  95  82
91  99  99  99  99  87    78  72  66  76  52  74
78  62  79  69  54  65    72  58  74  69  59  58
85  99  99  75  66  61
END DATA
COMPUTE READIFF = READ1 – READ2
COMPUTE LANGDIFF = LANG1 – LANG2
COMPUTE MATHDIFF = MATH1 – MATH2
LIST
MANOVA READIFF LANGDIFF MATHDIFF/
    PRINT = CELLINFO(MEANS)/
```

ANALYSIS OF VARIANCE – DESIGN 1
EFFECT . . . CONSTANT
Multivariate Tests of Significance (S = 1, M = 1/2, N = 6)

Test Name	Value	Exact F	Hypoth. DF	Error DF	Sig. of F
Pillais	.16341	.91155	3.00	14.00	.460
Hotellings	.19533	.91155	3.00	14.00	.460 ③
Wilks	.83659	.91155	3.00	14.00	.460
Roys	.16341				

Note . . . F statistics are exact.

EFFECT . . . CONSTANT (Cont.)
Univariate F-tests with (1.16) D. F.

Variable	Hypoth. SS	Error SS	Hypoth. MS	Error MS	F	Sig. of F
READIFF	8.47059	1219.52941	8.47059	76.22059	.11113	.743
LANGDIFF	49.47059	3777.52941	49.47059	236.09559	.20954	.653
MATHDIFF	564.94118	3489.05882	564.94118	218.06618	2.59069	.127

MANOVA. Note that three COMPUTE statements are used to create the three difference variables, on which the multivariate analysis will be done, and that it is these difference variables that are used in the MANOVA line. We are testing whether these 3 difference variables (considered jointly) differ significantly from the 0 vector, that is, whether the differences on all 3 variables are jointly 0.

Again we obtain a T^2 value, like for the single sample multivariate repeated measures analysis, however, the exact F transformation is somewhat different:

$$F = \frac{N - p}{(N - 1)p} \, T^2, \text{ with } p \text{ and } (N - p) \, df$$

where N is the number of matched pairs and p is the number of difference variables.

The printout in Table 13.6 shows that the instrumental group does not differ from the non-instrumental group on the set of three difference variables ($F = .9115$, $p < .46$). Thus, the classroom time taken by the instrumental group did not adversely affect their achievement in these three basic academic areas.

13.10   ONE BETWEEN AND ONE WITHIN FACTOR – A TREND ANALYSIS

We now consider a slightly more complex design, adding a grouping (between) variable. An investigator interested in verbal learning randomly assigns 16 subjects to two treatments. She obtains recall scores on verbal-material after 1, 2, 3, 4, and 5 days. Treatments is the grouping variable. She expects there to be a significant effect over time, but wishes a more focused assessment. She wants to mathematically model the form of the decline in verbal recall. For this, trend analysis is appropriate and in particular orthogonal (uncorrelated) polynomials are in order. If the decline in recall is essentially constant over the days, then a significant linear (straight line) trend, or first degree polynomial, will be found. On the other hand, if the decline in recall is slow over the first two days and then drops sharply over the remaining 3 days, a quadratic trend (part of a parabola), or second degree polynomial, will be found. Finally, if the decline is slow at first, then drops off sharply for the next few days and finally levels off, we will find a cubic trend, or third degree polynomial. We illustrate each of these cases:

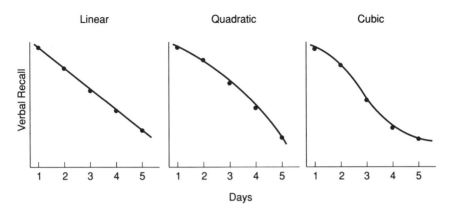

The fact that the polynomials are uncorrelated means that the linear, quadratic, cubic, and quartic components are partitioning distinct (different) parts of the variation in the data.

In Table 13.7 we present the SAS and SPSSX control lines for running the trend analysis on this verbal recall data. In Chapter 5, in discussing planned comparisons, we indicated that several types of contrasts are available in SPSSX MANOVA (Helmert, special, polynomial, etc.), and we also illustrated the use of the Helmert and special contrasts; here the polynomial contrast option is used. Recall these are built into the program, so that all we need do is request them, which is what has been done in the CONTRAST subcommand.

When several groups are involved, as in our verbal recall example, an *additional* assumption is homogeneity of the covariance matrices on the repeated measures for the groups. In our example the group sizes are equal, and in this case a violation of the equal covariance matrices assumption is not serious. That is, the test statistic is robust (with respect to type I error) against a violation of this assumption (cf. Stevens, 1986, Chapter 6). However, if the group sizes are substantially unequal, then a violation is serious, and we indicate in Table 6.5 what should be added to test the assumption.

Table 13.8 gives the means and standard deviations for the two groups on the 5 repeated measures. In Table 13.9 we present selected, annotated output from SPSSX MANOVA for the trend analysis. Results from that table show that the groups do not differ significantly ($F = .04$, $p < .837$) and that there is not a significant group by days interaction ($F = 1.2$, $p < .323$). There is, however, a quite significant days main effect, and in particular, the LINEAR and CUBIC trends are significant at the .05 level ($F = 239.14$, $p < .000$ and $F = 10.51$, $p < .006$ respectively). The linear trend is by far the most pronounced, and a graph of the means for the data

TABLE 13.7
SAS and SPSSX Control Lines for One Between and One Within Repeated
Measures Analysis

SAS (Release 5.16)		SPSSX (Release 2.2)
TITLE '1 BETW & 1 WITHIN';		TITLE '1 BETW & 1 WITHIN'
DATA TREND;		DATA LIST FREE/GPID Y1 Y2 Y3 Y4 Y5
INPUT GPID Y1 Y2 Y3 Y4 Y5;		BEGIN DATA
CARDS;		1 26 20 18 11 10
1 26 20 18 11 10		1 34 35 29 22 23
1 34 35 29 22 23		1 41 37 25 18 15
1 41 37 25 18 15		1 29 28 22 15 13
1 29 28 22 15 13		1 35 34 27 21 17
1 35 34 27 21 17		1 28 22 17 14 10
1 28 22 17 14 10		1 38 34 28 25 22
1 38 34 28 25 22		1 43 37 39 27 25
1 43 37 30 27 25		2 42 38 26 20 15
2 42 38 26 20 15		2 31 27 21 18 13
2 31 27 21 18 13		2 45 40 33 25 18
2 45 40 33 25 18		2 29 25 17 13 8
2 29 25 17 13 8		2 39 32 28 22 18
2 29 32 28 22 18		2 33 30 24 18 7
2 33 30 24 18 7		2 34 30 25 24 23
2 34 30 25 24 23		2 37 31 25 22 20
2 37 31 25 22 20		END DATA
PROC GLM;		MANOVA Y1 TO Y5 BY GPID (1,2)/
CLASS GPID;	③	WSFACTOR = DAY(5)/
MODEL Y1 Y2 Y3 Y4 Y5 = GPID;	④	CONTRAST (DAY) = POLYNOMIAL/
① REPEATED DAYS 5 (1 2 3 4 5)	③	WSDESIGN = DAY/
② POLYNOMIAL/SUMMARY;	⑤	RENAME = MEAN, LINEAR, QUAD,
		CUBIC, QUART/
		PRINT = TRANSFORM CELLINFO(MEANS)
	⑥	SIGNIF(AVERF UNIV)/
		ANALYSIS(REPEATED)/
	⑦	DESIGN = GPID/

① The REPEATED statement is fundamental for running repeated measures designs on SAS. The general form is REPEATED factorname levels (level values) transformation/options; Note that the level values are in parentheses. We are interested in polynomial contrasts on the repeated measures, and so that is what has been requested. Other transformations are available (HELMERT, PROFILE, etc. – see SAS USER's GUIDE:STATISTICS, Version 5, p. 454).

② SUMMARY here produces ANOVA tables for each contrast defined by the within subjects factors.

③ Recall again that the WSFACTOR (within subject factor) and the WSDESIGN (within subject design) subcommands are fundamental for running multivariate repeated measures analysis on SPSSX.

④ If we wish trend analysis on the DAY repeated measure variable, then all we need do is request POLYNOMIAL on the CONTRAST subcommand.

⑤ In this RENAME subcommand we are giving meaningful names to the polynomial contrasts being generated.

⑥ We *must* put UNIV within the SIGNIF keyword for the univariate tests to be printed out in repeated measures designs, and the univariate tests are *the* main thing of interest here, since they indicate whether there is a linear trend, a quadratic trend, etc.

⑦ It is important to realize that with SPSSX MANOVA there is a design subcommand (WSDESIGN) for the within or repeated measures factor(s) and a *separate* DESIGN subcommand for the between (grouping) factor(s).

TABLE 13.8
Means and Standard Deviations for One Between and
One Within Repeated Measures

```
CELL MEANS AND STANDARD DEVIATIONS
VARIABLE . . Y1
        FACTOR            CODE       MEAN      STD. DEV.      N

    GPID                   1        34.250       6.228        8
    GPID                   2        36.250       5.523        8
  FOR ENTIRE SAMPLE                 35.250       5.779       16
---------------------------------------------------------------
VARIABLE . . Y2
        FACTOR            CODE       MEAN      STD. DEV.      N

    GPID                   1        30.875       6.728        8
    GPID                   2        31.625       5.097        8
  FOR ENTIRE SAMPLE                 31.250       5.779       16
---------------------------------------------------------------
VARIABLE . . Y3
        FACTOR            CODE       MEAN      STD. DEV.      N

    GPID                   1        24.500       4.986        8
    GPID                   2        24.875       4.704        8
  FOR ENTIRE SAMPLE                 24.687       4.686       16
---------------------------------------------------------------
VARIABLE . . Y4
        FACTOR            CODE       MEAN      STD. DEV.      N

    GPID                   1        19.125       5.592        8
    GPID                   2        20.250       3.882        8
  FOR ENTIRE SAMPLE                 19.687       4.686       16
---------------------------------------------------------------
VARIABLE . . Y5
        FACTOR            CODE       MEAN      STD. DEV.      N

    GPID                   1        16.875       5.890        8
    GPID                   2        15.250       5.651        8
  FOR ENTIRE SAMPLE                 16.062       5.639       16
```

in Figure 13.1 shows this, although a cubic curve (with a few bends) will fit the data slightly better.

In concluding this example, the following from Myers (1979) is important,

TABLE 13.9
Selected Printout from SPSSX MANOVA for the Trend Analysis on the Verbal Recall Data

ORTHONORMALIZED TRANSFORMATION MATRIX (TRANSPOSED)

	MEAN	LINEAR		QUAD	CUBIC	QUART
Y1	.44721	−.63246		.53452	−.31623	.11952
Y2	.44721	−.31623		−.26726	.63246	−.47809
Y3	.44721	.00000	②	−.53452	.00000	.71714
Y4	.44721	.31623		−.26726	−.63246	−.47809
Y5	.44721	.63246		.53452	.31623	.11952

TESTS OF BETWEEN-SUBJECTS EFFECTS.

TESTS OF SIGNIFICANCE FOR MEAN USING UNIQUE SUMS OF SQUARES

SOURCE OF VARIATION	SS	DF	MS	F	SIG OF F
WITHIN CELLS	1764.67	14	126.05		
CONSTANT	51562.01	1	51562.01	409.07	.000
GPID	5.51	1	5.51	.04 ①	.837

TESTS INVOLVING 'DAYS' WITHIN-SUBJECT EFFECT.

MAUCHLY SPHERICITY TEST, W =	.09678
CHI-SQUARE APPROX. =	28.99686 WITH 9 D. F.
SIGNIFICANCE =	.001

GREENHOUSE-GEISSER EPSILON =	③ .44629
HUYNH-FELDT EPSILON =	.54366
LOWER-BOUND EPSILON =	.25000

EFFECT . . DAYS (CONT.)
UNIVARIATE F-TESTS WITH (1, 14) D. F.

①The group and group by days interaction are not significant, although the unadjusted DAYS main effect is significant at the .05 level.

②The last four columns of numbers are the coefficients for orthogonal polynomials, although they may look strange since each column is scaled such that the sum of the squared coefficients equals 1. Textbooks typically present the coefficients for 5 levels as follows:

Linear	−2	−1	0	1	2
Quadratic	2	−1	−2	−1	2
Cubic	−1	2	0	−2	1
Quartic	1	−4	6	−4	1

Compare, for example, *Fundamentals of Experimental Design*, Myers, 1979, p. 548.

③This value of $\hat{\varepsilon}$ indicates a severe violation of the sphericity assumption, although the adjusted univariate test is still easily significant at the .05 level.

(continued)

476

TABLE 13.9 (Continued)

VARIABLE	HYPOTH. MS	ERROR MS	F	SIG. OF F
LINEAR	3990.00625	16.68482	239.13988	.000
QUAD	6.11161	3.84375	1.59001	.228
CUBIC	24.80625	2.35982	10.51192	.006
QUART	4.25089	1.30446	3.25873	.093

These p values indicate significant linear and cubic trends at the .05 level.

TESTS INVOLVING 'DAYS' WITHIN-SUBJECT EFFECT.

AVERAGED TESTS OF SIGNIFICANCE FOR Y USING UNIQUE SUMS OF SQUARES

SOURCE OF VARIATION	SS	DF	MS	F	SIG OF F
WITHIN CELLS	338.70	56	6.05		
DAYS	4025.17	4	1006.29	166.38	.000
GPID BY DAYS	28.93	4	7.23	1.20	.323

Trend or orthogonal polynomial analyses should never be routinely applied whenever one or more independent variables are quantitative. . . . It is dangerous to identify statistical components freely with psychological processes. It is one thing to postulate a cubic component of A, to test for it, and to find it significant, thus substantiating the theory. It is another matter to assign psychological meaning to a significant component that has not been postulated on a priori grounds. (p. 456)

Now, suppose an investigator is in a part confirmatory and part exploratory study. He is conducting trend analyses on three different variables A, B, and C, and will be doing a total of 10 statistical tests. From previous research he is able to predict a linear trend on variable A, and from theoretical considerations he predicts a quadratic trend for variable C. He wishes to confirm these expectations; this is the confirmatory part of the study. He also wishes to determine if trends of any other nature are significant on variables A, B and C; this is the exploratory part of the study. A simple, but reasonable way, of maintaining control on overall type I error and yet having adequate power (at least for the predicted trends), would be to test each anticipated significant effect at the .05 level and test all other effects at the .005 level. Then, by the Bonferroni inequality, he is assured that

$$\text{overall } \alpha < .05 + .05 + 8(.005) = .14$$

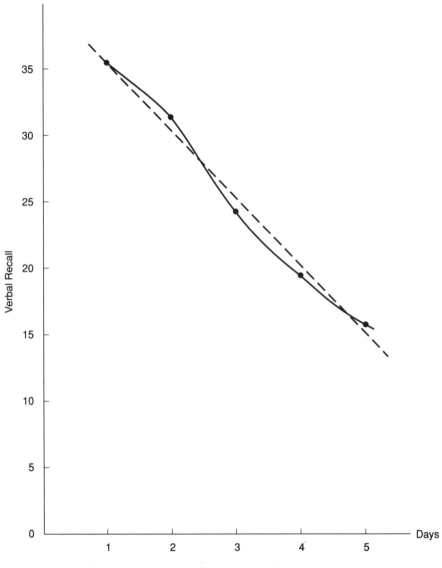

FIG. 13.1.   Linear and Cubic Plots for Verbal Recall Data

13.11   POST HOC PROCEDURES FOR THE ONE
BETWEEN AND ONE WITHIN DESIGN

In the one between and one within, or mixed model, repeated measures design, we have both the assumption of sphericity *and* homogeneity of the covariance matrices for the different levels of the between factor. This combination of assumptions has been called multisample sphericity. Keselman and Keselman (1988) conducted a Monte Carlo study examining how well four post hoc procedures controlled overall alpha under various violations of multisample sphericity. The four procedures were: the Tukey, a modified Tukey employing a nonpooled estimate of error, a Bonferroni t statistic, and a t statistic with a multivariate critical value. These procedures were also used in the Maxwell (1980) study of post hoc procedures for the single group repeated measures design.

Keselman and Keselman set the number of groups at 3 and considered 4 and 8 levels for the within (repeated) factor. They considered both equal and unequal group sizes for the between factor. Recall that ϵ quantifies departure from sphericity, and $\epsilon = 1$ means sphericity, with $1/(k - 1)$ indicating maximum departure from sphericity. They investigated $\epsilon = .75$ (a relatively mild departure) and $\epsilon = .40$ (a severe departure for the 4 level case, given the minimum value there would be .33). Selected results from their study are presented below for the four level within factor case.

		Tukey(pooled)	Bonferroni	Multivariate
$\epsilon = .75$	equal covariance matrices & gp sizes	6.34	3.46	1.70
	unequal covariance matrices, but equal group sizes	7.22	4.32	2.48
	unequal covariance matrices and gp sizes—larger variability with smaller group size	14.78	11.38	7.04
$\epsilon = .40$	equal covariance matrices & gp sizes	11.36	2.38	1.16
	unequal covariance matrices, but equal group sizes	10.08	2.70	1.56
	unequal covariance matrices and gp sizes—larger variability with smaller group size	17.80	6.34	3.94

The group sizes for the values presented above were 13, 10, and 7. The entries in the body of the table are to be compared against an overall alpha of .05.

The above results show that the Bonferroni approach keeps the overall alpha less than .05, provided you do not have *both* unequal group sizes and unequal covariance matrices. If you want to be confident that you will be rejecting falsely no more than your level of significance, then this is the procedure of choice. In my opinion, the Tukey procedure is acceptable for $\epsilon = .75$, as long as there are *equal* group sizes. For the other cases, the error rates for the Tukey are at least double the level of significance, and therefore not acceptable.

Recall that the pooled Tukey procedure for the single group repeated measures design was to reject if

$$|\bar{x}_i - \bar{x}_j| > q_{.05;k,(n-1)(k-1)} \sqrt{MS_{res}/n},$$

where n is the number of subjects, k is the number of levels and MS_{res} is the error term (Equation 1).

For the one between and one within design with J groups and k within levels, we declare two marginal means (means for the repeated measures levels over the J groups) different if

$$|\bar{x}_i - \bar{x}_j| > q_{.05;k,(N-J)(k-1)} \sqrt{MS_{kxs/J}/N} \tag{2}$$

where the mean square is the within subjects error term for the mixed model and N is total number of subjects.

13.12 ONE BETWEEN AND TWO WITHIN FACTORS

We consider both the univariate and multivariate analyses of a one between and two within repeated measures data set from Elashoff (1981). Two groups of subjects were given three different doses of two drugs. There are several different questions of interest in this study. Will the drugs be differentially effective for different groups? Is the effectiveness of the drugs dependent on dose level? Is the effectiveness of the drugs dependent on both dose level and on the group?

The control lines for obtaining the univariate and multivariate analyses on SPSSX MANOVA and on SAS GLM are given in Table 13.10. Because this is a fairly complex design, the schematic layout of it is given here:

	Dose	Drug 1			Drug 2		
		D1	D2	D3	D1	D2	D3
Gp 1	S_1	Y1	Y2	Y3	Y4	Y5	Y6
	S_2						
	:						
	S_8						
Gp 2	S_9						
	:						
	S_{16}						

Note that each subject is measured six times, and these constitute the dependent variables. There is a crossed design on the dose and drug variables. Recall also, as in our first example, that SIGNIF(AVERF) is used in the PRINT subcommand to obtain the univariate tests for SPSSX MANOVA. In Table 13.11 are the means and standard deviations for the variables.

Regarding Table 13.12, it is again very important for the reader to get a feel for the transformed variables, through which the various effects in the design are tested. It is these transformed variables that are grouped and tested for significance by the program. In the previous problem the four repeated measures were transformed into variates measuring linear, quadratic, and cubic trends, and each of these was tested for significance. To obtain some insight into what the transformed variates in Table 13.12 are contrasting, it is essential to refer to the schematic layout of the design in Table 13.10. The contrast variate in column 2 compares the first 3 repeated measures (corresponding to drug 1) against the last 3 repeated measures (corresponding to drug 2). Therefore, this variate is testing the drug main effect. The contrast variates in columns 3 and 4 *in combination* are testing the dose main effect. Why? First, there are three doses, thus only two degrees of freedom, and hence only two variates are needed. The variate in column 3 contrasts the first and fourth repeated measures (corresponding to dose level 1) against the third and sixth repeated measures (corresponding to dose level 3). The contrast variate in column 4 is orthogonal to the variate in column 3, and "soaks up" the remaining variation due to dose level. Notice that this variate does include dose level 2.

Examination of the significance tests in Table 13.12 show that the main effects for group and drug, as well as the group × drug interaction, are all significant at the .05 level. Let us examine what caused all this significance

TABLE 13.10
SAS and SPSSX Control Lines for One Between and Two Within
Repeated Measures Analysis

SAS (Release 5.16)	SPSSX (Release 2.2)
TITLE ' ELASHOFF DATA';	TITLE ' ELASHOFF DATA '
DATA ELAS;	DATA LIST FREE/GP Y1 Y2 Y3 Y4
INPUT GP Y1 Y2 Y3 Y4 Y5 Y6;	Y5 Y6
CARDS;	LIST
1 19 22 28 16 26 22	BEGIN DATA
1 11 19 30 12 18 28	1 19 22 28 16 26 22
1 20 24 24 24 22 29	1 11 19 30 12 18 28
1 21 25 25 15 10 26	1 20 24 24 24 22 29
1 18 24 29 19 26 28	1 21 25 25 15 10 26
1 17 23 28 15 23 22	1 18 24 29 19 26 28
1 20 23 23 26 21 28	1 17 23 28 15 23 22
1 14 20 29 25 29 29	1 20 23 23 26 21 28
2 16 20 24 30 34 36	1 14 20 29 25 29 29
2 26 26 26 24 30 32	2 16 20 24 30 34 36
2 22 27 23 33 36 45	2 26 26 26 24 30 32
2 16 18 29 27 26 34	2 22 27 23 33 36 45
2 19 21 20 22 22 21	2 16 18 29 27 26 34
2 20 25 25 29 29 33	2 19 21 20 22 22 21
2 21 22 23 27 26 35	2 20 25 25 29 29 33
2 17 20 22 23 26 28	2 21 22 23 27 26 35
PROC GLM;	2 17 20 22 23 26 28
CLASS GP;	END DATA
① MODEL Y1 Y2 Y3 Y4 Y5 Y6=GP;	MANOVA Y1 TO Y6 BY GP (1, 2) /
② REPEATED DRUG 2, DOSE 3;	③ WSFACTOR=DRUG (2), DOSE (3) /
	WSDESIGN/
	PRINT=TRANSFORM
	CELLINFO (MEANS)
	SIGNIF (AVERF)
	④ HOMOGENEITY (BOXM) /
	ANALYSIS (REPEATED) /
	DESIGN/

①Recall that in the MODEL statement the dependent variables, the repeated measures here, go on the left side and the classification or grouping variable(s) go on the right side.

②When there is more than one repeated measures factor, they *must* be separated by a comma, and the product of the levels of all factors must equal the number of dependent variables in the MODEL statement.

③The number of levels for each repeated measures factor is given in parentheses.

④This part of the PRINT subcommand requests the Box test, which is used to check the equality of covariance matrices assumption.

TABLE 13.11
Means and Standard Deviations for One Between and Two
Within Repeated Measures

CELL MEANS AND STANDARD DEVIATIONS

VARIABLE .. Y1

FACTOR	CODE	MEAN	STD. DEV.
GPID	1	17.50000	3.42261
GPID	2	19.62500	3.42000
FOR ENTIRE SAMPLE		18.56250	3.48270

VARIABLE .. Y2

FACTOR	CODE	MEAN	STD. DEV.
GPID	1	22.50000	2.07020
GPID	2	22.37500	3.24863
FOR ENTIRE SAMPLE		22.43750	2.63233

VARIABLE .. Y3

FACTOR	CODE	MEAN	STD. DEV.
GPID	1	27.00000	2.61861
GPID	2	24.00000	2.72554
FOR ENTIRE SAMPLE		25.50000	3.01109

VARIABLE .. Y4

FACTOR	CODE	MEAN	STD. DEV.
GPID	1	19.00000	5.34522
GPID	2	26.87500	3.75832
FOR ENTIRE SAMPLE		22.93750	6.03842

VARIABLE .. Y5

FACTOR	CODE	MEAN	STD. DEV.
GPID	1	21.87500	5.89037
GPID	2	28.62500	4.62717
FOR ENTIRE SAMPLE		25.25000	6.19139

VARIABLE .. Y6

FACTOR	CODE	MEAN	STD. DEV.
GPID	1	26.50000	2.92770
GPID	2	33.00000	6.84523
FOR ENTIRE SAMPLE		29.75000	6.09371

TABLE 13.12
Transformation Matrix and Group and Group × Drug Tests of
Significance

ORTHONORMALIZED TRANSFORMATION MATRIX (TRANSPOSED)

	1	2	3	4	5	6
1	.40825	.40825	.50000	−.28868	.50000	−.28868
2	.40825	.40825	.00000	.57735	.00000	.57735
3	.40825	.40825	−.50000	−.28868	−.50000	−.28868
4	.40825	−.40825	.50000	−.28868	−.50000	.28868
5	.40825	−.40825	.00000	.57735	.00000	−.57735
6	.40825	−.40825	−.50000	−.28868	.50000	.28868

Contrast variate for testing the drug main effect.

Contrast variates for testing the dose main effect.

Contrast variates for testing the drug × dose interaction.

TESTS OF SIGNIFICANCE FOR Y1 USING SEQUENTIAL SUMS OF SQUARES

SOURCE OF VARIATION	SUM OF SQUARES	DF	MEAN SQUARE	F	SIG. OF F
WITHIN CELLS	532.97917	14	38.06994		
CONSTANT	55632.51042	1	55632.51042	1461.32381	.000
GPID	270.01042	1	270.01042	7.09248	.019

This indicates the group main effect is significant at .05 level.

TESTS OF SIGNIFICANCE FOR Y2 USING SEQUENTIAL SUMS OF SQUARES

SOURCE OF VARIATION	SUM OF SQUARES	DF	MEAN SQUARE	F	SIG. OF F
WITHIN CELLS	375.64583	14	26.83185		
DRUG	348.84375	1	348.84375	13.00111	.003
GPID BY DRUG	326.34375	1	326.34375	12.16255	.004

These indicate that both the drug main effect and the group × drug interaction are significant at the .05 level.

so far. We take the means from Table 13.11 and insert them into the design yielding:

		DRUG					
		1			2		
	DOSE	1	2	3	1	2	3
GROUP 1		17.50	22.50	27.0	19.0	21.88	26.50
GROUP 2		19.63	22.38	24.0	26.88	28.63	33.0

Now, collapsing on dose, the group × drug design means are obtained:

	DRUG	
	1	2
GROUP 1	22.33	22.46
GROUP 2	22.00	29.50

The mean in cell 11 (22.33) is simply the average of 17.5, 22.5, and 27, while the mean in cell 12 (22.46) is the average of 19, 21.88, and 26.5, etc. It is now apparent that the outlier cell mean of 29.5 is what "caused" all the significance. For some reason drug 2 was not as effective with group 2 in inhibiting the response. We have indicated previously, especially in connection with multiple regression, how influential an individual subject's score can be in affecting the results. This example shows the same type of thing, only now the outlier is a mean.

In Table 13.13 we present the multivariate and univariate tests for the dose main effect and group × dose interaction effects. As indicated there, both the univariate and multivariate tests show the dose main effect significant at the .05 level, while both show the interaction effect is notsignificant. Table 13.14 gives the multivariate and univariate tests for the drug × dose and group × drug × dose interactions. Both the multivariate and univariate tests show that neither interaction is significant at the .05 level.

TABLE 13.13
Multivariate and Univarate Tests for Dose Main Effect and Group ×
Dose Interaction Effect

EFFECT .. DOSE

MULTIVARIATE TESTS OF SIGNIFICANCE (S = 1, M = 0, N = 5 1/2)

TEST NAME	VALUE	APPROX. F	HYPOTH. DF	ERROR DF	SIG. OF F
PILLAIS	.79534	25.26075	2.00	13.00	.000
HOTELLINGS	3.88627	25.26075	2.00	13.00	.000
WILKS	.20466	25.26075	2.00	13.00	.000
ROYS	.79534				

EFFECT .. GPID BY DOSE

MULTIVARIATE TESTS OF SIGNIFICANCE (S = 1, M = 0, N = 5 1/2)

TEST NAME	VALUE	APPROX. F	HYPOTH. DF	ERROR DF	SIG. OF F
PILLAIS	.18262	1.45223	2.00	13.00	.270
HOTELLINGS	.22342	1.45223	2.00	13.00	.270
WILKS	.81738	1.45223	2.00	13.00	.270
ROYS	.18262				

Univariate Tests

AVERAGED TESTS OF SIGNIFICANCE FOR Y USING SEQUENTIAL SUMS OF SQUARES

SOURCE OF VARIATION	SUM OF SQUARES	DF	MEAN SQUARE	F	SIG. OF F
WITHIN CELLS	290.95833	28	10.39137		
DOSE	758.77083	2	379.38542	36.50967	.000 ①
GPID BY DOSE	42.27083	2	21.13542	2.03394	.150

①These univariate tests of the dose main effect and group × dose interaction indicate that only the dose main effect is significant at the .05 level.
   The multivariate tests, given above, yield the same conclusions.

TABLE 13.14
Multivariate and Univariate Tests for Drug × Dose and Group × Drug × Dose Interaction

EFFECT .. GPID BY DRUG BY DOSE

MULTIVARIATE TESTS OF SIGNIFICANCE (S = 1, M = 0, N = 5 1/2)

TEST NAME	VALUE	APPROX. F	HYPOTH. DF	ERROR DF	SIG. OF F
PILLAIS	.14314	1.08583	2.00	13.00	.366
HOTELLINGS	.16705	1.08583	2.00	13.00	.366
WILKS	.85686	1.08583	2.00	13.00	.366
ROYS	.14314				

EFFECT .. DRUG BY DOSE

MULTIVARIATE TESTS OF SIGNIFICANCE (S = 1, M = 0, N = 5 1/2)

TEST NAME	VALUE	APPROX. F	HYPOTH. DF	ERROR DF	SIG. OF F
PILLAIS	.12604	.93739	2.00	13.00	.417
HOTELLINGS	.14421	.93739	2.00	13.00	.417
WILKS	.87396	.93739	2.00	13.00	.417
ROYS	.12604				

Univariate Tests

AVERAGED TESTS OF SIGNIFICANCE FOR Y USING SEQUENTIAL SUMS OF SQUARES

SOURCE OF VARIATION	SUM OF SQUARES	DF	MEAN SQUARE	F	SIG. OF F
WITHIN CELLS	247.79167	28	8.84970		
DRUG BY DOSE	12.06250	2	6.03125	.68152	.514
GPID BY DRUG BY DOSE	14.81250	2	7.40625	.83689	.444

Both the multivariate and univariate tests indicate that neither the drug × dose or group × drug × dose interaction effects are significant at the .05 level, since the probabilities are >.05.

Finally, Table 13.15 presents only the univariate results from SAS GLM. Actually, the univariate tests would be preferred here because both Greenhouse-Geisser epsilons are > .70.

13.13 TWO BETWEEN AND ONE WITHIN FACTORS

To illustrate how to run a two between and one within factor repeated measures design we consider hypothetical data from a study comparing the relative efficacy of a behavior modification approach to dieting versus a behavior modification + exercise approach (combination treatment) on weight loss for a group of overweight women. There is also a control group in this study. First, six each of women between 20 and 30 years old are randomly assigned to one of the three groups. Then, six each of women between 30 to 40 years old are randomly assigned to one of the three groups. The investigator wishes to determine whether age might moderate the effectiveness of the diet approach. Weight loss is measured two months, four months, and six months after the program begins. Schematically, the design is as follows:

		WGTLOSS1	WGTLOSS2	WGTLOSS3
GROUP	AGE			
CONTROL	20–30 YRS			
CONTROL	30–40 YRS			
BEH. MOD	20–30 YRS			
BEH. MOD.	30–40 YRS			
BEH. MOD + EXER.	20–30 YRS			
BEH. MOD + EXER.	30–40 YRS			

Treatment and age are the two grouping or between variables and time (over which the weight loss is measured) is the within variable. The SPSSX MANOVA control lines for running the analysis are given in Table 13.16.

Selected results from SPSSX MANOVA are given in Table 13.17. Looking first at the between subject effects at the top of the table, we see that only the diet main effect is significant at the .05 level ($F = 4.30$, $p < .023$).

Next, at the bottom of the printout, under

TESTS INVOLVING 'WGTLOSS' WITHIN SUBJECT EFFECT

we find that both wgtloss ($F = 84.57$, $p = .000$) and the diet by wgtloss interaction ($F = 4.88$, $p = .002$) are significant. Remember that these AVERAGED TESTS OF SIGNIFICANCE, as they are called by SPSSX, are in fact the univariate approach to repeated measures. SPSSX MANOVA does not print out by default the adjusted univariate tests (although they may be obtained by simply inserting GG AND HF in the SIGNIF part of the PRINT subcommand), but do note in the printout that "epsilons may be used to adjust degrees of freedom for the averaged results." In this case we needn't be concerned about adjusting because the Greenhouse-Geisser epsilon of .7749 and even more so, the Huynh-Feldt epsilon of .94883 indicate that sphericity is not a problem here. In this regard, note that the Mauchley test for sphericity is "highly" significant ($p = .008$) and seems to strongly indicate that sphericity is not tenable; however, on the basis of Monte Carlo studies, we recommend against using such statistical tests of sphericity.

TABLE 13.15
Univariate Analyses from SAS GLM for One Between and Two Within

UNIVARIATE TESTS OF HYPOTHESES FOR WITHIN SUBJECT EFFECTS

SOURCE	DF	TYPE III SS	MEAN SQUARE	F VALUE	PR > F
DRUG	1	348.84375000	348.84375000	13.00	0.0029
DRUG*GPID	1	326.34375000	326.34375000	12.16 ③	0.0036
ERROR (DRUG)	14	375.64583333 ⑤	26.83184524		

SOURCE	DF	TYPE III SS	MEAN SQUARE	F VALUE	PR > F
DOSE	2	758.77083333	379.38541667	36.51	0.0001
DOSE*GPID	2	42.27083333	21.13541667	2.03 ④	0.1497
ERROR (DOSE)	28	290.95833333 ⑤	10.39136905		

GREENHOUSE-GEISSER EPSILON = 0.8787
HUYNH-FELDT EPSILON = 1.0667

SOURCE	DF	TYPE III SS	MEAN SQUARE	F VALUE	PR > F
DRUG*DOSE	2	12.06250000	6.03125000	0.68	0.5140
DRUG*DOSE*GPID	2	14.81250000	7.40625000	0.84	0.4436
ERROR (DRUG*DOSE)	28	247.79166667 ⑤	8.84970238		

GREENHOUSE-GEISSER EPSILON = 0.7297 ①
HUYNH-FELDT EPSILON = 0.8513

TESTS OF HYPOTHESES FOR BETWEEN SUBJECTS EFFECTS

SOURCE	DF	TYPE III SS	MEAN SQUARE	F VALUE	PR > F
GPID	1	270.01041667	270.01041667	7.09	② 0.0185
ERROR	14	532.97916667 ⑤	38.06994048		

①Since both ê's are > .70, the univariate approach is preferred, since the type I error rate is controlled and it is more powerful than the multivariate approach.

②Groups differ significantly at the .05 level, since .0185 < .05.

③ & ④The drug main effect and drug by group interaction are significant at the .05 level, while the dose main effect is also significant at the .05 level.

⑤Note that 4 different error terms are involved in this design; an additional complication with complex repeated measures designs. The error terms are boxed.

In interpreting the significant effects, we construct from the means on the printout, the cell means for DIETS BY WGTLOSS combined over the age groups:

		WGTLOSS			
		1	2	3	ROW MEANS
	1	4.50	3.33	2.083	3.304
DIETS	2	5.33	3.917	2.250	3.832
	3	6.00	5.917	2.250	4.722
COLUMN MEANS		5.278	4.389	2.194	

Graphing the cell means shows rather nicely why the interaction effect was obtained

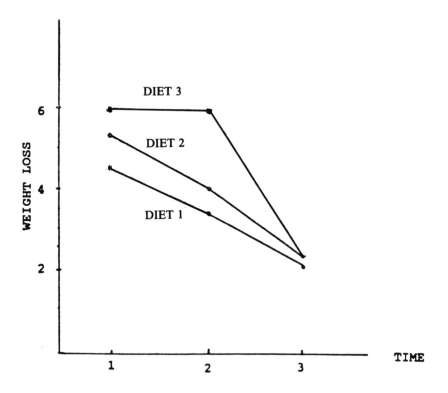

Recall that graphically an interaction is evidenced by nonparallel lines. In the above graph one can see that the profiles for diets 1 and 2 are essentially parallel; however, the profile for diet 3 is definitely not parallel with profiles for diets 1 and 2. And, in particular, it is the weight loss at time 2 that is making the profile for diet 3 distinctly non-parallel.

Table 13.16
Control Lines for a Two Between and One Within Design on SPSSX MANOVA

```
TITLE 'TWO BETWEEN AND ONE WITHIN DESIGN'
DATA LIST FREE/DIET AGE WGTLOSS1 WGTLOSS2 WGTLOSS3
LIST
BEGIN DATA
1 1 4 3 3   1 1 4 4 3   1 1 4 3 1   1 1 3 2 1
1 1 5 3 2   1 1 6 5 4   1 2 6 5 4   1 2 5 4 1
1 2 3 3 2   1 2 5 4 1   1 2 4 2 2   1 2 5 2 1
2 1 6 3 2   2 1 5 4 1   2 1 7 6 3   2 1 6 4 2
2 1 3 2 1   2 1 5 5 4   2 2 4 3 1   2 2 4 2 1
2 2 6 5 3   2 2 7 6 4   2 2 4 3 2   2 2 7 4 3
3 1 8 4 2   3 1 3 6 3   3 1 7 7 4   3 1 4 7 1
3 1 9 7 3   3 1 2 4 1   3 2 3 5 1   3 2 6 5 2
3 2 6 6 3   3 2 9 5 2   3 2 7 9 4   3 2 8 6 1
END DATA
MANOVA WGTLOSS1 TO WGTLOSS3 BY DIET(1,3) AGE(1,2)/
  WSFACTOR = WGTLOSS(3)/
  WSDESIGN = WGTLOSS/
  PRINT = CELLINFO(MEANS) SIGNIF(UNIV,AVERF)
  HOMOGENEITY(BOXM)/
  DESIGN/
```

The main effect for diet is telling us that the population row means are not equal, and from the above sample row means with the Tukey procedure, we conclude that diet 3 is significantly more effective than diet 1 over time. The weightloss main effect indicates that the population column means are not equal. The sample column means suggest, and the Tukey procedure for repeated measures confirms, that there is significantly greater weight loss after two and four months than there is after 6 months.

13.14   TWO BETWEEN AND TWO WITHIN FACTORS

This is a very complex design, an example of which appears in Bock (1975, pp. 483–484). The data was from a study by Morter, who was concerned about the comparability of the first and second responses on the form definiteness and form appropriateness variables of the Holtzman Inkblot procedure for a pre-adolescent group of subjects. The two between variables were grade level (4 and 7) and I. Q. (high and low); thus there was a crossed design on the subjects. The two within variables were form and time, with the design being crossed on the measures. The schematic layout for the design is given at the bottom of Table 13.18, which also gives the control lines for running the analysis on SPSSX MANOVA, along with the data.

It may be quite helpful for the reader to compare the control lines for this

Table 13.17
Selected Printout From SPSSX MANOVA for Two Between and One Within
Repeated Measures Design

TESTS OF BETWEEN-SUBJECTS EFFECTS.
TESTS OF SIGNIFICANCE FOR T1 USING UNIQUE SUMS OF SQUARES

SOURCE OF VARIATION	SS	DF	MS	F	SIG of F
WITHIN CELLS	128.83	30	4.29		
CONSTANT	1688.23	1	1688.23	393.12	.000
DIET	36.91	2	18.45	4.30	.023
AGE	.23	1	.23	.05	.818
DIET BY AGE	.80	2	.40	.09	.912

TESTS INVOLVING 'WGTLOSS' WITHIN-SUBJECT EFFECT.

MAUCHLY SPHERICITY TEST, W =	.71381
CHI-SQUARE APPROX. =	9.77706 WITH 2 D. F.
SIGNIFICANCE =	.008
GREENHOUSE-GEISSER EPSILON =	.77749
HUYNH-FELDT EPSILON =	.94883
LOWER-BOUND EPSILON	.50000

AVERAGE TESTS OF SIGNIFICANCE THAT FOLLOW MULTIVARIATE TESTS
ARE EQUIVALENT TO UNIVARIATE OR SPLIT-PLOT OR MIXED-MODEL
APPROACH TO REPEATED MEASURES.
EPSILONS MAY BE USED TO ADJUST D.F. FOR THE AVERAGE RESULTS.

TESTS INVOLVING 'WGTLOSS' WITHIN-SUBJECT EFFECT.
AVERAGED TESTS OF SIGNIFICANCE FOR WGTLOSS USING UNIQUE SUMS OF
SQUARES

SOURCE OF VARIATION	SS	DF	MS	F	SIG OF F
WITHIN CELLS	64.33	60	1.07		
WGTLOSS	181.35	2	90.68	84.57	.000
DIET BY WGTLOSS	20.93	4	5.23	4.88	.002
AGE BY WGTLOSS	1.80	2	.90	.84	.438
DIET BY AGE BY WGTLOSS	1.59	4	.40	.37	.828

example with those for the one between and two within example in Table
13.10, as they are quite similar. The main difference here is that there is an
additional between variable, hence an additional factor after the keyword
BY in the MANOVA command and three between effects in the DESIGN
subcommand. The reader is referred to Bock (1975) for an interpretation of
the results.

13.15 TOTALLY WITHIN DESIGNS

There are research situations where the *same* subjects are measured under
various treatment combinations, that is, where the same subjects are in each
cell of the design. This may be particularly the case when not many subjects
are available. We consider three examples to illustrate.

TABLE 13.18
Control Lines for Two Between and Two Within
Repeated Measures on SPSSX Manova

```
TITLE ' 2 BETWEEN & 2 WITHIN REPEATED MEASURES '
DATA LIST FREE/ GRADE IQ FD1 FD2 FA1 FA2
LIST
BEGIN DATA
 1  1   2   1   0   2  1  1  -7  -2  -2  -5  1  1  -3  -1  -3  -1
 1  1   1   1   0  -3  1  1   1  -1  -4  -2  1  1  -7   1  -4  -3
 1  2   0  -4  -9  -7  1  2  -1  -9  -9  -4  1  2  -6  -6   3  -4
 1  2  -2  -4  -4  -5  1  2  -2  -1  -3  -3  1  2  -9  -9  -3   1
 2  1   3   4   2  -3  2  1  -1  -1  -3  -3  2  1   2   2   2   0
 2  1   2   0  -2   0  2  1   0  -1   2   2  2  1   3   3  -4  -2
 2  1  -1   2   2  -1  2  1  -3  -2   3  -2
 2  2  -3  -2   5   2  2  2   2   3  -2  -3  2  2   2   4   1   3
 2  2   3   2  -5  -5  2  2  -4  -3  -3  -3  2  2   6   4  -9  -9
 2  2   2   1  -3   0  2  2  -1  -4  -2   0  2  2  -2  -1   2  -2
 2  2  -2  -4  -1   0
END DATA
```
① MANOVA FD1 TO FA2 BY GRADE(1,2) IQ(1,2)/
    WSFACTOR = FORM(2),TIME(2)/
    WSDESIGN = FORM,TIME,FORM BY TIME/
    PRINT = TRANSFORM CELLINFO(MEANS)
②   HOMOGENEITY(BOXM) SIGNIF(AVERF)/
②   DESIGN = GRADE,IQ, GRADE BY IQ/

---

① Below we give the experimental design schematically:

	FORM	FD		FA	
	TIME	1	2	1	2
GRADE 4	HI IQ				
	LOW IQ				
GRADE 7	HI IQ				
	LOW IQ				

② Again, as for the examples in Tables 13.7 and 13.11, there is a within S's design subcommand for the repeated measures factors, and a separate DESIGN subcommand for the between (grouping) factors. If we assume a full factorial model, as would be true in exploratory research, then these subcommands can be abbreviated to WSDESIGN/ and DESIGN/.

Example 1

A researcher in child development is interested in observing the same group of preschool children (all 4 years of age) in two situations at two different times (morning and afternoon) of the day. She is concerned with the extent of their social interaction, and will measure this by having two observers independently rate the amount of social interaction. The average of the two ratings will serve as the dependent variable. The within factors here are situation and time of day. There are 4 scores for each child: social interaction in situation 1 in the morning and afternoon, and social interaction in situation in the morning and afternoon. We denote the four scores by Y1, Y2, Y3, and Y4.

Such a totally within repeated measures design is easily setup on SPSSX MANOVA. The control lines are given below:

```
TITLE 'TWO WITHIN DESIGN'
DATA LIST FREE/Y1 Y2 Y3 Y4
BEGIN DATA

    DATA LINES

END DATA
MANOVA Y1 TO Y4/
   WSFACTOR = SIT(2),TIME(2)/
   WSDESIGN/
   PRINT = TRANSFORM CELLINFO(MEANS)/
   ANALYSIS(REPEATED)/
```

Note in this example that *only univariate* tests will be printed out by SPSSX for all three effects. This is because there is only one degree of freedom for each effect, and hence only one transformed variable for each effect.

Example 2

An investigator wants to examine automobile driving behavior as a function of three variables: time of day—morning and night; type of course—serpentine track, city streets and highway; and size of car—small and large. The dependent variable is the number of steering errors. There are 12 different treatment conditions in this study. To run an independent samples three-way ANOVA, he will need at least 10 subjects per cell for adequate power to detect interaction effects. This would mean a total of at least 120 drivers, which is probably not going to be practical. On the other hand, he may be able to quite easily obtain 15 drivers, and have each of them drive under all 12 conditions. If this is done, then we have a three within repeated measures design.

Example 3

A social psychologist is interested in determining how self reported anxiety level for 35–45 year old men varies as a function of situation, who they are with, and how many people are involved. A questionnaire will be administered to 20 such men, asking them to rate their anxiety level (on a Likert scale from 1 to 7) in 3 situations (going to the theater, going to a football game, and going to a dinner party), with primarily friends and primarily strangers, and with a total of 6 people and with 12 people. Thus, the men will be reporting anxiety for 12 different contexts. This is a three within, crossed repeated measures design, where situation (3 levels) is crossed with nature of group (2 levels) and with number in group (2 levels).

13.16 PLANNED COMPARISONS IN REPEATED MEASURES DESIGNS

Planned comparisons can also be easily setup on SPSSX MANOVA for repeated measures designs, although the WSFACTOR (within subject factor) subcommand must be included to indicate that the contrasts are being done on a repeated measures variable. To illustrate, we consider the setup of Helmert contrasts on a single group repeated measures design with data again from Bock (1975). The study involved the effect of 3 drugs on the duration of sleep of 10 mental patients. The drugs were given orally on alternate evenings, and the hours of sleep were compared with an intervening control night. Each of the drugs was tested a number of times with each patient. Thus, there are four levels for treatment, the control condition, and the three drugs. The first drug (level 2) was of a different type from the other two, which were of a similar type. Therefore, Helmert contrasts were appropriate. The control lines for running the contrasts, along with the significance tests for the contrasts, are given in Table 13.19.

There are two important additional points to be made regarding planned comparisons with repeated measures designs. First, SPSSX MANOVA requires that the comparisons be orthogonal for within subject factors. *If a non-orthogonal set of contrasts is input, then MANOVA will orthogonalize them (SPSSX User's Guide,* 3rd Ed., 1988, p. 609)* Secondly, it is *very important* that *separate* error terms are used for testing each of the planned comparisons for significance. Boik (1981) has shown that for even a very slight deviation from sphericity ($\epsilon = .90$), the use of a pooled error term can result in a type I error rate quite different from the level of significance. For $\epsilon = .90$ Boik showed, if testing at $\alpha = .05$, that the actual alpha for single degree of freedom contrasts ranged from .012 to .097. In some cases the pooled error term will underestimate the amount of error while for other

---

*There is a way to get around this problem. See Appendix C.

TABLE 13.19
Control Lines for Helmert Contrasts in a Single Group Repeated
Measures Design and Tests of Significance

TITLE ' HELMERT CONTRASTS FOR REPEATED MEASURES '
DATA LIST FREE/Y1 Y2 Y3 Y4
LIST
BEGIN DATA
.6 1.3 2.5 2.1   3 1.4 3.8 4.4   4.7 4.5 5.8 4.7
6.2 6.1 6.1 6.7   3.2 6.6 7.6 8.3   2.5 6.2 8 8.2
2.8 3.6 4.4 4.3   1.1 1.1 5.7 5.8   2.9 4.9 6.3 6.4
5.5 4.3 5.6 4.8
END DATA
MANOVA Y1 TO Y4/
① WSFACTOR = DRUGS(4)/
  CONTRAST(DRUGS) = HELMERT/
② WSDESIGN = DRUGS/
③ RENAME = MEAN,HELMERT1,HELMERT2,HELMERT3/
  PRINT = CELLINFO(MEANS) TRANSFORM/
  ANALYSIS(REPEATED)/

ORTHONORMALIZED TRANSFORMATION MATRIX (TRANSPOSED)

	1	2	3	4
1	.50000	.86603	.00000	.00000
2	.50000	−.28868	.81650	.00000
3	.50000	−.28868	−.40825	.70711
4	.50000	−.28868	−.40825	−.70711

UNIVARIATE F-TESTS WITH (1,9) D. F.

VARIABLE	HYPOTH. SS	HYPOTH. MS	ERROR MS	F		SIG. OF F
HELMERT1	24.29999	24.29999	2.76889	8.77608		.016
HELMERT2	16.53750	16.53750	1.08639	15.22245	④	.004
HELMERT3	.00050	.00050	.18272	.00274		.959

①②Recall that the WSFACTOR (within subjects factor) and WSDESIGN (within subjects design) subcommands must be included to indicate a repeated measures design; compare Table 13.2.

③We rename the variates being tested for significance for ease of reading of the output.

④These results indicate that the first two Helmert contrasts, defined by columns 2 and 3 in the transformation matrix above, are significant at the .05 level.

---

contrasts the error will be overestimated, resulting in a conservative test. Fortunately, in SPSSX MANOVA the error terms are separate for the contrasts (cf. Table 13.19). As O'Brien and Kaiser (1985) note, "The MANOVA approach handles sets of contrasts in such a way that each contrast in the set remains linked with just its specific error term. As a result, we avoid all problems associated with general (average) error terms" (p. 319).

13.17   PROFILE ANALYSIS

In profile analysis the interest is in comparing the performance of two or more groups on a battery of test scores (interest, achievement, personality). It is assumed that the tests are scaled similarly, or that they are commensurable. In profile analysis there are three questions to be asked of the data in the following order:

1. Are the profiles parallel? If the answer to this were yes for two groups, it would imply that one group scored uniformly better than the other on all variables.
2. If the profiles are parallel, then are they coincident? In other words, did the groups score the same on each variable?
3. If the profiles are coincident, then are the profiles level? In other words, are the means on all variables equal to the same constant.

Below we present *hypothetical* examples of parallel and nonparallel profiles: (the variables represent achievement in content areas)

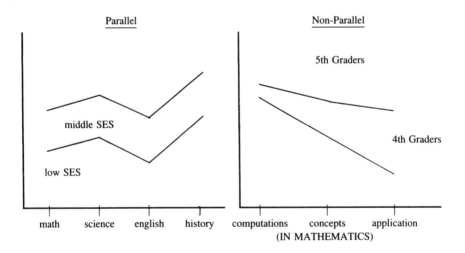

If the profiles are not parallel, then there is a group by variable interaction. That is, how much better one group does than another depends on the variable.

Why is it necessary that the tests be scaled similarly in order for the results of a profile analysis to be meaningfully interpreted? To illustrate, suppose we compared two groups on three variables, *A, B,* and *C,* two of which were on a 1 to 5 scale and the other on a 1 to 30 scale, i.e., not scaled similarily. Suppose the following graph resulted, suggesting nonparallel profiles:

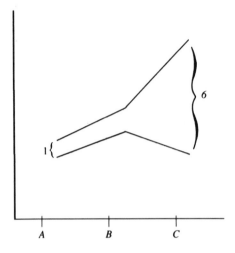

But the nonparallelism is a scaling artifact. The magnitude of superiority of group 1 for test A is $1/5$, which is exactly the same order of superiority on test C, i.e., $6/30 = 1/5$. A way of dealing with this problem if the tests are scaled differently is to convert first to some type of standard score (e.g., z or T) before proceeding with the profile analysis.

We now consider the running and interpretation of a profile analysis on SPSSX MANOVA, using some data from Johnson and Wichern (1982).

Example

In a study of love and marriage, a sample of husbands and wives were asked to respond to the following questions:

1. What is the level of passionate love you feel for your partner?
2. What is the level of passionate love that your partner feels for you?
3. What is the level of companionate love that you feel for your partner?
4. What is the level of companionate love that your partner feels for you?

The responses to all 4 questions were on a Likert type scale from 1 (none at all) to 5 (a tremendous amount). We wish to determine whether the profiles for the husbands and wives are parallel. There were 30 husbands and 30 wives that responded. The control lines for running the analysis on SPSSX are given in Table 13.20. The raw data is given on page 495 at the end of this chapter.

The test of parallelism appears in Table 13.21 and shows that parallelism is tenable at the .01 level, since the exact probability of .057 is greater than .01. Now, it is meaningful to proceed to the second question in profile analysis, and ask whether the profiles are coincident. The test for this is given in Table 13.22 and shows that the profiles can be considered coincident, i.e., the same. In other words, the differences for husbands and wives on the four variables can be considered due to sampling error. Finally, we ask whether husbands and wives scored the same on all 4 tests, i.e., the question of equal scale means. The test for equal scale means in Table 13.21 indicates this is not tenable. Reference to the univariate tests at the bottom of Table 13.21 shows that it is the difference in the way the subjects responded to scales 2 and 3 that was primarily responsible for the

TABLE 13.20
Control Lines for Profile Analysis of Husband and Wife Ratings

```
TITLE ' PROFILE ANALYSIS ON HUSBAND AND WIFE RATINGS'
DATA LIST FREE/ SPOUSE PASSYOU PASSPART COMPYOU COMPPART
LIST
BEGIN DATA

    DATA LINES

END DATA
REPORT VARS=PASSYOU PASSPART COMPYOU COMPPART/
    BREAK=SPOUSE/          ①
    SUMMARY=MEAN/
MANOVA PASSYOU TO COMPPART BY SPOUSE(1,2)/
    TRANSFORM=REPEATED/
    RENAME=AVERAGE DIF2AND1 DIF3 AND2 DIF4AND3 /
    PRINT=TRANSFORM /
    ANALYSIS=(DIF2AND1,DIF3AND2,DIF4AND3/ AVERAGE)/ ②
    DESIGN/
```

①The BREAK subcommand indicates what variable will define the subgroups (in this case husbands and wives). The SUMMARY subcommand tells the program what summary statistics we want printed for each subgroup; in this case we only want the means. See SPSSX User's Guide, 1983, Chap. 23.

②This subcommand defines two analyses. The first analysis, on the 3 difference variables before the / within the parentheses, answers questions 1 and 3 for the profile analysis. The second analysis, on the average variable, answers the question of coincident profiles. The general setup then of the ANALYSIS subcommand for k repeated measures in profile analysis would be

ANALYSIS=(DIF2AND1, DIF3AND2, . . . , DIFKANDK-1/ AVERAGE)/

For example, if $k=7$, then the ANALYSIS subcommand would be:

ANALYSIS=(DIF2AND1, DIF3AND2, DIF4AND3, DIF5AND4, DIF6AND5, DIF7AND6/ AVERAGE)/

TABLE 13.21
Test of Parallelism of Profiles for Husband and Wife Ratings

ORDER OF VARIABLES FOR ANALYSIS

	VARIATES	COVARIATES	NOT USED
	*DIF2AND1		AVERAGE
	*DIF3AND2		
	*DIF4AND3		
	3 DEPENDENT VARIABLES		
	0 COVARIATES		
	1 VARIABLE NOT USED		

NOTE.. "*" MARKS TRANSFORMED VARIABLES.

TRANSFORMATION MATRIX (TRANSPOSED)

	1	2	3	4
1	.25000	1.00000	.00000	.00000
2	.25000	−1.00000	1.00000	.00000
3	.25000	.00000	−1.00000	1.00000
4	.25000	.00000	.00000	−1.00000

EFFECT .. SPOUSE

MULTIVARIATE TESTS OF SIGNIFICANCE (S = 1, M = 1/2, N = 27)

TEST NAME	VALUE	APPROX. F	HYPOTH. DF	ERROR DF		SIG. OF F
PILLAIS	.12474	2.66027	3.00	56.00		.057
HOTELLINGS	.14251	2.66027	3.00	56.00	①	.057
WILKS	.87526	2.66027	3.00	56.00		.057
ROYS	.12474					

UNIVARIATE F-TESTS WITH (1,58) D. F.

VARIABLE	HYPOTH. SS	ERROR SS	HYPOTH. MS	ERROR MS	F	SIG. OF F
DIF2AND1	.81667	40.16667	.81667	.69253	1.17925	.282
DIF3AND2	.26667	50.46667	.26667	.87011	.30647	.582
DIF4AND3	.41667	4.56667	.41667	.07874	5.29197	.025

① This is the test of parallelism of the profiles, and indicates parallelism is tenable at the .01 level.

rejection of equal scale means. Note from the means at the top of Table 13.22 that the subjects scored somewhat higher on variable 3 than on variable 2.

13.18 DOUBLY MULTIVARIATE REPEATED MEASURES DESIGNS

In this section we consider a complex, but, not unusual in practice, repeated measures design, in which the same subjects are measured on several variables at each point in time, or on several variables for each treatment or condition. The following are three examples:

TABLE 13.22
Test of Coincidence of the Profiles and Equal Scale Means

SPOUSE	PASSYOU	PASSPART	COMPYOU	COMPPART
1.00				
MEAN	3.9000	3.9667	4.3333	4.4000
2.00				
MEAN	3.8333	4.1333	4.6333	4.5333

ORDER OF VARIABLES FOR ANALYSIS

VARIATES	COVARIATES	NOT USED
*AVERAGE		DIF2AND1
		DIF3AND2
		DIF4AND3

TESTS OF SIGNIFICANCE FOR AVERAGE USING SEQUENTIAL SUMS OF SQUARES

SOURCE OF VARIATION	SUM OF SQUARES	DF	MEAN SQUARE	F		SIG. OF F
WITHIN CELLS	9.04167	58	.15589			
CONSTANT	1066.81667	1	1066.81667	6843.35853		.000
SPOUSE	.26667	1	.26667	1.71060	①	.196

EFFECT .. CONSTANT

MULTIVARIATE TESTS OF SIGNIFICANCE (S = 1, M = 1/2, N = 27)

TEST NAME	VALUE	APPROX. F	HYPOTH. DF	ERROR DF		SIG. OF F
PILLAIS	.30301	8.11513	3.00	56.00		.000
HOTELLINGS	.43474	8.11513	3.00	56.00		.000
WILKS	.69699	8.11513	3.00	56.00	②	.000
ROYS	.30301					

UNIVARIATE F-TESTS WITH (1,58) D. F.

VARIABLE	HYPOTH. SS	ERROR SS	HYPOTH. MS	ERROR MS	F	SIG. OF F
DIF2AND1	2.01667	40.16667	2.01667	.69253	2.91203	.093
DIF3AND2	11.26667	50.46667	11.26667	.87011	12.94848	.001
DIF4AND3	.01667	4.56667	.01667	.07874	.21168	.647

①This indicates the profiles are coincident at the .01 level, since .196 > .01.
②This test indicates that equal scale means is not tenable at the .01 level, since .000 < .01.

1. We are interested in tracking elementary school children's achievement in math and reading, and we have their standardized test scores obtained in Grades 2, 4, 6, and 8. Here we have data for two variables, each measured at four points in time.

2. The *SPSSX User's Guide* (3rd ed., 1988, pp. 636–638) presents a second example of a doubly multivariate problem. There are 53 subjects measured on five types of tests on three occasions. In this example, there are also two between variables (group and gender). They show the complete control lines for running the analysis and explain selected printout.

3. A study by Wynd (1992) investigated the effect of stress reduction in preventing smoking relapse. Subjects were randomly assigned to an experimental group or control group. They were then invited to three abstinence booster sessions (three-part treatment) provided at 1-, 2-, and 3-month intervals. After each of these sessions, they were measured on three variables: imagery, stress, and smoking rate. I present the complete control lines from SPSSX MANOVA for analyzing the data from this study later on, and explain selected printout.

Why are the data from the above three situations considered to be *doubly* multivariate? Recall from Chapter 4 that I defined a multivariate problem as one involving several correlated dependent variables. In these cases, the problem is doubly multivariate because there is a correlational structure *within* each measure and a different correlational structure *across* the measures. For 1. above, the children's scores on math ability will be correlated across the grades, as will their verbal scores, but, in addition, there will be some correlation between their math and verbal scores.

Example Our example is the study in 3. by Wynd (1992), entitled "Relaxation imagery used for stress reduction in the prevention of smoking relapse." Subjects who had completed a local smoking cessation program were randomly assigned to either an experimental imagery group ($n = 29$) or an attention placebo control group ($n = 37$). Wynd described relaxation imagery as follows:

> During guided relaxation imagery training, subjects are instructed in deep-breathing techniques and progressive body muscle relaxation. An image of a peaceful scene (a beach, a mountain top, woodland scene) is then introduced by the therapist, for purposes of establishing full relaxation and a deep sense of calm. It is believed that through imagery the individual experiences perceptual changes that can produce new behavioral and lifestyle changes. (p. 295)

Wynd noted that several studies have demonstrated the successful use of imagery in reducing stress, and that because of this, the technique may be useful in changing risky behaviors, such as cigarette smoking. The subjects in the treatment group were invited to three abstinence booster sessions (three-part treatment) as described. Each session lasted 90 min. The agenda for the sessions, as presented in the paper, was:

Booster Session 1: Relapse prevention theories: managing stress, cravings, and urges. Deep-breathing exercises, progressive muscle relaxation, and imagery.

Booster Session 2: Additional stress management techniques. Imagery practice.

Booster Session 3: Exercise and weight management following smoking cessation. Imagery practice. Review and summary.

Smoking abstinence and relapse were measured through self-reported smoking rates and were validated by physiological measures of saliva thiocyanate levels. Stress was measured by the Perceived Stress Scale, a 14-item instrument designed to indicate subjective perceptions of stress in generalized life situations. Higher scores indicate more stress. Finally, creative imagery was measured with the Creative Imagination Scale, a 10-item scale measuring a subject's capacity for effectively using imagery to simulate reality. Higher scores indicate more creative imagery.

There is one between variable (group) in this study. It is a doubly multivariate repeated measures, because the subjects were measured on three variables (imagery, stress, and smoking rate) at each of three points in time. The complete SPSSX MANOVA control lines for the analysis are presented in Table 13.23. The cell means for the variables are given in Table 13.24.

Structurally, there is one between variable (groups) and one within variable (sessions), so there are three effects of interest: group main effect, session main effect, and group by session interaction effect. Because 10 subjects dropped out of the study, the notal n used for analysis was 66. I present selected, annotated printout for the group effect in Table 13.26, involving both the multivariate and univariate tests. Table 13.27 presents both the error and effect SSCP matrices, along with the *averaged* error and effect matrices and the averaged multivariate and univariate tests for the group by session interaction. Finally, similar output is in Table 13.28 for the session main effect.

The first major question to be answered is, "Did the three-part abstinence treatment make a difference?" Reference to Table 13.26 shows that the multivariate group effect is significant beyond the .01 level ($F = 10.9194$, $p < .001$), indicating that groups differ on the *set* of three variables. Reference to Table 13.24 shows that the differences are all in the right direction, i.e., the treatment group has more creative imagery, less stress, and a lower smoking rate.

If, however, the group by session interaction is significant, then we would have to qualify matters. Reference to Table 13.27 shows that the *averaged* multivariate test is significant beyond the .01 level. Also, all three univariate group by session interaction effects are significant beyond the .01 level. To interpret the nature of these three significant univariate interactions, it is very helpful to refer to Table 13.24, where the cell means

TABLE 13.23
SPSSX MANOVA Control Lines for Doubly Multivariate Repeated
Measures Analysis

TITLE 'DOUBLY MULT. REP. MEASURES ON WYND DATA'
① DATA LIST FREE/GPID CREAT1 CREAT2 CREAT3 STRESS1 STRESS2
   STRESS3 SMKRATE1 SMKRATE2 SMKRATE3
   BEGIN DATA

   DATA IN APPENDIX B

   END DATA
② MISSING VALUES ALL (−1)
③ MANOVA CREAT1 TO SMKRATE3 BY GPID(1,2)/
   WSFACTOR=SESSION(3)/
④   MEASURE=CREAT STRESS SMKRATE/
   WSDESIGN/
   PRINT=CELLINFO(MEANS) TRANSFORM SIGNIF(AVERF UNIV GG HF)
⑤   ERROR(SSCP) SIGNIF(HYPOTH)/
   DESIGN/

---

①Note that the three measures for the creative imagery variable are listed together and in the order they were obtained, similarily for stress, and then for smoking rate. This is important; as the SPSSX User's Guide (3rd ed., p. 636) noted, "Specify variables measuring a given attribute across occasions consecutively and in order."

②Because there were some missing data in this study and the code for missing data was −1, this command is used (cf. p. 29).

③The TO keyword is used to refer to the set of *consecutive* repeated measures variables.

④This MEASURE subcommand is used for labeling the averaged univariate results.

⑤This part of the PRINT subcommand is used to print the total ERROR SSCP matrix, the total HYPOTHESIS SSCP matrices, and the *averaged* SSCP error matrix and hypothesis matrices.

are given for each variable separately. For creative imagery, the control group was initially more creative in Session 2 and the gap widened even further for Session 3. For stress, the groups were about the same at Session 3. For stress, the groups were about the same at Session 1, but then the treatment group was much less stressed for Sessions 2 and 3. Finally, for smoking rate, there was not much of a difference at Session 2 (4.143 vs 3.710), but at Session 3, the gap was quite pronounced in favor of the treatment group.

13.19 SUMMARY OF MAJOR POINTS

1. Repeated measures designs are much more powerful than completely randomized designs, because the variability due to individual differences is

TABLE 13.24
Cell Means for Wynd Data on the Three Outcome Variables:
Creative Imagery, Stress, and Smoking Rate

| | | SESSION | | | |
		1	2	3	Group Means
	CREAT	14.857	26.114	28.686	23.219
TREAT	STRESS	27.829	23.457	23.200	24.83
	SMKRATE	0.0	4.143	3.057	2.4
	CREAT	17.097	18.484	19.806	18.462
CONTROL	STRESS	28.548	28.613	31.065	29.409
	SMKRATE	0.0	3.710	9.516	4.409
SESSION	CREAT	15.909	22.530	24.5154	
MEANS	STRESS	28.167	25.879	26.894	
	SMKRATE	0.0	3.939	6.091	

CREATIVE IMAGERY

| | SESSION | | |
	1	2	3
TREAT	14.857	26.114	28.686
CONTROL	17.097	18.484	19.806

STRESS

| | SESSION | | |
	1	2	3
TREAT	27.829	23.457	23.200
CONTROL	28.548	28.613	31.065

SMKRATE

| | SESSION | | |
	1	2	3
TREAT	0.0	4.143	3.057
CONTROL	0.0	3.710	9.516

removed from the error term, and individual differences are the major
reason for error variance.

2. Two major advantages of repeated measures designs are increased
precision (because of the smaller error term), and the fact that many less
subjects are needed than in a completely randomized design. Two potential
disadvantages are that the order of treatments may make a difference (this
can be dealt with by counterbalancing) and carryover effects.

3. Either a univariate or a multivariate approach can be used for
repeated measures analysis. The assumptions for a single group uni-

TABLE 13.25
Orthonormalized Transformation Matrix on the Variables for the Doubly Multivariate Problem

Orthonormalized Transformation Matrix (Transposed)

	①T1	②T2←CREAT→T3		①T4	②T5←STRESS→T6		①T7
CREAT1	.57735	.70711	-.40825	.00000	.00000	.00000	.00000
CREAT2	.57735	.00000	.81650	.00000	.00000	.00000	.00000
CREAT3	.57735	-.70711	-.40825	.00000	.00000	.00000	.00000
STRESS1	.00000	.00000	.00000	.57735	.70711	-.40825	.00000
STRESS2	.00000	.00000	.00000	.57735	.00000	.81650	.00000
STRESS3	.00000	.00000	.00000	.57735	-.70711	-.40825	.00000
SMKRATE1	.00000	.00000	.00000	.00000	.00000	.00000	.57735
SMKRATE2	.00000	.00000	.00000	.00000	.00000	.00000	.57735
SMKRATE3	.00000	.00000	.00000	.00000	.00000	.00000	.57735

	②T8←SMKRATE→T9	
CREAT1	.00000	.00000
CREAT2	.00000	.00000
CREAT3	.00000	.00000
STRESS1	.00000	.00000
STRESS2	.00000	.00000
STRESS3	.00000	.00000
SMKRATE1	.70711	-.40825
SMKRATE2	.00000	.81650
SMKRATE3	-.70711	-.40825

①T1, T4, and T7 all involve equal weighting on CREAT, STRESS, and SMKRATE across sessions, used to test the group effect.
②T2 and T3 are orthogonal contrasts on the CREAT variable, T5 and T6 are orthogonal contrasts on the STRESS variable, whereas T8 and T9 are orthogonal contrasts on the SMKRATE variable.

TABLE 13.26
Error and Effect SSCP Matrices and the Multivariate and Univariate Tests for the Between Group Effect

Tests involving Between-Subjects Effects., Denoted by **W** in the text.

WITHIN CELLS Sum-of-Squares and Cross-Products

	T1	T4	T7
T1	4141.08018		
T4	647.70630	5866.05407	
T7	−255.43656	3227.33978	6969.00645

EFFECT . . GPID
Adjusted Hypothesis Sum-of-Squares and Cross-Products. Denoted by **B** in the text.

	T1	T4	T7
T1	1115.87436		
T4	−1074.43357	1034.53179	
T7	−471.19980	453.70062	198.97335

Multivariate Tests of Significance (S = 1, M = ½, N = 30)

Test Name	Value	Exact F	Hypoth. DF	Error DF	Sig. of F
Pillais	.34570	10.91940	3.00	62.00	① .000
Hotellings	.52836	10.91940	3.00	62.00	.000
Wilks	.65430	10.91940	3.00	62.00	.000
Roys	.34570				

Note . . F statistics are exact.

Recall that Wilks's λ is given by $|\mathbf{W}|/|\mathbf{T}|$, where $\mathbf{T} = \mathbf{B} + \mathbf{W}$.
In this case, we have $|\mathbf{W}| = 1.21783 \times 10^{11}$ and $|\mathbf{T}| = 1.8613 \times 10^{11}$.

EFFECT . . GPID (Cont.)
Univariate F-tests with (1,64) D.F.

Variable	Hypoth. SS	Error SS	Hypoth. MS	Error MS	F	Sig. of F
T1	1115.87436	4141.08018	1115.87436	64.70438	17.24573	.000
T4	1034.53179	5866.05407	1034.53179	91.65709	11.28698	② .001
T7	198.97335	6969.00645	198.97335	108.89073	1.82728	.181

① The multivariate tests are significant beyond the .01 level, indicating the groups differ on the three variables, considered as a set. Reference to Table 13.24 shows that the differences are all in the right direction. The treatment group has more creative imagery, less stress, and a lower smoking rate.

② The univariate tests show, at the .01 level, that only the first two differences are significant.

TABLE 13.27
Error and Effect SSCP Matrices, Averaged Error and Effect SSCP Matrices and Averaged Multivariate and Univariate Tests for the Group by Session Interaction Effect

WITHIN CELLS Sum-of-Square and Cross-Products

	T2 CREAT	T3	T5 STRESS	T6	T8 SMKRATE	T9
T2	1411.67926					
T3	-424.55306	481.90230				
T5	262.43687	-38.69790	1468.95668			
T6	-18.42625	-92.08049	-815.12599	861.14962		
T8	42.49401	-108.42532	694.49954	-584.40033	3154.81382	
T9	-110.12970	138.45131	-318.86390	-272.04117	-610.57425	2358.48018

AVERAGED WITHIN CELLS Sum-of-Squares and Cross-Products

	CREAT	STRESS	SMKRATE
CREAT	1893.58157		
STRESS	170.35637	2330.10630	
SMKRATE	180.94531	422.45837	5513.29401

Each of the diagonal elements is just the sum of the diagonal elements in the above matrix (which involve contrasts on the given variable). Thus, 1893.58157 = 1411.67926 + 481.90230.

EFFECT .. GPID BY SESSION
Adjusted Hypothesis Sum-of-Squares and Cross-Products

	T2	T3	T5	T6	T8	T9
T2	1016.19953					
T3	-454.90886	203.64315				
T5	-652.98232	292.31213	419.58877			
T6	91.13740	-40.79830	-58.56243	8.17362		
T8	-590.31219	264.25740	379.31864	-52.94188	342.91345	
T9	-386.53150	173.03354	248.37468	-34.66590	224.53687	147.02487

EFFECT .. GPID BY SESSION
Adjusted Hypothesis Sum-of-Squares and Cross-Products

	CREAT	STRESS	SMKRATE
CREAT	1219.84268		
STRESS	-693.78062	427.76239	
SMKRATE	-417.27865	344.65274	489.93831

AVERAGED Multivariate Tests of Significance (S = 2, M = 0, N = ;62)

Test Name	Value	Approx. F	Hypoth. DF	Error DF	Sig. of F
Pillais	.53307	15.38365	6.00	254.00	.000 ①}
Hotellings	.96776	20.16162	6.00	250.00	.000
Wilks	.49429	17.73916	6.00	252.00	.000
Roys	.47554				

Note . . F statistic for Wilks's Lambda is exact.

EFFECT . . GPID BY SESSION (Cont.)
Univariate F-tests with (2,128) DF.

Variable	Hypoth. SS ②	Error SS	Hypoth. MS	Error MS	F	Sig. of F
CREAT	1219.84268	1893.58157	609.92134	14.79361	41.22871	.001 ③}
STRESS	427.76239	2330.10630	213.88119	18.20396	11.74916	.000
SMKRATE	489.93831	5513.29401	244.96916	43.07261	5.68735	.004

① These indicate a significant multivariate interaction beyond the .01 level.
② Note that the hypothesis and error sums of squares for the univariate tests are just the diagonal elements of the averaged within and hypothesis matrices.

③ These p values mean each of the individual variables has a Group × Session interaction effect. The nature of these interactions can be gauged by examining Table 13.24.

509

TABLE 13.28
Error and Effect SSCP Matrices, Averaged Error and Effect SSCP Matrices and Averaged Multivariate and Univariate Tests for the Session Main Effect

WITHIN CELLS Sum-of-Squares and Cross-Products

	T2	T3	T5	T6	T8	T9
T2	1411.67926					
T3	-424.55306	481.90230				
T5	262.43687	-38.69790	1468.95668			
T6	-18.42625	-92.08049	-815.12599	861.14962		
T8	42.49401	-108.42532	694.49954	-584.40033	3154.81382	
T9	-110.12970	138.45131	-318.86390	-272.04117	-610.57425	2358.48018

AVERAGED WITHIN CELLS Sum-of-Squares and Cross-Products

	CREAT	STRESS	SMKRATE
CREAT	1893.58157		
STRESS	170.35637	2330.10630	
SMKRATE	180.94531	422.45837	5513.29401

EFFECT .. SESSION
Adjusted Hypothesis Sum-of-Squares and Cross-Products

	T2	T3	T5	T6	T8	T9
T2	2248.19953					
T3	-686.75873	209.78456				
T5	-287.16414	87.72019	36.67968			
T6	510.25870	-155.86900	-65.17571	115.80998		
T8	1709.20296	-522.11116	-218.31772	387.92628	1299.42860	
T9	-245.79800	75.08405	31.39595	-55.78712	-186.86894	26.87335

EFFECT .. SESSION
Adjusted Hypothesis Sum-of-Squares and Cross-Products

	CREAT	STRESS	SMKRATE
CREAT	2457.98409		
STRESS	-443.03314	152.48966	
SMKRATE	1784.28701	-274.10484	1326.30195

AVERAGED Multivariate Tests of Significance (S = 2, M = 0, N = 62)

Test Name	Value	Approx. F	Hypoth. DF	Error DF	Sig. of F
Pillais	.64597	20.19595	6.00	254.00	.000
Hotellings	1.61818	33.71209	6.00	250.00	① .000
Wilks	.37423	26.65622	6.00	252.00	.000
Roys	.61302				

Note . . F statistic for Wilks's Lambda is exact.

EFFECT . . SESSION (Cont.)
Univariate F-tests with (2,128) DF.

Variable	Hypoth. SS	Error SS	Hypoth. MS	Error MS	F	Sig. of F
CREAT	2457.98409	1893.58157	1228.99204	14.79361	83.07589	.000
STRESS	152.48966	2330.10630	76.24483	18.20396	4.18837	② }.017
SMKRATE	1326.30195	5513.29401	663.15098	43.07261	15.39612	.000

① There is a significant multivariate session main effect at the .01 level.
② Only the CREAT and SMKRATE univariate tests are significant at the .01 level.

511

variate repeated measures analysis are (a) independence of the observations, (b) multivariate normality, and (c) sphericity (also called circularity). For the multivariate approach, the first two assumptions are still needed, but the sphericity assumption is *not* needed. Sphericity requires that the variances of the differences for *all pairs* of repeated measures are equal. Although statistical tests of sphericity exist, they are not recommended.

4. Under a violation of sphericity the Type I error rate for the univariate approach is inflated. However, a modified (adjusted) univariate approach, obtained by multiplying each of the degrees of freedom by $\hat{\varepsilon}$, yields an honest type I error rate.

5. Because both the modified (adjusted) univariate approach and the multivariate approach control the Type I error rate, the choice between them involves the issue of the power of the tests. As neither the adjusted univariate test or the multivariate test is usually most powerful, it is recommended that generally both tests be used, because they may differ in the treatment effects they will detect. The multivariate test, however, probably should be avoided when $n < k + 10$, because under this condition it's power will tend to be low.

6. If the sphericity assumption is tenable, then the Tukey procedure is a good post hoc technique for locating significant pairwise differences. If the sphericity assumption is not met, then the Bonferroni approach should be used. That is, do multiple *correlated t* tests, but use the Bonferroni inequality to keep the overall alpha level under control.

7. When several groups are involved, then an additional assumption is multisample sphericity, that is, that the covariance matrices for the groups on the transformed variables are equal. This can be checked with a test found in Anderson (1958, p. 259), which is available in SAS GLM and in BMDP2V. You should, however, remember our earlier caution on statistical tests for sphericity.

8. Designs with only within subject factors are fairly common in certain areas of research. These are designs where the *same* subjects are involved in every treatment combination or in each situation. Totally within designs are easily setup on SPSSX.

9. In testing contrasts with repeated measures designs it is imperative that a *different* error term be used for each contrast, since Boik (1981) showed that if a pooled error term is used the actual alpha will be quite different from the presumed level of significance.

10. In profile analysis we are comparing two or more groups of subjects on a battery of tests. It is assumed that the tests are scaled similarly. If they are not, then the scores must be converted to some type of standard score (e.g., z or T) for the analysis to be meaningful. Nonparallel profiles means there is a group by variable interaction, that is, how much better one group does than another depends on the variable.

EXERCISES—REPEATED MEASURES

1. In the multivariate analysis of the drug data we stated that H_0: $\mu_1 = \mu_2 = \mu_3 = \mu_4$ is equivalent to saying that $\mu_1 - \mu_2 = 0$ and $\mu_2 - \mu_3 = 0$ and $\mu_3 - \mu_4 = 0$. Show this is true.

2. Consider the following data set from a single sample repeated measures design with three repeated measures:

	Treatments		
S's	1	2	3
1	5	6	1
2	3	4	2
3	3	7	1
4	6	8	3
5	6	9	3
6	4	7	2
7	5	9	2

a) Do a univariate repeated measures analysis, using the procedure employed in the text. Do you reject at the .05 level?
b) Do a multivariate repeated measures analysis by hand (i.e., using a calculator) with the following difference variables: $y_1 - y_2$ and $y_2 - y_3$.
c) Run the data on SPSSX, obtaining both the univariate and multivariate results, to check the answers you obtained in (a) and (b).
d) Note the $(k - 1)$ transformed variables SPSSX uses in testing for the multivariate approach, and yet the same multivariate F is obtained. What point that we mentioned in the text does this illustrate?
e) Assume the sphericity assumption is tenable and employ the Tukey post hoc procedure at the .05 level to determine which pairs of treatments differ.

3. A school psychologist is testing the effectiveness of a stress management approach in reducing the state and trait anxiety for college students. The subjects are pretested and matched on these variables and then randomly assigned within each pair to either the stress management approach or to a control group. The following data are obtained:

	Stress Management		Control	
Pairs	State	Trait	State	Trait
1	41	38	46	35
2	48	41	47	50
3	34	33	39	36
4	31	40	28	38
5	26	23	35	19
6	37	31	40	30

Pairs	Stress Management		Control	
	State	Trait	State	Trait
7	44	32	46	45
8	53	47	58	53
9	46	41	47	48
10	34	38	39	39
11	33	39	36	41
12	50	45	54	40

a) Test at the .05 level, using the multivariate matched pairs analysis, whether the stress management approach was successful.

b) b) Which of the variables are contributing to multivariate significance?

4. Suppose that in the Elashoff drug example the two groups of subjects had been given the three different doses of two drugs under two different conditions. Then we would have a 1 between and three within design. What modifications in the control lines from Table 13.10 would be necessary to run this analysis?

5. Show that the covariance for the difference variables $(y_1 - y_2)$ and $(y_3 - y_4)$ in the drug data example is -8.6, and that the covariance for $(y_2 - y_3)$ and $(y_3 - y_4)$ is -19.

6. The extent of the departure from the sphericity assumption is measured by

$$\hat{\epsilon} = \frac{k^2 \, (\bar{s}_{ii} - \bar{s})^2}{(k - 1)(\sum\sum s_{ij}^2 - 2k\sum_i \bar{s}_i^2 + k^2 \bar{s}^2)}$$

where

$\bar{s}$ is the mean of all entries in the covariance matrix $\mathbf{S}$

$\bar{s}_{ii}$ is mean of entries on main diagonal of $\mathbf{S}$

$\bar{s}_i$ is mean of all entries in row i of $\mathbf{S}$

s_{ij} is ijth entry of $\mathbf{S}$

Find $\hat{\epsilon}$ for the following two covariance matrices:

(a) $\mathbf{S} = \begin{bmatrix} 76.8 & 53.2 & 29.2 & 69 \\ 53.2 & 42.8 & 15.8 & 47 \\ 29.2 & 15.8 & 14.8 & 27 \\ 69 & 47 & 27 & 64 \end{bmatrix}$ (answer $\hat{\epsilon} = .605$)

(b) $\mathbf{S} = \begin{bmatrix} 4 & 3 & 2 \\ 3 & 5 & 2 \\ 2 & 2 & 6 \end{bmatrix}$ (answer $\hat{\epsilon} = .83$)

From the magnitude of $\hat{\epsilon}$ in the above two cases, would you be concerned in either of above cases?

7. An equivalent way of stating the sphericity condition is to say that the variances of the difference variables for all pairs of treatments are equal. Thus, for three treatments, this would mean that

$$\sigma^2_{y_1-y_2} = \sigma^2_{y_1-y_3} = \sigma^2_{y_2-y_3}$$

where y_1, y_2 and y_3 represent the repeated measures for the three treatments.
   The formula expressing the variance of a difference variable in terms of the variances of the original variables and the covariance is:

$$\sigma^2_{y_i-y_j} = \sigma^2_{y_i} + \sigma^2_{y_j} - 2\sigma_{y_iy_j}$$

The above condition for sphericity then implies this is constant for all pairs (i and j) of treatments. Show that if uniformity holds, then sphericity will hold.

8. Twelve subjects were randomly assigned to two treatments. The following recall scores on verbal material after 1, 2, 3, 4, and 5 days were obtained:

		Days			
GPID	Y1	Y2	Y3	Y4	Y5
1.00	26.00	24.00	18.00	11.00	10.00
'1.00	34.00	35.00	29.00	22.00	23.00
1.00	41.00	37.00	25.00	18.00	15.00
1.00	29.00	28.00	22.00	15.00	13.00
1.00	35.00	34.00	27.00	21.00	17.00
1.00	28.00	25.00	16.00	11.00	10.00
2.00	42.00	38.00	26.00	20.00	15.00
2.00	31.00	30.00	21.00	15.00	13.00
2.00	45.00	40.00	33.00	25.00	18.00
2.00	29.00	27.00	17.00	11.00	8.00
2.00	39.00	36.00	26.00	20.00	18.00
2.00	33.00	32.00	22.00	12.00	7.00

Run the trend analysis on SPSSX MANOVA. Is there a significant group effect at the .05 level? Are any of the univariate interactions (linear × group, quadratic × group, etc.) significant at the .05 level? Which of the trends are significant at the .05 level for the days main effect? Which of these trends are most pronounced?

9. Consider the following covariance matrix:

$$\begin{array}{cccc} & y_1 & y_2 & y_3 \\ & \begin{array}{c} y_1 \\ \mathbf{S} = y_2 \\ y_3 \end{array} & \begin{bmatrix} 1.0 & .5 & 1.5 \\ .5 & 3.0 & 2.5 \\ 1.5 & 2.5 & 5.0 \end{bmatrix} \end{array}$$

Calculate the variances of the three difference variables: $y_1 - y_2$, $y_1 - y_3$ and $y_2 - y_3$. If the above represented the covariance matrix for a single group repeated measures design, what are the above results telling us concerning the sphericity condition? What do you think $\hat{\epsilon}$ will be equal to in this case?

10. Consider the following two data sets for 10 subjects on three repeated measures.

	DATA SET 1			DATA SET 2		
1	49	53	91	52	50	71
2	53	49	111	56	46	91
3	63	65	65	66	62	45
4	37	33	35	40	30	15
5	39	39	59	42	36	39
6	43	51	87	46	48	67
7	43	47	25	46	44	5
8	49	45	47	52	42	27
9	65	65	105	68	62	85
10	59	53	75	62	50	55

a) Run data set 1 on SPSSX MANOVA. Is the adjusted univariate test significant at the .05 level? Is the multivariate test significant at the .05 level? Relate these results to what was discussed in the chapter.

b) Run data set 2 on SPSSX MANOVA. Is the adjusted univariate test significant at the .05 level? Is the multivariate test significant at the .05 level? Relate these results to what was discussed in the chapter.

11. Some marketing researchers are conducting a study to evaluate both consumer beliefs and the stability of those beliefs about the following 4 brands of toothpaste: Crest, Colgate, Ultra Brite, and Gleem. The beliefs to be assessed are (1) good taste, (2) cavity prevention, and (3) breath protection. They also wish to determine the extent to which the beliefs are moderated by sex and by age (20–35, 36–50, and 51 and up). The subjects will be asked their beliefs at two points in time separated by a two month interval.

a) Set up schematically the appropriate repeated measures design.

b) Show the control lines necessary for running this design on SPSSX MANOVA in order to obtain both the univariate and multivariate tests.

PROFILE ANALYSIS DATA

SPOUSE	PASSYOU	PASSPART	COMPYOU	COMPPART
1.00	2.00	3.00	5.00	5.00
1.00	5.00	5.00	4.00	4.00
1.00	4.00	5.00	5.00	5.00
1.00	4.00	3.00	4.00	4.00
1.00	3.00	3.00	5.00	5.00
1.00	3.00	3.00	4.00	5.00
1.00	3.00	4.00	4.00	4.00
1.00	4.00	4.00	5.00	5.00
1.00	4.00	5.00	5.00	5.00
1.00	4.00	4.00	3.00	3.00
1.00	4.00	4.00	5.00	5.00
1.00	5.00	5.00	4.00	4.00
1.00	4.00	4.00	4.00	4.00
1.00	4.00	3.00	5.00	5.00
1.00	4.00	4.00	5.00	5.00
1.00	3.00	3.00	4.00	5.00
1.00	4.00	5.00	4.00	4.00
1.00	5.00	5.00	5.00	5.00
1.00	5.00	5.00	4.00	4.00
1.00	4.00	4.00	4.00	4.00
1.00	4.00	4.00	4.00	4.00
1.00	4.00	4.00	4.00	4.00
1.00	3.00	4.00	5.00	5.00
1.00	5.00	3.00	5.00	5.00
1.00	5.00	5.00	3.00	3.00
1.00	3.00	3.00	4.00	4.00
1.00	4.00	4.00	4.00	4.00
1.00	3.00	3.00	5.00	5.00
1.00	4.00	4.00	3.00	3.00
1.00	4.00	4.00	5.00	5.00
2.00	4.00	4.00	5.00	5.00
2.00	4.00	5.00	5.00	5.00
2.00	4.00	5.00	5.00	5.00
2.00	4.00	5.00	5.00	5.00
2.00	4.00	4.00	5.00	5.00
2.00	3.00	3.00	4.00	4.00
2.00	4.00	3.00	5.00	4.00
2.00	3.00	4.00	5.00	5.00
2.00	4.00	4.00	5.00	4.00
2.00	3.00	4.00	4.00	4.00
2.00	4.00	5.00	5.00	5.00
2.00	5.00	5.00	5.00	5.00
2.00	4.00	4.00	5.00	5.00
2.00	4.00	4.00	4.00	4.00
2.00	4.00	4.00	5.00	5.00
2.00	3.00	4.00	4.00	4.00
2.00	5.00	5.00	5.00	5.00
2.00	4.00	5.00	4.00	4.00
2.00	3.00	4.00	4.00	4.00
2.00	5.00	3.00	4.00	4.00
2.00	5.00	3.00	4.00	4.00
2.00	4.00	5.00	4.00	4.00
2.00	2.00	5.00	5.00	5.00
2.00	3.00	4.00	5.00	5.00
2.00	4.00	3.00	5.00	5.00
2.00	4.00	4.00	4.00	4.00
2.00	4.00	4.00	5.00	5.00
2.00	3.00	4.00	4.00	4.00
2.00	4.00	4.00	5.00	4.00
2.00	4.00	4.00	5.00	5.00

14 Categorical Data Analysis: The Log Linear Model

14.1 INTRODUCTION

The reader may recall from introductory statistics that one of the most elementary statistical tests is the two-way chi square. This test is appropriate if the subjects, or more generally entities, have been cross classified in two ways and the data is in the form of frequency counts. As an example, suppose we have taken a sample of 66 adults and wish to determine whether sex of adults is related to their approval or lack of approval of a television series. The results are as follows:

	Approval	No Approval
Male	22	16
Female	9	19

The null hypothesis for a two-way chi square is that the modes of classification are independent. In this case we have:

H_0: Sex is independent of approval of the television series. Based on the null hypothesis, expected cell frequencies (e_{ij}) are computed from

$$e_{ij} = \frac{\text{(row total) (column total)}}{n} \qquad (n \text{ is sample size})$$

and compared against the above observed frequencies (o_i) with the following chi square statistic:

$$\chi^2 = \Sigma \frac{(o_{ij} - e_{ij})^2}{e_{ij}}$$

518

Although the above is simple to handle statistically, how would we analyze the data if we also wished to examine the effect of location, as a possible moderator variable, on approval of the series, and had the following three-way contingency table?

	Rural			Urban	
	Approval	No Approval		Approval	No Approval
Female	3	7		6	12
Male	5	15		17	1

What most researchers have done in the past with such multiway contingency tables is to run several two-way analyses. This was encouraged by the statistical packages, which easily produced the chi squares for all two-way tables. But the reader should see that this is as unsatisfactory as having a three- or four-way ANOVA and only doing several two-way ANOVAs, for the following two reasons:

1. It doesn't enable one to detect three factor or higher order interactions.
2. It doesn't allow for the simultaneous examination of the pairwise relationships.

The log linear model is a way of handling multiway (i.e., more complex) contingency tables in a statistically sound way. Major advances by statisticians such as Goodman and Mosteller and their students in the 1960's and 1970's have made the log linear model accessible for applied workers. The model is available on all three major statistical packages (BMDP, SAS, and SPSSX).

Agresti (1990) has an excellent, comprehensive theoretical textbook on categorical data analysis, while Wickens (1989) and Kennedy (1983) have very good applied texts, written especially for social science researchers. Kennedy draws many analogies between log linear analysis and analysis of variance.

Multiway contingency tables are fairly common, especially with survey data. Below are two four-way tables:

A group of 362 patients receiving psychiatric care were cross classified according to four clinical indices, yielding this table:

		ACUTE DEPRESSION			
		YES		NO	
VALIDITY	SOLIDITY	INTROVERT	EXTROVERT	INTROVERT	EXTROVERT
	RIGID	15	23	25	14
ENERGETIC	HYSTERIC	9	14	46	47
	RIGID	30	22	22	8
PSYCHASTENIC	HYSTERIC	32	16	27	12

In a study of the relationship between car size and accident injuries, accidents were classified according to type of accident, severity, and whether the driver was ejected.

		ACCIDENT TYPE			
		COLLISION		ROLLOVER	
CAR WEIGHT	DRIVER EJECTED	NOT SEVERE	SEVERE	NOT SEVERE	SEVERE
SMALL	NO	350	150	60	112
	YES	26	23	19	80
STANDARD	NO	1878	1022	148	404
	YES	111	161	22	265

As the reader will see, the material in this chapter differs in several respects from that of all other chapters in the book:

1. The data now consist of frequency counts, rather than a score(s) for each subject on some dependent variable(s).
2. Whereas a linear model ($\mu_{ij} = \mu + \alpha_i + \beta_j + \alpha\beta_{ij}$ for ANOVA), or a linear combination of parameters for multiple regression was used in previous chapters, in multiway contingency tables the natural model is *multiplicative*. The *log*arithm is used to obtain a *linear* function of the parameters, hence the name log linear.
3. In log linear analysis, we are fitting a *series* of models to the data, whereas in ANOVA or regression one generally thinks of fitting *a* model to the data. Also, in log linear analysis we need to reverse our thinking on tests of significance. In log linear analysis, a test statistic that is not significant is good in the sense that the given model fits the data. In ANOVA or regression one generally wishes the statistic to be significant, indicating a significant main effect or interaction, or that a predictor variable contributes to significant variation on the dependent variable.
4. In multivariate analysis of variance, discriminant analysis, and repeated measures analysis the assumed underlying distribution was the multivariate normal, while with frequency data the appropriate distribution is the multinomial.

The first topic covered in the chapter concerns the sampling distributions, binomial and multinomial, that describe qualitative data, and the linkage of the multinomial to the two-way chi square. The log linear model is then developed for the two-way chi square (where it is not needed, but easiest to explain) and three-way tables, where the important concept of hierarchical models is introduced. Computer analysis is considered for two three-way data sets, where the process of model selection is illustrated. The notions of partial and marginal association are explained. Conditions under which it is valid to collapse to two-way tables are considered and the fundamental concept of the odds (cross product) ratio is discussed. A measure, the normed fit index, which can be very helpful in assessing model adequacy in very small or very large samples is considered. This measure is independent of sample size. The importance of cross validating the model(s) selected on an independent sample is emphasized. Three methods of selecting models for higher dimensional tables are given, and a computer analysis is illustrated for a four-way table. Both the BMDP and SPSSX statistical packages are illustrated. Finally, the use of contrasts (both planned and post hoc) in log linear analysis is discussed and an example given.

14.2 SAMPLING DISTRIBUTIONS: BINOMIAL AND MULTINOMIAL

The simplest case is where there are just two possible outcomes: heads or tails for flipping a coin, in favor or not in favor of a bond issue, obtaining a 6 or not obtaining a 6 in rolling a die. The event is dichotomous and we are interested in the probability of f_1 "successes" in n trials. It is assumed that the trials are *independent*, that is, what happens in any given trial is not dependent on what happened on a previous trial(s). This is important, as independence is needed to multiply probabilities and obtain the following Binomial Law:

$$P(f_1/n) = \frac{n!}{f_1! \, (n-f_1)!} \, P_1^{f_1} P_2^{n-f_1}$$

where P_1 is the probability of success and P_2 is the probability of failure, and $n! = n(n - 1)(n - 2) \cdot \cdot 2(1)$.

Example 1

What is the probability of obtaining 3 sixes in rolling a die 4 times? Because the probability of any face coming up for a fair die is 1/6, the probability of obtaining a 6 is 1/6 and the probability of not obtaining a 6 is 5/6. Since $n = 4$, $n! = 4! = 4\,3\,2\,1 = 24$. Therefore,

$$P(3/4) = \frac{4!}{3! \, 1!} \, (.1667)^3 \, (.8333)^1 = 4\,(.0039) = .0156$$

Thus the probability of obtaining 3 sixes is less than 2%, quite small, as you might have suspected.

The binomial distribution has been introduced first because it is of historical interest and because it is a special case of a more general distribution, the multinomial, which applies to k possible outcomes for a given trial. Let P_1 be the probability of the outcome being in category 1, P_2

the probability of the outcome being in category 2, P_3 the probability of being in category 3, etc. Then it can be shown that the probability of exactly f_1 occurrences in category 1, f_2 occurrences in category 2, etc., is given by

$$P(f_1,f_2, \ldots, f_k/n) = \frac{n!}{f_1! \, f_2! \, \cdot \cdot \, f_k!} \, P_1^{f_1} \, P_2^{f_2} \cdot \cdot \, P_k^{f_k}$$

This is the *multinomial law,* and it is important because it provides the *exact* sampling distribution for two-way and higher way contingency tables. The chi square test statistics that are presented in introductory statistics books for the one- and two-way chi square are approximations to the multinomial distribution. Before we relate the multinomial distribution to the two-way chi square, we give a few examples of its application in somewhat simpler situations.

Example 2

A die is thrown 10 times. What is the probability that a 1 will occur twice, a 3 three times, and anything else the other 5 times?

Here, $n = 10$ (number of trials), $f_1 = 2$, $f_2 = 3$ and $f_3 = 5$. Furthermore, the probability of a 1 is $P_1 = .1667$, the probability of a 3 is $P_2 = .1667$, and the probability of anything else is $P_3 = .667$. Therefore,

$$P(2,3,5/10) = \frac{10!}{2! \; 3! \; 5!} \, (.1667)^2 \, (.1667)^3 \, (.667)^5$$

$$= 2520 \, (.00013) \, (.132) = .043$$

Example 3

A city has 60% democrats, 30% republicans and 10% independents. If 6 individuals are chosen at random, what is the probability of getting 2 democrats, 1 republican, and 3 independents?

Here, $f_1 = 2$, $f_2 = 1$ and $f_3 = 3$, and the probability is:

$$P(2,1,3/6) = \frac{6!}{2! \; 1! \; 3!} \, (.60)^2 \, (.30)^1 \, (.1)^3 = .0065$$

In order to calculate the exact probabilities in each of the above examples, we needed to know the probability of the outcome in each category. In the first two examples this information was obtained from the fact that the probability of any face of a fair die coming up is 1/6, while in example 3 the probability of the outcome in each category (democrat, republican, or independent) was available from population information. To apply the multinomial law in the contingency table context, whether two-way, three-way, etc., we consider the cells as the categories, and think of it as a one-way layout. For example, with a 2 × 3 table, think of it as a one-way layout with 6 categories, or for a 2 × 2 × 3 table, think of it as a one-way layout with 12 categories. To calculate the probability of a certain frequency of subjects falling in each of the 6 cells of a 2 × 3 table, however, we must know the probability of the subject being in each cell (category). How does one obtain those probabilities? We consider an example to illustrate.

Example 4

A survey researcher is interested in determining how adults in a school district would vote on a bond issue. He also wants to determine if sex moderates the response. A sample of 40 adults yields the following observed cell frequencies:

	Favor	Oppose	Row Probs
Male	10	5	.375 = 15/40
Female	6	19	.625 = 25/40
Column Probs	.40	.60	

The null hypothesis being tested here is that sex is independent of type of response. But independence means that the probability of being in a given cell (category) is simply the product of the subject being in the ith row times the probability of the subject being in the jth column. From these row and column probabilities, then, it is a simple matter to obtain the probability of a subject being in each cell:

$$P_{11} = .375(.4) = .15, \; P_{12} = .375(.6) = .225$$

$$P_{21} = .625(.4) = .25, \; P_{22} = .625(.6) = .375$$

Therefore, the probability of obtaining this *specific* set of observed cell frequencies, assuming that the variables are independent, is given by the multinomial law as:

$$P\,(10,5,6,19/40) = \frac{40!}{10! \; 5! \; 6! \; 19!} \, (.15)^{10} \, (.225)^{5} \, (.25)^{6} \, (.375)^{19}$$

To obtain the sampling distribution, for hypothesis testing purposes, we would have to obtain the multinomial probabilities for all possible outcomes, a very tedious task at best. For example, for the two situations below

	Favor	Oppose			Favor	Oppose
Male	11	4		Male	9	6
Female	5	20		Female	7	18

the following probabilities would need to be calculated:

$$P(11,4,5,20/40) = \frac{40!}{11!\ 4!\ 5!\ 20!}\ (.15)^{11}\ (.225)^4\ (.25)^5\ (.375)^{20}$$

$$P(9,6,7,18/40) = \frac{40!}{9!\ 6!\ 7!\ 18!}\ (.15)^9\ (.225)^6\ (.25)^7\ (.375)^{18}$$

Fortunately, however, when sample size is fairly large, the chi square distribution provides a good approximation to the exact multinomial distribution, and can be used for testing hypotheses about frequency counts.

14.3   TWO WAY CHI SQUARE – LOG LINEAR FORMULATION

Although the log linear model is not really needed for the two-way chi square, it provides a simple setting in which to introduce some of the fundamental notions associated with log linear analysis for higher order designs. We illustrate three main ideas:

1. fitting a set of models to the data
2. the notion of effects for the log linear model
3. the notion of hierarchial models

Using a two-way ANOVA (which the reader has been exposed to), and then consider the parallel development for the two-way chi square.

Our two-way chi square involves 100 university undergraduates cross tabulated to determine whether there is an association between sex and attitude toward a constitutional amendment, while the two-way ANOVA examines the effect of sex and social class on achievement.

The data for both are presented below:

	CHI SQUARE			ANOVA		
	Attitude				Social Class	
	opposed	support			lower	middle	Row
Female	33	7	Female	60	50	55
Male	37	23	Male	40	30	35
			Column Means	50	40	45

The reader may recall that in ANOVA we can model the population cell means as a linear combination of effects as follows:

$$\mu_{ij} = \mu + \alpha_i + \beta_j + \alpha\beta_{ij}$$

and therefore the estimated cell means are given as

$$\bar{x}_{ij} = \underset{\substack{\text{grand} \\ \text{mean}}}{\bar{x}} + \underset{\text{main effects}}{\hat{\alpha}_i + \hat{\beta}_j} + \underset{\text{interaction}}{\hat{\alpha}\beta_{ij}}$$

where the estimated *main effects* for sex are given by:

$$\hat{\alpha}_1 = 55 - 45 = 10 \text{ and } \hat{\alpha}_2 = 35 - 45 = -10$$

i.e., row mean – grand mean for each level of sex.
The main effects for social class are given by:

$$\hat{\beta}_1 = 50 - 45 = 10 \text{ and } \hat{\beta}_2 = 40 - 45 = -5$$

i.e., column mean – grand mean in each case.

The *interaction effects* measure that part of the cell means that can not be explained by an overall effect and the main effects. Therefore, the estimated interaction effect for the ijth cell is:

$$\hat{\phi}_{ij} = \text{cell mean} - \text{grand mean} - \text{main effect of A} - \text{main effect of B}$$
$$= \bar{x}_{ij} - \bar{x} - (\bar{x}_{i\cdot} - \bar{x}) - (\bar{x}_{\cdot j} - \bar{x}) = \bar{x}_{ij} - \bar{x}_{i\cdot} - \bar{x}_{\cdot j} + \bar{x}$$

Recall also that for fixed effects models the sum of the interaction effects for every row and column must sum to 0. Thus, for this example, once we obtain the estimated interaction effect for cell 11, the others will be determined. The interaction effect for cell 11 is

$$\hat{\phi}_{11} = 60 - 55 - 50 + 45 = 0$$

Because of this, all the other cell interaction effects are 0.

Although ANOVA is not typically presented this way in textbooks, we could consider fitting various models to the data, ranging from a very simple model (grand mean), to a model involving a single main effect, a model involving all main effects, and finally the model with all effects. We could arrange these as a *hierarchical* set of models:

(1) $\bar{x}_{ij} = \bar{x}$ (most restricted)
(2) $\bar{x}_{ij} = \bar{x} + \hat{\alpha}_i$
(3) $\bar{x}_{ij} = \bar{x} + \hat{\alpha}_i + \hat{\beta}_j$
(4) $\bar{x}_{ij} = \bar{x} + \hat{\alpha}_i + \hat{\beta}_j + \hat{\alpha}\beta_{ij}$ (least restricted)

The arrangement is hierarchical, because as we proceed from most restricted to least restricted, the more restricted models become subsets of the lesser restricted models. For example, the most restricted model is a subset of model 2, because model 2 has the grand mean plus another effect, while model 2 is a subset of model 3, because model 3 has all the effects in model 2 plus β_j.

Now let us return to the two-way chi square. To express the expected cell frequencies here as a *linear* function of parameters we need to take the natural log of the expected frequencies. It is important to see why this is necessary. The reason is that for multidimensional contingency tables the *multiplicative* model is the natural one. To see why the multiplicative model is natural, it is easiest to illustrate with something the reader has already been exposed to. In the two-way chi square we are testing whether the two modes of classification are independent (this is the null hypothesis). But independence implies that the probability of an observation being in the ith row and the jth column is simply the *product* of the probability of being in the ith row (p_i) times the probability of being in the jth column (p_j), that is,

$$p_{ij} = p_i \cdot p_j$$

Recall that the expected cell frequency e_{ij} is given by $e_{ij} = N\,p_{ij} = N\,p_i \cdot p_j$. For our 2×2 example, let us denote the row totals by o_i+ and the column totals by o_{+j}. It then follows that $p_i = o_i+\,/\,N$ and $p_j = o_{+j}/N$, that is, the probability of being in the ith row is simply the number of observations in that row divided by the total number of observations, and similarly for columns. Therefore, we can rewrite the expected cell frequencies as:

$$e_{ij} = \frac{N\,o_{i+}\,o_{+j}}{N \cdot N} = (o_{i+}\,o_{+j})/N$$

and the expected frequencies are expressed as a multiplicative model. Using logs, however, we can transform the model to one that is *linear in the logs of the expected cell frequencies*. At this point it is important to recall the following rules regarding logs:

$\ln (ab) = \ln a + \ln b$ (log of product = sum of logs)

$\ln (a/b) = \ln a - \ln b$ (log of quotient = difference in logs)

$\ln a^b = b \ln a$

Now let us return to the expression for the expected cell frequencies under the main effects model and rewrite it in additive form using properties of logs:

$e_{ij} = o_i + o_{+j}/N$

$\ln e_{ij} = \ln o_{i+}\,o_{+j}/N$

$\ln e_{ij} = \ln o_{i+}\,o_{+j} - \ln N$ (log of quotient = diff. in logs)

$\ln e_{ij} = \ln o_{i+} + \ln o_{+j} - \ln N$ (log of prod. = sum of logs)

Thus, for cell 11 we have

$$\ln 28 = \ln 40 + \ln 70 - \ln 100$$

We now wish to define estimated effects for the two-way chi square that are analogous to what was done for the two-way ANOVA. In this case, however, we will be deviating the row and column *frequencies* about the grand mean of the expected frequencies.

$$\text{Main Effects for A:} = \underset{\text{row mean}}{\frac{\Sigma \ln e_{ij}}{J}} - \underset{\text{grand mean}}{\frac{\Sigma\Sigma \ln e_{ij}}{IJ}}$$

$$\text{Main Effects for B:} = \underset{\text{column mean}}{\frac{\Sigma \ln e_{ij}}{I}} - \underset{\text{grand mean}}{\frac{\Sigma\Sigma \ln e_{ij}}{IJ}}$$

$$\text{Interaction Effects:} = \ln e_{ij} - \frac{\Sigma \, \ln e_{ij}}{J} - \frac{\Sigma \ln e_{ij}}{I} + \frac{\Sigma\Sigma \ln e_{ij}}{IJ}$$

Now let us apply the above formulas to obtain the main effects for the attitude data presented at the beginning of this section. In the following table are given the natural logs of the expected frequencies under independence (the main effects model), along with the average natural logs for rows and columns. The effect parameters are then simply deviations of these averages from the grand mean of the natural logs.

| | Attitude | | Row | Row |
	Opposed	Support	Means	Effects
Female	3.332	2.485	2.909	−.202
	(28)	(12)		
Male	3.738	2.890	3.314	.203
Column Means	3.535	2.688	3.111	
Column Effects	.424	−.423	(grand mean)	

Both the sex main effect and joint main effect models were run on the SPSSX HILOGLINEAR procedure for the attitude data. The control lines for doing this, along with selected printout (including the parameter estimates), are given in Table 14.1. Note that only a single value is given for each parameter estimate for the main effect model in Table 14.1. The other value is immediately obtained, because the sum of the effects in each case must equal 0.

14.4   THREE-WAY TABLES

When the subjects are cross classified on three variables, then the log linear model can be used to test for a three-way interaction, as well as for all

TABLE 14.1
SPSSX Control Lines for Main Effects Model, Selected Printout,and Expected
Values for Models

TITLE 'LOG LINEAR MAIN EFFECT MODELS'
DATA LIST FREE/SEX ATTITUDE FREQ
WEIGHT BY FREQ
LOGLINEAR SEX(1,2) ATTITUDE(1,2)/
 PRINT =ESTIM/
 DESIGN =SEX/
 PRINT =ESTIM/
 DESIGN =SEX,ATTITUDE/
BEGIN DATA
1 1 33   1 2 7   2 1 37   2 2 23
END DATA

SEX MAIN EFFECT MODEL
  GOODNESS OF FIT TEST STATISTICS
               LIKELIHOOD RATION CHI SQUARE = 21.65063 DF =2 P =.000
                      PEARSON CHI SQUARE = 20.16667 DF =2 P =.000
  ESTIMATES FOR PARAMETERS
  SEX

PARAMETER	COEFF.	STD. ERR.	Z-VALUE
1	− .202735541	.10206	− 1.98637

SEX AND ATTITUDE MAIN EFFECTS MODEL
  GOODNESS OF FIT TEST STATISTICS
               LIKELIHOOD RATION CHI SQUARE = 5.19406 DF =1 P =.023
                      PEARSON CHI SQUARE = 4.96032 DF =1 P =.026
  ESTIMATES FOR PARAMETERS
  SEX

PARAMETER	COEFF.	STD. ERR.
1	− .2027325527	.10206

  ATTITUDE

PARAMETER	COEFF.	STD. ERR.
2	.4236488279	.10911

ORIGINAL DATA	EXPECTED VALUES UNDER THESE MODELS		
	EQUIPROBABILITY	SEX MAIN	SEX & ATTITUDE
ATTITUDE	ATTITUDE	ATTITUDE	ATTITUDE
M 33 7	M 25 25	M 20 20	M 28 12
F 37 23	F 25 25	F 30 30	F 42 18

two-way interactions and main effects. As with the two-way table, the
natural log of the expected cell frequencies is expressed as a linear
combination of effect parameters. In the two computer examples to be
considered we fit a series of models to the data, which range in complexity
from just the grand mean to a model with one or more main effects, to a
model with main effects and some two way interactions, and finally to the
saturated model (the model with all effects in it).

The other point to remember from the previous section is that we are examining only hierarchical models. A series of hierarchical models for a three-way table with factors A, B, and C is given in Table 14.2. Model 1 is called the most restricted model because only one parameter (the grand mean) is used to fit the data, while model 8 is called the least restricted or saturated model because all parameters are used to fit the data and they will fit the data perfectly. Recall also that the models are called hierarchical because the more restricted models are subsets of the less restricted models. For example, model 2 is a subset of model 4 since all the parameters in model 2 are in model 4. Similarily model 5 is a subset of model 7 since all parameters in model 5 are in model 7, which in addition has the ac and bc interaction parameters.

For Example 5, which uses Head Start data, we use basic probability theory to compute the expected cell frequencies for various models, showing how some of the printout from the package (BMDP4F) is obtained. The reader will see that two test statistics (the Likelihood ratio χ^2 and the Pearson χ^2) appear on the BMDP4F printout for testing each model for goodness of fit. The form of the Pearson χ^2 is exactly the same as for the two-way chi square. The complication is that when we get into three- or higher way tables, the computation of the expected frequencies becomes increasingly more difficult, depending on the model fitted. As a matter of fact, for certain models, probability theory can't be used to obtain the expected frequencies, rather an iterative routine is needed to obtain them. This is true for model 7 in Table 14.2 (see Bishop, Fienberg, & Holland, 1975, pp 83–84).

TABLE 14.2
A Set of Hierarchical Models for a General Three-Way Table
(factors A, B, and C)

Model No.	Log Linear Model	
1	$\ln \epsilon_{ijk} = \lambda$	BRACKET NOTATION
2	$\ln \epsilon_{ijk} = \lambda + \alpha_A$	[A]
3	$\ln \epsilon_{ijk} = \lambda + \alpha_A + \beta_B$	[A] [B]
4	$\ln \epsilon_{ijk} = \lambda + \alpha_A + \beta_B + \gamma_C$	[A] [B] [C]
5	$\ln \epsilon_{ijk} = \lambda + \alpha_A + \beta_B + \gamma_C + \phi_{AB}$	[A] [B] [C] [AB]
6	$\ln \epsilon_{ijk} = \lambda + \alpha_A + \beta_B + \gamma_C + \phi_{AB} + \phi_{AC}$	[A] [B] [C] [AB] [AC]
7	$\ln \epsilon_{ijk} = \lambda + \alpha_A + \beta_B + \gamma_C + \phi_{AB} + \phi_{AC} + \phi_{BC}$	[A] [B] [C] [AB] [AC] [BC]
8	$\ln \epsilon_{ijk} = \lambda + \alpha_A + \beta_B + \gamma_C + \phi_{AB} + \phi_{AC} + \phi_{BC} + \phi_{ABC}$	[A] [B] [C] [AB] [AC] [BC] [ABC]

λ, the α's, β's, γ's and ϕ's are parameters (population values). They, of course, must be estimated. Recall, from earlier in the chapter, that for a two way table the estimated main effect for ith row of factor A is given by α_i = average of natural logs − grand mean of natural logs of expected freqs for row i of expected freqs for all cells while the estimated main effect for the jth column of factor B is given by β_j = average of natural logs − grand mean of natural logs of expected freqs for jth col. of expected freqs for all cells. The estimated effects for the above three way table would proceed in an analogous fashion.

The data that was presented at the beginning of this chapter on approval versus non-approval of a television series has a significant three-way interaction present, and gives us an opportunity to discuss what this means in a contingency table, and to relate it to the interpretation of a three way interaction in ANOVA.

Example 5

This study involves 246 preschool children, 60 of which were in Head Start, the other 186 in a control group. They were classified as to the educational level of their parents (ninth, tenth and eleventh, or twelfth grade) and as to whether they failed or passed a test, yielding the following table.

Education	Treatment	Test Fail	Pass
Ninth	Head	11(111)	0(112)
	Cont	56(121)	15(122)
Tenth/Eleventh	Head	14(211)	8(212)
	Cont	44(221)	14(222)
Twelfth	Head	17(311)	10(312)
	Cont	35(321)	22(322)

The cell identification is in parentheses. The first number refers to the level of education, the second to the level for treatment and the third to the level for test. This data was run on BMDP4F. The control lines for doing so are presented in Table 14.3 and part of the printout is given in the same table. Note, as mentioned earlier, that two test statistics are given for testing each model for goodness of fit.

The results from the two statistics are generally quite similar, and we could use either. However, temporarily we use the Pearson for three reasons. First, the formula for it is intuitively easier to understand. Second, it is easier to compute than the likelihood ratio statistic. And third, there is evidence that the Pearson statistic is more accurate, especially when total sample size is small (Fienberg, 1980; Milligan, 1980). For example, Fienberg (1980) indicates that when $n = 100$ and one is testing for no second order interaction in a $3 \times 3 \times 3$ table at the .05 level, the actual $\alpha = .056$ for the Pearson, while the actual $\alpha = .104$ for the likelihood ratio test statistic. We said we will use the Pearson statistic temporarily, since when we get to *comparing models* there are technical reasons for preferring the likelihood ratio test statistic.

Note in Table 14.3 that all models are given. BMDP4F does this by default for three-way tables. It is important to remember that BMDP4F abbreviates the notation for hierarchical models. The program assumes that

Table 14.3
BMDP4F Control Lines and Selected Printout for Log Linear Analysis of
Head Start Data

PROBLEM TITLE IS 'HEAD START DATA'./
① INPUT VARIABLES=3. FORMAT IS FREE. TABLE IS 2,2,3./
② VARIABLE NAMES ARE TEST,TREAT,EDUC./
  TABLE INDICES ARE TEST,TREAT,EDUC. SYMBOLS ARE T,R,E./
  CATEGORY NAMES(1) ARE FAIL,PASS. CODES(1) ARE 1,2.
  NAMES(2) ARE HEAD,CONT. CODES(2) ARE 1,2.
  NAMES(3) ARE NINTH,TENELEV,TWELVE. CODES(3) ARE 1,2./
③ FIT ALL./
  END/
  11 0 56 15 14 8 44 14 17 10 35 22

***** ALL MODELS ARE REQUESTED—

MODEL	DF	LIKELIHOOD-RATIO CHISQ	PROB.	PEARSON CHISQ	PROB.
T.	10	91.04	0.0000	80.96	0.0000
R.	10	72.41	0.0000	63.32	0.0000
E.	9	140.02	0.0000	143.36	0.0000
T,R.	9	23.34	0.0055	18.54	0.0294
R,E.	8	72.31	0.0000	63.45	0.0000
E,T.	8	90.95	0.0000	80.90	0.0000
T,R,E.	7	23.24	0.0015	18.32	0.0106
TR.	8	23.19	0.0031	17.79	0.0229
TE.	6	62.77	0.0000	73.11	0.0000
RE.	6	63.24	0.0000	56.61	0.0000
T,RE.	5	14.17	0.0146	11.39	0.0442
R,TE.	5	15.06	0.0101	11.62	0.0404
E,TR.	6	23.09	0.0008	17.55	0.0074
TR,TE.	4	14.91	0.0049	11.23	0.0241
TE,RE.	3	5.99	0.1122	4.06	0.2552
RE,TR.	4	14.02	0.0072	11.08	0.0257
TR,TE,RE.	2	5.97	0.0504	4.11	0.1283

①The TABLE IS 2,2,3 refers to 2 levels for TEST by 2 levels for TREAT by 3 levels for EDUC.

②The variable that is listed first is the one whose subscripts vary most rapidly, and hence whose frequencies change most quickly. Note from the data display under Example 1 that the frequencies for TEST change first. Then the subscript for TREAT changes from 1 to 2 when we move to the second row of frequencies. Finally, the subscript for EDUC changes least rapidly (from 1 to 2) when we enter row 3 of the frequencies, i.e., the second level of education.

③The FIT ALL here refers to the fact that we are fitting all models to the data.

you realize if an interaction term is in the model, like TR for the present case, then all lower order relatives are also *automatically* included in that model. This implies in this case that the model specified by only TR really is the model [TR, R, T]. As another illustration, the model [R, TE] actually has the following effects in it: R, E, T, TE.

Now we wish to show the reader how the Pearson values in Table 14.3 are obtained for some of the models. We consider five different models, in increasing complexity:

1. T—single main effect model
2. T, R—two main effects in the model
3. T, R, E—all main effects (model of independence of factors)
4. R, TE—all main effects and single interaction effect
5. TE, RE—all main effects and two interaction effects

T—Single Main Effect Model

Here we are assuming the expected cell frequencies will vary only from FAIL to PASS, and that the expected frequencies will *not* vary by educational level or by treatment group. With six cells for each level of test, the expected frequencies are given by:

$$E_{ijk} = \frac{f_k}{6} = \frac{n \cdot p_k}{6}$$

where f_k is the frequency of observations in level k for TEST and p_k is the probability of being in level k of TEST. Because the frequency for level 1 of TEST $= f_1 = 177$, the expected frequencies for the 6 cells within FAIL $= E_{ij1} = 177/6 = 29.5$. The number of observations for level 2 (PASS) of TEST $= f_2 = 69$. Therefore, $E_{ij2} = 69/6 = 11.5$. Hence, the table of observed and expected frequencies is as follows:

		Test	
Education	Treatment	Fail	Pass
Ninth	Head	11(29.5)	0(11.5)
	Cont	56(29.5)	15(11.5)
Tenth/Eleventh	Head	14(29.5)	8(11.5)
	Cont	44(29.5)	14(11.5)
Twelfth	Head	17(29.5)	10(11.5)
	Cont	35(29.5)	22(11.5)

The Pearson chi square statistic is calculated as:

$$\chi^2 = \frac{(11-29.5)^2}{29.5} + \frac{(0-11.5)^2}{11.5} + \frac{(56-29.5)^2}{29.5} + \cdots + \frac{(22-11.5)^2}{11.5}$$

$\chi^2 = 80.958$, as indicated on the printout in Table 14.3.

The likelihood ratio chi square statistic is

$$L^2 = 2 \cdot \Sigma \, o_i \cdot \ln \, (o_i/e_i) = 2[11 \, \ln(11/29.5) + 0 \, \ln(0/11.5) +$$
$$56 \, \ln(56/29.5) + \ldots + 22 \, \ln(22/11.5)]$$

$$L^2 = 2 \cdot (-10.851 + 35.894 + 3.986 \ldots + 5.984 + 14.271) = 91.046$$

T, R Main Effects Model

Here we are assuming that both TEST and TREAT have a systematic, although *independent,* effect in determining the expected cell frequencies, and that the expected cell frequencies do not differ over educational level, because this effect is not in the model. Thus, the expected frequencies can be found by lumping educational levels together and applying the same formula used for the two way chi square, but then dividing by three to distribute the resulting expected frequencies over the three educational levels. The formula is

$$E_{ijk} = \frac{f_j f_k}{3n} = \frac{n \, p_j \, p_k}{3}$$

where f_j is the frequency of observations for level j of treatment and f_k is the frequency of observations for level k of TEST. Below we present the combined observed frequencies for the 3 educational levels, along with the calculated expected frequencies, given in parentheses:

	TEST		COLUMN
	FAIL	PASS	TOTAL
HEAD	42 (43.17)	18 (16.83)	60
CONT	135 (133.83)	51 (52.17)	186
ROW TOTAL	177	69	246

Now, to obtain the expected cell frequencies for each cell in the three-way design, we simply divide each of the above expected cell frequencies by 3, distributing them equally over the three educational levels. Thus, the chi square for this main effects model becomes:

$$\chi^2 = \frac{(11-14.39)^2}{14.39} + \frac{(0-5.61)^2}{5.61} + \frac{(56-44.61)^2}{44.61} + \ldots +$$

$$\frac{(35-44.61)^2}{44.61} + \frac{(22-17.39)^2}{17.39} = 18.546$$

as given on the printout in Table 14.3.

T, R, E Main Effects Model

Here we are assuming that TEST, TREAT, and EDUC all determine the expected cell frequencies, although they exert their influence independently of one another. Recall from basic probability theory that if independence is assumed we can multiply probabilities. Therefore, to find the probability that a given subject falls in some cell we simply multiply the probability of the subject being in the ith level for EDUC (p_i) by the probability of the subject being in jth level for TREAT (p_j) by the probability of the subject being in kth level for TEST (p_k). To determine the expected number of subjects in any cell we simply multiply by total sample size. Thus, the formula for obtaining the expected cell frequencies becomes:

$$E_{ijk} = n \, p_i \, p_j \, p_k$$

Below is the three-way table with level probabilities for each factor in parentheses (which is the number of observations in that level divided by total sample size) and the expected cell frequencies.

		TEST	
		FAIL (.72)	PASS (.28)
Ninth (.333)	HEAD (.244)	11 (14.39)	0 (5.6)
	CONT (.756)	56 (44.59)	15 (17.34)
Tenth/Eleventh (.325)	HEAD (.244)	14 (14.05)	8 (5.46)
	CONT (.756)	44 (43.52)	14 (16.924)
Twelfth (.341)	HEAD (.244)	17 (14.74)	10 (5.73)
	CONT (.756)	35 (45.66)	22 (17.76)

From the above formula then, note that $E_{111} = 14.39 = 246 \, (.333)(.244)(.72)$, and $E_{322} = 17.76 = 246 \, (.341)(.756)(.28)$.

Thus the chi square statistic for this model is:

$$\chi^2 = \frac{(11-14.39)^2}{14.39} + \frac{(0-5.6)^2}{5.6} + \frac{(56-44.59)^2}{44.59} + \ldots + \frac{(35-45.66)^2}{45.66}$$
$$+ \frac{(22-17.76)^2}{17.76}$$

$\chi^2 = 18.35$, as given on the printout in Table 14.3.

R, TE Model

For this model, since we are considering hierarchical models, all main effects are in the model as well as the marginal interaction TE. To obtain the expected cell frequencies we need the marginal table of frequencies for

TE (i.e., f_{ik}). But these need to be adjusted for the effect of R, which is operating independently of T and E since there are no TR or ER interactions in the model. Since R is operating independently, we simply multiply the f_{ik} by the probability of the subject being in either level of R. Therefore, the formula is

$$E_{ijk} = p_j f_{ik}$$

The two-way table of frequencies for test by educational level (TE), collapsed over the two treatment groups, is

	FAIL	PASS
Ninth	67	15
Tenth/Eleventh	58	22
Twelfth	52	32

Also, $p_1 = .244$ (probability of being in the HEAD group) and $p_2 = .756$ (probability of being in the control group). Below we present the table of observed and expected frequencies:

		FAIL	PASS
Ninth	HEAD (.244)	11 (16.35)	0 (3.66)
	CONT (.756)	56 (50.65)	15 (11.34)
Tenth/Eleventh	HEAD (.244)	14 (14.13)	8 (5.37)
	CONT (.756)	44 (43.85)	14 (16.63)
Twelfth	HEAD (.244)	17 (12.69)	10 (7.81)
	CONT (.756)	35 (39.31)	22 (24.19)

Therefore, from the above formula, we have for example

$$E_{111} = .244(67) = 16.35 \text{ and } E_{322} = .756(32) = 24.19.$$

The Pearson chi square statistic for this model is thus:

$$\chi^2 = \frac{(11-16.35)^2}{16.35} + \frac{(0-3.66)^2}{3.66} + \frac{(56-50.65)^2}{50.65} + \cdots + \frac{(35-39.31)^2}{39.31}$$
$$+ \frac{(22-24.19)^2}{24.19}$$

TE, RE Model

Since here we are fitting interactions, the probabilities of being in a given cell for the collapsed TE and RE tables is relevant. However, an adjustment for the probability of being in level i of E (education) is necessary.

The collapsed tables are

	TE			RE	
	FAIL	PASS		HEAD	CONT
Ninth	67	15	Ninth	11	71
Tenth/Eleventh	58	22	Tenth/Eleventh	22	58
Twelfth	52	32	Twelfth	27	57

The expected cell frequencies are calculated as:

$$E_{ijk} = \frac{n \, p_{ik} \, p_{ij}}{p_i} = \frac{f_{ik} \, f_{ij}}{f_i}$$

and thus a few sample expected frequencies are calculated as

$$E_{111} = 67(11)/82 = 8.99$$

$$E_{222} = 22(58)/80 = 15.95$$

and the full table of observed and expected cell frequencies is

		TEST	
		FAIL	PASS
Ninth	HEAD	11 (8.99)	0 (2.01)
	CONT	56 (58.01)	15 (12.99)
Tenth/Eleventh	HEAD	14 (15.95)	8 (6.05)
	CONT	44 (42.05)	14 (15.95)
Twelfth	HEAD	17 (16.714)	10 (10.286)
	CONT	35 (35.286)	22 (21.714)

Computation of the Pearson chi square statistic yields 4.05, within rounding error of the value on the printout.

14.5   MODEL SELECTION

Examination of Table 14.3 reveals, using the Pearson values, that only the models [TE,RE] and [TR,TE,RE] provide a good fit at the .05 level, since only in those cases are the probabilities $> .05$. Generally when one has more than one model that adequately fits the data, the most parsimonious model is chosen. That is, we prefer the simplest model that fits the data, which here is [TE, RE].

Generally, in comparing two or more *hierarchical* models that fit the data, the likelihood ratio chi square statistic is used. The difference between the two chi squares is referred to the chi square distribution with degrees of freedom equal to the difference in the degrees of freedom for the two models. There was no need to do this in the previous example since the likelihood ratio χ^2 for the more complicated model differed only very slightly from the χ^2 for the simpler model (5.97 vs. 5.99).

To illustrate how to use the likelihood χ^2 statistic for comparing models, we consider the results from a log linear analysis of a three-way table from Kennedy (1983, p. 108). Below are the likelihood ratio χ^2's from BMDP4F:

MODEL	DF	LIKELIHOOD CHISQ	PROB
T	6	42.91	.0000
E	6	46.58	.0000
S	6	8.39	.2109
T, E	5	42.55	.0000
E, S	5	8.03	.1546
S, T	5	4.36	.4984
T, E, S	4	4.00	.4057
TE	4	40.12	.0000
TS	4	3.34	.5032
ES	4	7.99	.0920
T, ES	3	3.96	.2655
E, TS	3	2.98	.3953
S, TE	3	1.57	.6664
TE, TS	2	0.54	.7623
TS, ES	2	2.94	.2304
ES, TE	2	1.53	.4655
TE, TS, ES	1	0.54	.4620

First we compare models [S] and [S,T], both of which fit the data at the .05 level. The difference in the likelihood chi squares is $8.39 - 4.36 = 4.03$, and the difference in the degrees of freedom for the two models is $6 - 5 = 1$. Because the critical value at the .05 level is 3.84, the difference is significant, indicating that [S,T] is the preferred model. Now let us compare the models [S,T] and [S,TE]. The difference in the chi squares is $4.36 - 1.57 = 2.79$, and the difference in degrees of freedom is $5 - 3 = 2$. This chi square is not significant since the critical value is 5.99, indicating that adding the TE interaction term and main effect E does not provide a better fit, and we should therefore stick with the simpler model, [S,T]. It is very important to note that comparing models with the likelihood chi square is only meaningful when they are hierarchically related — when one model is a subset of the other model. Note that this was the case in both of the above examples. In the first case the model [S] is a subset of the model [S,T], while in the second case the model [S,T] is a subset of the model [S,TE], in that the latter model actually contains the terms: S,T,E, and TE. On the other hand, we can not compare the models [E,S] and [TS], because the first model is not a subset of the second.

One of the advantages of hierarchical models is the availability of the above test for comparing models. With nonhierarchical models a statistical test for the difference between models does not exist. For this and other reasons, all the major texts on categorical data analysis deal almost exclusively with hierarchical models. If you find the need to use a

nonhierarchical model, they can be obtained from the SPSSX LOGLI-
NEAR program and from the SAS CATMOD program.

Before we turn to the next computer example, it will be helpful to
distinguish between three different types of association:

1. Marginal association—this is the association that exists between
   two variables A and B when we collapse over the levels of a third
   variable C.
2. Partial association—the association that exists between A and B
   after the effects of C are taken into account. If there is association
   between A and B for each level of C, then partial association exists.
3. Differential association—when the nature of the association between A and B is different for the levels of C. This is evidence for
   a significant three-way interaction.

Example 6 considers the following data:

	Rural		Urban	
	Approval	No Approval	Approval	No Approval
Female	3	7	6	12
Male	5	15	17	1

Note that the nature of the association between sex and approval is quite
different for the rural and urban areas, especially for males. We will see
shortly that there is a significant three-way interaction for this data. The
interpretation of a three-way interaction in ANOVA is somewhat analogous, except that in ANOVA means (rather than frequencies) are involved.
Consider a sex × treatment × social class design with the following profiles of means for the social classes:

	Lower		Middle	
	Treat 1	Treat 2	Treat 1	Treat 2
Males	60	53	71	65
Females	42	50	58	54

Here we have a three-way interaction since there is a strong ordinal
interaction for lower social class (males do much better than females for
Treat 1 but only slightly better for Treat 2) and no interaction for the middle
social class. That is, the profiles of means for the social classes are
significantly different.

14.6   COLLAPSIBILITY

In our analysis of the Head Start data (Table 14.3), it was found that the
three-way interaction was not significant, and that the model [TE,RE]

provided the most parsimonious fit to the data. The natural next step might appear to be that of reporting two-way tables for TE and RE, collapsing over the third variable, and discussing the results from these tables. But the question arises as to when we can validly collapse across a third variable. Bishop, Fienberg, and Holland (1975, pp 41–42) present an example, which we discuss shortly, to show that under certain conditions collapsing can lead to misleading interpretations.

Let A, B, and C be the factors for a three-way design. Then we can validly collapse AB over C if the following are met:

1. The three way interaction is not significant, i.e., $ABC = 0$.
2. Either A or B is independent of C, i.e., $AC = 0$ or $BC = 0$.

Similarly, we can validly collapse AC over B if $ABC = 0$ and either $AB = 0$ or $BC = 0$. Finally, BC can be collapsed over A if $ABC = 0$ and either $AB = 0$ or $AC = 0$.

Returning to the Head Start example, we see from the above that summarizing and discussing results from the TE table (collapsed over R) and the RE table (collapsed over T) will be valid if $TRE = 0$, which we know to be the case, and if either $TR = 0$ or $ER = 0$ for the first case. For the second case, collapsing will be valid if $TR = 0$ or $ET = O$. So for this particular example we can validly collapse in *both* cases if $TR = 0$. To determine if this is the case we take the data and combine over educational levels, yielding the following table for TR:

	Fail	Pass
Head Start	42	18
	(43.17)	(16.83)
Control	135	51
	(133.83)	(52.17)

The values in parentheses are the expected values. Calculation of the chi square yields $\chi^2 = .149$, which is clearly not significant. Thus, T is independent of R and we can validly collapse in both cases.

Now we return to the Bishop, et al. study (1975) mentioned earlier, which related survival of infants (variable 1) to the amount of prenatal care received by the mothers (variable 2). The mothers attended one of two clinics (variable 3). The three-dimensional table was:

		Infant Survival	
Clinic	Amount of care	Died	Survived
A	Less	3	176
	More	4	293
B	Less	17	197
	More	2	23

Let us examine the relationship between care and survival *within* each clinic using the cross product ratios. We find $\hat{\alpha}_A = 3(293)/4(176) = 1.2$ and $\hat{\alpha}_B = 17(23)/2(197) = 1$. Both of these are very close to 1, indicating that survival is unrelated to amount of care. Now, suppose someone had combined (collapsed) the information from the two clinics to examine the relationship between survival and amount of care. The combined table is

		Infant Survival	
		Died	Survived
	Less	20	373
Amount of Care			
	More	6	316

The cross product ratio for this table is 2.8, a considerable deviation from 1, indicating that survival is related to amount of care. This is erroneous, however, because it is not valid to collapse here. To validly collapse clinic would need to be independent of either amount of care or survival, but in fact clinic is dependent on both of these. The two-way table for clinic by survival is:

	Died	Survived
Clinic A	7	469
Clinic B	19	220

The chi square for this table is 19.06, which is significant at the .05 level. The reader should show that amount of care is also dependent on clinic.

Example 6

This example involves the survey data presented at the beginning of the chapter, which examined the effect of sex and geographic location on reaction to a television series.

	Rural		Urban	
	Approval	No Approval	Approval	No Approval
Female	3	7	6	12
Male	5	15	17	1

Cursory inspection of the above data reveals that the pattern of responses for rural males is very different from that for urban males. This data was run on BMDP4F and the results for all models is given in Table 14.4. Note that none of the models provide a satisfactory fit to the data at the .05 level. This means we need the saturated model to fit the data, and also implies that there is a significant three-way interaction effect. Recall that a significant three-way interaction means that the nature of the association (as revealed by the profile of frequency responses) is different for the levels

TABLE 14.4

Goodness of Fit Test Statistics for all Hierarchical Models for Sex by Location by Approval Data

***** ALL MODELS ARE REQUESTED –

MODEL	DF	LIKELIHOOD- RATIO CHISQ	PROB.	PEARSON CHISQ	PROB.
A.	6	29.85	0.0000	28.21	0.0001
L.	6	29.54	0.0000	27.29	0.0001
S.	6	28.57	0.0001	24.84	0.0004
A,L.	5	29.30	0.0000	26.90	0.0001
L,S.	5	28.02	0.0000	23.62	0.0003
S,A.	5	28.33	0.0000	24.45	0.0002
A,L,S.	4	27.78	0.0000	22.98	0.0001
AL.	4	19.94	0.0005	17.98	0.0012
AS.	4	23.97	0.0001	21.11	0.0003
LS.	4	26.15	0.0000	22.82	0.0001
A,L,S.	3	25.90	0.0000	22.66	0.0000
L,AS.	3	23.42	0.0000	20.74	0.0001
S,AL.	3	18.41	0.0004	16.85	0.0008
AL,AS.	2	14.05	0.0009	12.42	0.0020
AS,AL.	2	21.54	0.0000	18.77	0.0001
LS,AL.	2	16.54	0.0003	14.65	0.0007
AL,AS,LS.	1	8.03	0.0046	9.41	0.0022

of the third factor, chosen here to be location. The control lines for obtaining all models as well as for obtaining the χ^2 statistics for the sex × approval interaction (urbans) and the sex × approval interaction (rurals) are given in Table 14.5. Printout from that run (see Table 14.5) indicates that sex is independent of approval for rural subjects ($\chi^2 = .085$, $p < .77$) but that for urban urban subjects there is a strong interaction effect between sex and approval ($\chi^2 = 14.57, p < .0001$).

14.7 THE ODDS (CROSS PRODUCT) RATIO

At this point we wish to introduce a concept which many texts and authors use heavily in discussing log linear analysis, the odds ratio. For a 2 × 2 table the odds ratio is estimated as the product of the observed diagonal frequencies divided by the product of the non-diagonal frequencies:

$$\hat{\alpha} = (o_{11} \, o_{22})/(o_{12} \, o_{21})$$

If $\hat{\alpha}$ equals 1, then the variables (modes of classification) are independent. As a simple example to illustrate consider:

	Success	Failure
Treat 1	10	30
Treat 2	5	15

Here $\hat{\alpha} = 10(15)/30(5) = 1$. Note that the ratio of successes to failures is the *same* for both treatments, that is, it is independent of treatment. Or to put it in odds terms, the odds of succeeding are 1 in 4 regardless of treatment.

If the odds ratio is sufficiently deviant from 1, then we conclude that the modes of classification are dependent or associated. There is a statistical test for this, although we do not present it.

Let us use the odds ratio to characterize the differential association for rural and urban subjects in the previous example. For rurals the odds ratio is $\hat{\alpha}_1 = 3(15)/5(7) = 1.28$, while for urban subjects the odds ratio is given by $\hat{\alpha}_2 = 6(1)/17(2) = .03$. The ratio being near 1 for rurals implies independence, while the odds ratio being near 0 for urbans implies dependence. There is a statistical test for determining whether two such odds ratios are significantly different (Fienberg, 1980, p. 37). Significance for that test implies a three-way interaction effect. The test statistic is

$$z = \frac{\ln \hat{\alpha}_1 - \ln \hat{\alpha}_2}{\sqrt{s\hat{\alpha}_1^2 + s_{\hat{\alpha}_2}^2}}$$

where $s_{\hat{\alpha}_1}^2$ is the estimated variance of $\ln \hat{\alpha}_1$, and is given by

$$s_{\hat{\alpha}_1}^2 = 1/o_{11} + 1/o_{12} + 1/o_{21} + 1/o_{22}$$

If the three-way interaction is 0, then z has an approximate normal distribution with mean 0 and standard deviation of 1. Let us use this statistic to test the three-way interaction effect for the survey data. First, the

TABLE 14.5
BMDP4F Control Lines for Sex by Location by Approval Data with Observed and Expected Values for Each Geographic Region

---

```
PROBLEM TITLE IS 'THREE WAY LOG LINEAR'./
INPUT VARIABLES ARE 3. FORMAT IS FREE. TABLE IS 2,2,2./
VARIABLE NAMES ARE APPROV,LOCAT,SEX./
TABLE INDICES ARE APPROV,LOCAT,SEX.
SYMBOLS ARE A,L,S./
CATEGORY NAMES(1) ARE APPROV,UNAPPROV. CODES(1) ARE 1,2.
NAMES(2) ARE RURAL,URBAN. CODES(2) ARE 1,2.
NAMES(3) ARE FEMALE,MALE. CODES(3) ARE 1,2./
FIT ALL./
TABLE INDICES ARE APPROV,SEX. CONDITION IS LOCAT./  ①
PRINT OBSERVED.EXPECTED.STAN./
FIT ALL./
END/
3 7 6 12 5 15 17 1
```

---

① THE CONDITION IS LOCAT. part of the TABLE paragraph yields the APPROVAL BY SEX tables for each level of location.

(Continued)

TABLE 14.5 (*Continued*)

USING LEVEL   RURAL   OF VARIABLE 2 LOCAT
********   ********

SEX   APPROV

SEX	APPROV	UNAPPROV	TOTAL
FEMALE	3	7	10
MALE	5	15	20
TOTAL	8	22	30

MINIMUM ESTIMATED EXPECTED VALUE IS   2.67

STATISTIC	VALUE	D.F.	PROB.
PEARSON CHISQUARE	0.085	1	0.7703
YATES CORRECTED CHISQ.	0.000	1	1.0000

***** EXPECTEC VALUES – TABLE 2

SEX   APPROV

SEX	APPROV	UNAPPROV	TOTAL
FEMALE	2.7	7.3	10.0
MALE	5.3	14.7	20.0
TOTAL	8.0	22.0	30.0

***** STANDARDIZED DEVIATES = (OBS – EXP)/SQRT(EXP)

SEX   APPROV

SEX	APPROV	UNAPPROV	TOTAL
FEMALE	0.2	0.1	0.1
MALE	−0.1	0.1	−0.1
TOTAL	0.1	0.0	0.0

USING LEVEL   URBAN   OF VARIABLE 2 LOCAT
********   ********

SEX   APPROV

SEX	APPROV	UNAPPROV	TOTAL
FEMALE	6	12	18
MALE	17	1	18
TOTAL	23	13	36

MINIMUM ESTIMATED EXPECTED VALUE IS   6.50

STATISTIC	VALUE	D.F.	PROB.
PEARSON CHISQUARE	14.569	1	0.0001
YATES CORRECTED CHISQ.	12.040	1	0.0005

***** EXPECTEC VALUES – TABLE 2

SEX   APPROV

SEX	APPROV	UNAPPROV	TOTAL
FEMALE	11.5	6.5	18.0
MALE	11.5	6.5	18.0
TOTAL	23.0	13.0	36.0

***** STANDARDIZED DEVIATES = (OBS – EXP)/SQRT(EXP)

SEX   APPROV

SEX	APPROV	UNAPPROV	TOTAL
FEMALE	−1.6	2.2	0.5
MALE	1.6	−2.2	−0.5
TOTAL	0.0	0.0	0.0

denominator is just the square root of the sum of the reciprocals of the cell sizes:

$$\sqrt{s_{\hat{\alpha}_1}^2 + s_{\hat{\alpha}_2}^2} = \sqrt{1/3 + 1/5 + 1/7 + 1/15 + 1/6 + 1/17 + 1/12 + 1/1}$$

$$= \sqrt{2.045} = 1.43$$

Therefore, $z = (\ln 1.28 - \ln .03)/1.43 = 2.625$. We would reject at the .05 level, because the critical values are ± 1.96, and conclude that there is a significant three-way interaction.

14.8 NORMED FIT INDEX AND RESIDUAL ANALYSIS

The reader should recall our discussion in Chapter 1 on the strong effect sample size has on tests of significance. If sample size is large enough, almost any effect, whether in ANOVA, regression, or log linear analysis, will be declared significant. On the other hand, with small sample size important effects may not be declared significant because of inadequate power. Bonnett and Bentler (1983) comment on this problem in the context of model selection in log linear analysis:

> Sample size also has an undesirable effect on exploratory analyses when the formal test is the only criterion for model selection; overrestricted models tend to be selected in very small samples and underrestricted models tend to be selected in very large samples. Given the sample size dependency of the formal tests, goodness of fit information that is *independent* of sample size will surely be informative. (156, emphasis added)

Bonnett and Bentler describe a normed fit index $\hat{\Delta}$ that was originally proposed by Goodman (1971). We write it as follows:

$$\hat{\Delta} = \frac{\chi^2 \text{ (base model)} - \chi^2 \text{ (model being tested)}}{\chi^2 \text{ (base model)}}$$

Numerically, $\hat{\Delta}$ is bounded between 0 and 1, and it indicates the *percent improvement* in goodness of fit of the model being tested over the base model. The choice of base model is not fixed. It could be the model involving only the grand mean, or it could be the simpler of two models, both of which "fit" the data. To illustrate the latter, consider the following Pearson χ^2's from a run of data from Kennedy (1983, p. 108):

MODEL	DF	CHI SQUARE	PROB
T	6	39.53	.0000
E	6	46.45	.0000
S	6	8.00	.2381
T, E	5	39.19	.0000
E, S	5	7.91	.1614
S, T	5	4.58	.4688
T, E, S	4	4.13	.3883
TE	4	37.03	.0000
TS	4	3.28	.5121
ES	4	7.83	.0979
T, ES	3	3.99	.2622
E, TS	3	2.93	.4025
S, TE	3	1.60	.6588
TE, TS	2	.53	.7656
TS, ES	2	2.90	.2345
ES, TE	2	1.52	.4675
TE, TS, ES	1	.53	.4653

From the above it is clear that most of the models fit the data at the .05 level. The simplest model that fits the data involves the single main effect S. The next simplest, which involves a substantial drop in the chi square value, is the main effects model [S,T]. Using Goodman's $\hat{\Delta}$ we calculate percent improvement in goodness of fit for [S,T] over S:

$$\hat{\Delta} = (8 - 4.58)/8 = .43$$

Thus, we might prefer to adopt the model (S,T), although it is slightly more complicated, because of a substantial improvement in fit.

14.9 RESIDUAL ANALYSIS

In Chapter 3 on multiple regression we discussed the importance of residual analysis in assessing violations of assumptions, goodness of fit, and in identifying outliers. In log linear work analysis of residuals is also useful, for example, in identifying perhaps a single cell or small group of cells that may be responsible for a given model not fitting the data. The first point we need to make clear is that comparison of raw residuals could be quite misleading. Equal raw residuals may reflect quite different discrepancies if the expected values are different. For example, if the expected frequency for one cell is 100 and for another 10, and the raw residuals are $110 - 100 = 10$ and $20 - 10 = 10$, then it is intuitively clear that the deviation of 10 in the latter case reflects a larger percentage deviation. A means is needed of standardizing the residuals so that they can be meaningfully compared. Several types of standardized residuals have been developed. The one we illustrate is given on the BMDP4F output (Table 14.5), and is due to Haberman (1973). It is

$$\text{Standardized Residual} = \frac{\begin{array}{c}\text{observed} \\ \text{frequency}\end{array} - \begin{array}{c}\text{expected} \\ \text{frequency}\end{array}}{\sqrt{\text{expected frequency}}} = r_{ij}$$

Haberman has shown that if the conditions for the χ^2 approximation are met, then the distribution of the r_{ij} is approximately normal with a mean $= 0$ and a variance approaching 1. Thus, we can think of the r_{ij} as roughly standard normal deviates. Therefore, 95% of them should lie between -2 and 2. Hence any cell with a $|r_{ij}| > 2$ could be considered to be a "significant" residual, since these should only occur about 5% of the time. In a large table, 1 or 2 large residuals could be expected and should not be cause for alarm. However, a pattern of significant standardized residuals in a large table, or at least a few significant residuals in smaller tables, may well indicate the need for an additional term(s) in the model.

14.10   CROSS VALIDATION

We have been concerned previously in this chapter with selection of a model that fits the data well, and many procedures have been developed for this purpose. We have illustrated simultaneous procedures that test whether all effects of order k are 0, and use of tests of partial and marginal association. There are also backward and forward stepwise procedures (BMDP manual; Fienberg, 1980), analogous to what is done in stepwise regression. Thus, although there are many procedures for selecting a "good" model, the acid test is the generalizability of the model. That is, how well will the model chosen fit on an independent sample? This leads us once again into cross validation, which was emphasized in regression analysis and in discriminant analysis.

Interestingly, many of the texts dealing with log linear analysis (Agresti, 1990; Fienberg, 1980) don't even mention cross validation, or only allude to it briefly. However, Bonnett and Bentler (1983) point to the importance of cross validation in log linear analysis, and a small study by Stevens (1984) indicates there is reason for concern. Stevens randomly split in half 15 real data sets (the n for 13 of the sets was very large (>361). Those models which were most parsimonious and fit quite well ($p > .20$) were selected and then cross validated on the other half of the random split. In 7 of the 15 sets, the model(s) chosen did *not* cross validate. What makes this of even greater concern is that the original sample sizes were quite large.

Table 14.6
BMDP4F Control Lines for Validating the Model for Head Start Data on an Independent Sample

---

PROBLEM TITLE IS 'VALIDATING THE MODEL'./
INPUT VARIABLES = 3. FORMAT IS FREE. TABLE IS 2,2,3./
VARIABLE NAMES ARE TEST,TREAT,EDUC./
TABLE INDICES ARE TEST,TREAT,EDUC./
CATEGORY NAMES(1) ARE FAIL,PASS. CODES(1) ARE 1,2.
NAMES(2) ARE HEAD,CONT. CODES(2) ARE 1,2.
NAMES(3) ARE NINTH,TENELEV,TWEL. CODES(3) ARE 1,2,3./
①   FIT MODEL IS TE,RE./
    END/
    5 1 63 16
②   9 5 39 13
    11 13 41 19

OUTPUT

MODEL 1

MODEL	D.F.	LIKELIHOOD	RATIO	PEARSON	PROB	
	D.F.	CHI-SQUARE	PROB	CHI-SQUARE		
TE,RE	3	4.28	.2330	4.36	.2248	③

---

① In this FIT paragraph we are fitting a specific model, i.e., TE,RE to the data. Recall from Table 14.3 that this was the most parsimonious model that fit the other random part of the data.

② Recall from Table 14.3 that the frequencies for the
derivation sample were   11   0 56 15
                            14   8 44 14
                            17 10 35 22

③ Since this p > .05, it indicates that the model cross validated at the .05 level.

The model selected in Table 14.3 for the Head Start data was actually one half of a random split of that data. Recall that the model selected was [TE, RE]. The control lines for validating the model on the other half of the random split are given in Table 14.6. Incidentally, it is possible to validate more than one model (in a single run) in the FIT paragraph, and we illustrate that later.

14.11   HIGHER DIMENSIONAL TABLES—MODEL SELECTION

When we consider four- or five-way tables, the number of potential models increases rapidly into the thousands, and the packages no longer enable one to test all models. Some type of screening procedure is needed to limit the number of models to be tested from a practical point of view. Three ways of selecting models are:

1. Stepwise procedures—these are analogous to the corresponding procedures in multiple regression. Here, effects are successively added or deleted according to some "level of significance." Both forward and backward selection are available on the BMDP4F program, while only backward selection is available on the SPSSX HILOGLINEAR procedure. We illustrate the backward selection procedure later in this section.

2. Use a two-stage procedure suggested by Brown (1976). In the first stage, global tests are examined that determine whether all k factor interactions are simultaneously 0. Thus, for a four-way table, these would determine whether all main effects are 0, whether all two-way interactions are 0, whether all three-way interactions are 0, and finally whether the four-way interaction is 0. Then for those sets of interactions that are significant in Stage 1, examine specific effects for significant partial and marginal association. Retain for the final model only those specific effects for which *both* the partial and marginal association are significant at some preassigned significance level. We illustrate this procedure shortly.

3. Compare all effects against their standard errors and retain for the final model only those effects whose standardized values (i.e., effect/standard error) exceed some critical value. For a five-way table with 31 effects, it would be wise to either test at the .01 level, or to use the Bonferroni inequality, setting overall α at .10 or .15.

Example 7

To illustrate the Brown procedure, we consider one of the four-way data sets presented at the beginning of the chapter. That set involved 362 patients receiving psychiatric care who were classified according to four clinical indices. We fit some models to a random split of this data, and then cross-validate these models on the other half of the random split. The data for the first half of the random split is given in Table 14.7, along with part of the printout from BMDP4F. Suppose we have decided a priori to make each global test at the .05 level and to test each individual effect at the .01 level. Examination of the global tests reveals that all two-way interactions are not 0 (Pearson $\chi^2 = 31.54$, $p < .00002$). Although the test for the three-way interactions is not significant at the .05 level, the probability level is close enough to warrant further scrutiny. This is because, as Benedetti and Brown (1978) have noted, "A single large effect may go undetected in the presence of many small effects."

Now we move on to Stage 2 of the Brown procedure: examinaton of the individual effects. Table 14.8 shows that SV, DO, and DV all have significant partial and marginal association at the .01 level. A look at the three-way interaction effects indicates that what Brown and Benedetti suggested could happen may have happened here. That is, the SDO, SDV,

TABLE 14.7
Frequency Table for Clinical (Four-Way) Data and Global Tests from BMDP4F
that all k Factor Interactions are 0

***** OBSERVED FREQUENCY TABLE 1

VALID	SOLID	DEPRESS	STABIL		
			INT	EXT	TOTAL
ENERG	RIGID	YES	11	13	24
		NO	10	9	19
		TOTAL	21	22	43
	HYST	YES	5	5	10
		NO	19	24	43
		TOTAL	24	29	53
PSY	RIGID	YES	19	8	27
		NO	13	4	17
		TOTAL	32	12	44
	HYST	YES	16	10	26
		NO	10	5	15
		TOTAL	26	15	41

TOTAL OF THE OBSERVED FREQUENCY TABLE IS   181

***** THE RESULTS OF FITTING ALL K-FACTOR MARGINALS.
SIMULTANEOUS TEST THAT ALL K+1 AND HIGHER
FACTOR INTERACTIONS ARE ZERO.

K-FACTOR	D.F.	LR CHISQ	PROB.	PEARSON CHISQ	PROB.
0-MEAN	15	43.35	0.00014	44.33	0.00010
1	11	38.67	0.00006	39.77	0.00004
2	5	8.33	0.13921	8.23	0.14415
3	1	0.09	0.75939	0.09	0.75930
4	0	0.	1.	0.	1.

***** SIMULTANEOUS TEST THAT ALL K-FACTOR INTERACTIONS
ARE SIMULTANEOUSLY ZERO.
THE CHI-SQUARES ARE DIFFERENCES IN THE ABOVE TABLE.

K-FACTOR	D.F.	LR CHISQ	PROB.	PEARSON CHISQ	PROB.
1	4	4.67	0.32233	4.56	0.33570
2	6	30.35	0.00003	31.54	0.00002
3	4	8.23	0.08347	8.13	0.08682
4	1	0.09	0.75939	0.09	0.75930

and SOV interactions are clearly not significant (all probabilities $> .37$), while the DOV effect is significant at the .01 level. Of course, another possibility is that this effect is spurious (a Type I error), since the overall α for all individual tests is not that tight. Thus, we entertain two possible models for cross-validation:

TABLE 14.8
Tests of Individual Effects for Partial and Marginal Association for Clinical
(Four-Way) Data

***** ASSOCIATION OPTION SELECTED FOR ALL TERMS OF ORDER LESS THAN
OR EQUAL TO 4

		PARTIAL ASSOCIATION			MARGINAL ASSOCIATION		
EFFECT	D.F.	CHISQUARE	PROB	ITER	D.F.	CHISQUARE	PROB
S.	1	3.46	0.0627				
D.	1	0.27	0.6027				
O.	1	0.27	0.6028				
V.	1	0.67	0.4135				
SD.	1	0.28	0.5959	4	1	0.20	0.6539
SO.	1	0.91	0.3392	3	1	1.10	0.2938
SV.	1	8.36	0.0038	3	1	8.48	0.0036
DO.	1	6.85	0.0089	3	1	7.53	0.0061
DV.	1	12.65	0.0004	3	1	13.26	0.0003
OV.	1	0.00	1.0000	4	1	0.88	0.3486
SDO.	1	0.21	0.6484	3	1	0.79	0.3736
SDV.	1	0.13	0.7217	3	1	0.19	0.6604
SOV.	1	0.28	0.5984	4	1	0.21	0.6440
DOV.	1	6.53	0.0106	4	1	7.78	0.0053
SDOV.	1	0.09	0.7594				

The partial association tests are conditional tests of the particular k factor interaction, adjusted for all other effects of the same order. Thus, if we had three factors A, B, and C, the parial association test for AB examines the difference in fit for the model (AB, AC, BC) vs. the model (AC, BC).

The maginal association test are unconditional tests of interaction, i.e., they ignore the effect of other variables.

1. Model 1—SV, DO, DV
2. Model 2—SV, DO, DV, DOV

The control lines for validating these two models and the data for the other half of the random split are given in Table 14.9. Unfortunately, the Pearson χ^2's at the bottom of the table indicate that neither model cross-validates at the .05 level (remember that the probabilities need to be *greater* than .05 for adequate fit at the .05 level).

To illustrate the backward stepwise selection procedure, we ran the same clinical data on SPSSX HILOGINEAR. The control lines for doing so are given in Table 14.10. In Tables 14.11 and 14.12 is selected printout from SPSSX HILOGLINEAR showing the seven steps needed before a final model was arrived at. The final model is the same as Model 2 found with the Brown procedure.

Although we do not show an example illustrating Procedure 3, that of comparing all effects against their standard errors, Fienberg (1980, pp. 84–88) presents an example of this approach.

TABLE 14.9

Control Lines for Cross Validating Two Models for the Validity × Solidity × Depression × Stability Data Along With the Independent Sample Frequency Table

---

PROBLEM TITLE IS 'VALIDATING TWO MODELS FOR 4 WAY TABLE'./
INPUT VARIABLES ARE 4. FORMAT IS FREE. TABLE IS 2,2,2,2./
VARIABLE NAMES ARE STABIL,DEPRESS,SOLID,VALID./
SYMBOLS ARE S,D,O,V./
CATEGORY NAMES(1) ARE INT,EXT. CODES(1) ARE 1,2.
NAMES(2) ARE YES,NO. CODES(2) ARE 1,2.
NAMES(3) ARE RIGID,HYST. CODES(3) ARE 1,2.
NAMES(4) ARE ENERG,PSY. CODES(4) ARE 1,2./
FIT MODEL IS SV,DO,DV. MODEL IS SV,DO,DV,DOV./   ①
END/
4 10 15 5 4 9 27 23 11 14 9 4 16 6 17 7

****** OBSERVED FREQUENCY TABLE 1

VALID	SOLID	DEPRESS	STABIL		
			INT	EXT	TOTAL
ENERG	RIGID	YES	4	10	14
		NO	15	5	20
		TOTAL	19	15	34
	HYST	YES	4	9	13
		NO	27	23	50
		TOTAL	31	32	63
PSY	RIGID	YES	11	14	25
		NO	9	4	13
		TOTAL	20	18	38
	HYST	YES	16	6	22
		NO	17	7	24
		TOTAL	33	13	46

TOTAL OF THE OBSERVED FREQUENCY TABLE IS   181

MODEL	D.F.	LIKELIHOOD-RATIO CHI-SQUARE	PROB	PEARSON CHI-SQUARE	PROB
SV,DO,DV.	8	16.10	0.0409	15.54	0.0494
SV,DOV.	6	15.61	0.0160	15.35	0.0177

① Here we are fitting the two models derived on the other set of data (Table 14.7) to this new set of data.

TABLE 14.10
SPSSX HILOGLINEAR Control Lines for Backward Elimination on the Clinical
(four-way) Data

TITLE 'BACKWARD ELIMINATION ON CLINICAL DATA'
DATA LIST FREE/VALID SOLID DEPRESS STABIL FREQ
WEIGHT BY FREQ
HILOGLINEAR VALID(1,2) SOLID(1,2) DEPRESS(1,2) STABIL(1,2)/
METHOD = BACKWARD/
DESIGN/
BEGIN DATA
1 1 1 1 11   1 1 1 2 13   1 1 2 1 10   1 1 2 2 9
1 2 1 1 5   1 2 1 2 5   1 2 2 1 19   1 2 2 2 24
2 1 1 1 19   2 1 1 2 8   2 1 2 1 13   2 1 2 2 4
2 2 1 1 16   2 2 1 2 10   2 2 2 1 10   2 2 2 2 5
END DATA

In concluding this section, a couple of caveats are in order. The first
concerns *overfitting,* which can occur because of fitting too many parameters to the data. Both Bishop et al. (1975, p. 324) and Marascuilo and Busk
(1987, p. 452) have issued warnings on situations where a model appears to
fit so well that the chi-square value is considerably smaller than the
associated degrees of freedom. Marascuilo and Busk recommend that if
several models fit a set 0f data (some extremely well), one choose the model
with the chi-square value that is approximately equal to the associated
degrees of freedom. Overfitting could well be the reason, or one of the
reasons, why many results in log linear analysis do not cross-validate.

The other caveat is that there is *no best* method of model selection
(Fienberg, 1980, p. 56), nor is any of the methods guaranteed to find the
best possible model. As Freeman (1987) noted, "The analyst can only rely
on his or her judgement in deciding which model is the one that is most
appropriate for . . . the data" (p. 214).

14.12 CONTRASTS FOR THE LOG LINEAR MODEL

Recall that in ANOVA and MANOVA we used contrasts of two types:

1. Post hoc—these were used with procedures, such as Scheffe's or
   Tukey's, to identify which specific groups were responsible for
   global significance.
2. Planned—here we set up a priori specific comparisons among
   population means, which might well correspond to specific hypotheses being tested.

TABLE 14.11
Selected Printout from SPSSX HILOGLINEAR for Backward Elimination on Clinical Data

If Deleted Simple Effect is		DF	L.R. Chisq Change	Prob
VALID*SOLID*DEPRESS*STABIL	①	1	.094	.7594

Step 1

The best model has generating class
VALID*SOLID*DEPRESS
VALID*SOLID*STABIL
VALID*DEPRESS*STABIL ②
SOLID*DEPRESS*STABIL

Likelihood ratio chi square = .09382 DF = 1 P = .759

If Deleted Simple Effect is		DF	L.R. Chisq Change	Prob
VALID*SOLID*DEPRESS		1	6.532	.0106
VALID*SOLID*STABIL		1	.277	.5984
VALID*DEPRESS*STABIL	③	1	.127	.7217
SOLID*DEPRESS*STABIL		1	.208	.6484

Step 2

The best model has generating class
VALID*SOLID*DEPRESS
VALID*SOLID*STABIL ④
SOLID*DEPRESS*STABIL

Likelihood ratio chi square = .22066 DF = 2 P = .896

If Deleted Simple Effect is		DF	L.R. Chisq Change	Prob
VALID*SOLID*DEPRESS		1	6.792	.0092
VALID*SOLID*STABIL		1	.215	.6428
SOLID*DEPRESS*STABIL	⑤	1	.181	.6706

Step 3

The best model has generating class
VALID*SOLID*DEPRESS
VALID*SOLID*STABIL ⑥
DEPRESS*STABIL

Likelihood ratio chi square = .40156 DF = 3 P = .940

If Deleted Simple Effect is	DF	L.R. Chisq Change	Prob
VALID*SOLID*DEPRESS	1	7.709	.0055
VALID*SOLID*STABIL	1	.128	.7202
DEPRESS*STABIL	1	.212	.6455

Step 4

The best model has generating class
VALID*SOLID*DEPRESS
DEPRESS*STABIL
VALID*STABIL
SOLID*STABIL

Likelihood ratio chi square = .52983 DF = 4 P = .971

① First, the 4-way interaction is tested, and the change in chi-square is far short of significance, so that this effect can be safely dropped from the model.

② At this point, all four 3-way interactions are tested. The 3-way interaction that causes the *smallest* change in chi-square (assuming the change is not significant) is deleted from the model. The smallest change is for VALID*DEPRESS*STABIL (see ③). Note in STEP 2 (see ④) that this effect is no longer in the model.

⑤ Again, the effect that has the smallest change in chi-square is deleted from the model; here it is SOLID*DEPRESS*STABIL. Note that this effect is not present in STEP 3 (see ⑥).

TABLE 14.12
Selected Printout from SPSSX HILOGLINEAR for Backward Elimination on
Clinical Data (cont.)

If Deleted Simple Effect is	DF	L.R. Chisq Change	Prob
VALID*SOLID*DEPRESS	1	7.795	.0052
DEPRESS*STABIL	1	.297	.5857
VALID*STABIL	1	8.376	.0038
SOLID*STABIL	1	.929	.3350

Step 5
The best model has generating class
  VALID*SOLID*DEPRESS
  VALID*STABIL
  SOLID*STABIL
Likelihood ratio chi square = .82688 DF = 5 P = .975

If Deleted Simple Effect is	DF	L.R. Chisq Change	Prob
VALID*SOLID*DEPRESS	1	7.779	.0053
VALID*STABIL	1	8.137	.0043
SOLID*STABIL	1	.757	.3844

Step 6
The best model has generating class
  VALID*SOLID*DEPRESS
  VALID*STABIL
Likelihood ratio chi square = 1.58348 DF = 6 P = .954

If Deleted Simple Effect is	DF	L.R. Chisq Change	Prob
VALID*SOLID*DEPRESS	1	① 7.780	.0053
VALID*STABIL	1	8.482	.0036

Step 7
The best model has generating class
  VALID*SOLID*DEPRESS
  VALID*STABIL
Likelihood ratio chi square = 1.58348 DF = 6 P = .954
The final model has generating class
  VALID*SOLID*DEPRESS
  VALID*STABIL

①In STEP 6, when each of the effets is deleted from the model, there is a significant change in the chi-square value at the .01 level. That is why in STEP 7 the final model consists of these effects, and all lower order derivatives because of the hierarchy principle, since neither of them can be deleted.

In both of the above cases, the contrasts were on means and the condition for a contrast was that the sum of the coefficients equal 0. The same type of contrasts can be utilized in log linear analysis, thanks to work by Goodman (1970), except now we will be contrasting observed cell frequencies. We denote a contrast by L, and the estimated contrast by $\hat{L}$. An estimated contrast would look like this:

$$\hat{L} = c_1\ln o_1 + c_2\ln o_2 + c_3\ln o_3 + \ldots c_k\ln o_k$$

where $\Sigma c_i = 0$ and the o_i denote the observed frequencies. The squared standard error for a contrast is given by:

$$s_L^2 = \sum_{i=1}^{k} c_i^2 / o_i$$

For large sample size, it has been shown that $z = \hat{L}/\hat{s}_L$ is normally distributed with mean = 0 and standard deviation = 1 if the null hypothesis is true. For planned comparisons, one uses this fact, along with the Bonferroni inequality, to easily test the contrasts with overall α under control. For post hoc analysis with contrasts, that is, to determine which cells accounted for a significant main effect or interaction, the critical values are given by S, where $s = \sqrt{\chi^2_{df(effect)}}$. If it were a main effect with 3 degrees of freedom, then $s = \sqrt{\chi^2_{.05;3}} = \sqrt{7.815} = 2.80$, while if it were an interaction with 2 degrees of freedom, then $s = \sqrt{\chi^2_{.05;2}} = \sqrt{5.99} = 2.45$.

Example—Post Hoc Contrasts

To illustrate the use of contrasts, we consider data from a survey of a large American city where the respondents were asked the question, "Are the radio and TV networks doing a good job, just a fair job, or a poor job?" Responses were further broken down by color of respondent and the year in which the question was asked, yielding the following table:

		RESPONSE			
YEAR	COLOR	GOOD	FAIR	POOR	TOTAL
1959	BLACK	81	23	4	108
	WHITE	325	253	54	632
1971	BLACK	224	144	24	382
	WHITE	600	636	158	1394

The data were run on BMDP4F. The only model that fits the data at the .05 level involves all two-way interactions and all main effects (RC, RY, CY, $df = 2$, Pearson $\chi = 3.45$, $p < .1777$). Since it can be shown that each of the interactions is significant, it is not valid to examine contrasts on collapsed (marginal) frequencies. Rather, the contrasts ned to be done on the individual cell frequencies. We examine the Color by Response interaction more closely with contrasts. Below we present the Color by Response profiles for each year, along with the expected frequencies in parentheses:

	1959			1971		
	GOOD	FAIR	POOR	GOOD	FAIR	POOR
BLACK	81 (59)	23 (40)	4 (9)	224 (181)	144 (171)	24 (40)
WHITE	325 (347)	253 (236)	54 (49)	600 (643)	636 (609)	158 (142)
	$\chi^2 = 21.3, p < .05$			$\chi^2 = 26.76, p < .05$		

Examination of the expected frequencies shows why we obtained the strong Color by Response interaction for each year. Note that more Blacks than expected (under independence) rate the networks GOOD for each year and fewer Blacks than expected rate the networks FAIR or POOR, while the reverse is true for Whites. To see where the larger discrepancies are, after adjusting for differing expected frequencies, we present below the standardized results:

	1959			1971		
	GOOD	FAIR	POOR	GOOD	FAIR	POOR
BLACK	2.86	−2.69	−1.6	3.20	−2.06	−2.53
WHITE	−1.18	1.11	.714	−1.70	1.09	1.34

These residuals suggest that the following contrasts may indicate significant subsources of variation:

$$\hat{L}_1 = \ln 23 - \ln 253 - (\ln 144 - \ln 636)$$

$$\hat{L}_2 = \ln 81 - \ln 325 - (\ln 224 - \ln 600)$$

The latter contrast determines whether the gap between Blacks and Whites in responding GOOD is the same for the two years. Now we test the significance of each contrast:

$$\hat{L} = 3.125 - 5.533 - 4.97 + 6.455 = -.913$$

$$s_{\hat{L}_1}^2 = 1/23 + 1/253 + 1/144 + 1/636 = .056$$

Therefore, the z statistic for this contrast is:

$$z_1 = -.913/\sqrt{.056} = -3.85$$

For contrast two, we have:

$$\hat{L}_2 = 4.39 - 5.78 - 5.41 + 6.4 = -.40$$

$$s_{\hat{L}_2}^2 = 1/81 + 1/325 + 1/225 + 1/600 = .0212$$

Thus, the z statistic for Contrast 2 is:

$$z_2 = -.40/\sqrt{.0212} = -2.74$$

Both of these contrasts are significant at the .05 level, since the critical values are $\sqrt{\chi_{.05;2}} = \sqrt{5.99} = 2.45$.

14.13   LOGLINEAR ANALYSIS FOR ORDINAL DATA

We have treated all the factors as categorical or nominal in this chapter, and if we are talking about sex, race, religion, etc., then this is perfectly appropriate. Often, however, we have ordinal information, such as age, educational level, or achievement. With ordinal information, the analysis becomes more complicated, but using the underlying information in the ordering yields a more powerful analysis. For those who wish to pursue this further, Agresti has a good book (1984) and several articles on the topic. Also, in a book written more for social scientists, Wickens (1989) has a nice, extended chapter on handling ordered categories.

14.14 SAMPLING AND STRUCTURAL (FIXED) ZEROS

One must distinguish between two types of zero observed frequencies in multidimensional contingency tables. Sampling zeros can occur in large tables because of relatively small sample size. No subjects are found in some of the cells because the sample size waseither not large enough or not comprehensive enough. These are different from structural zeros that can occur because no individuals of the type are possible for a given cell (e.g., male obstetrical patients).

Sampling zeros do not occur very often with social science data; when they do occur, there are a couple of ways of handling them. First, one may be able to remove the zeros by combining levels for a factor. Second, one may add a small positive constant to each cell, which is a conservative measure. Goodman has recommended adding .5 for saturated models, and SPSSX LOGLINEAR *by default* adds .5 to each cell. BMDP4F also allows the user to add a small positive constant (e.g., .0001) by using DELTA = .00001 in the TABLE paragraph. Agresti (1990, pp. 249–250) has discussed adding a constant to cells, and notes that "For unsaturated models, this usually smooths the data too much . . . When there is a problem with existence or computations, it is often adequate to add an extremely small constant . . . This alleviates the problem but avoids over-smoothing the data before the fitting process." I would recommend adding a very small constant, such as .0001.

If there are structural zeros or cells that one wishes to identify as structural zeros, these are specific in the packages (see BMDP Manual, 1985, p.197 and SPSSX Manual, Release 3.0, 1988, p. 546) and then the cells corresponding to the zeros are removed from the analysis. We do not pursue this further here; however, Fienberg (1980, Chapter 8) has a nice discussion of several applications of structurally incomplete tables.

EXERCISES

1. Plackett presented the following data on a random sample of diabetic patients:

Family history of diabetes		Yes		No	
Dependence on Insulin Injections		Yes	No	Yes	No
	< 45	6	1	16	2
Age at Onset					
	> 45	6	36	8	48

Use the BMDP4F program to determine which log linear models fit the data at the .05 level. If more than one fits, which model would you select, and why?

2. McLean (1980) investigated the graduation rates of Black and White students in two Southern universities: historically one was Black, the other White. Research indicated that, in general, Black students tend to complete their undergraduate degree programs at a lower rate than White students. McLean, however, suspected that the differential rate of completion was moderated in part by the type of institution attended. Specifically, he suspected that differences between Black and White completion would be more pronounced in White universities than Black universities. He obtained the following data (G-graduated and NG-not graduated):

		BLACK UNIV (W)		BLACK UNIV (B)		WHITE UNIV (W)		WHITE UNIV (B)	
		G	NG	G	NG	G	NG	G	NG
	HI	10	22	55	90	114	146	5	5
ABIL									
	LO	4	18	71	222	46	66	3	19

a) Use Brown's procedure and backward selection to determine which models fit the data.
b) Does the evidence tend to support McLean's hunch that differential rate of completion is moderated by the type of institution attended?

3. In a survey of a large American city, respondents were asked the question: "Are the radio and TV networks doing a good job, just a fair job, or a poor job?" Data for the responses to this question were broken down by color of the respondent, and the question was asked in two separate years.

COLOR		BLACK			WHITE		
RESPONSE	GOOD	FAIR	POOR	GOOD	FAIR	POOR
1959	81	23	4	325	253	54
1971	224	144	24	600	636	158

a) Run SPSSX backward selection on this data. What model is selected?
b) Is it valid to collapse here, or do we need to use contrasts?

4. The table below classifies 168 polio cases from the 1950s by age of subject, paralytic status, and by whether the subjects had been injected with the Salk vaccine.

AGE	SALK VACCINE	PARALYSIS NO	YES
0–4	Yes	20	14
	No	10	24
5–9	Yes	15	12
	No	3	15
10–14	Yes	3	2
	No	3	2
15–19	Yes	7	4
	No	1	6
20–39	Yes	12	3
	No	7	5

a) Using the SPSSX HILOGLINEAR program, determine whether the model of complete independence fits the data at the .05 level.

b) Set up the appropriate probability model for complete independence, calculate the expected frequencies using this model, and then show how the Pearson chi square value on the printout was obtained.

5. The following data from Demo and Parker (1987) classifies subjects by race, gender, GPA and self esteem.

Gender	Cumulative GPA	Black High Self-Esteem	Black Low Self-Esteem	White High Self-Esteem	White Low Self-Esteem
Males	High	15	9	17	10
	Low	26	17	22	26
Females	High	13	22	22	32
	Low	24	23	3	17

a) Run backward elimination on the SPSSX HILOGLINEAR program. What model is selected?

b) One of the effects in the final model is SEX*ESTEEM. Is it valid to collapse over race and GPA in interpreting this effect? Explain.

6. The data below were used in a study of parole success involving 5587 parolees in Ohio between 1965 and 1972 (a 10% sample of all parolees during this period). The study involved a dichotomous response—success (no major parole violation) or failure (returned to prison)—based on a one

year followup. The predictors of parole success included here are: type of committed offense, age, prior record, and alcohol or drug dependency. The data were randomly split into two parts. The counts for the second part of the random split are given in parentheses, and this data is to be used as the validation sample.

	No drug or alcohol dependency				Drug and/or alcohol dependency			
	25 or older		Under 25		25 or older		Under 25	
	Person offense	Other offense	Person offense	Other offense	Person offense	Other offense	Person offense	Other offense
	No Prior Sentence of Any Kind							
Success	48	34	37	49	38	28	35	57
	(44)	(34)	(29)	(58)	(47)	(38)	(37)	(53)
Failure	1	5	7	11	3	8	5	18
	(1)	(7)	(7)	(5)	(1)	(2)	(4)	(24)
	Prior Sentence							
Success	117	259	131	319	197	435	107	291
	(111)	(253)	(131)	(320)	(202)	(392)	(103)	(294)
Failure	23	61	20	89	38	194	26	191
	(27)	(55)	(25)	(93)	(46)	(215)	(34)	(102)

a) Run backward elimination on this data. What model is selected?
b) Determine whether the model selected in (1) fits on the validation sample at the .05 level.

7. In section 14.6 we indicated that if A, B and C are the factors for a three-way design, then we can validly collapse AB over C if the following are met:

a) The three-way interaction is not significant, i.e., ABC = 0.
b) Either A or B is independent of C, i.e., AC = 0 or BC = 0.

What would be the generalization of the above for more than three factors? That is, what conditions would have to be met, for example, to validly collapse AB over C and D in a four-way design?

References

Agresti, A. (1984). *Analysis of ordinal categorical data.* New York: Wiley.

Agresti, A. (1990). *Categorical data analysis.* New York: Wiley.

Akaike, H. (1987). Factor analysis and the AIC. *Psychometrika, 52,* 317–332.

Ambrose, A. (1985). *The development and experimental application of programmed materials for teaching clarinet performance skills in college woodwind techniques courses.* Unpublished doctoral dissertation, University of Cincinnati, Cincinnati.

Anderson, D. A., & Carney, E. S. (1974). *Ridge regression estimation procedures applied to canonical correlation analysis.* Unpublished manuscript, Cornell University, Ithaca, NY.

Anderson, J. C., & Gerbing, D. W. (1984). The effect of sampling error on convergence, improper solutions, and goodness-of-fit indices for maximum likelihood confirmatory factor analysis. *Psychometrika, 49,* 155–173.

Anderson, N. H. (1963). Comparison of different populations: Resistance to extinction and transfer. *Psychological Bulletin, 70,* 162–179.

Anderson, T. W. (1958). *An introduction to multivariate statistical analysis.* New York: Wiley.

Anscombe, V. (1973). Graphs in statistical analysis. *American Statistician, 27,* 11–21.

Bandalos, D. L. (1993). Factors influencing the cross-validation of confirmatory factor analysis models. *Multivariate Behavioral Research, 28,* 351–374.

Barcikowski, R., & Stevens, J. P. (1975). A Monte Carlo study of the stability of canonical correlations, canonical weights and canonical variate-variable correlations. *Multivariate Behavioral Research, 10,* 353–364.

Barcikowski, R. S. (1981). Statistical power with group mean as the unit of analysis. *Journal of Educational Statistics, 6,* 267–285.

Barcikowski, R. S. (1983). *Comptuer packages and research design, Vol. 3: SPSS and SPSSX.* Washington, DC: University Press of America.

Barcikowski, R. S., & Robey, R. R. (1984). Decisions in a single group repeated measures analysis: Statistical tests and three computer packages. *The American Statistician, 38,* 248–250.

561

Barnett, D., & Zucker, K. (1975). The others-concept and friendly and cooperative behavior in children. *Psychology in the Schools, 12,* 495–501.

Barnett, V., & Lewis, T. (1978). *Outliers in statistical data.* New York: Wiley.

Becker, B. (1987). Applying tests of combined significance in Meta analysis. *Psychological Bulletin, 102,* 164–171.

Belsley, D. A., Kuh, E., & Welsch, R. (1980). *Regression diagnostics: Identifying influential data and sources of collinearity.* New York: Wiley.

Benedetti, J. K., & Brown, M. B. (1978). Strategies for the selection of log linear models. *Biometrics, 34,* 680–686.

Benson, J., & Bandalos, D. L. (1992). Second-order confirmatory factor analysis of the Reactions to Tests scale with cross- validation. *Multivariate Behavioral Research, 27,* 459–487.

Bentler, P. M. (1989). *EQS structural equations program manual.* Los Angeles: BMDP Statistical Software.

Bentler, P. M. (1992a). *EQS: Structural equations program manual.* Los Angeles: BMDP Statistical Software.

Bentler, P. M. (1992b). On the fit of models to covariance and methodology to the *Bulletin. Psychological Bulletin, 112,* 400–404.

Bentler, P. M., & Bonett, D. G. (1980). Significance tests and goodness of fit in the analysis of covariance structures. *Psychological Bulletin, 88,* 588–606.

Benton, S., Kraft, R., Groover, J., & Plake, B. (1984). Cognitive capacity differences among writers. *Journal of Educational Psychology, 76,* 820–834.

Bird, K. D. (1975). Simultaneous contrast testing procedures for multivariate experiments. *Multivariate Behavior Research, 10,* 343–351.

Bishop, Y., Fienberg, S., & Holland, P. (1975). *Discrete multivariate analysis: Theory and practice.* Cambridge, MA: MIT Press.

Block, J. (1995). A contrarian view of the five-factor model approach to personality description. *Psychological Bulletin,* 187–215.

BMDP. (1990). *BMDP statistical software.* Berkeley: University of California Press.

Bock, R. D. (1975). *Multivariate statistical methods in behavioral research.* New York: McGraw-Hill.

Bock, R. D., & Haggard, E. (1968). The use of multivariate analysis of variance in behavioral research. In D. K. Whitla (Ed.), *Handbook of measurement and assessment in behavioral sciences.* Reading, MA: Addison Wesley.

Boik, R. J. (1981). A priori tests in repeated measures design: Effects of nonsphericity. *Psychometrika, 46,* 241–255.

Bollen, K. A. (1989). *Structural equations with latent variables.* New York: Wiley.

Bollen, K. A., & Long, J. S. (1993). *Testing structural equation models.* Newbury Park, CA: Sage.

Bolton, B. (1971). A factor analytical study of communication skills and nonverbal abilities of deaf rehabilitation clients. *Multivariate Behavioral Research, 6,* 485–501.

Bonnett, D., & Bentler, P. (1983). Goodness of fit procedures for the evaluation and selection of log linear models. *Psychological Bulletin, 93,* 149–166.

Boomsma, A. (1982). The robustness of LISREL against small sample sizes in factor analysis models. In K. G. Jöreskog & H. Wold (Eds.), *Systems under indirect observation: Causality, structure, prediction* (pp. 149–173). Amsterdam: North-Holland.

Box, G. E. P. (1949). A general distribution theory for a class of likelihood criteria. *Biometrika, 36,* 317–346.

Box, G. E. P. (1954). Some theorems on quadratic forms applied in the study of analysis of variance problems: II. Effect of inequality of variance and of correlation between errors in the two-way classification. *Annals of Mathematical Statistics, 25,* 484–498.

Bradley, R., Caldwell, B., & Elardo, R. (1977). Home environment, social status and mental test performance. *Journal of Educational Psychology, 69,* 697–701.

Breckler, S. J. (1990). Applications of covariance structure modeling in psychology: Cause for concern? *Psychological Bulletin, 107,* 260–273.

Brown, M. B. (1976). Screening effects in multidimensional contingency tables. *Applied Statistics, 25,* 37–46.

Browne, M. W. (1968). A comparison of factor analytic techniques. *Psychometrika, 33,* 267–334.

Browne, M. W., & Cudeck, R. (1989). Single sample cross-validation indices for covariance structures. *Multivariate Behavioral Research, 24,* 445–455.

Bryant, J. L., & Paulson, A. S. (1976). An extension of Tukey's method of multiple comparisons to experimental design with random concomitant variables. *Biometrika,* 631–638.

Bryk, A. D., & Weisberg, H. I. (1977). Use of the nonequivalent control group design when subjects are growing. *Psychological Bulletin, 85,* 950–962.

Burket, G. R. (1964). A study of reduced rank models for multiple prediction. *Journal of Educational Psychology, 69,* 697–701.

Byrne, B. M. (1989). *A primer of LISREL: Basic applications and programming for confirmatory factor analytic models.* New York: Springer-Verlag.

Byrne, B. M. (1994). *Structural equation modeling with EQS and EQS/Windows: Basic concepts, applications, and programming.* Newbury Park, CA: Sage.

Carlson, J. E., & Timm, N. H. (1974). Analysis of non-orthogonal fixed effect designs. *Psychological Bulletin, 81,* 563–570.

Cattell, R. B. (1963). Theory of crystallized and fluid intelligence: A critical experiment. *Journal of Educational Psychology, 54,* 1–22.

Cattell, R. B. (1966). The meaning and strategic use of factor analysis. In R. B. Cattell (Ed.), *Handbook of multivariate experimental psychology* (pp. 174–243). Chicago: Rand McNally.

Cattell, R. B., & Jaspers, J. A. (1967). A general plasmode for factor analytic exercises and research. *Multivariate Behavior Research Monographs.*

Church, A., & Burke, P. (1994). Exploratory and confirmatory tests of the Big Five and Tellegen's three- and four-dimensional models. *Journal of Personality and Social Psychology, 66,* 93–114.

Cliff, N. (1983). Some cautions concerning the application of causal modeling methods. *Multivariate Behavioral Research, 18,* 115–126.

Cliff, N. (1987). *Analyzing multivariate data.* New York: Harcourt, Brace Jovanovich.

Cliff, N., & Hamburger, C. D. (1967). The study of sampling errors in factor analysis by means of artificial experiments. *Psychological Bulletin, 68,* 430–445.

Cliff, N., & Krus, D. J. (1976). Interpretation of canonical analysis: Rotated vs. unrotated solutions. *Psychometrika, 41,* 35–42.

Clifford, M. M. (1972). Effects of competition as a motivational technique in the classroom. *American Educational Research Journal, 9,* 123–134.

Cochran, W. G. (1957). Analysis of covariance: Its nature and uses. *Biometrics, 13,* 261–281.

Cohen, J. (1968). Multiple regression as a general data-analytic system. *Psychological Bulletin, 70,* 426–443.

Cohen, J. (1977). *Statistical power analysis for the behavioral sciences.* New York: Academic Press.

Cohen, J. (1990). Things I have learned (so far). *American Psychologist, 45,* 1304–1312.

Cohen, J., & Cohen, P. (1975). *Applied multiple regression/correlation analysis for the behavioral sciences.* Hillsdale, NJ: Lawrence Erlbaum Associates.

Cohen, J., & Cohen, P. (1983). *Applied multiple regression/correlation analysis for the behavioral sciences*. Hillsdale, NJ: Lawrence Erlbaum Associates.

Collier, R. O., Baker, F. B., Mandeville, C. K., & Hayes, T. F. (1967). Estimates of test size for several test procedures on conventional variance ratios in the repeated measures design. *Psychometrika, 32*, 339-353.

Comrey, A. L. (1985). A method for removing outliers to improve factor analytic results. *Multivariate Behavioral Research, 20*, 273-281.

Conover, W. J., Johnson, M. E., & Johnson, M. M. (1981). Composite study of tests for homogeneity of variances with applications to the outer continental shelf bidding data. *Technometrics, 23*, 351-361.

Cook, R. D. (1977). Detection of influential observations in linear regression. *Technometrics, 19*, 15-18.

Cook, R. D., & Weisberg, S. (1982). *Residuals and influence in regression*. New York: Chapman & Hall.

Cooley, W. W., & Lohnes, P. R. (1971). *Multivariate data analysis*. New York: Wiley.

Cramer, E., & Nicewander, W. A. (1979). Some symmetric, invariant measures of multivariate association. *Psychometrika, 44*, 43-54.

Crocker, L., & Benson, J. (1976). Achievement, guessing and risk-taking behavior under norm referenced and criterion referenced testing conditions. *American Educational Research Journal, 13*, 207-215.

Cronbach, L. J. (1975). Beyond the two disciplines of scientific psychology. *The American Psychologist, 30*, 116-127.

Crowder, R. (1975). *An investigation of the relationship between social I.Q. and vocational evaluation ratings with an adult trainable mental retardate work activity center population*. Unpublished doctoral dissertation, University of Cincinnati, Cincinnati.

Crystal, G. (1988). The wacky, wacky world of CEO pay. *Fortune, 117*, 68-78.

Cudeck, R., & Browne, M. W. (1983). Cross-validation of covariance structures. *Multivariate Behavioral Research, 18*, 147-167.

D'Agostino, R. B., & Tietjen, G. L. (1971). Simulation probability points of b2 in small samples. *Biometrika, 58*, 669-672.

D'Agostino, R. B., & Tietjen, G. L. (1973). Approaches to the null distribution of b1. *Biometrika, 60*, 169-173.

Dallal, G. (1988). Statistical microcomputing—Like it is. *The American Statistician, 42*, 212-216.

Daniel, C., & Wood, F. S. (1971). *Fitting equations to data*. New York: Wiley.

Daniels, R. L., & Stevens, J. P. (1976). The interaction between the internal-external locus of control and two methods of college instruction. *American Educational Research Journal, 13*, 103-113.

Darlington, R. B., Weinberg, S., & Walberg, H. (1973). Canonical variate analysis and related techniques. *Review of Educational Research, 43*, 433-454.

Davidson, M. L. (1972). Univariate versus multivariate tests in repeated measures experiments. *Psychological Bulletin, 77*, 446-452.

Draper, N. R., & Smith, H. (1981). *Applied regression analysis*. New York: Wiley.

Dizney, H., & Gromen, L. (1967). Predictive validity and differential achievement on three MLA Comparative Foreign Language tests. *Educational and Psychological Measurement, 27*, 1127-1130.

Dunnett, C. W. (1980). Pairwise multiple comparisons in the homogeneous variance, unequal sample size cases. *Journal of the American Statistical Association, 75*, 789-795.

Edwards, D. S. (1984). *Analysis of faculty perceptions of deans' leadership behavior and organizational climate in baccalaureate schools of nursing*. Unpublished doctoral dissertation, University of Cincinnati, Cincinnati.

Elashoff, J. D. (1969). Analysis of covariance: A delicate instrument. *American Educational Research Journal, 6*, 383-401.

Elashoff, J. D. (1981). Data for the panel session in software for repeated measures analysis of variance. *Proceedings of the Statistical Computing Section of the American Statistical Association.*

Everitt, B. S. (1979). A Monte Carlo investigation of the robustness of Hotelling's one and two sample T2 tests. *Journal of the American Statistical Association, 74,* 48–51.

Feshback, S., Adelman H., & Williamson, F. (1977). Prediction of reading and related academic problems. *Journal of Educational Psychology, 69,* 299–308.

Fienberg, S. (1980). *The analysis of cross classified categorical data.* Cambridge, MA: MIT Press.

Finn, J. (1974). *A general model for multivariate analysis.* New York: Holt, Rinehart & Winston.

Finn, J. (1978). Multivariance: *Univariate and multivariate analysis of variance, covariance and regression.* Chicago: National Educational Resources.

Fisher, R. A. (1936). The use of multiple measurement in taxonomic problems. *Annals of Eugenics, 7,* 179–188.

Frane, J. (1976). Some simple procedures for handling missing data in multivariate analysis. *Psychometrika, 41,* 409–415.

Freeman, D. (1987). *Applied categorical data analysis.* New York: Marcel Dekker.

Friedman, G., Lehrer, B., & Stevens, J. (1983). The effectiveness of self directed and lecture/discussion stress management approaches and the locus of control of teachers. *American Educational Research Journal, 20,* 563–580.

Gary, H. E. (1981). *The effects of departure from circularity on type I error rates and power for randomized block factorial experimental designs.* Unpublished doctoral dissertation, Baylor University, Houston, TX.

Gerbing, D. W., & Anderson, J. C. (1985). The effects of sampling error and model characteristics on parameter estimation for maximum likelihood confirmatory factor analysis. *Multivariate Behavioral Research, 20,* 255–271.

Glass, G. C., & Stanley, J. C. (1970). *Statistical methods in education and psychology.* Englewood Cliffs, NJ: Prentice-Hall.

Glass, G. C., & Stanley, J. C. (1984). *Statistical methods in education and psychology.* Englewood Cliffs, NJ: Prentice-Hall.

Gnanadesikan, R. (1977). *Methods for statistical analysis of multivariate observations.* New York: Wiley.

Glassnapp, D., & Poggio, J. (1985). *Essentials of statistical analysis for the behavioral sciences.* Columbus, OH: Charles Merrill.

Goldberg, L. (1990). An alternative "description of personality": Big Five factor structure. *Journal of Personality and Social Psychology, 59,* 1216–1229.

Golding, S., & Seidman, E. (1974). Analysis of multitrait-multimethod matrices: A two step principal components procedure. *Multivariate Behavioral Research, 9,* 479–496.

Goodman, L. (1970). The analysis of multidimensional contingency tables: Stepwise procedures and direct estimation methods for building models for multiple classifications. *Technometrics, 13,* 33–61.

Green, S. (1990). *Power analysis in repeated measures analysis of variance with heterogeneity correlated trials.* Paper presented at the annual meeting of the American Educational Research Association, Boston, MA.

Greenhouse, S. W., & Geisser, S. (1959). On methods in the analysis of profile data. *Psychometrika, 24,* 95–112.

Griesinger, W. (1977). *Short term group counseling of parents of handicapped children.* Unpublished doctoral dissertation, University of Cincinnati, Cincinnati.

Guadagnoli, E., & Velicer, W. (1988). Relation of sample size to the stability of component patterns. *Psychological Bulletin, 103,* 265–275.

Guttman, L. (1941). Mathematical and tabulation techniques. Supplementary study B. In P.

Horst (Ed.), *Prediction of personnel adjustment.* New York: Social Science Research Council.

Haase, R., Ellis, M., & Ladany, N. (1989). Multiple criteria for evaluating the magnitude of experimental effects. *Journal of Consulting Psychology, 36,* 511-516.

Haberman, S. J. (1973). The analysis of residuals in cross classified tables. *Biometrics, 29,* 205-220.

Hakstian, A. R. (1971). A comparative evaluation of several prominent methods of oblique factor transformation. *Psychometrika, 36,* 175-193.

Hakstian, A. R., Roed, J. C., & Lind, J. C. (1979). Two sample T procedures and the assumption of homogeneous covariance matrices. *Psychological Bulletin, 86,* 1255-1263.

Hakstian, A. R., Rogers, W. D., & Cattell, R. B. (1982). The behavior of numbers factors rules with simulated data. *Multivariate Behavioral Research, 17,* 193-219.

Harman, H. (1983). *Modern factor analysis.* Chicago: University of Chicago Press.

Harris, R. J. (1976). The invalidity of partitioned U tests in canonical correlation and multivariate analysis of variance. *Multivariate Behavioral Research, 11,* 353-365.

Hays, W. L. (1981). *Statistics* (3rd ed.). New York: Holt, Rinehart & Winston.

Hawkins, D. M. (1976). The subset problem in multivariate analysis of variance. *Journal of the Royal Statistical Society, 38,* 132-139.

Herzberg, P. A. (1969). The parameters of cross validation. *Psychometrika* (Monograph supplement, No. 16).

Hoaglin, D., & Welsch, R. (1978). The hat matrix in regression and ANOVA. *American Statistician, 32,* 17-22.

Hoerl, A. E., & Kennard, W. (1970). Ridge regression: Biased estimation for non-orthogonal problems. *Technometrics, 12,* 55-67.

Hogg, R. V. (1979). Statistical robustness. On view of its use in application today. *American Statistician, 33,* 108-115.

Holland, J. L. (1966). *The psychology of vocational choice.* Waltham, MA: Blaisdell.

Holloway, L. N., & Dunn, O. J. (1967). The robustness of Hotelling's T2. *Journal of the American Statistical Association,* 124-136.

Hopkins, J. W., & Clay, P. P. F. (1963). Some empirical distributions of bivariate T2 and homoscedasticity criterion M under unequal variance and leptokurtosis. *Journal of the American Statistical Association, 58,* 1048-1053.

Hotelling, H. (1931). The generalization of Student's ratio. *Annals of Mathematical Statistics,* 360-378.

Hoyle, R. (Ed.). (1995). *Structural equation modeling: Concepts, issues and applications.* Newbury Park, CA: Sage.

Huber, P. (1977). *Robust statistical procedures* (No. 27, Regional conference series in applied mathematics). Philadelphia: SIAM.

Huberty, C. J. (1975). The stability of three indices of relative variable contribution in discriminant analysis. *Journal of Experimental Education,* 59-64.Z

Huberty, C. J. (1984). Issues in the use and interpretation of discriminant analysis. *Psychological Bulletin, 95,* 156-171.

Huberty, C. J. (1989). Problems with stepwise methods—better alternatives. In B. Thompson (Ed.), *Advances in social science methodology* (Vol. 1, pp. 43-70).

Huberty, C. (1994). *Applied discriminant analysis.* New York: Wiley.

Huck, S., Cormier, W., & Bounds, W. (1974). *Reading statistics and research.* New York: Harper & Row.

Huck, S., & McLean, R. (1975). Using a repeated measures ANOVA to analyse the data from a pretest-posttest design: A potentially confusing task. *Psychological Bulletin, 82,* 511-518.

Huitema, B. (1980). *The analysis of covariance and alternatives.* New York: Wiley.

Hummel, T. J., & Sligo, J. (1971). Empirical comparison of univariate and multivariate analysis of variance procedures. *Psychological Bulletin, 76,* 49–57.

Hutchinson, S. R. (1994). *The stability of post hoc model modifications in covariance structure models.* Paper presented at the annual meeting of the American Educational Research Association, New Orleans, LA.

Huynh, H., & Feldt, L. (1976). Estimation of the Box correction for degrees of freedom from sample data in the randomized block and split plot designs. *Journal of Educational Statistics, 1,* 69–82.

Huynh, H., & Feldt, L. S. (1970). Conditions under which mean square ratios in repeated measurement designs have exact F distributions. *Journal of the American Statistical Association, 65,* 1582–1589.

Hykle, J., Stevens, J. P., & Markle, G. (1993). *Examining the statistical validity of studies comparing cooperative learning versus individualistic learning.* Paper presented at the annual meeting of the American Educational Research Association, Atlanta, Ga.

Ito, K. (1962). A comparison of the powers of two MANOVA tests. *Biometrika, 49,* 455–462.

Jacobson, N. S. (Ed.). (1988). Defining clinically significant change [Special issue]. *Behavioral Assessment, 10*(2).

James, L. R., Mulaik, S. A., & Brett, J. (1982). *Causal analysis: Models, assumptions, and data.* Beverly Hills, CA: Sage.

James, W., & Stein, C. (1961). Estimation with quadratic loss. In *Proceedings of the Fourth Berkeley Symposium on Mathematical Statistics and Probability* (Vol. 1, pp. 361–379). Berkeley: University of California.

Jennings, E. (1988). Models for pretest–posttest data: Repeated measures ANOVA revisted. *Journal of Educational Statistics, 13,* 273–280.

Johnson, N., & Wichern, D. (1988). *Applied multivariate statistical analysis.* Englewood Cliffs, NJ: Prentice-Hall.

Jones, L. V., Lindzey, G., & Coggelshall, P. (Eds.). (1982). *An assessment of research-doctorate programs in the United States: Social and behavioral sciences.* Washington, DC: National Acedemy Press.

Jöreskog, K. G. (1967). Some contributions to maximum likelihood factor analysis. *Psychometrika, 32,* 443–482.

Jöreskog, K. G. (1969). A general approach to confirmatory maximum likelihood factor analysis. *Psychometrika, 34,* 183–202.

Jöreskog, K. G. (1993). Testing structural equation models. In K. A. Bollen & J. S. Long (Eds.), *Testing structural equation models* (pp. 294–313). Newbury Park, CA: Sage.

Jöreskog, K. G., & Lawley, D. N. (1968). New methods in maximum likelihood factor analysis. *British Journal of Mathematical and Statistical Psychology, 21,* 85–96.

Jöreskog, K. G., & Sörbom, D. (1986). *LISREL IV: Analysis of linear structural relationships by maximum likelihood and least squares methods.* Mooresville, IN: Scientific Software.

Jöreskog, K. G., & Sörbom, D. (1988). *LISREL 7: A guide to the program and applications.* Chicago: Statistical Package for the Social Sciences.

Jöreskog, K. G., & Sörbom, D. (1993). *LISREL 8 user's reference guide.* Chicago: Scientific Software.

Kaiser, H. F. (1960). The application of electronic computers to factor analysis. *Educational and Psychological Measurement, 20,* 141–151.

Kennedy, J. (1983). *Analyzing qualitative data.* New York: Praeger.

Kenny, D., & Judd, C. (1986). Consequences of violating the independent assumption in analysis of variance. *Psychological Bulletin, 99,* 422–431.

Keppel, G. (1983). *Design and analysis: A researchers' handbook.* Englewood Cliffs, NJ: Prentice-Hall.

Kerlinger, F., & Pedhazur, E. (1973). *Multiple regression in behavioral research*. New York: Holt, Rinehart & Winston.

Keselman, H. J., Murray, R., & Rogan, J. (1976). Effect of very unequal group sizes on Tukey's multiple comparison test. *Educational and Psychological Measurement*.

Keselman, H. J., Rogan, J. C., Mendoza, J. L., & Breen, L. L. (1980). Testing the validity conditions of repeated measures F tests. *Psychological Bulletin, 87*, 479–481.

Kirk, R. E. (1982). *Experimental design: Procedures for the behavioral sciences*. Belmont, CA: Brooks-Cole.

Krasker, W. S. & R. E. Welsch (1979). "Efficient Bounded-Influence Regression Estimation Using Alternative Definitions of Sensitivity," Technical Report #3, Center for Computational Research in Economics and Management Science, Massachusetts Institute of Technology, Cambridge, Mass.

Kvet, E. (1982). *Excusing elementary students from regular classroom activities for the study of instrumental music: The effect of sixth grade reading, language and mathematics achievement*. Unpublished doctoral dissertation, University of Cincinnati, Cincinnati.

Lachenbruch, P. A. (1967). An almost unbiased method of obtaining confidence intervals for the probability of misclassification in discriminant analysis. *Biometrics, 23*, 639–645.

Lauter, J. (1978). Sample size requirements for the T^2 test of MANOVA (tables for one-way classification). *Biometrical Journal, 20*, 389–406.

Lawley, D. N. (1940). The estimation of factor loadings by the method of maximum likelihood. *Proceedings of the Royal Society of Edinburgh, 60*, 64.

Lehrer, B., & Schimoler, G. (1975). Cognitive skills underlying an inductive problem-solving strategy. *Journal of Experimental Education, 43*, 13–21.

Light, R. & Pillemer, D. (1984). *Summing Up: The Science of Reviewing Research*. Cambridge, Mass.: Harvard University Press.

Light, R., Singer, J., & Willett, J. (1990). *By design*. Cambridge, MA: Harvard University Press.

Lindeman, R. H., Merenda, P. F., & Gold, R. Z. (1980). *Introduction to bivariate and multivariate analysis*. Glenview, IL: Scott, Foresman.

Linn, R. L. (1968). A Monte Carlo approach to the number of factors problem. *Psychometrika, 33*, 37–71.

Loehlin, J. C. (1992). *Latent variable models: An introduction to factor, path, and structural analysis* (2nd ed.). Hillsdale, NJ: Lawrence Erlbaum Associates.

Lohnes, P. R. (1961). Test space and discriminant space classification models and related significance tests. *Educational and Psychological Measurement, 21*, 559–574.

Lord, F. (1969). Statistical adjustments when comparing pre-existing groups. *Psychological Bulletin, 70*, 162–179.

Lord, R., & Novick, M. (1968). *Statistical theories of mental test scores*. Reading, MA: Addison-Wesley.

MacCallum, R. (1986). Specification searchers in covariance structure modeling. *Psychological Bulletin, 100*, 107–120.

MacCallum, R. C., Roznowski, M., & Necowitz, L. B. (1992). Model modifications in covariance structure analysis: The problem of capitalization on chance. *Psychological Bulletin, 111*, 490–504.

MacCallum, D. C., Wegener, D. T., Uchino, B. N., & Fabrigar, L. R. (1993). The problem of equivalent models in applications of covariance structure analysis. *Psychological Bulletin, 114*, 185–199.

Mallows, C. L. (1973). Some comments on Cp. *Technometrics, 15*, 661–676.

Marascuilo, L., & Busk, P. (1987). Loglinear models: A way to study main effects and interactions for multidimensional contingency tables with categorical data. *Journal of Counseling Psychology, 34*, 443–455.

Maradia, K. V. (1971). The effect of non-normality on some multivariate tests and robustness to non-normality in the linear model. *Biometrika, 58,* 105–121.

Maxwell, S. E. (1980). Pairwise multiple comparisons in repeated measures designs. *Journal of Educational Statistics, 5,* 269–287.

Maxwell, S., & Delaney, H. (1990). *Designing experiments and analyzing data.* Belmont, CA: Wadsworth.

Maxwell, S., Delaney, H. D., & Manheimer, J. (1985). ANOVA of residuals and ANCOVA: Correcting an illusion by using model comparisons and graphs. *Journal of Educational Statistics, 95,* 136–147.

McLean, J. A. (1980). *Graduation and nongraduation rates of black and white freshmen entering two state universities in Virginia.* Unpublished doctoral dissertation, The Ohio State University.

McNeil, K., & Karr, S. (1972). Brief reports: Psycholinguistic performance as an indicator of modernization. *Multivariate Behavioral Research, 7,* 397–399.

Mendoza, J. L., Markos, V. H., & Gonter, R. (1978). A new perspective on sequential testing procedures in canonical analysis: A Monte Carlo evaluation. *Multivariate Behavioral Research, 13,* 371–382.

Meredith, W. (1964). Canonical correlation with fallible data. *Psychometrika, 29,* 55–65.

Merenda, P., Novack, H., & Bonaventure, E. (1976). Multivariate analysis of the California Test of mental maturity, primary forms. *Psychological Reports, 38,* 487–493.

Meyer, P. (1965). *Introductory probability and statistical applications.* Reading, MA: Addison-Wesley.

Miller, R. (1977). Developments in multiple comparisons, 1966–1976. *Journal of the American Statistical Association, 72,* 779–788.

Milligan, G. (1980). Factors that affect type I and type II error rates in the analysis of multidimensional contingency tables. *Psychological Bulletin, 87,* 238–244.

Moore, D., & McCabe, G. (1989). *Introduction to the practice of statistics.* New York: Freeman.

Morris, J. D. (1982). Ridge regression and some alternative weighting techniques: A comment on Darlington. *Psychological Bulletin, 91,* 203–210.

Morrison, D. F. (1976). *Multivariate statistical methods.* New York: McGraw-Hill.

Morrison, D. F. (1983). *Applied linear statistical methods.* Englewood Cliffs, NJ: Prentice-Hall.

Mosteller, F., & Tukey, J. W. (1977). *Data analysis and regression.* Reading, MA: Addison-Wesley.

Mulaik, S. A., James, L. R., Van Alstine, J., Bennett, N., Lind, S., & Stilwell, C. D. (1989). Evaluation of goodness of fit indices for structural equation models. *Psychological Bulletin, 105,* 430–445.

Myers, J. L. (1979). *Fundamentals of experimental design.* Boston: Allyn & Bacon.

Myers, R. (1990). *Classical and modern regression with applications* (2nd ed.). Boston, MA: Duxbury Press.

Nold, E., & Freedman, S. (1977). An analysis of readers' responses to essays. *Research in English Education.*

Norusis, M. (1988). *SPSS/PC+ Base Manual V2.0.* Chicago, IL: SPSS Inc.

Novince, L. (1977). *The contribution of cognitive restructuring to the effectiveness of behavior rehearsal in modifying social inhibition in females.* Unpublished doctoral dissertation, University of Cincinnati, Cincinnati.

Nunnally, J. (1978). *Psychometric theory.* New York: McGraw-Hill.

O'Brien, R., & Kaiser, M. (1985). MANOVA method for analyzing repeated measures designs: An extensive primer. *Psychological Bulletin,* 316–333.

O'Grady, K. (1982). Measures of explained variation: Cautions and limitations. *Psychological Bulletin, 92,* 766–777.

Olson, C. L. (1974). Comparative robustness of six tests in multivariate analysis of variance. *Journal of the American Statistical Association, 69,* 894–908.

Olson, C. L. (1976). On choosing a test statistic in MANOVA. *Psychological Bulletin, 83,* 579–586.

Overall, J. E., & Spiegel, D. K. (1969). Concerning least squares analysis of experimental data. *Psychological Bulletin, 72,* 311–322.

Park, C., & Dudycha, A. (1974). A cross validation approach to sample size determination for regression models. *Journal of the American Statistical Association, 69,* 214–218.

Pedhazur, E. (1982). *Multiple regression in behavioral research* (2nd ed.). New York: Holt, Rinehart & Winston.

Pedhazur, E., & Schmelkin, L. (1991). *Measurement, design, and analysis.* Hillsdale, NJ: Lawrence Erlbaum Associates.

Pillai, K., & Jayachandian, K. (1967). Power comparisons of tests of two multivariate hypothese based on four criteria. *Biometrika, 54,* 195–210.

Plackett, R. L. (1974). *The analysis of categorical data.* London, Griffin.

Plante, T., & Goldfarb, L. (1984). Concurrent validity for an activity vector analysis index of social adjustment. *Journal of Clinical Psychology, 40,* 1215–1218.

Pope, J., Lehrer, B., & Stevens, J. P. (1980). A multiphasic reading screening procedure. *Journal of Learning Disabilities, 13,* 98–102.

Porebski, O. R. (1966). Discriminatory and canonical analysis of technical college data. *British Journal of Mathematical and Statistical Psychology, 19,* 215–236.

Press, S. J., & Wilson, S. (1978). Choosing between logistic regression and discriminant analysis. *Journal of the American Statistical Association, 7,* 699–705.

Pruzek, R. M. (1971). Methods and problems in the analysis of multivariate data. *Review of Educational Research, 41,* 163–190.

Reichardt, C. (1979). The statistical analysis of data from nonequivalent group designs. In T. Cook & D. Campbell (Eds.), *Quasi-experimentation: Design and analysis issues for field settings.* Chicago: Rand McNally.

Rencher, A. C., & Larson, S. F. (1980). Bias in Wilk's A in stepwise discriminant analysis. *Technometrics, 22,* 349–356.

Rogan, J. C., Keselman, H. J., & Mendoza, J. L. (1979). Analysis of repeated measurements. *British Journal of Mathematical and Statistical Psychology, 32,* 269–286.

Rogosa, D. (1977). *Some results for the Johnson-Neyman technique.* Unpublished doctoral dissertation, Stanford University, Stanford, CA.

Rogosa, D. (1980). Comparing non-parallel regression lines. *Psychological Bulletin.*

Rosenthal, R., & Rosnow, R. (1984). *Essentials of behavioral research.* New York: McGraw-Hill.

Rouanet, H., & Lepine, D. (1970). Comparisons between treatments in a repeated measures design: ANOVA and multivariate methods. *British Journal of Mathematical and Statistical Psychology, 23,* 147–163.

Roy, J., & Bargmann, R. E. (1958). Tests of multiple independence and the associated confidence bounds. *Annals of Mathematical Statistics, 29,* 491–503.

Roy, S. N., & Bose, R. C. (1953). Simultaneous confidence interval estimation. *Annals of Mathematical Statistics, 24,* 513–536.

Rummel, R. J. (1970). *Applied factor analysis.* Evanston, IL: Northwestern University Press.

Sarason, I. G. (1984). Stress, anxiety, and cognitive interference: Reactions to tests. *Journal of Personality and Social Psychology, 46,* 929–938.

SAS Institute Inc. (1985). *SAS user's guide: Statistics.* Cary, NC: Author.

Scandura, T. (1984). *Multivariate analysis of covariance for a study of the effects of leadership training on work outcomes.* Unpublished research paper, University of Cincinnati, Cincinnati.

Scariano, S., & Davenport, J. (1987). The effects of violations of the independence assumption in the one way ANOVA. *The American Statistician, 41,* 123–129.

Schutz, W. (1977). *Leaders of schools: FIRO theory applied to administrators.* LaJolla, CA: University Associates.

Shanahan, T. (1984). Nature of the reading-writing relation: An exploratory multivariate analysis. *Journal of Educational Psychology, 76,* 466–477.

Sharp, G. (1981). Acquisition of lecturing skills by university teaching assistants: Some effects of interest, topic relevance and viewing a model videotape. *American Educational Research Journal, 18,* 491–502.

Shavelson, R., Hubner, J., & Stanton, G. (1976). Self concept: Validation of construct interpretations. *Review of Educational Research, 46,* 407–441.

Shiffler, R. (1988). Maximum z scores and outliers. *American Statistician, 42,* 79–80.

Shin, S. H. (1971). *Creativity, intelligence and achievement: A study of the relationship between creativity and intelligence, and their effects on achievement.* Unpublished doctoral dissertation, University of Pittsburgh, Pittsburgh.

Singer, J., & Willett, J. (1988). *Opening up the black box of recipe statistics: Putting the data back into data analysis.* Paper presented at the annual meeting of the American Educational Research Association, New Orleans, LA.

Stilbeck, W., Acousta, F., Yamamoto, J., & Evans, L. (1984). Self reported psychiatric symptoms among black, hispanic and white outpatients. *Journal of Clinical Psychology, 40,* 1184–1192.

Smart, J. C. (1976). Duties performed by department chairmen in Holland's model environments. *Journal of Educational Psychology, 68,* 194–204.

Smith, A. H. (1975). *A multivariate study of factor analyzed predictors of death anxiety in college students.* Unpublished doctoral dissertation, University of Cincinnati, Cincinnati.

SPSS, Inc. (1988). *SPSSX user's guide.* New York: McGraw-Hill.

Stein, C. (1960). Multiple regression. In I. Olkin (Ed.), *Contributions to probability and statistics, essays in honor of Harol Hotelling.* Stanford, CA: Stanford University Press.

Stevens, J. P. (1972). Four methods of analyzing between variation for the k group MANOVA problem. *Multivariate Behavioral Research, 7,* 499–522.

Stevens, J. P. (1979). Comment on Olson: Choosing a test statistic in multivariate analysis of variance. *Psychological Bulletin, 86,* 355–360.

Stevens, J. P. (1980). Power of the multivariate analysis of variance tests. *Psychological Bulletin, 88,* 728–737.

Stevens, J. P. (1984). *Cross validation in the loglinear model.* Paper presented at the annual meeting of the American Educational Research Association, New Orleans, LA.

Steiger, J. H. (1979). Factor indeterminancy in the 1930s and the 1970s: Some interesting parallels. *Psychometrika, 44,* 157–167.

Stewart, D., & Love, W. (1968). A general canonical correlation index. *Psychological Bulletin, 70,* 160–163.

Stoloff, P. H. (1967). An empirical evaluation of the effects of violating the assumption of homogeneity of covariance for the repeated measures design of the analysis of variance (Tech. Rep.). College Park, MD: University of Maryland.

Tatsuoka, M. M. (1971). *Multivariate analysis: Techniques for educational and psychological research.* New York: Wiley.

Tatsuoka, M. M. (1973). Multivariate analysis in behavioral research. In F. Kerlinger (Ed.), *Review of research in education.* Itasca, IL: F. F. Peacock.

Tetenbaum, T. (1975). The role of student needs and teacher orientations in student ratings of teachers. *American Educational Research Journal, 12,* 417–433.

Thorndike, R., & Hagen, E. (1977). *Measurement and evaluation in psychology and education.* New York: Wiley.

Timm, N. H. (1975). *Multivariate analysis with applications in education and psychology.* Monterey, CA: Brooks-Cole.

Tucker, L. R., Koopman, R. F., & Linn, R. L. (1969). Evaluation of factor analytic research procedures by means of simulated correlation matrices. *Psychometrika, 34,* 421–459.

Weinberg, S. L., & Darlington, R. B. (1976). Canonical analysis when the number of variables is large relative to sample size. *The Journal of Educational Statistics, 1,* 313–332.

Weisberg, S. (1985). *Applied linear regression.* New York: Wiley.

Wickens, T. (1989). *Multiway contingency tables analysis for the social sciences.* Hillsdale, NJ: Lawrence Erlbaum Associates.

Wilk, H. B., Shapiro, S. S., & Chen, H. J. (1965). A comparative study of various tests of normality. *Journal of the American Statistical Association, 63,* 1343–1372.

Wilkinson, L. (1979). Tests of significance in stepwise regression. *Psychological Bulletin, 86,* 168–174.

Winer, B. J. (1971). *Statistical principles in experimental design* (2nd ed.). New York: McGraw-Hill.

Wothke, W. (1993). Nonpositive definite matrices in structural modeling. In K. A. Bollen & J. S. Long (Eds.), *Testing structural equation models* (pp. 00–00). Newbury Park, CA: Sage.

Yao, Y. (1965). An approximate design of freedom solution to the multivariate Behrens-Fisher problem. *Biomtrika,* 139–147.

Zwick, R. (1985). Nonparametric one-way multivariate analysis of variance: A computational approach based on the Pillai-Bartlett trace. *Psychological Bulletin, 97,* 148–152.

APPENDIX A:
Statistical Tables

TABLE A
Percentile Points for χ^2 Distribution

df	.99	.98	.95	.90	.80	.70	.50	.30	.20	.10	.05	.02	.01	.001
1	.03157	.03628	.00393	.0158	.0642	.148	.455	1.074	1.642	2.706	3.841	5.412	6.635	10.827
2	.0201	.0404	.103	.211	.446	.713	1.386	2.408	3.219	4.605	5.991	7.824	9.210	13.815
3	.115	.185	.352	.584	1.005	1.424	2.366	3.665	4.642	6.251	7.815	9.837	11.345	16.268
4	.297	.429	.711	1.064	1.649	2.195	3.357	4.878	5.989	7.779	9.488	11.668	13.277	18.465
5	.554	.752	1.145	1.610	2.343	3.000	4.351	6.064	7.289	9.236	11.070	13.388	15.086	20.517
6	.872	1.134	1.635	2.204	3.070	3.828	5.348	7.231	8.558	10.645	12.592	15.033	16.812	22.457
7	1.239	1.564	2.167	2.833	3.822	4.671	6.346	8.383	9.803	12.017	14.067	16.622	18.475	24.322
8	1.646	2.032	2.733	3.490	4.594	5.527	7.344	9.524	11.030	13.362	15.507	18.168	20.090	26.125
9	2.088	2.532	3.325	4.168	5.380	6.393	8.343	10.656	12.242	14.684	16.919	19.679	21.666	27.877
10	2.558	3.059	3.940	4.865	6.179	7.267	9.342	11.781	13.442	15.987	18.307	21.161	23.209	29.588
11	3.053	3.609	4.575	5.578	6.989	8.148	10.341	12.899	14.631	17.275	19.675	22.618	24.725	31.264
12	3.571	4.178	5.226	6.304	7.807	9.034	11.340	14.011	15.812	18.549	21.026	24.054	26.217	32.909
13	4.107	4.765	5.892	7.042	8.634	9.926	12.340	15.119	16.985	19.812	22.362	25.472	27.688	34.528
14	4.660	5.368	6.571	7.790	9.467	10.821	13.339	16.222	18.151	21.064	23.685	26.873	29.141	36.123
15	5.229	5.985	7.261	8.547	10.307	11.721	14.339	17.322	19.311	22.307	24.996	28.259	30.578	37.697
16	5.812	6.614	7.962	9.312	11.152	12.624	15.338	18.418	20.465	23.542	26.296	29.633	32.000	39.252
17	6.408	7.255	8.672	10.085	12.002	13.531	16.338	19.511	21.615	24.769	27.587	30.995	33.409	40.790
18	7.015	7.906	9.390	10.865	12.857	14.440	17.338	20.601	22.760	25.989	28.869	32.346	34.805	42.312
19	7.633	8.567	10.117	11.651	13.716	15.352	18.338	21.689	23.900	27.204	30.144	33.687	36.191	43.820
20	8.260	9.237	10.851	12.443	14.578	16.266	19.337	22.775	25.038	28.412	31.410	35.020	37.566	45.315

Probability

df														
21	8.897	9.915	11.591	13.240	15.445	17.182	20.337	23.858	26.171	29.615	32.671	36.343	38.932	46.797
22	9.542	10.600	12.338	13.041	16.314	18.101	21.337	24.939	27.301	30.813	33.924	37.659	40.289	48.268
23	10.196	11.293	13.091	14.848	17.187	19.021	22.337	26.018	28.429	32.007	35.172	38.968	41.638	49.728
24	10.856	11.992	13.848	15.659	18.062	19.943	23.337	27.096	29.553	33.196	36.415	40.270	42.980	51.179
25	11.524	12.697	14.611	16.473	18.940	20.867	24.337	28.172	30.675	34.382	37.652	41.566	44.314	52.620
26	12.198	13.409	15.379	17.292	19.820	21.792	25.336	29.246	31.795	35.563	38.885	42.856	45.642	54.052
27	12.879	14.125	16.151	18.114	20.703	22.719	26.336	30.319	32.912	36.741	40.113	44.140	46.963	55.476
28	13.565	14.847	16.928	18.939	21.588	23.647	27.336	31.391	34.027	37.916	41.337	45.419	48.278	56.893
29	14.256	15.574	17.708	19.768	22.475	24.577	28.336	32.461	35.139	39.087	42.557	46.693	49.588	58.302
30	14.953	16.306	18.493	20.599	23.364	25.508	29.336	33.530	36.250	40.256	43.773	47.962	50.892	59.703

Note: For larger values of df, the expression $\sqrt{2\chi^2} - \sqrt{2df - 1}$ may be used as a normal deviate with unit variance, remembering that the probability for χ^2 corresponds with that of a single tail of the normal curve.

Source: Reproduced from E. F. Lindquist, *Design and Analysis of Experiments in Psychology and Education,* Houghton Mifflin, Boston, 1953, p. 29, with the permission of the publisher.

TABLE B
Critical Values for *t*

df	Level of significance for one-tailed test					
	.10	*.05*	*.025*	*.01*	*.005*	*.0005*
	Level of significance for two-tailed test					
	.20	*.10*	*.05*	*.02*	*.01*	*.001*
1	3.078	6.314	12.706	31.821	63.657	636.619
2	1.886	2.920	4.303	6.965	9.925	31.598
3	1.638	2.353	3.182	4.541	5.841	12.941
4	1.533	2.132	2.776	3.747	4.604	8.610
5	1.476	2.015	2.571	3.365	4.032	6.859
6	1.440	1.943	2.447	3.143	3.707	5.959
7	1.415	1.895	2.365	2.998	3.449	5.405
8	1.397	1.860	2.306	2.896	3.355	5.041
9	1.383	1.833	2.262	2.821	3.250	4.781
10	1.372	1.812	2.228	2.764	3.169	4.587
11	1.363	1.796	2.201	2.718	3.106	4.437
12	1.356	1.782	2.179	2.681	3.055	4.318
13	1.350	1.771	2.160	2.650	3.012	4.221
14	1.345	1.761	2.145	2.624	2.977	4.140
15	1.341	1.753	2.131	2.602	2.947	4.073
16	1.337	1.746	2.120	2.583	2.921	4.015
17	1.333	1.740	2.110	2.567	2.898	3.965
18	1.330	1.734	2.101	2.552	2.878	3.922
19	1.328	1.729	2.093	2.539	2.861	3.883
20	1.325	1.725	2.086	2.528	2.845	3.850
21	1.323	1.721	2.080	2.518	2.831	3.819
22	1.321	1.717	2.074	2.508	2.819	3.792
23	1.319	1.714	2.069	2.500	2.807	3.767
24	1.318	1.711	2.064	2.492	2.797	3.745
25	1.316	1.708	2.060	2.485	2.787	3.725
26	1.315	1.706	2.056	2.479	2.779	3.707
27	1.314	1.703	2.052	2.473	2.771	3.690
28	1.313	1.701	2.048	2.467	2.763	3.674
29	1.311	1.699	2.045	2.462	2.756	3.659
30	1.310	1.697	2.042	2.457	2.750	3.646
40	1.303	1.684	2.021	2.423	2.704	3.551
60	1.296	1.671	2.000	2.390	2.660	3.460
120	1.289	1.658	1.980	2.358	2.617	3.373
∞	1.282	1.645	1.960	2.326	2.576	3.291

Reproduced from E. F. Lindquist, *Design and Analysis of Experiments in Psychology and Education*, Boston: Houghton-Mifflin. Reprinted with permission of the publisher.

TABLE C
Critical Values for F

				df *for Numerator*					
df *error*	α	*1*	*2*	*3*	*4*	*5*	*6*	*8*	*12*
1	.01	4052	4999	5403	5625	5764	5859	5981	6106
	.05	161.45	199.50	215.71	224.58	230.16	233.99	238.88	243.91
	.10	39.86	49.50	53.59	55.83	57.24	58.20	59.44	60.70
	.20	9.47	12.00	13.06	13.73	14.01	14.26	14.59	14.90
2	.01	98.49	99.00	99.17	99.25	99.30	99.33	99.36	99.42
	.05	18.51	19.00	19.16	19.25	19.30	19.33	19.37	19.41
	.10	8.53	9.00	9.16	9.24	9.29	9.33	9.37	9.41
	.20	3.56	4.00	4.16	4.24	4.28	4.32	4.36	4.40
3	.001	167.5	148.5	141.1	137.1	134.6	132.8	130.6	128.3
	.01	34.12	30.81	29.46	28.71	28.24	27.91	27.49	27.05
	.05	10.13	9.55	9.28	9.12	9.01	8.94	8.84	8.74
	.10	5.54	5.46	5.39	5.34	5.31	5.28	5.25	5.22
	.20	2.68	2.89	2.94	2.96	2.97	2.97	2.98	2.98
4	.001	74.14	61.25	56.18	53.44	51.71	50.53	49.00	47.41
	.01	21.20	18.00	16.69	15.98	15.52	15.21	14.80	14.37
	.05	7.71	6.94	6.59	6.39	6.26	6.16	6.04	5.91
	.10	4.54	4.32	4.19	4.11	4.05	4.01	3.95	3.90
	.20	2.35	2.47	2.48	2.48	2.48	2.47	2.47	2.46
5	.001	47.04	36.61	33.20	31.09	29.75	28.84	27.64	26.42
	.01	16.26	13.27	12.06	11.39	10.97	10.67	10.29	9.89
	.05	6.61	5.79	5.41	5.19	5.05	4.95	4.82	4.68
	.10	4.06	3.78	3.62	3.52	3.45	3.40	3.34	3.27
	.20	2.18	2.26	2.25	2.24	2.23	2.22	2.20	2.18
6	.001	35.51	27.00	23.70	21.90	20.81	20.03	19.03	17.99
	.01	13.74	10.92	9.78	9.15	8.75	8.47	8.10	7.72
	.05	5.99	5.14	4.76	4.53	4.39	4.28	4.15	4.00
	.10	3.78	3.46	3.29	3.18	3.11	3.05	2.98	2.90
	.20	2.07	2.13	2.11	2.09	2.08	2.06	2.04	2.02
7	.001	29.22	21.69	18.77	17.19	16.21	15.52	14.63	13.71
	.01	12.25	9.55	8.45	7.85	7.46	7.19	6.84	6.47
	.05	5.59	4.74	4.35	4.12	3.97	3.87	3.73	3.57
	.10	3.59	3.26	3.07	2.96	2.88	2.83	2.75	2.67
	.20	2.00	2.04	2.02	1.99	1.97	1.96	1.93	1.91
8	.001	25.42	18.49	15.83	14.39	13.49	12.86	12.04	11.19
	.01	11.26	8.65	7.59	7.01	6.63	6.37	6.03	5.67
	.05	5.32	4.46	4.07	3.84	3.69	3.58	3.44	3.28
	.10	3.46	3.11	2.92	2.81	2.73	2.67	2.59	2.50
	.20	1.95	1.98	1.95	1.92	1.90	1.88	1.86	1.83
9	.001	22.86	16.39	13.90	12.56	11.71	11.13	10.37	9.57
	.01	10.56	8.02	6.99	6.42	6.06	5.80	5.47	5.11
	.05	5.12	4.26	3.86	3.63	3.48	3.37	3.23	3.07
	.10	3.36	3.01	2.81	2.69	2.61	2.55	2.47	2.38
	.20	1.91	1.94	1.90	1.87	1.85	1.83	1.80	1.76

(*cont.*)

TABLE C (Continued)

df error	α	\multicolumn{8}{c}{df for Numerator}
		1	2	3	4	5	6	8	12
10	.001	21.04	14.91	12.55	11.28	10.48	9.92	9.20	8.45
	.01	10.04	7.56	6.55	5.99	5.64	5.39	5.06	4.71
	.05	4.96	4.10	3.71	3.48	3.33	3.22	3.07	2.91
	.10	3.28	2.92	2.73	2.61	2.52	2.46	2.38	2.28
	.20	1.88	1.90	1.86	1.83	1.80	1.78	1.75	1.72
11	.001	19.69	13.81	11.56	10.35	9.58	9.05	8.35	7.63
	.01	9.65	7.20	6.22	5.67	5.32	5.07	4.74	4.40
	.05	4.84	3.98	3.59	3.36	3.20	3.09	2.95	2.79
	.10	3.23	2.86	2.66	2.54	2.45	2.39	2.30	2.21
	.20	1.86	1.87	1.83	1.80	1.77	1.75	1.72	1.68
12	.001	18.64	12.97	10.80	9.63	8.89	8.38	7.71	7.00
	.01	9.33	6.93	5.95	5.41	5.06	4.82	4.50	4.16
	.05	4.75	3.88	3.49	3.26	3.11	3.00	2.85	2.69
	.10	3.18	2.81	2.61	2.48	2.39	2.33	2.24	2.15
	.20	1.84	1.85	1.80	1.77	1.74	1.72	1.69	1.65
13	.001	17.81	12.31	10.21	9.07	8.35	7.86	7.21	6.52
	.01	9.07	6.70	5.74	5.20	4.86	4.62	4.30	3.96
	.05	4.67	3.80	3.41	3.18	3.02	2.92	2.77	2.60
	.10	3.14	2.76	2.56	2.43	2.35	2.28	2.20	2.10
	.20	1.82	1.83	1.78	1.75	1.72	1.69	1.66	1.62
14	.001	17.14	11.78	9.73	8.62	7.92	7.43	6.80	6.13
	.01	8.86	6.51	5.56	5.03	4.69	4.46	4.14	3.80
	.05	4.60	3.74	3.34	3.11	2.96	2.85	2.70	2.53
	.10	3.10	2.73	2.52	2.39	2.31	2.24	2.15	2.05
	.20	1.81	1.81	1.76	1.73	1.70	1.67	1.64	1.60
15	.001	16.59	11.34	9.34	8.25	7.57	7.09	6.47	5.81
	.01	8.68	6.36	5.42	4.89	4.56	4.32	4.00	3.67
	.05	4.54	3.68	3.29	3.06	2.90	2.79	2.64	2.48
	.10	3.07	2.70	2.49	2.36	2.27	2.21	2.12	2.02
	.20	1.80	1.79	1.75	1.71	1.68	1.66	1.62	1.58
16	.001	16.12	10.97	9.00	7.94	7.27	6.81	6.19	5.55
	.01	8.53	6.23	5.29	4.77	4.44	4.20	3.89	3.55
	.05	4.49	3.63	3.24	3.01	2.85	2.74	2.59	2.42
	.10	3.05	2.67	2.46	2.33	2.24	2.18	2.09	1.99
	.20	1.79	1.78	1.74	1.70	1.67	1.64	1.61	1.56
17	.001	15.72	10.66	8.73	7.68	7.02	6.56	5.96	5.32
	.01	8.40	6.11	5.18	4.67	4.34	4.10	3.79	3.45
	.05	4.45	3.59	3.20	2.96	2.81	2.70	2.55	2.38
	.10	3.03	2.64	2.44	2.31	2.22	2.15	2.06	1.96
	.20	1.78	1.77	1.72	1.68	1.65	1.63	1.59	1.55
18	.001	15.38	10.39	8.49	7.46	6.81	6.35	5.76	5.13
	.01	8.28	6.01	5.09	4.58	4.25	4.01	3.71	3.37
	.05	4.41	3.55	3.16	2.93	2.77	2.66	2.51	2.34
	.10	3.01	2.62	2.42	2.29	2.20	2.13	2.04	1.93
	.20	1.77	1.76	1.71	1.67	1.64	1.62	1.58	1.53

(cont.)

TABLE C (*Continued*)

df error	α	1	2	3	4	5	6	8	12
					df *for Numerator*				
19	.001	15.08	10.16	8.28	7.26	6.61	6.18	5.59	4.97
	.01	8.18	5.93	5.01	4.50	4.17	3.94	3.63	3.30
	.05	4.38	3.52	3.13	2.90	2.74	2.63	2.48	2.31
	.10	2.99	2.61	2.40	2.27	2.18	2.11	2.02	1.91
	.20	1.76	1.75	1.70	1.66	1.63	1.61	1.57	1.52
20	.001	14.82	9.95	8.10	7.10	6.46	6.02	5.44	4.82
	.01	8.10	5.85	4.94	4.43	4.10	3.87	3.56	3.23
	.05	4.35	3.49	3.10	2.87	2.71	2.60	2.45	2.28
	.10	2.97	2.59	2.38	2.25	2.16	2.09	2.00	1.89
	.20	1.76	1.75	1.70	1.65	1.62	1.60	1.56	1.51
21	.001	14.59	9.77	7.94	6.95	6.32	5.88	5.31	4.70
	.01	8.02	5.78	4.87	4.37	4.04	3.81	3.51	3.17
	.05	4.32	3.47	3.07	2.84	2.68	2.57	2.42	2.25
	.10	2.96	2.57	2.36	2.23	2.14	2.08	1.98	1.88
	.20	1.75	1.74	1.69	1.65	1.61	1.59	1.55	1.50
22	.001	14.38	9.61	7.80	6.81	6.19	5.76	5.19	4.58
	.01	7.94	5.72	4.82	4.31	3.99	3.76	3.45	3.12
	.05	4.30	3.44	3.05	2.82	2.66	2.55	2.40	2.23
	.10	2.95	2.56	2.35	2.22	2.13	2.06	1.97	1.86
	.20	1.75	1.73	1.68	1.64	1.61	1.58	1.54	1.49
23	.001	14.19	9.47	7.67	6.69	6.08	5.65	5.09	4.48
	.01	7.88	5.66	4.76	4.26	3.94	3.71	3.41	3.07
	.05	4.28	3.42	3.03	2.80	2.64	2.53	2.38	2.20
	.10	2.94	2.55	2.34	2.21	2.11	2.05	1.95	1.84
	.20	1.74	1.73	1.68	1.63	1.60	1.57	1.53	1.49
24	.001	14.03	9.34	7.55	6.59	5.98	5.55	4.99	4.39
	.01	7.82	5.61	4.72	4.22	3.90	3.67	3.36	3.03
	.05	4.26	3.40	3.01	2.78	2.62	2.51	2.36	2.18
	.10	2.93	2.54	2.33	2.19	2.10	2.04	1.94	1.83
	.20	1.74	1.72	1.67	1.63	1.59	1.57	1.53	1.48
25	.001	13.88	9.22	7.45	6.49	5.88	5.46	4.91	4.31
	.01	7.77	5.57	4.68	4.18	3.86	3.63	3.32	2.99
	.05	4.24	3.38	2.99	2.76	2.60	2.49	2.34	2.16
	.10	2.92	2.53	2.32	2.18	2.09	2.02	1.93	1.82
	.20	1.73	1.72	1.66	1.62	1.59	1.56	1.52	1.47
26	.001	13.74	9.12	7.36	6.41	5.80	5.38	4.83	4.24
	.01	7.72	5.53	4.64	4.14	3.82	3.59	3.29	2.96
	.05	4.22	3.37	2.98	2.74	2.59	2.47	2.32	2.15
	.10	2.91	2.52	2.31	2.17	2.08	2.01	1.92	1.81
	.20	1.73	1.71	1.66	1.62	1.58	1.56	1.52	1.47
27	.001	13.61	9.02	7.27	6.33	5.73	5.31	4.76	4.17
	.01	7.68	5.49	4.60	4.11	3.78	3.56	3.26	2.93
	.05	4.21	3.35	2.96	2.73	2.57	2.46	2.30	2.13
	.10	2.90	2.51	2.30	2.17	2.07	2.00	1.91	1.80
	.20	1.73	1.71	1.66	1.61	1.58	1.55	1.51	1.46

(*cont.*)

TABLE C (Continued)

df error	α	df for Numerator							
		1	2	3	4	5	6	8	12
28	.001	13.50	8.93	7.19	6.25	5.66	5.24	4.69	4.11
	.01	7.64	5.45	4.57	4.07	3.75	3.53	3.23	2.90
	.05	4.20	3.34	2.95	2.71	2.56	2.44	2.29	2.12
	.10	2.89	2.50	2.29	2.16	2.06	2.00	1.90	1.79
	.20	1.72	1.71	1.65	1.61	1.57	1.55	1.51	1.46
29	.001	13.39	8.85	7.12	6.19	5.59	5.18	4.64	4.05
	.01	7.60	5.42	4.54	4.04	3.73	3.50	3.20	2.87
	.05	4.18	3.33	2.93	2.70	2.54	2.43	2.28	2.10
	.10	2.89	2.50	2.28	2.15	2.06	1.99	1.89	1.78
	.20	1.72	1.70	1.65	1.60	1.57	1.54	1.50	1.45
30	.001	13.29	8.77	7.05	6.12	5.53	5.12	4.58	4.00
	.01	7.56	5.39	4.51	4.02	3.70	3.47	3.17	2.84
	.05	4.17	3.32	2.92	2.69	2.53	2.42	2.27	2.09
	.10	2.88	2.49	2.28	2.14	2.05	1.98	1.88	1.77
	.20	1.72	1.70	1.64	1.60	1.57	1.54	1.50	1.45
40	.001	12.61	8.25	6.60	5.70	5.13	4.73	4.21	3.64
	.01	7.31	5.18	4.31	3.83	3.51	3.29	2.99	2.66
	.05	4.08	3.23	·2.84	2.61	2.45	2.34	2.18	2.00
	.10	2.84	2.44	2.23	2.09	2.00	1.93	1.83	1.71
	.20	1.70	1.68	1.62	1.57	1.54	1.51	1.47	1.41
60	.001	11.97	7.76	6.17	5.31	4.76	4.37	3.87	3.31
	.01	7.08	4.98	4.13	3.65	3.34	3.12	2.82	2.50
	.05	4.00	3.15	2.76	2.52	2.37	2.25	2.10	1.92
	.10	2.79	2.39	2.18	2.04	1.95	1.87	1.77	1.66
	.20	1.68	1.65	1.59	1.55	1.51	1.48	1.44	1.38
120	.001	11.38	7.31	5.79	4.95	4.42	4.04	3.55	3.02
	.01	6.85	4.79	3.95	3.48	3.17	2.96	2.66	2.34
	.05	3.92	3.07	2.68	2.45	2.29	2.17	2.02	1.83
	.10	2.75	2.35	2.13	1.99	1.90	1.82	1.72	1.60
	.20	1.66	1.63	1.57	1.52	1.48	1.45	1.41	1.35
∞	.001	10.83	6.91	5.42	4.62	4.10	3.74	3.27	2.74
	.01	6.64	4.60	3.78	3.32	3.02	2.80	2.51	2.18
	.05	3.84	2.99	2.60	2.37	2.21	2.09	1.94	1.75
	.10	2.71	2.30	2.08	1.94	1.85	1.77	1.67	1.55
	.20	1.64	1.61	1.55	1.50	1.46	1.43	1.38	1.32

Source: Reproduced from E. F. Lindquist, *Design and Analysis of Experiments in Psychology and Education,* Houghton Mifflin, Boston, 1953, pp. 41–44, with the permission of the publisher.

TABLE D
Percentile Points of Studentized Range Statistic

90th Percentiles

number of groups

df error	2	3	4	5	6	7	8	9	10
1	8.929	13.44	16.36	18.49	20.15	21.51	22.64	23.62	24.48
2	4.130	5.733	6.773	7.538	8.139	8.633	9.049	9.409	9.725
3	3.328	4.467	5.199	5.738	6.162	6.511	6.806	7.062	7.287
4	3.015	3.976	4.586	5.035	5.388	5.679	5.926	6.139	6.327
5	2.850	3.717	4.264	4.664	4.979	5.238	5.458	5.648	5.816
6	2.748	3.559	4.065	4.435	4.726	4.966	5.168	5.344	5.499
7	2.680	3.451	3.931	4.280	4.555	4.780	4.972	5.137	5.283
8	2.630	3.374	3.834	4.169	4.431	4.646	4.829	4.987	5.126
9	2.592	3.316	3.761	4.084	4.337	4.545	4.721	4.873	5.007
10	2.563	3.270	3.704	4.018	4.264	4.465	4.636	4.783	4.913
11	2.540	3.234	3.658	3.965	4.205	4.401	4.568	4.711	4.838
12	2.521	3.204	3.621	3.922	4.156	4.349	4.511	4.652	4.776
13	2.505	3.179	3.589	3.885	4.116	4.305	4.464	4.602	4.724
14	2.491	3.158	3.563	3.854	4.081	4.267	4.424	4.560	4.680
15	2.479	3.140	3.540	3.828	4.052	4.235	4.390	4.524	4.641
16	2.469	3.124	3.520	3.804	4.026	4.207	4.360	4.492	4.608
17	2.460	3.110	3.503	3.784	4.004	4.183	4.334	4.464	4.579
18	2.452	3.098	3.488	3.767	3.984	4.161	4.311	4.440	4.554
19	2.445	3.087	3.474	3.751	3.966	4.142	4.290	4.418	4.531
20	2.439	3.078	3.462	3.736	3.950	4.124	4.271	4.398	4.510
24	2.420	3.047	3.423	3.692	3.900	4.070	4.213	4.336	4.445
30	2.400	3.017	3.386	3.648	3.851	4.016	4.155	4.275	4.381
40	2.381	2.988	3.349	3.605	3.803	3.963	4.099	4.215	4.317
60	2.363	2.959	3.312	3.562	3.755	3.911	4.042	4.155	4.254
120	2.344	2.930	3.276	3.520	3.707	3.859	3.987	4.096	4.191
∞	2.326	2.902	3.240	3.478	3.661	3.808	3.931	4.037	4.129

TABLE D (Continued)

95th Percentiles

df error	number of groups								
	2	3	4	5	6	7	8	9	10
1	17.97	26.98	32.82	37.08	40.41	43.12	45.40	47.36	49.07
2	6.085	8.331	9.798	10.88	11.74	12.44	13.03	13.54	13.99
3	4.501	5.910	6.825	7.502	8.037	8.478	8.853	9.177	9.462
4	3.927	5.040	5.757	6.287	6.707	7.053	7.347	7.602	7.826
5	3.635	4.602	5.218	5.673	6.033	6.330	6.582	6.802	6.995
6	3.461	4.339	4.896	5.305	5.628	5.895	6.122	6.319	6.493
7	3.344	4.165	4.681	5.060	5.359	5.606	5.815	5.998	6.158
8	3.261	4.041	4.529	4.886	5.167	5.399	5.597	5.767	5.918
9	3.199	3.949	4.415	4.756	5.024	5.244	5.432	5.595	5.739
10	3.151	3.877	4.327	4.654	4.912	5.124	5.305	5.461	5.599
11	3.113	3.820	4.256	4.574	4.823	5.028	5.202	5.353	5.487
12	3.082	3.773	4.199	4.508	4.751	4.950	5.119	5.265	5.395
13	3.055	3.735	4.151	4.453	4.690	4.885	5.049	5.192	5.318
14	3.033	3.702	4.111	4.407	4.639	4.829	4.990	5.131	5.254
15	3.014	3.674	4.076	4.367	4.595	4.782	4.940	5.077	5.198
16	2.998	3.649	4.046	4.333	4.557	4.741	4.897	5.031	5.150
17	2.984	3.628	4.020	4.303	4.524	4.705	4.858	4.991	5.108
18	2.971	3.609	3.997	4.277	4.495	4.673	4.824	4.956	5.071
19	2.960	3.593	3.977	4.253	4.469	4.645	4.794	4.924	5.038
20	2.950	3.578	3.958	4.232	4.445	4.620	4.768	4.896	5.008
24	2.919	3.532	3.901	4.166	4.373	4.541	4.684	4.807	4.915
30	2.888	3.486	3.845	4.102	4.302	4.464	4.602	4.720	4.824
40	2.858	3.442	3.791	4.039	4.232	4.389	4.521	4.635	4.735
60	2.829	3.399	3.737	3.977	4.163	4.314	4.441	4.550	4.646
120	2.800	3.356	3.685	3.917	4.096	4.241	4.363	4.468	4.560
∞	2.772	3.314	3.633	3.858	4.030	4.170	4.286	4.387	4.474

(cont.)

TABLE D (*Continued*)

97.5th Percentiles

number of groups

df error	2	3	4	5	6	7	8	9	10
1	35.99	54.00	65.69	74.22	80.87	86.29	90.85	94.77	98.20
2	8.776	11.94	14.01	15.54	16.75	17.74	18.58	19.31	19.95
3	5.907	7.661	8.808	9.660	10.34	10.89	11.37	11.78	12.14
4	4.943	6.244	7.088	7.716	8.213	8.625	8.976	9.279	9.548
5	4.474	5.558	6.257	6.775	7.186	7.527	7.816	8.068	8.291
6	4.199	5.158	5.772	6.226	6.586	6.884	7.138	7.359	7.554
7	4.018	4.897	5.455	5.868	6.194	6.464	6.695	6.895	7.072
8	3.892	4.714	5.233	5.616	5.919	6.169	6.382	6.568	6.732
9	3.797	4.578	5.069	5.430	5.715	5.950	6.151	6.325	6.479
10	3.725	4.474	4.943	5.287	5.558	5.782	5.972	6.138	6.285
11	3.667	4.391	4.843	5.173	5.433	5.648	5.831	5.989	6.130
12	3.620	4.325	4.762	5.081	5.332	5.540	5.716	5.869	6.004
13	3.582	4.269	4.694	5.004	5.248	5.449	5.620	5.769	5.900
14	3.550	4.222	4.638	4.940	5.178	5.374	5.540	5.684	5.811
15	3.522	4.182	4.589	4.885	5.118	5.309	5.471	5.612	5.737
16	3.498	4.148	4.548	4.838	5.066	5.253	5.412	5.550	5.672
17	3.477	4.118	4.512	4.797	5.020	5.204	5.361	5.496	5.615
18	3.458	4.092	4.480	4.761	4.981	5.162	5.315	5.448	5.565
19	3.442	4.068	4.451	4.728	4.945	5.123	5.275	5.405	5.521
20	3.427	4.047	4.426	4.700	4.914	5.089	5.238	5.368	5.481
24	3.381	3.983	4.347	4.610	4.816	4.984	5.126	5.250	5.358
30	3.337	3.919	4.271	4.523	4.720	4.881	5.017	5.134	5.238
40	3.294	3.858	4.197	4.439	4.627	4.780	4.910	5.022	5.120
60	3.251	3.798	4.124	4.356	4.536	4.682	4.806	4.912	5.006
120	3.210	3.739	4.053	4.276	4.447	4.587	4.704	4.805	4.894
∞	3.170	3.682	3.984	4.197	4.361	4.494	4.605	4.700	4.784

TABLE D (Continued)

99th Percentiles

number of groups

df error	2	3	4	5	6	7	8	9	10
1	90.03	135.0	164.3	185.6	202.2	215.8	227.2	237.0	245.6
2	14.04	19.02	22.29	24.72	26.63	28.20	29.53	30.68	31.69
3	8.261	10.62	12.17	13.33	14.24	15.00	15.64	16.20	16.69
4	6.512	8.120	9.173	9.958	10.58	11.10	11.55	11.93	12.27
5	5.702	6.976	7.804	8.421	8.913	9.321	9.669	9.972	10.24
6	5.243	6.331	7.033	7.556	7.973	8.318	8.613	8.869	9.097
7	4.949	5.919	6.543	7.005	7.373	7.679	7.939	8.166	8.368
8	4.746	5.635	6.204	6.625	6.960	7.237	7.474	7.681	7.863
9	4.596	5.428	5.957	6.348	6.658	6.915	7.134	7.325	7.495
10	4.482	5.270	5.769	6.136	6.428	6.669	6.875	7.055	7.213
11	4.392	5.146	5.621	5.970	6.247	6.476	6.672	6.842	6.992
12	4.320	5.046	5.502	5.836	6.101	6.321	6.507	6.670	6.814
13	4.260	4.964	5.404	5.727	5.981	6.192	6.372	6.528	6.667
14	4.210	4.895	5.322	5.634	5.881	6.085	6.258	6.409	6.543
15	4.168	4.836	5.252	5.556	5.796	5.994	6.162	6.309	6.439
16	4.131	4.786	5.192	5.489	5.722	5.915	6.079	6.222	6.349
17	4.099	4.742	5.140	5.430	5.659	5.847	6.007	6.147	6.270
18	4.071	4.703	5.094	5.379	5.603	5.788	5.944	6.081	6.201
19	4.046	4.670	5.054	5.334	5.554	5.735	5.889	6.022	6.141
20	4.024	4.639	5.018	5.294	5.510	5.688	5.839	5.970	6.087
24	3.956	4.546	4.907	5.168	5.374	5.542	5.685	5.809	5.919
30	3.889	4.455	4.799	5.048	5.242	5.401	5.536	5.653	5.756
40	3.825	4.367	4.696	4.931	5.114	5.265	5.392	5.502	5.599
60	3.762	4.282	4.595	4.818	4.991	5.133	5.253	5.356	5.447
120	3.702	4.200	4.497	4.709	4.872	5.005	5.118	5.214	5.299
∞	3.643	4.120	4.403	4.603	4.757	4.882	4.987	5.078	5.157

Reproduced from H. Harter, "Tables of Range and Studentized Range," *Annals of Mathematical Statistics*, 1960. Reprinted with permission.

TABLE E
Sample Size Needed in Three-Group MANOVA for Power = .70, .80
and .90 for α = .05 and α = .01

		Power =	α = .05			α = .01		
			.70	.80	.90	.70	.80	.90
Number of Variables		2	11	13	16	15	17	21
Effect Size		3	12	14	18	17	20	24
	$q^2 = 1.125$	4	14	16	19	19	22	26
Very Large	$d = 1.5$	5	15	17	21	20	23	28
	$c = 0.75$							
		6	16	18	22	22	25	29
		8	18	21	25	24	28	32
		10	20	23	27	27	30	35
		15	24	27	32	32	35	42
Large	$q^2 = 0.5$	2	21	26	33	31	36	44
	$d = 1$	3	25	29	37	35	42	50
	$c = 0.5$	4	27	33	42	38	44	54
		5	30	35	44	42	48	58
		6	32	38	48	44	52	62
		8	36	42	52	50	56	68
		10	39	46	56	54	62	74
		15	46	54	66	64	72	84
Moderate	$q^2 = 0.2813$	2	36	44	58	54	62	76
	$d = 0.75$	3	42	52	64	60	70	86
	$c = 0.375$	4	46	56	70	66	78	94
		5	50	60	76	72	82	100
		6	54	66	82	76	88	105
		8	60	72	90	84	98	120
		10	66	78	98	92	105	125
		15	78	92	115	110	125	145
Small	$q^2 = 0.125$	2	80	98	125	115	140	170
	$d = 0.5$	3	92	115	145	135	155	190
	$c = 0.25$	4	105	125	155	145	170	210
		5	110	135	170	155	185	220
		6	120	145	180	165	195	240
		8	135	160	200	185	220	260
		10	145	175	220	200	230	280
		15	170	210	250	240	270	320

(*cont.*)

TABLE E (*Continued*)
**Sample Size Needed for Four-Group MANOVA for Power = .70, .80
and .90 at α = .05 and α = .01**

			α = .05			α = .01		
		Power =	.70	.80	.90	.70	.80	.90
Number of Variables		2	12	14	17	17	19	23
Effect Size		3	14	16	20	19	22	26
	$q^2=1.125$	4	15	18	22	21	24	28
Very Large	$d=1.5$	5	16	19	23	23	26	30
	$c=0.4743$	6	18	21	25	24	27	32
		8	20	23	28	27	30	36
		10	22	25	30	29	33	39
		15	26	30	36	35	39	46
Large	$q^2=0.5$	2	24	29	37	34	40	50
	$d=1$	3	28	33	42	39	46	56
	$c=0.3162$	4	31	37	46	44	50	60
		5	34	40	50	48	54	64
		6	36	44	54	50	58	70
		8	42	48	60	56	64	76
		10	46	52	64	62	70	82
		15	54	62	76	72	82	96
Moderate	$q^2=0.2813$	2	42	50	64	60	70	86
	$d=0.75$	3	48	58	72	68	80	96
	$c=0.2372$	4	54	64	80	76	88	105
		5	58	70	86	82	94	115
		6	62	74	92	86	100	120
		8	70	84	105	96	115	135
		10	78	92	115	105	120	145
		15	92	110	130	125	145	170
Small	$q^2=0.125$	2	92	115	145	130	155	190
	$d=0.5$	3	105	130	165	150	175	220
	$c=0.1581$	4	120	145	180	165	195	240
		5	130	155	195	180	210	250
		6	140	165	210	190	220	270
		8	155	185	230	220	250	300
		10	170	200	250	240	270	320
		15	200	240	290	280	320	370

(*cont.*)

TABLE E (*Continued*)
**Sample Size Needed for Five Group MANOVA for Power = .70, .80 and
.90 at α = .05 and α = .01**

		Power =	α = .05			α = .01		
			.70	.80	.90	.70	.80	.90
Number of Variables		2	13	15	19	18	20	25
Effect Size		3	15	17	21	20	23	28
	$q^2 = 1.125$	4	16	19	23	22	26	30
Very Large	$d = 1.5$	5	18	21	25	24	28	33
	$c = 0.3354$							
		6	19	22	27	26	30	35
		8	22	25	30	29	33	39
		10	24	27	33	32	36	42
		15	28	33	39	38	44	50
Large	$q^2 = 0.5$	2	26	32	40	37	44	54
	$d = 1$	3	31	37	46	44	50	60
	$c = 0.2236$	4	34	42	50	48	56	66
		5	37	44	54	52	60	70
		6	40	48	58	56	64	76
		8	46	54	66	62	70	84
		10	50	58	72	68	78	90
		15	60	70	84	80	90	110
Moderate	$q^2 = 0.2813$	2	46	56	70	66	76	92
	$d = 0.75$	3	54	64	80	74	86	105
	$c = 0.1677$	4	60	72	88	82	96	115
		5	64	78	96	90	105	125
		6	70	82	105	96	110	135
		8	78	92	115	110	125	145
		10	86	105	125	120	135	160
		15	105	120	145	140	160	185
Small	$q^2 = 0.125$	2	100	125	155	145	170	210
	$d = 0.5$	3	120	145	180	165	195	240
	$c = 0.1118$	4	130	160	195	185	210	260
		5	145	170	220	200	230	280
		6	155	185	230	220	250	300
		8	175	210	260	240	280	330
		10	190	230	280	260	300	360
		15	230	270	330	310	350	420

TABLE E (*Continued*)
**Sample Size Needed for Six-Group MANOVA for Power = .70, .80 and
.90 at α = .05 and α = .01**

		Power =	$\alpha = .05$			$\alpha = .01$		
			.70	.80	.90	.70	.80	.90
Number of Variables		2	14	16	20	19	22	26
Effect Size		3	16	18	23	22	25	29
	$q^2=1.125$	4	18	21	25	24	27	32
Very Large	$d=1.5$	5	19	22	27	26	30	35
	$c=0.2535$	6	21	24	29	28	32	37
		8	23	27	33	31	35	42
		10	25	30	36	34	39	46
		15	30	35	42	42	46	54
Large	$q^2=0.5$	2	28	34	44	40	46	56
	$d=1$	3	33	39	50	46	54	64
	$c=0.1690$	4	37	44	54	52	60	70
		5	40	48	60	56	64	76
		6	44	52	64	60	68	82
		8	50	58	70	68	76	90
		10	54	64	78	74	84	98
		15	64	76	90	88	98	115
Moderate	$q^2=0.2813$	2	50	60	76	70	82	98
	$d=0.75$	3	58	70	86	80	94	115
	$c=0.1268$	4	64	76	96	90	105	125
		5	70	84	105	98	115	135
		6	76	90	110	105	120	145
		8	86	100	125	120	135	160
		10	94	110	135	130	145	175
		15	115	135	160	155	175	210
Small	$q^2=0.125$	2	110	135	170	155	180	220
	$d=0.5$	3	130	155	190	180	210	250
	$c=0.0845$	4	145	170	220	200	230	280
		5	155	185	230	220	250	300
		6	170	200	250	230	270	320
		8	190	230	280	260	300	350
		10	210	250	300	290	330	390
		15	250	290	360	340	380	460

[1]There exists a variate i such that $1/\sigma^2 \sum_{j=1}^{J} (\mu_{ij} - \mu_{i.}) \geq q^2$, where $\mu_{i.}$ is the total mean and σ^2 is variance. There exists a variate s such that $1/\sigma_i|\mu_{ij_1} - \mu_{ij_2}| \geq d$, for two groups j_1 and j_2. There exists a variate s such that for *all* pairs of groups 1 and m we have $1/\sigma_i|\mu_{i1} - \mu_{im}| \geq c$.

[2]The entries in the body of the table are the sample size required for *each* group for the power indicated. For example, for power = .80 at α = .05 for a large effect size with 4 variables, we would need 33 subjects per group.

Critical Values for F_{max} Statistic

df for * each variance	$1 - \alpha$	Number of Variances										
		2	3	4	5	6	7	8	9	10	11	12
2	.95	39.0	87.5	142	202	266	333	403	475	550	626	704
	.99	199	448	729	1036	1362	1705	2063	2432	2813	3204	3605
3	.95	15.4	27.8	39.2	50.7	62.0	72.9	83.5	93.9	104	114	124
	.99	47.5	85	120	151	184	216	249	281	310	337	361
4	.95	9.60	15.5	20.6	25.2	29.5	33.6	37.5	41.4	44.6	48.0	51.4
	.99	23.2	37.	49.	59.	69.	79.	89.	97.	106.	113.	120
5	.95	7.15	10.8	13.7	16.3	18.7	20.8	22.9	24.7	26.5	28.2	29.9
	.99	14.9	22.	28.	33.	38.	42.	46.	50.	54.	57	60
6	.95	5.82	8.38	10.4	12.1	13.7	15.0	16.3	17.5	18.6	19.7	20.7
	.99	11.1	15.5	19.1	22.	25.	27.	30.	32.	34.	36	37
7	.95	4.99	6.94	8.44	9.70	10.8	11.8	12.7	13.5	14.3	15.1	15.8
	.99	8.89	12.1	14.5	16.5	18.4	20.	22.	23.	24.	26	27
8	.95	4.43	6.00	7.18	8.12	9.03	9.78	10.5	11.1	11.7	12.2	12.7
	.99	7.50	9.9	11.7	13.2	14.5	15.8	16.9	17.9	18.9	19.8	21
9	.95	4.03	5.34	6.31	7.11	7.80	8.41	8.95	9.45	9.91	10.3	10.7
	.99	6.54	8.5	9.9	11.1	12.1	13.1	13.9	14.7	15.3	16.0	16.6
10	.95	3.72	4.85	5.67	6.34	6.92	7.42	7.87	8.28	8.66	9.01	9.34
	.99	5.85	7.4	8.6	9.6	10.4	11.1	11.8	12.4	12.9	13.4	13.9
12	.95	3.28	4.16	4.79	5.30	5.72	6.09	6.42	6.72	7.00	7.25	7.48
	.99	4.91	6.1	6.9	7.6	8.2	8.7	9.1	9.5	9.9	10.2	10.6
15	.95	2.86	3.54	4.01	4.37	4.68	4.95	5.19	5.40	5.59	5.77	5.93
	.99	4.07	4.9	5.5	6.0	6.4	6.7	7.1	7.3	7.5	7.8	8.0
20	.95	2.46	2.95	3.29	3.54	3.76	3.94	4.10	4.24	4.37	4.49	4.59
	.99	3.32	3.8	4.3	4.6	4.9	5.1	5.3	5.5	5.6	5.8	5.9
30	.95	2.07	2.40	2.61	2.78	2.91	3.02	3.12	3.21	3.29	3.36	3.39
	.99	2.63	3.0	3.3	3.4	3.6	3.7	3.8	3.9	4.0	4.1	4.2
60	.95	1.67	1.85	1.96	2.04	2.11	2.17	2.22	2.26	2.30	2.33	2.36
	.99	1.96	2.2	2.3	2.4	2.4	2.5	2.5	2.6	2.6	2.7	2.7

*Equal group size (n) is assumed in the table; hence $df = n - 1$. If group sizes are not equal, then use the harmonic mean (rounding off to the nearest integer) as the n.

TABLE G
Critical Values for Bryant-Paulson Procedure

Error df	Number of Covariates (C)	α	Number of Groups 2	3	4	5	6	7	8	10	12	16	20
3	1	.05	5.42	7.18	8.32	9.17	9.84	10.39	10.86	11.62	12.22	13.14	13.83
		.01	10.28	13.32	15.32	16.80	17.98	18.95	19.77	21.12	22.19	23.82	25.05
	2	.05	6.21	8.27	9.60	10.59	11.37	12.01	12.56	13.44	14.15	15.22	16.02
		.01	11.97	15.56	17.91	19.66	21.05	22.19	23.16	24.75	26.01	27.93	29.38
	3	.05	6.92	9.23	10.73	11.84	12.72	13.44	14.06	15.05	15.84	17.05	17.95
		.01	13.45	17.51	20.17	22.15	23.72	25.01	26.11	27.90	29.32	31.50	33.13
4	1	.05	4.51	5.84	6.69	7.32	7.82	8.23	8.58	9.15	9.61	10.30	10.82
		.01	7.68	9.64	10.93	11.89	12.65	13.28	13.82	14.70	15.40	16.48	17.29
	2	.05	5.04	6.54	7.51	8.23	8.80	9.26	9.66	10.31	10.83	11.61	12.21
		.01	8.69	10.95	12.43	13.54	14.41	15.14	15.76	16.77	17.58	18.81	19.74
	3	.05	5.51	7.18	8.25	9.05	9.67	10.19	10.63	11.35	11.92	12.79	13.45
		.01	9.59	12.11	13.77	15.00	15.98	16.79	17.47	18.60	19.50	20.87	21.91
5	1	.05	4.06	5.17	5.88	6.40	6.82	7.16	7.45	7.93	8.30	8.88	9.32
		.01	6.49	7.99	8.97	9.70	10.28	10.76	11.17	11.84	12.38	13.20	13.83
	2	.05	4.45	5.68	6.48	7.06	7.52	7.90	8.23	8.76	9.18	9.83	10.31
		.01	7.20	8.89	9.99	10.81	11.47	12.01	12.47	13.23	13.84	14.77	15.47
	3	.05	4.81	6.16	7.02	7.66	8.17	8.58	8.94	9.52	9.98	10.69	11.22
		.01	7.83	9.70	10.92	11.82	12.54	13.14	13.65	14.48	15.15	16.17	16.95
6	1	.05	3.79	4.78	5.40	5.86	6.23	6.53	6.78	7.20	7.53	8.04	8.43
		.01	5.83	7.08	7.88	8.48	8.96	9.36	9.70	10.25	10.70	11.38	11.90
	2	.05	4.10	5.18	5.87	6.37	6.77	7.10	7.38	7.84	8.21	8.77	9.20
		.01	6.36	7.75	8.64	9.31	9.85	10.29	10.66	11.28	11.77	12.54	13.11
	3	.05	4.38	5.55	6.30	6.84	7.28	7.64	7.94	8.44	8.83	9.44	9.90
		.01	6.85	8.36	9.34	10.07	10.65	11.13	11.54	12.22	12.75	13.59	14.21
7	1	.05	3.62	4.52	5.09	5.51	5.84	6.11	6.34	6.72	7.03	7.49	7.84
		.01	5.41	6.50	7.20	7.72	8.14	8.48	8.77	9.26	9.64	10.24	10.69
	2	.05	3.87	4.85	5.47	5.92	6.28	6.58	6.83	7.24	7.57	8.08	8.46
		.01	5.84	7.03	7.80	8.37	8.83	9.21	9.53	10.06	10.49	11.14	11.64
	3	.05	4.11	5.16	5.82	6.31	6.70	7.01	7.29	7.73	8.08	8.63	9.03
		.01	6.23	7.52	8.36	8.98	9.47	9.88	10.23	10.80	11.26	11.97	12.51
8	1	.05	3.49	4.34	4.87	5.26	5.57	5.82	6.03	6.39	6.67	7.10	7.43
		.01	5.12	6.11	6.74	7.20	7.58	7.88	8.15	8.58	8.92	9.46	9.87
	2	.05	3.70	4.61	5.19	5.61	5.94	6.21	6.44	6.82	7.12	7.59	7.94
		.01	5.48	6.54	7.23	7.74	8.14	8.48	8.76	9.23	9.61	10.19	10.63
	3	.05	3.91	4.88	5.49	5.93	6.29	6.58	6.83	7.23	7.55	8.05	8.42
		.01	5.81	6.95	7.69	8.23	8.67	9.03	9.33	9.84	10.24	10.87	11.34
10	1	.05	3.32	4.10	4.58	4.93	5.21	5.43	5.63	5.94	6.19	6.58	6.87
		.01	4.76	5.61	6.15	6.55	6.86	7.13	7.35	7.72	8.01	8.47	8.82
	2	.05	3.49	4.31	4.82	5.19	5.49	5.73	5.93	6.27	6.54	6.95	7.26
		.01	5.02	5.93	6.51	6.93	7.27	7.55	7.79	8.19	8.50	8.99	9.36
	3	.05	3.65	4.51	5.05	5.44	5.75	6.01	6.22	6.58	6.86	7.29	7.62
		.01	5.27	6.23	6.84	7.30	7.66	7.96	8.21	8.63	8.96	9.48	9.88

(cont.)

Error df	Number of Covariates (C)	α	Number of Groups 2	3	4	5	6	7	8	10	12	16	20
12	1	.05	3.22	3.95	4.40	4.73	4.98	5.19	5.37	5.67	5.90	6.26	6.53
		.01	4.54	5.31	5.79	6.15	6.43	6.67	6.87	7.20	7.46	7.87	8.18
	2	.05	3.35	4.12	4.59	4.93	5.20	5.43	5.62	5.92	6.17	6.55	6.83
		.01	4.74	5.56	6.07	6.45	6.75	7.00	7.21	7.56	7.84	8.27	8.60
	3	.05	3.48	4.28	4.78	5.14	5.42	5.65	5.85	6.17	6.43	6.82	7.12
		.01	4.94	5.80	6.34	6.74	7.05	7.31	7.54	7.90	8.20	8.65	9.00
14	1	.05	3.15	3.85	4.28	4.59	4.83	5.03	5.20	5.48	5.70	6.03	6.29
		.01	4.39	5.11	5.56	5.89	6.15	6.36	6.55	6.85	7.09	7.47	7.75
	2	.05	3.26	3.99	4.44	4.76	5.01	5.22	5.40	5.69	5.92	6.27	6.54
		.01	4.56	5.31	5.78	6.13	6.40	6.63	6.82	7.14	7.40	7.79	8.09
	3	.05	3.37	4.13	4.59	4.93	5.19	5.41	5.59	5.89	6.13	6.50	6.78
		.01	4.72	5.51	6.00	6.36	6.65	6.89	7.09	7.42	7.69	8.10	8.41
16	1	.05	3.10	3.77	4.19	4.49	4.72	4.91	5.07	5.34	5.55	5.87	6.12
		.01	4.28	4.96	5.39	5.70	5.95	6.15	6.32	6.60	6.83	7.18	7.45
	2	.05	3.19	3.90	4.32	4.63	4.88	5.07	5.24	5.52	5.74	6.07	6.33
		.01	4.42	5.14	5.58	5.90	6.16	6.37	6.55	6.85	7.08	7.45	7.73
	3	.05	3.29	4.01	4.46	4.78	5.03	5.23	5.41	5.69	5.92	6.27	6.53
		.01	4.56	5.30	5.76	6.10	6.37	6.59	6.77	7.08	7.33	7.71	8.00
18	1	.05	3.06	3.72	4.12	4.41	4.63	4.82	4.98	5.23	5.44	5.75	5.98
		.01	4.20	4.86	5.26	5.56	5.79	5.99	6.15	6.42	6.63	6.96	7.22
	2	.05	3.14	3.82	4.24	4.54	4.77	4.96	5.13	5.39	5.60	5.92	6.17
		.01	4.32	5.00	5.43	5.73	5.98	6.18	6.35	6.63	6.85	7.19	7.46
	3	.05	3.23	3.93	4.35	4.66	4.90	5.10	5.27	5.54	5.76	6.09	6.34
		.01	4.44	5.15	5.59	5.90	6.16	6.36	6.54	6.83	7.06	7.42	7.69
20	1	.05	3.03	3.67	4.07	4.35	4.57	4.75	4.90	5.15	5.35	5.65	5.88
		.01	4.14	4.77	5.17	5.45	5.68	5.86	6.02	6.27	6.48	6.80	7.04
	2	.05	3.10	3.77	4.17	4.46	4.69	4.88	5.03	5.29	5.49	5.81	6.04
		.01	4.25	4.90	5.31	5.60	5.84	6.03	6.19	6.46	6.67	7.00	7.25
	3	.05	3.18	3.86	4.28	4.57	4.81	5.00	5.16	5.42	5.63	5.96	6.20
		.01	4.35	5.03	5.45	5.75	5.99	6.19	6.36	6.63	6.85	7.19	7.45
24	1	.05	2.98	3.61	3.99	4.26	4.47	4.65	4.79	5.03	5.22	5.51	5.73
		.01	4.05	4.65	5.02	5.29	5.50	5.68	5.83	6.07	6.26	6.56	6.78
	2	.05	3.04	3.69	4.08	4.35	4.57	4.75	4.90	5.14	5.34	5.63	5.86
		.01	4.14	4.76	5.14	5.42	5.63	5.81	5.96	6.21	6.41	6.71	6.95
	3	.05	3.11	3.76	4.16	4.44	4.67	4.85	5.00	5.25	5.45	5.75	5.98
		.01	4.22	4.86	5.25	5.54	5.76	5.94	6.10	6.35	6.55	6.87	7.11
30	1	.05	2.94	3.55	3.91	4.18	4.38	4.54	4.69	4.91	5.09	5.37	5.58
		.01	3.96	4.54	4.89	5.14	5.34	5.50	5.64	5.87	6.05	6.32	6.53
	2	.05	2.99	3.61	3.98	4.25	4.46	4.62	4.77	5.00	5.18	5.46	5.68
		.01	4.03	4.62	4.98	5.24	5.44	5.61	5.75	5.98	6.16	6.44	6.66
	3	.05	3.04	3.67	4.05	4.32	4.53	4.70	4.85	5.08	5.27	5.56	5.78
		.01	4.10	4.70	5.06	5.33	5.54	5.71	5.85	6.08	6.27	6.56	6.78

(cont.)

TABLE G (Continued)

Error df	Number of Covariates (C)	α	\multicolumn{11}{c}{Number of Groups}
			2	3	4	5	6	7	8	10	12	16	20
40	1	.05	2.89	3.49	3.84	4.09	4.29	4.45	4.58	4.80	4.97	5.23	5.43
		.01	3.88	4.43	4.76	5.00	5.19	5.34	5.47	5.68	5.85	6.10	6.30
	2	.05	2.93	3.53	3.89	4.15	4.34	4.50	4.64	4.86	5.04	5.30	5.50
		.01	3.93	4.48	4.82	5.07	5.26	5.41	5.54	5.76	5.93	6.19	6.38
	3	.05	2.97	3.57	3.94	4.20	4.40	4.56	4.70	4.92	5.10	5.37	5.57
		.01	3.98	4.54	4.88	5.13	5.32	5.48	5.61	5.83	6.00	6.27	6.47
60	1	.05	2.85	3.43	3.77	4.01	4.20	4.35	4.48	4.69	4.85	5.10	5.29
		.01	3.79	4.32	4.64	4.86	5.04	5.18	5.30	5.50	5.65	5.89	6.07
	2	.05	2.88	3.46	3.80	4.05	4.24	4.39	4.52	4.73	4.89	5.14	5.33
		.01	3.83	4.36	4.68	4.90	5.08	5.22	5.35	5.54	5.70	5.94	6.12
	3	.05	2.90	3.49	3.83	4.08	4.27	4.43	4.56	4.77	4.93	5.19	5.38
		.01	3.86	4.39	4.72	4.95	5.12	5.27	5.39	5.59	5.75	6.00	6.18
120	1	.05	2.81	3.37	3.70	3.93	4.11	4.26	4.38	4.58	4.73	4.97	5.15
		.01	3.72	4.22	4.52	4.73	4.89	5.03	5.14	5.32	5.47	5.69	5.85
	2	.05	2.82	3.38	3.72	3.95	4.13	4.28	4.40	4.60	4.75	4.99	5.17
		.01	3.73	4.24	4.54	4.75	4.91	5.05	5.16	5.35	5.49	5.71	5.88
	3	.05	2.84	3.40	3.73	3.97	4.15	4.30	4.42	4.62	4.77	5.01	5.19
		.01	3.75	4.25	4.55	4.77	4.94	5.07	5.18	5.37	5.51	5.74	5.90

APPENDIX B:
Data Sets

DESCRIPTION OF NATIONAL ACADEMY OF SCIENCES DATA

The following data is from a 1982 National Academy of Sciences published report rating the "scholary quality" of research programs in the humanities, physical sciences and social sciences. The ratings were based on the rankings of quality and reputation made by senior faculty in the field who taught at institutions other than the one being rated.

The data to be presented are the quality ratings of 46 research doctorate programs in psychology, as well as six potential correlates of the quality ratings. Here is a description of the variables: QUALITY Mean rating of scholarly quality of program faculty NFACULTY Number of falculty members in program as of December 1980 NGRADS Number of program graduates from 1975 through 1980 PCTSUPP Percentage of program graduates from 1975-1979 that received fellowships or training grant support during their graduate education PCTGRANT Percent of faculty members holding research grants from the Alcohol, Drug Abuse and Mental Health Administration, the National Institute of Health or the National Science Foundation at any time during 1978-1980 NARTICLE Number of published articles attributed to program faculty members 1978-1980 PCTPUB Percent of faculty with one or more published articles from 1978-1980

OBS	NAME	QUALITY	NFACULTY	NGRADS	PCTSUPP	PCTGRANT	NARTICLE	PCTPUB
1	ADELPHI	12	13	19	16	8	14	39
2	ARIZONA – TUSCON	23	29	72	67	3	61	66
3	BOSTON UNIV	29	38	111	66	13	68	68
4	BROWN	36	16	28	52	63	49	75
5	U C BERKELEY	44	40	104	64	53	130	83
6	U C RIVERSIDE	21	14	28	59	29	65	79
7	CARNEGIE MELLON	40	44	16	81	35	79	82
8	UNIV OF CHICAGO	42	60	57	65	40	187	82
9	CLARK UNIV	24	16	18	87	19	32	75
10	COLUMBIA TEACHERS	30	37	41	43	8	50	54
11	DELAWARE, UNIV OF	20	20	45	26	25	49	50
12	DETROIT, UNIV OF	8	11	27	7	0	9	27
13	FLORIDA ST – TALAH	28	29	112	64	35	65	69
14	FULLER THEOL SEMIN	14	14	57	10	0	11	43
15	UNIV OF GEORGIA	27	38	167	28	13	196	84
16	HARVARD	46	27	113	62	52	173	85
17	HOUSTON, UNIV OF	29	32	122	51	119	79	69
18	UNIV ILLINOIS-CHAMP	42	56	116	56	32	208	73
19	IOWA, UNIV OF	33	32	54	49	10	120	69
20	KANSAS, UNIV OF	31	42	79	41	14	114	71
21	KENT STATE UNIV	23	30	76	22	20	87	67
22	LOUISIANA STATE	18	18	62	39	6	10	39
23	UNIV OF MARYLAND	29	41	98	41	12	101	66
24	MIAMI UNIV	21	23	52	33	4	59	78
25	U MICH – ANN ARB	45	111	222	64	32	274	70
26	U MISSOURI	25	26	63	39	23	160	89
27	U NEW HAMPSHIRE	18	16	24	4	31	39	63
28	NEW YORK UNIV	33	38	154	55	34	84	63
29	U NC – GREENSBORO	21	19	40	7	5	60	84
30	NORTHEASTERN	24	16	18	25	63	31	63
31	NOTRE DAME	15	13	29	23	15	62	85
32	OKLA ST – STILLWATER	15	23	41	51	4	24	57
33	PENN STATE	36	32	69	65	16	122	75
34	PRINCETON	38	21	38	28	48	92	91
35	UNIV OF ROCHESTER	32	28	90	70	36	117	61
36	SUNY ALBANY	27	22	52	10	27	114	86
37	ST LOUIS UNIVERSITY	16	20	80	46	10	19	40
38	UNIV SOUTH FLORIDA	26	32	41	13	6	64	56
39	STANFORD	48	26	81	70	58	155	100
40	TEMPLE	26	40	81	42	10	70	68
41	TEXAS TECH LUBBOCK	14	19	87	15	5	72	79
42	UNIV OF TOLEDO	12	17	26	9	6	15	59
43	UNIV OF UTAH, SALT L	29	29	71	74	17	85	76
44	VIRGINIA POLYTECH	34	27	20	0	29	79	57
45	WASHINGTON UNIV-ST. L	28	26	70	68	27	84	73
46	UNIV WISC – MADISON	39	36	59	57	67	172	83

Jones, L. V., Lindzey, G., & Coggeshall, P. (Eds.) (1982). *An Assessment of Research-Doctorate Programs in the United States: Social and Behavioral Sciences,* (Washington, DC: National Academy Press).

DESCRIPTION OF SESAME STREET DATA BASE

This data is part of a large data set that evaluated the impact of the first year of the Sesame Street television series. Sesame Street was concerned mainly with teaching preschool related skills to children in the 3–5 year age range, with special emphasis on reaching 4 year old disadvantaged children. The format of the show was designed to hold young children's attention through action oriented, short duration presentations teaching specific preschool cognitive skills and some social skills. Each show was one hour and involved much repetition of concepts within and across shows.

A main concern for the evaluation, which was carried out at Educational Testing Service, was that it would permit generalization to the populations of children of most interest to the producers of the program (the Children's Television Workshop). Five populations were of interest:

1. Three to five year old disadvantaged children from inner city areas in various parts of the country.
2. Four year old advantaged suburban children.
3. Advantaged rural children.
4. Disadvantaged rural children.
5. Disadvantaged Spanish speaking children.

Children representative of these populations were sampled from five different sites in the United States.

Both before and after viewing the series the children were tested on a variety of cognitive variables (variables 8 through 19 in the data set), including knowledge of body parts, knowledge about letters, knowledge about numbers, etc.

The variables are arranged on the file as follows:

Variable No.	Variable Name	Description
1	ID	Subject identification number
2	SITE	Five different sampling sites coded as 1,2,3,4 or 5.
3	SEX	Male - 1, Female - 2
4	AGE	in months
5	VIEWCAT	Viewing categories coded as a 1 if children rarely watched the show to a 4 if the children watched the show on average of more than 5 times a week

(Continued)

Variable No.	Variable Name	Description
6	SETTING	Setting in which Sesame Street was viewed, coded as 1 for home and coded as 2 for school
7	VIEWENC	A treatment condition in which some children were encouraged to view Sesame St (code - 1) and others were not (code - 2)
8	PREBODY	pretest on knowledge about body parts (maximum score - 32)—naming and functions of body parts
9	PRELET	pretest on knowledge about letters (maximum score - 58)—including recognizing letters, naming capital letters, matching letters in words
10	PREFORM	pretest on knowledge about forms (maximum score - 20)—recognizing and naming forms
11	PRENUMB	pretest on knowledge about numbers (maximum score - 54)—recognizing and naming numbers, counting, addition and subtraction
12	PRERELAT	pretest on knowledge of relational terms (maximum score - 17)—amount, size and position relationship
13	PRECLASF	pretest on knowledge of classification skills (maximum score - 24)—classifying by size, form, number and function
14	POSTBODY	posttest knowledge on body parts
15	POSTLET	posttest knowledge of letters
16	POSTFORM	posttest knowledge of forms
17	POSTNUMB	posttest knowledge of numbers
18	POSTREL	posttest knowledge of relations
19	POSTCLAS	posttest knowledge of classification skills
20	PEABODY	Mental age scores obtained from administration of the Peabody Picture Vocabulary Test as a pretest measure of vocabulary maturity

SESAME STREET DATA

ID	SITE	SEX	AGE	VIEWCAT	SETTING	VIEWENC	PREBODY	PRELET	PREFORM	PRENUMB	PRERELAT	PRECLASF	POSTBODY	POSTLET	POSTFORM	POSTNUMB	POSTREL	POSTCLAS	PEABODY
1	1	1	66	1	2	1	16	23	12	40	14	20	18	30	14	44	14	23	62
2	1	2	67	3	2	1	30	26	9	39	16	22	30	37	17	39	14	22	80
3	1	1	56	3	2	2	22	14	9	9	9	8	21	46	15	40	9	19	32
4	1	1	49	1	2	2	23	11	10	14	9	13	21	14	13	19	8	15	27
5	1	1	69	4	2	2	32	47	15	51	17	22	32	53	18	54	14	21	71
6	1	2	54	3	2	2	29	26	10	33	14	14	27	36	14	39	16	24	32
7	1	2	47	3	2	2	23	12	11	13	11	12	22	45	12	44	12	15	28
8	1	1	51	2	2	1	32	48	19	52	15	23	31	47	18	51	17	23	38
9	1	1	69	4	2	1	27	44	18	42	15	20	32	50	17	48	14	24	49
10	1	2	53	3	2	1	30	38	17	31	10	17	32	52	19	52	17	24	32
11	1	2	58	2	2	2	25	48	14	38	16	18	26	52	15	42	10	17	43
12	1	2	58	4	2	2	21	25	13	29	16	21	17	29	15	40	10	19	58
13	1	2	49	1	2	2	28	8	9	13	8	12	20	16	9	18	10	13	39
14	1	1	64	2	2	1	26	11	15	21	10	15	26	28	15	35	16	14	43
15	1	2	58	2	2	1	23	15	9	16	9	11	28	21	10	22	10	17	56
16	1	1	49	3	2	1	25	12	17	24	12	18	28	45	14	45	13	21	37
17	1	1	57	2	2	1	25	15	13	16	10	18	25	24	16	28	8	18	43
18	1	1	45	4	2	1	16	12	8	11	6	3	25	16	11	17	9	9	29
19	1	1	45	3	2	1	25	16	12	23	10	13	32	46	18	35	14	19	45
20	1	1	60	3	2	2	19	19	8	23	14	10	28	50	12	38	12	13	51
21	1	2	65	4	2	1	29	24	14	41	10	23	29	48	20	51	15	24	55
22	1	1	44	4	1	1	25	15	17	22	11	16	32	42	19	45	15	19	49
23	1	2	38	3	1	1	20	9	2	7	8	9	22	23	17	19	15	14	31
24	1	1	35	4	1	1	11	6	8	16	8	9	22	27	16	20	14	15	40
25	1	2	42	2	1	1	15	7	8	11	12	7	14	13	7	21	12	10	48
26	1	2	50	2	1	1	26	14	10	36	13	17	25	18	14	42	13	18	35
27	1	1	61	4	2	2	28	42	16	40	16	11	24	27	15	20	14	14	62
28	1	2	34	4	1	1	17	13	7	10	5	11	21	17	13	13	10	15	42
29	1	1	60	3	1	2	23	13	9	23	11	14	28	20	18	45	14	21	58
30	1	2	39	2	1	1	11	5	5	5	5	1	27	15	13	9	8	12	29
31	1	1	39	3	1	1	24	4	11	25	11	17	21	11	12	13	9	10	49
32	1	2	41	2	1	1	24	8	3	14	8	8	21	17	10	18	9	14	30
33	1	2	55	3	1	1	31	15	17	45	16	24	32	43	18	46	13	21	62
34	1	2	42	3	1	1	23	11	7	15	6	7	29	27	14	33	9	19	58
35	1	1	50	4	1	1	18	17	12	28	12	17	29	41	15	48	12	22	55
36	1	1	58	2	1	1	13	12	6	10	6	11	29	23	11	27	8	10	33
37	1	2	59	3	1	2	27	7	13	23	12	10	32	39	18	49	16	19	55
38	1	2	36	1	1	2	11	12	9	5	5	3	12	12	6	13	9	6	27
39	1	1	51	2	1	1	32	16	16	34	15	17	21	17	6	21	8	12	62
40	1	1	51	2	1	1	31	18	13	33	15	14	21	16	11	7	9	11	58
41	1	1	48	3	1	1	13	14	8	8	10	11	21	22	10	28	8	19	34
42	1	1	43	2	1	1	17	13	14	13	11	14	24	19	12	22	11	20	32
43	1	2	35	3	1	2	23	12	8	9	5	5	29	11	8	9	11	11	32
44	1	2	36	1	1	2	11	2	6	5	2	4	21	6	11	6	6	7	28

(Continued)

SESAME STREET DATA *(Continued)*

ID	SITE	SEX	AGE	VIEWCAT	SETTING	VIEWENC	PREBODY	PRELET	PREFORM	PRENUMB	PRERELAT	PRECLASF	POSTBODY	POSTLET	POSTFORM	POSTNUMB	POSTREL	POSTCLAS	PEABODY
45	1	2	39	2	1	2	20	18	6	4	4	6	19	8	11	22	10	10	29
46	1	1	45	4	1	2	14	13	9	16	9	12	29	48	17	48	14	19	35
47	1	1	58	3	1	2	30	38	15	45	14	18	32	48	19	46	14	23	67
48	1	2	38	3	1	1	13	10	7	8	5	7	26	36	14	20	10	16	29
49	1	2	57	4	1	1	26	15	11	22	10	15	24	20	18	28	12	18	35
50	1	1	49	3	1	2	26	35	10	47	13	17	26	13	7	12	11	14	67
51	1	1	55	1	2	2	24	11	10	18	8	10	20	10	14	23	10	10	39
52	1	2	44	4	2	2	25	39	18	41	9	21	30	47	20	50	11	23	90
53	1	1	56	1	2	2	13	11	6	15	10	11	15	13	9	13	10	6	46
54	1	2	48	2	2	2	17	11	9	14	8	9	26	32	15	27	11	11	39
55	1	1	50	2	2	2	16	10	8	9	7	6	21	15	17	17	12	15	34
56	1	1	52	1	2	2	16	15	6	13	11	13	19	14	14	18	7	16	38
57	1	2	51	2	2	1	24	14	10	20	10	17	28	21	17	36	19	17	34
58	1	2	58	1	2	2	25	17	17	23	14	15	25	16	19	28	4	20	37
59	1	2	48	3	2	2	13	10	10	13	9	7	27	15	14	23	11	12	33
60	1	1	54	4	2	2	16	13	10	10	9	7	19	20	14	19	12	11	36
61	2	1	52	4	2	2	20	35	15	21	8	20	27	48	19	47	15	22	49
62	2	2	48	1	2	2	20	12	11	13	7	11	28	19	17	17	11	17	53
63	2	1	55	4	2	2	28	13	10	29	11	12	30	31	19	45	15	22	65
64	2	1	55	2	2	2	23	16	5	32	10	13	28	28	15	46	13	17	55
65	2	2	55	2	1	2	30	27	11	39	12	17	32	40	19	52	17	23	85
66	2	2	56	1	1	1	26	18	10	30	12	9	29	46	13	44	13	17	43
67	2	2	50	3	2	1	31	15	10	24	11	20	31	43	18	52	14	23	65
68	2	1	51	3	2	1	28	19	14	37	13	15	32	47	19	48	15	22	75
69	2	1	58	3	2	2	30	14	17	37	13	20	28	38	15	36	16	18	85
70	2	2	55	4	2	2	27	10	10	12	14	16	31	42	16	31	13	20	40
71	2	2	41	4	1	2	24	22	14	42	14	21	30	49	19	50	14	22	58
72	2	2	51	4	1	2	20	13	11	22	11	15	27	17	11	20	14	14	42
73	2	1	52	4	2	1	29	13	9	18	10	10	30	23	17	28	12	17	69
74	2	2	54	3	2	1	30	26	13	23	10	17	32	42	12	37	12	19	58
75	2	1	47	4	1	1	19	12	11	16	11	12	28	43	18	38	14	17	37
76	2	1	50	4	1	1	31	30	15	47	15	19	23	48	19	49	13	20	62
77	2	2	55	4	1	1	31	13	18	39	15	24	31	51	19	50	14	23	99
78	2	1	50	3	2	1	32	27	13	29	13	12	31	45	19	53	16	23	75
79	2	2	57	2	2	1	31	19	14	36	13	11	32	50	17	47	15	22	82
80	2	2	55	4	2	2	20	12	9	16	11	18	30	30	14	18	12	16	47
81	2	2	55	4	2	2	26	14	8	24	13	12	30	45	19	43	15	24	62
82	2	1	50	3	2	1	30	44	15	45	12	11	32	53	19	52	15	23	67
83	2	1	52	3	2	1	26	13	11	34	12	12	30	45	17	43	13	21	40
84	2	2	45	2	2	1	28	12	9	16	7	8	28	21	14	32	9	17	41
85	2	2	52	3	2	1	24	14	8	18	8	7	28	43	12	41	13	15	56
86	2	1	53	4	1	1	26	17	15	32	13	16	27	37	15	31	14	23	73
87	2	2	53	4	2	2	29	10	17	23	13	15	32	51	19	48	16	21	85
88	2	2	53	2	2	2	23	12	12	15	11	17	28	20	15	19	8	19	59

(Continued)

SESAME STREET DATA (*Continued*)

ID	SITE	SEX	AGE	VIEWCAT	SETTING	VIEWENC	PREBODY	PRELET	PREFORM	PRENUMB	PRERELAT	PRECLASF	POSTBODY	POSTLET	POSTFORM	POSTNUMB	POSTREL	POSTCLAS	PEABODY
89	2	2	56	3	1	2	28	29	11	43	13	22	31	32	15	40	15	21	58
90	2	2	54	4	2	2	32	46	15	48	13	21	32	51	19	50	16	23	92
91	2	1	50	2	2	1	22	17	8	18	12	14	25	16	14	32	14	17	69
92	2	1	50	3	1	1	29	25	14	35	15	20	26	36	16	31	8	15	56
93	2	2	53	4	1	1	25	17	12	30	13	17	29	40	17	40	13	22	78
94	2	1	45	4	1	1	21	16	12	15	11	17	29	36	19	29	10	16	58
95	2	2	56	4	1	1	32	22	15	32	11	13	31	46	20	51	14	24	78
96	2	1	53	3	1	1	31	14	16	29	11	17	32	43	19	42	13	22	67
97	2	2	46	4	1	1	22	28	14	20	5	15	32	42	13	29	15	18	69
98	2	2	46	2	1	2	30	18	14	23	11	11	29	33	13	36	8	16	53
99	2	1	50	3	1	2	18	13	8	14	11	12	19	23	11	31	12	17	55
100	2	2	47	1	1	2	17	10	5	11	8	7	18	19	9	8	10	13	53
101	2	1	56	2	2	1	27	11	15	22	13	14	30	47	20	45	15	24	67
102	2	2	46	3	1	1	27	13	13	22	12	13	28	36	17	46	11	20	62
103	2	2	45	4	1	1	21	23	14	27	13	20	31	48	19	44	11	24	59
104	2	2	46	4	1	1	19	17	4	19	10	13	28	36	16	29	10	15	46
105	2	2	47	3	1	1	31	9	14	24	11	16	32	42	17	42	11	20	58
106	2	1	52	2	2	1	26	16	12	30	14	16	27	29	20	41	15	21	92
107	2	2	52	4	2	1	24	15	12	30	14	14	31	45	18	49	13	23	48
108	2	1	56	2	1	1	21	22	12	25	12	15	29	37	14	46	14	18	65
109	2	1	48	4	1	1	28	22	13	19	11	8	32	48	18	43	15	19	67
110	2	1	49	3	1	1	25	16	13	18	15	15	27	48	13	45	15	18	59
111	2	2	55	4	2	1	32	8	13	23	11	17	29	35	18	36	11	19	39
112	2	2	45	3	1	1	22	15	12	20	9	14	25	21	15	21	9	16	47
113	2	1	45	3	1	1	32	16	14	30	11	17	25	26	17	39	13	19	51
114	2	2	48	4	1	1	31	6	8	13	7	13	29	32	15	23	7	16	43
115	2	1	58	1	1	2	19	14	12	23	11	10	28	15	10	34	11	7	65
116	3	1	55	2	1	1	20	16	7	14	9	9	21	11	13	20	13	13	39
117	3	2	48	1	1	2	20	15	5	13	8	7	21	14	3	17	10	7	33
118	3	2	52	3	1	1	14	6	3	9	4	8	18	19	20	18	12	20	34
119	3	2	58	1	1	1	20	11	5	25	9	7	26	16	10	23	12	12	35
120	3	1	50	3	2	2	13	12	5	11	10	9	21	18	10	19	10	9	32
121	3	1	58	3	2	2	22	19	11	35	10	17	23	44	18	46	13	19	44
122	3	2	49	4	2	2	14	13	7	5	5	7	17	16	12	19	12	15	31
123	3	1	56	4	2	2	24	17	9	16	11	10	29	35	17	40	14	19	44
124	3	1	50	1	1	2	7	14	4	10	5	5	19	15	13	14	13	17	27
125	3	2	49	1	1	1	20	18	3	14	6	6	11	12	6	8	9	5	29
126	3	1	46	2	1	1	15	14	8	23	14	12	25	18	14	30	12	16	47
127	3	1	57	2	1	1	26	14	9	23	15	9	28	15	14	24	12	9	35
128	3	1	44	1	2	2	12	9	7	14	9	14	13	13	7	17	9	7	32
129	3	2	41	2	2	2	16	14	9	10	11	9	22	17	9	23	8	13	36
130	3	2	58	4	2	1	17	9	11	28	8	13	29	13	12	29	12	15	38
131	3	2	60	4	2	1	31	19	11	27	11	16	31	31	17	38	13	22	42

(*Continued*)

SESAME STREET DATA   *(Continued)*

ID	SITE	SEX	AGE	VIEWCAT	SETTING	VIEWENC	PREBODY	PRELET	PREFORM	PRENUMB	PRERELAT	PRECLASF	POSTBODY	POSTLET	POSTFORM	POSTNUMB	POSTREL	POSTCLAS	PEABODY
132	3	2	40	2	1	1	12	14	3	17	6	6	16	13	6	17	10	9	27
133	3	2	37	2	1	1	7	4	6	4	5	4	13	13	6	14	9	11	60
134	3	1	45	1	1	1	12	5	5	9	7	7	15	13	12	20	12	11	28
135	3	1	60	3	1	1	17	18	9	14	7	6	32	36	13	32	13	12	33
136	3	1	52	2	1	2	18	13	9	24	10	16	25	15	12	26	11	10	55
137	3	2	46	4	1	1	20	12	4	17	8	8	28	22	17	38	14	20	29
138	3	2	60	4	1	1	23	16	9	25	11	14	29	26	17	38	16	22	46
139	3	1	60	3	1	1	17	11	10	15	10	14	11	13	7	16	9	13	33
140	3	1	59	3	1	1	7	16	11	10	6	10	15	14	9	14	8	10	32
141	3	2	52	3	1	1	29	20	8	37	13	13	28	46	12	42	13	15	47
142	3	1	60	3	1	1	29	13	12	17	12	16	29	25	17	32	13	19	90
143	3	2	56	2	1	1	21	12	12	17	9	14	23	26	16	34	10	20	61
144	3	2	54	2	2	2	18	28	9	14	12	16	27	42	18	37	11	15	36
145	3	2	61	3	1	1	13	12	8	16	7	11	28	15	15	18	7	15	35
146	3	2	61	3	1	1	29	18	12	22	11	14	30	25	17	39	13	19	48
147	3	2	51	3	1	1	17	15	5	11	10	11	32	43	14	44	15	21	35
148	3	1	49	4	2	1	19	17	7	16	3	6	27	27	18	43	15	20	35
149	3	1	52	2	1	1	22	13	10	20	11	14	22	14	9	21	9	7	35
150	3	2	55	3	2	1	25	13	12	16	10	14	26	17	6	31	13	9	35
151	3	2	60	4	2	1	28	10	10	22	12	15	28	15	15	30	11	17	45
152	3	2	43	1	2	2	14	9	5	15	5	6	16	16	12	14	10	14	33
153	3	1	55	3	2	1	14	7	9	15	9	12	18	15	16	22	11	16	42
154	3	2	52	4	2	1	18	11	9	15	8	12	23	23	15	40	13	18	32
155	3	2	56	1	2	1	26	24	13	25	9	10	17	7	3	13	6	5	40
156	3	1	56	4	1	1	24	11	11	28	14	17	27	14	15	40	12	21	42
157	3	2	47	2	1	1	20	19	9	25	12	8	26	24	13	35	11	17	46
158	3	2	56	2	1	1	17	18	8	17	5	9	24	17	10	19	10	15	39
159	3	2	52	3	1	1	28	15	13	27	9	15	31	16	16	22	12	18	69
160	3	2	51	4	1	1	23	14	11	23	8	11	31	37	17	42	14	18	36
161	3	1	51	1	1	1	7	13	6	11	7	6	12	8	14	22	10	16	35
162	3	2	53	3	1	1	15	15	8	18	8	11	29	32	12	28	10	14	34
163	3	1	50	4	1	1	26	11	14	23	10	11	39	22	16	40	14	17	32
164	3	2	59	4	1	1	16	10	8	21	9	12	25	22	14	31	10	18	38
165	3	1	53	3	1	1	14	12	7	9	9	5	22	28	9	30	9	10	32
166	3	1	55	3	1	1	15	10	7	9	6	11	24	20	14	27	9	9	34
167	3	1	57	1	1	1	6	13	2	8	7	7	18	6	4	0	1	4	35
168	3	1	58	2	1	1	16	5	5	8	6	9	13	14	11	11	9	16	34
169	3	1	44	3	1	1	10	12	4	9	10	11	13	15	3	8	3	5	28
170	3	1	39	1	1	2	14	12	4	5	7	5	13	11	8	19	10	8	29
171	3	1	53	4	2	1	21	17	12	16	10	13	27	20	14	29	15	16	37
172	3	2	52	4	1	1	23	10	9	9	7	6	21	16	11	20	9	9	32
173	3	1	57	3	1	2	25	11	10	19	11	13	28	29	20	25	16	19	35
174	3	2	40	3	1	1	11	10	7	14	4	8	16	22	11	21	9	9	35

(Continued)

SESAME STREET DATA (*Continued*)

ID	SITE	SEX	AGE	VIEWCAT	SETTING	VIEWENC	PREBODY	PRELET	PREFORM	PRENUMB	PRERELAT	PRECLASF	POSTBODY	POSTLET	POSTFORM	POSTNUMB	POSTREL	POSTCLAS	PEABODY
175	3	2	47	2	1	1	16	13	7	7	6	9	22	13	4	18	11	9	32
176	3	1	51	2	1	1	25	19	11	24	12	8	26	20	15	24	11	13	47
177	3	1	48	2	1	1	11	7	4	14	3	13	11	12	8	27	11	10	35
178	3	2	49	1	1	2	15	16	6	9	4	7	20	16	7	17	10	5	35
179	3	1	50	2	1	1	12	8	5	17	8	10	18	19	12	13	12	17	30
180	4	2	53	1	2	2	10	13	4	13	7	8	19	16	9	16	7	11	35
181	4	2	52	1	2	2	13	15	8	19	8	9	21	11	8	16	7	11	39
182	4	1	51	1	2	2	19	12	9	17	8	12	27	16	12	27	11	16	39
183	4	1	52	1	2	2	20	16	12	22	11	17	25	19	14	26	11	15	36
184	4	1	46	1	2	2	13	3	3	1	4	4	24	11	10	13	11	13	27
185	4	2	51	1	2	2	21	19	12	25	13	14	24	15	11	25	8	14	45
186	4	2	47	1	2	2	19	12	13	27	8	11	24	14	15	21	7	13	28
187	4	2	51	3	2	1	25	13	12	21	12	16	31	16	15	25	11	18	40
188	4	2	54	1	2	1	8	20	5	8	7	6	14	13	11	11	8	10	47
189	4	2	54	2	2	1	12	4	9	4	7	6	17	13	10	12	9	8	36
190	4	1	57	2	2	1	24	11	10	28	12	11	30	24	18	26	14	16	39
191	4	1	53	2	2	1	17	12	8	9	5	11	26	13	11	20	10	15	39
192	4	2	50	2	2	1	20	16	8	18	9	13	28	25	15	15	9	12	43
193	4	2	57	1	2	2	28	23	16	33	14	11	26	25	16	42	14	11	69
194	4	2	58	1	2	2	31	30	12	44	14	17	32	43	16	44	11	13	69
195	4	2	58	1	2	2	28	29	9	33	14	8	29	44	9	44	15	10	38
196	4	2	53	1	2	2	19	19	14	24	11	16	21	13	9	31	10	16	39
197	4	2	49	1	2	2	20	17	7	13	9	10	30	15	6	21	10	9	30
198	4	2	51	1	2	2	10	1	2	2	4	0	13	0	0	0	0	0	34
199	4	1	58	1	2	2	22	13	9	13	10	9	18	18	11	13	11	8	36
200	4	2	51	1	2	2	18	12	4	10	5	9	17	10	8	14	5	10	48
201	4	2	53	1	2	2	21	17	9	18	9	11	28	15	9	19	12	9	49
202	4	2	56	3	2	1	29	17	17	32	10	20	30	33	17	38	12	20	49
203	4	2	51	3	1	1	19	11	10	19	8	7	22	19	11	39	11	21	37
204	4	1	47	1	1	1	23	12	11	14	11	13	29	15	13	22	14	16	45
205	4	2	54	4	1	1	23	14	12	23	8	15	28	41	16	35	16	22	46
206	4	1	54	4	1	1	17	15	6	15	4	11	24	30	13	42	17	20	32
207	4	2	46	1	1	1	22	14	7	15	3	14	29	24	18	36	13	23	30
208	4	2	52	2	1	1	20	15	14	19	5	13	27	45	16	38	17	22	35
209	4	2	48	1	1	1	24	18	5	21	9	11	23	17	10	16	15	9	36
210	4	1	49	2	1	2	17	21	7	23	9	4	13	14	13	35	15	13	45
211	4	1	58	1	1	2	14	7	3	17	13	6	22	15	11	23	13	9	59
212	4	1	46	3	1	2	18	13	10	11	7	9	22	14	13	23	10	13	42
213	4	1	57	1	1	2	27	19	11	20	10	15	27	19	8	29	23	11	41
214	4	1	48	4	1	2	27	12	15	23	11	16	27	17	13	27	13	10	39
215	4	2	52	2	1	2	23	8	9	16	12	8	20	16	13	23	10	12	94
216	4	1	57	2	1	1	29	17	12	24	12	16	31	32	12	17	9	10	55
217	4	1	46	3	1	1	18	9	10	12	9	14	24	18	11	13	8	10	28

(*Continued*)

SESAME STREET DATA   (*Continued*)

ID	SITE	SEX	AGE	VIEWCAT	SETTING	VIEWENC	PREBODY	PRELET	PREFORM	PRENUMB	PRERELAT	PRECLASF	POSTBODY	POSTLET	POSTFORM	POSTNUMB	POSTREL	POSTCLAS	PEABODY
218	4	1	55	2	1	1	14	12	8	14	11	11	27	40	18	35	16	21	32
219	4	1	44	3	1	1	8	11	6	10	6	9	31	23	15	18	10	13	28
220	4	1	56	1	2	2	26	15	12	29	11	12	25	23	13	40	12	16	59
221	4	2	44	2	1	1	14	14	12	10	10	12	25	23	16	26	13	12	27
222	4	1	59	4	1	1	28	17	12	27	10	11	31	46	19	29	16	20	61
223	5	1	48	2	1	1	16	8	8	9	8	8	24	11	9	11	8	7	35
224	5	1	56	2	1	1	22	17	11	23	14	13	30	20	17	38	13	21	58
225	5	2	58	2	1	1	20	18	8	26	11	10	30	44	12	40	13	21	59
226	5	2	53	1	1	1	15	11	2	8	10	5	18	19	10	14	6	8	34
227	5	2	53	1	1	1	26	16	8	14	10	9	28	13	12	18	10	11	41
228	5	2	65	1	1	2	15	16	5	24	12	12	22	15	12	26	11	19	44
229	5	1	46	1	1	2	15	5	5	4	9	4	15	13	10	10	8	11	41
230	5	1	49	1	1	2	19	12	12	16	13	15	28	16	14	36	14	16	59
231	5	1	55	1	1	2	21	40	8	36	9	10	27	49	13	47	9	17	53
232	5	2	46	2	1	1	20	9	6	17	10	11	29	13	12	23	12	8	31
233	5	2	58	4	1	1	30	55	19	52	15	23	31	54	19	54	15	23	78
234	5	1	47	4	1	1	18	13	9	20	8	11	28	34	17	33	11	18	43
235	5	1	53	4	1	1	26	25	14	36	13	13	30	44	19	43	15	23	90
236	5	2	51	2	1	1	30	15	8	12	10	10	30	33	12	45	12	20	49
237	5	1	49	4	1	1	17	16	12	15	8	15	25	26	15	20	12	11	41
238	5	1	43	2	1	1	16	13	6	11	8	9	22	19	10	10	9	7	30
239	5	2	60	3	1	1	23	16	9	33	14	16	29	35	18	50	13	23	69
240	5	1	51	4	1	1	21	11	10	27	10	12	25	32	17	47	11	19	65

DESCRIPTION OF NATIONAL MERIT DATA SET

This is data on 165 National Merit scholars. National Merit scholars are high school seniors who have generally scored in the top 1% on a series of very difficult cognitive tests, which are administered by Educational Testing Service. Thus, all the subjects in this data set are uniformly quite bright cognitively. However, they could differ considerably on personality variables. One of the variables that might "cause" them to differ on personality characteristics would be amount of their parents education. The first 90 cases in this data set are merit scholars whose parents had an eighth grade education or less, with the remaining 75 cases being merit scholars whose both parents had at least one college degree. They were measured with the Vocational Preference Inventory on a variety of variables; the three we focus on here are conventional (CONVEN), enterprising (ENTERP), and artistic (ARTISTIC). Some feeling for what these variables are measuring is obtained by examining the technical manual for the VPI (Consulting Psychologists, 1970) and the manuals "Clinical Interpretation" and "Conceptual Definition" for each variable. Below are parts of these for each of the variables:

Conventional

Clinical Interpretation: "Are conforming, status oriented, ethnocentric, not original . . . . Generally prefer subordinate roles. They seem to achieve their goals by conforming, living by the rules, and ordering their lives."
Conceptual Definition: " . . . a whole hearted uncritical acceptance of cultural values and attitudes, a living in the eyes of others with its emphasis on excessive self-control."

Enterprising

Clinical Interpretation: "Differ from CONVENTIONAL high scorers in their need for ambiguous verbal tasks rather than structured activity and a greater need for power . . . . Prefer social interaction as a medium of personal expression, but dislike well-defined language or work situations."
Conceptual Definition: " . . . dominance, risk taking, sociability, and enthusiasm."

Artistic

Clinical Interpretation: " . . . Tend to be original, imaginative, complex, unconventional and introverted."
Conceptual Definition: " . . . anxiety and immaturity, expressiveness, originality, unconventionality, erratic effort, and behavior."

NATIONAL MERIT DATA

GPID	CONVEN	ENTERP	ARTISTIC	GPID	CONVEN	ENTERP	ARTISTIC	GPID	CONVEN	ENTERP	ARTISTIC
1	0	0	4	1	3	3	0	1	0	0	1
1	3	3	4	1	1	3	6	1	4	3	3
1	0	0	5	1	0	1	0	1	1	2	0
1	1	1	1	1	1	3	0	1	0	0	4
1	2	0	3	1	1	2	5	1	2	2	7
1	1	3	2	1	4	3	6	1	2	0	0
1	2	0	4	1	1	0	1	1	4	3	0
1	4	1	1	1	0	0	0	1	0	3	4
1	4	1	1	1	0	0	0	1	4	2	0
1	4	3	8	1	7	8	8	1	1	2	1
1	0	6	5	1	2	0	4	1	0	0	4
1	2	3	8	1	1	0	5	1	6	4	3
1	0	1	0	1	3	0	8	1	0	1	13
1	1	4	4	1	2	0	5	1	1	0	5
1	2	0	0	1	2	3	8	1	8	2	1
1	1	0	0	1	1	1	3	1	1	0	0
1	1	1	6	1	4	4	0	1	1	1	0
1	5	4	5	1	4	3	6	1	2	1	4
1	1	1	5	1	0	7	8	1	1	4	4
1	8	5	4	1	3	1	6	1	4	2	3
2	0	2	5	2	0	0	2	2	0	0	3
2	4	4	0	2	2	1	1	2	2	3	2
2	1	1	0	2	0	3	5	2	2	3	3
2	0	1	4	2	0	0	1	2	0	5	2
2	0	0	1	2	0	2	0	2	0	1	5

(*Continued*)

NATIONAL MERIT DATA (*Continued*)

GPID	CONVEN	ENTERP	ARTISTIC	GPID	CONVEN	ENTERP	ARTISTIC	GPID	CONVEN	ENTERP	ARTISTIC
2	0	0	8	2	1	4	4	2	2	1	7
2	0	3	0	2	0	1	0	2	1	1	0
2	0	1	8	2	2	3	8	2	4	2	3
2	0	0	3	2	1	5	5	2	1	2	10
2	2	1	6	2	0	0	0	2	0	0	8
2	0	0	4	2	3	2	2	2	0	5	12
2	2	5	6	2	0	2	8	2	0	3	8
2	1	5	8	2	3	5	9	2	0	4	3
2	0	2	4	2	3	9	7	2	2	5	2
2	1	5	0	2	0	0	0	2	0	0	10
2	3	0	8	2	0	0	0	2	0	0	0
1	3	0	0	1	0	3	8	1	6	0	1
1	4	5	2	1	0	6	9	1	0	4	0
1	2	0	0	1	2	1	0	1	3	7	10
1	0	1	5	1	0	1	8	1	6	9	14
1	1	2	7	1	4	4	9	1	0	4	10
1	2	9	2	1	3	1	1	1	5	7	14
1	1	0	1	1	2	3	2	1	1	1	0
2	0	0	8	2	2	2	0	2	1	3	1
2	0	0	4	2	1	3	8	2	7	8	7
2	0	0	0	2	1	1	2	2	0	2	10
2	0	2	8	2	0	4	2	2	6	9	11
2	2	5	7	2	1	1	1	2	2	1	13
2	0	0	7	2	0	0	2	2	1	9	10
1	0	5	12	1	2	4	10	1	2	7	14
2	0	3	13	2	5	5	10	2	1	1	10
2	1	4	11	2	5	6	9	2	11	8	1
1	11	3	6	1	12	9	10	2	1	12	4
1	10	4	3	2	3	12	13	2	3	10	14
1	5	4	12	1	13	11	11	1	14	11	14

DESCRIPTION OF THE CARTOON DATA SET

This is a data set on 179 subjects from the *Minitab Handbook* (2nd ed., 1985), and is used with permission of the publisher. A short instructional slide presentation was developed, which dealt with the behavior of people in a group situation, and in particular the various roles or character types that group members often assume. The presentation consisted of a 5 minute lecture on tape, accompanied by 18 slides. Each role was identified by an animal. Each animal was shown on two slides: once in a cartoon sketch and once in a realistic picture. All 179 subjects saw all 18 slides, but a randomly selected half of them saw the slides in black and white while the other half saw the slides in color.

After seeing the slides, the subjects took a test on the material. The slides were presented in random order, and the subjects wrote down the character type represented by that slide. They received two scores: one for the number of cartoon characters correctly identified and one for the number of realistic characters correctly identified. Each score could range from 0 to 9, since there were 9 characters. Four weeks later the subjects were retested. Some subjects did not show up for the retest and that is indicated by a blank.

There are three groups of subjects in this study: (1) preprofessional personnel at three hospitals in Pennsylvania involved in an in-service training program, (2) professional personnel involved in the same training program, and (3) a group of Penn State undergraduate students. All these subjects were given the Otis Mental Ability Test, which yields a rough estimate of their natural ability.

The order in which the variables are arranged on the file is as follows:

Variable No.	Variable Name	Description
1	ID	Identification number
2	COLOR	0 = black and white, 1 = color (no participant saw both)
3	ED	Education: 0 = preprofessional, 1 = professional, 2 = college student
4	LOCATION	Location: 1 = hospital A, 2 = hospital B, 3 = hospital C, 4 = Penn State student
5	OTIS	OTIS score: from about 70 to about 130
6	CARTOON1	Score on cartoon test given immediately after presentation (possible scores are 0,1,2,. . .,9)
7	REAL1	Score on realistic test given immediately after presentation (possible scores are 0,1,2,. . .,9)
8	CARTOON2	Score on cartoon test given four weeks (delayed) after presentation (possible scores are 0,1,2,. . .,9; a blank is used for a missing observation)
9	REAL2	Score on realistic test given four weeks (delayed) after presentation (possible scores are 0,1,2,. . .,9; a blank is used for a missing observation)

CARTOON DATA

ID	COLOR	EDUC	LOC	OTIS	CARTOON1	REAL1	CARTOON2	REAL2
1	0	0	1	107	4	4		
2	0	0	2	106	9	9	6	5
3	0	0	2	94	4	2	3	0
4	0	0	2	121	8	8	6	8
5	0	0	3	86	5	5		
6	0	0	3	99	7	8	7	5
7	0	0	3	114	8	9	5	4
8	0	0	3	100	2	1		
9	0	0	3	85	3	2		
10	0	0	3	115	8	7	8	5
11	0	0	3	101	7	6		
12	0	0	3	84	7	5		
13	0	0	3	94	4	3		
14	0	0	3	87	1	3	2	0
15	0	0	3	104	9	9	5	6
16	0	0	3	104	5	6		
17	0	0	3	97	6	5		
18	0	0	3	91	1	0		
19	0	0	3	83	4	4		
20	0	0	3	93	0	0		
21	0	0	3	92	2	2		
22	0	0	3	91	5	2	3	1
23	0	0	3	88	2	1		
24	0	0	3	90	5	4	4	3
25	0	0	3	103	6	2		
26	0	0	3	93	9	9	8	4
27	0	0	3	106	2	0	6	3
28	1	0	1	98	3	3		
29	1	0	1	103	6	5	2	2
30	1	0	2	109	5	4	1	2
31	1	0	2	107	8	8		
32	1	0	2	108	8	8	7	6
33	1	0	2	107	3	2		
34	1	0	3	87	6	4	2	2
35	1	0	3	113	5	4	4	4
36	1	0	3	80	0	3	1	1
37	1	0	3	91	5	6		
38	1	0	3	102	8	9	5	5
39	1	0	3	83	4	1	2	1
40	1	0	3	108	9	9		
41	1	0	3	86	4	4		
42	1	0	3	96	6	3		
43	1	0	3	101	5	3		
44	1	0	3	97	6	3	4	4
45	1	0	3	88	3	1	2	0
46	1	0	3	104	4	2	2	0
47	1	0	3	87	7	3		
48	1	0	3	86	1	1		
49	1	0	3	90	6	5	4	1
50	1	0	3	102	6	2		
51	1	0	3	105	2	2		
52	1	0	3	115	7	8		
53	1	0	3	88	4	3		
54	1	0	3	111	8	8		
55	1	0	3	95	5	4		
56	1	0	3	104	5	5		
57	0	1	1	79	7	4	6	4
58	0	1	1	82	3	2		
59	0	1	1	123	8	8	7	5
60	0	1	1	106	9	7	8	6
61	0	1	1	125	9	9	4	3
62	0	1	1	98	7	6		
63	0	1	1	95	7	7	4	4
64	0	1	2	129	9	9	7	7
65	0	1	2	90	7	6	3	5
66	0	1	2	111	6	2	3	1
67	0	1	2	99	4	5	3	1
68	0	1	2	116	9	7	7	7
69	0	1	2	106	8	7	6	4
70	0	1	2	107	8	5		
71	0	1	2	100	7	6	2	1
72	0	1	2	124	8	9	3	5
73	0	1	3	98	6	7	1	1
74	0	1	3	124	9	6	6	5
75	0	1	3	84	1	4		
76	0	1	3	91	8	3		
77	0	1	3	118	6	6	3	4
78	0	1	3	102	6	4		
79	0	1	3	95	7	4		
80	0	1	3	90	4	3		
81	0	1	3	86	1	0		
82	0	1	3	104	6	4		
83	1	1	1	111	9	9	6	3
84	1	1	1	105	1	0		
85	1	1	1	110	1	0	0	0
86	1	1	1	80	0	0	0	0
87	1	1	1	78	4	1	1	1
88	1	1	2	120	9	9		
89	1	1	2	110	9	6	6	5
90	1	1	2	107	8	6		

(Continued)

CARTOON DATA (*Continued*)

ID	COLOR	EDUC	LOC	OTIS	CARTOON1	REAL1	CARTOON2	REAL2	ID	COLOR	EDUC	LOC	OTIS	CARTOON1	REAL1	CARTOON2	REAL2
91	1	1	2	125	7	8			135	0	2	4	121	9	8	7	8
92	1	1	2	117	9	9			136	0	2	4	125	9	8		
93	1	1	2	126	8	8	5	5	137	0	2	4	101	6	6	4	6
94	1	1	2	98	4	5			138	0	2	4	120	8	9	6	7
95	1	1	2	111	8	6			139	0	2	4	99	9	6		
96	1	1	2	110	8	7			140	0	2	4	128	8	9	8	7
97	1	1	2	120	9	7			141	0	2	4	129	8	6	5	2
98	1	1	2	114	8	7	6	4	142	0	2	4	125	8	6	7	4
99	1	1	2	117	6	7			143	0	2	4	107	8	8	8	5
100	1	1	3	105	7	6			144	0	2	4	102	8	7	6	4
101	1	1	3	97	6	6			145	0	2	4	125	9	8		
102	1	1	3	86	1	1			146	1	2	4	129	8	8		
103	1	1	3	111	7	5			147	1	2	4	122	3	0	2	3
104	1	1	3	93	1	0			148	1	2	4	124	7	6	6	7
105	1	1	3	115	8	7			149	1	2	4	115	8	8		
106	1	1	3	102	2	3	5	2	150	1	2	4	117	8	6	5	2
107	1	1	3	111	7	3	4	4	151	1	2	4	132	7	6	5	7
108	1	1	3	82	1	1			152	1	2	4	109	8	5	5	5
109	1	1	3	117	8	5	4	3	153	1	2	4	107	9	5	9	2
110	0	2	4	132	9	9			154	1	2	4	116	8	7	6	5
111	0	2	4	113	7	8			155	1	2	4	118	8	5	6	5
112	0	2	4	130	9	7	1	4	156	1	2	4	124	9	9	6	7
113	0	2	4	122	9	9	6	4	157	1	2	4	102	9	5	5	2
114	0	2	4	103	7	5	3	0	158	1	2	4	110	9	7	7	7
115	0	2	4	103	7	5	3	0	159	1	2	4	119	7	5	2	4
116	0	2	4	118	9	9			160	1	2	4	99	3	2	4	0
117	0	2	4	119	9	9	7	8	161	1	2	4	102	7	8	5	6
118	0	2	4	97	8	8	6	4	162	1	2	4	115	7	7		
119	0	2	4	123	9	9	7	4	163	1	2	4	105	8	6	3	0
120	0	2	4	113	8	7	6	6	164	1	2	4	104	7	6		
121	0	2	4	110	8	7	3	5	165	1	2	4	112	7	7		
122	0	2	4	119	8	7	6	6	166	1	2	4	117	9	9	6	5
123	0	2	4	116	5	7			167	1	2	4	108	9	9		
124	0	2	4	113	8	6	5	5	168	1	2	4	135	8	8	8	8
125	0	2	4	128	9	9			169	1	2	4	133	8	8	7	7
126	0	2	4	113	8	5	4	2	170	1	2	4	105	6	4	5	3
126	0	2	4	113	8	5	4	2	171	1	2	4	124	7	7	9	8
127	0	2	4	110	5	7			172	1	2	4	112	9	9	9	8
128	0	2	4	114	7	6	5	5	173	1	2	4	128	9	9	9	9
129	0	2	4	132	9	8	4	6	174	1	2	4	96	8	8	7	6
130	0	2	4	110	7	8	2	5	175	1	2	4	110	8	8	4	5
131	0	2	4	122	7	7	4	2	176	1	2	4	108	8	8	6	8
132	0	2	4	123	9	9	6	7	177	1	2	4	125	7	6	8	8
133	0	2	4	131	9	9	7	7	178	1	2	4	111	4	3	4	1
134	0	2	4	131	9	9	8	8	179	1	2	4	103	4	3	2	1

DESCRIPTION FOR WYND DATA SET

This study by Christine Wynd (*Journal of Advanced Nursing,* 1992, 204–302), investigated the effect of stress reduction in preventing smoking relapse. Subjects who had completed a local smoking cessation program were randomly assigned to either an experimental group or an attention placebo control group. The subjects in the treatment group were exposed to a three session treatment, and were measured on 3 variables at each session: creative imagery, stress and smoking rate. In the data listing I have abbreviated these variables as CRE, STR and SMR. The subjects in the experimental group are coded as 1 and those in the control group as 2. The fact that there are multiple measures for each session makes it a doubly multivariate problem.

GPID	CRE1	CRE2	CRE3	STR1	STR2	STR3	SMR1	SMR2	SMR3
1.00	8	27	30	19	16	16	0	0	0
1.00	10	−1	−1	24	−1	−1	0	20	20
1.00	6	30	30	23	40	44	0	20	10
1.00	14	20	24	19	15	12	0	0	0
1.00	20	33	34	40	27	27	0	0	0
1.00	18	−1	−1	32	−1	−1	0	25	25
1.00	22	16	18	21	25	24	0	0	0
1.00	6	36	36	22	22	22	0	0	0
1.00	18	21	24	33	22	20	0	0	0
1.00	8	24	28	38	25	24	0	0	0
1.00	12	29	30	28	21	22	0	0	0
1.00	14	26	28	21	18	18	0	0	0
1.00	26	−1	−1	33	−1	−1	0	0	0
1.00	22	33	34	38	28	28	0	0	0
1.00	18	26	28	33	35	30	0	0	0
1.00	6	20	26	27	21	20	0	0	0
1.00	10	33	34	30	29	27	0	20	20
1.00	16	35	36	37	27	26	0	0	0
1.00	24	−1	−1	40	−1	−1	0	40	40
1.00	22	32	34	30	28	24	0	0	0
1.00	22	26	32	30	36	30	0	25	25
1.00	30	32	34	32	25	24	0	0	0
1.00	14	27	30	30	24	24	0	0	0
1.00	14	29	30	28	21	27	0	0	0
1.00	12	19	28	26	29	33	0	35	20
1.00	18	21	28	9	11	10	0	0	0
1.00	20	28	30	20	15	17	0	0	0
1.00	20	26	20	38	21	19	0	0	0
1.00	22	26	34	39	24	22	0	0	0
1.00	6	22	26	22	22	20	0	0	0
1.00	12	23	24	30	10	15	0	0	0

GPID	CRE1	CRE2	CRE3	STR1	STR2	STR3	SMR1	SMR2	SMR3
1.00	10	22	18	34	34	35	0	20	20
1.00	26	27	32	25	25	22	0	0	0
1.00	8	27	30	28	21	22	0	0	0
1.00	20	24	30	23	18	18	0	0	0
1.00	12	26	36	29	22	20	0	0	0
1.00	10	23	20	25	16	17	0	0	0
1.00	14	20	18	26	23	24	0	0	0
1.00	8	25	30	21	25	29	0	25	12
2.00	10	16	22	26	31	32	0	0	0
2.00	20	−1	−1	28	−1	−1	0	20	20
2.00	22	24	26	29	28	31	0	0	0
2.00	14	16	18	31	29	30	0	0	0
2.00	18	20	20	44	36	40	0	25	25
2.00	18	21	24	25	40	40	0	0	15
2.00	10	16	22	37	30	34	0	0	0
2.00	26	27	28	25	30	36	0	0	0
2.00	6	9	12	36	38	38	0	0	20
2.00	20	−1	−1	22	−1	−1	0	10	10
2.00	22	23	24	24	25	24	0	0	0
2.00	6	7	8	13	33	30	0	0	30
2.00	10	−1	−1	29	−1	−1	0	40	40
2.00	16	19	22	32	28	36	0	30	30
2.00	18	16	16	30	25	30	0	0	0
2.00	16	16	16	35	37	35	0	0	30
2.00	24	22	24	13	28	28	0	0	20
2.00	8	9	10	31	23	30	0	0	0
2.00	22	−1	−1	33	−1	−1	0	40	40
2.00	22	23	24	23	28	26	0	0	25
2.00	14	18	22	25	21	24	0	0	0
2.00	16	16	16	26	23	28	0	0	0
2.00	16	18	22	32	36	35	0	0	0
2.00	16	18	20	23	30	30	0	20	20
2.00	34	28	22	30	30	31	0	0	10
2.00	14	12	10	30	31	30	0	0	10
2.00	20	18	16	29	24	26	0	0	0
2.00	18	24	30	38	37	38	0	0	30
2.00	14	−1	−1	29	−1	−1	0	25	25
2.00	22	23	24	27	22	22	0	0	0
2.00	22	24	16	45	35	42	0	40	30
2.00	10	20	22	34	22	32	0	0	0
2.00	22	22	28	22	24	30	0	0	0
2.00	24	−1	−1	20	−1	−1	0	26	26
2.00	22	21	20	20	19	23	0	0	0
2.00	18	18	18	25	29	28	0	0	0
2.00	10	9	12	25	15	24	0	0	0

APPENDIX C:
Obtaining Nonorthogonal Contrasts in Repeated Measures Designs*

This appendix features a KEYWORDS (an SPSS publication) article from 1993 on how to obtain nonorthogonal contrasts in repeated measures designs. The article first explains why SPSS is structured to orthogonalize any set of contrasts for repeated measures designs. The article then clearly explains how to obtain nonorthogonal contrasts for a single sample repeated measures, and indicates how to do so for some more complex repeated measures designs.

NONORTHOGONAL CONTRASTS ON WSFACTORS IN MANOVA

Many users have asked how to get SPSS MANOVA to produce nonorthogonal contrasts in repeated measures, or within-subjects, designs. The reason that nonorthogonal contrasts (such as the default DEVIATION, or the popular SIMPLE, or some SPECIAL user-requested contrasts) are not available when using WSFACTORS is that the averaged tests of significance require orthogonal contrasts, and the program has been structured to ensure that this is the case when WSFACTORS is used (users with SPSS Release 5.0 and later should note that DEVIATION is no longer the default contrast type for WSFACTORS).

MANOVA thus transforms the original dependent variables Y(1) to Y(K) into transformed variabled labeled T1 to TK (if no renaming is done), which

---

*Reprinted from KEYWORDS, number 52, 1993, copyright © by SSPS, Inc., Chicago.

represent orthonormal linear combinations of the original variables. The transformation matrix applied by MANOVA can be obtained by specifying PRINT = TRANSFORM. Note that the transformation matrix has been transposed for printing, so that the contrasts estimated by MANOVA are discerned by reading down the columns.

Here is an example, obtained by specifying a simple repeated measures MANOVA with four levels and no between-subjects factors. The following syntax produces the output in Figure 1:

MANOVA Y1 TO Y4
    /WSFACTORS = TIME(4)
    /PRINT = TRANSFORM

To see what contrasts have been obtained, simply read down the columns of the transformation matrix. Thus we have:

$$T1 = .500*Y1 + .500*Y2 + .500*Y3 + .500*Y4$$
$$T2 = .707*Y1 - .707*TY4$$
$$T3 = -.408*Y1 + .816*Y2 - .408*Y4$$
$$T4 = -.289*Y1 - .289*Y2 + .866*Y3 - .289*Y4$$

Three further points should be noted here. First, the coefficients of the linear combination used to form the transformed variables are scaled such that the transformation vectors are of unit length (normalized). This can be duplicated by first specifying the form of the contrasts using integers, then dividing each coefficient by the square root of the sum of the squared integer coefficients. For example:

$$T3 = (-1*Y1 + 2*Y2 - 1*Y4)/SQRT[(-1)**2 + 2**2 + (-1)**2]$$

Second, the first transformed variable (T1) is the constant term in the within-subjects model, a constant multiple of the mean of the original dependent variables. This will be used to test between-subjects effects if any are included in the model.

Orthonormalized Transformation Matrix (Transposed)			
	T1	**T2**	**T3**	**T4**
Y1	.500	.707	-.408	-.289
Y2	.500	.000	.816	-.289
Y3	.500	.000	.000	.866
Y4	.500	-.707	-.408	-.289

Figure 1

Finally, note that the contrasts generated here are not those that we requested (since we did not specify any contrasts, the default DEVIATION contrasts would be expected). An orthogonalization of a set of nonorthogonal contrasts changes the nature of the comparisons being made. It is thus very important when interpreting the univariate F-tests or the parameter estimates and their t-statistics to look at the transformation matrix when transformed variables are being used, so that the inferences being drawn are based on the contrasts actually estimated.

This is not the case with the multivariate tests. These are invariant to transformation, which means that any set of linearly independent contrasts will produce the same results. The averaged F-tests will be the same given any orthonormal set of contrasts.

Now that we know why we can't get the contrasts we want when running a design with WSFACTORS, let's see how to make MANOVA give us what we want. This is actually fairly simple. All that we have to do is get MANOVA to apply a nonorthogonal transformation matrix to our dependent variables. This can be achieved through the use of the TRANSFORM subcommand. What we do is remove the WSFACTORS subcommand (and anything else such as WSDESIGN or ANALYSIS(REPEATED) that refers to within-subjects designs) and transform the dependent variables ourselves.

For our example, the following syntax produces the transformation matrix given in Figure 2:

```
MANOVA Y1 TO Y4
   /TRANSFORM = DEVIATION
   /PRINT = TRANSFORM
   /ANALYSIS = (T1/T2 T3 T4)
```

Note that this transformation matrix has not been orthonormalized; it gives us the deviation contrasts we requested. You might be wondering what the purpose of the ANALYSIS subcommand is here. This subcommand separates the transformed variables into effects so that the multivariate tests

Transformation Matrix (Transposed)			
	T1	T2	T3	T4
Y1	1.000	.750	-.250	-.250
Y2	1.000	-.250	.750	-.250
Y3	1.000	-.250	-.250	.750
Y4	1.000	-.250	-.250	-.250

Figure 2

produced in this case are equivalent to those in the run where WSFAC-TORS was used. This serves two purposes. First, it allows us to check to make sure that we're still fitting the same model. Second, it helps us to identify the different effects on the output. In this case, we will have only effects labeled "CONSTANT," since we don't have any WSFACTORS as far as MANOVA is concerned. MANOVA is simply doing a multivariate analysis on transformed variables. This is the same thing as the WSFAC-TORS analysis, except that the labeling will not match for the listed effects.

In this example, we will look for effects labeled CONSTANT with T2, T3 and T4 as the variables used. These correspond to the TIME effect from the WSFACTORS run, as can be seen by comparing the multivariate tests, but the univariate tests now represent the contrasts that we wanted to see (as would the parameter estimates if we had printed them).

Often the design is more complex than a simple repeated measures analysis. Can this method be extended to any WSFACTORS design? The answer is yes. If there are multiple dependent variables to be transformed (as in a doubly multivariate repeated measures design), each set can be transformed in the same manner. For example, if variables A and B are each measured at three time points, resulting in A1, A2, A3, etc., the following MANOVA statements could be used:

```
MANOVA A1 A2 B1 B2 B3
  /TRANSFORM(A1 A2 A3/B1 B2 B3)=SIMPLE
  /PRINT=TRANSFORM
  /ANALYSIS=(T1 T4/T2 T3 T5 T6)
```

The TRANSFORM subcommand tells MANOVA to apply the same transformation matrix to each set of variables. The transformation matrix printed by MANOVA would then have a block diagonal structure, with two 3×3 matrices on the main diagonal and two 3×3 null matrices off the main diagonal. The ANALYSIS subcommand separates the two constants, T1 and T4, from the TIME variables, T2 and T3 (for A), and T5 and T6 (for B).

Another complication that may arise is the inclusion of between-subjects factors in analysis. The only real complication involved here is in interpreting the output. Printing the transformation matrix always allows us to see what the transformed variables represent, but there is also a way to identify specific effects without reference to the transformation matrix.

There are two keys to understanding the output from a MANOVA with a TRANSFORM subcommand: 1) The output will be divided into two sections: those which report statistics and tests for transformed variables T1, etc., which are the constants in the repeated measures model, used for testing between-subjects effects, and those which report statistics and tests for the other transformed variables (T2, T3, etc.), which are the contrasts among the dependent variables and measure the time or repeated measures effects; 2) Output that indicates transformed variable T1 has been used represents exactly the effect stated in the output. Output that indicates transformed variables T2, etc. have been used represents the interaction of whatever is listed on the output with the repeated measures factor (such as time).

In other words, an effect for CONSTANT using variates T2 and T3 is really the Time effect, and an effect FACTOR1 using T2 and T3 is really the FACTOR1 BY TIME interaction effect. If between-subjects effects have been specified, the CONSTANT term must be specified on the DESIGN subcommand in order to get the TIME effects. Also, the effects can always be identified by matching the multivariate results to those from the WSFACTORS approach as long as the effects have been properly separated with an ANALYSIS subcommand.

An example might help to make these principles more concrete. The following MANOVA commands produced the four sets of F-tests listed in Figure 3:

```
MANOVA Y1 TO Y4 BY A(1,2)
    /WSFACTORS = TIME(4)
```

The second run used TRANSFORM to analyze the same data, producing the output in Figure 4.

```
MANOVA Y1 TO Y4 BY A(1,2)
        /TRANSFORM = SIMPLE
        /ANALYSIS = (T1/T2 T3 T4)
        /DESIGN = CONSTANT, A
```

The first table in each run is the test for the between-subjects factor A. Note that the F-values and associated significances are identical. The sums of squares differ by a constant multiple due to the orthonormalization. The CONSTANT term in the TRANSFORM run is indeed the constant and is usually not of interest. The second and third tables in the WSFACTORS run contain only multivariate tests for the A BY TIME and A factors, respectively. The univariate tests here are not printed by default. The corresponding tables in the TRANSFORM output are labeled A and CONSTANT, with the header above indicating the variates T2, T3 and T4 are being analyzed. Note that the multivariate tests are exactly the same as those for the WSFACTORS run. This tells us that we have indeed fit the same model in both runs.

The application of our rule for interpreting the labeling in the TRANS-FORM run tells us that the second table represents A BY TIME and that the

```
#1--The A main effect
Tests of Between-Subjects Effects.

Tests of Significance for T1 using UNIQUE sums of squares

Source of Variation      SS       DF      MS       F    Sig of F
WITHIN CELLS          36.45       17     2.14
A                      3.79        1     3.79    1.77     .201
------------------------------------------------------------------
#2--The A BY TIME interaction effect

EFFECT .. A BY TIME
Multivariate Tests of Significance (S = 1, M = 1/2, N = 6 1/2)

Test Name     Value      Exact F    Hypoth.DF    Error DF    Sig. of F
Pillais      .59919     7.47478        3.00        15.00        .003
Hotellings  1.49496     7.47478        3.00        15.00        .003
Wilks        .40081     7.47478        3.00        15.00        .003
Roys         .59919
Note.. F statistics are exact.
------------------------------------------------------------------
#3--The TIME effect

EFFECT .. TIME

Multivariate Tests of Significance (S = 1, M = 1/2, N = 6 1/2)
Test Name     Value      Exact F    Hypoth.DF    Error DF    Sig. of F
Pillais      .29487     2.09085        3.00        15.00        .144
Hotellings   .41817     2.09085        3.00        15.00        .144
Wilks        .70513     2.09085        3.00        15.00        .144
Roys         .29487
Note.. F statistics are exact.
------------------------------------------------------------------
 #4--The averaged F-tests for TIME and A BY TIME

Tests involving 'TIME' Within-Subject Effect.

AVERAGED Tests of Significance for Y using UNIQUE sums of squares
Source of Variation      SS       DF      MS       F    Sig of F
WITHIN CELLS         231.32       51     4.54
TIME                  25.97        3     8.66    1.91     .140
A BY TIME             30.55        3    10.18    2.25     .094
```

Figure 3

third table represents CONSTANT BY TIME, which is simply TIME. Since
MANOVA is simply running a multivariate analysis with transformed
variables, as opposed to a WSFACTORS analysis, univariate F-tests are
printed by default. The univariate tests for TIME are generally the major

```
Order of Variables for Analysis
Variates      Covariates
T1
-----------------------------------------------------------------------
#1--The A main effect
Tests of Significance for T1 using UNIQUE sums of squares

Source of Variation    SS       DF      MS        F      Sig of F
WITHIN CELLS         145.79     17     8.58
CONSTANT            8360.21      1   8360.21    974.86     .000
A                     15.16      1     15.16      1.77     .201
-----------------------------------------------------------------------
Order of Variables for Analysis
      Variates      Covariates
      T2
      T3
      T4
-----------------------------------------------------------------------
#2--The A BY TIME interaction effect

EFFECT .. A
Multivariate Tests of Significance (S = 1, M = 1/2, N = 6 1/2)
Test Name      Value     Exact F   Hypoth. DF   Error DF  Sig. of F
Pillais        .59919    7.47478      3.00        15.00     .003
Hotellings    1.49496    7.47478      3.00        15.00     .003
Wilks          .40081    7.47478      3.00        15.00     .003
Roys           .59919
Note.. F statistics are exact.


EFFECT .. A
Univariate F-tests with (1,17) D. F.
Variable  Hypoth. SS  Error SS  Hypoth. MS  Error MS   F     Sig. of F
T2         18.73743  135.78889   18.73743   7.98758  2.34582   .144
T3          9.58129  227.15556    9.58129  13.36209   .71705   .409
T4          2.24795  108.48889    2.24795   6.38170   .35225   .561
-----------------------------------------------------------------------
#3--The TIME effect

EFFECT .. CONSTANT
Multivariate Tests of Significance (S = 1, M = 1/2, N = 6 1/2)
Test Name     Value  Exact F   Hypoth. DF   Error DF  Sig. of F
Pillais       .29487  2.09085      3.00        15.00     .144
Hotellings    .41817  2.09085      3.00        15.00     .144
Wilks         .70513  2.09085      3.00        15.00     .144
Roys          .29487
Note.. F statistics are exact.


EFFECT .. CONSTANT
Univariate F-tests with (1,17) D. F.
Variable  Hypoth. SS  Error SS  Hypoth. MS  Error MS   F     Sig. of F
T2         23.15848  135.78889   23.15848   7.98758  2.89931  .107
T3          4.94971  227.15556    4.94971  13.36209   .37043  .551
T4         45.19532  108.48889   45.19532   6.38170  7.08202  .016
```

Figure 4

source of interest, as they are usually the reason for the TRANSFORM run. The A BY TIME tests may be the tests of interest if interaction is present.

Finally, the WSFACTORS run presents the averaged F-tests, which are not available in the TRANSFORM run (and which would not be valid, since we have not used orthogonal contrasts). One further example setup might be helpful in order to clarify how we would proceed if we had multiple within-subject factors. This is probably the most complex and potentially time-consuming situation we will encounter when trying to get MANOVA to estimate nonorthogonal contrasts in within-subject designs, since we must know the entire contrast (transformation) matrix we want MANOVA to apply to our data. In this case we must use a SPECIAL transformation and spell out the entire transformation matrix (or at least the entire matrix for each dependent variable; if there are multiple dependent variables, we can tell MANOVA to apply the same transformation to each).

Let's look at a situation where we have a 2×3 WSDESIGN and we want to do SIMPLE contrasts on each of our WSFACTORS. The standard syntax for the WSFACTORS run would be:

```
MANOVA V1 TO V6
  /WSFACTORS = A(2) B(3)
```

The syntax for the TRANSFORM run would be:

```
MANOVA V1 TO V6
  /TRANSFORM = SPECIAL (1   1   1   1   1   1
                        1   1   1  -1  -1  -1
                        1   0  -1   1   0  -1
                        0   1  -1   0   1  -1
                        1   0  -1  -1   0   1
                        0   1  -1   0  -1   1)
  /PRINT = TRANSFORM
  /ANALYSIS = (T1/T2/T3 T4/T5 T6)
```

Note that the final two rows of the contrast matrix are simply coefficient by coefficient multiples of rows two and three and two and four, respectively. Also, the ANALYSIS subcommand here separates the effects into four groups: the CONSTANT and A effects (each with one degree of freedom), and the B and A BY B interaction effect (with two degrees of freedom). Once again, this separation allows us to compare the TRANSFORM output with appropriate parts of the WSFACTORS output.

Though this use of SPECIAL transformations can be somewhat tedious if there are many WSFACTORS or some of these factors have many levels, it is also very general and will allow us to obtain the desired contrasts for designs of any size.

Answer Section

ANSWERS FOR CHAPTER 2

1.

a) $\mathbf{A} + \mathbf{C} = \begin{bmatrix} 3 & 7 & 6 \\ 9 & 0 & 6 \end{bmatrix}$

(b) $\mathbf{A} + \mathbf{B}$ not meaningful - must be of the same dimension to add.

(c) $\mathbf{A}\,\mathbf{B} = \begin{bmatrix} 13 & 12 \\ 14 & 24 \end{bmatrix}$

(d) $\mathbf{A}\,\mathbf{C}$ not meaningful - number of rows of $\mathbf{C}$ is not equal to number of columns of $\mathbf{A}$.

e) $\boldsymbol{u}'\mathbf{D}\,\boldsymbol{u} = 70$

f) $\boldsymbol{u}'\,\boldsymbol{v} = 23$

g) $(\mathbf{A} + \mathbf{C})' = \begin{bmatrix} 3 & 9 \\ 7 & 0 \\ 6 & 6 \end{bmatrix}$

h) $3\,\mathbf{C} = \begin{bmatrix} 3 & 9 & 15 \\ 18 & 6 & 3 \end{bmatrix}$

i) $|\mathbf{D}| = 20$

j) $\mathbf{D}^{-1} = \dfrac{1}{20} \begin{bmatrix} 6 & -2 \\ -2 & 4 \end{bmatrix}$

k) $|\mathbf{E}| = 1 \begin{vmatrix} 3 & 1 \\ 1 & 10 \end{vmatrix} - (-1) \begin{vmatrix} -1 & 1 \\ 2 & 10 \end{vmatrix} + 2 \begin{vmatrix} -1 & 3 \\ 2 & 1 \end{vmatrix} = 3$

by expanding along the first row

The same answer (i.e., 3) should be obtained by expanding along *any* row or column.

l) $\mathbf{E}^{-1} = ?$ Matrix of cofactors $= \begin{bmatrix} 29 & 12 & -7 \\ 12 & 6 & -3 \\ -7 & -3 & 2 \end{bmatrix}$ $|\mathbf{E}| = 3$

Therefore, $\mathbf{E}^{-1} = \dfrac{1}{3} \begin{bmatrix} 29 & 12 & -7 \\ 12 & 6 & -3 \\ -7 & -3 & 2 \end{bmatrix}$

m) $\mathbf{u}' \, \mathbf{D}^{-1} \, \mathbf{u} = 30/20$

n) $\mathbf{B} \, \mathbf{A} = \begin{bmatrix} 8 & 0 & 11 \\ 7 & 6 & 7 \\ 18 & 4 & 23 \end{bmatrix}$

o) $\mathbf{X}' \, \mathbf{X} = \begin{bmatrix} 51 & 64 \\ 64 & 90 \end{bmatrix}$

2. $\begin{bmatrix} y_1 \\ y_2 \\ \vdots \\ y_N \end{bmatrix} = \begin{bmatrix} e_1 \\ e_2 \\ \vdots \\ e_N \end{bmatrix} + \begin{bmatrix} 1 & x_{11} & x_{12} & x_{13} \\ 1 & x_{21} & x_{22} & x_{23} \\ \multicolumn{4}{c}{\ldots\ldots} \\ 1 & x_{N1} & x_{N2} & x_{N3} \end{bmatrix} \begin{bmatrix} b_0 \\ b_1 \\ b_2 \\ b_3 \end{bmatrix}$

$\begin{array}{cccc} \mathbf{y} & \mathbf{e} & + & \mathbf{X} & \mathbf{b} \\ (N \times 1) & (N \times 1) & & (N \times 4) & (4 \times 1) \end{array}$

Single matrix equation is: $\mathbf{y} = \mathbf{e} + \mathbf{X} \, \mathbf{b}$

3. $\mathbf{S}$ (covariance matrix) $= \dfrac{1}{4} \begin{bmatrix} 26.8 & 24 & -14 \\ 24 & 24 & -14 \\ -14 & -14 & 52 \end{bmatrix}$

4.

a) $r_{12} = \dfrac{s_{12}}{s_1 s_2} \Rightarrow s_{12} = r_{12} \, s_1 s_2 = .80 \, (10)(7) = 56$

Therefore, $\mathbf{S} = \begin{bmatrix} 100 & 56 \\ 56 & 49 \end{bmatrix} \Rightarrow |\mathbf{S}| = 1{,}764$

b) $s_{12} = .20 \, (9)(6) = 10.8$

Therefore, $\mathbf{S} = \begin{bmatrix} 81 & 10.8 \\ 10.8 & 36 \end{bmatrix} \Rightarrow |\mathbf{S}| = 2799.36$

The fact that the generalized variance is larger for (b) might seem surprising, since the variances for both variables are larger for (a). However, the fact that the variables are highly correlated in (a) means that much of the variance in either variable can be accounted for by the other variable. This fact reduces the generalized variance for (a) considerably.

ANSWERS FOR CHAPTER 3

1.

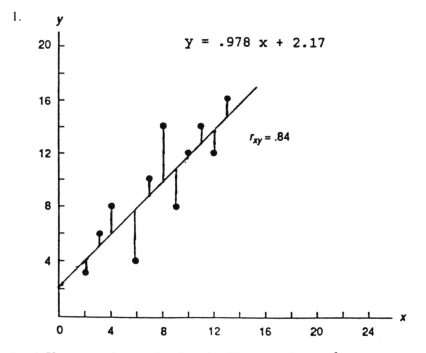

$$y = .978\ x + 2.17$$

$$r_{xy} = .84$$

3. a) If x_1 enters the equation first, it will account for $(.60)^2 \times 100$, or 36% of the variance on y.

b) To determine how much variance on y predictor x_1 will account for if entered second we need to partial out x_2. Hence we compute the following semi partial correlation:

$$r_{y1.2(s)} = \frac{r_{y1} - r_{y2}\ r_{12}}{\sqrt{1 - r_{12}^2}}$$

$$= \frac{.60 - .50(.80)}{\sqrt{1 - (.8)^2}} = .33$$

$$r_{y1.2(s)}^2 = (.33)^2 = .1089$$

Thus, x_1 accounts for about 11% of the variance if entered second.

c) Since x_1 and x_2 are strongly correlated (multicollinearity), when a predictor enters the equation influences greatly how much variance it will account for. Here when x_1 entered first it accounted for 36% of variance, while it only accounted for 11% when entered second.

4. The admissions official would use semi parital correlations to partial out the contributions of x_1 and x_2 first, and then determine how much unique variance in success x_3 and x_4 account for. In terms of the packages, one could achieve this by *forcing* x_1 and x_2 into the equation and assigning x_3 and x_4 the same level value to see which enters the equation next.

   An educated guess is that x_4 would probably have the greater incremental validity. Although x_4 has a smaller correlation with y (.46) than x_3 (.60), it is only weakly correlated with x_1 and x_2, whereas x_3 has strong correlations with x_1 and x_2 (.6 and .8). Thus, x_3 is quite redundant. Most of the variance in success that it accounts for is the same variance that x_1 and x_2 account for.

5. a) Show that the multiple correlation of .346 is not significant at the .05 level.

$$F = [(.346)^2/4)]/[(1-(.346)^2)/63] = .03/.014 = 2.14$$

The critical value at the .05 level is 2.52. Since $2.14 < 2.52$, we fail to reject the null hypothesis.

b)

$$F = \frac{[(.682)^2 - (.555)^2]/6}{[1-(.682)^2]/(57-11)} = \frac{.026}{.012} = 2.17$$

Since 2.17 is less than the critical value of 2.3, we conclude that the Home inventory variables do *not* significantly increase predictive power.

7. a) We can not have much faith in the reliability of the regression equations. It was indicated in the chapter that generally about 15 subjects per predictor are needed for a reliable equation. Here, in the second case the N/k ratio is $114/16 = 7/1$, far short of what is needed. In the first case we have a double capitilization on chance, with preselection (picking the 6 out of 16) and then the capitilization due to the mathematical maximiation property for multiple regression.

b) *Herzberg Formula*

$$\hat{\rho}_c^2 = 1 - (113/97)(112/96)(115/114)(1 - .32)$$

$$\hat{\rho}_c^2 = 1 - .933 = .067$$

Thus, if the equation were cross validated on many other samples from the same population we could expect to account for only about 7% of the variance on social adjustment.

9. TITLE 'CREATING NEW VARIABLES & STEPWISE AND BACK-
WARD REG.'
DATA LIST FREE/ X1 X2 X3 X4 X5 X6 X7 X8 X9 X10 X11 X12 X13
X14 X15
BEGIN DATA
   DATA LINES
END DATA
COMPUTE COMP1 = X7 + X8
COMPUTE COMP2 = X2 + X5 + X10
LIST
REGRESSION VARIABLES=X1 X3 X4 X11 TO X14 COMP1
COMP2/
DEPENDENT=X4/
METHOD=STEPWISE/
CASEWISE = ALL PRED RESID ZRESID LEVER COOK/
SCATTERPLOT(*RES,*PRE)/
DEPENDENT=X4/
METHOD=BACKWARD/
CASEWISE = ALL PRED RESID ZRESID LEVER COOK/
SCATTERPLOT(*RES,*PRE)/

10. TITLE 'USING FIXED FORMAT AND TESTING SET OF PREDS
AS BLOCK'
DATA LIST FIXED/X1 1 X2 2 X3 3-4 X4 5-6 X5 7-8 X6 9-11(2)
X7 12-14 X8 15-16
LIST
BEGIN DATA
   DATA LINES
END DATA
REGRESSION VARIABLES=X1 TO X8/
DEPENDENT=X8/
ENTER X1/ENTER X2/TEST(X3 X4 X5)

11. We simply need to refer to the Park and Dudycha table for 4 predictors, with $\alpha = .95$, and $\epsilon = .10$. Since the table does not provide for an estimate of $\rho^2 = .62$, we interpolate between the sample sizes needed for $\rho^2 = .50$ and $\rho^2 = .75$. Those sample sizes are 43 and 25. Since .62 is about halfway between .50 and .75, the sample size required is 34 subjects.

12. If we use the median value of 11, the Stein estimate of average cross validity power is

$$\rho_c^2 = 1 - \frac{(21)\,(20)\,(23)}{(10)\,(9)\,(22)}(1 - (.423)) = -1.81$$

Since this estimate is negative, we would accept 0 as the value, and conclude that the equation has essentially no generalizability.

14. a) PREBODY entered the equation first because it had the largest simple correlation (.650) with POSTBODY and it was significant at the .05 level.

b) PREFORM entered the equation second because it had the largest partial correlation with POSTBODY (.1948) and it was significant at the .05 level ($p = .0025$).

c) The regression coefficients defining the prediction equation are found in the bottom left hand corner of page 3; they yield the following equation

POSTBODY $= 13.062 + .435$ PREBODY $+ .292$ PREFORM

d) Multicollinearity is definitely present since the correlations among the predictors range from moderate (.453) to fairly strong (.718).

e) The Stein estimate of average cross validity power is

$$\rho_{c}^{2} = 1 - \frac{239\ (238)\ (241)}{234\ (233)\ (240)}\ (1 - (.445)\ ) = .418$$

This estimates that if we were to apply the prediction equation to many other samples from the same population, then we would expect *on the average* to account for 41.8% of the variance on POSTBODY.

f) The RSQCH is simply the squared semipartial correlation between PREFORM and POSTBODY with PREBODY partially only from PREFORM:

$$r_{(s)} = [.551 - .65(.68)]/\sqrt{1 - .68^2} = .149$$

Squaring, we obtain .022, which is the value on the printout within rounding error.

g) If a linear model is appropriate, then we would expect about only 5% of the standardized residuals to be greater than 2 in absolute value. In this case that number is $240(.05) = 12$. We see on page 5 of the printout that there are 10 standardized rediduals greater than 2.10772. There still could be a few more just slightly greater than 2 in absolute value. But this would still be right in the range of what we would expect.

h) We use 3k/n as the rough critical value for identifying an outlier on the set of predictors. This yields $3(2)/240 = .025$. Examination of the LEVERAGE values on page 5 shows that there are 7 outliers on the set of predictors.

i) There are no influential data points since none of the Cook distances even approach 1.

j) The plot is fairly random; however, there is some evidence indicating nonconstant variance. Notice how above the line of 0, as you move from left to right how the residuals funnel in (and there is a heavier concentration of them as each of the asterisks indicates 4 residuals at that location).

k) Although there is some positive skewness in the residuals, the deviation is not large enough to be of any concern.

ANSWERS FOR CHAPTER 4

1. a) This is a three-way univariate ANOVA, with sex, socioeconomic status, and teaching method as the factors and Lankton algebra test score as the dependent variable.

b) This is a multivariate study, a two-group MANOVA with reading speed and reading comprehension as the dependent variables.

c) This is a multiple regression study, with success on the job as the dependent variable and high school gpa and the personality variables as the predictors.

d) This is a factor analytic study, where the items are the variables being analyzed.

e) This is a multivariate study, and a complex repeated measures design (to be discussed in Chapter 13). There is one between or classification variable (social class) and one within variable (grade) and the subjects are measured on 3 dependent variables (reading comprehension, math ability, and science ability) at 3 points in time.

2. Because there are more variables (the items are the variables) here than subjects, the covariance matrix S is singular and can't be inverted. Another way of thinking about this is that there are no degrees of freedom for error since $N - p - 1 = 45 - 50 - 1 = -6$! The investigator must consider substantially reducing the number of variables for analysis by logically grouping items into subsets and using the subtest total scores as the dependent variables.

3. You should definitely not be impressed with these results. Since this is a 3-way design (call the factors A, B, and C) there are 7 statistical tests (7 effects — A, B, and C main effects, the AB, AC, and BC interactions and the three way interaction ABC) being done for each of the 5 dependent variables, making a total of 35 statistical tests that were done at the .05 level. The chance of 3 or 4 of these being type I errors is quite high. Yes, we could have more confidence if the significant effects had been hypothesized a priori. For then there would have been a empirical (theoretical) basis for expecting

the effects to be "real," which we would then be empirically confirming. Since there are 5 correlated dependent variables, a 3-way multivariate analysis of variance would have been a better way statistically of analyzing the data.

4. The within matrices for groups 1 and 2 are respectively:

$$\mathbf{W}_1 = \begin{bmatrix} 9.2 & -8 \\ -8 & 22 \end{bmatrix} \quad \mathbf{W}_2 = \begin{bmatrix} 2 & -1 \\ -1 & 2 \end{bmatrix}$$

Therefore the pooled within SSCP matrix is:

$$\mathbf{W} = \mathbf{W}_1 + \mathbf{W}_2 = \begin{bmatrix} 9.2 & -8 \\ -8 & 22 \end{bmatrix} + \begin{bmatrix} 2 & -1 \\ -1 & 2 \end{bmatrix} = \begin{bmatrix} 11.2 & -9 \\ -9 & 24 \end{bmatrix}$$

b) The pooled within covariance matrix $\mathbf{S}$ is given by:

$$\mathbf{S} = \frac{1}{N-k} \mathbf{W} - \frac{1}{8-2} \begin{bmatrix} 11.2 & -9 \\ -9 & 24 \end{bmatrix} = \begin{bmatrix} 1.87 & -1.5 \\ -1.5 & 4 \end{bmatrix}$$

1.87 is the variance for y_1 and 4 is the variance for y_2

-1.5 is the covariance for y_1 and y_2

c) Hotelling's T^2 is given by:

$$T^2 = \frac{n_1 n_2}{n_1 + n_2} (\bar{\mathbf{y}}_1 - \bar{\mathbf{y}}_2)' \mathbf{S}^{-1} (\bar{\mathbf{y}}_1 - \bar{\mathbf{y}}_2),$$

where $\bar{\mathbf{y}}_1$ and $\bar{\mathbf{y}}_2$ are the vectors of means for groups 1 and 2 and $\mathbf{S}^{-1}$ is the inverse of the covariance matrix.

$$\mathbf{S}^{-1} = \frac{1}{5.23} \begin{bmatrix} 4 & 1.50 \\ 1.5 & 1.87 \end{bmatrix} = \begin{bmatrix} .765 & .287 \\ .287 & .358 \end{bmatrix}$$

where 5.23 is the determinant of $\mathbf{S}$.

Now, the means for y_1 and y_2 in group 1 are 2.6 and 5, while the means for y_1 and y_2 in group 2 are 5 and 7. Thus,

$$\bar{\mathbf{y}}_1 - \bar{\mathbf{y}}_2 = \begin{pmatrix} 2.6 \\ 5.0 \end{pmatrix} - \begin{pmatrix} 5 \\ 7 \end{pmatrix} = \begin{pmatrix} -2.4 \\ -2.0 \end{pmatrix}$$

Therefore,

$$T^2 = \frac{5(3)}{8} (-2.4, -2) \begin{bmatrix} .765 & .287 \\ .287 & .358 \end{bmatrix} \begin{pmatrix} -2.4 \\ -2.0 \end{pmatrix} = 16.11$$

d) The multivariate null hypothesis is that the population mean vectors are equal, i.e., $\boldsymbol{\mu}_1 = \boldsymbol{\mu}_2$.

e) To test the multivariate null hypothesis we use the exact F transformation of T^2:

$$F = \frac{n_1 + n_2 - p - 1}{(n_1 + n_2 - 2)p} T^2 = \frac{8 - 2 - 1}{6\,(2)} (16.11) = 6.71$$

The critical value at the .05 level is:

$$F_{.05;\ p,\ N-p-1} = F_{.05;\ 2,5} = 5.79$$

Since $6.71 > 5.79$ we reject the multivariate null hypothesis and conclude that the groups differ on the set of 2 variables.

6. a) $s_1^2 = 9$, $s_2^2 = 4$ and $r_{12} = .70$ (given)

Also, the row vector of mean differences $\mathbf{d}' = (1, -.5)$.

To calculate T^2 we need the covariance matrix for the variables. We already have the variances, but need the covariance. But,

$$r_{12} = \frac{s_{12}}{s_1 s_2} \rightarrow s_{12} = r_{12}\, s_1 s_2 = (.70)(3)(2) = 4.2$$

Therefore,

$$\mathbf{S} = \begin{bmatrix} 9 & 4.2 \\ 4.2 & 4 \end{bmatrix} \Rightarrow \mathbf{S}^{-1} = \begin{bmatrix} .218 & -.229 \\ -.229 & .491 \end{bmatrix}$$

$$T^2 = \frac{(30)(30)}{60} (1, -.5) \begin{bmatrix} .218 & -.229 \\ -.229 & .491 \end{bmatrix} \begin{pmatrix} 1 \\ -.5 \end{pmatrix} = 8.565$$

$$F = \frac{60 - 3}{58\,(2)} (8.565) = 4.21$$

Critical value at .05 is 3.15; therefore the multivariate test is significant at the .05 level.

Univariate Tests

$$F_1 = t_1^2 = \frac{1^2}{9\left(\dfrac{1}{30} + \dfrac{1}{30}\right)} = 1/.6 = 1.66$$

$$F_2 = t_2^2 = \frac{(-.5)^2}{4\left(\dfrac{1}{30} + \dfrac{1}{30}\right)} = .25/.266 < 1$$

Critical value at $.05 = F_{.05;\ 1,58} = 4$; thus neither of the variables is significant in a univariate sense.

b) $r_{12} = .20 \Rightarrow s_{12} = .2\ (3)(2) = 1.2$

$$S = \begin{bmatrix} 9 & 1.2 \\ 1.2 & 4 \end{bmatrix} \Rightarrow S^{-1} = \begin{bmatrix} .116 & -.035 \\ -.035 & .260 \end{bmatrix}$$

$$T^2 = \frac{30(30)}{60}\ (1,\ -.5) \begin{bmatrix} .116 & -.035 \\ -.035 & .260 \end{bmatrix} \begin{pmatrix} 1 \\ -.5 \end{pmatrix} = 3.25$$

$$F = \frac{60 - 3}{58\ (2)}\ (3.25) = 1.597$$

Since 1.597 is less than the critical value of 3.15, the multivariate test is not significant.

The reason multivariate significance is not obtained here is that the generalized error variance against which significance is being tested is much greater here ($|S| = 34.56$) than it was in part (a), where $|S| = 18.36$.

9. Using Table 4.6 with $D^2 = .64$ (as a good approximation):

Variables	n	.64
3	25	.74
5	25	.68

Interpolating between the power values of .74 for 3 variables and .68 for 5 variables, we see that about 25 subjects per group will be needed for power $= .70$ for 4 variables.

12. a) The multivariate null hypothesis is rejected at the .05 level, since $F = 3.7488$, $p < .016$.

b) The value of Mahalanobis $D^2 = 5.144$, which is a very large multivariate effect size! Thus, it is not surprising that the multivariate null hypothesis was rejected. With an effect size this large, not many subjects per group are needed for excellent power.

c) Setting overall $\alpha = .05$, via the Bonferroni approach, means that each variable is tested for significance at the $.05/6 = .0083$ level of significance. From the printout then the following variables are significant:

Variable	F	prob.
Tone	13.97	.001
Rhythm	9.34	.006
Inton	13.86	.001
Artic	17.17	.000

ANSWERS FOR CHAPTER 5

1. a) The multivariate null hypothesis is that the population mean vectors for the 3 groups are equal, i.e., $\mu_1 = \mu_2 = \mu_3$. We do reject the multivariate null hypothesis at the .05 level since $F = 3.34$ (corresponding to Wilk's Λ), $p < .008$.

    b) Groups 1 and 2 are significantly different at the .05 level on the set of 3 variables since $F = 3.9247$, $p < .0206$. Also, groups 2 and 3 are significantly different since $F = 7.6099$, $p < .001$.

    c) Only variable $Y2$ is significant at the .01 level for groups 1 and 2, since the t for this variable is t(pooled) $= -3.42$, $p < .003$.

    Variables $Y2$ and $Y3$ are significant at the .01 level for groups 2 and 3, since t(pooled) for $Y3$ is 4.41, $p < .001$.

    d) Variables $Y2$ and $Y3$ are still significantly different for groups 1 and 2 with the Tukey confidence intervals, since the intervals do not cover 0.

    Variables $Y2$ and $Y3$ are still significantly different for groups 2 and 3, but $Y1$ is not significantly different since it's interval does cover 0.

3. We could not place a great deal of confidence in these results, since from the Bonferroni Inequality the probability of *at least one* spurious significant result could be as high as 12 (.05) $= .60$. Thus, most of these 4 significant results could be type I errors. The authors did not a priori hypothesize differences on the variables for which significance was found.

4. To show that the contrasts are orthogonal (since the group sizes are equal), it suffices to show that the sum of the products of the coefficients for each pair is 0:

    1 & 2: $1(0) + (-.25)(1) + (-.25)(1) + (-.25)(-1) + (-.25)(-1) = 0$
    1 & 3: $1(0) + (-.25)(1) + (-.25)(0) + (-.25)(0) + (-.25)(-1) = 0$
    1 & 4: $1(0) + (-.25)(0) + (-.25)(0) + (-.25)(1) + (-.25)(-1) = 0$
    2 & 3: $0(0) + 1(1) + 1(-1) + (-1)(0) + (-1)(0) = 0$
    2 & 4: $0(0) + 1(0) + 1(0) + (-1)(1) + (-1)(-1) = 0$
    3 & 4: $0(0) + 1(0) + (-1)(0) + 0(1) + 0(-1) = 0$

    b) To show that the set of contrasts are not orthogonal we need merely show that at least one of the pairs of contrasts is not orthogonal:
    1 & 2: $1(1) + (-.25)(-.50) + (-.25)(-.50) + (-.25)(0) + (-.25)(0)$ $\neq 0$

    c) Control lines for contrast set in part (a):

TITLE ' SPECIAL CONTRASTS FOR EXERCISE 4 '
DATA LIST FREE/ GPS Y1 Y2 Y3 Y4
LIST

```
·BEGIN DATA
    DATA LINES
END DATA
MANOVA Y1 TO Y4 BY GPS(1,5)/
  CONTRAST(GPS) = SPECIAL(1 1 1 1 1 1  −.25 −.25 −.25 −.25
  0 1 1 −1 −1 0 1  −1 0 0 0 0 0 1 −1)/
  PARTITION(GPS)/
  DESIGN = GPS(1),GPS(2),GPS(3),GPS(4)/
  PRINT = CELLINFO(MEANS)/
```

The control lines for the second contrast set in part (a) is exactly the same except for the CONTRAST subcommand which now is:

```
CONTRAST(GPS) = SPECIAL(1 1 1 1 1 1  −.25 −.25 −.25 −.25
1 −.5 −.5 0 0 1 0 0  −.5 −.5 0 1 1 −1 −1)/
```

7.

T_2			T_3	
y_1	y_2		y_1	y_2
4	8		7	6
5	6		8	7
6	7		10	8
$\bar{y}_{12} = 5$	$\bar{y}_{22} = 7$		9	5
			7	6
			$\bar{y}_{13} = 8.2$	$\bar{y}_{23} = 6.4$

Computation of W_2 for T_2

$$ss_1 = (4 - 5)^2 + (6 - 5)^2 = 2$$
$$ss_2 = (8 - 7)^2 + (6 - 7)^2 = 2$$
$$ss_{12} = ss_{21} = (4 - 5)(8 - 7) + (5 - 5)(6 - 7) + (6 - 5)(7 - 7) = -1$$

Therefore,

$$W_2 = \begin{bmatrix} 2 & -1 \\ -1 & 2 \end{bmatrix}$$

Computation of W_3 for T_3
$$
\begin{aligned}
ss_1 &= (7 - 8.2)^2 + (8 - 8.2)^2 + (10 - 8.2)^2 + (9 - 8.2)^2 \\
&\quad + (7 - 8.2)^2 \\
&= 1.44 + .04 + 3.24 + .64 + 1.44 = 6.8 \\
ss_2 &= (6 - 6.4)^2 + (7 - 6.4)^2 + (8 - 6.4)^2 + (5 - 6.4)^2 \\
&\quad + (6 - 6.4)^2 \\
&= .16 + .36 + 2.56 + 1.96 + .16 = 5.2
\end{aligned}
$$

$$ss_{12} = ss_{21} = (7 - 8.2)(6 - 6.4) + (8 - 8.2)(7 - 6.4)$$
$$+ (10 - 8.2)(8 - 6.4) + (9 - 8.2)(5 - 6.4)$$
$$+ (7 - 8.2)(6 - 6.4)$$
$$= .48 + (-.12) + 2.88 + (-1.12) + .48 = 2.6$$

Therefore,

$$\mathbf{W}_3 = \begin{bmatrix} 6.8 & 2.6 \\ 2.6 & 5.2 \end{bmatrix}$$

ANSWERS FOR CHAPTER 6

2. The actual type I error rate, using Table 6.2, is .42.

5. a) We would not be concerned here with respect to type I error (even though the test is significant), since the group sizes are equal and various studies have shown that for equal n the actual α is very close to the nominal α. If power was an issue, however, we could be concerned given the Holloway and Dunn results (Table 6.8).

b) Here we would be concerned with respect to type I error since the test is significant and the group sizes are sharply unequal. Since the large variability is associated with the small group size, the multivariate test statistics will be too liberal.

c) Here we probably need not be concerned with respect to type I error even though the test is significant. This is because of a somewhat cancelling out type effect. There is large variability associated with the largest group size (which produces a conservative test) but also large variability associated with one of the smallest group sizes (group 1), which would produce a liberal test.

7. The skewness and kurtosis values from the BMDPAM printout are:

	GROUP 1 (11)		GROUP 2 (8)		GROUP 3 (10)	
	skewness	kurtosis	skewness	kurtosis	skewness	kurtosis
$Y1$	.50	−1.29	.14	−1.65	.07	−1.77
$Y2$	−.37	−1.03	−.40	−1.22	−.09	−1.50
$Y3$	−.29	−1.43	.54	−1.34	−.07	−1.94

Critical value for skewness at .01 for group 1 is 1.54, for group 2 is 1.601 and for group 3 is 1.505. None of the values in above table exceed any of critical values in absolute value, hence there is no significant deviation on any of the variables due to skewness.

Recall that to use the critical values from Table 6.5 in testing for kurtosis we must first add 3 to each of the values from the BMDPAM printout. This yields:

	GROUP 1	GROUP 2	GROUP 3
$Y1$	1.71	1.35	1.23
$Y2$	1.97	1.78	1.50
$Y3$	1.57	1.66	1.06

Since the critical values for significant deviation due to leptokurtosis are all greater than 3, there clearly is no significant deviation of this type. The critical values for a significant deviation due to platykurtosis for groups 1, 2 and 3 respectively are 1.43, 1.31 and 1.39. If any of the values in above table are *less* than these critical values we have a significant deviation. There is no significant deviation for groups 1 and 2. We do, however, have significant deviations due to platykurtosis on variables $Y1$ and $Y3$ in group 3. The appropriate transformation (cf. Fig. 6.3) is $1/2 \log \dfrac{1 + x}{1 - x}$.

b) Test for homogeneity of covariance matrices assumption:

Box test $F = 1.00622$, $p < .440$

This test is not significant at .05 level. Since the group sizes were approximately equal, the multivariate test statistics are robust with respect to type I error, and the concern is with type II error.

ANSWERS FOR CHAPTER 7

1. a) The number of discriminant functions is $\min(k - 1, p) = \min(3 - 1, 3) = 2$

b) Only the first discriminant function is significant at the .05 level. The tests occur under DIMENSION REDUCTION ANALYSIS

ROOTS	F	SIG of F
1 to 2	3.34	.008
2 to 2	.184	.833

d) The vector of raw discriminant coefficients is

$$\mathbf{a}_1 = \begin{pmatrix} .47698 \\ -.77237 \\ -.83084 \end{pmatrix}$$

The **B** matrix, from the printout is:

$$\begin{bmatrix} 4.67798 & 8.71215 & 7.42010 \\ 8.71215 & 16.85415 & 14.27574 \\ 7.42010 & 14.27574 & 12.10131 \end{bmatrix}$$

Now, rounding off to 3 decimal places, we compute $\mathbf{a}_1' \mathbf{B} \mathbf{a}_1$

$$(.477, -.772, -.831) \begin{bmatrix} 4.678 & 8.712 & 7.420 \\ 8.712 & 16.854 & 14.276 \\ 7.420 & 14.276 & 12.101 \end{bmatrix} \begin{pmatrix} .477 \\ -.772 \\ -.831 \end{pmatrix}$$

$$\mathbf{a}_1' \mathbf{B} \mathbf{a}_1 = (-10.66, -20.719, -17.538) \begin{pmatrix} .477 \\ -.772 \\ -.831 \end{pmatrix} = 25.484$$

Now, rounding off the **W** matrix to 3 decimal places, we have

$$\mathbf{a}_1' \mathbf{W} \mathbf{a}_1 = (.477, -.772, -.831) \begin{bmatrix} 24.684 & 10.607 & 17.399 \\ 10.607 & 18.111 & 14.690 \\ 17.399 & 14.690 & 17.864 \end{bmatrix} \begin{pmatrix} .477 \\ -.772 \\ -.831 \end{pmatrix}$$

$$\mathbf{a}_1' \mathbf{W} \mathbf{a}_1 = (-10.873, -21.13, -17.886) \begin{pmatrix} .477 \\ -.772 \\ -.831 \end{pmatrix} = 25.989$$

Now, the largest eigenvalue is given by $\mathbf{a}_1' \mathbf{B} \mathbf{a}_1 / \mathbf{a}_1' \mathbf{W} \mathbf{a}_1$

$\phi_1 = 25.484/25.989 = .98057$

and this agrees with the value on the printout within rounding error.

3. a) Since there were 3 significant discriminant functions in the Smart study, the association is diffuse and the Pillai-Bartlett trace is most powerful (see 5.12).

b) In the Stevens study there was only 1 significant discriminant function (concentrated association), and in this case Roy's largest root has been shown to be most powerful (again see 5.12).

ANSWERS FOR CHAPTER 9

1. a) Control lines for Scandura MANCOVA on SPSSX MANOVA:

```
TITLE ' MANCOVA 2 GROUPS - 5 DEP VARS AND 3 COVARIATES '
DATA LIST FREE/ TRTMT2 HOPPOCKA LMXA ERSA QUANAFT QUALAFT MPS OLI
    DTT
LIST
BEGIN DATA
  DATA LINES
END DATA
MANOVA HOPPOCKA TO DTT BY TRTMT2(1,2)/
  ANALYSIS=HOPPOCKA LMXA ERSA QUANAFT WITH MPS OLI DTT/
  PRINT=PMEANS/
  DESIGN/
  ANALYSIS=HOPPOCKA LMXA ERSA QUANAFT QUALAFT/
  DESIGN=MPS+OLI+DTT,TRTMT2, MPS BY TRTMT2 + OLI BY TRTMT2 + DTT
  BY TRTMT2/
```

b) To determine whether covariance is appropriate two things need to be checked:

1. Is there a significant relationship between the dependent variables and the set of covariates, or equivalently is there a significant regression of the dependent variables on the covariates?
2. Is the homogeneity of the regression hyperplanes satisfied?

Under EFFECT . . . WITHIN CELLS REGRESSION are the multivariate tests for determining whether the two sets of variables are related. The multivariate F corresponding to Wilk's Λ shows there is a significant relationship at the .05 level ($F = 1.88, p < .027$). The test for the homogeneity of the regression hyperplanes appears under EFFECT . . . MPS BY TRTMT2 + OLI BY TRTMT2 + DTT BY TRTMT2. This test is not significant at the .05 level ($F = .956, p < .503$), meaning that the assumption *is* satisfied. Thus, from the above two results we see that covariance is appropriate.

c) The multivariate test for determining the 2 adjusted population mean vectors are equal appears under EFFECT . . . TRTMT2 The tests, which are equivalent (since there are only 2 groups), show significance at the .05 level ($F = 2.669, p < .029$).

d) The univariate tests show that only QUANAFT is significant at the .01 level ($F = 11.186, p < .001$).

e) The adjusted means for QUANAFT are .392 (for treatment group) and .323 (for control group), with the treatment group doing better.

4. Are there any differences on the SOCINT variable in Novince study using the Bryant Paulson 95% simultaneous confidence level? The following test statistic is appropriate (cf. Table 9.8).

$$BP = \frac{\overline{Y}_i^* - \overline{Y}_j^*}{\sqrt{MS_w^* \left[1 + \frac{1}{(J-1)} Tr(\mathbf{B}_x \mathbf{W}_x^{-1}) \right]/n}}$$

The adjusted means for the 3 groups for SOCINT are (Table 9.5):

TREAT 1: 103.087   TREAT 2: 76.119   TREAT 3: 108.158

The adjusted error term for SOCINT is 105.09 (Table 9.6), and recall that $Tr(\mathbf{B}_x \mathbf{W}_x^{-1}) = .307$. First we compare groups 1 and 2:

$$BP = \frac{103.087 - 76.119}{\sqrt{105.09 \left[1 + \frac{1}{2} (.307) \right]/11}}$$

$$= \frac{26.968}{\sqrt{105.09 \, (1.15)/11}} = \frac{26.968}{3.3146} = 8.136$$

Recall from the Novince example (no. 4) that the critical value $= 3.73$. Thus, we reject and conclude that groups 1 and 2 differ on SOCINT. Also, since the difference between the adjusted means for groups 2 and 3 is even larger, that difference will also be significant. Now we test the difference for groups 1 and 3:

$$BP = \frac{103.087 - 108.158}{3.3146} = -1.53$$

Since this is less (in absolute value) than the critical value of 3.73 groups 1 and 3 are not different.

6. a) From what is said we can not be confident that covariance is appropriate. First, no test is given indicating that there is a significant relationship between the 3 dependent variables and the covariates. Secondly, the test for the homogeneity of the regression hyperplanes is not given.

b) It would not have made a difference as to which multivariate test was used, since for two groups they are equivalent.

c) The post hoc procedure they are employing is the one using the Bonferroni Inequality, where for p dependent variables, if one wishes the overall α at .05, then each variable is tested at the $.05/p$ level of significance.

d) According to Huitema's inequality there are not enough subjects to have confidence in the reliability of the adjusted means. Since there are $J = 2$ groups and $N = 30$ subjects total, the number of covariates C should be limited so that

$$\frac{C + (2-1)}{30} < .10 \Rightarrow C < 2$$

ANSWERS FOR CHAPTER 11

1. a) Denote the linear combination for 2 variables as

$$y = a_1 x_1 + a_2 x_2$$

$$\text{var}(y) = (a_1, a_2) \begin{bmatrix} s_1^2 & s_{12} \\ s_{12} & s_2^2 \end{bmatrix} \begin{pmatrix} a_1 \\ a_2 \end{pmatrix}$$

$$= a_1^2 s_1^2 + 2 a_1 a_2 s_{12} + a_2^2 s_2^2$$

Denote the linear combination for 3 variables as

$$y_1 = a_1 x_1 + a_2 x_2 + a_3 x_3$$

$$\text{var}(y_1) = (a_1, a_2, a_3) \begin{bmatrix} s_1^2 & s_{12} & s_{13} \\ s_{12} & s_2^2 & s_{23} \\ s_{13} & s_{23} & s_3^2 \end{bmatrix} \begin{pmatrix} a_1 \\ a_2 \\ a_3 \end{pmatrix}$$

After all the matrix multiplication and combining of like terms the following is obtained:

$$\text{var}(y_1) = a_1^2 s_1^2 + a_2^2 s_2^2 + a_3^2 s_3^2 + 2 a_1 a_2 s_{12}$$
$$+ 2 a_1 a_3 s_{13} + 2 a_2 a_3 s_{23}$$

(b)

$$S = \begin{bmatrix} 451.4 & 271.2 & 168.7 \\ 271.2 & 171.7 & 103.3 \\ 168.7 & 103.3 & 66.7 \end{bmatrix}$$

s_{12} ↗ s_{13} ↓ s_{23} ↓

$y_1 = .81 x_1 + .50 x_2 + .31 x_3$

$\downarrow$ a_1 $\downarrow$ a_2 $\downarrow$ a_3

Now, plugging into the above formula for variance:

$$\text{var}(y_1) = (.81)^2 (451.4) + (.5)^2 (171.7)$$
$$+ (.31)^2 (66.7)$$

$$+ \ 2(.81)(.5) \ (271.2) \ + \ 2(81)(.31)(168.7)$$
$$+ \ 2(.5)(.31)(103.3)$$
$$\text{var}(y_1) \ = \ 296.16 \ + \ 42.925 \ + \ 6.41 \ + \ 84.72$$
$$+ \ 219.67 \ + \ 32.023 \ = \ 681.9$$

3. In Case 1 it is not necessary to apply Barltett's sphericity test since 8 of correlations are at least moderate ($>.40$) in size. In Case 2, on the other hand, only 1 of the 15 correlations is moderate (.40), and almost all the others are very small. Thus here Bartlett's sphericity test is advisable. Using the Lawley approximation, we have:

$$\chi^2 \ = \ \left\{ 110 \ - \ \frac{2(6) \ + \ 5}{6} \right\}$$
$$[(.29)^2 \ + \ (.18)^2 \ + \ (.04)^2 \ + \ \ldots \ + \ (-.14)^2 \ + \ (.12)^2]$$
$$\chi^2 \ = \ (107.1667)(.4467) \ = \ 47.87$$

The critical value at $\alpha \ = \ .01$ is 30.58 (df $= \ 1/2 \ (6)(5) \ = \ 15$). We reject and therefore conclude that the variables are correlated in the population.

5. a) Variance accounted for by component 1 : 57.43%
   Variance accounted for by component 2 : 35.92%
   b) Variance accounted for by varimax factor 1 : 50.44%
   Variance accounted for by varimax factor 2 : 42.96%
   c) The variance accounted for by the varimax rotated factors is spread out more evenly than for the components.
   d) The total amount of variance accounted for by the 2 components (93.35%) is the same, within rounding error, as that accounted for by the two varimax rotated factors (93.4%).

7. The first varimax factor is a manual communication construct, while the second varimax factor is an oral communication construct.
   b) The empirical clustering of the variables which load very high on varimax factor 1 (C_5, C_6, C_9 and C_{10}) is consistent with how the variables correlate in the original correlation matrix. The simple correlations for each pair of the above 4 variables ranges from .86 to .94.

ANSWERS FOR CHAPTER 12

1. Four features that canonical correlation and principal components have in common:
   a) both are mathematical maximization procedures

b) both use uncorrelated linear combinations of the variables

c) both provide for an additive partitioning; in components analysis an additive partitioning of the total variance, and in canonical correlation an additive partitioning of the between association.

d) correlations between the original variables and the linear combinations are used in both procedures for interpretation purposes.

3. a) The association between the 2 sets of variables is weak, since 17 of the 26 simple correlations are less than .30.

b) Only the largest canonical correlation is significant at the .05 level - from the printout:

Chi-Sq	df	prob
92.96	36	.0000
21.70	25	.6533

c) The following are the loadings from the printout:

CREATIVITY		ACHIEVEMENT	
Ideaflu	.227	Know	.669
Flexib	.412	Compre	.578
Assocflu	.629	Applic	.374
Exprflu	.796	Anal	.390
Orig	.686	Synth	.910
Elab	.703	Eval	.542

The canonical correlation basically links the ability to synthesis (the loading of .910 dominates the achievement loadings) to last 4 creativity variables, which have loadings of the same order of magnitude.

d) Since only the largest canonical correlation was significant, about 20 subjects per variable are needed for reliable results, i.e., about $20(12) = 240$ subjects. So, the above results, based on an N of 116, must be treated somewhat tenuously.

e) The redundancy index for the creativity variables given the achievement variables is obtained from the following values on the printout:

Av. Sq. Loading times Sqed Can Correl (1st Set)
.17787
.00906
.00931
.00222
.00063
.00019
.19928

This indicates that about 20% of the variance on the set of creativity variables is accounted for by the set of achievement variables.

f) The squared canonical correlations are given on the printout, and yield the following value for the Cramer-Nicewander index:

$$\frac{.48148 + .10569 + .06623 + .01286 + .00468 + .00917}{6} = .112$$

This indicates that the "variance" overlap between the two sets of variables is only about 11%, and is more accurate than the redundancy index since that index ignores the correlations among the dependent variables. And there are several significant correlations among the creativity variables, eight in the weak to moderate range (.32 to .46) and one strong correlation (.71).

6. The criterion of $10(p+q) + 50$ is not a conservative one according to the results of Barcikowski and Stevens. This criterion would imply, for example, if $p = 10$ and $q = 20$, that $10(10+20) + 50 = 350$ subjects are needed for reliable results. From Barcikowski and Stevens, on the other hand, about $30(20) = 600$ subjects are needed for reliable results, and more than that would be required if interpreting more than 1 canonical correlation.

ANSWERS FOR CHAPTER 13

2 . a) Univariate repeated measures analysis:

S	Treats 1	2	3	Row Means
1	5	6	1	4.0
2	3	4	2	3.0
3	3	7	1	3.667
4	6	8	3	5.667
5	6	9	3	6.0
6	4	7	2	4.333
7	5	9	2	5.333
Col means	4.571	7.143	2.0	4.571 (grand mean)

$$SS_b = 7[(4.571 - 4.571)^2 + (7.143 - 4.571)^2 + (2 - 4.571)^2]$$

$$SS_b = 7[6.615 + 6.61] = 92.575$$

$$SS_w = (5 - 4.571)^2 + (3 - 4.571)^2 + \ldots + (5 - 4.571)^2$$
$$+ (6 - 7.143)^2 + (4 - 7.143)^2 + \ldots + (9 - 7.143)^2$$
$$+ (1 - 2)^2 + (2 - 2)^2 + \ldots + (2 - 2)^2$$

$$SS_w = 32.57$$

$$SS_{b1} = 3[(4 - 4.571)^2 + (3 - 4.571)^2 + \ldots + (5.333 - 4.571)^2]$$

$$SS_{b1} = 22.476$$

Therefore,

$$SS_{res} = SS_w - SS_{b1} = 32.57 - 22.476 = 10.094$$

$$MS_{res} = SS_{res} / (n - 1)(k - 1) = 10.094/(7 - 1)(3 - 1) = .841$$

$$MS_b = SS_b / (k - 1) = 92.575/2 = 46.288$$

$$F = 46.288/.841 = 55.039$$

Critical value $F_{.05;2,12} = 3.88$

Thus, the treatments are significantly different at .05 level.
b) Multivariate repeated measures analysis using the difference variables $y_1 - y_2$ and $y_2 - y_3$:

$y_1 - y_2$	$y_2 - y_3$
-1	5
-1	2
-4	6
-2	5
-3	6
-3	5
-4	7

Means	-2.571	5.143
Variances	1.619	2.476

Calculation for the covariance of $(y_1 - y_2)$ and $(y_2 - y_3)$:

$$s_{y1-y2,y2-y3} = \frac{(-1 + 2.571)(5 - 5.143) + (-1 + 2.571)(2 - 5.143)}{6}$$
$$\frac{+ (-4 + 2.571)(6 - 5.143) + \ldots + (-4 + 2.571)(7 - 5.143)}{6}$$

$$= -9.429/6 = -1.571$$

Thus, the covariance matrix S for the difference variables is:

$$S = \begin{bmatrix} 1.619 & -1.571 \\ -1.571 & 2.476 \end{bmatrix}$$

We need the inverse of this covariance matrix:

$$S^{-1} = \frac{1}{1.541} \begin{bmatrix} 2.476 & 1.571 \\ 1.571 & 1.619 \end{bmatrix} = \begin{bmatrix} 1.607 & 1.019 \\ 1.019 & 1.051 \end{bmatrix}$$

$$T^2 = 7 \, (-2.571, 5.143) \begin{bmatrix} 1.607 & 1.019 \\ 1.019 & 1.051 \end{bmatrix} \begin{pmatrix} -2.571 \\ 5.143 \end{pmatrix} = 80.298$$

$$F = \frac{n - k + 1}{(n - 1)(k - 1)} T^2 = \frac{7 - 3 + 1}{6 \, (2)} (80.298) = 33.45$$

c) When the analysis is run on SPSSX MANOVA the following univariate and multivariate results are obtained:

Univariate—Under AVERAGED TESTS OF SIGNIFICANCE

	SUM OF SQUARES	F	SIG OF F
WITHIN CELLS	10.095		
TREAT	92.571	55.02	.000

Multivariate—F = 33.402

Both of these results agree, within rounding error, with those calculated in (a) and (b).

d) The transformed variables used by SPSSX (in columns 2 and 3 of the TRANSFORMATION MATRIX) are

$$.70711y_1 - .70711y_3 \text{ and } -.40825y_1 + .8165y_2 - .40825y_3$$

The point this illustrates is that there are other choices, than adjacent difference variables, which will yield the same multivariate test statistic. This is due to the invariance property of the Hotelling T^2 statistic.

e) A pair of means is significantly different at the .05 level with the Tukey procedure if:

$$|\bar{y}_i - \bar{y}_j| > q_{.05; \, k, \, (n-1)(k-1)} \sqrt{\frac{MS_{res}}{n}}$$

Here, $q_{.05;3,12} = 3.773$ and $MS_{res} = .84127$ (from printout).

Thus, a pairs of means will be significantly different if

$$|\bar{y}_i - \bar{y}_j| > 3.773 \sqrt{\frac{.84127}{7}} = 1.308$$

The means are $\bar{y}_1 = 4.571$, $\bar{y}_2 = 7.143$ and $\bar{y}_3 = 2.0$.

The differences between each pair of means exceeds 1.308 in absolute value and hence all pairs of treatments differ.

4. The design would look as follows:

| | | Condition 1 | | | | | | Condition 2 | | | | |
| | | Drug 1 | | | Drug 2 | | | Drug 1 | | | Drug 2 | |
Dose		1	2	3	'1	2	3	1	2	3	1	2	3
	s_1	y_1	y_2	y_3	y_4	y_5	y_6	y_7	y_8	y_9	y_{10}	y_{11}	y_{12}
	s_2												
Gp1													
	s_8												
	s_9	. . . . . .			. . . . . .			. . . . .			. . .		
	s_{10}												
Gp 2													
	s_{16}												

Note that each subject is measured 12 times, so that there are 12 variables. The SPSSX MANOVA control lines now are:

```
TITLE ' GROUP BY CONDITION BY DRUG BY DOSE '
DATA LIST FREE/Y1 Y2 Y3 Y4 Y5 Y6 Y7 Y8 Y9 Y10 Y11 Y12 GPID
LIST
```

```
BEGIN DATA
   DATA LINES
END DATA
MANOVA Y1 TO Y12 BY GPID(1,2)/
   WSFACTOR = COND(2),DRUG(2),DOSE(3)/
   WSDESIGN/
   PRINT = TRANSFORM HOMOGENEITY (BOXM) ERROR(COR) SINGIF(AVERF)
   CELLINFO(MEANS)/
   ANALYSIS(REPEATED)/
   DESIGN/
```

6. b)

$$S = \begin{bmatrix} 4 & 3 & 2 \\ 3 & 5 & 2 \\ 2 & 2 & 6 \end{bmatrix} \begin{matrix} \bar{s}_i \\ 3 \\ 3.33 \\ 3.33 \end{matrix}$$

Here,

$$k = 3, \bar{s} = 3.222, \bar{s}_{ii} = (4 + 5 + 6)/3 = 5$$

$$\sum\sum s_{ij}^2 = 4^2 + 3^2 + 2^2 + \ldots + 2^2 + 6^2 = 111$$

$$\hat{\epsilon} = \frac{9\,(5 - 3.222)^2}{2[111 - 2(3)\,\{9 + 11.09 + 11.09\} + 9\,(10.381)]}$$

$$\hat{\epsilon} = \frac{28.45}{2[111 - 187.08 + 93.43]} = .82$$

7. Show that uniformity implies sphericity. Uniformity means that all the variances are equal, i.e.,

$$\sigma_{y_1}^2 = \sigma_{y_2}^2 = \ldots = \sigma_{y_k}^2 = \sigma^2$$

Uniformity also means that all the covariances are equal, i.e.,

$$\sigma_{y_1 y_2} = \sigma_{y_1 y_3} = \ldots = \sigma_{y_{k-1} y_k} = \sigma_{com}$$

The variance of the difference variable for ith and jth treatments is:

$$\sigma_{y_i - y_j}^2 = \sigma_{y_i}^2 + \sigma_{y_j}^2 - 2\,\sigma_{y_i y_j}$$

But, from above, if uniformity holds then $\sigma_{y_i}^2 = \sigma_{y_j}^2$ and also $\sigma_{y_i y_j} = \sigma_{com}$. Thus, the variance for every difference variable is the same (which is the sphericity condition), namely $2\sigma^2 - 2\,\sigma_{com}$.

8. The group effect is not significant at the .05 level ($F = .327$, $p < .580$). Which of the trends are significant at the .05 level for the DAYS main effect? From the printout we have:
EFFECT ... DAYS

Univariate F tests

Variable	F	Sig of F
Linear	343.86	.000
Quad	.14	.714
Cubic	129.13	.000
Quart	9.27	.012

From the above, the linear, cubic, and quartic trends are significant at .05. However, from the F ratios clearly the linear and cubic trends are most pronounced.

Are any of the univariate interactions (linear by group, etc.) significant at the .05 level?

From the printout we have:

EFFECT . . . GPID BY DAYS

Univariate F tests

Variable	F	Sig of F
Linear	5.45	.042
Quad	.14	.714
Cubic	.206	.659
Quart	1.91	.196

Thus, only the linear by group interaction is significant at .05. This means the slope of the lines is different for the 2 groups.

11. The design schematically would look as follows:

		Time 1				Time 2		
	Cr	Col	Ub	Gl	Cr	Col	Ub	Gl
Brand								
Belief	1 2 3 4 5 6 7 8 9	10 11	12 13	14 15	16 17	18 19	20 21	22 23 24

AGE	
20–35	
M 36–50	
51 & ↑	
20–35	
F 36–50	
51 & ↑	

Note that each subject is measured 24 times. Thus, there are 24 variables for the analysis.

Control lines for SPSSX MANOVA (2 between and 3 within variables)

```
TITLE ' SEX BY AGE BY TIME BY BRAND BY BELIEF '
DATA LIST FREE/ Y1 Y2 Y3 Y4 Y5 Y6 Y7 Y8 Y9 Y10 Y11 Y12 Y13 Y14 Y15 Y16 Y17
    Y18 Y19 Y20 Y21 Y22 Y23 Y24 SEX AGE
LIST
BEGIN DATA
     DATA LINES
END DATA
MANOVA Y1 TO Y24 BY SEX(1,2) AGE(1,3)/
  WSFACTOR = TIME(2),BRAND(4),BELIEF(3)/
  WSDESIGN/
  PRINT = TRANSFORM HOMOGENEITY(BOXM) SIGNIF(AVERF) CELLINFO(MEANS)/
  ANALYSIS(REPEATED)/
  DESIGN/
```

ANSWERS FOR CHAPTER 14

3. a) Control lines for the 3 way run are given below:

```
TITLE ' THREE WAY LOGLINEAR ON SURVEY DATA '
DATA LIST FREE/YEAR COLOR RESPONSE FREQ
WEIGHT BY FREQ
BEGIN DATA
1 1 1 81 1 1 2 23 1 1 3 4 1 2 1 325 1 2 2 253 1 2 3 54
2 1 1 224 2 1 2 144 2 1 3 24 2 2 1 600 2 2 2 636 2 2 3 158
END DATA
HILOGLINEAR YEAR(1,2) COLOR(1,2) RESPONSE(1,3)/
  METHOD = BACKWARD/
  DESIGN/
```

Model selected: [YEAR*COLOR, YEAR*RESPONSE, COLOR*RESPONSE]

b) Since the model selected has all two way interactions, it is not valid to collapse on any category. Thus, the contrasts need to be done on the cell frequencies.

5. a) Control lines for the 4 way run are given below:

```
TITLE ' FOUR WAY LOGLINEAR - FROM AGRESTI, P. 202 '
DATA LIST FREE/SEX GPA RACE ESTEEM FREQ
WEIGHT BY FREQ
HILOGLINEAR SEX(1,2) GPA(1,2) RACE(1,2) ESTEEM(1,2)/
  METHOD = BACKWARD/
  DESIGN/
```

```
BEGIN DATA
1 1 1 1 15   1 1 1 2 9   1 1 2 1 17   1 1 2 2 10
1 2 1 1 26   1 2 1 2 17   1 2 2 1 22   1 2 2 2 26
2 1 1 1 13   2 1 1 2 22   2 1 2 1 22   2 1 2 2 32
2 2 1 1 24   2 2 1 2 23   2 2 2 1 3    2 2 2 2 17
END DATA
```

The model selected is: [SEX*GPA*RACE, GPA*RACE*ESTEEM, SEX*ESTEEM]

   b) Is it valid to collapse over race and gpa in interpreting the SEX*ESTEEM interaction? The answer is no. Although, superficially it may seem okay since there are no SEX*ESTEEM*RACE or SEX*ESTEEM*GPA interactions in the model, from exercise 7 we also need either sex to be independent of both race and gpa (which it is not since we have the SEX*RACE*GPA interaction effect) or esteem to be independent of both race and gpa (which it is not since we have GPA*RACE*ESTEEM in the model).

6 a) Control lines for the 5 way run are given below:

```
TITLE ' FIVE WAY LOGLINEAR - DATA FROM FEINBERG '
DATA LIST FREE/SENT SUCCFAIL DRUGALCH AGE OFFENSE FREQ
WEIGHT BY FREQ
HILOGLINEAR SENT(1,2) SUCCFAIL(1,2) DRUGALCH(1,2)
   AGE(1,2) OFFENSE(1,2)/
   METHOD=BACKWARD/
   CRITERIA MAXSTEPS(20)/
   DESIGN/
BEGIN DATA
1 1 1 1 1 48    1 1 1 1 2 34    1 1 1 2 1 37    1 1 1 2 2 49
1 1 2 1 1 38    1 1 2 1 2 28    1 1 2 2 1 35    1 1 2 2 2 57
1 2 1 1 1 1     1 2 1 1 2 5     1 2 1 2 1 7     1 2 1 2 2 11
1 2 2 1 1 3     1 2 2 1 2 8     1 2 2 2 1 5     1 2 2 2 2 18
2 1 1 1 1 17    2 1 1 1 2 259   2 1 1 2 1 131   2 1 1 2 2 319
2 1 2 1 1 197   2 1 2 1 2 435   2 1 2 2 1 107   2 1 2 2 2 291
2 2 1 1 1 23    2 2 1 1 2 61    2 2 1 2 1 20    2 2 1 2 2 89
2 2 2 1 1 38    2 2 2 1 2 194   2 2 2 2 1 27    2 2 2 2 2 101
END DATA
```

The model selected is:

[SENT*DRUGALCH*AGE,SENT*SUCCFAIL*AGE,SENT*AGE* OFFENSE, SUCCFAIL*OFFENSE, SUCCFAIL*DRUGALCH]

   b) To test this model on the validation data, enter the validation data and replace METHOD=BACKWARD/ with the following DESIGN subcommand:

DESIGN = SENT*DRUGALCH*AGE SENT*SUCCFAIL*AGE
SENT*AGE*OFFENSE SUCCFAIL*OFFENSE
SUCCFAIL*DRUGALCH/

The model does not cross validate since, for example, the Pearson chi square is 38.09984, with a p value less than .001.

7. The collapsibility conditions to validly collapse AB over C and D are several. We need ABCD = 0, as well as ABC = ABD = 0. Note that if either ABC or ABD is not 0, then the association for AB is different for the levels of C or D, and it obviously would not make sense to combine over those levels. In addition, either A must be independent of both C and D, or B must be independent of both C and D. In symbols, all of this means that at least one of the following models holds:

[AB, BCD] or [AB, ACD]

See Agresti (1990, pp. 145–146).

Author Index

Subject Index